Encyclopedia
of the
American Presidency

Editorial Board

Encyclopedia
of the
American Presidency

Editors

LEONARD W. LEVY
LOUIS FISHER

Volume 4

SIMON & SCHUSTER

A Paramount Communications Company

New York   London   Toronto   Sydney   Tokyo   Singapore

Simon & Schuster
Academic Reference Division
15 Columbus Circle
New York, New York 10023

A Paramount Communications Company

Printed in the United States of America

printing number
2   3   4   5   6   7   8   9   10

Library of Congress Cataloging-in-Publication Data

Encyclopedia of the American presidency

Leonard W. Levy, Louis Fisher, editors.
v. cm.

Includes bibliographical references and index.

1. Presidents—United States—Encyclopedias.   2.
Presidents—United States—Biography.   I. Levy, Leonard
Williams, 1923–   .   II. Fisher, Louis.
JK511.E53 1994   353.03'13'03—dc20   93-13574 CIP

ISBN 0-13-275983-7 (Set)
0-13-275975-6 (Vol. 4)

The paper used in this publication meets the minimum
requirements of the American National Standard for
Information Sciences—Permanence of Paper for Printed Library
Materials ANSI Z39.48-1984.

Abbreviations Used in This Work

Ala. Alabama
Ariz. Arizona
Ark. Arkansas
Art. Article
b. born
c. circa, about, approximately
Calif. California
cf. confer, compare
chap. chapter (pl., chaps.)
CIO Congress of Industrial Organizations
Cong. Congress
Colo. Colorado
Conn. Connecticut
d. died
D Democrat, Democratic
D.C. District of Columbia
Del. Delaware
diss. dissertation
DR Democratic-Republican
ed. editor (pl., eds); edition
e.g. exempli gratia, for example
enl. enlarged
esp. especially
et al. et alii, and others
etc. et cetera, and so forth

exp. expanded
f. and following (pl., ff.)
F Federalist
Fla. Florida
Ga. Georgia
GOP Grand Old Party (Republican Party)
H.R. House of Representatives
I Independent
ibid. ibidem, in the same place (as the one immediately preceding)
Ida. Idaho
i.e. id est, that is
Ill. Illinois
Ind. Indiana
IRS Internal Revenue Service
Kan. Kansas
Ky. Kentucky
La. Louisiana
M.A. Master of Arts
Mass. Massachusetts
Me. Maine
Mich. Michigan
Minn. Minnesota

Miss. Mississippi
Mo. Missouri
Mont. Montana
n. note
N.C. North Carolina
n.d. no date
N.Dak. North Dakota
Neb. Nebraska
Nev. Nevada
N.H. New Hampshire
N.J. New Jersey
N.Mex. New Mexico
no. number (pl., nos.)
n.p. no place
n.s. new series
N.Y. New York
Okla. Oklahoma
Ore. Oregon
p. page (pl., pp.)
Pa. Pennsylvania
pt. part (pl., pts.)
R Republican
rev. revised
R.I. Rhode Island
S. Senate
S.C. South Carolina

S.Dak. South Dakota
sec. section (pl., secs.)
ser. series
ses. session
supp. supplement
Tenn. Tennessee
Tex. Texas
U.N. United Nations
U.S. United States, United States Reports
USA United States Army
USAF United States Air Force
USN United States Navy
U.S.S.R. Union of Soviet Socialist Republics
v. versus
Va. Virginia
vol. volume (pl., vols.)
Vt. Vermont
W Whig
Wash. Washington
Wis. Wisconsin
W.Va. West Virginia
Wyo. Wyoming

S

SAINT LAWRENCE SEAWAY. The seaway is a 2,350-mile waterway from the Atlantic Ocean to the western end of Lake Superior and the southern shores of Lakes Erie and Michigan. The Great Lakes, the Saint Lawrence River, and their connecting channels posed serious problems in United States–Canadian relations for more than two centuries. These problems concerned matters of sovereignty, boundaries, shipping rights, power plants and energy production, and financing and managing the construction of dams, locks, and other facilities. After the boundary and early shipping issues were addressed in a series of treaties with Great Britain (1783, 1794, and 1814), attention was turned to free navigation (Treaty of Washington, 1854) and demilitarization (Rush-Bagot Agreement, 1817; TREATY OF WASHINGTON, 1871). A convention in 1909 provided for the regulation of boundary waters and created machinery for the settlement of disputes, and two years later an International Joint Commission was established to deal with these matters and to propose recommendations for navigation improvements.

Subsequently, from the administration of Warren G. Harding to that of Dwight D. Eisenhower, policy and diplomacy turned to developing a joint United States–Canadian Great Lakes–Saint Lawrence Seaway, opening this extensive waterway to ocean-going shipping. This turned out to be a complex economic, political, and legal issue in relations between the United States and Canada, the President and Congress, and the federal government and the states.

A Great Lakes–Saint Lawrence Waterway Treaty, signed in 1932, was opposed by powerful interest groups and was defeated by the Senate in 1934. President Franklin D. Roosevelt then switched to the EXECUTIVE AGREEMENT process, and a new understanding, signed in 1941, created a Great Lakes–Saint Lawrence Basin Commission to deal with navigation and electric-power production. It languished during WORLD WAR II, and in 1948 it was also defeated by the Senate.

Except for a treaty concerning the Niagara River (1950), all other arrangements concerning the waterway since 1940 were consummated by exchanges of notes. The principal agreements—signed in 1940, 1952, and 1954—provided for the development of the seaway project. All told, the United States and Canada were party to more than fifteen treaties, agreements, and ancillary arrangements.

Concurrent legislation by Congress and the Canadian Parliament was required to implement these agreements. Despite persistent presidential urging for favorable congressional action, it was not until Canada enacted a bill in 1951 to proceed with the project unilaterally (which would have subjected the waterway to Canadian control) that Congress finally took action. Eisenhower submitted a new proposal to Congress in 1953, and the Wiley-Dondero Act was passed and signed in May 1954 (68 Stat. 92). The project was finally completed, and President Eisenhower and Queen Elizabeth II dedicated the seaway in a special ceremony on 26 June 1959.

This project, which cost hundreds of millions of dollars, required the deepening and widening of maritime channels; the construction of dams, locks, and power plants; and the creation of both U.S. and Canadian development and management agencies. It is a self-liquidating venture.

BIBLIOGRAPHY

Baxter, Richard R. *Documents on the St. Lawrence Seaway: A Selection.* 1960.

Sussman, Gennifer. *The St. Lawrence Seaway.* 1978.

U.S. Senate. *St. Lawrence Seaway Manual.* 83d Cong., 2d sess., 1954. S. Doc. No. 165.

ELMER PLISCHKE

SALARIES, EXECUTIVE. Top-level executive branch policymakers and managers receive salaries that are set and adjusted on a relatively automatic basis under the provisions of the Ethics Reform Act of 1989 (103 Stat. 1716).

The annual adjustment would be in effect as of 1 January of any given year and would be calculated by using the rate of change in the private sector wages and salaries element of the Employment Cost Index (Bureau of Labor Statistics) in a December to December span of time, ending on 31 December—twelve months prior to the effective date. Once that rate of change is established, the adjustment rate is determined by subtracting 0.5 from the rate of change. It was thought that this further reduction would demonstrate that the salaries for officials are not intended to keep direct pace with those in the private sector.

A second adjustment is possible pursuant to the review and recommendations of the Citizens' Commission on Compensation and Public Service [*see* QUADRENNIAL SALARY COMMISSION]. The review is conducted every fourth fiscal year.

Prior to 1964, Congress established salaries on the basis of individual positions within the various departments and agencies. In an effort to bring uniformity to the salary system, Congress established the executive schedule, a five-level salary system that ranges from secretaries of the departments (level I) to members of minor boards and commissions. Most of the positions on the executive schedule are filled by presidential appointment with the ADVICE AND CONSENT of the Senate. Recognizing the necessity to adjust the salaries periodically, Congress would act to do so through specific legislative enactment. However, rising problems of salary compression in the lower ranks, along with recruitment and retention, brought about in 1975 the establishment of a system of adjustments tied to the annual comparability adjustments established for the rank and file general schedule salaries.

Any discussion of quadrennial or annual "automatic" salary adjustments should contain the caveat that, at any time, Congress can legislate to withhold funding the adjustment or to change the mechanism of adjust-

Executive Schedule, 1993[a]

Level	Type of Office	Salary
Level I	Cabinet officers	$148,400
Level II	Deputy secretaries of departments, secretaries of military departments, and heads of major agencies	133,600
Level III	Under secretaries of departments, heads of middle-level agencies	123,100
Level IV	Assistant secretaries and general counsels of departments, heads of minor agencies, members of certain boards and commissions	115,700
Level V	Administrators, commissioners, directors, and members of boards, commissions, or units of agencies	108,200

[a]The Executive Schedule is the ranking of salaries for five levels of executive-branch officials. The salaries shown here are effective as of 1 January 1993. Prepared by Sharon Stiver Gressle.

ment either temporarily or permanently. This congressional interference became almost expected during the period between 1975 and 1989.

It is common for Congress, when establishing a position not on the executive schedule, to link the salary to one of the executive schedule levels. For example, several legislative and judicial branch officials' salaries are set either at "a rate not to exceed" or "a rate equal to Level." Whole salary systems are also statutorily linked to the executive schedule. For example, the Senior Executive Service, a cadre of senior managers (primarily career personnel), has a salary system that comprises six levels and is adjusted solely at the discretion of the President. However, Congress in establishing the system required that the salaries not exceed that paid at level IV. Other systems with similar limitations are those for the general schedule (GS ranks) administrative law judges, members of contract boards of appeals, Title 5 positions classified above a GS-15, the foreign service, and the special medical professional schedules.

It is generally accepted that people serving in policy-making positions within an administration will likely be making substantial financial sacrifices. Public service, it is argued, nevertheless gives one a sense of satisfaction in having served the nation. Striking the balance between the earning power sacrificed by a private sector executive and a salary level reasonably acceptable to the American public is a delicate exercise. The political reality, one must remember, is that

Executive Salaries, 1789–1993

Year	President	Vice President	Percent of President's Salary	Cabinet Members	Percent of President's Salary	Chief Justice	Percent of President's Salary	Members of Congress	Percent of President's Salary
1789	$ 25,000	$ 5,000	20.00	$ 3,500	14.00	$ 4,000	16.00		
1799				5,000	20.00				
1819				6,000	24.00	5,000	20.00		
1853		8,000	32.00	8,000	32.00				
1855						6,500	26.00		
1856								$ 3,000	12.00
1866								5,000	20.00
1871						8,500	34.00		
1873	50,000	10,000	20.00	10,000	20.00	10,500	21.00	7,500	15.00
1874		8,000	16.00	8,000	16.00			5,000	10.00
1903						13,000	26.00		
1907		12,000	24.00	12,000	24.00				
1909	75,000	12,000	16.00	12,000	16.00	13,000	17.00	7,500	10.00
1911						15,000	20.00		
1925		15,000	20.00	15,000	20.00			10,000	13.30
1926						20,500	27.00		
1946		20,000	26.60			25,500	34.00		
1947								12,500	16.67
1949	100,000	30,000	30.00	22,500	22.50	25,500	25.50	12,500	12.50
1955		35,000	35.00			35,500	35.50	22,500	22.50
1956				25,000	25.00				
1964		43,000	43.00	35,000	35.00	40,000	40.00		
1965								30,000	30.00
1969	200,000	62,500	31.25	60,000	30.00	62,500	31.25	42,500	21.25
1975		65,600	32.80	63,000	31.50	65,600	32.80	44,600	22.30
1976				66,000	33.00	68,800	34.40		
1977		75,000	37.50			75,000	37.50	57,500	28.75
1979		79,125	39.56	69,630	34.82	84,700	42.35	60,662	30.33
1980						92,400	46.20		
1981						96,800	48.40		
1982		91,000	45.50	80,100	40.05	100,700	50.35	69,800[a]	34.90
1984		94,600	47.30	83,300	41.65	104,700	52.35	72,600	36.30
1985		97,900	48.95	86,200	43.10	108,400	54.20	75,100	37.55
1987		115,000	57.50	99,500	49.75	115,000	57.50	89,500	44.75
1990		124,000	62.00	107,300	53.65	124,000	62.00	98,400[a]	49.20
1991		160,600	80.30	138,900	69.45	160,600	80.30	125,100[a]	62.55
1992		166,200	83.10	142,800	71.90	166,200	83.10	129,500	64.75
1993		171,500	85.75	148,400	74.20	171,500	85.75	133,600	66.80

[a] House and Senate salaries varied during these years; the higher salary is used in this table.
Prepared by Sharon Stiver Gressle.

these salaries are directly linked to congressional salaries (after 1994, level II and members of Congress must be at the same rate). Therefore, the executive schedule will always be affected by the perception by members of Congress as to what the electorate will accept.

There are two other types of executive salaries for which there is almost no accountability. Organizations that are statutorily established by or are supported through licensing, user fees, and other types of non-appropriated income have no statutory limits on the salaries that can be paid to the members of their boards of directors or top officials. In a few instances, there is, however, a partial limitation. For example, the executive director of the Tennessee Valley Authority is on the executive schedule while the members of the TVA board of directors are under no limitations. In addition, those organizations that are established by statute, such as the Federal Defense Research Centers, and are funded primarily through long-term project contracts, that is, appropriated funds, have no limit or accountability as to salary and benefit levels.

BIBLIOGRAPHY

Hartman, Robert W., and Arnold R. Weber, eds. *The Rewards of Public Service: Compensating Top Federal Officials.* 1980.

U.S. House of Representatives. Committee on Post Office and Civil Service. *Current Salary Schedules of Federal Officers and Employees Together with a History of Salary and Retirement Annuity Adjustments.* 101st Cong., 2d sess., 1990. Committee Print 101–8.

U.S. President's Panel on Federal Compensation. *Staff Report.* 1976.

SHARON STIVER GRESSLE

SALARIES, PRESIDENTIAL. The President receives an annual taxable salary of $200,000. Also available to the President is an annual taxable expense allowance of $50,000. The compensation levels have been in effect since January 1969.

Although the President is provided with quarters in the WHITE HOUSE, all personal and family expenses are expected to be borne by the President. For example, the food served in the family apartments is billed to the President.

The original salary established for the President in 1789 was $25,000 per annum. Over the course of time, the salary has been increased to the following rates: $50,000 per annum (1873), $75,000 per annum (1909), and, prior to the current rate, $100,000 per annum (1949).

Article II, Section 1, of the U.S. Constitution provides that "The President shall, at stated Times, receive for his Services, a Compensation, which shall neither be encreased nor diminished during the Period for which he shall have been elected, and he shall not receive within that Period any other Emolument from the United States, or any of them." In other words, there cannot be a change in a President's salary during the course of his term of office.

Both Presidents Harry S. Truman and Lyndon B. Johnson were incumbents at the time the acts estab-lishing the 1949 and 1969 increases were signed and they stood to benefit from those changes. However, the acts were effective as of 20 January, Inauguration Day. That met the requirement that the change not come "during the Period for which he shall have been elected." They were each beginning new terms.

With the substantial increases in 1987 and 1991, in salary for the Vice President, Chief Justice, and other top federal officials, coupled with the annual cost-of-living adjustments for those positions, a crisis of some note faced the Congress prior to the 1993 inauguration. The differential between the salary of the President and that of top federal officials had rapidly diminished. In 1789, the First Congress established the salary of the Vice President at 20 percent of that of the President. As of 1 January 1993, the salary of the Vice President was $171,500, or 86 percent of the President's salary. 20 January 1993 or 20 January 1997 would be the only opportunities left in the twentieth century to adjust the President's salary. Given the economic circumstances, the climate was not conducive to a substantial change in the salary rate for the 1993 date. However, if a 3 percent cost-of-living adjustment for the Vice President and other top officials were projected over the course of the following four years, January 1997 would have the salaries of the Vice President, Chief Justice, and Speaker of the House of Representatives within 3.5 percent of that of the President. The cost-of-living adjustments for top officials that went into effect with fair regularity during the 1980s largely contributed to shorter range. The appropriate salary differential between the President and the Vice President and other officials would probably be more than 20 percent and less than 96.5 percent.

The 1969 adjustment followed a suggestion in the 1968 report of the Commission on Executive, Legislative, and Judicial Salaries that the President's salary be increased to $200,000. The 1989 Commission on Executive, Legislative, and Judicial Salaries suggested that the President's salary be increased to $350,000.

The alternative to congressional action on the President's salary would be freezing the salaries of the Vice President and the other top officials. For a year or two, this would be acceptable. Soon thereafter, however, there would be the problem of salary compression on schedules limited by certain officials' salary rates.

[*See also* SALARIES, EXECUTIVE].

BIBLIOGRAPHY

Hartman, Robert W., and Arnold R. Weber, eds. *The Rewards of Public Service: Compensating Top Federal Officials.* 1980.

U.S. House of Representatives. Committee on Post Office and Civil

Service. *Current Salary Schedules of Federal Officers and Employees Together with a History of Salary and Retirement Adjustments.* 101st Cong., 2d sess. 1990. Committee Print 101-8.

SHARON STIVER GRESSLE

SALARIES, VICE PRESIDENTIAL. As of 1 January 1993, the salary of the Vice President of the United States was $171,500. The salary of the Vice President can be adjusted under one of three mechanisms. First, Congress can legislate a change in salary. Second, the salary is eligible for whatever automatic adjustments are made based on changes in the Bureau of Labor Statistics' Employment Cost Index. Third, the Vice President's salary is one of the pay rates studied every fourth fiscal year by the Citizens' Commission on Compensation and Public Service [*see* Quadrennial Salary Commission]. Pursuant to the recommendations of the commission and those of the President and to the approval of the Congress, the salaries within the purview of the commission can be adjusted.

In 1789, the salary of the Vice President was $5,000. That represented 20 percent of the President's salary of $25,000 per annum. As of 1993, the Vice President's salary was over 83 percent of the President's salary of $200,000.

The Vice President is not eligible for a set pension similar to that of the President. However, as president of the Senate, the Vice President is eligible to contribute to the retirement program available to members of Congress. There must be a minimum of five years of service during which contributions were made in order to become vested in the system. A Vice President serving only one term but with other congressional service would likely be eligible for that pension system. The benefits are calculated on the basis of high-three-year average salary, years in service, and level of contribution.

The Vice President may enroll in the Federal Health Benefits Program, which provides family coverage as well. It is a contributory program under which each member may select a specific health plan for coverage. At the discretion of the secretaries of the armed forces, the Vice President and that individual's immediate family may be eligible for care, on a minimal reimbursable basis, in military health care facilities.

Traditionally offices have been maintained for the Vice President both in the Old Executive Office Building and in the U.S. Capitol Building. The Vice President also maintains staff in the Capitol in addition to staff serving in the executive branch.

In 1974 legislation was approved that provided that the former residence of the Chief of Naval Operations on the grounds of the Naval Observatory in Washington, D.C., would be established as the official residence of the Vice President. This action followed decades of discussion as to the advisability of having such a residence and as to the most suitable establishment. Vice President and Mrs. Nelson A. Rockefeller were the first to occupy the house in this capacity, moving there in 1975. The navy is responsible for maintaining and staffing the residence; the Vice President pays for his and his family's food. Private donations were sought during the late 1980s for renovations needed to accommodate the family of Vice President Dan Quayle. They were the first vice presidential family with young children to occupy the residence.

[*See also* SALARIES, EXECUTIVE; SALARIES, PRESIDENTIAL.]

BIBLIOGRAPHY

Hartman, Robert W., and Arnold R. Weber, eds. *The Rewards of Public Service: Compensating Top Federal Officials.* 1980.

U.S. House of Representatives. Committee on Post Office and Civil Service. *Current Salary Schedules of Federal Officials and Employees Together with a History of Salary and Retirement Adjustments.* 101st Cong., 2d sess. 1990. Committee Print 101-8.

President's Panel on Federal Compensation. *Report.* 1975.

SHARON STIVER GRESSLE

SALT (STRATEGIC ARMS LIMITATION TALKS). A series of bilateral (United States–Soviet Union) negotiations aimed at curbing the long-standing, expensive, and dangerous superpower competition in intercontinental-range NUCLEAR WEAPONS, the Strategic Arms Limitation Talks (SALT) were initiated by President Lyndon B. Johnson in 1967. The first round of talks was deferred due to the Soviet invasion of Czechoslovakia in August 1968. President Richard M. Nixon resumed the deliberations, and formal negotiations opened in Helsinki, Finland, on 17 November 1969.

The first series of talks, termed SALT I, lasted for two and a half years and culminated in the signature, by President Nixon and Soviet general secretary Leonid I. Brezhnev, of two major agreements. The ABM (ANTIBALLISTIC MISSILE SYSTEM) TREATY regulated each side's pursuit of defensive systems that could intercept intercontinental ballistic missiles (ICBMs) or submarine-launched ballistic missiles (SLBMs). The Interim Agreement on Strategic Offensive Arms essentially "froze" the size of the two sides' arsenals of ICBMs and SLBMs for a five-year period, during which time the parties were to negotiate a more comprehensive, durable accord to reduce the overall weapons ceilings.

President Gerald Ford continued the SALT negotiations, reaching a major breakthrough at the Vladivostok, U.S.S.R., summit meeting in November 1974. At the summit, the outlines of a SALT II treaty to contain tighter restrictions on strategic offenses were worked out. The negotiations toward a complete accord, however, stretched on well past the original expectations, and the next formal arms reduction treaty was signed by President Jimmy Carter on 18 June 1979. The SALT II treaty capped each country's arsenal at 2,400 weapons (including ICBMs, SLBMs, and heavy bombers), to be reduced to a common ceiling of 2,250 weapons two years later. The SALT II treaty was a massive document, by far the longest and most detailed weapons agreement of its time, and it incorporated unprecedented verification mechanisms to ensure that each country could be confident that its rival was complying with its reciprocal obligations.

The SALT II treaty, however, never entered into force. While the Senate ratification hearings were pending, and as domestic controversy about the agreement was broiling, the Soviet Union invaded Afghanistan, and President Carter requested that the Senate defer its consideration of the pact.

President Ronald Reagan had campaigned against the SALT II treaty, arguing that it was "fatally flawed" and should be superseded by a START (STRATEGIC ARMS REDUCTION TALKS) agreement that would contain "deep cuts" in strategic arsenals, not merely cosmetic controls. Nevertheless, Reagan stated that he would continue to abide by the SALT II standards (as well as by the terms of the SALT I Interim Agreement, which had expired in 1977 but which the parties had continued to honor in the interval), so long as the U.S.S.R. did the same. In 1986, alleging persistent Soviet violations of the SALT accords, President Reagan terminated United States compliance.

The SALT negotiations inaugurated a new era of DETENTE between the United States and the Soviet Union, breaking away from the exchange of ritualistic, empty disarmament proposals that the two sides had exchanged—largely for public relations purposes— throughout the 1950s and 1960s. SALT became the centerpiece of the East-West dialogue, linked to a variety of other bilateral and multilateral issues, such as human rights, relations with African surrogate states, and the Soviet presence in CUBA. Observers disagree about whether the SALT accords actually constrained the two sides' arsenals or whether they simply embodied agreements not to undertake programs that neither country wanted, in any case, to pursue. The ABM treaty, at least, did shut off incipient competition in defensive systems, and the overall ARMS CONTROL process surely resulted in a diminution of tensions, fears, and military expenditures for both protagonists and around the globe.

BIBLIOGRAPHY

Smith, Gerard. *Doubletalk: The Story of SALT I.* 1985.
Talbott, Strobe. *Endgame: The Inside Story of SALT II.* 1979.
U.S. Arms Control and Disarmament Agency. *Arms Control and Disarmament Agreements: Texts and Histories of the Negotiations.* 1990.

DAVID A. KOPLOW

SALUTE, PRESIDENTIAL. Presidents of the United States are customarily honored with a twenty-one gun salute, four drum rolls and flourishes, and band renditions of either the national anthem or "Hail to the Chief" on their arrival, as well as their departure, from ceremonies not held at the White House or away from nation's capital. For ceremonies in Washington, the Presidential Salute Battery, a component of the Third U.S. Infantry ("The Old Guard"), fires twenty-one rounds at five-second intervals from a battery of three cannons. In other locations, the salute is carried out by local military units. A twenty-one gun salute, the highest number of firings given in honor of any American, is also rendered to former Presidents and Presidents-elect, as well as certain visiting dignitaries including a sovereign, a chief of state, and members of a reigning royal family.

Writers have speculated that the twenty-one volley salute, like many American customs, was acquired from the British. The exact origin of the tradition, however, remains shrouded in history, devoid of documentation. Legend has it that a gunfire salute is an ancient ceremony and prior to the War of Independence, the British compelled weaker nations to salute the ships of the Royal Navy when they sailed past foreign military installations. A seven-gun salute was recognized as the British national salute and foreign batteries on shore were obliged to fire three volleys in return for each one of the Royal Navy's seven.

Later, when gunpowder improved and was easier to maintain on a ship, the British sea salute was made equal to the shore salute—twenty-one volleys being the highest national honor. Other nations, however, continued to use a differing number of volleys. Finally, on 18 August 1875, the United States accepted a British proposal that salutes be returned "gun for gun." Subsequently, the international salute of all nations became twenty-one guns.

During the nation's first half century, American Presidents were given the national salute, which consisted of one volley for each state. The number varied from seventeen firings in 1810, when the national salute was first authorized, to twenty-six in 1841, when army regulations permanently set the presidential salute at twenty-one guns. The less famous national salute of the United States, which has always consisted of one volley for each state, now numbers fifty.

BIBLIOGRAPHY

Lovette, Leland P. *Naval Customs, Traditions, and Usage.* 1959.
Mack, William P., and Royal W. Connell. *Naval Ceremonies, Customs, and Traditions.* 1980.
Moss, James A. *Officers' Manual.* 1943.

STEPHEN W. STATHIS

SAVINGS AND LOAN DEBACLE. The savings and loan (S&L) debacle will ultimately involve the failure of roughly fifteen hundred S&Ls and the consequent payout of nearly $200 billion to depositors by the Federal government. The industry's condition arose from regulatory constraints that hampered its response to economic change in the 1960s and 1970s. By the time the constraints were removed, many institutions were insolvent. They continued to operate and generate more losses, however, because of the incentives provided by deposit insurance and the reluctance of the government to close them. Throughout much of the episode, responsibility for the industry was consigned to independent agencies; presidential involvement was largely weak and desultory.

The Savings and Loan Industry. The debacle's roots lay in the NEW DEAL reformulation of the S&L industry. Prior to the reforms of the 1930s, S&L depositors had to wait for their account to mature before they could withdraw their savings. Mortgages were not twenty- to thirty-year loans repaid in even monthly installments; they commonly matured in seven to twelve years, and frequently featured a balloon payment of principal at the end.

Although not faced with depositor runs of the sort experienced by banks, in the early 1930s S&Ls suffered as members withdrew their savings and mortgage holders defaulted on loans. The Federal government intervened in 1932 when President Hoover signed into law the Federal Home Loan Bank System. Initially a facility to provide funds to S&Ls in need of liquidity, the new the Federal Home Loan Bank Board (FHLBB) acquired power to charter and regulate federal S&Ls under the Roosevelt administration in 1933.

Further involvement came with federal deposit insurance. Deposit insurance was the only significant legislation of the hundred days neither requested nor supported by President Roosevelt (enactment of the insurance system for banks in 1933 owed more to Vice President JOHN NANCE GARNER, whose parliamentary maneuvering advanced the legislation in the Senate). When the Federal Savings and Loan Deposit Insurance Corporation (FSLIC) was created in 1934, the independent FHLBB acquired regulatory power over state-chartered institutions that chose to be insured.

Federal and state regulations were stringent. S&Ls were almost exclusively limited to investing in long-term home mortgages. Federally chartered S&Ls were prohibited from issuing mortgages with balloon payments or with variable interest rates. Most of the funds lent by S&Ls were obtained from passbook savings accounts. And in most instances, S&L operations were confined within narrow geographical bounds.

Thus, following the 1930s, S&Ls occupied a protected niche in financial markets. They paid low interest rates on money that could in practice be withdrawn by depositors on demand. They received higher rates on mortgages that took up to thirty years to be repaid. As long as the rate at which they lent exceeded that at which they borrowed, they prospered and grew.

But during the 1960s, interest rates rose in response to the rise in inflation. S&Ls were under pressure to pay higher rates to depositors: if they did not, depositors could take their funds elsewhere. Yet S&L portfolios were full of mortgage loans made when interest rates were lower. Profits began to slip.

Rather than loosen regulatory constraints so the industry could adjust to changing circumstances, the government tightened them. With the backing of the Johnson administration, the Federal Reserve Board (Fed) was authorized in 1966 to limit interest rates paid by S&Ls in the same manner as on banks. This policy kept the rates that S&Ls paid from rising, but caused deposit withdrawals whenever credit markets were tight and rates on alternative investments high.

The incentives created by rising interest rates spawned financial innovations that provided other alternatives for depositors. These alternatives affected not only S&Ls but banks as well. Deposit-taking institutions of all types lost ground within the financial services industry, and S&Ls were locked into a money-losing segment of that declining market.

Interest rates continued to increase through the 1970s. A set of proposals to restructure the industry were advanced by President Nixon in 1973 and President Ford in 1975. Congress rejected both attempts. The FHLBB and the Fed started loosening the regulatory grip on their own, an effort that Congress hindered by adding new interest-rate ceilings and discouraging the FHLBB from permitting federally chartered S&Ls to offer variable-rate mortgages. Also, in 1979 a federal court declared that the regulatory authorities had exceeded their power in loosening controls on the industry; DEREGULATION could not be achieved administratively.

Later in 1979, President Carter proposed deregulating the financial services industry. In 1980, legislation was finally enacted to phase out interest-rate ceilings for all depository institutions. Federal S&Ls were granted limited power to invest in consumer and commercial or business loans, to make residential real estate loans, and to offer credit cards.

Further relief came under President Reagan. In 1982, legislation accelerated the phase-out of interest ceilings. Federally chartered S&Ls were allowed to offer checking accounts, to increase the percentage of their asset holdings in consumer and business loans, and to invest in loans secured by commercial real estate. These actions were supplemented by deregulatory moves of the FHLBB. In addition, several states deregulated state-chartered institutions.

Disintegration and Debacle. Deregulation caused dislocations. The industry had excess capacity, so it had to consolidate. In addition, poor management (a consequence of protection) prevented many S&Ls from adjusting effectively to the rigors of competition. This is typical of deregulated industries. In the case of S&Ls, however, the government stood ready to absorb some of the resulting losses through deposit insurance.

Moreover, deregulation came too late for many S&Ls. Their net worth had already eroded to the point that they were insolvent or nearly so. Thus, by the time they were deregulated, a number of them owed their depositors nearly as much—or more—than they were in turn owed by borrowers. In other industries, firms suffering from similar balance-sheet deterioration would have been forced into bankruptcy court. But deposit insurance—by guaranteeing that depositors would not withdraw their deposits in fear of losing their money—eliminated the market pressures that otherwise would have forced the institutions to close.

Had the government promptly closed them, its losses would have been limited. But instead, the FHLBB engaged in forbearance, the policy of permitting institutions with little (or negative) net worth to operate. Thus, the institutions were bailed out in the sense that a government loan guarantee kept them in business past the time that normal market forces would have closed them down.

Institutions in which there is little net worth are ones in which owners have little left to lose of their original investment. But if big profits can be earned on new lending, the institution can recover and become solvent again. With little or nothing left to lose and everything to gain, ailing S&Ls made risky loans in an attempt to recover solvency. The overall losses inherent in such a strategy were compounded by added susceptibility to fraud. As a result, S&Ls sustained huge loan defaults.

The FHLBB faced a dilemma. Insolvent institutions would incur new losses unless closed. They could not be closed unless money was paid to honor the deposit guarantees. But once losses accumulated, there were not enough funds to honor the guarantees. Although FSLIC was a government-owned corporation whose obligations were not explicitly backed by the "full faith and credit" of the United States, it could not be allowed to default on the guarantees. Deposit insurance is essential for economic stability. A default would have precipitated a financial panic.

In 1986, the Reagan administration proposed that FSLIC borrow $15 billion to be repaid out of higher premiums. The proposal died in the ninety-ninth Congress. The following year, the proposal was taken up again. In 1987, $11 billion was authorized.

Because these funds were inadequate, the losses grew. FSLIC dealt with the problem by disposing of S&Ls in convoluted ways that conserved cash, but added to costs in the longer run. Finally, President Bush proposed to bring the ongoing bailout of the industry to an end with a $50 billion cleanup enacted in 1989.

Even before the legislation was passed, estimates of the approaching cleanup rose above $50 billion. However, the complicated method of financing, necessary for keeping the expenditure off the budget, prevented a larger sum from being substituted. Consequently, to continue the cleanup the Bush administration had to return two times in 1991 for additional funds. In 1992, Congress rejected a new request for more money, leaving the cleanup incomplete and permitting the bailout of some institutions to continue. In 1993 the Clinton administration requested $45 billion to complete the cleanup and capitalize a new insurance fund for S&Ls.

The expensive cleanup finally generated public awareness of the bailout, but the resulting indignation was largely misdirected. The effort to end the bailout was confused with the bailout itself, and the cleanup money was popularly believed to be going to owners and managers of institutions instead of to depositors. The losses were more often blamed on fraud and deregulation rather than on regulation, interest rates, and forbearance.

BIBLIOGRAPHY

Barth, James R. *The Great Savings and Loan Debacle.* 1991.
Kane, Edward J. *The S&L Insurance Mess: How Did It Happen?* 1989.
White, Lawrence J. *The S&L Debacle: Public Policy Lessons for Bank and Thrift Regulation.* 1991.
Woodward, G. Thomas. *Origins and Development of the Savings and Loan Situation.* Congressional Research Service report. 1990.

G. THOMAS WOODWARD

SCHECHTER POULTRY CORP. v. UNITED STATES

295 U.S. 495 (1935). The *Schechter* case tested the validity of the main agency of Franklin D. Roosevelt's program to achieve industrial recovery from the Great Depression. Enacted in the hundred days of 1933, the NATIONAL INDUSTRIAL RECOVERY ACT (NIRA) authorized trade associations to adopt industry-wide agreements (codes) on wages, hours, prices, and trade practices under the supervision of a new government agency, the National Recovery Administration (NRA). The law also sanctioned collective bargaining and authorized huge expenditures for public works.

Though the act gave a temporary lift to the economy, it soon faltered, and Roosevelt, who initially sought to postpone a court test, realized after a time that a number of businesses would defy the government unless the law was legitimated. By happenstance, the critical challenge came not from a major industry but from a relatively minor enterprise. The government charged the Schechter brothers, who ran the second largest kosher poultry operation in Brooklyn, of violating the wages-and-hours provisions of the NRA code and of unfair trade practices. In particular, they were accused of selling thousands of pounds of diseased chickens, a practice that was not only deleterious in itself but that also had an unfortunate economic effect in depressing the chicken market. The Schechters were found guilty and sentenced to brief jail terms. When they appealed, the Second Circuit Court, renowned for the presence of Learned Hand and his brother, Augustus Hand, upheld the conviction on wages-and-hours violations but reversed on trade practices.

On 27 May 1935, a day New Dealers were to call Black Monday, the Supreme Court, in one of three 9 to 0 decisions against the government, struck down the National Industrial Recovery Act. Chief Justice CHARLES EVANS HUGHES denied the government's claim that the emergence of the Great Depression was germane to assessing the validity of the statute and noted that extraconstitutional assertions of power were precluded by the Tenth Amendment. The act, he said, like the section of it that had been struck down in PANAMA REFINING CO. v. RYAN (1935), constituted an improper DELEGATION OF LEGISLATIVE POWER to the executive, for it gave the President "virtually unfettered" discretion to draft what were in essence "penal statutes" and authorized codemakers to "roam at will." Though he did not clearly articulate this concern, the Chief Justice appeared also to have been distressed that the actual decision-making power lay not with the President but with private business groups that were given executive sanction.

Hughes, gratuitously, went on to find the statute invalid for yet another reason: the Live Poultry Code imposed penalties on transactions that were in intrastate commerce, and hence beyond the scope of federal authority. He rejected the government's claim that since nearly all of the poultry reached New York markets from other states, it is interstate commerce, for once the chickens reached the slaughterhouse, they had "come to a permanent rest" within New York State. Nor, he added, could the operations of the Schechters be said to "affect" interstate commerce. Any impact they might have had on interstate commerce, he declared, drawing on a distinction from the opinion in *United States v. E. C. Knight* (1895) was only "indirect," and "if the commerce clause were construed to reach all enterprises and transactions which could be said to have an indirect effect upon interstate commerce, the federal government would embrace practically all the activities of the people."

Justice Benjamin Cardozo, joined by Justice Harlan Fiske Stone, concurred. Unlike the situation in the hot oil case (*Panama*), where, he recalled, he thought the Court had gone "too far," he found the delegation of powers in the live-poultry industry "delegation running riot." There was yet "another objection, far-reaching and incurable," Justice Cardozo added: the national government could not regulate labor in intrastate business, though, unlike Hughes, he acknowledged that "the law is not indifferent to considerations of degree."

The *Schechter* ruling had a devastating impact on Roosevelt and his policies. By obliterating the Recovery Act, it knocked out the centerpiece of Roosevelt's program. Furthermore, Hughes's opinion, in raising more than one constitutional objection, suggested that the Court was determined to be a roadblock to the NEW DEAL, and indicated a conception of the commerce power so circumscribed that it was not clear how much scope for the national government was left. The fact that the decision was unanimous—with even the so-called liberals on the bench in agreement—added to Roosevelt's concern. At a press conference that created a national controversy, the President accused the Court of returning the country to a "horse and buggy" conception of interstate commerce. He was gratified when, two years later, the Court, in *NLRB v. Jones and Laughlin*, without specifically repudiating *Schechter*, adopted a very broad reading of the commerce power that, in essence, repudiated the earlier opinion.

BIBLIOGRAPHY

Hawley, Ellis Wayne. *The New Deal and the Problem of Monopoly*. 1966.

Stern, Robert L. "The Commerce Clause and the National Economy, 1933–1946." *Harvard Law Review* 59 (1946): 645–693.

WILLIAM E. LEUCHTENBURG

SCHEDULE C POSITIONS. A category of positions in the executive branch that are political appointments and thus outside the merit system are called Schedule C positions. In 1952 after twenty years of Democratic control of the presidency, Dwight D. Eisenhower was elected and the REPUBLICAN PARTY returned to power. The Republicans felt that they needed additional leverage to ensure that the executive branch would have control over policy. Their suspicion was that most high-level positions in the Civil Service had been filled by those sympathetic to Democratic policy goals and that the new President needed more flexibility to name loyal Republicans to top posts. On 31 March 1953, therefore, Eisenhower issued Executive Order 10440, establishing a new schedule of positions—Schedule C positions—that would be separate from the regular civil-service merit system. These positions were to be distinguished from Schedule A and Schedule B positions, which were technically outside the merit system though most often filled through merit principles. (Schedule A included positions for which it was not practicable to hold examinations—e.g., seasonal employees and undercover agents as well as lawyers. Schedule B positions, though based on merit, included jobs for which it was impracticable to hold open competitive examinations—for example, student-trainee positions and positions for which professional reputation was an essential prerequisite.) Schedules A and B had included some positions that were in fact presidential political hires. These would now be transferred to the newly established Schedule C.

The justification for Schedule C positions is that an administration needs people who are the President's political partisans in key positions in the bureaucracy. According to chapter 213 of the *Federal Personnel Manual*, Schedule C positions must be "of a confidential or policy-determining character." They must involve "making or approving substantive policy recommendations" or work that can only be done "by someone with a thorough knowledge of and sympathy with the goals, priorities, and preferences of an official who has a confidential or policymaking relationship with the President or the agency head."

During the period immediately following their establishment, Schedule C positions were primarily bureau chiefs and their assistants, general counsels of agencies, directors of information, and heads of major staff units in agencies—that is, those at the higher levels of departments and agencies. But the category also came to include lower-level positions, such as secretaries and chauffeurs, that necessarily had a confidential relationship with political officials.

There were about 870 Schedule C positions in 1953; by 1954, about 1,200. In 1966 President Lyndon Baines Johnson, in Executive Order 11315, separated out the higher-level Schedule C positions by creating Non-career Executive Assignments at GS levels 16 to 18. These later became noncareer SENIOR EXECUTIVE SERVICE positions with the passage of the CIVIL SERVICE REFORM ACT of 1978. In 1968 there were about twelve hundred Schedule C positions (GS 15 and below), and by the 1980s there were about eighteen hundred. The bulk of these were at GS levels 13 to 15 (i.e., middle management). Schedule C positions originally allowed agency heads to make their own choices for major nonpresidential policy appointments in their departments, but in the 1980s the White House took control of many of the Schedule C positions and often presented agency heads with lists of loyal campaign workers for whom jobs were expected to be found.

BIBLIOGRAPHY

Henry, Laurin L. *Presidential Transitions.* 1960.
Rosen, Bernard. *The Merit System in the United States Civil Service.* 1975.
Van Riper, Paul P. *History of the United States Civil Service.* 1958.

JAMES P. PFIFFNER

SCIENCE ADVISER. The institution of the function of science adviser to the U.S. President ranks among the most important innovations in governmental organization. At the first science ministerial of the twenty-four-member Organization for Economic Cooperation and Development in 1962, the United States was the only country to be represented by a full-time science adviser to the head of government. Thirty years later, almost all member countries were represented by science advisers of corresponding rank at the OECD science ministerial meeting in 1992.

Since WORLD WAR II, Presidents recognized the importance of having a science adviser to provide independent advice. President Franklin D. Roosevelt looked to Vannevar Bush as head of the wartime Office of Scientific Research and Development. Following a report by William T. Golden President Truman established the first science advisory mechanism in the EXECUTIVE OFFICE OF THE PRESIDENT (EOP) with a science advisory committee reporting to the President through the Director of the Office of Defense Mobilization (ODM). Its chairman, Oliver Buckley, also had direct access to the President, although he seldom used such access. This arrangement was continued during the first Eisenhower Administration, when Lee A. DuBridge and Isidor I. Rabi served as part-time chairmen.

The launching of Sputnik in 1957 moved President Eisenhower to recognize the need for independent counsel in matters involving science-and-technology. Such an adviser would work with senior White House staff groups to handle science-and-technology issues relating to policy and program priorities and budgetary choices and mobilize the best science-and-technology expertise in support of presidential decision making.

President Eisenhower elevated the ODM Science Advisory Committee (chaired by the science adviser) to report directly to him. He sought its advice in responding to Sputnik and to the competing proposals of the military services. The adviser and the President's Science Advisory Committee (PSAC) played a key role in the organization of the National Aeronautics and Space Administration, the Arms Control and Disarmament Agency, and the establishment of the Director of Defense Research and Engineering and the Advanced Research Projects Agency in the DEPARTMENT OF DEFENSE. They advised on crucial questions regarding technical intelligence and the possibilities for a nuclear-test ban.

President Kennedy institutionalized the presidential science-advisory function by establishing the Office of Science and Technology (OST) in the EOP, adding the title of Director of OST to that of Special Assistant to the President. The portfolio of his science adviser, Jerome B. Wiesner, was broadened to include health, civilian science and technology, and the environment.

During the Johnson and Nixon administrations, the science adviser was deeply involved in national-security issues particularly as related to the VIETNAM WAR, ARMS CONTROL, and the treaty to eliminate biological weapons. After his reelection in 1972, President Nixon abolished both OST and PSAC, an action attributed to opposition by PSAC members to the President's positions on ballistic missile defense and the development of the supersonic transport, as well as the general disaffection of the academic community toward the Vietnam War. The science adviser's duties were added to those of the director of the National Science Foundation, who concentrated on energy research and development, industrial research and development, and agricultural research.

The OST function was resurrected in the EOP by an act of Congress in 1976 in the form of the OFFICE OF SCIENCE AND TECHNOLOGY POLICY, and President Ford reestablished the position of Special Assistant to the President for S&T. President Carter's science adviser dealt with questions such as the MX missile, the test ban, space policy, and air quality standards. President Reagan's advisers addressed issues concerning support of basic research, the aerospace plane, Stealth technology, and the Strategic Defense Initiative.

President Bush elevated the position to CABINET rank as Assistant to the President for S&T. Bush reestablished the science advisory committee as the President's Council of Advisers on Science and Technology (PCAST). His science advisor, D. Allan Bromley was instrumental in revitalizing the Federal Coordinating Council for Science and technology, in framing national technology policies, and in forging governmentwide research-and-development programs having presidential priority, including high-performance computing, global climate change, advanced materials, and biotechnology. In the Clinton administration, the importance of the science-advisory role was signified by the appointment of the science adviser very early in the administration at the same time as the appointment of Cabinet officers.

Although the science adviser's role as a senior member of the presidential staff was firmly reinforced during the Bush administration, the vicissitudes in science advising during the past fifty years underscore the fragility of the function and its critical dependence on the direct interest and involvement of the President.

[See also SCIENCE POLICY.]

Science Advisers

President	Science Adviser
33 Truman	Oliver E. Buckley, 1951–1952
	Lee A. DuBridge, 1952–1953
34 Eisenhower	Lee A. DuBridge, 1953–1956
	Isidor I. Rabi, 1956–1957
	James R. Killian, Jr., 1957–1959
	George B. Kistiakowsky, 1959–1961
35 Kennedy	Jerome B. Wiesner, 1961–1963
36 L. B. Johnson	Jerome B. Wiesner, 1963–1964
	Donald F. Hornig, 1964–1969
37 Nixon	Lee A. DuBridge, 1969–1970
	Edward E. David, Jr., 1970–1973
	H. Guyford Stever, 1973–1974
38 Ford	H. Guyford Stever, 1974–1976
39 Carter	Frank Press, 1977–1981
40 Reagan	George A. Keyworth II, 1981–1986
	John P. McTague, 1986
	William R. Graham, 1987–1989
41 Bush	D. Allan Bromley, 1989–1993
42 Clinton	John H. Gibbons, 1993–

BIBLIOGRAPHY

Beckler, David Z. "A Decision Maker's Guide to Science Advising." In *Worldwide Science and Technology Advice to the Highest Levels of Governments.* Edited by William T. Golden. 1991.

Bronk, Detlev W. "Science Advice in the White House: The Genesis of the President's Science Advisers and the National Science Foundation." *Science* 186 (11 October 1974): 116-121. Reprinted in *Science Advice to the President*. Edited by William T. Golden. 2d ed. Forthcoming.

Golden, William T., ed. *Science and Technology Advice to the President, Congress, and Judiciary*. 2d ed. Forthcoming.

Killian, James R. *Sputnik, Scientists, and Eisenhower*. 1977.

Kistiakowsky, George B. *A Scientist at the White House*. 1976.

Wiesner, Jerome. *Where Science and Politics Meet*. 1965.

DAVID Z. BECKLER and WILLIAM T. GOLDEN

SCIENCE POLICY. The earliest expression of national science policy is contained in Article I, Section 8, of the Constitution, which established the patent system "to advance the Progress of Science and the useful Arts." Its underlying objectives were to encourage invention for economic development and to promote scientific and technical advance through public disclosure.

The term *science policy* is sometimes used as shorthand for science-and-technology policy, particularly in Western European countries. Thus, the President's Science Advisory Committee (PSAC), which existed from 1957 to 1972, dealt with technology policy as well as science policy. It was reconstituted by President Bush in 1969 with a new name, the President's Council of Advisers on Science and Technology. On the other hand, the Assistant to the President for Science and Technology is commonly referred to as the President's SCIENCE ADVISER.

There is no single, comprehensive U.S. science policy, but presidential policymaking attempts to interrelate and balance the various science-policy objectives in the overall national interest. National science policies are usually expressed indirectly through budgetary and other concrete measures that reflect presidential objectives tempered by congressional actions and initiatives. An exception is the statement of national policy for science and technology included in the National Science, Engineering, and Technology Policy and Priorities Act of 1976, which established the OF-FICE OF SCIENCE AND TECHNOLOGY POLICY (OSTP) in the EXECUTIVE OFFICE OF THE PRESIDENT (EOP). This policy declaration per se has made little imprint on federal science-and-technology programs and policies.

Although science policy and technology policy are closely interrelated, there are important differences. For example, policies designed to assure a strong academic science and manpower base—called policies for science—are different from policies to promote technological development for economic, NATIONAL SE-CURITY, energy, space, health care, and other objectives—called science in policy.

The most enduring science-and-technology policies are embodied in legislation establishing government institutions. During the first hundred years of the Republic, government policy for the support of science and technology was institutionalized in the creation of federal departments and agencies authorized to support research and development in carrying out their missions, such as the War and Navy departments, the Public Health Service, the Geological Survey, the Agricultural Research Service, and the National Bureau of Standards.

The institutionalization of federal science-and-technology policy intensified after WORLD WAR II with the establishment of the National Science Foundation, the National Institutes of Health, the ATOMIC ENERGY COMMISSION, the National Aeronautics and Space Administration, the Defence Advanced Research Projects Agency, and the Environmental Protection Agency. A pluralistic approach in supporting research and development was a deliberate science-and-technology policy. Pluralism has been viewed as a source of strength in concentrating science-and-technology efforts to achieve specific objectives and in mobilizing public support for federal investments in research and development. However, the resulting policy and program fragmentation complicates the task of framing coherent science-and-technology policies that transcend individual departmental and agency missions.

Wars have led to major changes in national science policy. The National Academy of Sciences was established by congressional charter in 1862 in response to a need to reach outside of government for science advice during the CIVIL WAR. The need for systematic, broad-based scientific advice during WORLD WAR I resulted in the organization of the National Research Council as the operating arm of the National Academy of Sciences. The Office of Scientific Research and Development was established in the EOP in 1942 to mobilize the nation's best scientists and engineers and research teams in World War II.

The war and its aftermath fundamentally altered U.S. science and technology policy in two significant respects. First, it forged a new relationship between the federal government and the scientific community that was essential to marshal the nation's most advanced science-and-technology capabilities in support of the war effort. The new partnership between grassroots scientists and engineers and the federal bureaucracy induced a sea change in the process of formulating national science policies that influenced postwar national-security policies and the growth of science-based industries. Second, the war established a publicly accepted rationale for federal support of basic scientific research. It was recognized that the successful development of nuclear and other sophisticated weapons depended on European advances in fundamental scientific research, a dangerous dependency for the United States. Vannevar Bush's *Science: the Endless Frontier* (1945) helped legitimize the role of the federal government in supporting university-based scientific research and led to the creation of the National Science Foundation in 1950.

The new relationship between science and government during the war shaped the postwar presidential science advisory structure and the formal incorporation of outside scientific and technical advice in presidential policy-making. This was an innovation in government organization of historic dimensions, bringing directly to the office of the President the views and policy recommendations of grass-roots scientists, engineers, and technologists in the front ranks of their peers.

The KOREAN WAR prompted President Truman's decision to establish a science advisory committee and science adviser as recommended in a report to him by William T. Golden. Because of its emphasis on the national-security aspects of science-and-technology policies, it was decided that the committee should report to the President primarily, but not exclusively, through the Director of the Office of Defense Mobilization (ODM). Prepared at President Eisenhower's request, the committee's landmark report to the NATIONAL SECURITY COUNCIL (NSC), " Meeting the Threat of Surprise Attack," caused a profound review of the military-strategic relationships between the United States and the Soviet Union. The report also resulted in new policies and programs to maintain American readiness and military superiority, including the unprecedented NSC decision to accord highest national priority to the development of the intercontinental ballistic missile.

Moved by public concern over the launching of Sputnik in 1957, President Eisenhower transformed the ODM Science Advisory Committee into the President's Science Advisory Committee and appointed a full-time Special Assistant to the President for Science and Technology on the WHITE HOUSE STAFF, as advocated in the 1950 Golden report to President Truman. The Science Advisory Committee recommended the creation of a civilian-based space agency, building on the outstanding capabilities of the National Advisory Committee for Aeronautics. Its involvement in the nuclear-test ban issue led to the establishment of the ARMS CONTROL AND DISARMAMENT AGENCY and to the atmospheric test-ban treaty. In the late 1960s the committee provided the technical assessment that prompted President Nixon's initiative for a worldwide ban on biological warfare.

Earlier preoccupation with the national-security dimensions of science-and-technology policy gradually gave way to other science-policy concerns. Although science-and-technology-related national-security issues held center stage during the VIETNAM WAR, from the mid 1960s, policies for preserving environmental quality, strengthening biomedical research, achieving energy independence, and improving science education moved closer to the center. The White House science advisory structure was terminated by President Nixon in 1972, and the responsibilities of presidential science adviser were delegated to the Director of the National Science Foundation. The science advisory structure reemerged in 1976 by legislative action that established the Office of Science and Technology Policy in the EOP and by the appointment by President Ford of a full-time Special Assistant to the President for Science and Technology. However, the President's Science Advisory Committee (PSAC) was not reinstated as a continuing advisory mechanism.

After 1976, White House science-and-technology-policy advisers turned their attention to the domestic and international concerns that persisted into the 1990s. With the brief exception of SDI (STRATEGIC DEFENSE INITIATIVE), the national-security-policy function of the science-advisory mechanism was largely curtailed after the demise of PSAC. With the end of the COLD WAR, the function could reemerge with different objectives. Science-and-technology policies played an important role in moving toward a single national science-and-technology base that can serve both national-security and domestic purposes.

The appointment of the President's Council of Advisers on Science and Technology (PSAC by a different name) by President Bush in 1989 returned the science-policy apparatus to its original structure, but with a different policy agenda for the science adviser. Foremost were science-and-technology policies and programs to deal with the weakening of international competitiveness of American high-technology companies and environmental deterioration on a global as well as a local scale. The need to integrate policies for science and technology into a broad array of national policies (including economic, regulatory, trade, international, and other policies) became more pressing and difficult for a science-and-technology advisory mechanism primarily concerned with federal research-and-development programs. Technology policy became a captive of ideological differences and embroiled in unenlightened debates over "industrial policy" and "picking winners," despite the first White House statement of federal technology policy and the science adviser's success in defending government support of generic and precompetitive research. The large federal deficit and severe constraints on discretionary funding (including a large component of research and development) evoked calls for setting priorities for research and development including striking a balance between large scientific programs and facilities and supporting investigator-initiated research projects. The strong ties between the federal government and the great research universities, envisaged by the Vannevar Bush report and cemented by the National Science Foundation, weakened in the face of financial constraints and political pressures for selective support, and by concerns about charges for overhead costs of conducting federally financed research.

Science-and-technology policy was at a crossroads at the end of 1992. While aimed at preserving and enhancing the strength of American science and technology, it was increasingly recognized that such policies must be more fully integrated with other national policies to achieve long-range national goals and objectives. The Clinton administration has given unprecedented political emphasis to technology policy as a prime mover for economic growth and job creation. This requires a new level of analytical skill and ability to communicate among economists, social scientists, legal and other professions, and the public at large.

BIBLIOGRAPHY

Beckler, David. "The Precarious Life of Science in the White House." *Daedalus* (Summer 1974): 115–134.

Bush, Vannevar. *Science: the Endless Frontier.* 1945.

Dupree, Hunter. *Science in the Federal Government: A History of Policies and Activities to 1940.* 1957.

Golden, William T. *Government Military-Scientific Research: Review for the President of the United States, 1950–51.* Typescript. 1951. Basic documents including precept, report, and memoranda, including interviews with about 150 appropriate individuals.

Herken, Gregg. *Cardinal Choices: Presidential Science Advising from the Atomic Bomb to SDI.* 1992.

Stein, Jeffrey. *A History of Science Policy in the United States, 1940–1985.* Report prepared for the Task Force on Science Policy, Committee on Science and Technology, U.S. House of Representatives. 1986.

DAVID Z. BECKLER and WILLIAM T. GOLDEN

SCOTT, WINFIELD (1786–1866), military officer, Whig presidential nominee in 1852. A Virginia lawyer, Scott entered the army in 1809. During the WAR OF 1812 he was captured once, wounded in battle, and had two horses killed under him. He began the war as a lieutenant-colonel and ended as a brevetted major-general and a national hero. After the war Scott saw action in various INDIAN campaigns. In the 1830s he personally represented President Jackson in South Carolina during the NULLIFICATION controversy, organized the Cherokee removal, and acted as a diplomat and negotiator in avoiding a war on the Maine-Canada border. In 1841 he became general-in-chief of the army.

WHIG PARTY politicians began to consider Scott for the presidency starting in 1839. He was a famous war hero with political and diplomatic skills and no obvious political enemies. He was also a southerner who had lived in the North.

When the MEXICAN WAR began Scott made Zachary Taylor the senior field commander. Taylor's success was mixed; he won battles, but seemed unable to win the war fast enough to suit President Polk. Polk was loath to give Scott any direct role in the fighting because he did not want to enhance Scott's presidential prospects for 1848. Polk wanted to send a reliable Democrat to Mexico and even attempted to create a rank above Scott's, to be filled by Senator Thomas Hart Benton. This plan failed mostly because Benton had no military experience. In November 1846 Polk reluctantly sent Scott to the front, accompanied by a group of political generals—all loyal Democrats. In March Scott landed in Veracruz. By mid September Scott had led the army in a series of victories, culminating with the capture of Mexico City. Despite these victories Polk and the Democratic general Gideon J. Pillow undermined Scott's record. Scott took a short leave from the army and by the time Scott's name was cleared, and the country aware of the honors he deserved, General Taylor had the Whig presidential locked up. By 1852 Scott's reputation was restored and he had been promoted to lieutenant general, a rank previously held only by George Washington.

In the 1852 Whig convention President Millard Fillmore initially received all but one of the southern votes, Scott carried the Mid-Atlantic states and the Midwest, and DANIEL WEBSTER had a smattering of votes, mostly from New England. The northerners, Webster and Fillmore, supported the COMPROMISE OF 1850, including the Fugitive Slave Law. Scott, the southerner, was supported by the antislavery wing of the party, led by WILLIAM H. SEWARD. Voting began on a Friday night and ended the following Monday, when Scott received the nomination on the fifty-third ballot. Scott was saddled with a platform that thoroughly endorsed the Compromise of 1850; the Whig Party was saddled with a political novice too independent to take advice from party leaders. The party was deeply divided over SLAVERY, the Compromise of 1850, and personal enmity among the leaders and their followers. In the general election Franklin Pierce carried all but four states and virtually destroyed the Whig Party. Scott was that party's last national candidate.

After the election Scott remained in the army. In 1857 he fruitlessly opposed the Mormon War of 1857 and in 1859 he traveled to the West Coast and effectively negotiated with Britain over border disputes in the Northwest. During the secession winter of 1860–1861 he unsuccessfully urged President James Buchanan to reinforce southern forts. When Abraham Lincoln came into office Scott helped organize the defenses of Washington. Despite his Virginia origins, Scott remained loyal to his uniform and country. Scott's plan for defeating the Confederacy—the Anaconda plan—called for massive troops and a slow, methodical squeezing of the rebel states. In the spring of 1861 this plan was politically unthinkable. Lincoln turned to younger generals, with unrealistic notions of quickly seizing Richmond and ending the war. Scott opposed the early attack on Virginia, which resulted in the Union rout at First Manassas. Yet, even that defeat might have been avoided if the field commanders had followed Scott's orders and plans. In the panic that followed the battle, Scott remained calm, issuing orders and reorganizing defenses. As he had been doing since Lincoln took office, Scott worked twelve to fourteen hours daily, creating and saving the army. In October the seventy-five-year-old Scott resigned, leaving the war to younger men, who ignored his advice and plans. Ironically, Union victory was achieved only when Lincoln, Grant, and Sherman began to adopt Scott's overall strategy for the war.

BIBLIOGRAPHY

Elliott, Charles Winslow. *Winfield Scott: The Soldier and the Man.* 1937.

Smith, Arthur D. Howden. *Old Fuss and Feathers: The Life and Exploits of Lt-General Winfield Scott.* 1937.

PAUL FINKELMAN

SDI (STRATEGIC DEFENSE INITIATIVE).

A military research and development program inaugurated by President Ronald Reagan on 23 March 1983, the Strategic Defense Initiative (SDI) was an effort to move beyond the traditional strategic doctrine of deterrence through "mutual assured destruction" that dominated United States–Soviet Union relations throughout most of the COLD WAR. Under Reagan's original vision, SDI would seek to develop a

shield against incoming missiles that would render an attacker's warheads "impotent and obsolete." Opponents in Congress and elsewhere quickly criticized the revolutionary idea as impractical, wasteful, and destabilizing and attached the enduring label "Star Wars" to the program.

SDI greatly expanded the preexisting research program into defensive technologies, which had been permitted under the 1972 ABM (ANTIBALLISTIC MISSILE SYSTEM) TREATY. Annual funding rose to approximately $4 billion throughout the 1980s and early 1990s, although each year legislators fought a pitched battle with DEPARTMENT OF DEFENSE officials regarding program funding and limitations.

A variety of candidate technologies was investigated for performance of the antiballistic missile mission. Many of the early proposals were space-based, envisioning a swarm of predatory satellites that could stay passively in orbit for years and suddenly activate during a missile attack, firing bursts of high-energy lasers or subatomic particles at attacking missiles while they were still in outer space, far from American territory.

These space-based versions of SDI were especially controversial because of their enormous costs and problematic legality. Estimates typically ranged upwards of $100 billion for the complete system, and even then there were doubts about the technology's ability to accomplish the several significant, unprecedented tasks simultaneously. Many of these satellite versions of SDI would have relied on nuclear explosions outside the atmosphere, in violation of the Outer Space treaty (1967) and the Limited Test Ban treaty (1963). Moreover, the traditional understanding of the ABM treaty was much less permissive regarding development and testing of mobile or space-based defensive systems as compared to fixed, ground-based hardware. The Reagan administration then propounded a "new interpretation" of the ABM treaty to attempt to legalize more advanced work on space interceptors, but this effort at TREATY REINTERPRETATION generated its own political maelstrom.

Other versions of SDI largely abandoned the reliance on such exotic technology, focusing instead on advanced versions of familiar kinetic-energy projectiles, such as miniature land-based interceptor missiles. Even these more modest efforts were highly controversial and technologically problematic. Development schedules repeatedly stretched out, cost estimates inexorably rose, and the ultimate goals of the program were scaled back.

Support for the notion of ballistic-missile defense received a significant boost during the 1991 GULF WAR, with the apparent success of American Patriot missiles in destroying Iraqi Scud missiles. Critics, however, asserted that the actual interception ratio of the Patriot system had been greatly overstated and that, in any case, the task of negating a few slow, obsolescent Iraqi Scuds was incommensurately different from the original SDI assignment of precluding a well-timed, coordinated massive onslaught of state-of-the-art ICBMs.

BIBLIOGRAPHY

Boffey, Philip M., William J. Broad, Leslie Gelb, Charles Mohr, and Holcomb B. Noble. *Claiming the Heavens.* 1988.
Simon, Jeffrey, ed. *Security Implications of SDI: Will We Be More Secure in 2010?* 1990.
U.S. Congress. Office of Technology Assessment. *Ballistic Missile Defense Technologies.* 1985.

DAVID A. KOPLOW

SEAL, PRESIDENTIAL. The use and design of the seal of the President of the United States, unlike those of most U.S. government seals, owes more to custom and tradition than law. Although the early history of the seal remains obscure, it is known that American Chief Executives at least since Millard Fillmore have apparently used such a device.

Fillmore's seal was made by Edward Stabler, a Sandy Spring, Maryland, steel engraver, from a crude sketch drawn by the President. An actual impression of the 1850 seal created by Stabler has not survived. Neither has the die been found of the subsequent seal, the coat of arms of which was used until 1945. Heraldic scholars, however, have determined that this second seal bore the device of the coat of arms used for the first time shortly after Rutherford B. Hayes's inauguration in March 1877.

Hayes's coat of arms consisted of an eagle facing to its left with its wings raised. Arranged between the eagle's wings at the highest point was an arc of cloud puffs, below which were seven stars arranged in a curved line, followed by a single segment of scroll on which *E Pluribus Unum* was inscribed in plain roman capital letters directly above the eagle's head. Six more stars were arranged behind the eagle's head. The eagle's talons grasped thirteen arrows and an olive branch.

Exactly when the encircling legend, "Seal of the President of the United States," was added is not clear, but it probably dates from at least the late 1880s. Also late in the nineteenth century, the arc of stars was expanded from seven to nine and four more stars were placed behind the eagle's head.

An EXECUTIVE ORDER signed by President Harry S. Truman on 25 October 1945 changed the design of the presidential seal so that the eagle's head faced toward its right rather than its left. This change was apparently made so the seal would conform to heraldic custom. President Truman also decided that the eagle on the seal should be in the bird's natural colors rather than white, and placed a simple circle of forty-eight stars around the coat of arms.

President Dwight Eisenhower, in 1959 and 1960 executive orders, added two additional stars to the circle surrounding the coat of arms to reflect the admission of Alaska and Hawaii as states. A 1972 executive order, signed by President Richard M. Nixon, detailed rules governing the use of the seal. Further clarification of the rules was provided by President Gerald B. Ford in a 1976 executive order.

BIBLIOGRAPHY

Patterson, Richard S., and Richardson Dougall. *The Eagle and the Shield.* 1976.

STEPHEN W. STATHIS

SEATO TREATY. The Southeast Asia Collective Defense Treaty entered into force on 19 February 1955. Southeast Asia Treaty Organization (SEATO) members included the United States, Australia, France, New Zealand, Pakistan, the PHILIPPINES, Thailand, and the United Kingdom. Article IV provides that each party recognizes that armed aggression in the treaty area against any of the parties that "would endanger its own peace and safety, and agrees that it will in that event act to meet the common danger in accordance with its constitutional processes." Measures taken under that article shall be immediately reported to the Security Council of the UNITED NATIONS.

The SEATO Treaty, like other Pacific-area MUTUAL SECURITY TREATIES ratified over the previous thirty years, did not provide that an attack on one party was to be regarded as an attack on all. Secretary of State DEAN ACHESON reported to President Dwight D. Eisenhower that the treaty language "leaves to the judgment of each country the type of action to be taken in the event an armed attack occurs. There is, of course, a wide range of defensive measures which might be appropriate depending upon the circumstances." Eisenhower transmitted Acheson's report to the Senate. In executive session hearings before the Senate Foreign Relations Committee, Secretary of State JOHN FOSTER DULLES (Acheson's successor) explained why the Pacific-area treaties did not contain the provision present in the NATO TREATY and RIO TREATY to the effect that an attack on one was to be regarded as an attack on all. That language, Dulles said, had created "doubts and uncertainties" concerning the treaties' "constitutional effect." Moreover, he explained that the treaty created an obligation for consultation but not an obligation for action. During floor debate, Senator Walter George said that the treaty left "no doubt that the constitutional powers of the Congress and the President are exactly where they stood before." The treaty, George said, "has no effect whatsoever on the thorny question of whether, how, and under what circumstances the President might involve the United States in warfare without the approval of Congress." The United States is not automatically obligated to provide military force in the event of an armed attack. No significant discussion of the issue occurred.

BIBLIOGRAPHY

Glennon, Michael J. *Constitutional Diplomacy.* 1990.
Glennon, Michael J. "United States Mutual Security Treaties: The Commitment Myth." *Columbia Journal of Transnational Law* 24 (1986): 509–552.

MICHAEL J. GLENNON

SECESSION. After the election of Abraham Lincoln as the first Republican President on 5 November 1860, several southern states moved to secede from the Union between 20 December 1860 and 21 May 1861. Secessionist theories had arisen early in American history and could be plausibly associated with founders as prominent as Thomas Jefferson. By 1860 the doctrine, as enunciated by Virginia Senator James M. Mason, stated that

> our Federal system was a confederation of sovereign powers, not a consolidation of States into one people, and, as a consequence, whenever a State considered the compact broken, and in a manner to endanger her safety, such State stood remitted, as in sovereign right, to determine for herself . . . both the mode and measure of redress.

The extended debate over the subject had made clear how to proceed: states, claiming original sovereignty that was never surrendered, would call conventions of the people to enact secession.

The South Carolina legislature announced popular elections for a state convention within a week of hearing the election results, and the delegates chosen unanimously passed a secession ordinance on 20 December. Mississippi seceded on 9 January, Florida on 10 January, Alabama on 11 January, Georgia on 19 January, and Louisiana on 26 January. The Texas state convention passed a secession ordinance on 1 February, but submitted it to a referendum on 23

February, at which time it passed 44,317 to 13,020. Virginia's and Arkansas's conventions were dominated by antisecessionists, and North Carolina and Tennessee at first rejected the idea of holding conventions.

Grounds for resistance had been well articulated by President Andrew Jackson in his Proclamation on NULLIFICATION of 10 December 1832. In preparing his inaugural address of 4 March 1861, Lincoln apparently consulted that document along with the Constitution, DANIEL WEBSTER's Reply to Hayne, and HENRY CLAY's famous speech on the COMPROMISE OF 1850. Lincoln declared: "I hold, that in contemplation of universal law, and of the Constitution, the Union of these States is perpetual. Perpetuity is implied, if not expressed, in the fundamental law of all national governments. It is safe to assert that no government proper, ever had a provision in its organic law for its own termination."

"Descending" from such "general principles," Lincoln argued that "in legal contemplation, the Union is perpetual." It was

> much older than the Constitution. It was formed in fact, by the Articles of Association in 1774. . . . matured and continued by the Declaration of Independence in 1776. . . . further matured and the faith of all the then thirteen States expressly plighted and enjoined, that it should be perpetual, by the Articles of Confederation in 1778. . . . And finally, in 1787, one of the declared objects for ordaining and establishing the Constitution, was "to form a more perfect union."

Lincoln added practical arguments as well. "Plainly," he said,

> the central idea of secession, is the essence of anarchy. A majority, held in restraint by constitutional checks, and limitations, and always changing easily, with deliberate changes of popular opinions and sentiments, is the only true sovereign of a free people. . . . Unanimity is impossible; the rule of a minority, as a permanent arrangement, is wholly inadmissible; so that, rejecting the majority principle, anarchy, or despotism in some form is all that is left.

After the fall of Fort Sumter and the President's proclamation of 15 April, calling for 75,000 men to "suppress" the insurrection, Virginia seceded on 17 April (a 23 May referendum approved 96,750 to 32,134), followed by Arkansas and Tennessee on 6 May (a Tennessee referendum on 8 June went 104,913 for and 47,238 against), and North Carolina on 20 May. All the states acted through special conventions except Tennessee, whose secession ordinance was an act of the legislature.

In his message to the special session of Congress convened on 4 July 1861, Lincoln said, "It may well be questioned whether there is, to-day, a majority of the legally qualified voters of any State, except perhaps South Carolina, in favor of disunion." This statement could hardly have been true: qualified voters elected secessionist majorities to the Deep South conventions; Texas's secession was approved by a vote of the people; and more recent events drove four more states out.

Still, Lincoln's idea had power, and historians to this day debate the depth of popularity for secession, the social forces behind the movement, and the psychological state of southern public opinion after Lincoln's election.

BIBLIOGRAPHY

Carpenter, Jesse T. *The South as a Conscious Minority, 1789–1861: A Study in Political Thought.* 1930.
Stampp, Kenneth M. "The Concept of a Perpetual Union." In *The Imperiled Union: Essays on the Background of the Civil War.* 1980.
Wooster, Ralph A. *The Secession Conventions of the South.* 1962.

MARK E. NEELY, JR.

SECRET AGENTS. See PRIVATE ENVOYS.

SECRET SERVICE. The United States Secret Service, now well known for its function of PROTECTION OF PRESIDENTS, originated as a small anticounterfeiting organization in the DEPARTMENT OF THE TREASURY near the end of the CIVIL WAR. It was established by Secretary of the Treasury Hugh McCulloch on 5 July 1865, based on an earlier decision made at the last CABINET meeting held by Abraham Lincoln.

From extremely modest origins, the Secret Service has grown to an organization of 4,600 employees with a budget of $475 million (in fiscal year 1992). In addition to anticounterfeiting, it is responsible for detecting and suppressing forgery and for investigating frauds connected with Treasury electronic funds transfers, credit cards, computer access, and federally insured financial institutions. Its protective duties, which started a century ago, were initially either authorized by the Secretary of the Treasury or acquired directly on an ad hoc basis at the request of Presidents or their advisers. The specific assignments were ratified in annual appropriations acts usually only after the detail was already in place. These short-term arrangements were finally given statutory permanency in 1951, when Congress first codified the service's authority (18 U.S.C. 3056).

Secret Service protection of the President and others began with President Grover Cleveland and his family in 1894. The service acquired this responsibility in part because of its nationwide investigative and intelligence-gathering capability and the absence of competing organizations at the time (a Bureau of Investigation, for instance, did not exist in the DEPARTMENT OF JUSTICE until 1908). Presidential protection was regularized for Theodore Roosevelt following the assassination of William McKinley in 1901 and was first given statutory recognition in 1906.

The protective assignments, which have been added piecemeal over the years, now include: the Vice President (or other officer next in order of succession if the vice presidency is vacant); the President's and Vice President's immediate families; President-elect and Vice President–elect and their immediate families; major candidates for the presidency and vice presidency (and their spouses within 120 days of the election); and former Presidents, their spouses (until remarriage), and their minor children (until the age of sixteen). In addition, the service provides security for visiting heads of foreign states or governments (and their spouses) and other distinguished visitors as well as official representatives of the United States performing special missions abroad.

As part of the Secret Service, the Uniformed Division—which superseded the Executive Protective Service and its predecessor, the White House Police—has its own protective mandate in public law (2 U.S.C. 202). It is charged with protecting the President, Vice President, and members of their immediate families; the WHITE HOUSE and any building in which presidential offices are located; the Vice President's official residence; the Treasury building and grounds; and foreign diplomatic missions located in the Washington, D.C., metropolitan area.

Collectively, these protective assignments account for an estimated 40 percent of the Secret Service's budget in most years, rising to about 60 percent during presidential election years, when the number of protectees and extent of security details increase substantially.

BIBLIOGRAPHY

Bowen, Walter S., and Harry Edward Neal. *The United States Secret Service.* 1960.
Jeffreys-Jones, Rhodri. *American Espionage: From Secret Service to CIA.* 1977.
Kaiser, Frederick M. "Origins of Secret Service Protection of the President." *Presidential Studies Quarterly* 18 (1988): 101–127.
U.S. President's Commission on the Assassination of President John F. Kennedy (Warren Commission). *Report.* 1964.
U.S. Secret Service. *Moments in History, 1865–1990.* 1990.

FREDERICK M. KAISER

SECURITY CLEARANCES. Security clearances, held by about 3.2 million federal and private-sector contract employees, are used to determine whether an employee is "reliable, trustworthy, of good conduct and character, and of complete and unswerving loyalty to the United States" (Executive Order 10450). The appropriate level of clearance, along with an official need to know certain information, is required to gain access to NATIONAL SECURITY information classified at the confidential, secret, or top-secret level. The employing agency adjudicates the clearance, that is, it judges whether an applicant or employee meets the criteria and standards. The determination is based on a check of federal-agency records and, for higher levels, a background investigation (or periodic reinvestigation for already cleared employees).

The security clearance program—a fragmented system with authority dispersed among agencies and decentralized within them—is still governed for the most part by EXECUTIVE ORDERS issued by President Dwight D. Eisenhower. The Supreme Court affirmed the President's inherent authority to control such access in 1988. The majority opinion in *Navy v. Egan* noted that the "President, after all, is the 'COMMANDER IN CHIEF of the Army and Navy of the United States.' . . . His authority to classify and control access to information bearing on national security and to determine whether an individual is sufficiently trustworthy . . . flows primarily from this constitutional investment of power in the President."

Executive Order 10450 on "Security Requirements for Government Employment," issued by President Eisenhower in 1953, covers direct employees of the government. Under it, the OFFICE OF PERSONNEL MANAGEMENT (OPM), the successor to the Civil Service Commission, is the lead agency for conducting background investigations for the competitive CIVIL SERVICE. OPM also has government-side policy-making and oversight responsibilities under the order. The employing agency is the lead for conducting background investigations for personnel in the excepted service, such as agents in the CENTRAL INTELLIGENCE AGENCY and FEDERAL BUREAU OF INVESTIGATION. The Defense Investigative Service handles background investigations for the DEPARTMENT OF DEFENSE and thus conducts the largest number of investigations.

A second executive order—E.O. 10865, "Safeguarding Classified Information in Industry," issued by President Eisenhower in 1960 and amended by him the next year just before he left office—applies to private-sector employees needing access to such information. It forms the basis for the Defense Industrial Security Program.

Both the Reagan and Bush administrations considered revising or replacing the two governing orders. At the end of his term, President Bush issued E.O. 12829 establishing a new National Security Program for private-sector contractors. Prodded in part by the defense industry because of the high costs associated with the ongoing system, it sets uniform standards for protecting classified information and is applicable to all contracting agencies.

Added to or reinforcing these executive orders are authorities in other presidential orders and directives, public law, and agency regulations. One of the most important is a directive from the Director of Central Intelligence (DCI) setting minimum standards for access to Sensitive Compartmented Information (SCI). This covers intelligence sources and methods and is based on the DCI's mandate in the 1947 NATIONAL SECURITY ACT to prevent their unauthorized disclosure (50 U.S.C. 403). Other authority is included in the 1946 Atomic Energy Act, as amended (42 U.S.C. 2161–2169 and 2274). It established the category of "restricted data"—referring to NUCLEAR WEAPONS and special nuclear materials—and provides the basis for security clearances in the now-defunct Atomic Energy Commission and its successor, the DEPARTMENT OF ENERGY.

In addition, President Ronald Reagan's 1986 executive order (E.O. 12564) promoting a "Drug-Free Federal Workplace" ties its goal directly to preventing the use of illegal drugs by employees who require "access to sensitive information" and who would otherwise "pose a serious risk to national security." Drug-testing requirements for federal employees with access to classified material was narrowly upheld in a 5 to 4 Supreme Court decision in 1989 (*National Treasury Employees Union v. Von Raab*). President Bush issued National Security Directive 63 in 1992, calling for a single-scope background investigation for access to top secret and sensitive compartmented information.

An offshoot of the security-clearance system was a highly controversial National Security Decision Directive 84 (NSDD-84), issued by President Reagan in 1983. Designed primarily to combat leaks of classified information from the executive, NSDD-84 called for a dramatic escalation of POLYGRAPH TESTS for security-clearance holders and set in motion the process to draft a new executive order on personnel security clearances. Both of these initiatives raised substantial opposition. Congress restricted the number of lie detectors used in screening employees, because of their fallibility and projected costs. And legislators, as well as civil liberties organizations and employee unions, criticized the eventual draft order, which was then put on hold, in part because of its failure to protect due process rights of employees.

The current security-clearance system has been criticized both for failing to govern access effectively and efficiently and for causing unnecessary and oppressive demands on individuals.

Among the identified problems is the inordinately large number of personnel required to have clearances. This overloads the clearance system, spreads the investigative agencies too thinly, and increases the costs of running the government and operating programs; moreover, because agencies do not accept a background investigation conducted elsewhere, employees need a separate investigation when transferring to or working under contract with a different agency. These conditions result in delays in clearing an individual and in incomplete or inadequate investigations, multiple investigations, and postponed reinvestigations. The failure to conduct reinvestigations on schedule was found to be a major factor in some of the espionage cases in 1985, which resulted in an unprecedented number of indictments and prosecutions.

Critics have also condemned the absence of minimum due-process rights and other procedural safeguards for appealing a denial or revocation of a security clearance. Because agencies have substantial discretion over the process, there may be no guarantee of even a written notification of an unfavorable determination let alone a right to legal counsel during the appeal.

BIBLIOGRAPHY

Kaiser, Frederick M. "The Impact of Overclassification on Personnel and Information Security." *Government Information Quarterly* 3 (1986): 251–269.

U.S. Department of Defense Commission To Review DOD Security Policies and Procedures. *Keeping the Nation's Secrets.* 1985.

U.S. General Accounting Office. *Information Security: Update of Data on Employees Affected by Federal Security Programs.* 1989.

U.S. Senate. Permanent Subcommittee on Investigations. *Federal Government Security Clearance Programs.* 99th Cong., 1st Sess. 1985.

U.S. Senate. Select Committee on Intelligence. *Meeting the Espionage Challenge: A Review of United States Counterintelligence and Security Programs.* 99th Cong., 2d Sess. 1986.

FREDERICK M. KAISER

SEDITION ACT. See Alien and Sedition Acts.

SEERY v. UNITED STATES 127 F. Supp. 601 (1955). *Seery v. United States* was one of a series of cases in the mid 1950s in which the federal courts limited the scope and effects of EXECUTIVE AGREEMENTS.

The opera singer Maria Jeritza Seery, a naturalized American citizen, sought compensation for damages that occurred when the United States Army seized a luxurious estate she owned in Austria for use as an officers' club after WORLD WAR II, from 1945 to 1947. The United States entered into an agreement with Austria in 1947 in which the United States paid $15.4 million to Austria to settle all claims resulting from the American occupation of Austria and Austrian officials offered Madame Jeritza $600. She then sued the United States government, asserting that it could not, by international agreement, negate her right under the Fifth Amendment to just compensation for the taking of her property for public use.

Defending itself before the U.S. Court of Claims, the government cited the Supreme Court's decisions in UNITED STATES v. BELMONT (1937) and UNITED STATES v. PINK (1942) to support its contention that executive agreements like the one with Austria, even though not approved by the Senate, were similar to treaties and part of the supreme law of the land. Madame Jeritza's attorneys argued that those decisions were not relevant because the executive agreements involved had not deprived American citizens of any of their constitutionally protected rights. They asserted that neither treaties nor executive agreements could authorize government actions that the Constitution prohibited.

Since this case involved an executive agreement, the court of claims did not consider the legal status of treaties that conflicted with the Constitution. The judges ruled, however, that since executive agreements were not even mentioned in the text of the Constitution, and since they were entered into by the President alone, without the participation of either the Senate or Congress as a whole, such agreements could not impair or destroy the constitutional rights of American citizens.

Madame Jeritza was eventually awarded $11,000 in damages, and the Supreme Court refused to grant certiorari when the government tried to appeal the decision.

The ruling in *Seery v. United States* made it clear that executive agreements in conflict with the Constitution were invalid. Along with the Supreme Court's decision in REID v. COVERT in 1957, this verdict defused much of the concern about treaties and executive agreements that had led to the BRICKER AMENDMENT controversy.

BIBLIOGRAPHY

Oliver, Covey. "Executive Agreements and Emanations from the Fifth Amendment." *American Journal of International Law* 49 (1955): 362–366.

Roche, Clayton. "Constitutional Law: Executive Agreements: Effect

When in Conflict with Constitutional Rights." *California Law Review* 43 (1955): 525–530.

DUANE TANANBAUM

SENIOR EXECUTIVE SERVICE (SES). The centerpiece of President Jimmy Carter's Civil Service Reform Act of 1978 (CSRA) was the Senior Executive Service. Modeled on both the British higher civil service and the top management level in the private sector, the SES was intended to create a mobile, flexible, and elite cadre of government managers.

Reforms such as the SES had been proposed for a number of years. The second of the Hoover Commissions reported in 1955, for example, that senior managers in the career civil service should be assigned a broader, more flexible role in government. It was left to Carter's Personnel Management Project, however, to create a formal proposal for such a group. To move from the rigidities of the traditional civil service system to this more flexible cadre, the CSR Act proposed to eliminate most of the "supergrade" (GS 16–18) and executive schedule positions in the federal service. In their place would be the Senior Executive Service, a group entered only by contract, whose members would not be covered by many of the traditional civil service protections and securities.

The problem that the SES was intended to address was complex. Solutions to some aspects of the problem conflicted with solutions to other components. For example, the presidential desire for improved political responsiveness was in tension with the "higher civil service" concept of expanded flexibility and discretion for senior managers. Other aspects of the problem addressed by the SES included a too-narrow, program-linked view of policy and management objectives and the lack of generalized management skills within the civil service. In addition, reformers wished to rectify the problem created by the link between the salaries of top managers in government and those of members of Congress. As managers advanced up the career ladder, they quickly—often at a relatively early age—reached a pay ceiling imposed by Congress that prevented them from receiving appropriate pay. While managers' pay remained capped at this level, that of their subordinates continued to advance, creating serious pay compression problems.

Title IV of the Civil Service Reform Act, which created the Senior Executive Service, contained the following provisions: First, all persons in a supergrade or executive schedule position at the time the legislation was passed were eligible for membership in the SES (about eight thousand positions). Second, govern-ment-wide, 10 percent of the positions were reserved for political appointments. Third, members entered the SES through a contract that committed them to increased opportunity for mobility and flexibility but removed some career civil service protections. Fourth, SES members were eligible to compete for financial bonuses and awards based on individual performance; the legislation provided that 50 percent of any agency's SES members would be eligible to receive an award each year. Fifth, the SES would be a rank-in-person system, rather than the rank-in-position system then in place throughout the civil service, meaning that SES members would carry their rank to whatever positions they accepted or were assigned. Sixth, SES members would also be eligible for increased training and development opportunities as well as sabbatical leaves.

The SES was implemented quickly. Nearly 98 percent of those eligible for initial membership in the SES joined, but this high number reflected dissatisfaction with pay restrictions rather than enthusiasm for the reform. The SES encountered difficulties almost at once. Congress was dissatisfied with the outcomes of the first performance review and award process; within six months of the SES's implementation Congress cut the number of SES members eligible for annual awards by half, and the Office of Personnel Management (OPM), using its discretionary authority, reduced the total by another 5 percent.

In addition, the budget cuts and staff reductions of the early years of the administration of Ronald Reagan created a turbulence in the federal government that quickly overshadowed efforts at civil-service reform. The SES continued to play a key role in efforts to improve presidential management of the career bureaucracy, however. Presidential management strategies such as "jigsaw puzzle management," advocated by presidential advisers from the Heritage Foundation, utilized the political appointees in the SES to control decision points inside the bureaucracy that had previously been inaccessible to political appointees. The mobility provisions of the SES were utilized to move career managers to different—and generally less influential—positions. Very few career members of the SES moved into policy-making positions, and those who did left government service after brief policy stints.

Of equal significance, a large number of career members of the SES retired or resigned from government in the years 1979 to 1984. Some chose to retire at the end of the "high three" years of benefit calculations. This permitted retirement benefits to be based on the three highest-salary years of the SES member. Many scientific and technical experts left government for better-paying jobs in the private sector. Others, however, left because of the "bureaucrat bashing" so pervasive in Washington and because of a perceived politicization of the top levels of the career bureaucracy. In the early years of the SES, the often-negative experiences of its members caused many junior members of the career bureaucracy to become disenchanted as well. The formation of the Senior Executive Association, which functioned as a quasi union for senior executives, was further evidence that the CSRA had not created an elite cadre of senior policy advisers.

The experience of the SES in the late 1980s and early 1990s was more positive. This was due, in part, to a move away from what one observer termed the "halcyon promise" of the legislation to more realistic expectations for performance and progress. It was also due to a decision by the Office of Personnel Management to take more direct responsibility for the success of the SES. Perhaps most significantly, however, pay increases for senior executives were approved in 1987 and again in 1990 (the latter becoming effective in 1991). Changes also occurred in the bonus system. In 1984, the OPM increased the number eligible for awards in each agency to 35 percent of that agency's total SES membership. In 1987 that limit was removed, and in 1989 40 percent of the total membership received a bonus.

Important changes occurred in other areas as well. One of President George Bush's first speeches was to members of the SES in Washington; in that speech Bush affirmed the importance of excellent career civil servants to good government. Partly because of difficulties in recruiting political appointees, the Bush administration relied more heavily on career civil servants to fill important management positions.

Nonetheless, in the early 1990s problems remained for the SES. Compensation levels remain tied to those of Congress; despite pay increases, agencies employing large numbers of top-level scientific and technical personnel asked to be removed from the SES to increase compensation levels for these critical employees. Provisions of the Ethics Reform Act of 1989 provided for recertification of SES members' performance qualifications every four years. There were also lingering fears of potential for increased politicization.

BIBLIOGRAPHY

Harper, Kirke. "The Senior Executive Service after Twelve Years." In *The Promise and Paradox of Civil Service Reform.* Edited by Patricia W. Ingraham and David Rosenbloom. 1992.

Huddleston, Mark. *The Government's Managers.* 1987.

Huddleston, Mark. "To the Threshold of Reform: The Senior Executive Service and America's Search for a Higher Civil Service." In *The Promise and Paradox of Civil Service Reform.* Edited by Patricia W. Ingraham and David Rosenbloom. 1992.

Rosen, Bernard. "Uncertainty in the Senior Executive Service." *Public Administration Review* 42 (March–April 1981): 203–206.

PATRICIA W. INGRAHAM

SEPARATION OF POWERS. The separation of powers is the principal theory that informs the allocation of powers among the branches of the national government. Its centrality to the government's structure is indicated by the opening phrases of the first three articles of the Constitution, each of which vests a basic category of power (legislative, executive, and judicial) in a distinct and independent branch (a Congress, a President, and a Supreme Court).

The Theory of Separation. As understood by the major authors of the Constitution, the theory of the separation of powers contains two basic elements. First, it holds that political power is divided naturally into fairly distinct powers, each of which can be defined according to a general function. In the evolution of the theory from Locke to Montesquieu, there were debates on exactly what these powers are. But by the time of the founding of the Republic, it was accepted that there were three powers: a legislative power, meaning a power to make laws; a judicial power, meaning a power to assess penalties (criminal or civil) and apply law (including the Constitution) in cases and controversies; and an EXECUTIVE POWER, meaning a power to carry out law and, more broadly, to act with discretion for the nation, especially in crises or in FOREIGN AFFAIRS, where laws either cannot apply or would conflict with the national interest.

Separation of powers theory assisted the Founders in understanding the character of these powers and their respective roles in governing. In particular, the great expositors of the theory had stressed the importance of the executive power, showing that good government requires a command institution capable of exercising broad discretion. This teaching stood in sharp contrast to the prevailing Whig, or antiexecutive, view that informed most of the state constitutions. Separation of powers theory for the Founders was thus directly connected to the establishment of a strong and independent executive office.

The second element of the separation of powers theory holds that there are fundamental benefits that derive from housing the core of each power in a distinct institution that has a capacity to act on its own. One benefit is safety for liberty and freedom from despotism, which results from avoiding a concentration of power in the hands of a single person or institution. Separation of powers provides a rationale for dispersing power. Above all, the separation of the judicial power of determining punishment from the powers of legislating and executing affords an essential protection for individual rights. Unlike the ANTI-FEDERALISTS, the Founders were willing to grant broad powers to the national government because they were confident that the division of powers inside the government was an adequate check against despotism.

Another benefit of separating powers is governmental efficiency, at least in one respect. Because the powers are different in character, exercising them well requires different qualities. Separation allows each institution to be structured to carry out its own function. Thus, the bulk of the legislative power can be placed in a body that provides for broad representation and that ensures deliberation, while the core of the executive power can be housed in an institution that is headed by a single individual and is capable of "decision, activity, secrecy, and dispatch" (FEDERALIST 70).

The Founders' use of the theory of separation of powers has been widely misunderstood. Contrary to the simpler and more rhetorically satisfactory arguments of their opponents, the Founders insisted that nothing in the theory demanded a total or complete separation. The theory is not a mathematical formula that aims, in James Madison's words, at "beauty or the symmetry of form," but a political doctrine designed to secure important benefits. These benefits require a basic, but not a total, separation.

Shared Powers. The separation of powers, while it is fundamental to the whole constitutional design, is not the only theory that governs the allocation of powers. The Founders relied on other, supplemental considerations to justify placing parts of certain powers outside of their "home" institution. Powers were shared for four reasons: to enable each branch to maintain its independence (as in the President's VETO power); to assure conformity to the basic spirit of popular government (as in the Congress's power to declare war [see WAR, DECLARATION OF]); to encourage temperate governmental decisions (as in the Senate's power to confirm judges and other federal officers); and to endow the government as a whole with a greater capacity for coherent action (as in the President's power to inform Congress, make recommendations, and employ the veto). The first three of these reasons rely on a notion of CHECKS AND BALANCES to impose further restraints on power, but the last one provides the structural possibility for presidential leadership and is designed to enhance the energy of the government.

Congress's powers are not the exact equivalent of the legislative power, and the President's powers are not the exact equivalent of the executive power. Certain parts of the traditional executive power have been removed from the exclusive control of the President (such as declaring war and making appointments [see APPOINTMENT POWER]), while parts of other powers have been given to the President. The fact that powers are shared, however, does not reduce the significance of the separation of powers as the foundation on which the national government rests. Both the structure of the government (three distinct branches with no overlapping personnel) and the principal vesting of power in each branch derives from the theory of the separation of powers. That theory remains essential to an understanding of the powers of each institution. Thus Article II, Section 1, which vests "the executive power" in the President, constitutes a positive and meaningful grant of power. As interpreted by many Presidents, this grant gives the President the full executive power, that is, including a power to act for the nation in foreign affairs and in emergencies, qualified only insofar as parts of that power have been explicitly removed or assigned elsewhere.

Reinterpretations. The theory of the separation of powers has been a source of profound controversy. The Founders' view of the theory survives in and through interpretation of parts of the Constitution, but their overall understanding of the theory has been obscured, if not lost, over the course of American history. It has been largely replaced by the very different understandings of the theory of two other schools of thought: the Anti-Federalists and the progressives.

Anti-Federalists. The Anti-Federalists claimed to have opposed the Constitution in part because it violated the separation of powers. For the Anti-Federalists, the theory of separation of powers demanded a complete separation. All of each power and only each power had to be placed in its "home" institution. If separation was good, then strict separation must be better.

The Anti-Federalists invoked the theory, however, only when objecting to a strong and independent presidency. Although they were true to their own logic in those instances where the President was granted parts of the legislative power, their overriding concern was less to separate powers than to limit the power of the presidency. It is here, in fact, that one reaches the heart of the debate, for which the separation of powers theory was employed as a stalking horse. The fundamental division was less over the strictness of the separation than over the nature and respective importance of the three powers.

For the Anti-Federalists, the key to the allocation of power was to assure legislative supremacy. The legislative branch, in their view, was the only true representative of the people. All "motion" in government should derive from the legislature. They conceived the executive power very narrowly as a ministerial power to carry out the legislature's will. Any discretionary power the President might exercise should come from explicit grants accorded to him by statute. For them, the separation of powers was another name for legislative supremacy.

Progressives. Woodrow Wilson developed the other major school of thought on the separation of powers, which was embraced at the beginning of the twentieth century by many progressive thinkers. Wilson began by accepting the new orthodoxy that the Constitution embodied a pure theory of the separation of powers. "The government of the United States," he wrote, "was constructed upon the whig theory of political dynamics." But whereas the WHIG PARTY celebrated this fact, Wilson declared it to be the fatal flaw of the whole design. The separation of powers impedes strong, effective, and democratic government, which is synonymous with unified leadership under a powerful executive. The Constitution must be changed to overcome the separation of powers. Varying this position slightly for practical reasons, Wilson later argued that while the Constitution was based on Whig theory, it has been written in a way that allowed it to be stretched and reinterpreted. A theory of strong presidential leadership, though contrary to the spirit of the separation of powers, could nevertheless be grafted onto the Constitution.

Most theoretical discussions of the separation of powers in the twentieth century have accepted one or the other of Wilson's views about the character of the Constitution and its relationship to the separation of powers. Even those who quibble with the notion of pure separation accept the more fundamental point that the constitutional allocation of powers is incompatible with a strong presidency. The Constitution was intended to fracture power, which makes governance difficult under modern conditions. What has changed since Wilson's time, however, is the judgment of whether the Constitution so understood is good or bad. In the aftermath of the VIETNAM WAR, many abandoned their preference for a Wilsonian presidency in favor of the Whig-like idea of the separation of powers.

Maintaining Separation. A final issue about the constitutional allocation of powers relates to the question of how a balance among the institutions can be maintained over time. Who or what will police the separation? The American tradition has supplied three answers.

The first was Thomas Jefferson's curious idea that no policing system internal to the government is feasible and that therefore a balance can only be assured by the people acting through a constitutional convention every generation. Dismissed by most as too radical, this idea nevertheless reemerged in modified form during the election of 1800. Jefferson established the precedent that major issues relating to the balance of power among the institutions can be submitted to the people during a presidential election, and that some kind of mandate can be claimed by the victor to reduce or enlarge the power of one of the institutions. This approach has been used on several occasions in American history when the constitutional balance of powers has been an important campaign issue.

A second answer, favored by the founders, is to rely on the structure of the government and the incentives those in each branch have to protect their institutional power. As Madison wrote, "Ambition must be made to counteract ambition." (*Federalist* 51) The solution to conflicting claims among the branches is the outcome of their struggle, a struggle in which each institution has the words of the Constitution, its specific powers, and its base of influence with the American people. This method of resolving conflicts has probably been the predominant one, having prevailed in such areas as the WAR POWER and EXECUTIVE PRIVILEGE.

A final answer is judicial review, where the Supreme Court serves as the umpire and resolves constitutional disputes according to a definitive, legal interpretation of the meaning of the Constitution. This method has played an important role in a few instances, such as matters relating to the REMOVAL POWER and the so-called LEGISLATIVE VETO, although even in these areas the conflicts between Congress and the President are resolved primarily outside the courts through a sophisticated system of political accommodations. Those who believe that judicial decisions are (or should be) the principal means of resolving constitutional questions relating to the allocation of powers have an overly legalistic understanding of the Constitution. The historical record clearly demonstrates the greater importance, and perhaps the greater flexibility, of the other two mechanisms for resolving constitutional disputes. Both of these mechanisms view the Constitution as a document to be interpreted and enforced through the political process.

BIBLIOGRAPHY

Bessette, Joseph, and Jeffrey Tulis, eds. *The Presidency in the Constitutional Order*. 1981.

Fisher, Louis. *Constitutional Conflicts between Congress and the President*. 3d ed. 1991.

Mansfield, Harvey. *Taming the Prince*. 1989.

Vile, M. J. C. *Constitutionalism and the Separation of Powers*. 1967.

JAMES CEASER

SEQUESTRATION. Sequestration is the cancellation of budgetary resources pursuant to procedures set forth by the 1985 GRAMM-RUDMAN-HOLLINGS ACTS (GRH). Sequestered funds are, with certain exceptions, no longer available for obligation or expenditure. A sequester is implemented according to a formula that prescribes the amounts to be cancelled and the share to be drawn from each category of resources. GRH provides for a sequester when the estimated deficit at the start of the fiscal year exceeds that year's target deficit by more than a preset margin. The 1990 BUDGET ENFORCEMENT ACT (BEA) added sequesters for breaching any discretionary spending caps and for revenue or direct spending legislation that causes a net increase in the deficit.

Automatic Rules and Political Discretion. Sequestration arose out of extended conflict between the President and Congress over BUDGET POLICY and high deficits averaging $146 billion during the 1982–1985 fiscal years. When GRH was enacted, it was viewed as a means of breaking the impasse by substituting automatic, self-implementing rules for discretionary action by elected officials. The expectation was that by agreeing in advance on specific procedures, the President and Congress would reduce the deficit, even when they disagreed about what should be done.

The budgetary record of the 1986–1990 period indicates that the threat of a sequester diminished budgetary conflict somewhat but did not control the deficit. Conflict abated after GRH was enacted because the President and Congress shared an interest in averting a sequester or minimizing its impact. But the deficit crisis was not resolved because the only truly automatic features of the GRH process were the cutbacks made after sequestration was ordered. Everything occurring before that point, including the critical determination of whether a sequester should be triggered, was subject to political judgment. The GRH sequester, for an excess deficit, was especially prone to manipulation because it was based on the projected rather than the actual deficit and could be triggered only within the first 15 days of the fiscal year. The sequester process was inactive during the remaining 350 days of the fiscal year, even if new legislation added to the deficit. These characteristics made the GRH sequester vulnerable to bookkeeping tricks, such as shifting expenditures to the year in progress (when it was too late for a sequester) or to the year after next (too early for the sequester process to begin). They also enabled politicians to avoid a sequester by fabricating unrealistically optimistic economic projections or by misestimating the impact of revenue or expenditure legislation.

Sequestration was used only sparingly during the 1986–1990 period. A limited sequester was imposed during 1986; the automatic cancellation of budget resources was deactivated during the following year by a Supreme Court decision; a sequester was averted in 1988 and 1989 by legislation raising the deficit targets; and a small, partial-year sequester was implemented in 1990. The limited sequesters hardly dented the deficit, which averaged $40 billion above target during the five years before GRH was superseded by the BEA in 1990.

BEA introduced a complex array of sequesters to guard against deficit-raising legislation throughout the year. BEA sequesters can be triggered at three different times: at the end of the session when the impact of the year's legislation is estimated; during the next session when the impact of new revenue or spending legislation is assessed; and during the last quarter of the fiscal year when any required sequester is taken from the next year's resources. BEA sequesters do not apply when the excess deficit results from existing rather than new legislation or when the new legislation is designated as emergency action by the President and Congress. Except for an inconsequential sequester during BEA's first year, no funds have been cancelled pursuant to these rules.

Sequestration and Presidential Power. The sequestration process both empowers and constrains the President. A sequester can be activated only by presidential order, but once he determines that an excess deficit exists, the President must withdraw resources according to detailed rules and procedures set forth in law. Thus, the President has considerable discretion in determining whether a sequester is to occur, but hardly any in determining how it is carried out.

The 1985 GRH provided for a sequester to be ordered pursuant to a determination of an excess deficit by the COMPTROLLER GENERAL. In BOWSHER V. SYNAR (1986), however, the Supreme Court ruled that as a legislative officer, the Comptroller General could not exercise this executive power. Congress amended GRH in 1987 to give the President exclusive power to determine whether a sequester is to be ordered. But Congress balanced this grant of presidential power with further restrictions on the manner in which a sequester is to be implemented. The formula enacted in the 1985 law provided for half of the cancelled resources to be taken from defense and half from nondefense. Within each of these categories, equal percentage cutbacks were to be made in each program, project, or activity. This formula was retained in 1987, but additional rules were enacted for computing the amount to be cut. Constrained in how he could implement a sequester, the President contrived to avoid exercising the power.

BIBLIOGRAPHY

Schier, Steven. *A Decade of Deficits*. 1992.
White, Joseph, and Aaron Wildavsky. *The Deficit and the Public Interest: The Search for Responsible Budgeting in the 1980s*. 1989.

ALLEN SCHICK

SEWARD, WILLIAM H. (1801–1872), Secretary of State. A native of upstate New York, William Henry Seward became a lawyer and politician, moving from the National Republican to the ANTI-MASONIC PARTY and then WHIG PARTY before becoming a Republican in 1855. An early antislavery advocate, he harbored little respect for those who hated "men for the marks which God set upon them to commend them to our pity and our care." As a U.S. Senator, he opposed the COMPROMISE OF 1850 on antislavery grounds and declared that a "higher law than the Constitution" demanded the exclusion of SLAVERY from the territories; Democrats would taunt antislavery men with that phrase for years. In 1858 Seward called the sectional crisis an "irrepressible conflict," another much-quoted statement, interpreted by Democrats to mean that the Republicans were fomenting civil war.

Widely regarded as the most likely Republican nominee for President in 1860, Seward nevertheless lost the nomination to Abraham Lincoln. The New Yorker's reputation for antislavery radicalism hurt him with some crucial state delegations, such as those of Indiana and Illinois, while his consistent record of fairness toward Catholics damaged him with Pennsylvanians, who needed to woo former Know-Nothing voters.

Lincoln, seeking a strong Cabinet containing his major Republican rivals, obtained Seward's agreement to become Secretary of State. Despite his reputation for radicalism, Seward wanted the administration to follow a conciliatory policy toward the South. He pursued devious policies in the secession crisis and made statements to southern emissaries that did not represent Lincoln's views—telling them, for example, that Fort Sumter in Charleston harbor would be evacuated.

When the rest of the Cabinet joined Lincoln on 29 March 1861 in supporting a move to resupply Fort Sumter, Seward drafted a desperate memorandum, dated 1 April, suggesting the administration had no policy, "either domestic or foreign," and urging provocation of an incident with a foreign country to reunite America. Execution of this policy might, he said,

"devolve . . . on some member of the Cabinet." Lincoln replied that his administration had a policy; moreover, if a new one were adopted, he—Lincoln—"must do it." Once the CIVIL WAR began, Seward adopted the views that slavery was doomed if the North won and that the administration should focus on saving the Union. He had long been an aggressive nationalist and held little sympathy for northern dissenters.

As Secretary of State, Seward achieved the administration's goal of keeping Great Britain and France from recognizing and significantly aiding the Confederacy. He became so valuable to Lincoln that in December 1862 the President skillfully protected him from an attempt by Republican Senators who deemed Seward too conservative to force his removal from the Cabinet.

In the summer of 1862, Seward persuaded Lincoln to delay announcement of the EMANCIPATION PROCLAMATION until a Union battlefield victory to ensure that the policy exuded strength rather than desperation. This indifference to the pace of black freedom foretold Seward's role in Andrew Johnson's Cabinet, in which he served loyally even though Johnson was attempting to frustrate reconstruction of the southern social order. As a diplomat, Seward remained successful; through the ALASKA PURCHASE TREATY, Seward added an area to the United States larger than the territory gained after the MEXICAN WAR.

BIBLIOGRAPHY

Van Deusen, Glyndon G. *William Henry Seward*. 1967.

MARK E. NEELY, JR.

SEYMOUR, HORATIO (1810–1886), governor of New York, Democratic presidential nominee in 1868. Born in Pompey Hill, New York, Horatio Seymour was trained as a lawyer. Influential nationally from mid century to his death in 1886, he received his political education in the highly complex and competitive environment of New York party politics. An adroit professional, Seymour fought to preserve the DEMOCRATIC PARTY through one of its most difficult eras.

Seymour was a New York assemblyman from 1841 to 1842 and again in 1844 (in 1842 he served as mayor of Utica). Seymour became a chief proponent of state canal development. Serving as speaker of the assembly from 1845 to 1847, Seymour watched as territorial expansionism, the MEXICAN WAR, INTERNAL IMPROVEMENTS, and the new state constitution divided the party. Seymour was an adamant anti-abolitionist. He did believe, however, that in the long run the SLAVERY system could not compete against free labor.

Seymour narrowly lost the New York governorship in 1850; he won in 1852 but lost his reelection bid in 1854. As governor Seymour improved the state's penal system and spoke out against temperance, vetoing a state prohibition bill. In national politics, he positioned himself as a pro-Union Democrat, denouncing nativism, antislavery politics, and temperance. He supported James Buchanan in 1856, and, declining to enter into the race himself, pushed for STEPHEN A. DOUGLAS in 1860, believing Douglas to be the only candidate who could keep the party together. He favored the Crittenden Compromise and advocated putting it to a national vote as a way of avoiding SECESSION.

Seymour's path during the CIVIL WAR was complicated by his opposition to Abraham Lincoln's administration. Elected governor again in 1862, Seymour did his best to fulfill the state's military obligations and quotas. He criticized Lincoln's expansive use of wartime powers. He spoke out particularly against the army's arrest of Clement Vallandigham, the peace or COPPERHEAD Democrat. Seymour criticized Lincoln's EMANCIPATION PROCLAMATION and doubted that the federal draft of 1863 was constitutional. During the famous New York draft riots, Seymour quelled the riots, but also gave a pro-riot speech in New York. He told his audience that he requested a suspension of the draft until a court had ruled on it. HORACE GREELEY excoriated Seymour for his handling of the draft riots, particularly Seymour's salutation of "My Friends" during his speech.

At the war's end, the Democrats stood as the minority party. Officially retired to Utica, Seymour emerged as a conservative critic of Republican RECONSTRUCTION. Privately he worked to salvage the party. In 1867, many Democrats had hopes of drafting Ulysses S. Grant for the party's presidential nomination. After Grant chose the Republicans, the Democrats were left with several substitutes: antiwar Democrat George Pendleton, Thomas Hendricks, and Chief Justice SALMON P. CHASE. Seymour himself endorsed Chase, although Chase had been a member of Lincoln's Cabinet and a RADICAL REPUBLICAN (though once a Democrat). A deadlocked convention, however, picked Seymour. After much demurring, he accepted. Francis Blair, Jr., was his running mate.

The presidential election of 1868 turned on the issue of Reconstruction. Seymour argued that the South's economic rehabilitation must precede black civil rights. He insisted, further, that suffrage was a state and not a national issue. Running mate Blair

embarrassed the ticket with blatantly white supremacist speeches. Throughout the South, the Democratic Party organized a campaign of intimidation and violence (sometimes in alliance with the KU KLUX KLAN) aimed at newly enfranchised black voters and others in the Republican coalition. Grant won the presidency in 1868 with a plurality of 300,000, although Seymour may well have won a majority of white votes. Seymour's performance was respectable, particularly in view of Mississippi's, Texas's, and Virginia's absence (normally Democratic states). In the South, the Republicans won Alabama, South Carolina, and Arkansas; the Democrats, Georgia and Louisiana.

After his defeat in 1868, Seymour remained active in party organizing but refrained from seeking office. With SAMUEL J. TILDEN, he launched a successful reform campaign against Boss William Marcy Tweed and Tammany Hall. Seymour opposed the presidential compromise arrived at by the ELECTORAL COMMISSION in 1877. His friend and protégé Grover Cleveland won in 1882.

BIBLIOGRAPHY

Alexander, DeAlva. *A Political History of the State of New York.* 1909.
Foner, Eric. *A Short History of Reconstruction.* 1990.
Keller, Morton. *Affairs of State.* 1977.
Mitchell, Stewart. *Horatio Seymour of New York.* 1938.

JOHN F. WALSH

SHERMAN, JAMES S. (1855–1912), businessman, mayor, Representative, twenty-seventh Vice President of the United States (1909–1912). James Sherman grew up in a political environment in Utica, New York. His father served in the New York State legislature and for ten years as a tally clerk in the U.S. House of Representatives. Nicknamed "Sunny Jim" because of his genial nature, Sherman graduated from Hamilton College (1878), where he earned a reputation as a debater and declaimer. After being awarded a law degree by the same college and gaining admission to the bar, he practiced law in Utica from 1879 to 1907. In 1881 he married Carrie Babcock, of Utica; they had three sons. Upon the death of his father, he became president of both a canning company and a bank that his father had established. His political career began when he was elected mayor of Utica at the age of twenty-eight. In 1886 he was elected to Congress and served from 1893 to 1908.

While in Congress, Sherman was chairman of the Committee on Indian Affairs for twelve years and served on many other committees. He also served as right-hand man to Speakers Thomas Reed, David B.

Henderson (who defeated him for the speakership), and Joseph Cannon and often presided over the House when it sat as a committee of the whole. Yet, no major legislation bears his name. Meanwhile he served his county Republican committee; chaired the New York State Republican Convention (1895, 1900, 1908); was chairman of the National Republican Congressional Committee (1908); was a delegate to the Republican national convention (1892); and was also a trustee of Hamilton College.

At the Republican national convention in 1908, President Theodore Roosevelt maneuvered to have William Howard Taft chosen as his successor. With Taft agreeing, Roosevelt also tried to have a midwestern progressive (insurgent) named as Vice President. However, conservative delegates balked and named Sherman.

By objecting to progressive reforms, Taft stood to lose to insurgents and Democrats in the congressional elections of 1910 and to lose to Roosevelt if he entered the presidential race in 1912. Roosevelt hoped to be chosen as the temporary chairman of the New York Republican state convention and to obtain a progressive platform. Upon learning that Taft intended to meet with Roosevelt to smooth over their differences, Sherman advised Taft that Roosevelt would speak against him and carry the state convention. Taft decided against a meeting, and Sherman became the temporary chairman.

In the late spring of 1910, Taft launched a campaign against congressional insurgents and sent Sherman to aid conservative Wisconsin Republicans to purge Sen. Robert M. La Follette from the party. He failed. In 1912, again at Taft's insistence, Sherman spoke against Wisconsin progressives and in favor of regular Republicans.

The Republican national convention of 1912 renamed Taft and, at his urging, Sherman also. Roosevelt thereupon organized the Progressive (Bull Moose) Party. When Sherman died less than a week before the election, Taft named Nicholas Butler as his running mate.

BIBLIOGRAPHY

Coletta, Paolo E. *The Presidency of William Howard Taft.* 1973.
Dunn, Arthur Wallace. *From Harrison to Harding: A Personal Narrative, Covering a Third of a Century 1888–1921.* 2 vols. 1922.
Pringle, Henry F. *The Life and Times of William Howard Taft.* 2 vols. 1939.

PAOLO E. COLETTA

SHERMAN, JOHN (1823–1900), Representative, Senator, Secretary of the Treasury, Secretary of State,

contender for the Republican presidential nomination in the 1880s. Sherman was born into a frontier family in north central Ohio. As a youth he abandoned schooling to become a surveyor and to supervise the construction of canals. In 1840, he changed his career to pursue law and, in the years that followed, became a successful attorney while acquiring a modest fortune from real estate development. The sectional crisis sharpened Sherman's interest in politics and, after attaining prominence in local Whig affairs, he was elected to Congress in 1854. He became a Republican and served in the national House of Representatives from 1855 to 1861, and then in the Senate until 1877. He became Secretary of the Treasury under President Rutherford B. Hayes (1877–1881), returned to the Senate until 1897, and ended his career as Secretary of State under President William McKinley (1897–1898). This record was especially impressive given the turbulence of Ohio politics of the day, which involved conflicting ethnic concerns and differing commercial, labor, and manufacturing interests. Nonetheless, Sherman mastered this volatile situation through the use of able local lieutenants, by paying close attention to his constituents' needs, and by relying on his national reputation as a unifier of local factions. His caution and his shrewdness were later to become legendary. Once while on a trip home for political reasons he remarked that he was going to "mend some fences" at his farm in Mansfield; the phrase entered the national political vocabulary. His serious mien made him appear to be a statesman rather than a politician, a public figure instead of a personality. It was his fate to evoke admiration rather than affection, and critics called him "the Ohio Icicle."

Sherman's reputation rested on the ability to frame complex financial legislation that would pass Congress. He helped shape the Morrill Tariff Act of 1861 and remained a staunch protectionist, as his state's constituencies demanded. He favored paying Civil War bills with higher taxes, but acquiesced in issuing paper money and long-term bonds. He believed that they would be redeemed in gold easily with peace time prosperity. As Secretary of the Treasury he redeemed paper "greenback" currency in gold and refunded much of the public debt to the government's advantage. Sherman was clearly wise in the ways of Congress and political administration, understood safe public finance, and was adept at compromise.

Sherman hoped that these achievements would carry him to the White House. He was the Hayes administration's candidate in 1880, and was mentioned in 1884, but made his principal bid in 1888. His strength then rested on southern delegations who were important in nominating a candidate even if they could not deliver votes in the election. He commanded some loyalty among other delegates who favored his financial record, western origins, and sobriety. In the end, Sherman could not overcome the party elements who disliked his financial policies and his lack of dynamism. The nod went to Senator Benjamin Harrison of Indiana, who was as colorless as Sherman, but who had done less and thus evoked less criticism. Mentioned again in 1892, he declined to seek the nomination.

Sherman continued to be an elder statesman in the Senate, where he fathered two more famous pieces of legislation in 1890. The Sherman Silver Purchase Act was a compromise between monetary factions and aimed to sustain the price of domestic silver without threatening gold redemption. The SHERMAN ANTITRUST ACT sought to prevent monopolies without fostering excessive government interference in the market economy.

In 1897, Sherman accepted President McKinley's offer to become Secretary of State, a post that offered Sherman an honorable conclusion to public life. The office was chiefly ceremonial, since the President was accustomed to conducting his own foreign policies. Sherman ultimately disagreed with McKinley over the coming war with Spain, and resigned before the conflict began. Sherman's career illustrated the political maxim that achievement was not always a road to the presidency since it inevitably created both friends and enemies. Although he well understood that a strong political record was the best credential only when allied with a compelling personality or popular issue, Sherman, who throughout his career always affected indifference, never quite recovered from losing the great prize.

BIBLIOGRAPHY

Burton, Theodore E. *John Sherman.* 1906.

Kerr, Winfield Scott. *John Sherman, His Life and Public Services.* 2 vols. 1908.

Sherman, John. *Recollections of Forty Years in the House, Senate, and Cabinet.* 2 vols. 1895.

H. WAYNE MORGAN

SHERMAN ANTITRUST ACT (1890).

Ohio's Republican Senator JOHN SHERMAN launched the case for federal antitrust legislation before his Senate colleagues in March 1890 with these words:

The popular mind is agitated with problems that may disturb social order, and among them all none is more threatening than the inequality of condition, of wealth, and opportunity that has grown within a single generation out of the concentration of capital into vast combinations to control production and trade and to break down competition. . . . If we will not endure a king as a political power we should not endure a king over the production, transportation, and sale of any of the necessaries of life.

Three months later, on 2 July 1890, President Benjamin Harrison signed into law the Sherman Antitrust Act, the nation's first federal antitrust statute. The act contains two major provisions: section 1, an anticartel provision, prohibits "contracts, combinations and conspiracies in restraint of trade"; section 2, ostensibly addressing concentrated, anticompetitive market structures, prohibits "monopolization" and "attempts to monopolize" trade or commerce among the several states or with foreign nations.

The Sherman Act empowers the ATTORNEY GENERAL to file either criminal or civil suits to enforce the law. In criminal suits, conviction is deemed a felony, with penalties ranging up to three years of imprisonment and maximum fines of $350,000 for convicted individuals and $10 million for convicted firms. In civil suits, the government can seek injunctions to stop monopolistic behavior or, in the extreme, to transform the structure of the defendant firm through dissolution, divorcement, or divestiture—trustbusting in the literal sense. In addition, the act affords private plaintiffs the right to file antitrust suits of their own; if successful, they are entitled to recover three times the damages they demonstrate to have suffered because of Sherman Antitrust Act violations.

As an anticartel policy, section 1 of the act has been singularly effective. The courts have long adhered to a strict, per se prohibition against price-fixing, bid rigging, territorial market and customer allocations, and other blatantly anticompetitive agreements. Such agreements have been ruled to be in and of themselves illegal—regardless of any extenuating circumstances or the avowed intentions of the conspirators in adopting them. Commencing in the 1970s, government enforcement of section 1 was considerably broadened in cases challenging restrictions on price competition and advertising in the professions (dentistry, medicine, law) and even the Ivy League colleges, as well as in cases involving professional sports and state and local government activities.

As an antimonopoly policy, by contrast, section 2 of the act has gone through a tortuous history. The language of this section has been subject to elastic interpretation, with courts, government enforcers, and analysts having grappled over the years with defining and debating the difference between *monopoly* (about which the statute is silent) and *monopolization* (which the statute forbids but does not define). Section 2 has been bedeviled by a conflict between distrust of concentrated power, on the one hand, and a fear of attacking successful firms, on the other. At bottom, this persistent controversy has turned on the question whether it is market dominance and the possession of concentrated market power that is objectionable in a competitive free-enterprise system, or, alternatively, whether it is the abuse of market power—rather than its possession—that constitutes the core problem to be addressed. Debate has further swirled about the appropriate definition of "bad" behavior—whether it requires brutal, vicious acts and practices or whether it should be evaluated in terms of poor economic performance (inefficiency, technological backwardness, excessive prices). As a result, the nation's ANTITRUST POLICY has vacillated with the composition of the courts and the philosophical inclinations of the administrations charged with enforcing it. At times, lenient and even lax enforcement of section 2, coupled with stringent enforcement of section 1 in prosecuting cartels, has had the effect of encouraging mergers and monopolies—a singularly perverse result to be achieved by an antitrust statute.

[See also BUSINESS POLICY; CLAYTON ACT.]

BIBLIOGRAPHY

Adams, Walter, and James W. Brock. Antitrust Economics on Trial: A Dialogue on the New Laissez-Faire. 1991.

Adams, Walter, and James W. Brock. The Bigness Complex: Industry, Labor and Government in the American Economy. 1986.

Kovaleff, Theodore P., ed. "Symposium on the 100th Anniversary of the Sherman Act and the 75th Anniversary of the Clayton Act." Antitrust Bulletin. 35 (1990).

Millon, David. "The Sherman Act and the Balance of Power." Southern California Law Review 61 (1988): 1219–1292.

Thorelli, Hans B. The Federal Antitrust Policy. 1955.

WALTER ADAMS and JAMES W. BROCK

SHULTZ, GEORGE P. (b. 1920), Secretary of Labor, Director of the Office of Management and Budget, Secretary of the Treasury, Secretary of State. As Richard M. Nixon's first Secretary of Labor, Shultz instituted the so-called Philadelphia plan, obligating construction companies with federal contracts to hire a specific quota of nonwhite workers. As the economy stagnated in 1970, Nixon appointed Shultz as the director of the newly formed OFFICE OF MANAGEMENT AND BUDGET. The President consulted Shultz on formulation of his New Economic Policy in August 1971. Although Shultz later regretted having advised Nixon to impose wage and price controls, he set up the Cost of Living Council to implement the controls. Shultz became Secretary of the Treasury in May 1972, remaining until March 1974. Shultz was untouched by the growing WATERGATE AFFAIR, but Nixon and his White House aides came to distrust Shultz as insufficiently zealous in pursuit of their political agenda.

After leaving government, Shultz taught business at Stanford University and worked for the Bechtel Group, a large international engineering and construction concern. When Alexander Haig resigned as Secretary of State in June 1982, Ronald Reagan, eager to restore confidence in his foreign policy, named Shultz to succeed Haig. Shultz's calm demeanor, vast experience in international economics, and his ability to get along with people of different backgrounds and opinions, made him an effective diplomat. He advocated a more forceful U.S. presence in the Middle East in the wake of Israel's 1982 invasion of Lebanon. In September of that year, he arranged for an American peacekeeping force to go to Beirut. In the wake of an attack on a U.S. Marine barrack in October 1983, Shultz became an outspoken advocate of strong measures against terrorism. Reagan's indifference to the daily management of public affairs left his subordinates free to squabble among themselves. Shultz complained that Secretary of Defense CASPAR W. WEINBERGER did not choose aggressively to confront terrorists. The Secretary of State also opposed the plans of national security advisers Robert McFarlane and John Poindexter and their subordinate Oliver North to sell arms to Iran in exchange for the return of U.S. hostages held in Lebanon. In the later years of the Reagan administration, Shultz fostered better relations between the United States and the Soviet Union, helping to negotiate the INF (INTERMEDIATE-RANGE NUCLEAR FORCES) TREATY of December 1987.

BIBLIOGRAPHY

Ambrose, Stephen E. Nixon: The Triumph of a Politician, 1962–1972. 1989.

Cannon, Lou. President Reagan: The Role of a Lifetime. 1991.

Shultz, George P. Turmoil and Triumph: My Years as Secretary of State. 1993.

ROBERT D. SCHULZINGER

SIGNING STATEMENTS, PRESIDENTIAL. Approval of major legislation is usually accompanied by a signing statement in which the President gives his reasons for approval. When bills passed by Congress are presented to Presidents for final consideration, Presidents usually issue messages to explain their decisions. Article I, Section 7 of the Constitution requires Presidents to include written explanations with vetoed bills when they are returned to the house of origin in Congress. Even though pocket-vetoed bills are not returned to Congress, Presidents have traditionally issued a memorandum of disapproval explaining their decision. When Presidents approve of legislation submitted to them, however, they are only required to sign the bill into law. According to Section 7, when the President is presented with a bill, "if he approve he shall sign it." For important legislation, however, Presidents often prepare signing statements to publicize, explain, or justify their decisions. These statements may praise or criticize the legislation in question, and they are important primarily for their political, rather than legal, significance. As the Supreme Court noted in *La Abra Silver Mining Co. v. United States* (1899), "It has properly been the practice of the President to inform Congress by message of his approval of bills, so that the fact may be recorded." In the twentieth century, bill-signing ceremonies have been used as occasions to recognize the efforts of key members of Congress or others with particular interest in the legislation in question.

One ambiguity regarding bill signing persisted throughout the nineteenth century. During the country's first hundred years, the prevailing belief and consequent practice was that Presidents did not possess the authority to sign bills when Congress was not in session, since bill signing was considered a part of the legislative process. This belief led Presidents to travel to the Capitol on the last day of a congressional session to sign those bills that were not to be vetoed. Abraham Lincoln was the first president to violate this practice, although Congress later objected and repassed the bill in question during the following session. Grover Cleveland became the first President to refuse to travel to Capitol Hill during the final days of congressional sessions, but the issue was not finally resolved until the Supreme Court ruled in the *La Abra* case that Presidents could indeed sign bills after a congressional recess as long as signing occurred within ten days of bill presentation. This ruling was extended to all adjournments in *Edwards v. United States* (1932).

In the 1980s, a significant controversy arose concerning the legal significance of presidential signing statements. Prior to the 1980s, Presidents who maintained doubts about some aspect of a bill they planned to sign would usually note their disapproval in their signing statement and perhaps urge further legislative or other action. On occasion, they would use signing statements to impose their interpretation of a statute. Under President Ronald Reagan this practice became systematic. He argued that signing statements could serve as a basis of statutory interpretation—that is, he

sought to use signing statements to reinterpret the meaning of the legislation he was signing into law. For example, in his signing statement accompanying enactment of the Immigration Reform and Control Act of 1986, he attempted to reinterpret the statute's standards concerning when an alien would be eligible for permanent citizenship. Reagan made a similar effort by proposing in the signing statement accompanying the Safe Drinking Water Act of 1986 that the Environmental Protection Agency was in fact not required to enforce provisions of the act, even though the bill stipulated such enforcement. Symptomatic of this view was the successful effort of Reagan's Attorney General, EDWIN MEESE III, to have signing statements included in the *U.S. Code Congressional and Administrative News*—something that had never been done before. This effort spawned criticism that the President was intruding improperly on Congress's exclusive power to assign meaning to the legislation it drafts, since the examination of legislative intent is a frequent means used by courts to interpret statutes. To grant legal or constitutional weight to presidential signing statements, according to critics, would in effect grant the President the power to substitute presidential judgment for that of Congress and to rewrite legislation after it had been passed by Congress. Critics also argue that this practice usurps the judicial power to interpret the laws passed by Congress. This Reagan administration practice was continued by George Bush, who also tried to impose his constitutional interpretation on legislation in signing statements.

BIBLIOGRAPHY

Alston, Chuck. "Bush Crusades on Many Fronts to Retake President's Turf." *CQ Weekly Report*, 3 February 1990, pp. 291–295.

Garber, Marc N., and Kurt A. Wimmer. "Presidential Signing Statements as Interpretations of Legislative Intent." *Harvard Journal on Legislation* 24 (1987): 363–395.

Rogers, Lindsay. "The Power of the President to Sign Bills after Congress Has Adjourned." *Yale Law Journal* 30 (1920): 1–22.

ROBERT J. SPITZER

SITUATION ROOMS. Only since the early 1960s has there been an area in the White House dedicated to supporting the President's role as COMMANDER IN CHIEF. Franklin D. Roosevelt did have a Map Room during WORLD WAR II, but it was not until 1962, with the advent of secure electronic communications and display technology, that a situation room was established in the White House in which the President's command responsibilities were centered.

Today, copies of all important incoming and outgoing diplomatic, military, and intelligence communications are transmitted to the situation room by the operations centers in the departments of State and Defense and the CENTRAL INTELLIGENCE AGENCY (CIA); NATIONAL SECURITY messages signed by or destined personally for the President or the NATIONAL SECURITY ADVISER are also handled there. The threshold of what is defined as important can be raised or lowered by the White House; in a crisis, even tactical data are demanded. Staff, many of whom are on detail from Defense, State, and the CIA, are on duty on a twenty-four hour basis to summarize the material received. Display boards are used; during the VIETNAM WAR a sand table of a battlefield was constructed for Lyndon Baines Johnson.

In 1992 there were two situation rooms in the White House. The earlier one was a rather cramped area, with a small conference room, in the basement of the west wing. In 1982 Ronald Reagan created a second "sit room" by making over what used to be the Secretary of State's office in the OLD EXECUTIVE OFFICE BUILDING. Its conference room can seat sixty; closed-circuit TV cameras connect it with the situation room in the west wing. At the center of the newer room's east wall is a screen, and behind it are four rooms of computing and projection equipment that can handle any kind of graphic or textual display. The computers receive, search, sort, relay to individual officers' work-stations, print out, file, and index the flow of data and will even signal when a critical message comes in. The situation rooms have vastly expanded the ability of the President and White House national security aides to monitor and control not only the strategic but, if desired, even the most detailed tactical aspects of U.S. operations abroad. Military and diplomatic old-timers blanch at the intrusiveness of this central White House management (which is especially meticulous in crises) but one must remember that, after all, the President *is* Commander in Chief.

BIBLIOGRAPHY

Karnow, Stanley. *Vietnam: A History.* 1983.
Kissinger, Henry. *White House Years.* 1979.
Patterson, Bradley H., Jr. *The Ring of Power: The White House Staff and Its Expanding Role in Government.* 1988.

BRADLEY H. PATTERSON, JR.

SIX-YEAR PRESIDENTIAL TERM. Proposals to limit presidential tenure to a single term, and to lengthen that term from four to six years, have been advanced repeatedly since the time of Andrew Jackson. Many Presidents, beginning with Jackson, have supported the single-term limitation, and most of those the six-year term as well. In 1867, the issue reached the stage of Senate floor debate, and in 1913 the Senate approved a constitutional amendment by the necessary two-thirds vote but it was not considered by the House.

Debate centered originally on the single-term question, with the length of the term a subsidiary issue. Jackson himself was neutral regarding the four- or six-year term, and the single-term proponents were divided in the 1867 Senate debate. But in 1913 the Senate voted decisively for six rather than four years, and since then the two propositions have usually been coupled.

Advocates of a one-term limit have emphasized the contention that, as Senator John D. Works of California put it in the 1913 debate, the effort to reelect a President "is a prolific source of political corruption, neglect of official duty, and betrayal of trust on the part of public servants." According to Works and other Senators, Theodore Roosevelt in 1904 and William Howard Taft in 1912 had mobilized thousands of federal officeholders into a political army and had turned the White House into a campaign headquarters, immobilizing government for a year or more. Even the just-defeated President Taft conceded that his administration had lost "part of its effectiveness for the public good by this diversion to political effort for at least a year."

These arguments were brought up to date, and augmented, in the early 1980s by the Committee for a Single Six-Year Presidential Term, which cited supporting statements by Presidents Eisenhower, Johnson, Nixon, Ford, and Carter, and included high officials of all of those administrations, as well as President Reagan's, in its leadership. Said Johnson in his memoirs: "The old belief that a President can carry out the responsibilities of his office and at the same time undergo the rigors of campaigning is, in my opinion, no longer valid."

Others have charged Presidents with manipulating the economy to bring it to a peak in the reelection year and have claimed that the desire for reelection leads to presidential timidity when tough but unpopular decisions are needed. They have argued that a President ineligible for reelection would stand higher with the people and with Congress because he would be credited with acting in the public, rather than partisan or personal interest. Carter said many of his actions were unjustly suspected as being "campaign ploys," and ineligibility for reelection would have "strengthened my hand with the Congress."

Opponents of the term limit reply that presidential behavior would be changed far less than the proponents claim. Presidents ending their second terms have often worked nearly as hard to elect their chosen successors—and so vindicate their own records—as they did for their own reelections. Far from standing apart from politics, Presidents Eisenhower and Reagan (both made ineligible for a third term by the TWENTY-SECOND AMENDMENT) were highly partisan in their second terms, as were Jefferson, Jackson, Theodore Roosevelt, Woodrow Wilson (until his incapacitation), and Harry Truman.

The opportunity for reelection keeps a President responsive to the people as he should be, it is argued. And if he becomes a LAME-DUCK PRESIDENT immediately upon inauguration, he will lose—not gain—influence in Congress. Data from the Eisenhower and Reagan periods show declines in support for the President among members of their own REPUBLICAN PARTY in Congress during those Presidents' second terms. Loss of congressional support makes it harder, not easier, for Presidents to make tough but unpopular decisions.

Opponents have directed their most effective attack not at the one-term limit but at the six-year term. They summarize their case simply: Six years is too long for a bad President, too short for a good one.

Of the twenty-nine Presidents who have sought a second term (through 1984, and including those who served a partial first term) fourteen have been rejected. An extended term would only, it is argued, have continued those unsuccessful presidencies. Some, notably Andrew Johnson and Herbert Hoover, had been discredited and reduced to futility long before their single terms had ended and had even aroused such hatred that two more years of inept leadership might have brought violence, with its threat to every institution. In the absence of any mechanism for removing Presidents who have failed but are innocent of the "high crimes and misdemeanors" required for IMPEACHMENT, a four-year term presents more than sufficient risk, opponents contend. Six years for an incompetent, erratic, or listless President would have been disastrous on several past occasions, and could be again.

Moreover, the midterm election usually results in a loss of congressional strength by the President's party and hence in a setback to PRESIDENTIAL LEADERSHIP. At present, the weakening of the presidency following the midterm election lasts only two years until the next presidential election gives a winning candidate a fresh mandate and a new HONEYMOON PERIOD with the public and the Congress. With a six-year term, the President's period of weakness would be extended to four years—or two-thirds of the term rather than half. This could be shortened to three years, however, if House terms were lengthened to three years and Senators divided into two classes with one from each state elected each three years, as has been proposed by some advocates of the six-year term.

In any case, the issue has been quiescent since the early 1980s. Despite its support by an impressive array of former Presidents and high administration officials, the Committee for a Single-Six-Year Presidential Term failed to arouse widespread public backing or even interest, and suspended its efforts.

BIBLIOGRAPHY

Foundation for the Study of Presidential and Congressional Terms. *Presidential and Congressional Term Limitation: The Issue that Stays Alive.* 1980.

The Jefferson Foundation. "So Great a Power to Any Single Person." In *Reforming American Government: The Bicentennial Papers of the Committee on the Constitutional System.* Edited by Donald L. Robinson. 1985.

Sundquist, James L. *Constitutional Reform and Effective Government.* Rev. ed. 1992. Chapters 2 and 5.

U.S. Senate. Subcommittee on Constitutional Amendments. Judiciary Committee. *Single Six-Year Term for President.* 92d Cong., 1st sess. 1971.

JAMES L. SUNDQUIST

SLAVERY. Because slavery was a source of profound conflict in American society, it inevitably had an impact on the presidency and on presidential politics. In the early days of the republic its influence, though deeply rooted, was muted and secondary. After 1820, however, slavery assumed rapidly growing importance in presidential politics and policy-making, and decisions regarding slavery directly affected the prestige and power of several Chief Executives. Ultimately, an exercise of presidential power began the destruction of slavery during the CIVIL WAR.

A Sectional Issue. At the founding of the nation, slavery was one of the important interests that states or sections sought to defend. Nevertheless, slavery's influence was not predominant at this point. A consensus prevailed that the institution was a necessary evil, and many Founding Fathers assumed that its gradual disappearance at some indefinite point in the future would be welcome.

The South's interest in slavery appeared in the Constitution in clauses counting three-fifths of the slaves for purposes of representation and taxation, requiring the return of FUGITIVE SLAVES, and forbidding a prohibition of the international slave trade before 1808. Some southerners approvingly noted the federal government's ability to assist a state in putting down domestic insurrections. The preference of southern leaders like Thomas Jefferson for strict construction also bore a relationship to the protection of slavery. But these issues neither dominated politics nor prevented southern congressmen like JOHN C. CALHOUN from being fervid nationalists following the WAR OF 1812.

The debates over the admission of Missouri in 1820 [see MISSOURI COMPROMISE], however, revealed that a change of great potential import was occurring. Southern congressmen expressed with unaccustomed sharpness their determination that no one outside the South would be permitted to tamper with slavery. Soon political and intellectual leaders from the South suggested, and then proclaimed, that slavery was not an evil but a positive good. This change, and the rise of ABOLITIONISM in the North in the 1830s, set the stage for national political conflict over slavery.

Before the formation of the REPUBLICAN PARTY, both major parties—the WHIG PARTY and DEMOCRATIC PARTY—tried to avoid open sectional clashes over slavery. Martin Van Buren of New York played an especially important role in this regard. His influence in the 1820s and 1830s shaped a Democratic Party whose leaders were often western men holding views acceptable to the South. A believer in Jefferson's ideal of limited government, Van Buren saw the South as the strongest bastion of republicanism and viewed slavery as both a secondary issue and an institution that had many sincere critics among Jefferson's southern followers. Van Buren's influence with Andrew Jackson helped keep many potentially divisive issues connected to slavery out of national politics. During his own term as President Van Buren declined to support the annexation of Texas, knowing it would occasion conflict.

The Texas Question and Popular Sovereignty. The Texas question, however, would not go away. When John Tyler became President in 1841, he decided that the acquisition of Texas would add "lustre" to his name, although he realized there would be trouble. "Slavery—I know that is the objection," Tyler wrote. In fact, the addition of such a large slaveholding republic proved quite unpopular in the North, especially after Secretary of State Calhoun linked Texas to the protection of slavery. In an aggressive letter to British officials in 1844, Calhoun assailed Great Britain for alleged antislavery designs on Texas and suggested that the executive branch wanted to annex Texas primarily to preserve slavery. Anger over Calhoun's letter led to the Senate's rejection of an annexation treaty by a vote of 16 to 35 [see TEXAS, ANNEXATION OF].

Strong feelings about slavery's expansion influenced presidential politics in 1844, as southern Democrats blocked the nomination of Martin Van Buren because he had failed to show enough enthusiasm for Texas. The Democrats nominated instead James K. Polk of Tennessee, who avidly desired new territory both in the southwest and in Oregon. Polk defeated the Whig's HENRY CLAY, who opposed expansion. At this point outgoing President Tyler convinced Congress to take the unusual step of admitting Texas by joint resolution, which required only a simple majority in both houses. Mexico immediately broke relations with the United States.

President Polk negotiated with Great Britain a settlement of conflicting claims to Oregon [see OREGON TREATY], but in 1846 war with Mexico had begun. Although U.S. forces were successful in the field, the MEXICAN WAR proved deeply divisive at home. Historian David Potter has written that in much of the country "it was regarded as a war of unjustified aggression on behalf of the evil institution of slavery." Moreover, in August 1846 Democrat David Wilmot of Pennsylvania proposed that "neither slavery nor involuntary servitude shall ever exist" in any territory to be won from Mexico. The WILMOT PROVISO, which he offered to benefit "the sons of toil, of my own race and own color," immediately aroused bitter controversy. It never passed the Congress, but the legislatures of fourteen northern states eventually endorsed it. Thereafter, the question of whether slavery would be allowed in the territories was at the center of national politics.

In 1848 Democratic presidential aspirant LEWIS CASS advanced an idea that became known as popular sovereignty. Cass hoped to defuse the explosive slavery issue and move disputes away from the nation's capital. Although Congress would ultimately have to approve statehood for a territory, it should "in the meantime," Cass said, allow settlers "to regulate their own concerns in their own way." These simple words were actually quite ambiguous. Southerners understood them to mean that a territory's residents ultimately would decide for or against slavery but could take no action to bar slavery before assuming statehood. Northerners argued the position later championed by STEPHEN A. DOUGLAS—that self-government was a fundamental American principle, and that residents in a territory could choose to have slavery or prohibit it.

In the 1848 presidential race, the ambiguity of Cass's idea allowed Democrats to argue for their candidate one way in the North and another way in the South; but it was not enough. War hero Zachary Taylor won the election for the Whigs, aided by unusually strong support from southern voters who felt reassured by the fact that Taylor was a slaveholder. To the South's displeasure, however, President Taylor favored the admission of California as a free state, a step that would upset the sectional balance of power in the Senate. Representatives from nine southern states met in Nashville to demand that slavery should have a chance in California, or at least the southern part of it. Efforts to settle this conflict led eventually to the COMPROMISE OF 1850.

Despite its apparent importance, the Compromise of 1850 failed to resolve disputes over slavery. A key provision of the compromise bills allowed the newly formed territories of New Mexico and Utah to legislate on "all rightful subjects . . . consistent with the Constitution." This formula seemed to endorse popular sovereignty, but it retained all the ambiguities of that concept, for North and South differed over what could constitutionally be done. The compromise's fugitive slave law also laid the foundation for new bitterness. Northern antislavery forces soon objected that the law violated basic American rights and encouraged federal officials to hand over alleged fugitives, whether they were or were not slaves.

A Political Earthquake. Controversies over slavery plagued the presidency of Franklin Pierce, a northern Democrat whose principles mirrored those of Van Buren. Elected after pledging to support the Compromise of 1850, Pierce saw his administration run aground on the shoals of sectional issues related to slavery. In 1854 Pierce sent marines, cavalry, and artillery to Boston to ensure the return of fugitive slave Anthony Burns. This striking display of federal power in support of slavery only alarmed northerners; textile manufacturer Amos A. Lawrence wrote that "we went to bed one night old fashioned, conservative, Compromise Union Whigs & waked up stark mad Abolitionists." Pierce's unsuccessful efforts to purchase CUBA from Spain increased fears that the Slave Power was taking over the nation's government. His proposal to build a transcontinental railroad likewise fell victim to sectional differences.

But when Pierce gave his support to Stephen Douglas's KANSAS-NEBRASKA ACT, he unwittingly multiplied sectional conflict over slavery. This bill established two new territories on the Great Plains and in them repealed the prohibition on slavery in that region that had been established in the Missouri Compromise. After an enormous struggle in Congress, the bill passed with overwhelming southern support. Its repeal of the Missouri Compromise, however, caused a political earthquake in the North. Thousands of northerners were alarmed because slavery could now

spread into a vast territory where it had long been prohibited. Their fears hastened the demise of the Whig party and led to the organization of the new Republican Party, dedicated to opposing the expansion of slavery in the territories. Slavery now had become the dominant issue in American politics, and for the next four years the two-party system would function to accentuate, rather than suppress, conflict over slavery.

Democrat James Buchanan of Pennsylvania, who won the White House in 1856, soon learned that policies pleasing to the South inflamed northern fears over slavery. Buchanan encouraged the Supreme Court to rule on the Dred Scott case [see DRED SCOTT V. SANDFORD], in hopes that a ruling from the high court might settle territorial issues. Chief Justice Roger Taney, backed by a majority of southern justices, ruled that Negroes were not citizens, that slaves did not gain their freedom by residence in free states or territories, and that Congress never had possessed the power to ban slavery from the territories. This endorsement of the most uncompromising southern positions further alarmed many northerners.

When Buchanan supported the admission of Kansas under the Lecompton Constitution, he exacerbated these northern fears. The bloody conflicts in Kansas were complicated, but it was quite clear that most residents wanted the territory to become a free state. Proslavery forces, however, controlled the writing of the Lecompton Constitution, which guaranteed that slavery would continue at least for those slaves already in the territory and their descendants. Kansans were not to be given a chance to vote for or against slavery in toto, despite earlier statements by Buchanan to the effect that the bona fide residents must be allowed to decide their social institutions.

This was too much even for Stephen Douglas, who was normally a loyal Democrat and who needed southern support in his bid for the 1860 presidential nomination. Douglas broke with Buchanan on the issue and led the successful fight to block the admission of Kansas. Angered by his stand, southern Democrats turned against Douglas; in 1860 they would split the Democratic party rather than accept his nomination for President. Meanwhile, many northern voters saw in the struggle still more evidence that slavery was gaining control over the federal government.

Emancipation. These developments contributed greatly to the victory of Lincoln's Republican Party in the 1860 presidential contest. Republicans appealed to a broad spectrum of voters with platform planks stressing economic development, free homesteads, and other issues, but the core of the party's platform was opposition to the extension of slavery. Although Lincoln and his party stated explicitly that they would not interfere with slavery in the states where it existed, they insisted that the institution must not be allowed to expand. In many speeches Lincoln also had underscored fears that slavery's advocates were trying to "push it forward, till it shall become lawful in *all* the states . . . *North* as well as *South.*" These fears, plus the Republicans' other appeals, enabled the party to win the 1860 election by gaining an ELECTORAL-COLLEGE majority in the northern states.

Slavery proved to be a central issue for Lincoln's presidency despite numerous efforts to keep it in the background. When the Civil War began, both President and Congress made clear that the war was being fought to preserve the Union, not to alter the status of slavery. Initially, Lincoln's government directed that slaves who escaped into Union lines be returned to their owners. In May 1862 Lincoln countermanded General David Hunter's proclamation of freedom for slaves in Georgia, South Carolina, and Florida, and he made no attempt to use the powers that Congress had given him to emancipate slaves through the Confiscation Acts. To some who proposed the use of slaves as soldiers, Lincoln even expressed doubt that the slaves could be effective or reliable in a military role.

By the summer of 1862, however, Lincoln had changed his views and decided that the war for the Union must also become a war against slavery. He read a draft of his emancipation proclamation to the Cabinet, which persuaded him to delay its issuance until after a notable Union victory. In September, therefore, after the battle of Antietam, Lincoln issued the Preliminary Emancipation Proclamation, warning the South that unless it returned to the Union he would declare its slaves free on 1 January 1863. With the arrival of the new year, Lincoln declared that "all persons held as slaves" in areas designated as in rebellion "are, and henceforward shall be, free." His proclamation stated that this unprecedented action came "by virtue of the power in me vested as commander-in-chief . . . in time of actual armed rebellion."

The Emancipation Proclamation contained complex ambiguities, for its duration as a "war measure" might be subject to challenge, and it excluded all areas of the Confederacy that were in fact under federal control. It represented, nevertheless, the decisive step toward liberation of the slaves. The Thirteenth Amendment, passed with Lincoln's encouragement and ratified in 1865, completed the legal destruction of slavery, but the nation had embarked on this policy through an act of executive authority, just as former President John Quincy Adams once predicted. Eman-

cipation brought new strength to the federal armies, identified the Union with the cause of human liberty, and linked the presidency with the protection and expansion of freedom.

In the GETTYSBURG ADDRESS Lincoln called on his listeners to resolve "that this nation shall have a new birth of freedom" as a result of the war. Presidential power was, in fact, the agent of freedom's rebirth. Through strong action in prosecuting the war and initiating the destruction of slavery, Lincoln created new expectations about the President's role and the nation's responsibility in defending liberty. Whereas the American Revolution had sought to protect citizens from oppressive central power, the Civil War promoted positive ideas of liberty and government. In this new conception, the nation helped individuals to realize their rights and surmount the constraining bonds of custom, prejudice, or law. The destruction of slavery brought broader notions of both liberty and presidential leadership.

BIBLIOGRAPHY

Brown, Richard H. "The Missouri Crisis, Slavery, and the Politics of Jacksonianism." *South Atlantic Quarterly* 65, no. 1 (Winter, 1966): 55–72.

Fehrenbacher, Don E. *The Dred Scott Case.* 1978.

Foner, Eric. *Free Soil, Free Labor, Free Men.* 1970.

McPherson, James M. *Abraham Lincoln and the Second American Revolution.* 1990.

Potter, David M. *The Impending Crisis.* 1976.

Robinson, Donald L. *Slavery in the Structure of American Politics, 1765–1820.* 1971.

Smith, Justin H. *The Annexation of Texas.* 1941.

PAUL D. ESCOTT

SLIDELL'S MISSION. John Slidell's mission to Mexico in November 1845 revealed President James K. Polk's determination to obtain California—by purchase if possible, by force if necessary. A peaceful acquisition required negotiation, but with the American decision to annex Texas in March 1845 Mexico recalled its minister [*see* TEXAS, ANNEXATION OF]. Suddenly in September Polk's agent in Mexico, William S. Parrott, informed the administration that Mexico was prepared to resume diplomatic relations. The President reacted by appointing John Slidell of Louisiana as minister to Mexico. The State Department hurriedly prepared the necessary instructions, troubled by rumors of the impending collapse of the peacefully disposed José Joaquin Herrera regime. Upon receiving his orders in Pensacola, Slidell departed for Vera Cruz. By early December he had taken up residence in Mexico City.

Slidell's instructions revealed Polk's territorial designs. For $40 million and the cancellation of all American claims against Mexico he hoped to acquire a boundary along the Rio Grande to the thirty-second parallel and then west to the Pacific. His primary objective was frontage on the distant ocean that included San Francisco and Monterey, but possibly San Diego as well. He assumed that Mexico, because of its military and financial helplessness, would accept a negotiated settlement. To Mexican officials Slidell's presence in the capital seemed no less than an American attempt to impose a new boundary under the threat of force. Herrera refused to respond. Slidell understood what a settlement would require, observing in late December that Mexico's resistance would continue "until the Mexican people shall be convinced by hostile demonstrations, that our differences must be settled promptly, either by negotiation or the sword." In January the Herrera government fell to General Mariano Peredes who also declined to negotiate. With the failure of his mission Slidell, like the President, advocated war.

[*See also* MEXICAN WAR.]

BIBLIOGRAPHY

Graebner, Norman A. *Empire on the Pacific: A Study in American Continental Expansion.* 1955.

Pletcher, David M. *The Diplomacy of Annexation: Texas, Oregon, and the Mexican War.* 1973.

NORMAN A. GRAEBNER

SLOGANS, CAMPAIGN. See CAMPAIGN SLOGANS.

SMITH, ALFRED E. (1873–1944), governor of New York, Democratic presidential nominee in 1928. Al Smith's progressive record as governor (1919–1921; 1923–1929) in a conservative era catapulted him to the leadership of the eastern, urban wing of the national DEMOCRATIC PARTY. A product of a political machine, New York City's Tammany Hall, he nevertheless stood for efficiency and economy in government, social and labor reform, and reform in education and penal institutions. He also championed hospital and housing construction, establishment of a park system, and public development of water power resources. Smith was a devout Catholic, but he displayed ecumenism in both appointments and program development. His first presidential bid came in 1924, when at the Democratic national convention in New York City's Madison Square Garden he challenged for the nomination the former Secretary of the Treasury

William G. McAdoo, leader of the southern-western, rural wing of the party. A prolonged and bitterly divided convention resulted in both men's withdrawal and the nomination of JOHN W. DAVIS. At this juncture Smith had not carved out a national program, though he vigorously opposed PROHIBITION, attacked Republican protectionism, and favored a Wilson-type of internationalism. He considered himself a STATES' RIGHTS Democrat in the tradition of Thomas Jefferson.

By 1928, the Democratic party's southern-western wing lacked effective leadership, and Smith, having been overwhelmingly reelected governor two years earlier, emerged as the odds-on favorite to win the presidential nomination. He avoided discussing national issues until he was nominated in Houston on the first ballot, then proceeded to map out a program, sometimes following the PARTY PLATFORM, other times deviating from it. He advocated revision of the Volstead Act and championed regulation by the states of alcoholic beverages. His selection of the "wet" Catholic businessman John J. Raskob as Democratic national chairman not only confirmed his dislike of prohibition but also his determination to face the religious issue squarely and to mollify the business community in a prosperous era.

Much of the Smith canvass, indeed, was defensive and was directed at the powerful religious campaign waged against him as the first Catholic to run for the presidency. His economic program differed little from that of the Republican candidate Herbert C. Hoover. He eschewed the concentration of power in Washington and supported a business-like tariff. On agriculture and water power he assumed a more advanced position than Hoover but failed to satisfy fully the respective constituent groups. Smith tried throughout to capitalize on his image as a progressive and humanitarian, but his New York demeanor and accent, his expressed loyalty to Tammany Hall, and his sometimes provincial behavior rendered his effort less successful than he had hoped. In the fall he suffered a crushing electoral defeat. Although he had chosen Arkansas Senator Joseph T. Robinson as his vice presidential running mate, he lost several southern states on the religious issue and perhaps on prohibition. Elsewhere he was unable to overcome Republican prosperity but managed to win traditionally Republican Massachusetts and Rhode Island and most of the nation's largest cities, where he captured a substantial percentage of the ethnic vote.

After 1928, Smith drifted more toward conservatism. At first he renounced further political ambition, but when the presidential movement of Governor Franklin D. Roosevelt of New York gained momentum, he proclaimed his availability for the 1932 Democratic nomination. The two former allies had a falling out. Roosevelt's failure as governor to consult with Smith on program and patronage, his alleged radical tendencies, and his reputation as a compromiser moved Smith, now a successful businessman as head of the Empire State Corporation, to lead a stop-Roosevelt effort at the 1932 Democratic national convention in Chicago. Having failed he reluctantly endorsed Roosevelt's candidacy, but within one year became a critic of the NEW DEAL. Smith attacked centralization and bureaucracy in Washington, ridiculed the government's monetary policy as being unsound, and assailed federal intrusion in the free enterprise system. He also impugned Roosevelt's judgment and the President's capacity for firm and steady leadership. In 1934, he joined other disillusioned Democrats in the formation of the American Liberty League, an organization financed mainly by Smith's business friends John J. Raskob and the duPont brothers, which championed the restoration of Jefferson-Jackson principles and railed against the "socialist-Marxist state" in Washington. An extension of his long-held position on the role of the federal government, Smith's statements in behalf of the conservative cause led him to oppose Roosevelt's reelection in 1936 and 1940. Issues relating to WORLD WAR II drew him closer to Roosevelt once again and the two had a partial rapprochement shortly before Smith's death.

BIBLIOGRAPHY

Burner, David, *The Politics of Provincialism: The Democratic Party in Transition, 1918–1932.* 1968.

Josephson, Matthew, and Hannah Josephson. *Al Smith: Hero of the Cities.* 1969.

Lichtman, Allan J. *Prejudice and the Old Politics: The Presidential Election of 1928.* 1979.

O'Connor, Richard. *The First Hurrah: A Biography of Alfred E. Smith.* 1970.

Schwarz, Jordan A. "Al Smith in the Thirties." *New York History* 45 (1964): 316–330.

ROBERT F. WESSER

SMOOT-HAWLEY TARIFF ACT (1930). Herbert Hoover adhered to the Republican protectionist tradition reimplemented by the FORDNEY-MCCUMBER TARIFF ACT of 1922. He wished to revitalize the Tariff Commission—an administrative device allowing the President to raise or lower tariffs by as much as 50 percent—and shared progressive beliefs that the commission was better able than Congress to fine-tune tariff protectionism. Elected with western support, Hoover advocated duty increases on agricultural im-

ports as part of a legislative program intended to alleviate the farm depression of the 1920s. Otherwise, Hoover foresaw only "limited changes" to the existing tariff.

House deliberations on tariff revision, directed by Ellis Hawley (R-Ore.), chairperson of the Ways and Means Committee, proceeded without effective leadership from the administration. Protectionist Republicans engaged in a flurry of logrolling, substantially increasing duties on both agricultural and industrial products. Senate insurgents, led by William Borah (R-Id.), narrowly lost in an effort to rescind all industrial duty increases. Insurgents also opposed the Tariff Commission, but Hoover interceded to save it. He failed, however, to halt the feeding frenzy of rate increases led by Reed Smoot (R-Utah) and other Republican arch-protectionists.

Hoover, who had sought the act's agricultural-product-duty increases, was disappointed that the duties on so many manufactured products were increased as well. In signing the bill, he highlighted the continuation of flexible tariff provisions and suggested that any gross tariff inequities could be cured by the Tariff Commission.

The act continued a pattern of economic nationalism already apparent in the international economy before its passage and invited protectionist retaliation from Canada and Europe. It represented a setback to internationalist efforts to mitigate depression conditions, impairing European exports at a time when Europe already suffered from crushing international debt burdens and massive trade imbalances.

BIBLIOGRAPHY

Fausold, Martin L. *The Presidency of Herbert C. Hoover.* 1985.

Taussig, F. W. *The Tariff History of the United States.* 8th ed. 1931.

Warren, Harris Gaylord. *Herbert Hoover and the Great Depression.* 1959.

RALPH MITZENMACHER

SNEPP v. UNITED STATES 444 U.S. 507 (1980). *Snepp* was concerned with the government's authority to forbid the publication of classified material by former government employees. On 19 February 1980, a majority of the Supreme Court of the United States in a per curiam decision reversed a Court of Appeals, Fourth Circuit, decision that the authority of the CENTRAL INTELLIGENCE AGENCY (CIA) to prohibit the publication of classified material by its former employees did not extend to the censorship of unclassified material. This decision arose out of the circumstances surrounding the publication of a book titled *Decent Interval.* Its author, Frank Snepp, while working for the CIA, had signed an employee agreement in 1968 that he would submit to the agency any material he intended to publish for prepublication review. The purpose of the contractual requirement was to prevent the publication of classified material. Despite the fact that Snepp's book did not contain classified material, the agency took action against Snepp because he breached the requirement to submit his manuscript for review. The Supreme Court majority upheld a decision of the District Court for Eastern Virginia (rejected by the Fourth Circuit) to impose a constructive trust over the profits derived from the sale of Snepp's book.

Justice John Paul Stevens, supported by Justices William Brennan and Thurgood Marshall, wrote a strong dissenting opinion, characterizing the majority's decision as granting "the Government unprecedented and drastic relief in the form of a constructive trust over the profits" derived from Snepp's book. He further argued that the remedy "is not supported by statute, by the contract, or by the common law." Stevens argued that there is a clear distinction between violation of the obligation not to disclose confidential information (which the CIA conceded Snepp did not violate) and the duty to submit material for prepublication review (which Snepp did violate). Stevens made clear that he believed that the CIA's resentment of criticism might well have resulted in curtailment of Snepp's right to publish even if Snepp had submitted his manuscript for prepublication review. Thus the underlying issue for Stevens was whether the statutes authorized the executive branch to use its protection of secrets to stifle criticism. The punative nature of the majority's remedy also provoked strong criticism from Justice Stevens. He noted pointedly that because Snepp had not gained any profits as a result of his breach of the prepublication agreement, "the Government, rather than Snepp, will be unjustly enriched if he is required to disgorge profits attributed entirely to his own legitimate activity."

The most serious consequence of the majority's decision is, according to Stevens, the adoption of a drastic new punative remedy, which may be used "to enforce a special prior restraint on a citizen's right to criticize his government."

Justice Stevens's emphasis on governmental suppression of dissent and criticism identified one of the most serious long-range problems involving the scope of executive authority. Where executive authority can invoke national security, criticism of such authority can increasingly be muted by invocation of the real or alleged need for secrecy as the subsequent IRAN-CONTRA AFFAIR underscored.

BIBLIOGRAPHY

Koffler, Joseph H., and Gershman, Bennett L. "The New Seditious Libel." *Cornell Law Review* 69 (1984): 816.
Sunstein, Cass R. "Government Control of Information." *California Law Review* 74 (1986): 889.

JOHN R. SCHMIDHAUSER

SOCIAL SECURITY. Old-age insurance, known as social security, was one of the provisions of the Social Security Act, which President Franklin D. Roosevelt signed into law on 14 August 1935. The act began the modern programs of unemployment compensation, welfare, and public health as well as providing old-age benefits. Old-age insurance was a federally administered program in which the government collected contributions of 1 percent of the first $3,000 of an employee's wages from both employers and employees and paid pensions to the employees on their retirement. Tax collections were to begin in January 1937, and the first benefits were to be paid in 1942.

Origin. Roosevelt had played the key role in creating the act. In June 1934, he asked Labor Secretary FRANCES PERKINS to chair a cabinet-level Committee on Economic Security that, together with a staff headed by two Wisconsin state officials, made the crucial decisions to recommend a federal social insurance program for old age financed through payroll taxes. The President himself changed the financing provisions of the legislation to reflect his preference for a fully funded law that would never have to rely on general revenues. He contrasted this contributory approach favorably with other currently popular plans, such as Dr. Francis Everett Townsend's proposals to pay everyone over sixty a pension of $200 a month. The President resisted congressional attempts both to abandon social insurance in favor of noncontributory welfare grants to the elderly and to permit those with liberal private pension plans to withdraw from social security.

Having used his political clout to secure passage of the law, Roosevelt entrusted the management of the program to Perkins and to the independent, three-person Social Security Board. The President appointed John Winant, a Republican, as the board's first chairman. When Winant quit in the fall of 1936 to devote his time to defending the program from political attacks, Roosevelt replaced him with Arthur Altmeyer, who guided the program until 1953.

Social security surfaced as a campaign issue in 1936, when Republican candidate ALFRED M. LANDON criticized the program as "unjust, unworkable, stupidly drafted, and wastefully financed." In response to such criticism, Roosevelt agreed to a plan, devised by the Social Security Board and passed by Congress in 1939, to reduce the amount of money held in reserve to finance benefits, to initiate benefits earlier than planned, and to broaden benefits to include special benefits for workers' wives and for the dependents of workers who died before retirement age.

Amendments and Adjustments. President Harry S. Truman concentrated on passage of national health insurance and transformed it from a secondary political concern to a highly visible partisan political issue. In the process, he called attention to disability insurance as part of a comprehensive program to reduce the income lost during or because of illness. As his health and disability proposals stalled in Congress, he continued to advocate the expansion of other forms of social security and called repeatedly for retirement benefits at age 60 for women, higher benefit levels for everyone, and expanded coverage that included agricultural workers. In May 1948 he urged Congress to pass these items.

On 28 August 1950, Truman signed major amendments to the Social Security Act that had been written by Altmeyer and his associates in the Social Security Administration, the successor agency to the Social Security Board. These important amendments raised benefit levels above those available through state welfare programs and ended the competition between state-run, noncontributory welfare programs for the elderly and social security. They also expanded coverage to reach non-farm self-employed people.

President Dwight D. Eisenhower inherited a social security program that, because of the 1950 amendments, was popular and well entrenched in Washington. He vowed to bring social security coverage to farm workers and others not receiving benefits. Despite this intention, his election raised the possibility that alternatives to contributory social insurance might receive serious consideration at the presidential level. Eisenhower's victory coincided with the adoption by the Chamber of Commerce of a plan to cover all elderly people with payroll taxes set at a level to fund the program on a current basis and without allowing surplus revenues to develop. The Chamber of Commerce also called for the abolition of state welfare programs for the elderly. Oveta Culp Hobby and NELSON A. ROCKEFELLER, in charge of the newly created Department of Health, Education, and Welfare, consulted with Chamber of Commerce officials and other conservative critics of the program, such as Representative Carl Curtis (R-Neb.). These critics urged the President to abandon the contributory features of social security and simply to "blanket in" those elderly

people who were not receiving benefits. By the fall of 1953, Eisenhower had decided to reject this approach, and, as he told stockbroker Edward Hutton in October, "to build upon the system that has been in effect for almost twenty years." The President proposed and secured passage in September 1954 of a law that preserved the existing system, raised benefit levels, and extended social security coverage to farmers.

Although Eisenhower replaced many key officials (including Altmeyer) in the Social Security Administration with his own appointees, he failed to check the advance of social security. After 1954, he lost control over social security policy. Congress passed disability insurance—early retirement pensions for those who had contributed to the social security system and could prove they were "unable to engage in substantial gainful employment"—over his opposition in 1956. Congressional Democrats, urged on by organized labor, began to contemplate passage of Medicare, that is, health insurance for social security beneficiaries. They argued that retirement benefits could never be raised high enough to cover the costs of catastrophic illness. Eisenhower, preferring health-insurance coverage that relied on private insurance companies, opposed Medicare.

Presidents John F. Kennedy and Lyndon B. Johnson both worked for the passage of Medicare. Kennedy appointed Wilbur Cohen, an old associate of Arthur Altmeyer's, to a key post in the Department of Health, Education, and Welfare, and he selected Robert Ball, a Democrat and strong proponent of program expansion, to become the new Commissioner of Social Security. Although Kennedy pressed the matter, Congress refused to pass Medicare, which remained on the legislative agenda at the time of Kennedy's death. Johnson pursued the matter with his customary vigor and, after the President's decisive victory in 1964, Wilbur Mills (D-Ark.) the cautious head of the House Ways and Means Committee, acquiesced to its passage.

Medicare became a reality on 30 July 1965. Johnson traveled to Independence, Missouri, to sign the legislation in Truman's presence—a moment that marked the high point in the acceptance of contributory social insurance.

Issues of Finance. In the 1970s, financing issues came to dominate the policy agenda, and Presidents reluctantly responded to them. In 1977, President Jimmy Carter tried to assert control over social security policy-making and to introduce general revenues and differential tax rates on employers and employees into the program. Carter's proposals underscored his desire to correct a deficit that had developed because of the economy's poor performance and a 1972 decision to index benefits to the rate of inflation. Congress rejected Carter's proposals and instead elected higher social security taxes on both employers and employees.

Even this infusion of money could not ease the system's financial problems. After proposals put forward in May 1981 to reduce benefits for early retirees did not receive serious congressional consideration, President Ronald Reagan appointed a National Commission on Social Security Reform on 16 December 1981. Delaying the start of its substantive work until after the 1982 election, this commission eventually became a forum for hard bargaining among congressional leaders, the Reagan administration, and representatives of organized labor and big business. By 15 January 1984, an inner group of commission members, including former commissioner Robert Ball, had fashioned a compromise that Reagan staffer JAMES A. BAKER III endorsed on behalf of the President. This compromise became the basis for the 1984 Social Security Amendments, which Congress passed in April. The new law preserved the basic contributory character of social security on which Roosevelt had insisted in 1935. It included a one-time suspension of the cost-of-living adjustment, which permanently reduced social security benefits. The new law also raised tax levels by accelerating the effective dates of previously passed tax increases.

In 1984 Reagan also agreed to legislation that preserved the rights of people on the disability rolls. The President had attempted to purge the rolls of people who did not meet the law's strict definition of disability, only to encounter intense opposition from Congress and from advocates of disabled people. The new law made it impossible to remove someone from the rolls unless the government could demonstrate that the person's medical condition had improved.

After 1984, social security faded as a presidential issue. Republicans Reagan and George Bush preferred not to debate matters on which agreement had been reached in 1984. Congress objected to reserve-funding plans that allowed a large surplus to develop in the social security trust funds, but the Presidents, dependent on social security taxes for current operating revenues, chose not to endorse plans, such as that of Senator Daniel P. Moynihan (D-N.Y.), to reduce social security taxes. Fears about the system's ability to fund the retirement of the baby boom generation went largely unheeded, and social security continued to function as America's largest and most successful social welfare program.

BIBLIOGRAPHY

Achenbaum, W. Andrew. *Social Security: Visions and Revisions.* 1986.

Berkowitz, Edward D. *America's Welfare State: From Roosevelt to Reagan.* 1991.

Derthick, Martha. *Policymaking for Social Security.* 1979.

EDWARD D. BERKOWITZ

SOFAER DOCTRINE. While serving as State Department legal adviser, Abraham Sofaer defended the Reagan Administration's reinterpretation of the 1972 ABM (ANTIBALLISTIC MISSILE SYSTEM) TREATY. When President Ronald Reagan inaugurated the STRATEGIC DEFENSE INITIATIVE in 1983, some Senators argued that the SDI's development and deployment would contravene the Senate's original understanding of the ABM Treaty when it consented to that treaty in 1972. The Reagan administration originally agreed with this position, indicating that it would only "research" the SDI, but not "develop" or "deploy" it without renegotiating the treaty. But subsequently, the administration announced that it would reinterpret the ABM Treaty as permitting the SDI's development. That TREATY REINTERPRETATION drew upon not only an innovative reading of one ABM Treaty provision, but also upon an agreed statement that was appended to the treaty after the Senate had consented to the accord. When testifying at joint hearings of the Senate Committee on Foreign Relations and the Senate Committee on the Judiciary, Sofaer articulated what has since been called the Sofaer Doctrine: "When [the Senate] gives its advice and consent to a treaty, it is to the treaty that was made, irrespective of the explanations it is provided" by the executive branch. This doctrine applies apparently even if the executive branch withheld information (such as the agreed statement) from the Senate. If the Senate had originally understood the ABM Treaty as prohibiting an "exotic" missile system such as the SDI, it should have expressly established that understanding as a written condition to its ratification of the treaty. Sofaer emphasized that if the President followed the Senate's unwritten assumptions about a treaty, he might violate the United States' express obligations to another country under the treaty and international law. Sofaer thus concluded that President Reagan had the constitutional authority to reinterpret the ABM Treaty. The Senate, however, countered that the treaty reinterpretation diminished its constitutional role of giving advice and consent to treaties that the President makes. Because Article II of the Constitution gives the Senate a supervisory role in the exercise of the TREATY-MAKING POWER, it logically allows for senatorial participation in the remaking, renegotiation, or reinterpretation of a treaty. President Reagan eventually announced that he would "voluntarily" adhere to the ABM Treaty's original interpretation.

But in 1987, the Senate and executive branch also debated the President's authority to reinterpret the Treaty on the Elimination of Intermediate-range and Shorter-range Missiles (INF TREATY). The Senate attached the Biden condition to its ratification of the INF Treaty. A counterweight to the Sofaer Doctrine, the Biden condition provides that the "United States shall interpret the Treaty in accordance with the common understanding of the Treaty shared by the President and the Senate at the time the Senate gave its advice and consent to ratification." The executive branch exchanged instruments with the Soviet Union ratifying the INF Treaty and containing the Biden condition. But shortly thereafter, President Reagan disavowed the Senate's condition as a violation of his constitutional authority to administer treaties and other federal laws. The reinterpretation issue has fueled political controversy, but the federal courts have never decided this issue as a matter of constitutional law. Sofaer has adhered to the doctrine named after him; but his recent writings recognize the political wisdom in having the executive branch work cooperatively with the Senate on treaty making and treaty reinterpretation.

BIBLIOGRAPHY

Randall, Kenneth C. "The Treaty Power." *Ohio State Law Journal* 51 (1990): 1089–1126.

Sofaer, Abraham D. "The ABM Treaty and the Strategic Defense Initiative." *Harvard Law Review* 99 (1986): 1972–1985.

Symposium. "Arms Control Treaty Reinterpretation." *University of Pennsylvania Law Review* 137 (1989): 1351–1557.

KENNETH C. RANDALL

SOLICITOR GENERAL. The Office of Solicitor General in the DEPARTMENT OF JUSTICE was created, along with the Department itself, in 1870. Before that time, the ATTORNEY GENERAL was not the head of a department; rather, he functioned as an individual who for many years had his own private practice in addition to his responsibilities as the government's legal representative. As those responsibilities grew, the Attorney General had to rely increasingly on outside counsel. After the CIVIL WAR, the burden of the office and the annual expense of outside counsel had increased to the point that Congress decided to create the Department of Justice and to provide for the appointment of "a Solicitor General, learned in the law, to assist the Attorney General in the performance of his duties." From 1870 to the present day, the Solicitor General is the only person in the federal government required by statute to be "learned in the law."

Since the creation of the office, thirty-nine persons have served as Solicitor General, including one who later became President (William Howard Taft), several who later served on the Supreme Court (Taft, Stanley Reed, ROBERT JACKSON, and Thurgood Marshall), or who held other important federal offices in the executive and judicial branches (FRANCIS BIDDLE, Charles Fahy, and Simon Sobeloff), and many other prominent lawyers, such as JOHN W. DAVIS, Erwin Griswold, and Archibald Cox.

The duties of the Solicitor General have never been spelled out in detail in the governing statutes. Rather, they have evolved over the years, and are now made more specific in regulations issued by the Attorney General. Most important among these duties is the Solicitor General's responsibility for the representation of the United States, its officers and agencies, in the Supreme Court of the United States. Thus, with few exceptions applicable to certain independent agencies, the Solicitor General must give his approval before a case that the government has lost in a lower court may be taken to the Supreme Court for review. The Solicitor General is also responsible for the briefing and oral argument of cases accepted for review in that Court. Other important duties include the requirement of authorization for appeal from any decision in a federal court that is adverse to the government, for the filing by the United States (or any officer or agency) of a brief amicus curiae (friend of the court) in any court, of a petition for rehearing *en banc* (before the full appeals court rather than before a three-judge panel) in a federal court of appeals, or of a petition for intervention in any judicial proceeding.

Since the Solicitor General's Office is relatively small—totaling in 1992 some twenty lawyers and additional support staff—the office invariably draws on the work of lawyers in other divisions of the Justice Department or other government agencies. But at least two lawyers in the Solicitor General's Office work on almost every matter before it is brought to the Solicitor General for decision or review. With the exception of one of the deputies who serves as counselor to the Solicitor General, these lawyers are career civil servants selected solely on the basis of professional ability and without regard to political views or affiliation.

The Solicitor General is called on by the nature of his position and authority to play a number of roles, and the range and variety of his responsibilities is a source of some tension. One of his tasks, which is of low visibility but of great importance to the working of

Solicitors General

President	Solicitor General
18 Grant	Benjamin H. Bristow, 1870–1872 Samuel F. Phillips, 1872–1877
19 Hayes	Samuel F. Phillips, 1877–1881
20 Garfield	Samuel F. Phillips, 1881
21 Arthur	Samuel F. Phillips, 1881–1885
22 Cleveland	John Goode, 1885–1886 George A. Jenks, 1886–1889
23 B. Harrison	Orlow Chapman, 1889–1890 William Howard Taft, 1890–1892 Charles H. Aldrich, 1892–1893
24 Cleveland	Lawrence Maxwell, Jr., 1893–1895 Holmes Conrad, 1895–1897
25 McKinley	John K. Richards, 1897–1901
26 T. Roosevelt	John K. Richards, 1901–1903 Henry M. Hoyt, 1903–1909
27 Taft	Lloyd Wheaton Bowers, 1909–1910 Frederick W. Lehmann, 1910–1912 William Marshall Bullitt, 1912–1913
28 Wilson	John William Davis, 1913–1918 Alexander King, 1918–1920 William L. Frierson, 1920–1921
29 Harding	James M. Beck, 1921–1923
30 Coolidge	James M. Beck, 1923–1925 William D. Mitchell, 1925–1929

President	Solicitor General
31 Hoover	Charles Evans Hughes, Jr., 1929–1930 Thomas D. Thatcher, 1930–1933
32 F. D. Roosevelt	James Crawford Biggs, 1933–1935 Stanley Reed, 1935–1938 Robert H. Jackson, 1938–1940 Francis Biddle, 1940–1941 Charles Fahy, 1941–1945
33 Truman	J. Howard McGrath, 1945–1946 Philip B. Perlman, 1947–1952 Walter J. Cummings, Jr., 1952–1953
34 Eisenhower	Walter J. Cummings, Jr., 1953 Simon E. Sobeloff, 1954–1956 J. Lee Rankin, 1956–1961
35 Kennedy	Archibald Cox, 1961–1963
36 L. B. Johnson	Archibald Cox, 1963–1965 Thurgood Marshall, 1965–1967 Erwin N. Griswold, 1967–1969
37 Nixon	Erwin N. Griswold, 1969–1973 Robert H. Bork, 1973–1974
38 Ford	Robert H. Bork, 1974–1977
39 Carter	Wade H. McCree, 1977–1981
40 Reagan	Rex E. Lee, 1981–1985 Charles Fried, 1985–1989
41 Bush	Kenneth W. Starr, 1989–1993
42 Clinton	Drew S. Days, 1993–

government, is to deal with intragovernmental conflict with respect to the positions to be taken, and the arguments made, in the Supreme Court. On some occasions, such a conflict arises wholly between divisions in the Department of Justice itself, but the conflict may be broader and manysided, embracing other EXECUTIVE DEPARTMENTS or one or more of the independent agencies. These conflicts are often resolved through a process in which all sides are heard and every effort to reach accommodation is explored. Sometimes, the disagreement is one of policy that cannot be resolved without executive action at a higher level. And sometimes, especially when one of the independent agencies is a party to the disagreement, the conflict will not be fully resolved at the executive level but will be disclosed to the Court. This may be done through the use of an amicus curiae brief, either on behalf of the independent agency or, if the agency itself is a party to the case, on behalf of the United States. On at least one occasion—in *St. Regis Paper Co. v. United States* (1961)—the disagreement was disclosed to the Court by the Solicitor General himself, who presented both the argument for the DEPARTMENT OF COMMERCE on one side of the issue and for the Federal Trade Commission on the other.

Another source of tension—and one that in the 1980s and 1990s engendered considerable debate—arises from the Solicitor General's role as an advocate and his role as an "officer of the court." To some extent, this tension exists for every lawyer, but in the case of the Solicitor General, it is intensified by the difficulty of identifying the "client" and by the significance of the continuing relationship between the Solicitor General and the courts, and particularly the Supreme Court. Although the Solicitor General is appointed by the President, and may be overruled or removed by him, and also reports to the Attorney General, he is at the same time charged with representing the United States as a professional "learned in the law." The Supreme Court not only relies heavily on the accuracy and completeness of his submissions but also on his judgment and discretion in selecting the cases in which review is sought. And Congress looks to his office to defend the constitutionality of its legislation and to see that the laws it has enacted are applied in accordance with their expressed purposes, even when the executive may be reluctant to do so.

On rare but significant occasions, these responsibilities have led the Solicitor General to confess to the Supreme Court that a lower court has committed an error in the government's favor, to refuse to sign a brief that the Attorney General or an independent agency wishes to submit, or to disagree with the desire of others in the executive branch to take a position that he believes is unwarranted in law. More frequently, it has led him to refuse requests to seek Supreme Court or lower court review because he does not view the cases as worthy of the reviewing court's attention.

The tension between the Solicitor General's role as advocate and his broader responsibilities can never be fully resolved, and indeed the existence of that tension serves important purposes. The processes and professionalism of the Solicitor General's Office tend to moderate the more extreme views that are part of every administration. Even (or especially) at a time when the line between law and policy is increasingly viewed as indistinct, the Solicitor General's insistence on full and accurate disclosure, and on observing the bounds of appropriate argument, carries many benefits. It serves both the judiciary by helping the judges to evaluate the cases worthy of review and by assuring that the arguments made will be responsible and useful to the court, and the executive by increasing the likelihood that the courts will respond favorably to the government's petitions and arguments. Finally, the duty of the Solicitor General to represent the United States, and not simply his superiors in the executive branch, helps to assure that the interest of the legislative branch will be effectively presented to the Court without the need for separate representation, except in those rare instances when legislative action is viewed as threatening the constitutional prerogatives of the executive itself.

BIBLIOGRAPHY

Caplan, Lincoln. *The Tenth Justice.* 1987.
Fried, Charles. *Order and Law.* 1991.
Griswold, Erwin N. *Ould Fields, New Corne.* 1992.
Salokar, Rebecca Mae. *The Solicitor General: The Politics of Law.* 1992.
"Symposium: The Role and Function of the United States Solicitor General." *Loyola of Los Angeles Law Review* 21 (1987): 1047–1272.

DAVID L. SHAPIRO

SORENSEN, THEODORE (b. 1928), presidential adviser. Few advisers influenced the presidency of John F. Kennedy more than Theodore C. Sorensen. He had served as Senator Kennedy's chief administrative assistant and as his key speechwriter during the 1960 presidential campaign. Sorensen wrote much of Kennedy's acclaimed inaugural address. As President Kennedy's youthful special WHITE HOUSE COUNSEL, he continued to draft important addresses, including the United Nations speech of September 1961, which emphasized the futility of war; the much-publicized American University address of 10 June 1963, which called for "genuine" peace; and the moving speech of 11 June 1963, which focused on the moral dimension of the civil rights struggle. Sorensen was an unusually skilled wordsmith who contributed to the lofty eloquence of the Kennedy presidency and committed Kennedy to positions and policies consistent with the President's liberal political philosophy. Much of Sorensen's progressivism was influenced by the social philosophy of Senator George Norris of Sorensen's home state of Nebraska.

As special counsel, the hard-driving Sorensen also oversaw most of the President's paperwork, supervised staff assignments, played a major role in implementing economic policy, drafted many of the key messages to Congress for the Kennedy legislative agenda, and worked closely with department heads in formulating the domestic program. Even though Kennedy never employed a WHITE HOUSE CHIEF OF STAFF, Sorensen came close to assuming that role. He also continued to ghostwrite books and articles for Kennedy. It is with good reason that Kennedy called Sorensen his "intellectual blood bank."

Following the fiasco of the BAY OF PIGS INVASION of April 1961, Kennedy also sought Sorensen's advice in foreign policy matters. A proponent of restraint and caution, Sorensen favored a naval blockade instead of an air strike during the CUBAN MISSILE CRISIS and urged internal reforms regarding the Ngo Dinh Diem government of South Vietnam as a way to limit American military activity in the VIETNAM WAR. Completely devoted to Kennedy, Sorensen resigned following Kennedy's assassination and in 1965 published *Kennedy*, an intimate and favorable biography.

BIBLIOGRAPHY

Giglio, James N. *The Presidency of John F. Kennedy.* 1991.
Parmet, Herbert S. *JFK: The Presidency of John F. Kennedy.* 1983.
Sorensen, Theodore C. *Kennedy.* 1965.

JAMES N. GIGLIO

SPACE POLICY. Important presidential decisions about space preceded the first United States space launch in 1958. In fact, many argue that the United States would have placed the first satellite in orbit were it not for President Dwight D. Eisenhower's insistence that a new "civilian" launch vehicle be developed separately from the ballistic missile program. Army development of ballistic missiles proceeded independently from the Naval Research Laboratory's development of the Vanguard satellite launch vehicle. Requests by the army team, headed by Wernher von Braun, during 1956 and 1957 to use their Jupiter C missile to launch satellites were repeatedly denied.

Consequently, the Soviets won the distinction of launching the world's first satellite, *Sputnik 1*, on 4 October 1957. That launch propelled the U.S. space program forward and made politics a centerpiece of its existence since that time.

Post-Sputnik Competition. The Vanguard program, previously a low priority, suddenly became the focus of attention and was pushed to achieve a launch. The first attempt ended disastrously as the rocket rose three feet off the pad and exploded in flames. Fortunately the Eisenhower administration had reconsidered von Braun's efforts, and on 31 January 1958, *Explorer 1* became America's first satellite atop von Braun's missile.

President Eisenhower, who had announced U.S. plans to build and launch satellites (on 29 July 1955) as part of U.S. activities in support of the 1957–1958 International Geophysical Year, and Congress quickly moved to establish separate military and civilian space programs through enactment of the National Aeronautics and Space Act of 1958. The act created the National Aeronautics and Space Administration (NASA) to conduct a civilian space program while military space activities were placed under the Department of Defense (DOD).

In the spring of 1961, President John F. Kennedy faced many immediate challenges, including challenges in the space program. The Soviet Union scored another space first on 12 April 1961 with the launch of the first man (Yuri Gagarin) into space. Coming on the heels of the BAY OF PIGS INVASION President Kennedy found himself eager to restore a positive image for the United States. Three weeks after Gagarin's flight, Alan Shepard became the first American in space (though his flight was only suborbital). Kennedy went before Congress three weeks later and called on the nation to commit itself to the goal of landing a man on the moon and returning him safely to earth by the end of the decade. The moon race was on.

The space program blossomed, with programs initiated not only in human spaceflight, but space science and space applications (communications and weather, for example). The Department of Defense's modest space budget provided for the development of, among other things, a major tool of the COLD WAR era—reconnaissance satellites. With military satellites came development of an antisatellite (ASAT) system of nuclear-tipped missiles based in the Pacific.

The thrust into space lost no momentum as President Lyndon B. Johnson assumed office. Johnson had been instrumental in drafting and passing the space act while in the Senate. One of his major contributions was language encouraging international cooperation in space. His interest continued both as Vice President (where he chaired the interagency National Aeronautics and Space Council) and President. His consistent support of the Apollo program, even in the wake of the deaths of the first Apollo crew in 1967, kept the nation on course to achieve Kennedy's goal. Scientific and applications programs also grew.

Johnson supported military space efforts, too, commenting in 1967 that the dividends of military space operations to the United States were equal to ten times everything that had been spent on space. His announcement that the Pacific-based ASAT system was operational in 1964 was surprisingly candid considering the highly classified nature of military space activities.

A Decade of Retrenchment. On 20 July 1969, Neil Armstrong and Edwin "Buzz" Aldrin set foot on the lunar surface, fulfilling Kennedy's quest and winning the moon race. But times had changed. Richard M. Nixon was President and no fan of a space program so closely linked with Kennedy's memory. The nation's attention was focused on the VIETNAM WAR and solving domestic problems. The moon race had been won, and the public's interest in space waned. A 1969 report chaired by Vice President SPIRO T. AGNEW on post-Apollo goals was not well received. Two and a half years later, Nixon finally approved a small portion of the plan—building a reusable vehicle for taking people and cargo back and forth to space, ostensibly at much less cost than conventional rockets. To win his support, NASA had to cut in half the estimated cost of the program.

This program, the space shuttle, became NASA's main initiative for the 1970s. The agency's budget was reduced significantly and funding for new space projects, military and civilian, was hard to find. Nixon, in fact, abolished the policy-making Space Council in 1973. The extent to which the political aura surrounding space had changed was highlighted by the 1975 U.S. Soviet Apollo-Soyuz Test Project where DETENTE, rather than competition, was showcased.

In general, the 1970s was a decade of retrenchment. In 1978, space policy emerged from hibernation with two directives issued by President Jimmy Carter, but they contained no bold initiatives. Carter made a notable contribution to military space objectives, however, directing development of a new ASAT device to replace the Pacific-based system, which had been terminated in 1975. Simultaneously, he engaged the

Soviet Union in ASAT limitation talks, but the Soviet invasion of Afghanistan cooled the climate for ARMS CONTROL and the talks ended.

A New Momentum. President Ronald Reagan's first space policy action was to abrogate an agreement with the European Space Agency on the International Solar Polar Mission (ISPM), which was to involve two spacecraft (one built by each side) to observe simultaneously the sun's north and south poles. For budgetary reasons, Reagan canceled the U.S. probe, the first time the United States essentially withdrew from an international space program (though other parts of the agreement—to launch the European probe, for example—were honored). This action initially labeled him as an opponent of the space program, but as his tenure proceeded, he steadily increased both the NASA and the DEPARTMENT OF DEFENSE (DOD) space budgets (DOD's surpassed NASA's for the first time in 1982). Reagan issued many space policies, from broad pronouncements on military and civilian space themes, to focused policies on specific topics such as the commercial space launch industry.

Reagan's most visible legacies are the space station program and the nascent commercial space business. He approved NASA's plan to build a new space station in 1984 and directed that it be built with international partners. The space station became the centerpiece of NASA's program. Reagan's support of NASA was undiminished following the 28 January 1986 explosion of the space shuttle *Challenger*, though it did lead to major revisions in U.S. launch policy. His administration championed the privatization of government space programs and the birth of commercial space activities, diversifying government responsibility for space by enlarging the role of the DEPARTMENT OF COMMERCE and placing the DEPARTMENT OF TRANSPORTATION in charge of the commercial space-launch-services industry.

Reagan's 1983 "Star Wars" speech laid the groundwork for the STRATEGIC DEFENSE INITIATIVE (SDI) program to develop a system for ballistic missile defense (BMD). Though not a space program per se, the prospect of basing weapons in space for strategic defense sparked debate over the apparent militarization of space. Whether or not SDI weapons ultimately are based in space, any BMD system will rely on satellites for tasks such as early warning.

The DOD space budget grew from $4.8 billion in 1981 to $17.7 billion in 1988, only a small portion of which is attributable to SDI. DOD (and intelligence community) space activities across the board grew substantially. The ASAT program begun by President Carter continued through the Reagan term, only to be canceled in 1988 because of congressional opposition to the prospect of an arms race in space.

Budgetary Constraints and a Changing World. The dramatic changes in the geopolitical landscape since 1989 and the fiscal environment affected prospects for DOD's space program under President George Bush. The focus of some space programs, especially communications and early warning, changed to support tactical (regional) conflicts rather than a strategic confrontation with the Soviet Union. This shift was partially based on experience from the GULF WAR, which many dub the first space war where a wide range of space assets were available to the United States and its allies. Although President Bush initiated a new ASAT program, its progress was slowed by fiscal constraints and unclear justification.

The budget situation also affected the civilian space program. President Bush issued several space policy guidelines, but his most dramatic was a speech on 20 July 1989, the twentieth anniversary of the first Apollo landing on the moon, announcing that America would lead the way in human exploration of the solar system—a return to the moon, and then on to Mars. The program, called the Space Exploration Initiative (SEI), coincided with deepening fiscal constraints, and little progress was made in the first several years.

The space program has been enmeshed in politics since its very beginning. The level of interest and support of the President has been, and will continue to be, crucial to the conduct of U.S. space activities.

BIBLIOGRAPHY

Burrows, William E. *Deep Black: Space Espionage and National Security.* 1986.

Logsdon, John M. *The Decision to Go to the Moon: Project Apollo and the National Interest.* 1970.

Mark, Hans. *The Space Station: A Personal Journey.* 1987.

McDougall, Walter A. *. . . The Heavens and the Earth: A Political History of the Space Age.* 1985.

U.S. Congress. House. Committee on Science and Technology. *United States Civilian Space Programs: 1958–1978.* 2 vols. 97th Cong., 1st sess. 1981. 98th Cong., 1st sess. 1983.

Von Braun, Wernher, Frederick I. Ordway III, and Dave Dooling. *Space Travel: A History (An Update of History of Rocketry and Space Travel).* 1985.

MARCIA S. SMITH

SPANISH-AMERICAN WAR. The Spanish-American War (1898) marked an important transition in the presidency; it foreshadowed a shift from a foreign policy of isolation to one of intervention, reflecting the nation's acquisition of great-power status and the onset of challenges to NATIONAL SECURITY from Europe and Asia. The war stemmed from Spain's refusal to grant independence to CUBA. After a Cuban insurgency began in 1895, President Grover Cleveland exerted pressure for a peaceful settlement. His successor, William McKinley, became more and more involved in efforts to arrange home rule for Cuba. The Spanish government granted limited autonomy late in 1897, but on 15 February 1898 the American battleship *Maine* blew up in Havana harbor. Many Americans incorrectly assumed that Spain was responsible; this feeling stimulated widespread public support for Cuban independence. McKinley sought a diplomatic settlement, wishing to pursue a domestic political agenda, but, when Spain dallied, he was compelled to act. His sole war aim was Cuban independence.

McKinley's preoccupation with gaining a peaceful settlement inhibited prewar preparations; however, after hostilities began on 21 April 1898, he energetically directed military and diplomatic activity, proving adept at relating strategic designs to political goals. He sought to end the war quickly with the least possible expenditure of blood and treasure, adopting a peripheral strategy that made use of his modest but competent navy to attack Spain's colonies in the Caribbean Sea and the western Pacific. This decision established theaters of war where the United States possessed significant superiority of force and Spain was at a disadvantage. Command of the sea would determine the outcome.

Conduct of the War. The navy conducted the first wartime operations. Rear Adm. William T. Sampson established a blockade of Havana as soon as the war began, and he extended it as his North Atlantic Squadron grew in strength and awaited the arrival of a Spanish squadron under Adm. Pascual Cervera. After the Cervera's squadron made landfall at Santiago de Cuba on 19 May, Sampson's ships blockaded them. Meanwhile, Commodore George Dewey's Asiatic Squadron destroyed a weak Spanish squadron at Manila on May 1. This victory accomplished McKinley's goals—to provide a base for Dewey, to preclude Spanish commerce raiding in the Pacific, and to press Spain toward early negotiations.

These naval achievements guided the employment of the army. When news of Dewey's victory reached him, McKinley decided to send an expeditionary force to Manila, thereby maintaining pressure on Spain to negotiate soon. He had not as yet decided the disposition of the PHILIPPINES. After Cervera was bottled up at Santiago de Cuba, McKinley ordered an expeditionary force to that city, recognizing that the destruction of Cervera's squadron would assure the United States

general and lasting command of the Caribbean Sea. It was still not feasible to attack the main Spanish garrison in Havana because the volunteer army needed for this extensive operation was not ready.

These decisions led to an important diplomatic initiative. McKinley signaled his war aims to Spain through a friendly neutral power, Great Britain, indicating that besides Cuban independence he sought U.S. annexation of PUERTO RICO and Guam in lieu of a monetary indemnity to defray war costs. He did not specify his attitude toward the Philippines because of uncertainty created by the resumption of Filipino insurgency against Spain.

Despite unavoidable confusion, given the need to move quickly, an expeditionary forced led by Maj. Gen. William Shafter reached Santiago de Cuba late in June; it attacked 1 July. The troops did not succeed in storming the city, but they occupied strong positions on the San Juan Heights, forcing the Spanish governor-general in Cuba to order Cervera out of the harbor. When Cervera's five vessels sortied on 3 July, Sampson's squadron destroyed them all. Shafter then laid siege to Santiago de Cuba, which was forced to capitulate on 17 July. As soon as the city was secured, Maj. Gen. Nelson Miles led an expedition to Puerto Rico. It encountered little opposition and had almost conquered the island when the war ended.

During June and July an army expedition led by Maj. Gen. Wesley Merritt arrived at Manila, which was also threatened by Filipino insurgents. Dewey managed to negotiate a shadowy agreement with the Spanish governor-general, providing for capitulation of the Spanish garrison after a brief show of force intended to preserve Spanish honor. In return, the Americans were to prevent the Filipino insurgents from penetrating the walled city, where Spanish noncombatants had taken refuge. Merritt attacked Manila on 13 August, encountering token opposition, and soon the city capitulated. Merritt occupied Manila and kept the insurgents at bay.

The Peace Settlement. McKinley's plan to wage a brief conflict and to force an early Spanish defeat worked perfectly. After the embarrassment to Spanish arms at Santiago de Cuba, the Madrid government sought peace, negotiating with McKinley in Washington through the good offices of the French ambassador there, Jules Cambon. On 12 August, Cambon and McKinley signed a protocol that ended the war, provided for Cuba's independence, and guaranteed American annexation of Puerto Rico and Guam. The only outstanding issue, disposition of the Philippines, was left to a peace conference that began in September in Paris.

McKinley did not wish to annex the Philippines, preferring either to take nothing or to gain a naval base. Nonetheless, growing public support forced his hand, as it had in April. To retain control of his administration, he decided to annex the entire Philippine archipelago. Although defeated Spain could not resist this initiative, the Philippine insurgents, led by Emilio Aguinaldo, proved unwilling to accept American control. The result was the Philippine War, which ended with the defeat of the insurgents in July 1902.

McKinley's conduct during 1898 reflected the necessity for strong presidential leadership in wartime. He was forced to respond to public pressure exerted through Congress in deciding to go to war and in resolving to annex the Philippines after the victory. Withal, he managed wartime policy and strategy expertly, ending the war quickly and cheaply.

BIBLIOGRAPHY

Chadwick, French E. *The Relations of the United States and Spain: The Spanish-American War.* 2 vols. 1911.

Cosmas, Graham A. *An Army for Empire: The United States Army in the Spanish-American War.* 1971.

Leech, Margaret. *In the Days of McKinley.* 1959.

Trask, David F. *The War with Spain in 1898.* 1981.

Welch, Richard E. *Response to Imperialism: The United States and the Philippine-American War, 1899–1902.* 1979.

DAVID F. TRASK

SPECIAL COUNSEL. See White House Counsels.

SPECIAL ENVOYS. See Private Envoys.

SPECIAL PROSECUTOR. See Independent Counsel.

SPECIE CIRCULAR. The Specie Circular ordered that after 1836 the government would receive only gold and silver (specie) in payment for public land, except from actual settlers. Speculation in land during the 1830s had reached such a high level that the General Land Office in charge of sales could not keep up with it. Some $25 million in land sales were recorded in 1836, creating an enormous surplus in the treasury. By the time President Andrew Jackson acted on the matter, land sales had reached $5 million a month. "Doing a land-office business" entered the national vocabulary as a result. Most of the sales involved paper money from banks that had little or no assets to back it up. Fraud regularly occurred because some speculators drove up the price of land beyond its worth before unloading it on unsuspecting settlers. The quantity of paper money used in land sales had increased more than 50 percent over an eighteen-month period.

To check what was becoming a wild inflation of currency, President Jackson in an EXECUTIVE ORDER, issued the Specie Circular on 11 July 1836 through the Secretary of the Treasury. It stated that after August 15, nothing but specie would be accepted by the government in payment for public land, except from settlers actually on the land. The authority for this action was a resolution of 1816 whereby the Secretary of the Treasury was authorized to use his discretionary power to receive or reject the notes of specie-paying banks in payment of dues owed the government.

The circular was another forceful exercise of EXECUTIVE POWER by Jackson. Senator Thomas Hart Benton of Missouri, one of Jackson's closest supporters, said that it demonstrated "the foresight, the decision, and the invincible firmness of General Jackson." But it also showed a callous disregard for Congress, inasmuch as Jackson knew there was strong opposition to it and that Congress might even pass legislation to counteract it. Consequently he waited until Congress adjourned for the summer before issuing the Specie Circular.

BIBLIOGRAPHY

Feller, Daniel. *Public Lands and Jacksonian Politics.* 1984.

Rohrbough, Malcom J. *The Land Office Business: The Settlement and Administration of American Public Lands, 1789–1837.* 1969.

ROBERT V. REMINI

SPEECHWRITERS, PRESIDENTIAL. In an age when Presidents must generate public support to achieve legislative and administrative goals, the message of the President matters. Policy success depends on a President's ability to articulate themes that will attract public interest. Because speeches are an important resource for galvanizing presidential electoral and policy support, a White House unit is devoted to preparing the spoken (and written) presidential word.

Presidential speechwriters have been a regular feature of the White House Staff since Judson Welliver joined the administration of Warren G. Harding. While Presidents since Harding's time have varied their use of speechwriters, they have all turned to them for assistance. Prior to the development of a White House speechwriting staff in the 1920s, persons working in the departments were detailed to the White House to prepare presidential remarks, although they remained on their departmental payrolls.

The organization of the speechwriting operation generally reflects the type of organization found in a particular White House. If a President prefers a loosely structured White House, speechwriters are likely to report directly to him, as was true during the Lyndon B. Johnson administration. A tightly organized staff structure, as seen in the early Ronald Reagan White House, integrates speechwriting with other staff units. There is a partisan component to the speechwriting operation. In Republican administrations the unit is more likely to be tied to the long-range communications planning operations, while in Democratic administrations the unit tends to be more loosely tied either to the President directly or to the daily communication operations.

When the BROWNLOW COMMITTEE recommended the appointment of several presidential assistants—a recommendation that led to the creation in 1939 of the EXECUTIVE OFFICE OF THE PRESIDENT (EOP) and an enhanced White House staff—it spoke of presidential assistants' having to have "passion for anonymity." While for many years assistants maintained a low profile, they ultimately became more conspicuous. Speechwriters are among the White House staff members who have made the transition from behind-the-scenes players to front-stage personalities. When President Reagan was leaving office and George Bush was preparing to take over, both had the same speechwriter, Peggy Noonan. She is generally credited with writing the farewell address of Reagan and the INAUGURAL ADDRESS of Bush. Several Reagan speechwriters left office to take visible communications positions: Patrick Buchanan became a television commentator and a 1992 presidential candidate; David Gergen took an editorial position at *U.S. News and World Report* and became a frequent guest on television news programs.

The speechwriting operation is responsible for preparing major addresses, such as the annual STATE OF THE UNION MESSAGE, as well as shorter remarks at Rose Garden ceremonies held outside the OVAL OFFICE. The material prepared by speechwriters falls into three basic categories: major speeches, remarks delivered at ceremonial appearances, and written statements. The critical speeches of an administration, such as the inaugural address(es), annual state of the union messages, UNITED NATIONS speeches, and addresses delivered to joint sessions of Congress, involve the work of staff in the speechwriting office and throughout the White House, who review drafts for policy implications. The state of the union address also has to contend with the contributions of members of the CABINET, who seek to advance their own policy interests. Speechwriters often specialize, with some writing the ideological speeches (as was the case with Tony Dolan in the Reagan years) and others tapped for their particular policy specialty or their ability to write humorous remarks (e.g., Peter Benchley in the Johnson administration).

While Presidents are responsible for the remarks contained in a speech, individual speechwriters can play a significant role in developing content. It is almost impossible to separate policy from the words used to promote it. Bryce Harlow, a senior staff member in the Dwight D. Eisenhower White House, observed, "The speechwriters in the White House can have a very, very substantial influence on policy, either by the methodology of presentation of the material or by the inclusion or exclusion of ideas, and by the fact that he has to work so intimately with the President." A memorandum in the Carter Library illustrates the point. In the Jimmy Carter administration, speechwriter James Fallows used his position to lobby senior administration staff on policy questions. In April 1978 he urged Press Secretary Jody Powell to alter the position of the State Department toward a settlement in Southern Rhodesia, even though he recognized that his effort represented an end run around the White House staffing system.

The usefulness of the speechwriting operation depends upon the President and the message he has to offer. Speechwriters can make a President appear more articulate, but the effectiveness of the speech depends on the President's delivery. In 1986 Peggy Noonan produced a moving speech to honor the astronauts killed in the destruction of the space shuttle *Challenger*, yet that speech had a special impact because of Reagan's capacity to understand and convey the depth of national mourning.

BIBLIOGRAPHY

Anderson, Patrick. *The President's Men.* 1968.

Cornwell, Elmer. *Presidential Leadership of Public Opinion.* 1965.

Deaver, Michael K., with Mickey Herskowitz. *Behind the Scenes.* 1987.

Fallows, James. "The Passionless Presidency." *Atlantic Monthly* 239 (January 1979): 33–47; 243 (May 1979): 33–48.

Grossman, Michael Baruch, and Martha Joynt Kumar. *Portraying the President: The White House and the News Media.* 1981.

Kernell, Samuel. *Going Public: New Strategies of Presidential Leadership.* 1985.

Noonan, Peggy. *What I Saw at the Revolution: A Political Life in the Reagan Era.* 1990.

Patterson, Bradley H., Jr. *The Ring of Power: The White House Staff and Its Expanding Role in Government.* 1988.

Safire, William. *Before the Fall: An Inside View of the Pre-Watergate White House.* 1975.

Tulis, Jeffrey. *The Rhetorical Presidency.* 1987.

MARTHA KUMAR

SPENDING POWER. Although the Constitution appears to grant Congress complete authority to decide how to spend the taxpayers' money, history offers many instructive lessons that the spending power is often shared with the President and other executive officials. Congress alone appropriates funds; actual expenditures depend to a substantial extent on decisions made within the executive branch.

Constitutional Principles. The Framers were familiar with the efforts of English monarchs to rely on extraparliamentary sources of revenue for military expeditions and other operations of government. Partly because of those transgressions, England lurched into a civil war and Charles I lost both his throne and his head. The establishment of democratic government is tied directly to legislative control over spending.

The Constitution attempted to avoid a repetition of British civil war and bloodshed by vesting the power of the purse squarely in Congress. Under Article I, Section 9, "No Money shall be drawn from the Treasury, but in Consequence of Appropriations made by Law." In FEDERALIST 48, James Madison explained that "the legislative department alone has access to the pockets of the people." The power of the purse, Madison said in *Federalist* 58, represents the "most compleat and effectual weapon with which any constitution can arm the immediate representatives of the people, for obtaining a redress of every grievance, and for carrying into effect every just and salutary measure."

The Framers did more than place the power of the purse with Congress. They deliberately divided government by making the President the COMMANDER IN CHIEF and reserving to Congress the power to finance military expeditions. The Framers rejected a government in which a single branch could both make war and fund it. As George Mason advised his colleagues at the constitutional convention in 1787, the "purse & the sword ought never to get into the same hands whether Legislative or Executive."

The congressional power of the purse is not unlimited. Congress cannot use appropriations bills to enact bills of attainder, to restrict the President's PARDON POWER, or to establish a religion. The Constitution prohibits Congress from diminishing the salaries of the President or federal judges. Congress would overstep its boundaries if it refused to appropriate funds for the President to receive foreign ambassadors or to negotiate treaties. Congress may add conditions and provisos to appropriations bills, but conditions are invalid if they attempt to achieve unconstitutional results.

Lump Sums versus Itemization. In the early years, the Federalists advocated lump-sum appropriations and executive-spending discretion, while the Democratic-Republicans championed line-itemization and legislative control. President Thomas Jefferson's Secretary of the Treasury, ALBERT GALLATIN, advocated "specific appropriations for each object of a distinct nature." Jefferson went beyond that, in his first message to Congress, by announcing that it would be prudent to appropriate "specific sums to every specific purpose susceptible of definition." ALEXANDER HAMILTON promptly called that guideline "preposterous." Nothing could be "more wild or of more inconvenient tendency," he said, than to adopt Jefferson's proposal.

Once in office, Gallatin and Jefferson appreciated the need for lump-sum appropriations. In an 1802 report to Congress, Gallatin cautioned against excessive subdivision of the appropriations, especially in the case of the War and Navy departments. Jefferson himself recognized that "too minute a specification has its evil as well as too general one," and thought it better for Congress to appropriate in gross while trusting in executive discretion. It was preferable, he said, to make a temporary trust to the President, which could be "put an end to if abused."

Contingencies and Emergencies. During periods of war and national depression, Congress delegates broad spending power to the President. A CIVIL WAR act provided for $50 million to pay two- and three-year volunteers, $26 million for subsistence, $14 million for army transportation and supplies, and another $76 million for assorted items, to be divided among them "as the exigencies of the service may require." On the eve of the SPANISH-AMERICAN WAR, President William McKinley asked from Congress and received $50 million "for the national defense, and for each and every purpose connected therewith, to be expended at the discretion of the President."

Emergency relief programs during the Great Depression set aside billions to be spent at the President's discretion. An act of 1934 appropriated $950 million for emergency relief programs and the civil works program, making the money available "for such projects and/or purposes and under such rules and regulations as the President in his discretion may prescribe." The Emergency Relief Appropriation Act of 1935 appropriated $4.8 billion to be used "in the discretion and under the direction of the President." A study published at the start of President Franklin D. Roosevelt's second term estimated that Congress, since 4 March 1933, had given him discretionary authority over $15.4 billion. That compared to a total of $1.6 billion in discretionary spending power given to all previous Presidents.

Executive Commitments. Constitutional principles

imply that Congress is the branch that decides to commit the nation's resources, but Presidents and executive officials have found it expedient at times to enter into financial obligations not authorized by Congress. In 1796, during debate on JAY'S TREATY, the House of Representatives warned both the President and the Senate that the TREATY-MAKING POWER could not be used to usurp the constitutional prerogatives of the House, such as the authority to regulate trade. The House adopted a resolution stating that the House retained full discretion in deciding whether to provide appropriations and legislation to carry treaties into effect.

Another early conflict arose from President Jefferson's decision to accept an offer from France to sell the whole of Louisiana for $11,250,000—plus an additional $3,750,000 to cover private claims against France—even though the offer exceeded instructions established by Congress [see LOUISIANA PURCHASE]. After members of Congress reviewed the facts submitted by Jefferson, they appropriated the additional funds. Jefferson also relied on EXECUTIVE PREROGATIVE in 1807 after a British vessel fired on the American ship *Chesapeake*. Without statutory authority he ordered military purchases for the emergency and disclosed his actions to Congress when it returned. "To have awaited a previous and special sanction by law," he said, "would have lost occasions which might not be retrieved."

In 1861, after the firing on Fort Sumter, and while Congress was adjourned, President Abraham Lincoln directed Secretary of the Treasury SALMON P. CHASE to advance $2 million to three private citizens, the money to be used for "military and naval measures necessary for the defense and support of the Government." When Congress returned, it passed legislation authorizing Lincoln's initiatives.

During the administration of Franklin D. Roosevelt, Congress discovered that he had created agencies by EXECUTIVE ORDER and was using appropriated funds to finance agency activities that lacked statutory support. An amendment known as the Russell Rider was adopted in 1944 to prohibit the use of any appropriation for an agency unless Congress had specifically authorized the expenditure of funds by the agency. That restriction remains part of current law.

In a number of instances the President has presented Congress with a fait accompli and in effect compelled it to appropriate the necessary funds. The commitment of troops in the KOREAN WAR by President Harry S. Truman in 1950 is one example. Despite the provisions of the UNITED NATIONS PARTICIPATION ACT of 1946, no attempt was made to obtain congressional approval before sending military troops. President George Bush threatened to take unilateral military action against Iraq in 1991 in the PERSIAN GULF WAR, arguing that he did not need advance authorization from Congress. In the end, however, he asked for and received legislative support.

Transfer Authority. Congress recognizes that Presidents need limited authority to shift funds from one appropriations account to another (transfer authority). In 1793, Secretary of the Treasury Alexander Hamilton found himself in the middle of a controversy over transfers of funds. Congressman William Giles of Virginia presented a number of resolutions that charged Hamilton with improper use of funds, implying that he had transferred funds illegally. Giles argued that laws making specific appropriations of money "should be strictly observed by the administrator of the finances thereof." Congressman William Smith of South Carolina rebutted Giles point by point, insisting that the administration ought to be free to depart from congressional appropriations whenever it would improve the public safety or credit. The House voted down the Giles resolutions.

Over the years, Congress has allowed Presidents to transfer funds not only when it was in recess but while it was in session. Secretary of the Treasury WILLIAM H. CRAWFORD told Congress in 1817 that transfers helped legislators by informing them where appropriations had been deficient and where redundant, thus providing an instructive guide for future appropriations bills. He warned that if Congress terminated transfer authority, agencies would submit inflated budget estimates as a technique for cushioning against unexpected and unpredictable expenses. Congress restricted transfer authority by limiting the activity to a total dollar amount and by placing a percentage limit on the funds that could be taken from one account and added to another.

During periods of great emergency, Congress delegates broad transfer authority to the executive branch. The 1932 Economy Act cut federal spending so hastily and in such indiscriminate fashion that Congress permitted the administration to transfer funds from one agency to another to minimize the damage. As much as 12 percent could be transferred, provided that no appropriation was increased by more than 15 percent. The LEND LEASE ACT of 1941 appropriated $7 billion for ordnance, aircraft, tanks, and for other categories of defense. The President could transfer as much as 20 percent of the appropriations from one category to another, provided that no appropriation was increased by more than 30 percent.

During the VIETNAM WAR, President Richard M.

Nixon expanded the conflict by moving into Cambodia in 1970. Initially he financed that decision by transferring funds from foreign assistance accounts. Three years later, after a fierce bombing of Cambodia had depleted a number of DEFENSE DEPARTMENT accounts, he requested additional transfer authority to restore funds to those accounts. He asked Congress to increase the transfer authority for the Defense Department from $750 million to $1.25 billion. That request precipitated a confrontation between the branches, eventually leading Congress to delete all funds for the war in Southeast Asia.

Reprogramming. Through a highly decentralized and informal system, Congress allows the executive branch to shift funds within an appropriation account. In return for this flexibility, executive officials must tell designated congressional committees about pending reprogrammings and, in some cases, receive their prior approval. These agency-committee agreements are usually defined by informal, nonstatutory guidelines.

Each year executive agencies come before Congress to justify their budget estimates, setting forth in great detail the purposes to which funds are to be applied. Requests are then modified by committee and congressional action, as explained in committee reports and by floor amendments. However, most of the detailed information in agency justification sheets, committee reports, and floor action is omitted from the appropriation bill. The funds are grouped together to form lump-sum appropriation accounts.

Judged by the statute itself, appropriations appear to give the executive branch great discretion to spend within the lump sum. Nevertheless, the mass of material surrounding and supporting the appropriation—the nonstatutory controls—implies a high degree of itemization. Agencies are expected to keep faith with Congress by spending the money in accordance with their original departmental justifications, as amended by committee and floor action. Through such actions the integrity of the budget process is preserved.

Congress understands that it is often necessary and desirable for agencies to depart from budget justifications. Agencies must estimate many months and sometimes years in advance of the time that they are called upon to spend the funds. As the budget year unfolds, new and better applications of money come to light. Good management requires some reprogramming.

Nevertheless, reprogramming authority can be easily abused. An agency can request money for a popular program, knowing that Congress will provide the funds. Later it can ask its review committees to use the money for a program that might not have passed

the scrutiny of the full Congress. Even more abusive is the use of reprogramming to finance a program that had been presented to Congress and denied. Appropriations acts typically contain language to prevent these abuses. A 1991 statute provides: "No part of the funds in this Act shall be available to prepare or present a request to the Committees on Appropriations for reprogramming of funds, unless for higher priority items, based on unforeseen military requirements, than those for which originally appropriated and in no case where the item for which reprogramming is requested has been denied by the Congress" (105 Stat. 1173, sec. 8010).

The expenditure process, by its every nature, requires substantial discretion for administrators. They need to exercise judgment and take responsibility for their actions, but those actions ought to be directed toward executing congressional, not administrative, policy.

[*See also* IMPOUNDMENT; LOBBYING WITH APPROPRIATED MONEY ACT; STATEMENT AND ACCOUNT CLAUSE; UNVOUCHERED EXPENSES.]

BIBLIOGRAPHY

Fisher, Louis. *Presidential Spending Power.* 1975.
Fisher, Louis. "How Tightly Can Congress Draw the Purse Strings?" *American Journal of International Law* 83 (1989): 758–766.
Nobleman, Eli E. "Financial Aspects of Congressional Participation in Foreign Relations." *The Annals* 289 (1953): 145–164.
Sidak, J. Gregory. "The President's Power of the Purse." *Duke Law Journal* (1989): 1162–1253.
Stith, Kate. "Congress's Power of the Purse." *Yale Law Journal* 97 (1988): 1343–1396.
Wilmerding, Lucius, Jr. *The Spending Power.* 1943.

LOUIS FISHER

SPOILS SYSTEM. See PATRONAGE.

SQUARE DEAL. Theodore Roosevelt once told a protégé who tended to be precise and pedantic that political speeches should be watercolors, not etchings. His 1903 speech, which introduced "square deal" into America's political lexicon, was a watercolor: strong on general principles; weak on specifics. This, however, was very useful from the standpoint of Roosevelt's political career from 1903 to 1913, as he evolved, in his own terms, from "an enlightened conservative" to a "radical liberal." Roosevelt then could claim that while his means may have changed as he began to advocate far more concentration of authority in the hands of the executive to intervene in the national economy, his principles were invariable. Those principles—

Roosevelt's vision of what presidential domestic policy should be—were the essence of his "square deal."

Roosevelt first used the term "square deal" in a speech entitled "Class Government," delivered at the New York State Fair in September 1903. "Square" simply meant "fair," and "deal" was an analogue to a card game.

The President, according to Roosevelt in 1903, should not divide the rewards for economic enterprise to ensure that all players receive certain shares, large or small. The speech, consequently, is laced with praise for "individual initiative," labor, effort, and "the chance to work hard at work worth doing." It furthermore maintained that "the recognition of this government as being either for the poor as such or for the rich as such, would prove fatal to the Republic."

Roosevelt then was advocating regulatory responsibilities for the President, not the philosophy of the so-called distributive state. None of the participants in the American economy—be it capital, labor, or consumers—would receive a special advantage. Instead, they would all play "square," that is fairly. If that were done, according to Roosevelt's political persuasion, each would contribute to the common good of the nation by working automatically "for the benefit of the people as a whole."

Of course, virtually no employer, worker, or consumer was (or ever is) against fair play, in principle. The debate was about details. However, for Roosevelt to specify exactly what actions are fair, and what ones are not, is to make a speech into an etching. It is also to assume that he knew precisely what was and was not fair, when he did not know. Roosevelt said that "honesty, decency, fair-dealing and common sense" were "essential to all of us, as we deal with the complex industrial problems of the day." But his 1903 speech gave little indication how those attributes would settle those complex problems.

He did, however, specifically propose a bureau of corporations to oversee interstate business, which he would place within the federal Department of Commerce and Labor. When the bureau was born later that year, it had official power to investigate big business and informal power to regulate economic activity. If business ignored the bureau's guidance about prices, wages, and working conditions, it could recommend that the President file an antitrust suit. If that suit did nothing else, it could tie business up in a lengthy and expensive litigation, whose ultimate outcome was very difficult to predict. For this reason, certain businessmen, like J. P. Morgan, preferred to deal with the Bureau of Corporations, than with an antitrust suit and the courts.

When Roosevelt coined the term "square deal," he had not yet been elected President in his own right, having ascended to the White House when President William McKinley—a rather conservative man—was assassinated. Under those circumstances, Roosevelt had no mandate for domestic policy beyond a rather vague saying: "square deal." Once elected in 1904, his policies steadily became more progressive as he added elements of economic redistribution to the foundation of business regulation. In the next ten years, Roosevelt would advocate a broadened pension program for veterans and federal workman's compensation as well as health and old age insurance—all entitlements being debated in the federal government ninety years later.

Roosevelt, nonetheless, remained true to his vision that government should be an impartial broker, not a committed partisan. As he wrote in 1911, when talking about the tariff, "we want . . . a square deal for the wage earner, a square deal for the employer, and a square deal for the general public."

BIBLIOGRAPHY

Blum, John Morton. *The Republican Roosevelt*. 1963.
Goldman, Eric F. *Rendezvous with Destiny*. 1956.
Link, Arthur S., and Richard L. McCormick. *Progressivism*. 1983.
Mowry, George E. *The Era of Theodore Roosevelt and the Birth of Modern America, 1900–1912*. 1958.
Wiebe, Robert. *The Search for Order, 1877–1920*. 1967.

MICHAEL D. PEARLMAN

STAMPS COMMEMORATING PRESIDENTS. Since 1847, when the second adhesive U.S. postage stamp to be issued featured Gilbert Stuart's familiar portrait of George Washington, every deceased President has been depicted on at least two or more stamps. (Portrayal of living persons on stamps has been prohibited by law since 1866.)

Eight Presidents—George Washington, Thomas Jefferson, James Madison, Andrew Jackson, Zachary Taylor, Abraham Lincoln, Ulysses S. Grant, and James A. Garfield—were commemorated prior to 1900. Benjamin Harrison joined this select group in 1902. Eight other Presidents were added during the 1920s, but a dozen still had not been featured on a stamp when Franklin D. Roosevelt became President. The unremembered included John Adams, John Quincy Adams, Chester A. Arthur, James Buchanan, Martin Van Buren, Calvin Coolidge, Millard Fillmore, William Henry Harrison, Andrew Johnson, Franklin Pierce, James K. Polk, and John Tyler. (John Adams had appeared on a 1-cent post card issued in 1898.)

In 1938, through the efforts of Roosevelt, a lifelong stamp collector, all twenty-nine of the deceased Presidents were included in a special presidential series. In 1986, nearly a half century after the first presidential series was released, the postal service issued a new series, honoring the thirty-five men who served as President from George Washington through Lyndon B. Johnson.

Of the approximately 570 individuals featured on U.S. postage stamps between 1847 and 1991, thirty-five were Presidents and four were First Ladies— MARTHA WASHINGTON, DOLLEY MADISON, ELEANOR ROOSEVELT, and ABIGAIL ADAMS. Washington, the individual most frequently so honored has been on eighty stamps, twice as many as Postmaster Benjamin Franklin (forty). Among the Presidents the most commemorated after Washington were Lincoln, Jefferson, Jackson, Franklin D. Roosevelt, and Theodore Roosevelt respectively. American Presidents have also proved popular subjects on foreign stamps, with more than eighty countries having issued Franklin D. Roosevelt philatelia.

Of the fourteen Vice Presidents on U.S. stamps, only three—GEORGE CLINTON, ELBRIDGE GERRY, and HUBERT H. HUMPHREY—never attained the presidency. Clinton and Gerry appeared on stamps reproducing John Trumbull's painting, *The Declaration of Independence*. Humphrey's issue, the first to be dedicated entirely to a former Vice President, was released in 1991. Unsuccessful presidential candidates remembered with stamps include HENRY CLAY, George Clinton, STEPHEN A. DOUGLAS, JOHN C. FREMONT, HORACE GREELEY, CHARLES EVANS HUGHES, JOHN JAY, RUFUS KING, CHARLES C. PINCKNEY, WINFIELD SCOTT, ALFRED E. SMITH, ADLAI E. STEVENSON (1900–1965), and DANIEL WEBSTER.

BIBLIOGRAPHY

Lehnus, Donald J. *Angels to Zeppelins: A Guide to Persons, Objects, Topics, and Themes on United States Postage Stamps, 1847–1980.* 1982.

Thomas, Richard. *Linn's Who's Who on U.S. Postage Stamps.* 1991.

STEPHEN W. STATHIS

STANTON, EDWIN M. (1814–1869), Attorney General, Secretary of War. Edwin McMasters Stanton was born in Steubenville, Ohio, on 19 December 1814. Stanton entered Kenyon College in 1831, but he failed to finish a degree. He turned to law, beginning practice in 1836.

Stanton attained a strong professional reputation as a lawyer. In 1846, he moved to Pittsburgh and then to Washington, D.C. in 1856. Appointed special prosecutor to the United States government, Stanton's painstaking care of the land claims arising out of the MEXICAN WAR brought him much distinction. On 20 December 1860, James Buchanan chose him ATTORNEY GENERAL. Before his appointment Stanton had shown little interest in electoral politics. A supporter of JOHN C. BRECKINRIDGE during the election of 1860, Stanton was a pro-Union Democrat. During the winter of 1860–1861, Stanton, among Buchanan's Cabinet officers, strongly supported the provisioning of Fort Sumter, briefing incoming Republicans on the matter.

At the outset of the Lincoln administration, Stanton became General GEORGE B. MCCLELLAN's legal adviser and assistant to Secretary of War Simon Cameron. With Cameron, Stanton wrote a report arguing that slaves should be armed for the Union. Abraham Lincoln removed Cameron for this report and picked Stanton to replace him as Secretary of War. Stanton took over the WAR DEPARTMENT in January 1862.

An efficient if imperious administrator, Stanton was a strong Secretary of War. Reforming the administrative structure of the department, Stanton, along with Quartermaster General Montgomery Meigs, regularized the flow of men and matériel needed for the war and reduced the fraud and abuses endemic to early requisitioning. Stanton broke with McLellan after the general's apparent slowness to attack. Stanton gained respect for Lincoln as the war went on.

Stanton remained as Secretary of War in Andrew Johnson's administration, although relations with the new President soon became strained. Stanton increasingly sided with congressional RADICAL REPUBLICANS on RECONSTRUCTION, favoring the FREEDMEN'S BUREAU, punishment of the South (notably the Military Reconstruction acts of 1867), and reprisals against JEFFERSON DAVIS.

Stanton's position within the Johnson Cabinet became the constitutional pretext for the Radical Republican attempt to remove the President. The TENURE OF OFFICE ACT (1867) obliged the President to keep executive officials until the Senate had approved a successor. The act was a severe limitation on EXECUTIVE PREROGATIVE, and Johnson adamantly opposed it. Johnson demanded that Stanton leave his post in August 1867, while Congress was in recess. Citing the act, Stanton declined until Congress could meet again in December. In early 1868 Johnson suspended Stanton and appointed Alonzo Thomas; Stanton replied by ordering Thomas's arrest and barricading himself in his office building. Congress responded to Johnson's defiance of the Tenure of Office Act by impeaching the President in February 1868 [see IMPEACHMENT OF ANDREW JOHNSON]. With Chief Justice

Salmon P. Chase sitting as presiding officer, Johnson was then tried in the Senate. By one vote, the Senate failed to sustain Johnson's impeachment. Stanton subsequently relinquished the office.

President S. Ulysses Grant chose Stanton to become a Supreme Court Justice in 1869. Stanton died on 24 December 1869, before he could take his seat.

BIBLIOGRAPHY

Benedict, Michael Les. *The Impeachment and Trial of Andrew Johnson.* 1973.
Flower, Frank. *Edwin McMasters Stanton.* 1909.
Keller, Morton. *Affairs of State.* 1977.
Pratt, Fletcher. *Stanton, Lincoln's Secretary of War.* 1953.

JOHN F. WALSH

START (STRATEGIC ARMS REDUCTION TALKS).

During the 1980 presidential election campaign, Ronald Reagan repeatedly criticized the pending SALT (STRATEGIC ARMS LIMITATION TALKS) II treaty as inadequate because it failed to incorporate "real" ARMS CONTROL, merely capping—rather than cutting—the levels of strategic NUCLEAR WEAPONS on both sides. Once in office, President Reagan dramatized his new objective by abandoning the traditional Strategic Arms Limitation Talks (SALT) in favor of a new set of Strategic Arms Reduction Talks (START).

Bilateral START negotiations (covering land-based and sea-based intercontinental ballistic missiles, strategic bombers, and other long-range nuclear weapons) continued into the administration of President George Bush. Finally, after nine years of intermittent negotiations, the treaty was signed on 31 July 1991. The START agreement was the most massive arms-control accord ever undertaken, containing reams of details in various supporting documents, such as elaborate protocols governing the process of intrusive on-site inspection, the mechanisms for dismantling excess weaponry, and the exchange of data regarding weapons systems.

In August 1991, however, almost immediately after the START signing ceremony, the Soviet Union was shaken by a coup attempt in which hard-line communists unsuccessfully attempted Mikhail Gorbachev's ouster. This fiasco set in train the dissolution of the Soviet Union and the resurgence of American apprehensions about the stability and safety of its erstwhile negotiating partner. It also directly jeopardized the START treaty by challenging the familiar notion about who was sitting across the negotiating table from the United States. Instead of one integrated, tightly controlled superpower, there were suddenly four newly independent republics with strategic nuclear weapons on their soil: Ukraine, Belarus, Kazakhstan, and Russia. The next several months were devoted to resolution of this uncertainty, and in May 1992, a tentative modus vivendi was reached, with the three smaller republics agreeing to dismantle or transfer to Russia all their strategic nuclear weapons. Russia will become the sole "successor state" to the former Soviet Union for the purpose of START and other disarmament accords, and the other three republics would eventually become nuclear-weapons-free.

At the same time, however, the START agreement was also imperiled from a different direction. In 1991 and 1992, President Bush and Soviet president Gorbachev and then Russian president Boris Yeltsin engaged in a series of unilateral arms reduction measures, exchanging overlapping proposals for additional deep cuts in strategic weaponry. The goals of these initiatives far surpassed those of the START agreement, leading some to argue that the 1991 document was obsolete even before it was ratified and that, instead of attempting to bring the treaty into force, the parties should leapfrog over it, proceeding directly to the more substantial measures. Bush administration officials maintained, however, that the treaty should be sustained because it incorporated a structure of verification and a mechanism for regularizing future reductions. They contended that once this overall treaty format was brought into force, future negotiations on subsequent deeper cuts could proceed more expeditiously. At the same time, they conceded that the 1991 START agreement might be the last of its kind—that is, the last effort to deal comprehensively with a whole series of arms control measures in a single, laboriously drafted treaty text.

BIBLIOGRAPHY

Kartchner, Kerry M. *Negotiating START: Strategic Arms Reduction Talks and the Quest for Strategic Stability.* 1992.
Talbott, Strobe. *Deadly Gambits: The Reagan Administration and the Stalemate in Nuclear Arms Control.* 1984.

DAVID A. KOPLOW

STAR WARS.
See SDI (STRATEGIC DEFENSE INITIATIVE).

STASSEN, HAROLD
(b. 1907), governor of Minnesota, nine-time candidate for the Republican presidential nomination. A member of the moderate, internationalist wing of the REPUBLICAN PARTY, Harold Edward Stassen served as a U.S. delegate to the inaugural conference of the UNITED NATIONS in San Fran-

cisco. Stassen came closest to the Republican nomination in 1948, receiving 157 first-ballot votes at the convention but eventually losing to Thomas E. Dewey.

Stassen failed to win the nomination again in 1952, losing to the extremely popular Dwight D. Eisenhower. As Eisenhower's Mutual Security Administrator and Director of the Foreign Operations Administration, Stassen pursued his internationalist positions on foreign aid. In an increasingly polarized COLD WAR atmosphere, Stassen's positions were much more liberal than Eisenhower's. Stassen clashed with Senator Joseph McCarthy over McCarthy's privately arranged deal with Greek shipowners not to trade with communist nations. Despite Stassen's liberalism, however, in 1955 Eisenhower made him special adviser on disarmament matters.

Stassen's greatest political blunder came in the 1956 election campaign. In May 1956, Stassen recommended to Eisenhower to replace Vice President Richard M. Nixon with Christian Herter, the governor of Massachusetts. Eisenhower made no clear statement on Nixon's viability. In July, Stassen publicly asked Nixon to give up his place on the ticket. Party leaders rallied behind Nixon and isolated Stassen, who was obliged to second the renomination of Nixon at the convention. In 1957, Stassen unsuccessfully sought the Republican nomination for governor of Pennsylvania. Stassen name was placed in nomination for the presidency at Republican national conventions from 1960 through 1980, but he no longer possessed any significant power base.

BIBLIOGRAPHY

Parmet, Herbert S. *Eisenhower and the American Crusades.* 1972.
Schlesinger, Arthur M., Jr., and Fred L. Israel. *History of American Presidential Elections.* Vol. 4. 1971.

JOHN F. WALSH

STATE, DEPARTMENT OF. The Secretary of State is the first-ranking CABINET member. Though small in size relative to other Cabinet agencies, the State Department performs the critically important services of implementing the foreign policy of the United States.

History of the Department. The State Department was the first executive department created after adoption of the Constitution. The act creating the Department of Foreign Affairs and the Office of Secretary was signed into law on 27 July 1789 and directed the secretary to run the department "in such manner as the President of the United States shall, from time to time order or instruct." Two months later, Congress added important domestic functions, chiefly correspondence with the states, publication of acts of Congress (and later the census), maintenance of a library (forerunner of the Library of Congress), registration of copyrights and patents, and the keeping of the Great Seal of the United States. The addition of these domestic responsibilities (most long since assigned to other agencies) led in 1789 to the changing of the the the Department's name to the Department of State.

Thomas Jefferson, the first secretary of the department, instituted some of the department's most enduring functions. He dispatched consuls abroad and required them to report on commercial, political, and military developments and to alert American merchants and vessels to the same. Jefferson was also responsible for distinguishing between diplomatic and consular functions: the former involving the conduct of political relations with other countries and the latter concerned with commercial matters and the affairs of U.S. citizens abroad. The diplomatic and consular services functioned separately until they were joined in 1924.

The department grew slowly during the nineteenth century because of U.S. policies of isolation and NEUTRALITY toward both Europe and the Americas. In 1833, the first departmental reorganization led to the appointment of a chief clerk, who was given responsibility for managing the department on a daily basis, and the creation of seven bureaus including a diplomatic and a consular bureau to communicate with overseas posts. A second reorganization in 1870 established four geographic bureaus (two diplomatic and two consular) and five functional bureaus.

At the turn of the century, U.S. interventions abroad and American territorial acquisitions expanded the department's duties. The two world wars further increased departmental responsibilities, chiefly in the areas of assistance to American citizens aboard; political, military, and economic reporting; acting as representatives of other states fighting as belligerents in enemy countries; refugee aid; and POW exchanges.

In 1944, a major reorganization was began by Edward Stettinius, then Undersecretary of State. Later, as Secretary of State, Stettinius issued a departmental order grouping similar functions together and assigning responsibility for related offices to the undersecretary or one of the six assistant secretaries. A number of new functional bureaus were created for trade relations, cultural diplomacy, and public information, and new offices responsible for management and policy planning were added. The Interim Research and Intelligence Service, now the Bureau of Intelligence and Research, was established in 1945. The increasing

Secretaries of State

President	Secretary of State
1 Washington	Thomas Jefferson, 1789–1793 Edmund Randolph, 1794–1795 Timothy Pickering, 1795–1797
2 J. Adams	Timothy Pickering, 1797–1800 John Marshall, 1800–1801
3 Jefferson	James Madison, 1801–1809
4 Madison	Robert Smith, 1809–1811 James Monroe, 1811–1817
5 Monroe	John Quincy Adams, 1817–1825
6 J. Q. Adams	Henry Clay, 1825–1829
7 Jackson	Martin Van Buren, 1829–1831 Edward Livingston, 1831–1833 Louis McLane, 1833–1834 John Forsyth, 1834–1837
8 Van Buren	John Forsyth, 1837–1841
9 W. H. Harrison	Daniel Webster, 1841
10 Tyler	Daniel Webster, 1841–1843 Abel P. Upshur, 1843–1844 John C. Calhoun, 1844–1845
11 Polk	James Buchanan, 1845–1849
12 Taylor	John M. Clayton, 1849–1850
13 Fillmore	John M. Clayton, 1850 Daniel Webster, 1850–1852 Edward Everett, 1852–1853
14 Pierce	William L. Marcy, 1853–1857
15 Buchanan	Lewis Cass, 1857–1860 Jeremiah S. Black, 1860–1861
16 Lincoln	William H. Seward, 1861–1865
17 A. Johnson	William H. Seward, 1865–1869
18 Grant	Elihu B. Washburne, 1869 Hamilton Fish, 1869–1877
19 Hayes	William M. Evarts, 1877–1881
20 Garfield	James G. Blaine, 1881
21 Arthur	James G. Blaine, 1881 Frederick T. Frelinghuysen, 1881–1885
22 Cleveland	Thomas F. Bayard, 1885–1889
23 B. Harrison	James Blaine, 1889–1892

President	Secretary of State
23 B. Harrison	John W. Foster, 1892–1893
24 Cleveland	Walter Q. Gresham, 1893–1895 Richard Olney, 1895–1897
25 McKinley	John Sherman, 1897–1898 William R. Day, 1898 John Hay, 1898–1901
26 T. Roosevelt	John Hay, 1901–1905 Elihu Root, 1905–1909 Robert Bacon, 1909
27 Taft	Philander C. Knox, 1909–1913
28 Wilson	William Jennings Bryan, 1913–1915 Robert Lansing, 1915–1920 Bainbridge Colby, 1920–1921
29 Harding	Charles Evans Hughes, 1921–1923
30 Coolidge	Charles Evans Hughes, 1923–1925 Frank B. Kellogg, 1925–1929
31 Hoover	Henry L. Stimson, 1929–1933
32 F. D. Roosevelt	Cordell Hull, 1933–1944 Edward R. Stettinius, Jr., 1944–1945
33 Truman	Edward R. Stettinius, Jr., 1945 James F. Byrnes, 1945–1947 George C. Marshall, 1947–1949 Dean G. Acheson, 1949–1953
34 Eisenhower	John Foster Dulles, 1953–1959 Christian A. Herter, 1959–1961
35 Kennedy	Dean Rusk, 1961–1963
36 L. B. Johnson	Dean Rusk, 1963–1969
37 Nixon	William P. Rogers, 1969–1973 Henry A. Kissinger, 1973–1974
38 Ford	Henry A. Kissinger, 1974–1977
39 Carter	Cyrus R. Vance, 1977–1980 Edmund S. Muskie, 1980–1981
40 Reagan	Alexander Haig, 1981–1982 George P. Shultz, 1982–1989
41 Bush	James A. Baker III, 1989–1992 Lawrence S. Eagleburger, 1992–1993
42 Clinton	Warren M. Christopher, 1993–

importance of economics in foreign relations was reflected in the department's absorption of several temporary wartime economic agencies and the addition of an Undersecretary for Economics in 1946.

Beginning at the turn of the century, efforts were made to professionalize the FOREIGN SERVICE. Competitive exams for the consular service were initiated in 1895, and a merit system (including competitive entrance exams for all diplomatic and consular positions except minister and ambassador) followed in 1906. The Lowden Act of 1911 allowed the U.S. government to purchase buildings overseas to house foreign missions, relieving the financial strain on envoys and ensuring functional and dignified quarters for all

officials irrespective of private wealth. The Rodgers Act of 1924 and the Foreign Service Act of 1946 continued improvements in the conditions affecting foreign service personnel, especially in the areas of entrance and promotion within the service, rotations from post, expenses and benefits, home leave, and retirement.

A number of developments since WORLD WAR II have had major impact on the department. First, the NATIONAL SECURITY ACT of 1947 concentrated responsibility for coordination of NATIONAL SECURITY POLICY in the White House under the direction of a NATIONAL SECURITY ADVISER. Since then, while the influence of the department has varied, it clearly no longer has exclusive executive authority for FOREIGN AFFAIRS. Despite this development, or perhaps in response to it, the role of the Secretary of State expanded as many holders of the office personally committed themselves to diplomatic initiatives, heightening the U.S. profile in the Middle East, for example, or focusing on U.S.-Soviet relations.

In 1949, President Harry S. Truman launched a new era in U.S. foreign assistance when he announced a large aid package aimed at helping underdeveloped countries expand their economies and participate in international markets [see POINT FOUR PROGRAM]. In the 1990s, foreign economic and military aid made up the largest portion of the foreign affairs budget. While in absolute terms the United States gave more foreign aid than any other country, the absolute amount given has declined steadily and as a percentage of gross national product is smaller than that given by any of the other major noncommunist donors. Foreign affairs spending declined from 12 percent of federal expenditures in the years immediately after the war to less than 2 percent in 1993.

Finally, the dramatic rise in international terrorism had a profound impact on the department. From 1965 to 1992, eighty-six State Department personnel were killed, including U.S. ambassadors to Guatemala, Sudan, Cyprus, Lebanon, Afghanistan, and Pakistan. The department became increasingly involved in efforts to combat international terrorism through intelligence, coordination with other governments, security measures, and legal proceedings such as the indictment of two suspects in the bombing of Pan Am Flight 103 over Lockerbie, Scotland, in 1988 and subsequent efforts to gain their extradition and trial.

Relationship with Congress. The struggle among the branches for control of the U.S. government, anticipated by the Framers, has been very evident in the area of foreign affairs. Foreign affairs were originally conducted by committees and single executives under the close control of the Continental Congress. The Constitution made the direction of foreign affairs predominantly the province of the President. Article II designated the President as COMMANDER IN CHIEF, with the power to make treaties, to nominate executive officials (including the Secretary of State and all U.S. ambassadors), and to receive foreign ambassadors [see AMBASSADORS, RECEIVING AND APPOINTING]. To prevent absolute executive power over foreign affairs, the Constitution gave Congress several powers, including the power to regulate foreign commerce, declare war, appropriate funds, ratify treaties, and approve executive appointments. Through the exercise of these powers, Congress has always been able to exercise control over the Department of State and its activities by limiting spending, creating (and abolishing) positions, confirming nominations to high positions within the department, investigating activities, and legislating national polices.

Throughout American history, Congress has sporadically utilized all these powers. In the late twentieth century, however, Congress systematically utilized its powers to control the department. Among the most significant features of Congress's control are (1) specific approval of the number and description of all high-ranking jobs, including creation of an Inspector General, independent of the Secretary of State, to investigate misconduct; (2) predesignation of recipients for the majority of all U.S. foreign aid—as high as 96 percent in one foreign-aid program—leaving the department with discretion over the allocation of a very small portion of such funds; and (3) prohibitions on the extension of humanitarian or military assistance aimed specifically at countries found to engage in activities considered by Congress to be detrimental to U.S. interests (such as terrorism or development of a nuclear device).

Department officials continue to have control over day-to-day diplomacy, which permits the exercise of broad discretion in seeking settlements of disputes or advancement of U.S. interests. Congress has even exercised power, however, over these aspects of department activity. On virtually every issue of public note, for example, negotiators must routinely keep interested legislators and committees informed of their actions and plans. Congress and individual legislators use their power over legislation, appointments, and investigations to demand information about diplomatic activities, including communications with foreign officials and internal deliberations. These demands are routinely resisted, but such information is obtained in many cases. Finally, in some areas of great public visibility, legislators have became observers at negotiating sessions, particularly in arms control but also increasingly in environmental and trade issues. While department personnel continue to control such negotiations, Congress has become a real presence, not merely in the final approval or implementation of policies or treaties but also in their development. Although these trends pose difficulties for the department, they also carry advantages: interested legislators become more informed, contribute to the solutions ultimately adopted, and are more likely to grant approval when called on to do so.

Executive-Branch Competition. Historically, the State Department's control over the management and implementation of foreign policy has cut across all areas of governmental concern. Presidents since

George Washington have used PRIVATE ENVOYS, special agents, or designated negotiators to handle specific problems. Most negotiations as well as ongoing relationships with foreign governments have been handled, however, by the State Department through its control of diplomatic posts and communications.

Over the years, various circumstances have caused control over important areas of foreign affairs to shift from the State Department to other executive agencies. Revolutionary improvements in communications and travel have deprived the State Department of the virtual monopoly it once possessed over contact with foreign officials abroad. In addition, the handling of specific areas of diplomatic activity has become increasingly complex, demanding specialization and expertise. The executive agencies responsible for such subjects as commerce, taxation, defense, intelligence, crime, and the regulation of specific areas such as communication, securities, and environment have been faced with the increasing globalization of their areas of concern. Domestic economic planning, for example, requires an understanding of foreign trends and policies and results in plans for international coordination, cooperation, and negotiation. Similarly, domestic crime, especially federal crime, increasingly contains international sources or components in such areas as narcotics trafficking, terrorism, and financial fraud. Finally, in competing with one another, executive-branch officials are no less prone to pursue their personal ambitions and the aggrandizement of their positions than are executive and legislative officials in competition with each other. Consequently, executive officials in departments other than State have competed for influence and control over the foreign aspects of their areas of responsibility.

These trends and activities have significantly shifted foreign-affairs responsibility from the State Department to the executive agencies, especially the National Security Council and the OFFICE OF THE U.S. TRADE REPRESENTATIVE. Several agencies have direct liaison with their counterparts in foreign countries.

The effects of multiagency involvement in foreign affairs are offset to a considerable extent by State Department participation in many of the foreign activities of other agencies. But the effects of this dispersal of foreign affairs authority go beyond the mere shift of responsibility from one set of executive officials to another. Agencies with specialized responsibility tend to take positions that are driven strongly by their own special, sometimes relatively narrow, responsibilities, whereas State Department officials tend to take a broader view of the nation's interests. Criminal law enforcement provides one example. Prosecutors understandably seek to prosecute all crime, without regard to the political consequences, as, for example, when U.S. prosecutors pursued Manuel Noriega of PANAMA. In such situations, the State Department tends to give greater weight than does the JUSTICE DEPARTMENT to other factors, such as diplomatic immunity and respect for the sovereignty and sensibilities of foreign states and the UNITED NATIONS. The President, the NSC Adviser and staff, have increasingly become the arbiters of such conflicting agendas.

BIBLIOGRAPHY

Bemis, Samuel Flagg. *A Diplomatic History of the United States.* 1936.
Eberstadt, Nicholas. *Foreign Aid and American Purpose.* 1988.
Stuart, Graham H. *The Department of State: A History of Its Organization, Procedure and Personnel.* 1949.
Trask, David F. *A Short History of the U.S. Department of State, 1781–1981.* 1981.

ABRAHAM D. SOFAER

STATEMENT AND ACCOUNT CLAUSE.

Found in Article I, Section 9, clause 7, of the Constitution, the statement and account clause requires that "a regular Statement and Account of the Receipts and Expenditures of all public Money shall be published from time to time." In the absence of a visible and explicit budget process, the Framers realized that the public would have a difficult time evaluating the wisdom with which funds were spent. Holding officials accountable for their use of taxpayers' money—a fundamental tenet of democratic government—would be next to impossible without an open record of expenditures.

This belief in the accountability of public financing has been reiterated in modern laws. The Secretary of the Treasury, for instance, is directed by statute to publish reports on the outcome of financial operations in the federal government "for the information of the President, the Congress, and the public" (31 U.S.C. 66b[a] [1970]). Similarly, the Budget and Accounting Procedures Act of 1950 states that the government shall provide "full disclosure of the results of financial operations" (64 Stat. 834, sec. 111, codified at 31 U.S.C. 65 [1970]).

Debate among the Framers on the question of openness in public financing was ambiguous. Some delegates to the CONSTITUTIONAL CONVENTION in Philadelphia believed that openness would be all but "impossible in many cases," as GOUVERNEUR MORRIS put it. Others, such as RUFUS KING, suggested that openness, if that word meant tracing every last shilling in detail, would prove to be "impractical." On the matter of when to report to the public, James Madison reasoned that an accounting should be provided on a regular basis but with some flexibility as to the exact timing; others proposed a fixed annual reporting time. The delegates adopted Madison's prescription of "from time to time."

In contrast to this advocacy of openness, the history of public financing in the United States often points to concealment. Budget experts estimate that billions of dollars in federal funds are hidden from public view each year—and even from their governmental surrogates, members of Congress. The estimated $30 billion expended in recent years by the U.S. INTELLIGENCE COMMUNITY, for example, remains concealed from all but a few legislators on the House and Senate intelligence committees. The list of additional covert expenditures is long.

Experts and laypeople agree that exigencies of diplomacy, military security, and sensitive intelligence operations may necessitate secret expenditures on occasion, but, increasingly, observers of American government wonder whether the nation has accepted too many instances of covert financing. When public scrutiny no longer plays a role in key spending decisions, critics question the viability of the democratic process.

BIBLIOGRAPHY

Fisher, Louis. *Presidential Spending Power*. 1975.
Glennon, Michael J. *Constitutional Diplomacy*. 1990.
U.S. Senate Select Committee on Intelligence. "Whether Disclosure of Funds Authorized for Intelligence Activities Is in the Public Interest," *Hearings*. 95th Cong., 1st sess., 1977.

LOCH K. JOHNSON

STATE OF THE UNION MESSAGES. Article 2, Section 3 of the Constitution stipulates that the President "shall from time to time give to the Congress information of the State of the Union and recommend to their Consideration such Measures as he shall judge necessary and expedient."

So uncontroversial was this notion that the CHIEF EXECUTIVE should offer Congress his assessment of the state of the union and recommend legislation for its consideration that it had occasioned no debate in the CONSTITUTIONAL CONVENTION. "No objection has been made to this class of authorities," wrote ALEXANDER HAMILTON in FEDERALIST 77, "nor could they possibly admit of any."

Although the Constitution specifies that the state of the union message be delivered "from time to time," Presidents read that as an invitation to transmit the PRESIDENT'S AGENDA to Congress each year. For all of the

nineteenth and most of the twentieth century, the resulting rhetorical form was known as the President's annual message. Taking its name from its constitutional function, in the mid 1940s, Presidents and presidential scholars began identifying the address as the "state of the union" message.

On 8 January 1790, faced with an unprecedented rhetorical situation, George Washington responded to the constitutional enjoinder by delivering a speech rooted in the monarch's speech from the throne. So obvious was Washington's dependence on the "king's speech" that an observer wrote: "It is evident from the President's speech that he wishes everything to fall into the British mode of business." (The monarch's statement of "cause of summons," known as the "King's Speech," was delivered after a majority of the members of Parliament had been sworn in. In the hands of a powerful ruler, the address constituted a legislative mandate.)

The Congress, which had rejected as too monarchial the title "His Highness the President of the United States of America and Protector of the Rights of the Same" reacted to Washington's first annual message as parliament traditionally had responded to the king's speech, and drafted, debated, and designated a delegation to deliver an echoing speech in response. After repeating the President's requests, the echoing speech pledged congressional cooperation. Should fortune eradicate the annual messages of Washington and Adams, scholars could reconstruct them from their mirror images, the reply speeches. "No man can turn over the Journals of the First Six Congresses of the United States," noted John Randolph, "without being fairly sickened with the adulation often replied by the Houses of Congress."

As the state of the union messages became more controversial, debate over the content and tone of the replies increased. Nonetheless, the practice continued through the Sixth Congress in 1800. In 1801, Thomas Jefferson assumed the presidency and pledged to a "return to simple, republican forms of Government." His messages, delivered by messenger in writing, invited no congressional response. "By sending a message, instead of making a speech at the opening of the session," he confided to a colleague, "I have prevented the bloody conflict [to] which the making an answer would have committed them. They consequently were able to set into real business at once."

So interwoven was the oral delivery of the state of the union message and the distasteful British tradition, however, that Woodrow Wilson, a student of history and the first President to deliver the address orally since John Adams, felt the need to divorce the delivered address from its monarchical past. Wilson let it be known that he did not expect a formal answer from Congress except in enactment of the legislation he proposed.

"I am very glad indeed to have this opportunity to address the two Houses directly and to verify for myself the impression that the President of the United States is a person, not a mere department of the Government hailing Congress from some isolated island of jealous power, sending messages, not speaking naturally and with his own voice—that he is a human being trying to cooperate with other human beings in a common service," Wilson told the assembled members of Congress.

Until the advent of radio, the message was transmitted to the public by the print press. Partisan papers reprinted the message in toto. Opponents of the President attacked each address with vigor. These exchanges occasioned the historian Charles Beard to observe that the annual message was "the one great public document of the United States which is widely read and discussed. Congressional debates receive scant notice, but the President's message is ordinarily printed in full in nearly every metropolitan daily, and is the subject of general editorial comment throughout the length and breadth of the land. It stirs the country: it often affects Congressional elections; and it may establish grand policy."

In the state of the union message, the President has the opportunity to exercise LEGISLATIVE LEADERSHIP by linking national history to present assessments and to make recommendations for future policy. The address affords him the opportunity to appeal for popular and congressional support of his legislative agenda. At the same time, in the television age, the address provides the public with a view of two of the three branches of government each acknowledging the prerogatives of the other, and thus maintaining institutional integrity.

The addresses differ in the number and kind of recommendations they marshall. Some have outlined only general programs, leaving the legislative details to Congress; others have laid out specific policy proposals. Some are lengthy catalogs of unrelated topics; others are focussed discussions of a handful of legislative priorities.

But throughout the presidency, these addresses have, in the words of the historian Arthur M. Schlesinger, Jr., functioned as "both an instrument and an index of PRESIDENTIAL LEADERSHIP." In the hands of a forceful President, the address shapes the country's sense of itself. So, for example, in state of the union messages James Monroe promulgated the MONROE DOCTRINE, Abraham Lincoln prophesied that "in giving freedom to the slave we assure freedom to the free," Franklin D. Roosevelt committed the country to FOUR FREEDOMS, and Lyndon B. Johnson forecast the GREAT SOCIETY. But the addresses also have served venal ends. Ulysses S. Grant's final annual message is a sometimes snivelling apologia; Andrew Johnson used the message to whine and inveigh about RECONSTRUCTION. More recently, the 1984 speech was employed by Ronald Reagan as a de facto announcement of his candidacy for reelection.

The issues addressed in the state of the union messages reflect the development of the nation. The messages of the Founders focused on constituent policies, such as abiding entangling alliances and encouraging manufacturing and policies to build the nation state. Throughout the nineteenth century, the messages centered on such distributive issues as development of land and harbors. In the late nineteenth century, questions of regulating resources emerged, with the creation, for example, of the Interstate Commerce Commission in 1887. During the NEW DEAL, the messages took on social and economic themes. After Roosevelt's time, the four types coexisted in various combinations.

Although their content and form vary widely, most of the state of the union messages embody the structure implied in the Constitution: they assess the state of the union and offer either general or specific recommendations in response to that assessment. These functions increase the likelihood that the speech will shape the national agenda.

For Wilson, the address was a powerful vehicle of presidential leadership. "If the President has personal force and cares to exercise it," he wrote, "there is a tremendous difference between his message and the views of any other citizen either outside Congress or in it; . . . the whole country reads them and feels the writer speaks with an authority and a responsibility which the people themselves have given him."

BIBLIOGRAPHY

Campbell, Karlyn Kohrs, and Kathleen Hall Jamieson. *Deeds Done in Words: Presidential Rhetoric and the Genres of Governance.* 1990.

Gilbert, Sheldon, et al. "The State of the Union Address and the Press Agenda." *Journalism Quarterly* 1980: 584–588.

Jamieson, Kathleen M. "Antecedent Genre as Rhetorical Constraint." *Quarterly Journal of Speech* 61 (1975): 406–415.

Schlesinger, Arthur M., ed. *The State of the Union Messages of the Presidents, 1790–1966.* 3 vols. 1966.

KATHLEEN HALL JAMIESON

STATES' RIGHTS. The states' rights tradition in American politics is traceable to the nation's earliest debates concerning the character and development of the polity. Over the years it has provided many occasions for serious constitutional discourse and philosophical reflection, but it is as a rhetorical weapon in the service of particular interests that it is chiefly known. Long associated with state-centered claims of sovereignty, the doctrine as used in the political arena has acquired a less restricted meaning applicable to local assertions of policy prerogative in a constitutional system committed to FEDERALISM. The presidency, as an institution of the national government, has therefore always been deeply involved in the battles to determine the bounds of states' rights.

To understand the nature of this involvement, a distinction must be made between Presidents and the presidency. While individual Chief Executives have from time to time supported the cause of states' rights, evolution in the office of the presidency is closely associated with a long-term decline in the fortunes of the doctrine. Thus, even in the case of stalwart defenders of states' rights such as Presidents Thomas Jefferson and Andrew Jackson, specific actions taken to advance the status of the states were ultimately overshadowed by these leaders' successful efforts to transform and strengthen the presidency in ways that left the national government in a stronger position vis-à-vis the states. While the results of this transformation have only slowly manifested themselves in this competitive domain, the presidency in the late twentieth century has clearly fulfilled its potential as the principal vehicle for achieving the nationalization of American politics.

Inherent Powers. This evolution could not have come about had the advocates of small-state interests prevailed at the Constitutional Convention. One such advocate, William Paterson of New Jersey, had submitted a plan reflecting the view, strongly held in the smaller states, that the Articles of Confederation required only modest changes. One element of Paterson's plan provided that the national executive could be removed from office by Congress if such action were called for by a majority of the state governors. Had this proposal been adopted, the Articles' failed combination of weak executive power and sovereign states would have been perpetuated. Instead, the Framers opted to rectify the deficiencies of a weak executive, and in Article II of the Constitution they established, over the objections of the most vociferous advocates of state sovereignty, the legal basis for a strong presidency. ALEXANDER HAMILTON's classic observation in FEDERALIST 70 expresses the sentiment of the ultimately prevailing view: "Energy in the Executive is a leading character of the definition of good government."

President George Washington's decisive action in 1794 in quelling the WHISKEY REBELLION in western Pennsylvania suggested the potential to which such energy might be put in relation to the states, but the fact that in the nation's first century the presidency played only a relatively modest role in national policymaking meant that this potential was for a long time barely tapped. The constitutional doctrine of INHERENT POWER was not advanced in any systematic way until the twentieth century, but its foundations had been established from the first in the Constitution. Thus, the constitutional status of the executive has always embodied at least a latent challenge to the states' rights position and to its twin assumptions of the Constitution as a compact among sovereign states and of a federal government possessing only the powers specifically enumerated to it. While exertions of inherent executive power have been most often evaluated within a SEPARATION OF POWERS context in which the Congress has been the other major player, a comprehensive assessment of the cumulative impact of these efforts on the distribution of constitutional authority must also take into account their role in helping to delineate the residual powers of the states. What is clear is that the triumph of the doctrine of implied powers, whether in association with the legislative or the executive branch of the national government, has produced a contraction in the scope of states' rights.

Jefferson and Jackson. The role of the presidency in shaping the limits of state power should not be viewed in strictly constitutional terms. This point is nowhere better illustrated than in the presidencies of Jefferson and Jackson, both of whom defended the constitutional prerogatives of the states, while setting into motion political forces that had enormous impact on the subsequent erosion of these prerogatives. Thus Jefferson, principal author of the Kentucky Resolutions of 1799, provided the first articulation of the doctrine of NULLIFICATION. His voice was later associated in the South with the most unequivocal and extreme version of states' rights philosophy. Jefferson's views in this area became more moderate over the years, but as his fierce criticism of Chief Justice John Marshall's nationalist sentiments in *McCulloch v. Maryland* (1819) indicates, his concerns about the autonomy of the states remained steadfast. Yet as President, Jefferson's embargo laws and his purchase of Louisiana represented a massive repudiation of his earlier views, not least because his failure to consult with the states in advance was thought by many of them to have violated their sovereignty.

In the long run, however, it is Jefferson's decisive role in the development of the political party system that may constitute his greatest legacy as far as strengthening the presidency at the expense of the states is concerned. Andrew Jackson and Martin Van Buren were instrumental in carrying forward this aspect of Jefferson's legacy; Jackson was the first President to claim a mandate from the people as a whole. More than anything else, the development of the plebiscitarian character of the presidency has provided a nationalistic focus to that office. Jackson himself used his mandate to pursue a states' rights agenda; indeed, he employed the powers of the presidency—for example, the VETO—to constrain the activities of the national government. But while his vision of the polity was largely state-centered, he created a model of the energetic popularly based CHIEF EXECUTIVE that would ultimately advance the centralizing thrust of policy-making in the twentieth century.

However solicitous he was of the prerogatives of the states, Jackson's most profound contribution to the states' rights debate is inscribed in his defense of the Union against the threat of nullification. South Carolina's assertion, in the face of the TARIFF OF ABOMINATIONS (1828), of a right to declare that enactment null and void and, if necessary, to withdraw from the Union and to establish an independent state prompted Jackson to enunciate a passionate Hamiltonian repudiation of the doctrine of state sovereignty and of its corollary right of SECESSION. His equation of secession with revolution, and of disunion with treason, laid the groundwork for President Abraham Lincoln's actions a generation later: "Nullification means insurrection and war. . . . Can anyone of common sense believe the absurdity that . . . a state has a right to secede and destroy this Union and the liberty of our country with it?" With this sentiment Lincoln was in total agreement; his theory of the perpetual Union was a refinement of the Jacksonian argument and was ultimately embraced by the Supreme Court in *Texas v. White* (1869), in which the Court offered its most definitive rejection of the constitutional premises of John Taylor and JOHN C. CALHOUN: "What can be indissoluble if a perpetual Union, made more perfect, is not? . . . The Constitution, in all its provisions, looks to an indestructible Union, composed of indestructible States."

Lincoln's achievement in saving the Union greatly increased the powers of the presidency, but, perhaps more important, it elevated it to a position of moral preeminence. Henceforth, the President would be looked to for moral leadership, which, alas, has not always been forthcoming. But even in the case of Presidents who have been reluctant to assume this mantle of leadership, the Lincoln legacy of defending a moral principle embodied in the nation as a whole

has survived. Thus, a century after the DRED SCOTT V. SANDFORD (1857) decision, a southern governor, Orval Faubus, proclaimed his resistance to the enforcement of constitutionally mandated racial equality in the public schools by saying: "The question now is whether the head of a sovereign state can exercise his constitutional powers and discretion in maintaining peace and good order within his jurisdiction, being accountable to his own good conscience and to his own people." The answer was provided by the federal troops sent to Little Rock by President Dwight Eisenhower, whose sense of duty eventually prevailed over whatever doubts he may have had as to the wisdom of the Supreme Court's decision in *Brown v. Board of Education* (1954) [*see* LITTLE ROCK CRISIS].

Enforcement of Rights. What is now routine but once was not, executive enforcement of judicially mandated individual rights, has its roots in the CIVIL WAR's constitutional legacy of a radically altered status for the states in the federal system. The postwar amendments codified an older view associated with advocates of natural rights philosophy and jurisprudence, who had always insisted that fundamental rights could not logically be subordinated to states' rights. Since fundamental rights, correctly understood, possess a universal dimension, it was thought by some to be basically incoherent to hold them applicable to one level of government but not another. For this reason, nationalism made much more sense than states' rights.

With the emergence of the modern presidency from its passive nineteenth-century policy-making role vis-à-vis Congress, executive initiative came to characterize the ascendance of the national government in twentieth-century politics, and this in turn accelerated the enforcement of the new constitutional agenda. Theodore Roosevelt's conception of EXECUTIVE POWER as limited only by express constitutional or congressional restrictions meant that the powers reserved to the states could not effectively be established in advance of presidential performance. Woodrow Wilson, in much the same spirit, saw the President as the "unifying force in our complex system, the leader of both the party and the nation." In his view the President was to be an active agent of reform, employing his national mandate to pursue policies that would in the past have been thwarted by forces committed to deeply entrenched states' rights assumptions.

The fortunes of states' rights in relation to the evolution of the twentieth-century presidency was illuminated by the political scientist E. E. Schattschneider's classic account of the "long-standing struggle between the conflicting tendencies toward the privatization and socialization of conflict." According to

Schattschneider, "ideas concerning equality, consistency, equal protection of the laws, justice, liberty, freedom of movement, freedom of speech and association, and civil rights tend to socialize conflict." In terms of the competition between levels of government, these ideas have historically been resisted by limiting the scope of conflict to the political arena of states' rights. In contrast the presidency, shaped over the years into its present plebiscitory form as the only institutional voice for a national constituency, has become the central instrument for the expansion of the scope of conflict in American politics. Hence it bears a major responsibility for the steady decline of states' rights.

President Franklin Roosevelt's NEW DEAL marks the critical moment when this expansion acquired a legitimacy that would henceforth create an expectation for activist national government. Speaking of the Framers, Roosevelt said: "When they considered the fundamental powers of the new national government, they used generality, implication, and statement of mere objectives as intentional phrases which flexible statesmanship of the future, within the Constitution, could adapt to time and circumstance." Roosevelt's leadership of Congress and his appointments to the Supreme Court established the model by which future Presidents would be judged in the exercise of statesmanship in the pursuit of a national agenda. [see JUDGES, APPOINTMENT OF]. In particular, the greatly expanded executive branch became the beneficiary of an irrevocable shift in the focal point of economic and social policy from the states to the national government. Accompanying the expansion in the scope of conflict was a growing realization that, within the federal government, only the executive commanded the resources and the expertise necessary to provide specific policy-making focus for the increasingly complex governmental tasks at hand.

While the shift has been irrevocable in the sense that the states can never recapture the limelight they enjoyed in earlier years, the struggle between the forces of privatization and socialization still continues. Disillusionment with Washington-centered government has in recent decades provided a more receptive political audience for the rhetoric of states' rights. President Richard Nixon, for example, proposed a "New Federalism in which power, funds, and responsibility flow from Washington to the States and to the people." But the reality has been that even in administrations such as that of President Ronald Reagan, in which deference to states' rights existed as a matter of clear principle, the New Deal transformation of the political and constitutional landscape of federalism has only marginally been affected by presidential action.

The continuing contests over states' rights may very well be shaped in a more definitive way by what Presidents do indirectly through their appointments to the federal judiciary than by what they are likely to accomplish directly through their own actions. In the late twentieth century, the Supreme Court has been bitterly divided over the question of what some Justices considered to be unwarranted interference in the constitutional prerogatives of the states. The narrowness of the split on the Court highlights the crucial role of the President in the appointment process and, ultimately, in influencing the future course of federalism. Historically, too, a full accounting of the presidential role in the debate over states' rights should acknowledge the contributions of such Presidents as John Adams, Andrew Jackson, and Dwight Eisenhower for their selection of Justices who have had a profound impact on the ebb and flow of states' rights doctrine. To the extent, therefore, that the survival of this doctrine is entwined in the constitutional politics of the Supreme Court, attention to this matter might most profitably be directed to electoral politics at the presidential level.

BIBLIOGRAPHY

Ackerman, Bruce. *We the People: Foundations*. 1991.

Corwin, Edward S. *The President: Office and Powers*. 1957.

Goldwin, Robert A., ed. *A Nation of States: Essays on the American Federal System*. 1965.

Mason, Alpheus Thomas, and Richard H. Leach. *In Quest of Freedom: American Thought and Practice*. 1959.

Schattschneider, E. E. *The Semisovereign People: A Realist's View of Democracy in America*. 1960.

GARY JEFFREY JACOBSOHN

STEEL-SEIZURE CONTROVERSY. For discussion of President Harry S. Truman's seizure of steel mills in 1952, see EXECUTIVE ORDER 10340 and YOUNGSTOWN SHEET & TUBE CO. v. SAWYER.

STEVENSON, ADLAI E. (1835–1914), twenty-third Vice President of the United States (1893–1897). Adlai Ewing Stevenson was born in Kentucky, where his family owned a small plantation and a few slaves. In the early 1850s, they moved to Bloomington, Illinois, where the young Stevenson began his education. He later taught school, attended Illinois Wesleyan University, and enrolled for two years at Centre College in Danville, Kentucky. He left college before graduating, studied law, and practiced in Metamora, Illinois. Like most small-town lawyers, Stevenson was not a specialist but a good general practitioner. He quickly became well known for his even temperament and geniality.

Politics interested Stevenson, who was always a loyal Democrat. He campaigned for STEPHEN A. DOUGLAS for the Senate in 1858 and for the presidency in 1860, and he supported GEORGE B. MCCLELLAN in 1864. He favored monetary inflation and a low tariff, which appealed to many disaffected Democrats in rural Illinois. The panic of 1873 produced a Democratic congressional landslide in 1874, and Stevenson was one of the beneficiaries, winning a seat in the House of Representatives. He was defeated for reelection two years later but gained a second term in 1878, this time with support from local GREENBACK PARTY elements. His work in Congress was unexceptional, though he continued to accumulate friends and the goodwill of party leaders.

In 1885 President Grover Cleveland named him First Assistant Postmaster General. Cleveland's was the first Democratic administration since James Buchanan's. Federal officeholders had no tenure, and local postmasters were vital in any party organization, so Stevenson duly replaced thousands of untenured Republican postmasters with faithful Democrats. In 1889 the departing Cleveland nominated Stevenson to the Supreme Court of the District of Columbia. The Republican majority in the Senate had not forgotten Stevenson's work in the Post Office, however, and declined to confirm him. Stevenson continued to work for Cleveland and was in the Illinois delegation to the national convention of 1892 that renominated the former President for another term. Stevenson then became a logical choice as a running mate for a number of reasons: he might help carry a doubtful major western state; he was known to the party's leaders; and he worked well with other politicians. The idea that he might succeed to the presidency seemed remote. Geography was more important than chance. The ticket won.

The vice presidency brought Stevenson few duties except to preside over the Senate. He differed from Cleveland on the currency issue, remaining an inflationist while the President was a militant supporter of the gold standard. But, as in the past, he did not push his views. For one moment, however, his succession did seem possible, with potentially dangerous consequences for the party. Cleveland underwent an operation for cancer of the jaw in the summer of 1893, just as the administration faced the volatile question of maintaining the gold standard. The President's aides kept the operation secret, lest public discussion of Cleveland's possible death and Stevenson's succession cause a panic on the bond and stock markets or produce a run on the gold reserve. Cleveland survived and maintained gold redemption.

In a show of bipartisanship, in 1897 President William McKinley named the former Vice President to a commission that studied the feasibility of adopting international bimetallism. In 1900, Stevenson joined WILLIAM JENNINGS BRYAN on the Democratic ticket. In 1908, despite his age, he almost won the governorship of Illinois, which attested to his residual appeal for many of that state's Democrats.

Stevenson was a typical secondary party leader of the period. He appealed to many factions in an important, politically volatile state, while espousing ideas that were acceptable to many Democrats elsewhere. He lacked the drive, ambition, or willingness to make enemies necessary to develop a national career. But he appeared suited to the vice presidency at a time when the office did not seem to be a stepping-stone to the presidency, either through succession or political advancement.

BIBLIOGRAPHY

Stevenson, Adlai. *Something of Men I Have Known.* 1909.

H. WAYNE MORGAN

STEVENSON, ADLAI E. (1900–1965), governor, Democratic presidential nominee in 1952 and 1956, ambassador. Adlai Ewing Stevenson was born in Los Angeles to a distinguished Illinois family. He graduated from Princeton University in 1922, attended Harvard Law School for two years, worked for his family's newspaper, the Bloomington, Illinois, *Daily Pantagraph,* and received a law degree in 1926. Stevenson practiced law privately in Chicago until 1941, when he was appointed special assistant to Secretary of the Navy Frank Knox. In 1945, after Stevenson was named personal assistant to Secretary of State Edward Stettinius, he assisted in planning the UNITED NATIONS. In 1945 he served as a senior adviser of the U.S. delegation to the first session of the U.N. General Assembly.

In 1948 Stevenson was elected governor of Illinois. He reformed the state police by establishing a merit system, attacked organized gambling, doubled state spending on education, and sponsored public works. The eloquence and courage he displayed as governor made him the obvious choice of the Democratic national convention in 1952, which nominated him for the presidency after three ballots. It was that rarity in modern politics, a genuine draft, for Stevenson did not wish to run against the enormously popular Dwight D. Eisenhower. But he reluctantly answered his party's call, choosing as his running mate Senator John Sparkman of Alabama.

Although Stevenson at first admired Eisenhower, he loathed the general's running mate, Senator Richard M. Nixon of California, who during the campaign added to his reputation as a red-baiter at Stevenson's expense by saying, for example, "Stevenson holds a Ph.D. degree from [Dean] Acheson's College of Cowardly Communist Containment." Despite his hatred, Stevenson said little about Nixon during the campaign, trying instead—without much success—to engage Eisenhower on the issues. Eisenhower's failure to defend his patron General GEORGE C. MARSHALL against the attacks on Marshall's character by Senator Joseph McCarthy of Wisconsin, disgusted Stevenson [see MC-CARTHYISM].

Less and less did he regard Eisenhower as fit to be President, and he began campaigning against him zealously and with increased effectiveness. But Stevenson could not overcome the handicap of having to run on the record of President Harry S. Truman, whose popularity was then at its lowest, and his chances were diminished by the KOREAN WAR, which Americans desperately wished to see ended. Eisenhower's vow to go to Korea if elected ensured his victory in November, although Stevenson's share of the popular vote was a respectable twenty-seven million to Eisenhower's nearly thirty-four million.

Although he had been relatively conservative during his first presidential race, Stevenson evolved into a liberal over the next four years. No longer reluctant to run, he fought for the nomination in 1956, and, after receiving it, he allowed the convention to choose his running mate; Senator Estes Kefauver of Tennessee won narrowly over Senator John F. Kennedy of Massachusetts. Stevenson's most daring proposals—to end both the draft and nuclear testing—were of no help to his campaign. Indeed, they are thought to have cost him as many as three million votes. Stevenson's endorsement of the Supreme Court's decision banning racially segregated schools hurt him in the South. Stevenson called for a broad range of liberal measures including federal aid to education (at that time a controversial issue), aid for economically depressed areas, support for health care, and expanded social security benefits and housing for the elderly. Many of his proposals would eventually become law, and it is fair to say that Stevenson laid down a good part of the agenda that Democratic Presidents and Congresses would later pursue.

His admirable program notwithstanding, Stevenson could not overcome either Eisenhower's great personal appeal or that fact that the country was prosperous and at peace. The eruption of war in the Middle East and revolution in Hungary, both crises breaking out late in the campaign, made Eisenhower's proven leadership an invaluable campaign asset. Because he was so far behind, Stevenson tried in his final speech to make an issue of the President's health, which had been poor. This was unworthy of him and did not affect the election. Eisenhower's margin of victory amounted to almost ten million votes, 35.6 million compared with Stevenson's 26 million.

As his reward for long service to the DEMOCRATIC PARTY Stevenson became U.S. Ambassador to the United Nations in 1961, holding the office until his death of a heart attack in 1965. Stevenson's most important contribution was made during the CUBAN MISSILE CRISIS of 1962. While he was publicly condemning the Soviets for introducing weapons of mass destruction into CUBA, privately he stood up against the hawkish members of ExCom, President Kennedy's special advisory committee. Stevenson thereby helped the administration find a peaceful way out of the most dangerous confrontation of the nuclear age.

BIBLIOGRAPHY

"Adlai Stevenson: The Man from Libertyville." A film written, produced, and directed by Andrew Schlesinger. 1990.

Davis, Kenneth Sydney. *The Politics of Honor: A Biography of Adlai E. Stevenson.* 1967.

Johnson, Walter, ed. *The Papers of Adlai E. Stevenson.* 8 vols. 1972–1979.

Martin, John Bartlow. *Adlai Stevenson and the World: The Life of Adlai E. Stevenson.* 1977.

Martin, John Bartlow. *Adlai Stevenson of Illinois: The Life of Adlai E. Stevenson.* 1976.

WILLIAM L. O'NEILL

STEWARDSHIP THEORY. When the anthracite coal strike of 1902 threatened both the nation's and his administration's well-being, President Theodore Roosevelt wrote that he could not conduct his presidency "on the Buchanan principle of striving to find some constitutional reason for inaction." Instead, as he stated in his *Autobiography* (1913), his tenure illustrated "the Jackson-Lincoln theory of the Presidency." The *Autobiography*, written after Roosevelt left office, contains the fullest exposition of his stewardship theory, incorporating his views of EXECUTIVE POWER.

According to the theory, the President is bound to do all he can for the people and nation without specific authorization, unless the action contemplated is forbidden by the Constitution or by law. The stewardship theory is among the most sweeping claims of power a President has ever articulated as well as an accurate prophecy, uttered early in the twentieth century, of what the presidency would become later in that century.

In Roosevelt's formulation, the President represents the national interest rather than merely individual preferences or the interests of the coalition of groups that elected him. Consequently, he can rightly exercise the sovereign powers of the nation, including those residual powers that are not enumerated in the Constitution, or assigned to any branch. With the people, the Constitution, and the President joined in common bond, Presidents need not defer to a congressional majority nor to their own party. Roosevelt's stewardship theory is a prescription for government by EXECUTIVE PREROGATIVE, with the President acting independently rather than according to the collaborative processes incorporated in the Constitution.

Despite his expansive view of presidential power, Roosevelt, in practice, and sometimes in theory, considerably circumscribed it. Because the President is so powerful, Roosevelt wrote to Henry Cabot Lodge, he should be closely watched by the people and held to strict accountability. ELIHU ROOT, Roosevelt's Secretary of War and later his Secretary of State, noted that "Theodore is a bit of a bluffer occasionally, and at the same time he had the nerve to go on—to take a chance his statements would have a deciding effect, and, if not, to go on and trust the country would back him up." Others remarked about Roosevelt's expansive verbalizing and his timidity of deed. Although Roosevelt celebrated and exaggerated his trustbusting efforts, his more modest successor, President William Howard Taft, was decidedly more successful in that area.

The chief application of the stewardship theory was to the anthracite-coal strike, the first labor-management dispute that a President attempted to mediate personally. Roosevelt was aided by the nation's premier financier, J. P. Morgan, who pressured the coal operators into submitting the dispute to an arbitration commission, whose membership the President chose. Heeding a call that he appoint an "eminent sociologist," to the commission, Roosevelt selected a union official. Fortunately for Roosevelt, the arbitrators' decision was accepted by both miners and owners. Had it not been accepted, Roosevelt planned to seize the mines and run them as a receiver, which, his Attorney General advised would be illegal. In this instance, the stewardship theory moved government away from its habit of siding with management in labor disputes.

Preeminent among the critics of the theory was Taft, who ridiculed the notion that the President possesses a constitutional warrant to don the role of "a Universal Providence," and who assailed claims of "a residual executive power" as thoroughly "unsafe." In ruling on President Harry S. Truman's seizure of the steel mills in 1952, Judge David A. Pine of the federal district court of the District of Columbia commented that Roosevelt's stewardship claims "do not comport with our recognized theory of government, but with a theory with which our government of laws and not of men is constantly at war."

[See also PRESIDENCY, PRESIDENTIAL CONCEPTIONS OF THE.]

BIBLIOGRAPHY

Andrews, Wayne, ed. *The Autobiography of Theodore Roosevelt.* 1975.
Harbaugh, William Henry. *Power and Responsibility: The Life and Times of Theodore Roosevelt.* 1961.

LOUIS W. KOENIG

STIMSON, HENRY L. (1867–1950), Secretary of War, Secretary of State. Educated at Yale University and at Harvard Law School, Henry L. Stimson was a preeminent New York lawyer who frequently undertook the duties of appointive office. On the single occasion when he ran for public office, for the governorship of New York on the Republican ticket in 1910, he was roundly defeated.

Stimson liked to recall that he served every American President from Theodore Roosevelt to Harry S. Truman, save for Warren G. Harding, although in one instance this was merely in military service as a colonel in WORLD WAR I. Theodore Roosevelt appointed him U.S. district attorney in New York City, and Stimson enlivened that office by gathering a group of young assistants that included FELIX FRANKFURTER. William H. Taft appointed Stimson Secretary of War. Stimson championed the army's chief of staff, Major General Leonard Wood, against a powerful War Department rival, so as to strengthen the general staff system. President Calvin Coolidge used Stimson's talents to bring peace to rival factions in Nicaragua in 1927 and afterward made him governor general of the Philippines. President Herbert Hoover appointed him Secretary of State. In 1940, Franklin D. Roosevelt sought bipartisanship in the Cabinet by again making Stimson Secretary of War; he held that office into the Truman administration.

Stimson's accomplishments were considerable, but perhaps fewer and less glorious than he imagined. For instance, though General Wood triumphed during Taft's administration, he lost out to subordinate War Department generals during the presidency of Woodrow Wilson. Stimson did do well in Nicaragua and the Philippines, although Theodore Roosevelt's brand of

American imperialism ultimately waned. As Secretary of State Stimson was largely unsuccessful, through an inability to get along with President Hoover. Stimson inclined toward an aggressive posture in U.S. foreign policy; Hoover, preoccupied with the Great Depression, could not tolerate use of American forces abroad. The only accomplishment of Stimson's several efforts to contain Japanese expansion in Manchuria was the so-called Stimson Doctrine, by which the United States refused to recognize the political entities that resulted from aggression. Stimson took an interest in limiting naval armaments, a vain enterprise, as its effect was to limit the arms of the Western democracies while the Japanese soon withdrew from the restrictions of the London Naval Treaty of 1930. By the end of the Hoover administration Stimson was virtually estranged from the President.

Stimson joined the Cabinet of Franklin D. Roosevelt in 1940 as WORLD WAR II was intensifying in Europe. In army matters Stimson followed the lead of Chief of Staff GEORGE C. MARSHALL. He took interest in the wartime nuclear project and removed the historically important Japanese city of Kyoto from the list of possible atomic-bomb targets. By the end of the war, age had brought his energies to a low ebb.

[*See also* ATOMIC BOMB, USE OF.]

BIBLIOGRAPHY

Current, Richard N. *Secretary Stimson: A Study in Statecraft.* 1954.

Morison, Elting E. *Turmoil and Tradition: A Study of the Life and Times of Henry L. Stimson.* 1960.

Stimson, Henry L., and McGeorge Bundy. *On Active Service in Peace and War.* 1948.

ROBERT H. FERRELL

STRATEGIC DEFENSE INITIATIVE. See SDI (STRATEGIC DEFENSE INITIATIVE).

STRATEGIC PRESIDENCY. A President who has a strong, definite agenda to accomplish must carefully plan how to approach the first term in office. Despite many factors beyond presidential control, presidents can enhance their chances for success by acting strategically. Having a strategy means having a long-term perspective or vision that is different from dealing with emergencies or gaining short-term political advantage. A strategic approach shows an appreciation for the fragility of presidential power—a fragility that stems from constitutional design, from public expectations that are out of proportion to the President's power to deliver, and from the fickleness of public opinion.

While many Presidents may have acted strategically, the term *strategic presidency* is specifically associated with modern Presidents' self-conscious approach to presidential power. In his 1960 book *Presidential Power and the Modern Presidents*, Richard Neustadt emphasizes the importance of personal reputation rather than formal powers as a key element of a President's ability to succeed. The series of shortened or one-term presidencies of John F. Kennedy, Lyndon B. Johnson, Richard M. Nixon, Gerald Ford, and Jimmy Carter made observers of the presidency sensitive to the uncertainty of presidential success and the need for Presidents to act coherently to achieve their goals.

The elements of a strategic approach include early planning for PRESIDENTIAL TRANSITION, starting quickly with the agenda, setting priorities, and using political capital carefully.

Carter was the first President to shift significant resources from his campaign effort to a planning operation for transition. In the summer of 1976 he set up an operation to prepare policy options and to compile lists of potential presidential appointees. This unprecedented effort contributed some important personnel to Carter's administration, though its effects were undermined by personal rivalries and other problems early in his administration.

In the spring of 1980 candidate Ronald Reagan also initiated a transition-planning effort for personnel and policy. But the main contributions of the Reagan administration to the strategic approach to the presidency were its actions during his first year in office. David Stockman had been laying out budget options and Pendleton James had been planning personnel selection well before the election. One of the strategic choices of the new administration was to set very clear priorities in its policy goals, deciding to focus most of its efforts on its economic agenda: tax cuts, domestic spending reduction, and increases in defense spending. Once its goals were set, it moved quickly to accomplish them. The success of the Reagan agenda in his first year was at least partially a result of its careful planning and a strategic approach to its policy agenda.

The strategic approach is sensitive to the fact that the presidency moves through political time and that as time passes, opportunities diminish. One of the tenets of this approach is that there is a narrow window of opportunity at the beginning of a new administration during which the President will have the best opportunity to accomplish policy goals. A new President enjoys a HONEYMOON PERIOD with the public, and public approval ratings are characteristically high. Early in the administration the President can take advantage of the mandate of the voters, regardless of how close the election may have been. But, barring unforeseen good luck, public approval ratings will soon begin to fall, and the claimed mandate will dissipate. Though Congress will not give a new President a free ride, it will at least be open to the new President's initiatives. Late in the first year of an administration, however, members of Congress will begin to think about upcoming midterm elections and will begin to be less sympathetic to presidential requests.

Related to the need to move quickly is the importance of choosing priorities among the many campaign promises and pressing issues facing the nation. There is no way a President can address all important needs, so it is necessary to choose a small number to set as administration priorities. A failure to choose priorities can confuse the public and diffuse the efforts of the President's allies in Congress.

A strategic approach to the presidency does not guarantee success, and a President's most important actions may come in response to unforeseen foreign or domestic events. What a strategic approach can do, however, is to increase the probability that the policy goals of a new President will be achieved.

[See also PRESIDENCY, PRESIDENTIAL CONCEPTIONS OF THE; THEORIES OF THE PRESIDENCY.]

BIBLIOGRAPHY

Heineman, Ben W., and Curtis A. Hessler. *Memorandum for the President: A Strategic Approach to Domestic Affairs in the 1980s.* 1980.

Light, Paul C. *The President's Agenda: Domestic Policy Choice from Kennedy to Carter.* 1982.

Neustadt, Richard E. *Presidential Power and the Modern Presidents.* 1st ed. 1960. 1990.

Neustadt, Richard E., and Ernest R. May. *Thinking in Time: The Uses of History for Decision Makers.* 1986.

Pfiffner, James P. *The Strategic Presidency.* 1988.

JAMES P. PFIFFNER

STRONG PRESIDENT. The strong President is at the opposite end of the spectrum from the LITERALIST PRESIDENT. Strong Presidents are typified by George Washington, Andrew Jackson, Abraham Lincoln, Woodrow Wilson, Theodore and Franklin D. Roosevelt, Lyndon B. Johnson, Ronald Reagan. Richard Nixon was a strong President in foreign affairs, but less so in domestic affairs. Strong Presidents are more recurrent in the twentieth century than in the nineteenth, and, altogether, they comprise a minority of Presidents. The Constitution's general phrasing of EXECUTIVE POWER allows for reinterpretation, which can foster a strong presidency. In addition, the advent of the United States as a world power has spurred the strong presidency.

A strong President is one who responds to the nation's problems and can effect his program. The United States, born in an unfriendly world, was aided by Washington's exceptional leadership. With the decline of the Federalists, the republic was transformed into a more popular government. The crisis of the Civil War was managed chiefly by the strong leadership of Lincoln. Twentieth-century Presidents, such as Franklin D. Roosevelt and Lyndon B. Johnson, were initiators of key economic regulations and social services.

The strong President interprets his powers broadly. He is prone to stretch precedents set by earlier incumbents to the point where the legality of his acts may be questioned. The executive power, with which the Constitution entrusts him, is pushed to far limits, accompanied by extreme formulations of his legal powers, such as Lincoln's war power claim, a hybrid of the President's power as COMMANDER IN CHIEF and of his duty to defend the Constitution and to execute faithfully the laws. When faced with formidable problems such as waging war, overcoming the Great Depression, or resolving labor-management disputes in key industries, the strong President is apt to claim inherent power to act—the power to do everything except that which the Constitution forbids—rather than rely on enumerated powers, or those that provide a specific warrant for action.

The strong President is one who makes his claims of power prevail by skillfully gaining support for such claims from Congress, the courts, and the public. His chances for success increase if he constructively manages the problems to which his claimed powers are addressed. Lincoln's unprecedented exertions of power were followed by his successes in gaining support for his actions. Congress by legislation ratified much of what he did, the courts approved, and the President's performance passed scrutiny in the elections of 1862 and 1864.

The strong presidency is best sustained by a President of exceptional political skill and persuasive leadership. Performing under constraints of a democracy and in a weak party system, the strong President exploits his opportunities for publicity, his veto, his power over budget and expenditure, his power of appointment. The strong President is a principal unifying force in a diffuse political system and pluralistic society. The strong President's most potent wellspring of power is his capacity to incorporate popular concerns and aspirations. "If he rightly interprets the national thought and insists upon it," wrote Woodrow

Wilson, "he is irresistible; and the country never feels the zest for action so much as when its President is of such insight and calibre."

Times of crisis and change afford the best opportunity for a strong President. His orientation is not to the past but to the future.

The rise of a strong presidency may occur with the assent of the other governmental branches. The presidency gains strength when Congress delegates power to the CHIEF EXECUTIVE. In wartime, economic depression, or an energy crisis, for example, Congress has been prone to delegate powers to the President with few constraints. The courts contribute to presidential strength when they determine that questions of presidential power, including those affecting Congress, are political questions, and thus inappropriate for judicial determination. The bureaucracy often contributes to the strong presidency by forfeit. The bureaucracy's ingrained disinclination to innovate, heightens dependence on the presidency to present new policy.

As a wielder of great power, the strong President faces temptations of excess, of straying beyond democratic bounds, even to the point of subverting political processes and sanctioning criminal conduct. The WATERGATE AFFAIR entailed break-ins and burglaries and violations of Fourth Amendment protections against illegal searches and seizures. The IRAN-CONTRA AFFAIR during the Reagan presidency involved the subversion of Congress's constitutional power to appropriate monies. The strong presidency can put a strain on the checks and balances the Framers erected to keep the office within safe bounds.

[See also PRESIDENCY, PRESIDENTIAL CONCEPTIONS OF THE; THEORIES OF THE PRESIDENCY.]

BIBLIOGRAPHY

Burns, James MacGregor. *Presidential Government.* 1965.
Cronin, Thomas E. *The State of the Presidency.* 1980.
Koenig, Louis W. *The Chief Executive.* 5th rev. ed. 1986.
Neustadt, Richard E. *Presidential Power.* 1960.
Pious, Richard M. *The American Presidency.* 1979.
Schlesinger, Arthur M. *The Imperial Presidency.* 1973.

LOUIS W. KOENIG

SUBDELEGATION. Congress regularly delegates legislative power to the President and administrative officials. In turn, the President, by necessity, must transfer much of the authority conveyed to him to his subordinates. Similarly, legislative authority given to agency heads to make regulatory decisions is regularly shifted to subordinates. The subdelegation of power by the President has been an important means of building the modern presidency and the EXECUTIVE OFFICE OF THE PRESIDENT.

The courts have generally upheld the President's power to subdelegate statutory duties to subordinates. In a leading case, *Williams v. United States* (1843), the Supreme Court ruled that the President need not personally authorize every disbursement of public funds even though a statute had so provided: the President need not "perform in person the numerous detail . . . which . . . he is, in a correct sense, by the Constitution and laws required and expected to perform."

Delegation and subdelegation challenge constitutional principles that powers delegated to government by the people cannot be further delegated and that officials who exercise policy-making powers be ultimately accountable to the people, but such delegation is widely viewed as an inescapable characteristic of a large national government. The issue of subdelegation was raised in the 1930s during the passage of the NATIONAL INDUSTRIAL RECOVERY ACT, but was overshadowed by the dispute over the delegation of legislative power in that act.

Throughout the twentieth century, Congress increasingly provided for subdelegation through express statutory language. In 1950, responding to a study that found the President was responsible for functions mandated by more than eleven hundred laws, Congress expressly provided for subdelegation of power from the President to department and agency officials. The Subdelegation Act of 1950 (64 Stat. 419, 3 U.S.C. 301) authorizes the President to empower the department or agency heads in the executive branch, or any official who is required to be appointed by and with the advice and consent of the Senate, to perform any function that is vested in the President by law. However, such subdelegation does not relieve the President of his responsibility in office for the acts of "any such head or other official designated by him to perform such functions." The delegation must be in writing, published in the *Federal Register*, cannot be precluded by statute, and can be revoked at any time. It does not relieve the President of his constitutional responsibilities for the actions taken by these officials. Congress can, by law, prohibit the President from delegating functions assigned to him to others.

[See also DELEGATION OF LEGISLATIVE POWER.]

BIBLIOGRAPHY

Fisher, Louis. *Constitutional Conflicts between Congress and the President.* 1991.
Schubert, Glendon A., Jr. "Judicial Review of the Subdelegation of Presidential Power." *Journal of Politics* 12 (1950): 668.

Schubert, Glendon A., Jr. "The Presidential Subdelegation Act of 1950." *Journal of Politics* 13 (1951): 647.

GARY C. BRYNER

SUCCESSION, PRESIDENTIAL.

SUCCESSION, PRESIDENTIAL. Between October 1973 and December 1974, the United States underwent a series of unprecedented political experiences. A concerned citizenry viewed the events accompanying SPIRO T. AGNEW's resignation as Vice President, Gerald R. Ford's nomination and appointment as his successor, the sad, swift transition from Richard M. Nixon to Gerald Ford, and then NELSON A. ROCKEFELLER's selection as VICE PRESIDENT. Few if any Americans, however, doubted that the transfer of power in each instance would come about in an orderly manner. Nor was the legitimacy of these transitions at issue.

Still, hardly any aspect of the American presidency, has proved more challenging to lawmakers than succession. The Constitution, as well as three constitutional amendments (the TWELFTH AMENDMENT, 1804; the TWENTIETH AMENDMENT 1933; and the TWENTY-FIFTH AMENDMENT, 1967), the PRESIDENTIAL SUCCESSION ACT of 1947, and political party rules govern different succession possibilities.

The importance of the process is evidenced by the nine Vice Presidents who reached the White House through succession. Four—John Tyler (1841), Millard Fillmore (1850), Calvin Coolidge (1923), and Harry S. Truman (1945)—assumed the presidential mantle when the incumbent died. Four others—Andrew Johnson (1865), Chester A. Arthur (1881), Theodore Roosevelt (1901), and Lyndon B. Johnson (1963)—became President following a PRESIDENTIAL ASSASSINATION. A unique resignation occasioned Gerald R. Ford's (1974) occupancy of the White House.

In the Constitution. At the CONSTITUTIONAL CONVENTION in 1787, the question of succession was discussed late in the proceedings and given relatively little consideration. ALEXANDER HAMILTON offered a proposal on 18 June calling for a successor to the President as part of his plan for a national executive who would serve for life, but it was never debated.

Hamilton's idea was revived by the Committee of Detail in its report of 6 August, which provided that if a President was removed from office, died, resigned, or was disabled, the President of the Senate would exercise those duties until another President was chosen or the disability removed. Dissatisfaction with the provision was voiced when it was discussed on 27 August, and the question was delayed until 4 September, when the Committee on Postponed Matters offered a revised proposal. The new language had the Vice President for the first time exercising the duties of CHIEF EXECUTIVE in the case of removal, death, absence, resignation, or inability of the President, "until another President could be chosen, or until the inability of the President be removed." Subsequent amendments, approved three days later, provided additional details concerning both presidential and vice presidential vacancies, including as well a provision for a special election.

Most delegates apparently wanted both provisions to be included in the Constitution. Sometime between 8 and 12 September, however, while the Committee on Detail worked to produce a final draft, that intention was lost. The merging of the 4 September motion for the Vice President to succeed the President, and the subsequent motions of 7 September resulted in grammatical ambiguities. The committee's final draft, which, with minor modifications by the Convention, became Article II, Section 2, clause 6, of the Constitution, provided that:

> In case of the Removal of the President from Office, or of his Death, Resignation, or Inability to discharge the Powers and Duties of the said Office, the Same shall devolve on the Vice President, and Congress may by Law provide for the Case of Removal, Death, Resignation, or Inability, both of the President and Vice President, declaring what Officer shall then act as President, and such Officer shall act accordingly, until the Disability be removed, or a President shall be elected.

Left unclear was whether "the Same" in this provision referred to "the said Office" (the presidency) or, as the delegates intended, only its "Power and Duties." Also uncertain was whether there was to be a special election.

Fifty-two years later, when President William Henry Harrison died just one month after his 4 March 1841 inauguration, the CABINET and many others felt Vice President John Tyler should only be an acting President until a special election could be held. Tyler, however, acted quickly and decisively, assuming both the duties and powers of the office. After arriving in Washington, he took the presidential oath, delivered a message to the American people on the constitutionality of his succession and policies that would guide his administration, and moved into the White House.

When Congress convened in mid May 1841, both Houses by "overwhelming majorities," resolved, in the words of the *New York Daily Express*, that "John Tyler, late vice president [had] become, by the death of General Harrison, 'President of the United States,' and not vice president exercising the office of president." The TYLER PRECEDENT paved the way for all future Vice Presidents to complete the unexpired portion of a President's term in instances of death, impeachment, or resignation. In 1967, Congress confirmed this historical practice with the Twenty-fifth Amendment.

Succession Acts. The Framers also left unanswered what would happen when both the President and Vice President were unable to discharge their duties. This responsibility was left to Congress to handle by law. The Presidential Succession Act of 1792, the first attempt to extend the succession line called for the president pro tem of the Senate, followed by the Speaker of the House, to "act as President" when both the presidency and vice presidency were vacant. A special election for a full four-year term was to be held the following November if the double vacancy occurred prior to the last six months of a presidential term. Opponents of the act thought the Secretary of State, rather than a congressional officer, was a more appropriate successor.

On 18 April 1853, when WILLIAM R. KING became the third of seven Vice Presidents to die in office, a month-and-a-half after taking the oath, considerable attention was directed at the unsatisfactory nature of the Succession Act. Concern focused principally on the fact that for periods of considerable length there was neither a president pro tem of the Senate nor a Speaker of the House available as a successor if something happened to the President and Vice President.

The Senate Judiciary Committee in 1856 recommended extending the succession line to include the Chief Justice of the Supreme Court and Associate Justices of the Court, but nothing came of the proposal. President Andrew Johnson's 1868 plea for a revision of the act, shortly after he narrowly escaped removal from office [see IMPEACHMENT OF ANDREW JOHNSON], likewise attracted little attention. Chester A. Arthur, shortly after becoming President following James A. Garfield's death in September 1881, asked Congress to address the uncertainties associated with succession, but a lengthy Senate debate produced no action. Twice in 1883 the Senate approved legislation establishing succession by Cabinet officers.

Not until Vice President THOMAS A. HENDRICKS died in 1885, however, was the House prompted to concur. Hendrick's death on 25 November was especially troublesome because Congress was not in session and there was neither a president pro tem nor Speaker to act as a successor if something happened to President Grover Cleveland. A new Speaker and president pro tem were not chosen until 7 December, when the Forty-ninth Congress convened. Had Cleveland died during the interim, a special session of Congress could not have been called since there would be no Chief Executive to call it or sign legislation addressing the emergency.

President Cleveland in his first annual message on 8 December stressed that such a possibility was intolerable and needed immediate resolution. Congress acted quickly. The Senate after vigorous debate, approved by voice vote a new succession act sponsored by Senator George F. Hoar on 17 December 1885. The House followed suit on 15 January 1886, by a 186 to 72 vote.

The Succession of Act of 1886 provided that in case of the impeachment, death, resignation, or inability of both the President and Vice President, the line of succession then passed to the Secretary of State and other Cabinet officers in the order of the creation of the departments. Although the act did not make provision for a new election, as was done in the 1792 act, a clause was included that allowed Congress to call such an election if it was deemed appropriate.

Two primary factors—the danger of not having a presidential successor and the desirability of assuring continuity in policy—brought about adoption of the act. While it was under consideration, there was no Vice President and the president pro tem, JOHN SHERMAN, a Republican, stood next in line for the presidency, which the Democrats had recently won. Arguments against the act stressed that it violated democratic principles by allowing the President to appoint his potential successors, and it was unclear if the succession was temporary or permanent.

When Harry S. Truman became President in April 1945, following Franklin D. Roosevelt's death, he inherited as potential successors a Secretary of State, followed by a Secretary of the Treasury, who had never held an elective office. Truman was particularly concerned about the nation being without a Vice President for almost four years.

Two months after he assumed office, and again in early 1947, Truman sent special messages to Congress calling for a revision of the 1886 act. Congress responded in mid 1947 by approving a new law incorporating virtually all Truman's suggestions. It placed the Speaker of the House and then the president pro tem in the succession line, followed by officers of the Cabinet. Only Truman's recommendation that a special election be held for the remainder of the unexpired term failed to gain approval.

Presidential Disability. The nature of the Vice President's role when the President was physically or mentally unable to discharge the duties of his office remained unaddressed until 1958. When Presidents James A. Garfield, Grover Cleveland, and Woodrow Wilson suffered serious disabling illnesses, little consideration was given to having the Vice President act as President.

Garfield was incapacitated by an assassin's bullet for two and a half months before his 19 September 1881 death. During the interim, the Cabinet concluded that a PRESIDENTIAL DISABILITY did not exist, despite the fact that he was prohibited by his physician from conducting any official business.

On 1 July 1893, President Cleveland secretly underwent a major operation for cancer of the mouth on board the yacht *Oneida*. Cleveland spent the next two months recuperating. Even though a severe financial crisis gripped the nation, neither Vice President ADLAI E. STEVENSON (1835–1914) nor most of the Cabinet were ever apprised of the seriousness of Cleveland's disability. After President Wilson suffered a stroke on 2 October 1919, he remained a semi-invalid for the remaining seventeen months of his second term. During most of that period, the President's wife, EDITH WILSON, his personal physician, and private secretary ran the government. Presidential disability became an issue again early in 1958 when President Dwight D. Eisenhower suffered his third serious illness in three years, any one of which could have been seriously disabling if not fatal. Eisenhower became convinced, he wrote in *The White House Years*, that "specific arrangements" needed to be made "for the Vice President to succeed to [the presidency] if [he] should incur a disability that precluded proper performance of duty over any period of significant length."

At a 26 February 1958 press conference, Eisenhower disclosed that he had a "clear understanding" with Vice President Richard M. Nixon on what to do if he became unable to perform his duties. The arrangement called for Nixon "to serve as Acting President, exercising the powers and duties of the Office until the inability had ended." Determination of inability would be made "if possible," by the President. If the inability prevented the "President from so communicating with the Vice President," Nixon would make the determination "after such consultation as seems to him appropriate under the circumstances." In each instance, the President "would determine when the inability had ended." Presidents John F. Kennedy and Lyndon B. Johnson entered into similar agreements with their potential successors prior to the ratification of the Twenty-fifth Amendment on 10 February 1967.

The Twenty-fifth Amendment. Under the Twenty-fifth Amendment, the Vice President assumes the President's power and responsibilities if the President informs Congress that he is unable to perform his duties, the Vice President then is acting President until the President informs Congress that he is capable of resuming his duties, or if the Vice President and a majority of the "principal officers of the executive branch," or any other body designated by Congress, determine that the President is incapacitated, the Vice President then becomes acting President until the

President informs Congress that the disability has been removed. In the latter instance, if the group determining the existence of a disability informs Congress within four days that the disability still exists contrary to the President's opinion, the Vice President continues as acting President and Congress has twenty-one days to resolve the issue, the decision to be made by a two-thirds majority of each House.

It also authorizes the President, whenever there is a vacancy in the office of Vice President, to nominate a replacement, who becomes Vice President when confirmed by a majority of both Houses of Congress. Gerald R. Ford was nominated to be Vice President under this clause in 1973, and when Ford succeeded Richard M. Nixon as President in 1974, he nominated Nelson A. Rockefeller to be his successor. For the first time in the nation's history, there was a President and Vice President neither of whom were elected by the people.

Between Election and Inauguration. Despite three different succession acts, and three constitutional amendments, the selection process is still dependent, to a certain extent, upon political party rules. Neither the Constitution nor federal statutes provide for the contingency of a presidential or vice presidential candidate dying, withdrawing, or being disqualified between election day and the day the ELECTORAL COLLEGE meets five weeks later. The rules of the Democratic and Republican parties, however, empower their national committees to fill such vacancies. If the presidential candidate dies, the elevation of the vice presidential candidate would be likely but not certain.

Constitutional scholars have differing opinions on the question of succession between the time the electors meet and the counting of electoral votes by Congress on 6 January. They suggest at least two possible scenarios that might occur if a presidential candidate selected by a majority of the electors dies, withdraws, or is disqualified during this period.

Congress could declare that the candidate who received a majority of the votes for President was elected, even if he had died or resigned, and then the Vice President-elect would assume the presidency under the Twentieth Amendment. It could also declare that no qualified candidate for President had received a majority of the votes cast and the election would accordingly be determined by the House of Representatives under the provisions of the Twelfth Amendment.

If the President-elect dies between 6 January and Inauguration Day (20 January), the Vice President-elect becomes President-elect under the Twentieth Amendment. In the event a President has not been chosen, or a President-elect is disabled, found to be constitutionally unqualified, or refuses to accept the office, the Vice President in the meantime acts as President.

BIBLIOGRAPHY

Feerick, John D. *The Twenty-fifth Amendment*. 1976.
Silva, Ruth. *Presidential Succession*. 1951.
Stathis, Stephen W. "Presidential Disability Agreements Prior to the 25th Amendment." *Presidential Studies Quarterly* 12 (1982): 208–215.
Thompson, Kenneth W. *Papers on Presidential Disability and the Twenty-fifth Amendment*. 2 vols. 1991.

STEPHEN W. STATHIS

SUPPLY-SIDE ECONOMICS. In the history of economic thought the term *supply-side economics* is used in two different senses. Coined in 1976, supply-side economics, narrowly defined, refers only to that part of economic policy that deals with the effect of tax rates on economic activity and how changes in those tax rates, especially personal income tax rates, affect people's incentives to work, save, and invest. But during the 1980s, supply-side economics came to represent a much broader, comprehensive set of economic policies—also often referred to as Reaganomics—that were espoused and implemented by Ronald Reagan during his presidency. Today when most people speak of supply-side economics they are referring specifically to the economic policies that were enacted by law and government regulatory policies between 1981 and 1990.

In this broader, more widely used definition the goal of supply-side economic policy was twofold: to create jobs and to stimulate economic growth. Supply-side economics consists of five key elements, each one complementing and strengthening the others: The first of these fundamental principles of supply-side economics is to *control the growth of federal spending* so that it is reasonable and prudent, generally construed to be in the range of 4 or 5 percent growth per year. No cuts in overall federal spending, however, were ever proposed or implemented during the 1980s. Of equal importance is the *reduction of income tax rates* for individuals and the acceleration and simplification of investment depreciation schedules for business. Tax-rate reduction is considered essential to job creation and economic growth because of the vital impact that tax rates have on incentives to work, save, and invest.

Another integral part of supply-side economics is *regulatory reform:* the comprehensive review of all government regulations affecting economic growth and prompt changes or repeal when those regulations are found to be excessive or counterproductive. Although beyond the scope of the executive branch, the establishment of a stable and sound MONETARY POLICY is also considered an essential part of supply-side economic policy, and every effort is made to ensure this—consistent with the independence of the Federal Reserve System. Finally, one of the least noted but perhaps most important element of supply-side economic policy is its goal of *constancy and stability*: restoring economic confidence by following a consistent national economic policy that does not change from month to month.

Supply-side economic policy was controversial because it became the central battleground for the Democrats and Republicans in the 1980s. Some of the myths from those political battles persist. The most common misconception about supply-side economics is that it claimed that one could raise more tax revenues immediately by cutting tax rates. Obviously it could not, and it did not. What was true was that tax revenues did not decline by the full amount of the tax-rate cut because of the additional stimulus to the economy that the cut fostered. Studies conducted by Lawrence Lindsey at Harvard University in the late 1980s showed as much as 50 percent of the tax revenue being recouped after a few years. In fact, the amount of taxes paid by taxpayers with adjusted gross incomes over $200,000 a year increased by 25 percent.

How well supply-side economics performed during the seven or eight years of its heyday will probably not be answered satisfactorily for decades. Marginal individual income tax rates, the tax rate paid on the highest amount earned, declined dramatically from 70 percent to 28 percent. A number of regulatory reforms were enacted, the most notable being the repeal of all controls on the pricing and distribution of gasoline and oil. Few new regulations were enacted. Monetary policy was remarkably stable and consistent. And the basic economic policy, once in place, did not change.

On the other hand, federal spending was not stringently controlled; the rate of growth slowed somewhat from the 1970s but federal spending still increased by hundreds of billions of dollars. In 1980, total federal spending was $591 billion a year. By 1988, annual federal spending had jumped to $1.064 trillion, an increase of $473 billion. During this time, annual defense spending increased by $156 billion, leaving more than two-thirds of the increased spending to nondefense areas, primarily social welfare programs such as SOCIAL SECURITY, Medicare, and other health and welfare programs.

The detractors of supply-side economic policy will

point to the fact that the federal deficits and the national debt swelled to record levels as federal spending continued to increase rapidly, almost doubling during Reagan's two terms of office, and that defense spending increased too much and social welfare spending increased too little. The supporters of supply-side economics will argue that, in spite of the failure to control federal spending sufficiently, almost 19 million new jobs were created, economic growth was positive for eight straight years (the longest peacetime economic expansion in U.S. history), that inflation dropped to low levels, interest rates fell dramatically, the poverty rate declined, and the value of the stock market nearly tripled.

Part of the controversial nature of supply-side economics stems from its origins. The ideas were crafted by a diverse group of intellectuals, politicians, and economists who were not part of the establishment. They included unconventional economists such as Robert Mundell of Columbia University and Arthur Laffer of the University of Southern California; economic consultants Norman Ture, Alan Reynolds, and Jude Wanniski; intellectuals Irving Kristol and Paul Craig Roberts; government economists Steve Entin and Bruce Bartlett; an editor from the *Wall Street Journal*, Robert Bartley; and politicians such as Jack Kemp and Ronald Reagan. They were joined by a few major establishment economists—most notably Milton Friedman, Paul McCracken, GEORGE SHULTZ, and Alan Greenspan—as the policy was refined and transformed into national economic policy.

BIBLIOGRAPHY

Anderson, Martin, *Revolution*. 1988.
Bartley, Robert L. *The Seven Fat Years: And How to Do It Again*. 1992.
Roberts, Paul Craig. *The Supply-Side Revolution: An Insider's Account of Policymaking in Washington*. 1984.

MARTIN ANDERSON

SUPREME COURT DECISIONS ON THE PRESIDENCY. In MARBURY V. MADISON (1803), the Supreme Court established the power of the federal courts to review the constitutionality of executive branch actions. The Court concluded that the judiciary could determine whether Secretary of State James Madison, at the obvious direction of President Thomas Jefferson, acted improperly in denying William Marbury his commission to serve as a justice of the peace. Although the Court dismissed the case for a lack of jurisdiction, the decision forcefully established the ability of the Supreme Court to review presidential actions.

In the two centuries after *Marbury*, the Supreme Court reviewed countless challenges to presidential actions. A striking pattern emerged. In cases involving FOREIGN AFFAIRS, the President almost always prevailed. But in cases involving domestic affairs, the result was less predictable. The Court employed a functional approach, finding for the President unless the President was usurping the powers granted to another branch of government or preventing another branch from carrying out its tasks.

Foreign Affairs. In the realm of FOREIGN AFFAIRS, the Supreme Court has been highly deferential to the President. The President virtually always wins constitutional challenges to the conduct of foreign policy either because the Court rules in his favor on the merits or because the Court deems the matter to pose a nonjusticiable political question. The latter approach dismisses the case and in practical result allows the President's conduct to continue.

The most forceful expression of this deference to the President was in UNITED STATES V. CURTISS-WRIGHT EXPORT CORP. (1936). Congress adopted a joint resolution allowing the President to ban arms sales to countries involved in the Chaco border dispute—a war between Bolivia and Paraguay—if he concluded that such a prohibition might shorten the hostilities. After the President issued a PROCLAMATION outlawing sales, the defendant company argued that Congress had impermissibly delegated legislative power to the executive. The case was considered by the Supreme Court at a time when it was aggressively limiting the ability of Congress to delegate legislative power in the domestic arena. In *Curtiss-Wright*, however, the Court upheld the delegation and declared that the President has broad INHERENT POWERS in the realm of foreign affairs.

In an opinion by Justice George Sutherland, the Court stated that foreign and domestic powers are "different, both in respect of their origin and their nature." The Court explained that domestic powers were granted by the states to Congress and therefore Congress possesses only that authority specifically enumerated in the Constitution. But because foreign policy powers are inherent to the executive, the President's authority is not narrowly constrained to that which is specifically enumerated. Justice Sutherland wrote,

> The investment of the federal government with the powers of external sovereignty did not depend on the affirmative grants of the Constitution. The powers to declare and wage war, to conclude peace, to make treaties, to maintain diplomatic relations with other sovereignties, if they had never been mentioned in the Constitution, would have vested in the federal government as necessary concomitants of sovereignty.

Many scholars have criticized the Court's conclusion in *Curtiss-Wright* that the President has broad inherent powers in the area of foreign affairs. Such unlimited authority is incompatible with a government of limited powers. The Constitution is not silent on foreign policy, but instead enumerates authority with regard to subjects such as regulating foreign commerce, making treaties, and waging war. This express detailing of powers would be unnecessary if the President has the inherent authority ascribed in *Curtiss-Wright*. Perhaps because of these criticisms the Supreme Court has not relied expressly on *Curtiss-Wright* very often in its subsequent decisions. But the ultimate conclusion of *Curtiss-Wright* has very much been in evidence: the judiciary defers to the President with regard to foreign policy decisions.

For example, never in U.S. history has the Supreme Court invalidated the President's action as COMMANDER IN CHIEF in using troops in a foreign country [*see* WAR POWERS]. In the PRIZE CASES (1863), the Supreme Court upheld inherent presidential power to repel invasion or rebellion without prior legislative authorization. In upholding President Abraham Lincoln's blockade of southern ports following the attack on Fort Sumter in 1861, the Court declared, "This Court must be governed by the decisions and acts of the political department of the government to which the power was entrusted."

More than a century later, the Supreme Court repeatedly refused to hear challenges to the constitutionality of the VIETNAM WAR. More than a dozen lawsuits were filed arguing that the President was impermissibly waging war without a congressional DECLARATION OF WAR as required by Article I of the Constitution. In almost all of these cases, the lower federal court dismissed the matter as posing a nonjusticiable political question and the Supreme Court denied review.

In 1973, Congress adopted the WAR POWERS RESOLUTION to limit the duration of American participation in foreign wars without congressional approval. In addition to imposing reporting and consulation requirements on the President, the War Powers Resolution states that troops may not be used in hostilities beyond sixty days—which the President can extend by thirty days—without congressional approval. Although Presidents repeatedly have maintained that this is unconstitutional, there never has been a judicial ruling.

The Court's deference to the President in the area of war making is paralleled by its upholding executive actions concerning agreements with foreign nations. Article II, Section 2, of the Constitution authorizes the President to negotiate treaties that are effective when approved by two-thirds of the Senate. The President, however, has been accorded broad powers to negotiate foreign policy matters via EXECUTIVE AGREEMENTS—agreements between the President and a foreign nation that do not require Senate approval.

In UNITED STATES V. BELMONT (1937) and UNITED STATES V. PINK (1942), the Court upheld executive agreements arising out of the United States' recognition of the Soviet Union in 1937. The executive agreement assigned to the United States all Soviet claims against Americans who held funds of Russian companies seized after the revolution. In *Belmont*, the Court declared that the agreement was "within the competence of the President . . . and the Executive had the authority to speak as the sole organ." In *Pink*, the Court emphasized that executive agreements have the same effect as treaties under the supremacy clause of the Constitution.

In DAMES & MOORE V. REGAN (1981), the Supreme Court upheld an executive agreement whereby the United States lifted a freeze on Iranian assets in the United States in exchange for the release of American hostages in Iran [*see* IRANIAN HOSTAGE CRISIS]. Although there are certainly limits on executive agreements—they cannot violate the Constitution or federal laws (for example, in REID V. COVERT, invalidating an executive agreement as violating the Constitution)—there is no doubt that the Supreme Court has accorded great discretion to the President in this area.

Most cases before the Supreme Court concerning treaties have involved conflicts between state laws and treaties, not issues of presidential power. However, when such questions of executive authority have been before the Court, the President has prevailed. In GOLDWATER V. CARTER (1979), a constitutional challenge was brought to the President's termination of the United States treaty with Nationalist China (Taiwan) as part of the recognition of the People's Republic of China. Senator BARRY GOLDWATER argued that the termination of a treaty, like the repeal of a statute, requires Congressional approval. The Court's plurality opinion, authored by Justice William H. Rehnquist, found that the challenge posed a nonjusticiable political question. Justice Lewis F. Powell in a concurring opinion would have dismissed the case as not being ripe because Congress had not acted to disapprove the President's action. Other Justices, joining in an opinion by Justice William J. Brennan, would have allowed the President's actions as within the scope of executive power.

Domestic Affairs. Thus, the consistent pattern has been that presidential actions in the realm of foreign affairs have been upheld by the Supreme Court. The record in the domestic arena is much more mixed and therefore harder to summarize. In general, the Supreme Court has taken a functional approach. The Court has invalidated presidential actions that have usurped the powers of another branch of government or that have prevented another branch from carrying out its tasks. Correspondingly, the Court has sided with the President and invalidated legislative actions that have usurped or interfered with presidential powers.

YOUNGSTOWN SHEET & TUBE CO. V. SAWYER (1952) is perhaps the most famous instance of judicial invalidation of a presidential action for exceeding the scope of executive powers and usurping the authority of other branches of government. In response to a strike in the steel industry during the KOREAN WAR, President Harry S. Truman ordered the Secretary of Commerce to seize and operate the steel industry. The Supreme Court invalidated this action, with many Justices emphasizing the conscious decision by Congress to deny statutory authority for such presidential seizures of industry. In essence, the President was assuming the legislative power. Moreover, as Justice William O. Douglas explained in a concurring opinion, the President's action was a taking of property that obligated Congress to appropriate funds for compensation, thus usurping Congress's spending power.

In an often-cited concurring opinion, Justice Robert Jackson outlined three types of executive action. He explained that the President's authority is the strongest when he is acting pursuant to statutory authority. The President then has all the powers of the executive and all those of the legislature behind him. In contrast, the President's authority is weakest when the President is acting against congressional will. The President's conduct is then permissible only if constitutionally authorized as part of the executive's power. In the middle are actions neither approved nor disapproved by Congress. Although Jackson's analysis was illuminating in *Youngstown* in light of Congress's express decision to deny authority for presidential seizures, in general its usefulness is limited by its failure to offer any criteria for determining the hard cases, that is, to render judgment on when the President has inherent authority to act without express constitutional or statutory provisions.

The Supreme Court also has invalidated presidential acts that prevent other branches from carrying out their tasks and responsibilities. UNITED STATES V. NIXON (1974) is illustrative. The Watergate special prosecutor, Archibald Cox, sought to compel President Richard M. Nixon to produce tapes of conversations to be used as evidence in a prosecution of individuals involved in the cover-up of the WATERGATE AFFAIR. The President invoked EXECUTIVE PRIVILEGE as a defense against producing the tapes.

Executive privilege had a legacy tracing back to the earliest days of the nation. In 1796, President George Washington asserted executive privilege as the basis for refusing to furnish the House of Representatives with requested correspondence and other documents in connection with the negotiation of JAY'S TREATY. In *United States v. Burr* (1807), Chief Justice John Marshall, sitting as a circuit judge, ruled that courts could compel the President to deliver documents sought in the treason trial of AARON BURR. In the twentieth century, in *Chicago & Southern Air Lines v. Waterman Security Steamship Corp.* (1948), the Supreme Court held that the President could keep secret materials "from intelligence services whose reports are not and ought not to be published to the world."

In *Nixon*, however, the Supreme Court held that executive privilege was limited by the need for evidence at a criminal trial. The Court explained that the President's need for confidentiality "must yield to the demonstrated, specific need for evidence in a pending criminal trial." The President's claim of executive privilege was invalid because it prevented the judiciary from carrying out its function of fairly trying criminal defendants.

The Supreme Court has followed a similar functional approach in evaluating presidential claims that the actions of other branches violate EXECUTIVE PREROGATIVES. Legislative or judicial actions that assume presidential power have been invalidated. For example, in BOWSHER V. SYNAR (1986), the Supreme Court held that Congress cannot delegate executive power to itself or its officers. *Bowsher* concerned the first of the GRAMM-RUDMAN-HOLLINGS ACTS, which sought to eliminate the federal budget deficit by 1991. The act prescribed the maximum allowable deficit for each of five years and authorized the COMPTROLLER GENERAL, a congressional officer, to impose across-the-board spending cuts if the deficit exceeded the ceiling. The Supreme Court ruled that the law was unconstitutional because it had granted the executive power—the authority to implement the law—to a legislative official.

Similarly, legislative or judicial actions that prevent the President from carrying out the duties of the office are ruled unconstitutional. In NIXON V. FITZGERALD (1982), for example, the Court held that the President has absolute immunity to civil suits for money damages for actions taken in office. The Court reasoned that allowing such judicial relief would impede effective presidential actions.

The Supreme Court's treatment of the appointment and REMOVAL POWER also illustrates its functional approach to the presidency. Article II of the Constitution prescribes the APPOINTMENT POWER. Under its terms, the President, with the ADVICE AND CONSENT of the Senate, appoints ambassadors, Supreme Court Justices, and all officers of the United States. Congress, however, may vest the appointment of "inferior officers" in the President, DEPARTMENTAL SECRETARIES, or judges of the lower federal courts. In BUCKLEY V. VALEO (1976), the Court held that it was unconstitutional for Congress to authorize the Speaker of the House and the president pro tem of the Senate to appoint members of the Federal Election Commission because this usurped presidential appointment power.

In MORRISON V. OLSON (1988), the Supreme Court held that it was constitutional for Congress to vest the appointment of the INDEPENDENT COUNSEL in a panel of federal court judges, because Article II of the Constitution allows the federal courts to appoint "inferior officers." The Court reasoned that an independent counsel was an inferior officer because he or she could be fired by the ATTORNEY GENERAL for just cause. The Court also emphasized the functional need for independent counsels responsible for investigating alleged misconduct in the executive branch to remain independent of direct executive control.

Although the Constitution is quite specific about the appointment power, it is silent about the ability of the President to remove government officials. One of the most important constitutional controversies in American history—the IMPEACHMENT OF ANDREW JOHNSON—concerned the removal power. Following the CIVIL WAR, Congress attempted to limit the powers of President Andrew Johnson, a southerner from Tennessee who became President after Lincoln's assassination. Congress adopted the TENURE OF OFFICE ACT, which prevented Johnson from firing Cabinet officials. After Johnson fired Secretary of State EDWIN M. STANTON for blatant insubordination, articles of IMPEACHMENT were immediately drawn and passed by the House of Representatives. The vote in the Senate, however, was one vote short of the two-thirds majority needed for convicting and removing Johnson from office.

The Supreme Court did not consider the removal power fully until MYERS V. UNITED STATES (1926). In *Myers*, the Court declared unconstitutional a law that limited the ability of the President to remove postmasters without Senate consent. The Court concluded that "the President has the exclusive power of removing executive officers of the United States whom he has appointed by and with the advice and consent of the Senate."

But subsequently the Court made it clear that Congress can limit presidential removal for offices where independence from the President would be desirable. In HUMPHREY'S EXECUTOR V. UNITED STATES (1935), the Court held that Congress could limit the removal of commissioners of the Federal Trade Commission. The Court later explained in WIENER V. UNITED STATES (1958) that the difference between *Myers* and *Humphrey's Executor* is "the difference in functions between those who are part of the executive establishment and those whose tasks require absolute freedom from executive interference." The Court's approach is thus expressly functional, allowing presidential removal for officers that should be accountable to the President, but permitting restrictions on removal where independence is desirable.

Although the Supreme Court's analysis of presidential powers in the domestic realm has generally been functional, there are instances in which the Court has taken a far more formalistic approach. INS V. CHADHA (1983) is a paradigm of formalistic judicial reasoning that attempts to reason directly from the text of the Constitution without consideration of functional policy considerations. *Chadha* involved the constitutionality of the LEGISLATIVE VETO—a technique whereby Congress attempts to overrule an executive action by a resolution of one or both houses of Congress.

The legislative veto originated in the 1930s as a method of congressional oversight of executive agency actions. Although traditionally there has been a rule that Congress cannot delegate legislative power, the reality has been that even extremely broad delegations have virtually always been upheld. There was a brief time in the mid 1930s when the Supreme Court invalidated laws as being excessive delegations of power (PANAMA REFINING CO. V. RYAN [1935]; SCHECHTER POULTRY CORP. V. UNITED STATES [1935]). But since then, not a single federal law has been declared unconstitutional as an impermissible delegation of power. Congress devised the legislative veto as a method of checking administrative actions. Specifically, Congress grants power to an agency but the law provides that Congress can overturn the executive action by passing a resolution. Under some laws, a resolution of one chamber or even a committee is sufficient to reverse an executive action.

In *Chadha*, the Supreme Court declared legislative vetos unconstitutional. The Court, in an opinion by Chief Justice Warren E. Burger, reasoned in a syllogism. The Court said that all legislative action requires bicameralism, passage by both chambers of Congress, and presentment, giving the bill to the President for signature or veto. The Court then explained that a legislative veto is legislative action because it is Congress acting to alter the status quo. The Court thus concluded that legislative vetos are unconstitutional because there is not bicameralism or presentment. Chief Justice Burger's opinion relied entirely on the language in the text of the Constitution and quotations from THE FEDERALIST. The Court expressly declared that functional considerations were irrelevant.

Chadha has been criticized for its very formalistic approach, which is different from the Court's more usual functional analysis in SEPARATION OF POWERS cases. For functional reasons the Court has allowed very broad delegations of legislative power to executive agencies. Therefore, critics have argued that the Court erred in eschewing this functional approach in appraising a legislative check on the exercise of delegated power.

Examining Supreme Court decisions concerning presidential powers does not, of course, exhaust the manner in which the Supreme Court and Presidents have interacted over time. The most obvious relationship between Presidents and the Court is in the President's power of APPOINTMENT OF JUDGES. By choosing new Justices, with the approval of the Senate, a President can change the course of constitutional law for decades after the end of his term.

Presidents often have been openly critical of, even hostile to, Supreme Court decisions. The Jefferson administration criticized the decision in *Marbury* for permitting the Court to oversee the executive branch. Lincoln was highly critical of the Court's decision in DRED SCOTT V. SANDFORD (1857), which invalidated the MISSOURI COMPROMISE. Perhaps the most notable confrontation between a President and the Supreme Court occurred in the 1930s when President Franklin D. Roosevelt proposed a COURT-PACKING PLAN to assure approval of NEW DEAL legislation.

After numerous decisions invalidating New Deal programs, Roosevelt proposed legislation to allow the President to appoint one new Justice for every sitting Justice over age seventy, up to a maximum of fifteen. The result would have been an immediate pro–New Deal majority on the Court. The proposal was widely criticized as a threat to judicial independence. The reform was made unnecessary when Justice Owen Roberts changed his vote and began upholding New Deal legislation. Although it will never be known for sure whether Roberts was influenced by the Court-packing controversy, his action always will be known as the "switch in time that saved nine."

Ultimately, the interaction between the President and the Supreme Court is a function of many different factors: the ideology of the President and the Court;

the political climate of the time; the issue, especially whether it involves domestic policy or foreign affairs. Although the Court often has been deferential to the President, it also has been willing to enforce separation of powers and invalidate presidential actions.

[*See also* TREATY-MAKING POWER.]

BIBLIOGRAPHY

Bickel, Alexander. "Congress, the President, and the Power to Wage War." *Chicago-Kent Law Review* 48 (1971): 131–147.

Henkin, Louis. *Foreign Affairs and the Constitution*. 1972.

Lofgren, Charles. "*United States v. Curtiss Wright Export Corp.*: A Historical Reassessment." *Yale Law Journal* 83 (1973): 1–32.

Miller, Arthur. "An Inquiry into the Relevance of the Intentions of the Founding Fathers, with Special Emphasis upon the Doctrine of Separation of Powers." *Arkansas Law Review* 27 (1973): 583–602.

Strauss, Peter. "The Place of Agencies in Government: Separation of Powers and the Fourth Branch." *Columbia Law Review* 84 (1984): 573–669.

Tribe, Laurence. *American Constitutional Law*. 2d ed. 1988.

Van Alstyne, William. "A Political and Constitutional Review of *United States v. Nixon*." *UCLA Law Review* 22 (1974): 116–140.

ERWIN CHEMERINSKY

SUPREME COURT JUSTICES' PERSONAL RELATIONS WITH PRESIDENT. According to "the myth of the cult of the robe," Supreme Court Justices are "legal monks" removed from political life. Justice FELIX FRANKFURTER maintained, "When a priest enters a monastery, he must leave—or ought to leave—all sorts of worldly desires behind him. And this Court has no excuse for being unless it's a monastery." Yet Frankfurter was on intimate terms with President Franklin D. Roosevelt, frequently offering him advice on a range of public policy issues. Nor was he alone in maintaining or trying to cultivate relations with a President. More than seventy of the 106 who had, as of 1992, sat on the high bench advised Presidents about the APPOINTMENT OF JUDGES, patronage appointments, proposed legislation, and other matters of domestic and foreign policy. The reality is that members of the Court are political actors who may find it difficult to refrain from continuing close associations with or offering advice to Presidents.

Supreme Court Justices' relations with Presidents depend on a number of factors, but much depends on a Justice's association with a President prior to his or her appointment to the Court. Chief Justice Fred M. Vinson was an intimate adviser of President Harry S. Truman before joining the Court and continued to confer with him by telephone in the evenings and on fishing trips they took together in Key West, Florida.

Justice ABE FORTAS had an even closer personal and working relationship with President Lyndon B. Johnson. They had been friends for more than thirty years before Johnson named Fortas to the Court in 1965. While on the Court, Fortas remained among Johnson's elite group of foreign policy advisers. He regularly attended White House meetings on the conduct of the VIETNAM WAR, FISCAL POLICIES, labor legislation, ELECTORAL REFORM, and campaign financing and gave advice on other issues of domestic policy. Justice Fortas also helped write Johnson's speeches and messages to Congress on civil rights and criminal justice reform, along with recommending individuals for appointments to the Department of Justice and the federal bench.

In the nineteenth century, Justices typically had close relations with Presidents, particularly when they belonged to the same political party. The Washington, D.C., community was small and intimate, and the justices spent only a few months there each year. When in the capital during Court sessions Justices frequently socialized with the President and others in his administration at formal dinners and other gatherings. Besides such socializing, Presidents often consulted with Justices privately about public affairs. Although in 1793 the Jay Court refused President George Washington's request for an advisory opinion on the constitutionality of a treaty, responding that there were "strong arguments against the propriety of our extrajudicially deciding such questions," members of the Court did not feel precluded from giving their individual views on issues of public policy to the President.

Presidents were also inclined during the nineteenth century to elevate high-ranking members of their administrations and closest advisers to the Court. In 1801, after unsuccessfully offering the Chief Justiceship to several other leading members of the FEDERALIST PARTY, President John Adams appointed his Secretary of State, JOHN MARSHALL, to the center chair on the Court. When it fell to President Andrew Jackson in 1835 to name Chief Justice Marshall's successor, he immediately turned to his longtime supporter and Secretary of the Treasury, ROGER B. TANEY. President Abraham Lincoln, in turn, appointed his Secretary of the Treasury, SALMON P. CHASE, to fill Taney's seat in 1864.

The lines between permissible and impermissible communications, judicial and extrajudicial activities, and Justices' public and private lives were not as sharply drawn in the nineteenth century as they became during the twentieth. For instance, in response to presidential requests Chief Justices JOHN JAY and John Marshall served for brief periods as Secretary of

State, and Justice Oliver Ellsworth accepted the post of minister to France. During the CIVIL WAR era, Justice Samuel Nelson was an intermediary relaying peace proposals to the Confederacy, while Justice Stephen J. Field reported to Lincoln on conditions in the West when he returned to the capital from his circuit-riding duties in California.

In the early part of the twentieth century, several Justices maintained close contacts with Presidents and accepted extrajudicial assignments. Chief Justice William Howard Taft, the only former President to serve on the Court, ambitiously pursued a broad range of extrajudicial activities. He helped shape the 1924 REPUBLICAN PARTY platform and regularly consulted with Republican Presidents Warren G. Harding and Calvin Coolidge on patronage appointments, judicial reform, pending legislation, and even military expenditures. Both before and after his appointment to the Court in 1916, Louis D. Brandeis was a trusted confidant of progressive President Woodrow Wilson, and he later assumed a similar role with Franklin D. Roosevelt during Roosevelt's first term in the White House.

With the development of the institutionalized presidency in the twentieth century, Presidents' relations with Justices changed. The emergence of a larger WHITE HOUSE STAFF, greater delegation of presidential responsibilities, and increased demands on their time affected Presidents' relations with and reliance on Justices. Too, since the NEW DEAL, Presidents have tended to delegate the task of judicial selection to their Attorneys General, and this has also affected their relationships with members of the Court. Democratic and Republican Presidents have tended to differ, however, both in their approaches to judicial appointments and in their relations with Justices.

President Franklin D. Roosevelt's close association with his nine appointees was reminiscent of the practice of earlier Presidents and remained a model for later Democratic Presidents. Roosevelt considered his appointments to the Court a personal prerogative, and he elevated some of his most faithful supporters to the bench. Moreover, neither Roosevelt nor his appointees thought that judicial service ruled out their continued consultations. Justice Frankfurter was not alone in maintaining his personal and professional connections with the President: Justices Hugo L. Black, William O. Douglas, Stanley Reed, and Harlan F. Stone also advised Roosevelt on judicial appointments and other questions of public policy. Justice Frank Murphy frequently met with Roosevelt to discuss the conduct of the war effort in the Pacific during WORLD WAR II, and Justice JAMES F. BYRNES, during his one-year stay on the bench, continued to offer Roosevelt counsel on the drafting and constitutionality of pending legislation.

Besides naming Chief Justice Vinson, Truman elevated two other old friends from Congress, Harold Burton and Sherman Minton, along with his Attorney General, Tom Clark. John F. Kennedy named Byron White and Arthur Goldberg to the Court: both came from his administration and both had played active roles in Kennedy's presidential campaign and were well known to the President and his brother, Attorney General ROBERT F. KENNEDY. Johnson turned to his trusted friend Abe Fortas and, for politically symbolic reasons, also nominated his SOLICITOR GENERAL—the first African American to sit on the Court, Thurgood Marshall. Because these Democratic Presidents named close friends and ardent supporters to the Court, they also tended to maintain collegial relations with them.

By contrast, Republican Presidents since Dwight D. Eisenhower have delegated much of the responsibility for screening possible candidates and recommending nominees for the Court to their Attorneys General. Eisenhower knew his first appointee, Chief Justice Earl Warren, but relied on the advice of his Attorney General when making his other three appointments. Similarly, Richard M. Nixon had known his first appointee, Warren Burger, from the 1952 Republican Party national convention and from their work in the Eisenhower administration. But Nixon did not know Burger well. Nor did Nixon know his other three appointees—Justices Harry Blackmun, Lewis F. Powell, Jr., and William H. Rehnquist—before nominating them. When Gerald Ford succeeded Nixon in the OVAL OFFICE, he too turned to his Attorney General to find a noncontroversial and moderately conservative nominee, and ended up elevating a little-known federal appellate court judge, John Paul Stevens, in 1975. Ronald Reagan considered judicial appointments symbolic of his presidential power and instrumental to achieving his social policy agenda. He therefore relied not only on his Attorney General but also on senior White House staff to screen potential nominees rigorously. Reagan picked his Justices on the basis of his staff's recommendations and had little or no prior association with his four appointees. George Bush likewise relied on his White House staff and first met his two appointees, David H. Souter and Clarence Thomas, just days before he announced their nominations. As a result, these Republican Presidents and their Justices shared only formal, though convivial, relations—not the intimate working relations that some Justices have had with Democratic Presidents.

Even those Justices who do not have an established relationship with the occupant of the Oval Office may build friendships and even an advisory role with Presidents. Justice Harlan Fiske Stone, who was appointed to the Court in 1925 by his former college classmate President Calvin Coolidge, became an intimate consultant to Republican President Herbert Hoover, joining his "Medicine Ball Cabinet," at which policy issues—and an exercise ball—were thrown around. When Roosevelt succeeded Hoover in office, Stone thought that his advisory role would end, but he developed a relationship with Roosevelt and continued to offer advice on the Department of Justice's litigation strategies and on problems facing the Court. When Chief Justice CHARLES EVANS HUGHES retired in 1941, Roosevelt elevated Stone to Chief Justice.

Few Justices have deemed it either important or proper for them to try to develop influence with Presidents. Frankfurter's relations with Roosevelt were extraordinary, though his constant meddling sometimes backfired, and Roosevelt came to consider him somewhat of a pest. Justice Douglas was another exception: he had wide-ranging interests, traveled the world during the Court's summer recesses, and regularly sent Presidents letters concerning his observations on domestic and foreign affairs. Douglas frequently communicated with Presidents Truman, Kennedy, and Johnson about concerns ranging from saving the redwoods in California and protecting the environment, to increased Soviet influence in the Middle East, to the wisdom of diplomatic recognition of the People's Republic of China. Such advisory relationships with Presidents are, however, far from the norm. Most Justices have considered it improper and imprudent for them to consult with Presidents about issues of public policy, particularly after the public outcry over revelations of Justice Fortas's extrajudicial activities forced him to resign from the Court in 1969.

Recent Presidents have also generally deemed it improper for them to seek advice from sitting members of the Court. Still, on rare occasions they have privately sought Justices' advice. Eisenhower reportedly met with Chief Justice Warren and on several occasions asked his Attorney General to consult with Warren about cases pending before the Court. Both the Kennedy and Johnson administrations went to Warren for advice on judicial appointments and other matters. Presidents Nixon, Ford, and Reagan received advice from Chief Justice Burger on judicial appointees, including appointments to the Supreme Court.

Among the members of the Court, Chief Justices have rather consistently sought to advise Presidents on judicial appointments as well as on other matters affecting the courts and the administration of justice. As titular head of the federal judiciary, the Chief Justice has administrative responsibilities shared by no other Justice and occupies a unique position from which to evaluate the work of lower court judges and to oversee the operation of the judicial system. Chief Justices Taft and Burger aggressively promoted their ideas for judicial reform. The relations that Justices have with occupants of the Oval Office have been affected not only by personal associations but also by the growth in the size of the presidency, by each President's approach to judicial appointments, and by evolving standards of judicial conduct.

BIBLIOGRAPHY

Abraham, Henry J. *Justices and Presidents*. 3d rev. ed 1992.
Cibes, William J., Jr. *Extra-Judicial Activities of Justices of the United States Supreme Court, 1790–1960*. 1975.
Frankfurter, Felix. *From the Diaries of Felix Frankfurter*. 1974.
Murphy, Bruce. *Fortas: The Rise and Ruin of a Supreme Court Justice*. 1988.
O'Brien, David M. *Storm Center: The Supreme Court in American Politics*. 3d rev. ed. 1993.

DAVID M. O'BRIEN

SUPREME COURT NOMINEES NOT CONFIRMED. The appointment of Supreme Court Justices is a power shared by the President and the Senate. The Constitution requires that the President "shall nominate, and by and with the Advice and Consent of the Senate shall appoint . . . Judges of the supreme Court." Recent scholarship has focused on nominations refused confirmation by the Senate and the factors accounting for these refusals.

Of the 143 nominations that Presidents have made to the Supreme Court by 1993, twenty-six (approximately 18 percent) have failed to gain Senate confirmation. The Senate's refusal rate has increased sharply when one or both of the following unfavorable conditions have been present: the President's party was in the minority in the Senate and/or the nomination was forwarded to the Senate in the last year of a President's term. Nominations made when neither unfavorable condition was present were rejected at a rate of only 10 percent (9 of 92) while those made when one unfavorable condition was present were turned down at a rate of 19 percent (7 of 37); those forced to confront both unfavorable conditions were denied confirmation at an astounding rate of 71 percent (10 of 14). Five unsuccessful nominations between 1968 and 1987 occurred when one of the two unfavorable conditions was present. Lyndon B.

Johnson's unsuccessful nomination of Abe Fortas to be Chief Justice was sent to the Senate during Johnson's last year in office. Richard M. Nixon's unsuccessful nominations of Clement F. Haynsworth, Jr., and G. Harrold Carswell as well as Ronald Reagan's failed nominations of Robert H. Bork and Douglas H. Ginsburg occurred when these Presidents' Republican Party was in the minority in the Senate.

Analysis of failed nominations has led scholars to conclude that several significant factors have consistently contributed to the Senate's refusing to confirm Supreme Court nominees. Most notable among these factors are the nominee's views or ideology, the timing of the nomination, and the President's management of the confirmation process.

Ideology. Agreement or disagreement with a Supreme Court nominee's political philosophy, or ideology, has generally been the most important factor determining whether a Senator will support the nomination. For example, one study found that in the recent unsuccessful nomination of conservative Robert Bork, Senators classified as liberals supported confirmation at a rate of 8 percent (4 of 50) while those noted as conservatives favored confirmation at a rate of 76 percent (38 of 50).

Presidents and Senators know that Justices of the Supreme Court play a crucial role in shaping public policy through the decisions handed down by the Court and that the most significant element influencing these decisions is the Justices' ideology. Consequently, in attempting to further their policy goals, Presidents generally seek to appoint people sympathetic to their own ideology. Because not all Senators are likely to be sympathetic to a Presidents' views, opposition can surface every time a nomination is made. Given the link between party affiliation and political ideology, the extent of this opposition can be approximately determined by the party composition in the Senate. Not surprisingly, any President whose party is in the minority in the Senate will generally face more extensive ideological opposition and greater risk of refusal than one whose party is in the majority. Accordingly, Supreme Court nominations forwarded to the Senate when the President's party is in the minority are likely to be turned down at a higher rate than those submitted when the Chief Executive's party is in the majority.

Timing. Analysis of the Senate's handling of nominations made during the last year of a President's term has revealed the role that timing has played in many refusals to confirm. In these nominations, Senators opposed to confirmation for whatever reason become more emboldened in their opposition because of the

Unsuccessful Supreme Court Nominations

Nominating President	Nominee	Approximate Date of Nomination	Outcome
Washington, F	John Rutledge, F	5 November 1795	Rejected (10–14)
Madison, DR	Alexander Wolcott, DR	4 February 1811	Rejected (9–24)
J. Q. Adams, DR	John Crittenden, W	18 December 1828	Postponed
Jackson, D	Roger Taney, D	5 January 1835	Postponed
Tyler, D	John Spencer, W	9 January 1844	Rejected (21–26)
	Reuben Walworth, D	3 March 1844	Postponed/Withdrawn
	Edward King, D	5 June 1844	Postponed/Withdrawn
	John Read, D	7 February 1845	No action
Polk, D	George Woodward, D	23 December 1845	Rejected (20–29)
Fillmore, W	Edward Bradford, W	16 August 1852	No action
	George Badger, W	10 January 1853	Postponed
	William Micou, W	24 February 1853	No action
Buchanan, D	Jeremiah Black, D	6 February 1861	Postponed
A. Johnson, D	Henry Stanbery, R	16 April 1866	No action
Grant, R	Ebenezer Hoar, R	15 December 1869	Rejected (24–33)
	George Williams, R	2 December 1873	Withdrawn
Hayes, R	Stanley Matthews, R	26 January 1881	No action
Cleveland, D	William Hornblower, D	19 September 1893	Rejected (24–30)
	Wheeler Peckham, D	22 January 1894	Rejected (32–41)
Hoover, R	John Parker, R	21 March 1930	Rejected (39–41)
L. B. Johnson, D	Abe Fortas, D	26 June 1968	Withdrawn
Nixon, R	Clement F. Haynsworth, Jr., R	18 August 1969	Rejected (45–55)
	G. Harrold Carswell, R	19 January 1970	Rejected (45–51)
Reagan, R	Robert H. Bork, R	2 July 1987	Rejected (42–58)
	Douglas H. Ginsburg, R	20 October 1987	Withdrawn

[a]John Rutledge was confirmed by the Senate as an Associate Justice in September 1789, but never sat on any Supreme Court cases. He did serve on circuit duty before resigning in February 1791. In 1795, as a recess appointee, he presided as Chief Justice and participated in several cases, but the Senate rejected him for a lifetime term in December 1795.

[b]Roger Taney was nominated as Associate Justice in January 1835; the nomination was postponed. The following year, Jackson nominated him to be Chief Justice and the Senate confirmed him.

[c]The Senate took no action on the nomination of Matthews in the final days of the Hayes administration in early 1881; Garfield renominated Matthews in March 1881; the Senate confirmed him.

[d]Johnson nominated Associate Justice Fortas to be Chief Justice; the nomination was withdrawn in the face of Senate opposition.

Abbreviations: F, Federalist; DR, Democratic-Republican; D, Democrat; R, Republican; W, Whig.

Prepared by John Massaro.

increased likelihood of defeating the nomination. Opposition is seen as effective because Senators realize that any delay in considering the nomination can permanently block confirmation because the President will soon be leaving office. Indeed, in some instances nominations occurring near the end of a President's term, notably Lyndon Baines Johnson's 1968 attempt to appoint ABE FORTAS as Chief Justice, have enabled a small group of Senators to employ a filibuster to block a direct vote on the nomination.

Management. Poor presidential management—the lack of prudence, astuteness, and skill on the President's part as he oversees the confirmation process—has also been a factor in unsuccessful Supreme Court nominations. While presidential management has many dimensions, the President's major managerial responsibility is to select a nominee capable of gaining Senate approval, and a careless President can needlessly increase opposition to confirmation by selecting a nominee vulnerable to charges, for example, that the person lacks the requisite ethical sensitivity, legal competence, or judicial temperament to serve on the Supreme Court.

Selecting a vulnerable nominee can provide Senators with an additional and sometimes decisive basis for opposing the nomination: Senators sympathetic to the nominee's views and ordinarily inclined to support the nomination can be led to vote against confirmation because of these charges. This was true in the critical votes cast by some conservative Republicans against

Richard M. Nixon's 1969 and 1970 nominations of conservative Republicans Clement F. Haynsworth, Jr., on grounds of the nominee's alleged lack of ethical sensitivity, and G. Harrold Carswell, on the basis of the nominee's reported lack of competence.

While charges relating to ethics, competence, and temperament can be important in generating legitimate opposition, their most significant impact lies in their use as cover issues masking antagonism stemming from ideological concerns. Senators who openly base their opposition on ideological grounds run the risk of alienating some of their constituents if only because every Senator's constituency is to some extent divided along ideological lines. But because there is virtually unanimous agreement within each Senator's constituency that a would-be Supreme Court Justice should possess a requisite degree of ethical sensitivity, competence, and judicial temperament, opposing a nomination on these more acceptable, less contentious grounds will offend fewer, if any, of the Senator's constituents and be less politically risky.

BIBLIOGRAPHY

Abraham, Henry J. *Justices and Presidents: A Political History of Appointments to the Supreme Court.* 2d ed. 1985.

Bronner, Ethan. *Battle for Justice: How the Bork Nomination Shook America.* 1990.

Massaro, John. *Supremely Political: The Role of Ideology and Presidential Management in Unsuccessful Supreme Court Nominations.* 1990.

O'Brien, David M. *Judicial Roulette: Report of the Twentieth Century Fund Task Force on Judicial Selection: Background Paper by David M. O'Brien.* 1988.

Tribe, Laurence H. *God Save This Honorable Court.* 1985.

JOHN MASSARO

T

TAFT, WILLIAM HOWARD (1857–1930), twenty-seventh President of the United States (1909–1913), Chief Justice of the United States (1921–1930). William Howard Taft rose to power in the REPUBLICAN PARTY through the appointive political route. Before his election to the presidency, he had never been elected to a legislative or executive office in his entire career, serving primarily in judicial offices. Hand-picked as Theodore Roosevelt's successor—a "forced succession to the presidency" the DEMOCRATIC PARTY platform charged—Taft suddenly found himself a fish out of water, deficient in many of the skills of popular leadership, facing both the growing social protests of the progressive movement as well as the insatiable ambition of his predecessor, a "histrionic genius" who refused to leave the political stage.

Early Career. Born into the politically prominent family of Alphonso Taft of Cincinnati, Ohio, Secretary of War and Attorney General in the Grant administrations, Taft inherited his father's Republican connections and activism, as well as his father's frustrated ambition for a seat on the Supreme Court. Taft followed in his father's footsteps as an undergraduate at Yale. He graduated second in his class, but, perhaps more important to his later rise to national prominence, he was inducted into the prestigious Skull and Bones Society, which his father had helped found. He then returned to Ohio to attend the University of Cincinnati law school, graduating in 1880. His rise in politics was rapid—assistant county prosecutor of Hamilton County (1880); assistant county solicitor of Hamilton County (1885); the Superior Court of Ohio (1887), to which he won an additional five-year term in 1888 (the only popularly elected office he would ever hold before 1908); Solicitor General of the United States in the Harrison administration (1890); federal judge for the Sixth Judicial Circuit (1892); first Governor General of the PHILIPPINES (1900); and, finally, Secretary of War (1903) in the Theodore Roosevelt administration.

Taft's life-long ambition for the United States Supreme Court was widely known in the Republican Party. When President William McKinley persuaded Taft to give up a lifetime position as a federal judge in 1900 to become the first civilian Governor General of the Philippines, the President assured Taft, "you shall not suffer." Taft interpreted that statement as a promise of a Supreme Court appointment, perhaps the Chief Justiceship itself if it should become vacant.

But McKinley was assassinated in September 1901, and Theodore Roosevelt, a long-time admirer and friend of Taft, became President. Trying to ensure his own nomination for the presidency in 1904 by eliminating a potential rival, Roosevelt twice offered Taft a seat on the Supreme Court in the fall of 1902. Taft, however, had become genuinely committed to the welfare of the Philippine people, and his task of establishing a sound civilian government had not been completed. Also, he and his ambitious family were very aware that he was increasingly mentioned in national circles as a potential presidential candidate of the future.

Acutely aware of his rising political stature nationally, Taft nevertheless would have preferred the Chief Justiceship at this point in his career. Chief Justices, however, had always been appointed from outside of the Supreme Court itself. For Taft to have accepted an Associate Justiceship without a clear promise of promotion would have left Roosevelt free to follow tradition and bypass him. And since there was a distinct possibility that the aging Chief Justice, Melville Fuller, would be retiring, Taft declined the two Roosevelt offers. However, by April 1903, Taft, recovering from a life-threatening illness brought on by service in the Philippines, accepted Roosevelt's offer to become Secretary of War where he could continue to oversee Philippine policy as well as position himself for higher office. He became one of the President's closest and most loyal lieutenants.

When President Roosevelt shocked the nation upon his reelection in 1904 and publicly announced that he would not seek another term, Taft immediately became his most likely successor. In March 1906, Roosevelt again offered him an appointment to the Supreme Court. Taft again declined. He had set his sights firmly on the White House. Only an offer of the Chief Justiceship itself would have deflected him from the presidency at this point in his career.

Two Controversies. In his second term, Roosevelt proceeded to groom Taft as his successor and maneuver his followers into supporting Taft's nomination and election in 1908. Roosevelt believed Taft would loyally continue his administration's domestic and foreign policies without change. Upon his election, however, Taft demonstrated that he would run his own administration in his own way. He had intimated to Roosevelt that he would like to keep most of the Cabinet members, but once elected, he moved to place his own appointees in positions of trust, many of whom were prominent corporation lawyers. While Roosevelt had stirred the conscience of the nation through his preaching of progressive reform, Taft believed the special function of his administration would be "to complete and perfect the machinery" of government necessary to achieve the progressive ideals of his predecessor, while interfering "with legitimate business as little as possible."

Two major issues arose in Taft's first year that overshadowed all others—the PAYNE-ALDRICH TARIFF ACT and the BALLINGER-PINCHOT AFFAIR. Taft mishandled both issues, and never recovered politically from the damage to his reputation and administration.

The tariff. The issue of tariff reform had bedeviled Roosevelt throughout his presidency, but he had finessed it by doing nothing. Taft's official biographer, Henry Pringle, labelled the tariff issue as Roosevelt's "legacy of doom." Roosevelt had avoided the tariff issue because he knew it would have exacerbated tensions within the Republican Party and led to electoral defeat for the party. The history of recent tariff reform had indicated that, whenever rate schedules

were opened to the insatiable pressures of Congressmen from localities, revision inevitably got out of hand, created serious political problems for the incumbent party, and produced a defeat for the in-party at the next election. A new President could only hope to confront the issue immediately and hope that the political damage from revision could be repaired or forgotten by the next presidential election. Roosevelt was aware of the daunting political odds against which his successor would have to struggle. Wishing to give Taft a free hand and to avoid the inevitable political fallout from tariff revision, the former President set sail for Africa in December 1908, to return a year later just in time to participate in the 1910 midterm elections.

The Republican Party had traditionally been a high tariff party, but popular opinion continued to build for a reduction in rates and an end to unjustified subsidies to the business community and "the trusts." Although Roosevelt repeatedly warned Taft not to raise popular expectations about downward revision that could not be realized, Taft made reform the major campaign issue and immediately after his inauguration convened a special session of Congress in March 1909 to deliver on his campaign promise. Progressive Republicans, anticipating a clarion call to do battle for downward revision, were sadly disappointed by Taft's uninspiring message to Congress calling perfunctorily for revision.

Reopening the tariff issue inevitably led to intensive lobbying on over one thousand rate schedules by the affected interests. Logrolling was the order of the day, and any pretence at scientific rate making was belied by the uncontrolled chaos loosed by tariff makers in Congress. Rather than take an active role in trying to shape the bill before it was reported out of committee in both houses, Taft, a neophyte in dealing with Congress and tariff rates, deliberately chose a "policy of harmony" with Speaker of the House Joseph Cannon and Senate Majority Leader Nelson Aldrich of Rhode Island rather than an alliance with progressive Republican Congressmen—Insurgents, as they would come to be called because of their direct assault on the policies and power of the established Republican leadership. Cannon and Aldrich represented approximately 80 percent of the regular Republicans in Congress. If Taft hoped to enact his party promises into law, he believed he had no choice but to cast his lot with the regular Republican leaders, even though he initially had severe reservations about them. Roosevelt had done the same in his early years as President. In return for his hands off strategy, the leadership promised to shepherd the bill through Congress and then give the President an opportunity to influence the bill in conference committee. Roosevelt who had ended his presidency openly feuding with the same standpat leadership, would have, in all likelihood, chosen a more active strategy of trying to influence the bill in its early stages, very likely taking tariff issues over the heads of the leadership to the people, or even vetoing an unacceptable bill. But Taft, conciliatory by nature and not eager to upset business confidence in his administration, avoided the high-risk strategy of confrontation. He believed that he could achieve more in the long run by cooperating with the leadership, and that open warfare, which he had witnessed in the latter stages of the Roosevelt administration, was a sign of presidential weakness, not strength.

The result of his policy of harmony was a highly flawed bill, a far cry from the genuine downward revision he had promised. Insurgent Republicans refused to support the final product. Although the President was able to wrest some last-minute concessions out of the conference committee, he refused to veto the final bill. The congressional leadership and the tariff-making process of the Congress had trapped him. Not only was he stuck with a bill with higher rates than he had promised, but he was also tarnished by the public alliance he had forged with the leadership, an alliance that enraged progressive Republicans in Congress who found themselves increasingly at odds with their own President and the congressional leadership on other issues as well.

What the Insurgents could not readily fathom in Taft was his reverence for the rule of law and the judicial system and his fetish for party loyalty. A Republican loyalist from birth, Taft had made his way up the Republican political ladder in Ohio and Washington by demonstrating, not only intelligence, hard work, good judgment, and a cheerful disposition, but loyalty. He had learned to subordinate his own personal desires throughout his career for the greater good of the party or the nation. Thus, when he encountered the Insurgent Republicans who saw law and the judiciary only as obstacles to the attainment of their progressive ends, who refused to subordinate themselves to the welfare of the party and its leaders, and who castigated their President as a reactionary because he was so committed to working within the legal system he so revered, Taft found it difficult to cooperate with this new breed of Republican.

Taft toured the West in September 1909 to defend his record. At Winona, Minnesota, he further angered progressives by unnecessarily praising the Payne-Aldrich Tariff Act as "the best tariff bill that the Republican party ever passed." He continued to defend his Winona remarks throughout his western tour, further alienating the progressive wing of his party. Taft increasingly relied upon the entrenched leadership of Congress, even cooperating with it in attempting to discipline the unruly Insurgents by withholding patronage and, more significantly, trying behind the scenes to purge them from the party in the 1910 elections.

The Ballinger-Pinchot affair. The Ballinger-Pinchot controversy, which began in the fall of 1909, further exacerbated Taft's problems with progressive Republicans, and eventually Theodore Roosevelt himself. Gifford Pinchot, Chief Forester in the Department of Agriculture, had enjoyed a special personal relationship with Roosevelt that gave him influence on conservation issues out of all proportion to his actual office. In retaining Pinchot, Taft promised Roosevelt that he would use the Chief Forester likewise as "a kind of conscience" on conservation issues. However, Secretary of the Interior Richard Ballinger, acting on behalf of the President who wanted a public lands withdrawal policy that would withstand legal challenge, began to return some land to the public domain that had previously been withdrawn by executive order. Roosevelt's withdrawal policy was based upon a 1902 statute that only authorized the withdrawal of water power sites. Roosevelt had interpreted the statute generously as authorizing the extensive withdrawal of public land, not so much for power sites, but for general conservation purposes. Rather than seeking a change in the federal legislation to guarantee the legality of his executive orders, Roosevelt simply bypassed Congress and acted on his broad interpretation of the statute in question. When Taft, supposedly a supporter of conservation who had never publicly questioned the withdrawal policy before, suddenly revealed himself as having serious doubts about the legality of what Roosevelt had done, Pinchot was outraged. Although he prevailed upon Taft to stop returning the withdrawn land to the public domain until Congress could legalize Roosevelt's actions, Pinchot and other conservationists felt Taft had betrayed them and Roosevelt. They launched a guerrilla war against Ballinger and, by implication, Taft himself.

Seizing upon charges of Ballinger's corruption by Louis Glavis, a minor official of the General Land Office, Pinchot charged further that Ballinger had been party to a fraudulent attempt by the Morgan-Guggenheim banking syndicate to seize federal coal lands in Alaska. The resulting public furor over the charges and countercharges, and Pinchot's eventual sensational public acknowledgement of his deliberate insubordination on behalf of the higher cause of conservation, gave the President no choice but to fire the Chief Forester in December 1909. Pinchot was now a genuine martyr, and Ballinger, by contrast, had become a symbol in the public mind of Taft's alleged alliance with special interests. Taft felt that Ballinger had been unjustly attacked and refused to encourage his departure. By retaining Ballinger for another year, Taft unnecessarily increased the political damage to his relations with the progressive wing of his party.

Domestic Policies. Taft's alliance with the congressional leadership, however, did pay some legislative dividends. As the Sixty-first Congress neared adjournment in June 1910, Taft could point to a number of campaign promises and policies that had been enacted into law—a postal savings bank, the MANN-ELKINS ACT strengthening the power of the Interstate Commerce Commission, legislation legalizing the Roosevelt policy of withdrawing public lands, a new Tariff Board that promised to make tariff making more scientific and less political, campaign finance reform, continued appropriations for the Roosevelt policy of naval expansion, and, although not an original campaign promise, even a constitutional amendment approving the income tax.

But the return of Roosevelt to New York in June 1910 from Africa quickly deflected public attention away from these solid achievements. The former President received one of the most enthusiastic and tumultuous welcomes ever given a public figure in American politics. Already suffering from constant comparisons to his popular predecessor, Taft found himself unable to recover from his early mistakes or heal the rift in the party that Roosevelt's return only widened.

Roosevelt was disturbed by what he viewed as his lieutenant's ineptness, independence, and less-than-progressive record. He found the Republican Party badly divided, with the Insurgents and Regulars more interested in defeating each other than in cooperating to maintain party dominance. This was his heaviest count against Taft. Unwilling to endorse the Taft record as he campaigned for Republicans in the midterm elections of 1910, Roosevelt increasingly became a rallying point for disenchanted progressives who urged him to return to power in 1912. Taft, suspicious of Roosevelt's motives, watched and waited as the rift between them widened. The prospect of a Roosevelt challenge for the Republican nomination in 1912 cast a pall of pessimism and paranoia over the White House for the duration of the Taft presidency.

Republicans suffered a stunning defeat in the 1910 midterm elections. For the first time in sixteen years, the House went Democratic, 228 Democrats to 160 Republicans. An eighty-vote Republican majority evaporated, replaced by a sixty-eight-vote Democratic majority. In the Senate, Republicans lost seats, but held on to a 51 to 40 majority. Standpat Republicans everywhere were the big losers, while the Insurgent Republicans, whom Taft had attempted to purge because of their disloyalty, were all reelected. When informed of the Democratic Party landslide and Insurgent triumphs, Taft was shocked. "It was," he lamented, "not only a landslide but a tidal wave and holocaust all rolled into one general cataclysm." Defeat in 1912 appeared certain.

The Democratic Party gains of 1910 seriously eroded Taft's ability to push his own domestic legislation through a House dominated by Democrats and Insurgent Republicans. Much of the President's attention turned to subjects more within his control. By executive order, he incorporated seventy thousand federal employees under the merit system, and would have covered all employees up to the level of bureau chiefs if the law had permitted. With respect to antitrust policy, Taft and Attorney General George Wickersham enforced the antitrust laws more vigorously and indiscriminately than had Roosevelt, alienating many in the business community in the process. Taft's record, in fact, was better than that of his precedessor, with twice as many suits brought than in the previous administration.

More significant for the presidency as an institution, Taft tackled the chaotic budget-making process of the national government, particularly the practice of the departments that submitted independent budgets to the Congress with little or no coordination from the White House. He successfully sought the creation of a Commission on Economy and Efficiency to introduce more modern business practices to government and persisted in trying to gain executive control of the budget-making process. In June 1912 he sent Congress a special message on the need for budgetary reform and requested legislation that would require the President to formulate and present an annual budget to the Congress. Although the Democrats in the House balked at Taft's attempt to assert greater control over the budget, his recommendations eventually became the basis for the BUDGET AND ACCOUNTING ACT of 1921 and set the stage for greater executive control over the budget-making process for the rest of the twentieth century.

Foreign Affairs. In the lame-duck session of December 1910, President Taft sought to push through a reciprocity agreement with Canada that would have lowered U.S.-Canadian trade barriers and repaired some of the high tariff damage of the Payne-Aldrich Tariff Act, particularly among progressives in the

West and newspaper publishers who had sought lower rates on pulp paper. Taft's great objective was commercial union with Canada. The agreement, however, required implementing legislation from Congress. The lame-duck Republican Congress balked at the low tariff agreement and adjourned, daring the President to commit political suicide by convening a special session of the newly elected Congress. Taft rose to the challenge and summoned a special session of the new Congress in March 1911. He was determined not to let this historic opportunity for a closer commercial union with Canada slip from his grasp. Although he prevailed upon a majority of Democrats to support the agreement (a majority of Republicans were opposed), reciprocity died when the government of Sir Wilfred Laurier was defeated at the polls by a rising tide of Canadian nationalism and protectionism.

A Canadian reciprocity agreement was only part of the Taft administration's vigorous pursuit of American political and commercial expansion. One of the best-prepared men in the field of foreign affairs ever to serve in the White House, Taft was eager to see America assume her rightful place in the international community as an active and constructive world power. His Philippine experience, Far Eastern travels, and trouble-shooting experiences as Secretary of War had given him a broader understanding of international politics and economics than almost any leader of his generation. Arguing that the older American foreign policy of nonentanglement was outdated, Taft continued to support the Roosevelt policy of naval expansion, the construction of the Panama Canal, and the general policy of previous Republican administrations of increasing American influence on the world stage. Taft especially believed in McKinley's goal of vigorous commercial expansion throughout the world. Rather than relying heavily on military force or threats of force, Taft preferred to pursue American political objectives by promoting American commercial activity in areas of special interest to the United States. He described his Central American policy of commercial expansion, for example, as one of substituting "dollars for bullets" to produce political stability in the region. Unlike his more controversial record on domestic issues that produced a party schism between regular and progressive Republicans, Taft continued the internationalist McKinley-Roosevelt foreign policies with much less controversy.

If there was any significant difference between the Taft and Roosevelt foreign policies, it lay in Taft's legalistic and pacifist approach. Picking up where Roosevelt and Secretaries of State JOHN HAY and ELIHU ROOT had left off, Taft also promoted arbitration treaties with other major powers as a vehicle for resolving international disputes and promoting world peace. Believing that the rule of law could be applied to international relations, he advocated even more comprehensive arbitration agreements than those negotiated by the previous Secretaries of State. In March 1910, before the American Arbitration and Peace League, he boldly challenged the controversial notion that questions of national honor could not be submitted to an international tribunal for settlement. "I don't see any more reason why matters of national honor should not be referred to a court of arbitration any more than matters of property or national proprietorship," he argued. Finding arbitration and the peace issue to be a source of popular support, he pressed the matter and soon found Great Britain and France responding favorably. Treaties embodying the President's expansive view—"the great jewel" of his administration he described them—were negotiated in August 1911 and submitted to the Senate. But as his successor Woodrow Wilson would later learn regarding the LEAGUE OF NATIONS Covenant, a nationalistic Senate proved all too ready to attach reservations to protect the prerogatives of the Senate and the sovereignty of the United States. The reservations were so severe that Taft refused to submit the final treaties to France and Great Britain for ratification. His strong support for arbitrating questions of national honor, however, represented a significant challenge to U.S. nationalism and the game of power politics being played by the world powers and was far in advance of the times.

Taft's handling of revolutionary disturbances along the U.S.–Mexican border in the fall of 1911 again illustrated the President's pacifist and statesmanlike nature. When border disturbances led to the loss of a number of American lives on American soil, Taft mobilized American troops along the Mexican border but refused to order any military incursions into Mexico proper against the elements responsible for the violence. Despite nationalist calls for stronger military measures against Mexico, including from Roosevelt himself, Taft followed a policy of watchful waiting, believing that any intervention in Mexico would actually jeopardize the lives of forty thousand Americans living there. Officially, he publicly maintained, "I seriously doubt whether I have such authority [to intervene] under any circumstances, and if I had, I would not exercise it without express Congressional approval." The President, who felt that intervention was absolutely the wrong policy, used this convenient legal argument to blunt criticisms of his calculated inaction. There was no doubt, however, that if the revolution in Mexico had begun to threaten American lives, Taft would not have hesitated to use whatever military force necessary to protect them. Impetuous military action might have enhanced his own popularity within the Republican Party and the nation, and possibly even guaranteed him reelection, but, with the Philippine experience fresh in his mind, Taft chose to place the national interest and American lives above his own political fortunes. He would not play to what he contemptuously called the "peanut gallery." His actions have provided us with a clear case study of the inherent limitations of the Richard Neustadt theory of presidential power and demonstrated that there are instances, rare though they may be, where personal or presidential power considerations are clearly irrelevant when a President must protect the national interest and American lives.

The Supreme Court. One facet of the Taft presidency that has attracted little attention, primarily because Taft himself chose to deemphasize it, was his remarkable record of six appointments to the Supreme Court to fill five vacancies—Horace Lurton, CHARLES EVANS HUGHES, Edward White (from Associate Justice to Chief Justice), Willis VanDevanter, Joseph Lamar, and Mahlon Pitney. One cannot understand Taft unless one recognizes his ambition to serve on the Court, especially as Chief Justice, and his reverence for the law and the American judicial system. The Court that Taft inherited in 1909 had several members of advanced age and deteriorating health. Following a deliberate policy of nonpartisanship as well as a southern strategy, Taft maintained the 6 to 3 nominal Republican-Democratic balance on the Court, which he inherited, while adding to its southern representation. He packed the Court with practical conservatives like himself who were sensitive to the need for national regulatory legislation, but who, otherwise, provided no dramatic new departures from the general conservative orientation of the Court. Those appointments clearly provided Taft with his most gratifying moments as President.

Taft elevated the sixty–five-year-old Southern Democrat Edward White from Associate Justice to Chief Justice instead of Charles Evans Hughes, the much younger (forty-eight) former governor of New York. Hughes had virtually been promised the position when originally appointed to the Court, but, at the eleventh hour, Taft bowed to internal pressures from the Court and the Senate to elevate a more experienced jurist. "Hughes is young enough to wait," Taft concluded, as he offered the prize to White. Already anticipating defeat in 1912, Taft also kept alive his dream of becoming Chief Justice, finally realized in

1921 when his fellow Ohioan President Warren G. Harding appointed him to the office. Before his resignation from the Supreme Court and death in 1930, Taft helped engineer President Herbert Hoover's appointment of Hughes as Chief Justice, thus fulfilling, belatedly, his original promise to Hughes to make him Chief Justice.

The End of a Presidency. What historians have remembered most about the Taft presidency, however, was his clash with Roosevelt for the Republican nomination in 1912, a struggle that split the Republican Party, produced the PROGRESSIVE (BULL MOOSE) PARTY candidacy of Roosevelt, and paved the way for the victory of Woodrow Wilson. Unwilling to step aside for an increasingly strident and populist Theodore Roosevelt, Taft fought a rear-guard action to retain control of the Republican Party. He considered it more important to purge the party of the increasingly radical progressives supporting Roosevelt than to win reelection. By defeating Roosevelt's attempt to return to the White House, Taft guaranteed that his rival would never again be able to mount a serious challenge for his party's nomination. In the process, Taft sought to preserve the Republican Party as a bastion of constitutional conservatism, committed especially to "the principle of the absolute independence of the judiciary."

The epic struggle of 1912 spawned two conflicting theories of the presidency—the stewardship and literalist-constitutional. Smarting from defeat at the Republican convention and in the general election of 1912, Roosevelt immediately launched an attack on Taft in his *Autobigraphy* (1913), accusing him of being a weak, legalistic, Buchanan-like President. Roosevelt had not one good word to say about his successor and former friend and ally. Roosevelt tried to win by pen what he had been unable to win by sword. Decrying what he alleged was Taft's weak presidency, Roosevelt advocated instead the STEWARDSHIP THEORY of presidential leadership, a theory that maintains that the President can do anything necessary for the public good as long as it is not forbidden by the Constitution or by law.

Taft responded to Roosevelt's criticisms in *Our Chief Magistrate and His Powers* (1916) and advanced the constitutional-literalist theory of presidential power [*see* LITERALIST PRESIDENT]. Unlike the stewardship theory, which accords the President whatever inherent powers he finds necessary to address national problems, Taft argued that the President has no "undefined residuum of power" to roam at will doing good. The President may have "influence," which of course he should use to promote the common good, but he does not possess an undefined, uncontrolled, and unlimited array of inherent legal powers. Although he clearly believed the President possessed very broad implied powers, Taft maintained generally that presidential actions must nevertheless be rooted in the specific grants of power in the Constitution. As long as a President could plausibly base his actions on a specific clause of the Constitution such as the executive power, take care, or commander in chief clause, Taft was more than willing to sanction the exercise of EXECUTIVE POWER necessary to meet virtually any national crisis. He found no difficulty, for example, in supporting Lincoln's broad assertions of presidential power during the CIVIL WAR, assertions that were generally linked to specific grants of executive power in the Constitution. Taft did not find fault with Roosevelt's presidency itself but disagreed with Roosevelt's post-presidential rhetoric and legal ignorance.

Taft's literalist view of presidential power is an overreaction to the self-serving rhetoric of a defeated rival. A more balanced view of Taft's philosophy requires a look at his extraordinary opinion in *Myers v. United States* (1926) in which he upheld the power of a President to remove a first-class postmaster appointed by the President. The President, Taft asserted, not only has the power to remove a postmaster whom he has appointed, Congress through the TENURE OF OFFICE ACT of 1867 and subsequent acts cannot limit that power by requiring Senate consent to removals. Given the broad grant of executive power and the take care clause, the President, Taft asserted, even has the power to remove members of the independent regulatory commissions who are not performing their responsibilities properly. In short, a President can fire independent commission members for essentially political reasons. This assertion of executive removal power was so expansive that a later Court in HUMPHREY'S EXECUTOR V. UNITED STATES (1935) found it necessary to limit the *Myers* ruling to the specific facts of the case and to recognize Congress's legitimate power to protect independent commission members from removal for purely political reasons, former President Taft's obiter dicta in *Myers* to the contrary notwithstanding.

Now permanent fixtures in the literature and the national debate on presidential power, the stewardship and literalist theories reflect the ambivalence of Americans about strong Presidents, an ambivalence that yearns for a strong leader in times of crisis, but a leader who respects the principles of constitutional democracy as well. William Howard Taft's contribution to that ongoing debate has been his most enduring legacy to our understanding of his own term as well as the American presidency in general.

BIBLIOGRAPHY

Anderson, Donald F. *William Howard Taft: A Conservative's Conception of the Presidency.* 1973.
Anderson, Judith I. *William Howard Taft, An Intimate History.* 1981.
Butt, Archibald Willingham. *Taft and Roosevelt: The Intimate Letters of Archie Butt.* 2 vols. 1930.
Coletta, Paolo E. *The Presidency of William Howard Taft.* 1973.
Manners, William. *TR and Will: A Friendship that Split the Republican Party.* 1969.
Mason, Alpheus T. *William Howard Taft: Chief Justice.* 1965.
Pringle, Henry F. *The Life and Times of William Howard Taft.* 2 vols. 1939.
Taft, William Howard. *Our Chief Magistrate and His Powers.* 1916. Rep. 1967.

DONALD F. ANDERSON

TAFT COMMISSION. The Taft Commission was the second presidentially initiated effort at ADMINISTRATIVE REFORMS OF THE PRESIDENCY. President William Howard Taft initiated the President's Inquiry in re Efficiency and Economy in September 1910. With a $100,000 appropriation, Taft hired Dr. Frederick Cleveland, of the New York Bureau of Efficiency, and a small staff to recommend administrative reforms. In March 1911, Taft expanded the study, creating the Taft Commission, formally titled the Commission on Economy and Efficiency. Cleveland chaired the commission, which had five other members: Merritt O. Chance, auditor of the Post Office; Harvey S. Chase, a public accountant; Frank J. Goodnow, professor of public administration at Columbia University; Walter Warwick, auditor of the Panama Canal Commission; and William F. Willoughby, a political scientist and assistant director of the Bureau of the Census.

Congress had dominated administrative reform in the nineteenth century, but Theodore Roosevelt's KEEP COMMISSION had broken that monopoly in 1905. The Taft Commission's importance lies primarily in the aims of its recommendations, which embodied a conception of administrative reform that made the President centrally responsible for the executive branch.

The commission produced three kinds of recommendations. First, it recommended improvements in details of governmental administrative practices. These included suggestions for improved personnel records, better accounting systems, and improvements in the distribution of government publications. Second, the commission addressed the overall organization of the executive branch, making recommendations for CABINET-department reorganization with the rationale that departmental administration would be improved by grouping together agencies that had similar purposes. Third, the commission addressed the absence of a budget system in government. Noting the deficits that had appeared during the decade, the commission recommended an executive budget to guide congressional appropriations and a budget bureau to aid the President in formulating an executive budget.

The commission continued its work through the end of the Taft administration in March 1913. It was crippled by congressional refusal to fund its activities fully. Congress rejected requests for larger appropriations in 1911 and 1912, only granting the commission $75,000 in each of those years. A number of the commission's recommendations for change in detailed administrative processes were implemented by Taft, but few of its recommendations for department reorganization were adopted, and its recommendation for an executive budget was quickly rejected by Congress as a threat to its prerogatives. The Taft Commission was, however, a harbinger of a changing executive branch. In 1921 Congress passed the BUDGET AND ACCOUNTING ACT, which created an executive budget, and the commission's vision of departmental reorganization ultimately became a hallmark of twentieth-century administrative reform.

BIBLIOGRAPHY

Arnold, Peri E. *Making the Managerial Presidency.* 1986.
Skowronek, Stephen. *Building a New American State.* 1982.

PERI E. ARNOLD

TAFT-HARTLEY ACT (1947). In the wake of the widespread postwar strikes of 1946, Congress passed the Labor-Management Relations Act, known as the Taft-Hartley Act, in June 1947. Republican sponsors Senator Robert Taft (Ohio) and Representative Fred Hartley (Ind.) succeeded in pushing through a law that substantially altered the WAGNER ACT (National Labor Relations Act) of 1935 and moved national labor policy in a probusiness direction. Though the bill passed in large measure because of public discontent with extensive labor militancy, organized labor and its congressional allies persuaded President Harry S. Truman, a Democrat, to veto the bill, a veto that the Republican-dominated Congress of 1946 quickly overrode. Though the President had earlier favored some type of legislative restrictions on labor militancy, Truman's decision to back organized labor marked a turning point in his domestic policy and subsequently served as the centerpiece of his 1948 reelection campaign. While the Truman administration failed in its efforts to repeal the Taft-Hartley Act in 1949, the veto and repeal drive resolidified the political alliance between organized labor and the Democratic presidency. In later years the issue of amendment of the Taft-Hartley Act would again surface from time to time and enter in presidential politics, but wholesale repeal was never again a realistic possibility.

Truman's decision to veto the "Slave Labor Law," as its opponents swiftly dubbed it, signaled his acceptance of the progressive mantel of the NEW DEAL heritage in domestic policy. Truman touted his Taft-Hartley veto and promised repeal of the despised law to rally support among workers and union members during his 1948 whistle-stop reelection campaign. This served to reinvigorate the sometimes troubled alliance between the President and organized labor, and indeed the response of the labor movement contributed heavily to Truman's surprise victory over THOMAS E. DEWEY. The repeal of the Taft-Hartley Act thereafter became a part of the President's FAIR DEAL domestic reform program of 1949. Nevertheless, despite this presidential backing, a conservative coalition of southern Democrats and Republicans refused to interpret Truman's reelection as a mandate to repeal Taft-Hartley. In a closely fought contest, they succeeded in not only heading off repeal but also forestalling substantial prolabor amendments.

In years afterward, from time to time organized labor, usually through its influence on Democratic Presidents, mounted Taft-Hartley revision campaigns aimed at various aspects of the law. In 1965–1966, for example, the AFL-CIO labor federation won the support of President Lyndon B. Johnson, a Democrat, in its efforts to repeal section 14(b) of the law, the provision that allowed states to pass antiunion right-to-work laws. In return for labor's lobbying work on behalf of Johnson's GREAT SOCIETY program, the President sought repeal on two separate occasions, but once again the drive collapsed in the face of a conservative filibuster in the Senate. Similarly, in 1977–1978 President Jimmy Carter, also a Democrat, assisted organized labor by attempting to win passage of the Labor Law Reform bill, a set of proposals that would have made modest administrative changes in the Taft-Hartley Act. Carter's willingness to do so again stemmed from the necessity of enlisting labor's lobbying energies in support of his troubled domestic agenda. Unfortunately for the labor movement, this bill met the same fate as the repeal of section 14(b). Thus, in sum, over the years a Democratic presidential candidate's or executive's stance on prolabor Taft-Hartley revision has thus become a quid pro quo for the intensity of organized labor's electoral and/or legislative backing in the national political arena, even though outright repeal is no longer contemplated.

BIBLIOGRAPHY

Lee, R. Alton. *Truman and Taft-Hartley: A Question of Mandate.* 1966.
Gall, Gilbert J. *The Politics of Right to Work: The Labor Federations as Special Interests, 1943–1979.* 1988.

GILBERT J. GALL

TANEY, ROGER B. (1777–1864), Secretary of the Treasury, Chief Justice of the United States. Born in Maryland and educated at Dickinson College, Roger Brooke Taney practiced law, served in the Maryland legislature, joined the DEMOCRATIC PARTY, and supported the election of Andrew Jackson in 1828. He was appointed Attorney General in the Jackson administration in July 1831 and quickly became Jackson's closest adviser in the Cabinet.

In particular, his intense opposition to the Second BANK OF THE UNITED STATES earned Jackson's respect and gratitude. His experience as counsel to a state bank led him to oppose the national bank, and when a recharter was introduced into Congress just prior to the presidential election of 1832, he accused the bank of attempting to interfere in the political process and control the outcome of the election. When the recharter bill passed Congress, Taney encouraged Jackson to veto the bill and he had a hand in drafting the veto message. After Jackson's triumphant reelection in 1832, Taney sided with the President in favoring the removal of the government's deposits from the bank. When the Secretary of the Treasury, William Duane, refused to obey Jackson's order to remove the deposits, the President appointed Taney in his place. In September 1833, Taney ordered government moneys removed from the national bank. Future government monies were deposited in selected state banks which the opposition party called pet banks.

Outraged by what it considered an unconstitutional arrogation of power by the Chief Executive, the Senate, led by HENRY CLAY, passed motions of censure against Jackson and Taney. It was the only time a President was censured by a branch of Congress.

Jackson wrote a protest message to the Senate denying its right to take such action and Taney had a hand in its composition. Then, when Taney's nomination as Secretary of the Treasury formally came before the Senate, it was defeated in June 1834. Jackson attempted to reward him for his loyalty and service by nominating him as an associate justice of the Supreme Court in January 1835, but again the Senate rejected him. A little more than a year later Jackson nominated him to replace John Marshall, recently deceased, as Chief Justice. Through deft management and an increase in voting strength among Democrats in the Senate, the nomination was confirmed on 15 March 1836.

When Jackson decided to end his presidential career with a farewell address similar to George Washington's FAREWELL ADDRESS, he enlisted Taney's help in its composition. That address, among many other things, attempted to explain the meaning of what is now popularly called Jacksonian Democracy. The definition was simple: the people are sovereign; their will is absolute; and liberty can only survive if defended by the virtuous.

Taney's distinguished career as a jurist—marred only by the infamous decision in DRED SCOTT V. SANDFORD (1857)—reflected his commitment to, and belief in, Jacksonian Democracy. In *Charles River Bridge Company v. Warren Bridge Company* (1837) he held that rights not specifically granted by a corporation charter could not be inferred. The rights of private property, he declared, while absolutely guarded did not mean that the rights of communities can be ignored.

Taney's *Dred Scott* decision also reflected his commitments as a Southerner and slave-holder. The decision went a long way toward increasing sectional conflict and probably hastened the coming of the CIVIL WAR. His decision in EX PARTE MERRYMAN was an important reaffirmation of the rights of civilians, even during wartime.

BIBLIOGRAPHY

Lewis, H. H. Walker. *Without Fear or Favor: A Biography of Chief Justice Roger Brooke Taney.* 1965.
Swisher, Carl B. *Roger B. Taney.* 1935.

ROBERT V. REMINI

TARIFF ACT OF 1789. The Tariff Act of 1789 represented Congress's first exercise of its power to tax under the new Constitution. The act imposed specific duties (i.e., duties based on quantity of imports, not valuation) on a variety of articles. It also included ad valorem duties (duties calculated according to the value of an item) on other imports, generally at the rate of 5 percent of value but ranging upwards to 15 percent in certain cases. There was a short list of free goods.

Primarily a revenue measure, the act also set forth its purpose as "the encouragement and protection of manufactures." Debate in Congress focused on the issue of protectionism and disclosed regional differences. Most southern representatives opposed protection, but Representative James Madison, who had introduced the measure in the House, agreed that those manufacturers enjoying protection under prior state tariffs ought to receive continued protection under the new national legislation.

Madison's original proposal included a system of tonnage duties that would favor American shipping interests and that would also discriminate against those nations, especially Britain, having no commercial treaties with the United States. The House passed Madison's tonnage proposals, but the Senate, more responsive to northern commercial interests reluctant to declare commercial warfare on England, rejected the concept of discrimination among foreign nations. The Tonnage Act of 1789, adopted as a separate measure, favored American over foreign vessels but did not include Madison's proposed discrimination against England.

President George Washington, whose management of MOUNT VERNON disclosed his own preference for economic self-reliance and local manufactures, made no official public comment concerning the subject of tariff and tonnage duties. Nevertheless, he was privately annoyed that the Tonnage Act failed to include provisions discriminating against England. Washington considered allowing the tariff and tonnage acts to become law without his signature, but he did sign both measures.

BIBLIOGRAPHY

Brant, Irving. *James Madison, Father of the Constitution, 1787–1800*. 1950.
Flexner, James Thomas. *George Washington and the New Nation (1783–1793)*. 1969.
Miller, John C. *The Federalist Era, 1789–1801*. 1960.
Stanwood, Edward. *American Tariff Controversies in the Nineteenth Century*. Vol. 1. Repr. 1967.

RALPH MITZENMACHER

TARIFF ACT OF 1816. Prior to 1808, agricultural and mercantile activities dominated the American economy, and Americans satisfied their demand for manufactures largely through imports. After 1808, the EMBARGO ACTS and Non-Intercourse Acts and then the WAR OF 1812 restricted American access to British manufactures, and Americans turned to local manufactures as an important aspect of the domestic economy.

After the war, attention turned to downward revision of wartime tariff schedules. Congressional debate centered on the effect of tariff revisions on America's incipient manufacturing sector and the desirability of protective tariffs.

Under the Tariff Act of 1816, American products receiving protection included, among others, cotton manufactures, woolens, and iron. The most protectionist aspects of the act were limited in duration—the highest duties were subject to automatic decreases in 1819—reflecting the belief that American manufacturers could quickly become competitive with their foreign rivals. The higher protective ad valorem duties (duties calculated on an item's value; e.g., 25 percent on woolens and cotton cloth) were actually lower than wartime rates, and it is doubtful that these rates were sufficient to provide the intended protective affect. The act did initiate minimum valuations on cotton cloth imports, thereby increasing effective protection for those goods.

President James Madison, who had been the original author of the mildly protective Tariff Act of 1789, generally espoused free trade principles during his congressional career. Nevertheless, Madison's foreign policy predilections during the 1790s included consistent support for discriminatory measures directed against Britain. By Madison's service as President, the Democratic-Republican political base included manufacturing interests. The protective aspects of the Tariff Act of 1816 received firm support in Madison's seventh annual message to Congress, in 1815, in language reminiscent of ALEXANDER HAMILTON's *Report on Manufactures*.

BIBLIOGRAPHY

Brant, Irving. *James Madison, Commander in Chief, 1812–1836*. 1961.
Stanwood, Edward. *American Tariff Controversies in the Nineteenth Century*. Vol. 1. Repr. 1967.
Taussig, F. W. *The Tariff History of the United States*. 8th ed. 1931.

RALPH MITZENMACHER

TARIFF ACT OF 1832. The tariff of 1832 was a little less protectionist than its 1828 predecessor, but its rates were still high. There was so much opposition by southerners to the rates imposed by the so-called TARIFF OF ABOMINATIONS (1828) that President Andrew Jackson, in his annual message to the Congress in 1831, called for a revision of the rates. Furthermore, revenues had increased to such an extent that the national debt would be paid off within the next few years. Thus a new tariff, said the President, with a more just and equitable schedule of rates should be passed. Louis McLane, the Secretary of the Treasury, acted upon Jackson's recommendation and submitted a report to Congress advising a reduction in duties from approximately 45 percent to 27 percent. Southern extremists demanded further cuts while protectionists sought to maintain as many high rates on manufactured products as possible. The McLane proposal was something of a compromise between these two positions.

The House Committee on Manufactures, chaired by John Quincy Adams of Massachusetts, brought forward a bill that deleted a few articles from the protected list and generally lowered or removed duties on noncompetitive goods. But, by and large, the bill retained high rates on all the other commodities previously protected. The bill passed the House on 16 May despite southern opposition.

When the bill came to the Senate, HENRY CLAY of Kentucky, leader of the party opposed to President Jackson, gave the bill his full support since he had had a hand in the schedule of rates determined by the House committee. The final terms of the Tariff of 1832 reduced revenues by approximately $5 million and reduced rates overall by approximately 25 percent. But high protective rates were kept on woolens, iron, and cotton. It remained a relatively high tariff, which many southerners still regarded as excessive. Jackson signed the bill on 14 July 1832.

BIBLIOGRAPHY

Remini, Robert V. *Henry Clay: Statesman for the Union.* 1991.
Remini, Robert V. *Andrew Jackson and the Course of American Freedom, 1822–1833.* 1981.

ROBERT V. REMINI

TARIFF ACT OF 1833. The Tariff Act of 1833 was a compromise between the high rates of earlier acts and the low rates of a proposed bill. South Carolina's NULLIFICATION of the TARIFF OF ABOMINATIONS (1828) and the TARIFF ACT OF 1832 and its threat to secede brought quick action by President Andrew Jackson to find a solution that would avoid bloodshed and civil war. In his annual message to Congress in December 1832, the President requested legislation that would lower the tariff rates to a more equitable level. At the same time he began preparations to use military force to put down any acts of insurrection by the rebellious state.

Within two weeks, a bill was readied by the Secretary of the Treasury, Louis McLane, and delivered to the chairman of the House Ways and Means Committee, Gulian C. Verplanck of New York. The committee then presented the Verplanck bill to the House on 8 January 1833.

According to this bill, the tariff rates would be cut in half to approximate the duties imposed by the TARIFF ACT OF 1816. The reductions would come over a two-year period, the first half in 1834, the second in 1835. Many believed that such a bill would find favor with the South Carolina nullifiers.

But politics played a key role in the enactment of a new schedule of rates. HENRY CLAY, the great advocate of tariff protection, joined forces with JOHN C. CALHOUN, the author of the nullification doctrine, in order to block Jackson's intended use of force to coerce South Carolina into compliance with federal law. What Clay proposed was an abandonment of the principle of protection and the gradual reduction of tariff rates over a ten-year period. The deepest cuts would not come until the end of the period, at which time the duties would stand at a uniform 20 percent, ad valorem. Calhoun agreed to this "compromise" and it passed Congress; the President signed it on 2 March 1833. South Carolina capitulated and repealed its Ordinance of Nullification.

BIBLIOGRAPHY

Peterson, Merrill D. *The Olive Branch and Sword: The Compromise of 1833.* 1982.
Remini, Robert V. *Henry Clay: Statesman for the Union.* 1991.
Remini, Robert V. *Andrew Jackson and the Course of American Democracy, 1833–1845.* 1984.

ROBERT V. REMINI

TARIFF ACT OF 1857. Spurred by California gold, American imports rose dramatically during the early 1850s, and even the moderate WALKER TARIFF ACT of 1846 generated large Treasury surpluses. Concerned about the surplus, both President Franklin Pierce and his Secretary of Treasury, Kentuckian James Guthrie, proposed tariff reductions in each year of the Pierce administration. Pierce opposed INTERNAL IMPROVEMENTS and feared that Treasury surpluses would be diverted to increased federal spending. Pierce was also mindful that, notwithstanding Guthrie's efforts to effect early partial retirement of the MEXICAN WAR debt, continuing surpluses resulted in a lockup of American specie reserves within the INDEPENDENT TREASURY to the detriment of ongoing economic activity.

Congress, little disposed to accept presidential leadership and diverted by continued controversy over the status of SLAVERY in the territories under the KANSAS-NEBRASKA ACT, failed to act on the administration's proposal for tariff reduction until early 1857. The Tariff Act of 1857 effected an average reduction in ad valorem rates (rates calculated on an item's value) of 20 percent. It also expanded the free list and admitted most raw wool imports competitive with home grown wool without duty.

The tariff debate of 1857 highlighted fissures within the protective movement that had long been apparent. Woolen manufacturers, wounded by tariff reductions in effect since 1846, could not realistically seek rate increases on imported woolens and instead lobbied for reduction of the rate applicable to imported raw wool. The free wool provision of the 1857 act effected an ad hoc alliance between southern democrats and New England manufacturing interests but generated opposition from wool growers in the North and West.

Iron producers also objected to diminished protection under the revised tariff. Republicans, having avoided any position on tariffs and protectionism in their national platform of 1856, perceived new discontent with Democratic policies in the critical iron-producing state of Pennsylvania. Commencing in 1857, Republican appeals to Pennsylvania and the West were increasingly protectionist.

BIBLIOGRAPHY

Nichols, Roy F. *Franklin Pierce: Young Hickory of the Granite Hills.* 1958.
Stampp, Kenneth M. *America in 1857: A Nation on the Brink.* 1990.
Stanwood, Edward. *American Tariff Controversies in the Nineteenth Century.* Vol. 2. Repr. 1967.

RALPH MITZENMACHER

TARIFF OF ABOMINATIONS (1828). The tariff, used as a polical weapon by the Democrats, laid heavy duties on certain items, which pleased states in the North and West and displeased Federalist New England. Although manufacturers had received a measure of protection in the Tariff Act of 1824, the rates did not go far enough to satisfy them. So a convention of manufacturers and farmers met in Harrisburg, Pennsylvania, on 30 July 1827 and petitioned Congress to raise import duties on flax, hemp, iron, distilled spirits, and several other commodities. Leaders of the DEMOCRATIC PARTY in Congress realized that the issue might be used to attract votes for their presidential candidate, Andrew Jackson, in the next election, especially in the North and West. So they concocted and introduced a bill that provided protection for products from these areas in order to appeal to farmers and manufacturers in those states where Jackson needed additional support. New England products received little protection because that section of the country was committed to the incumbent President, John Quincy Adams. What resulted was a bill with heavy duties on such raw materials as hemp, flax, molasses, and sail duck that favored the interest of western farmers; and a duty on iron that was aimed at pleasing manufacturers in Pennsylvania. Rates on raw wool were also raised; but while they delighted sheep herders they angered woolen manufacturers, most of whom were in New England. To make matters worse, the duty on imported manufactured woolen products was kept low. Thus, this lopsided bill favored the interests of such states as New York, Pennsylvania, Kentucky, Missouri, and Ohio and discriminated against those in New England. Since the South was totally committed to Jackson, its interests did not come under serious consideration. After much tinkering with individual rates, the bill passed both houses of Congress by narrow margins. Southerners, who hated all tariffs because they forced them to purchase needed manufactured goods on a closed market and sell their cotton on an open market, denounced it as a "Tariff of Abominations."

BIBLIOGRAPHY

Remini, Robert V. "Martin Van Buren and the Tariff of Abominations." *American Historical Review* 63 (1958): 903–917.
Remini, Robert V. *Martin Van Buren and the Making of the Democratic Party.* 1959.

ROBERT V. REMINI

TARIFF POLICY. Numerous governmental interests, including revenue, economic development, and foreign policy, are affected by tariff policy. Tariff controversies have been politically significant, occasionally influencing presidential elections and frequently coloring PRESIDENTIAL-CONGRESSIONAL RELATIONS. Three distinct periods mark the history of presidential tariff policy. From 1789 to 1860, Congress dominated tariff-making and the tariff became an important political symbol. From 1861 to 1932, Congress and the President increasingly struggled for control over tariff matters in an era of expanding protectionism. After 1933, Congress delegated substantial tariff-making powers to the President, and tariff barriers to free trade notably declined.

Congressional Domination. Important tariff policy themes surfaced under George Washington. The TARIFF ACT OF 1789 established the tariff as the government's principal revenue source (it continued to be among the most potent revenue producers until WORLD WAR I). Congressional debate in 1789, and then ALEXANDER HAMILTON's 1791 Report on Manufactures, also focused attention on the tariff as a protectionist device. Foreign policy intruded as James Madison proposed, and the Senate rejected, tariff discrimination against Britain. Political response to these issues foreshadowed sectional and party divisions. Manufacturers in northern and mid-Atlantic states sought protection over the objections of New England merchants and southern agrarians. Federalists were identified with high tariffs and Republicans with low tariffs, although sectional ties often blurred party distinctions. Washington's hands-off approach to the legislative process established tariff policy firmly within the ambit of congressional control.

Tariff rates increased and revenues skyrocketed during the trade boom of the Napoleonic Wars, but the issue of protectionism did not rise to prominence again until 1816. Democratic-Republicans now counted artisans and manufacturers among their constituency and adopted an almost Hamiltonian outlook on America's infant industries. Madison, influenced by protectionists ALBERT GALLATIN and Alexander Dallas, favored the protective TARIFF ACT OF 1816, which was supported by some on the grounds of nationalism (including JOHN C. CALHOUN) who would become bitter foes of protectionism. The ties of nationalism frayed visibly in 1824, as a more protective tariff was passed over southern protest. By 1828, sectional differences exploded as the so-called TARIFF OF ABOMINATIONS increased tariffs to their highest antebellum level. John Quincy Adams, a lukewarm protectionist whose CABINET included archprotectionists HENRY CLAY and Richard Rush, paid the highest political price for the new tariff in the election of 1828, even though the act itself was the invention of Adams's political enemies in Congress, notably Martin Van Buren.

The tariff became a defining political issue after 1828. Andrew Jackson actively sought tariff reductions when it became clear that the TARIFF ACT OF 1832 would not quell southern discontent, as became so apparent in the NULLIFICATION crisis of 1832–1833. Jackson gladly accepted the TARIFF ACT OF 1833, the product of congressional compromise engineered by Clay and Calhoun, even though it did not impose immediate tariff reductions as large as those proposed by the administration. Whigs adopted protectionism as a component of Clay's AMERICAN SYSTEM and passed the more protective Tariff Act of 1842. Thereafter, James K. Polk raised tariff discourse to constitutional heights, arguing that congressional tax power permits revenue tariffs only, not protective tariffs. The fruits of Polk's reduction effort, the WALKER TARIFF ACT OF 1846, substantially reduced the Whig tariff. In 1857, motivated by Treasury surpluses as much as by constitutional principle, Democrats passed a new tariff cutting rates by 20 percent below Walker tariff duties.

Republican legislators ushered in a high-tariff era commencing with the MORRILL TARIFF ACT OF 1861. CIVIL WAR tariffs, coupled with massive wartime internal taxes, were not particularly protective in effect. But, after the war, Congress quickly dismantled the wartime system of internal levies while leaving the Morrill tariffs substantially intact. Pressures developed in the late 1860s and the 1870s for tariff reform. Protectionist Chester A. Arthur, forced to deal with Treasury surpluses and mindful of growing reform sentiment, in 1881 recommended establishment of a Tariff Commission to outline a path to tariff moderation. The commission's efforts proved fruitless when the Tariff Act of 1883 made no appreciable dent in the protective system. Further unsuccessful reform efforts in the 1880s, a decade distinguished by periodic Democratic control of the House of Representatives, demonstrated that the DEMOCRATIC PARTY had itself developed a cadre of protectionists more intent on pursuing local interests than in honoring the Party's low-tariff principles.

Congressional-Executive Struggle. An era of struggle between Congress and the executive for control of tariff policy followed. Grover Cleveland—highlighting the relationship between high tariffs, high consumer prices, and trust—devoted his entire annual message of 1887 to the call for tariff reform but could not win approval from the Republican Senate for the MILLS TARIFF ACT of 1888. Benjamin Harrison, elected in 1888 on a high-tariff platform, was able to secure passage of the highly protective McKINLEY TARIFF ACT of 1890. But Cleveland, whose reelection in 1892 was largely attributable to public distaste for the McKinley tariff, suffered frustration when Senate Democrats stubbornly blocked the most reformist aspects of the WILSON-GORMAN TARIFF ACT of 1894. Indeed, this pattern of conflict between the President and Senate resurfaced repeatedly: over the DINGLEY TARIFF ACT of 1897, when the Senate imposed even higher tariffs than had been sought by William McKinley; over the PAYNE-ALDRICH TARIFF ACT of 1909, when William Howard Taft's call for modest reform was dashed by Senate conservatives; and over the SMOOT-HAWLEY TARIFF ACT of 1930, when Herbert Hoover's proposal for "limited changes" increasing agricultural tariffs was distorted by Senate log rolling, greatly increasing duties at the outset of worldwide depression. During this age of increasing protectionism, only Woodrow Wilson demonstrated effective presidential leadership in tariff matters, using the powers of publicity and patronage to force moderate tariff reduction in the UNDERWOOD TARIFF ACT of 1913.

Yet, even as congressional protectionism reigned supreme, new tools of executive activism appeared to affect tariff-making. Benjamin Harrison and McKinley, recognizing the link between tariffs, trade, and foreign policy, obtained authority to negotiate reciprocal trade agreements moderating the protective tariffs of 1890 and 1897. Later, just prior to passage of the FORDNEY-McCUMBER TARIFF ACT of 1922, Warren G. Harding coupled his call for increased protectionism with a proposal that the Tariff Commission be endowed with new administrative powers permitting tariff reductions without legislative action. Hoover wrongly believed that the commission would effectively moderate Smoot-Hawley tariffs, but he correctly recognized that tariff matters were no longer the exclusive province of Congress.

Presidential Domination. Tariff policy changed dramatically during the NEW DEAL. Secretary of State CORDELL HULL seized upon the RECIPROCAL TRADE AGREEMENT as a tariff reduction device. This approach, adopted in the Reciprocal Trade Agreements Act of 1934, permitted the Franklin D. Roosevelt administration to negotiate EXECUTIVE AGREEMENTS with foreign governments reducing Smoot-Hawley tariffs by up to 50 percent. Such agreements required neither Senate treaty ratification nor congressional implementation. Congress extended this form of presidential authority numerous times after 1934, sometimes balking (under Dwight D. Eisenhower, for example, when Republican conservatives opposed further dismantling of tariff protection) and sometimes imposing restrictive conditions. But reciprocity extensions also increased presidential authority as executive discretion to lower tariffs became applicable to tariff rates previously lowered through the reciprocity process.

Bilateralism turned to multilateralism after WORLD WAR II. Harry S. Truman, as part of the overriding effort to fashion a framework for resumed international economic relations, agreed in 1947 to consolidate a series of bilateral agreements negotiated among twenty-three countries into a unified agreement, the GATT (GENERAL AGREEMENT ON TARIFFS AND TRADE). The ongoing GATT approach to tariff reduction, fostered by multinational application of most-favored-nation provisions, has since been extended in a series of negotiating "rounds" to include more than one hundred contracting parties.

But GATT hardly broke all barriers to international free trade. European nations established a free trade bloc, the European Economic Community (later the European Community), erecting tariff and nontariff barriers against outside penetration often conflicting with GATT requirements. John F. Kennedy recognized the dilemma for American interests most clearly when, in proposing the TRADE EXPANSION ACT of 1962, he sought to enhance American trade relations with Europe while expanding U.S. involvement within GATT. The problem of European economic nationalism continued to trouble Kennedy's successors, notably Richard M. Nixon and George Bush.

The astounding reduction of tariffs under GATT reshaped but did not eliminate American protectionism. Postwar Presidents—buffeted by repetitive congressional harping over perceived unfair trade practices by other countries, widening trade deficits, and erosion of American manufacturing—consistently asserted the ideals of international free trade while cooperating in the erection of comprehensive nontariff import barriers (e.g., import quotas, producer subsidies, and antidumping and countervailing duties) covering such diverse items as beef, steel, textiles, petroleum, and automobiles. And tariff restrictionism took a new tack as Congress authorized the President, in the Trade Acts of 1962 and 1974, to withhold most-favored-nation benefits from nations possessing nonmarket economies and not conforming to American human rights ideals.

Uncertainty over the future course of trade policy infused the election of 1992 and its aftermath. In the last year of his administration, Bush resisted congressional threats to China's most-favored-nation status, completed negotiations with Canada and Mexico for a North American Free Trade Agreement (NAFTA), and moved aggressively to seek mitigation of European Community agricultural protectionism in the stalled GATT process. President-elect Bill Clinton, professedly internationalist but also mindful of the protectionist bent of labor, considered a hard-line approach to China, and expressed conditional support for NAFTA, but he said little concerning ongoing GATT negotiations. Hovering over presidential transition was uncertainty whether Clinton would retain the full measure of executive autonomy over trade matters enjoyed by each of his predecessors since the New Deal or whether Congress would reassert its own authority on behalf of workers, farmers, and industries suffering the impact of the globalization of the American economy.

BIBLIOGRAPHY

Metzger, Stanley D. *Lowering Nontariff Barriers: U.S. Law, Practice, and Negotiating Objectives.* 1974.

Stanwood, Edward. *American Tariff Controversies in the Nineteenth Century.* 2 vols. Repr. 1967.

Taussig, F. W. *The Tariff History of the United States.* 8th ed. 1931.

Terrill, Tom E. *The Tariff, Politics, and American Foreign Policy 1874–1901.* 1973.

Van der Wee, Herman. *Prosperity and Upheaval: The World Economy, 1945–1980.* 1987.

RALPH MITZENMACHER

TAX POLICY. Federal tax policy poses three questions for Presidents. First, what should the overall level of taxation be? (Or, put another way, how large should government be?) Second, should taxes in the aggregate be reduced to stimulate economic growth or increased to combat inflation? And, third, how should the tax burden be distributed? The first two questions are hard to avoid. Every year, a President must submit a budget in which the overall level of spending, taxation, and borrowing is explicitly spelled out. Presidents also have an unavoidable responsibility for macroeconomic policy, not least because the public tends to hold Presidents accountable for the general state of the economy.

The third question—concerning the distribution of the tax burden within a given revenue level—*is* avoidable. Economic stimulus or restraint can be achieved by across-the-board tax changes that leave the relative distribution of the tax burden unchanged. Outside events do not force the issue of distribution onto the presidential agenda, nor do a President's regular duties require him to address it. Congress could push it onto the agenda, but it rarely does. Given the third question's inherent contentiousness—unless the overall level of taxation is being reduced, all decisions about distribution produce losers—it is not surprising that most Presidents avoid dealing with it except in symbolic or narrowly partisan ways.

Symbolic and partisan uses of the issue of tax distribution are of course commonplace for both Presidents and Congress. Since the income tax was instituted in 1913, Democrats have sought to increase the tax burden on the wealthy and large corporations while reducing it for lower-income individuals. "Closing loopholes" and "tax fairness" have been DEMOCRATIC PARTY staples. Republicans have sought to reduce the tax burden on higher-income individuals and business in order to stimulate investment and economic growth.

What rarely appear, however, are comprehensive presidential proposals for major structural reform that address accumulated inequities, inefficiencies, and complexities in a way that is both coherent and balanced. In short, Presidents rarely propose the kind of tax reform that tax policy experts like. This is in itself unremarkable. People who run for election have different goals from those who do not. What is puzzling is that Presidents sometimes do propose such comprehensive reforms, and that once—in 1986—such a reform was not only proposed but enacted.

Before exploring that puzzle by briefly reviewing the history of presidential involvement in tax reform, it is necessary to present an important subtheme that

partly explains why presidential forays into redistributional tax reform ever occur at all.

The Role of Experts. Federal tax policy in the latter half of the twentieth century saw the development of an unusually thorough and coherent body of knowledge and proposals for reform. Economists, lawyers, administrators, and government officials worked together for decades to develop these underpinnings for reform efforts. More importantly, there developed a longstanding tradition of expert's moving back and forth between government positions and academia, law firms, and accounting firms. The TREASURY DEPARTMENT's economic and legal tax offices and Congress's Joint Committee on Taxation are institutionalized embodiments of the policy goals of tax experts for tax reform. The staffs of these offices have a deep sense of their responsibility to the elected officials for whom they work. But they also have a strong professional commitment to advance what they consider good tax policy.

The well-developed set of criteria by which these experts define good tax policy includes especially these three: *equity* (i.e., that taxpayers in like circumstances should be taxed alike and, more controversially, that taxpayers with higher incomes should be taxed at a higher rate), *efficiency* (i.e., that taxation should interfere as little as possible with free-market economic decisions), and *simplicity* (i.e., that taxes should be as easy to understand and administer as possible). These criteria frequently conflict, and they often carry less weight with the public and elected officials than they do with tax policy experts. But they provide the basic starting point for most expert judgments about tax issues and for the advice that policy experts give elected officials. The work of these experts is frequently visible in the story that follows.

Federal Tax Policy before 1932. Before the Sixteenth Amendment authorized a federal income tax in 1913, more than 90 percent of federal revenues came from excise taxes and tariffs. Total revenues were modest, exceeding $500 million a year only twice before 1900. Federal income taxes were in 1862 and 1864 enacted to finance the CIVIL WAR, but these taxes were repealed in 1872. Another federal income tax was enacted in 1894 to help offset the decline in federal revenues brought about by the depression of 1893. The U.S. Supreme Court declared it unconstitutional in *Pollock v. Farmers' Loan & Trust Co.* (1895).

Congress had approved a constitutional amendment to allow an individual income tax in 1909. Following the Sixteenth Amendment's ratification in 1913, the financial demands of WORLD WAR I led to heavy reliance on individual and corporate income taxes, which averaged nearly 60 percent of total federal revenues from 1917 to 1920. With the end of the war and following a Republican sweep of the Congress and the presidency in 1920, President Warren G. Harding and his Treasury Secretary, Andrew W. Mellon, set about reducing the federal income tax. Individual and corporate income taxes dropped from 4.8 percent of gross national product (GNP) in 1920 to 2.3 percent in 1924.

Tax Reform from Roosevelt to Bush. Total federal revenues remained low up until World War II, never exceeding 8 percent of GNP (compared to 19 percent in the early 1990s). Individual and corporate income taxes accounted for less than 3 percent of GNP on the eve of World War II (compared to 10 percent in the early 1990s).

Roosevelt. President Franklin D. Roosevelt's main forays into tax reform were the heavily symbolic Revenue Acts of 1935 and 1936. Attacking "entrenched greed" and "economic royalists," Roosevelt proposed and Congress enacted legislation with dramatically higher tax rates that applied to fewer than 1 percent of individual taxpayers as well as a tax on the "undistributed profits" of corporations, which Congress sharply watered down in 1938 and repealed in 1939.

By far the most important tax legislation of the Roosevelt presidency was the Revenue Act of 1942, which converted the individual income tax from a class tax to a mass tax in order to finance World War II. The number of individual income tax returns jumped from fewer than 15 million in 1941 to more than 43 million in 1944, and individual income taxes rose from 1 percent of GNP in 1941 to nearly 10 percent in 1944. The legislation, which had broad bipartisan support, was driven overwhelmingly by the need to raise revenue for the war.

Truman. Truman's presidency was marked by continuing controversy over the overall level of taxation. Individual and corporate taxes were cut following World War II but raised again to finance the Korean War, prompting major partisan conflicts over each bill. While some of the debate over the level of taxation was conducted in terms of proposals for structural reform (for example, Truman sought to repeal the oil depletion allowance), decisions turned primarily on whether Republican or Democratic constituencies would be benefited or harmed by the changing levels of taxation. Again, reform proposals from Treasury and congressional experts were either brushed aside by the Congress or used as proxies in the main fight over whose political ox would be gored.

Eisenhower. The main tax-policy story of Eisenhower's presidency was that there was no story. Nothing much happened, apart from a (mostly technical) experts' rewrite of the tax code in 1954. With spending, inflation, and taxes all at relatively low and stable levels during the 1950s, there were no external forces to push tax policy onto the presidential agenda. The President himself had little apparent interest in structural reform or redistribution of the tax burden. The top tax-policy job in the Treasury Department became a part-time position.

Kennedy. The Kennedy administration provided a sharp contrast to the preceding eight years. President Kennedy, having promised in the 1960 campaign to "get the country moving again," proposed a reduction in business taxes in 1961, followed by a major across-the-board reduction in individual income taxes in 1963. Each of these economic stimulus proposals was accompanied by extensive proposals for structural reform and loophole-closing. The reform proposals were developed in the Treasury Department by Stanley Surrey, for years a prominent tax-reform advocate at the Harvard Law School, whom Kennedy had appointed to the top Treasury tax position. Kennedy's reform proposals ran into heavy opposition in Congress, however. Like the earlier reform proposals of Roosevelt and Truman they quickly fell away, leaving in place, however, the tax-reducing economic stimulus measures, which were enacted in 1962 and 1964.

Johnson. President Lyndon B. Johnson, perhaps reflecting his long congressional experience, had little interest in structural tax reform proposals. His Treasury Department, however, under Surrey's direction, continued internal work on reform proposals and consulted regularly with the chief of staff of the congressional Joint Committee on Taxation, Laurence Woodworth. As Johnson was leaving the presidency in early 1969, Surrey's four volumes of tax reform studies and proposals, which embodied the loophole-closing reform vision of Democratic policy experts, were delivered to Congress at its request and with no endorsement from President Johnson.

Johnson's outgoing Treasury Secretary, Joseph Barr, did appear at a congressional hearing with some data from Surrey, however. Barr pointed to 155 taxpayers with incomes of over $200,000, including 21 with incomes of over $1 million, who had paid no income taxes for 1967 and predicted a "taxpayers revolt" unless something was done about it. With individual income taxes at a post–World War II high because of President Johnson's 1968 Vietnam War surtax, and with congressional Democrats eager to gain partisan advantage over a new Republican President, Congress moved quickly to take up this invitation.

Nixon and Ford. In less than a year, President Richard M. Nixon was presented with the Tax Reform Act of 1969, a combination of tax cuts and loophole-closing structural reforms that relied heavily on the Surrey proposals, including repeal of the business investment tax credit, higher taxes on capital gains, a minimum tax on the wealthy, and tax reductions for lower-income individuals. Given the momentum it had developed with the public and in Congress, Nixon had little choice but to sign it. The 1969 act was the high-water mark for structural tax reformers until 1986.

During the remainder of the Nixon and Gerald Ford presidencies, the main initiative for making tax policy shifted to the democratic Congress. Congressionally initiated reform bills were enacted in 1975 and 1976, following the general thrust of the 1969 Surrey papers. The reform pendulum was swinging, however. As inflation pushed more taxpayers into higher tax brackets and eroded tax incentives for business investment, overall tax burdens began to grow. The tax cuts enacted every two years or so in the 1970s were barely enough to offset the effects of inflation.

Carter. President Jimmy Carter took office in 1977 proclaiming that the federal income tax was "a disgrace to the human race" and promising fundamental reform. It didn't happen. The Revenue Act of 1978, which originated in the Carter Treasury as a continuation of the liberal tax reform thrust of ten years before (with many of the junior staff people from the Surrey years now in senior roles), turned into a major defeat for this brand of tax reform by the time Congress had finished with it. Capital gains taxes were sharply reduced, business taxes were cut, individual tax cuts went mainly to middle- and upper-income taxpayers, and many special-interest tax preferences were created and expanded.

Reagan. When President Ronald Reagan took office in 1981, individual income taxes had reached their highest level since World War II: 9.6 percent of GNP, up from 8.2 percent just four years before. A major income tax cut was almost inevitable. President Reagan's 1981 tax proposals threw down the gauntlet to congressional Democrats, sharply reducing taxes on high-income individuals and corporations and forcefully extending the pro–business-investment thrust that had begun in 1978. With a newly Republican Senate and a conservative majority in the House, the President got almost everything he wanted in the Economic Recovery Tax Act of 1981.

Congressional Democrats soon began to recoup their 1981 losses, however, pushing through tax legislation in 1982 and 1984 that undid or scaled back much of what the 1981 act had done. A major impetus for the 1982 and 1984 tax increases was the explosion in the federal deficit that followed the 1981 act. Again, Treasury and congressional experts took the opportunity to achieve some technical reform goals. President Reagan and Congress thus arrived at the beginning of the 1984 presidential election year with rough equilibrium restored and few major pressures for further tax reform.

How then did President Reagan come two years later to sign the most significant tax reform bill in American history? The initial impetus came from the Reagan administration's fear that the Democrats might make tax reform an issue in the 1984 campaign, prompting the President to announce a Treasury Department "study" of tax reform in his 1984 state of the union address. As it turned out, Democratic nominee WALTER F. MONDALE pledged not tax reform but a tax increase, effectively removing most of the pressure for reform.

Second, when the Treasury's study emerged after the election, President Reagan was nonetheless so beguiled by the low top tax rate for individuals (35 percent, down from 70 percent when he first took office) that he found the rest of the package irresistible. The rest of the package included a set of loophole-closing proposals modeled closely on the reform agenda that tax policy experts and liberal reformers had been developing for four decades, along with a $20-billion-a-year tax increase for corporations that was used to finance a tax cut for individuals. Democrats loved it, but the President seemed not to notice the departures from Republican dogma.

The main congressional proponent of tax reform, Sen. Bill Bradley (D-N.J.), managed to establish the proposition that tax reform should be "neutral" both fiscally (with no overall tax increase or reduction) and distributionally (with no change in the individual tax burden by income class). This drained from the issue the partisan and ideological controversies that had stymied past structural reform efforts.

The decades of tax policy study, analysis, and debate that had formed a consensus among experts on the outlines of good tax policy strongly shaped elite and media views. Key Democratic and Republican congressional leaders concluded that their reputations would be enhanced by a successful tax reform effort. Finally, the professional tax staffs at the Treasury and the congressional Joint Committee on Taxation played a key role in nurturing a bill that was in many respects the culmination of the goals tax policy experts had sought for nearly half a century.

Bush. Tax controversies never stuck to Ronald Reagan's "Teflon" presidency, but they became his successor's tar baby. After pledging "Read my lips: No new taxes" throughout his 1988 election campaign, President George Bush was pushed into raising taxes by a Democratic Congress in 1990. A large share of the increases fell on upper-income Republicans and so-called Reagan Democrats, who were not mollified by the President's 1992 apology for going back on his pledge nor reassured by his promise never to do it again. Bush's repeated calls for reduced capital gains taxes were flicked away by the Democratic Congress, leading Republican constituencies to doubt his effectiveness and Democratic constituencies to question his sense of fairness.

Reagan's Success. Kennedy, Carter, and Reagan were the only Presidents to propose comprehensive tax reforms since the income tax became a truly mass tax during World War II. All three were strongly influenced by the institutionalized tax policy experts in the Treasury Department. But only one, President Reagan, was successful. The reform proposals of Kennedy and Carter were quickly brushed aside by the Congress. What made the difference?

The key difference is that Reagan—the most conservative President since Calvin Coolidge—proposed an essentially Democratic tax reform bill. Reagan's strong support gave political cover to moderates of both parties in Congress and garnered Republican support on party-loyalty grounds that would not otherwise have been forthcoming. When this was combined with the bill's fiscal and distributional neutrality, most of the ideology was drained from the issue. Without the ideological overlay that had blocked all previous efforts, the bill became virtually unstoppable. As one Senator commented, "It breathes its own air."

Could something like this happen again in tax policy, or in other policy areas? Perhaps, but it would likely require another President like Ronald Reagan, whose commitment to a few clear and simple goals was enough to override the contradictions and inconsistencies that trouble Presidents who pay closer attention to details.

BIBLIOGRAPHY

Birnbaum, Jeffrey H., and Alan S. Murray. *Showdown at Gucci Gulch.* 1987.
Conlan, Timothy J., Margaret T. Wrightson, and David R. Beam. *Taxing Choices: The Politics of Tax Reform.* 1990.
Leff, Mark. *The Limits of Symbolic Reform: The New Deal and Taxation, 1933–1939.* 1985.
Pechman, Joseph A. *Federal Tax Policy.* 5th ed. 1987.
Steuerle, C. Eugene. *The Tax Decade: How Taxes Came to Dominate the Public Agenda.* 1992.
Verdier, James M. "The President, Congress, and Tax Reform: Patterns over Three Decades." *Annals of the American Academy of Political and Social Science* 499 (September 1988): 114–123.
Witte, John F. *The Politics and Development of the Federal Income Tax.* 1985.

JAMES M. VERDIER

TAYLOR, ZACHARY (1784–1850), twelfth President of the United States (1849–1850). Taylor was born into a distinguished Virginia family but reared in frontier Kentucky. He was educated primarily at home. His father, a revolutionary war officer and important Kentucky official, gave him a small plantation from which Taylor ultimately went on to accumulate a sizable fortune in slaves and plantations centered in Louisiana. He was a kind slavemaster, who on at least one occasion gave his slaves a cash Christmas gift.

Military Career. In 1807 he enlisted in the army and quickly rose to become a captain. In 1810 he began a long and happy marriage with Margaret Mackall Smith, daughter of a rich planter. In 1812 he was promoted to brevet major for heroic action in defending Fort Harrison, Indiana Territory, against a superior force of Shawnees led by Tecumseh. He spent the next several years as a commander building roads and forts on various frontiers. From 1828 to 1837, as a colonel, he commanded various forts in present-day Minnesota, Wisconsin, Iowa, and Illinois and won high praise for his activities during the Black Hawk War, although he considered it an unnecessary conflict.

Taylor respected the INDIANS and insisted that treaties with them be honored, which made him unpopular when he prevented white encroachment on Indian lands. He built and staffed a school for Indians and often complained because the War Department ignored his suggestions for improving Indian relations and refused to send the money to meet existing treaty commitments.

Promoted to brevet brigadier general during the hapless Seminole War in Florida, Taylor stirred up opposition in Washington by trying to use thirty-three bloodhounds acquired from Cuba by the Florida government. The dogs proved to be useless, and Taylor always insisted that the muzzled dogs were used only to find the Indians and not to "worry" them. In dealing with Indians who assisted him and those who surrendered to be transported westward, Taylor honored every agreement to the letter. Large numbers of escaped slaves had joined the Seminoles, but Taylor refused to seize blacks claimed by Seminoles. He also would not return any runaway slaves to alleged owners unless they could prove their ownership, which was difficult, and through his efforts between three and four hundred blacks accompanied Seminoles to their new homes in present-day Oklahoma. During the presidential campaign of 1848 Taylor's dealings with the blacks in Florida were cited as evidence that he would not promote the expansion of SLAVERY.

In 1841 Taylor assumed command of the Second Military Department at Fort Smith, Arkansas, and immediately denounced the construction of the fort as an unnecessary monument to financial waste. He skillfully kept the peace among the different Indian tribes transported there by the government and protected them from the warlike prairie tribes and Texas raiding parties. He abandoned Fort Wayne because it occupied some of the best land of the Cherokees and interfered with the farms of the half-breeds. When angry settlers complained about their vulnerability to Indian massacres, he denounced their complaints as nonsense created entirely by greed.

Taylor was always on a frontier at election time and never voted, but he was an ardent Whig and supporter of HENRY CLAY. Though a large slaveholder he rejected as nonsense JOHN C. CALHOUN's argument that Texas must be annexed to preserve and perpetuate slavery. He carried out the orders that provoked the MEXICAN WAR, but he personally opposed both the ANNEXATION OF TEXAS and the seizure of additional territory from Mexico.

On 12 January 1846 Taylor, leading a small army, was ordered to the Rio Grande River. It was the southern boundary claimed by Texas, but was in fact more than one hundred miles south of the previous boundary of the Mexican state of Texas. He assured the Mexican commander at Matamoros that his advance was not an act of aggression, but no Mexican could have considered it otherwise. When the Mexicans ordered him to retreat northward, he blockaded the river and stopped all supplies bound for Matamoros. On 24 April 1846 a large Mexican force killed sixty-three American dragoons north of the river and the Mexican War began.

Taylor promptly won battles at Palo Alto and Resaca de la Palma against much larger Mexican armies and became a national hero overnight. While waiting for badly needed reinforcements at Matamoros, Taylor insisted upon protecting the civil and religious rights of the Mexican people and would not even use private home for hospital purposes without the consent of the owners. He had his surgeons attend the enemy wounded and even contributed several hundred dollars of his own money for their support.

Taylor has been faulted for lacking the killer instinct

that would have led him to pursue and crush the Mexican armies after his victories, but his alternatives in a strange country with untrained soldiers were much less simple in 1846 than they look today. He ultimately got part of his army to Monterrey, but only after herculean efforts and the deaths of thousands from disease. He has also been criticized for inadequate sanitary measures, but ignorance should not be confused with negligence. The germ theory of disease had not yet been formulated, and thirsty troops did not know they should not drink the contaminated water.

Taylor took Monterrey with only six thousand men in bloody hand-to-hand street fighting. The Mexican commander surrendered in exchange for a promise that for eight weeks Taylor would not advance beyond a mountain behind which the Mexican army was allowed to retire. Taylor agreed and explained later that the Mexicans had assured him their government was ready to end the war. He would not have soldiers killed for nothing; another attack on the city would kill women and children; and anyway, he needed eight weeks to prepare for another advance.

Harsh criticism of this decision—instead of praise for the victory—from the President and the Secretary of War convinced Taylor that President James K. Polk and General WINFIELD SCOTT were conspiring against him. Worried about Taylor as a possible 1848 presidential candidate, Polk selected Scott for an invasion at Veracruz and left Taylor with only six thousand largely inexperienced men. Hearing a rumor that Polk had died, Taylor wrote that he "would as soon have heard of his death, if true, as that of any other individual in the whole Union."

Ignoring Scott's order to fall back to a more defensible position at Monterrey, Taylor marched boldly against Mexican general Antonio López de Santa Anna, who was advancing with twenty thousand troops and would have to be met in any case. At Buena Vista, he flamboyantly rejected the Mexican demand for surrender within the hour and defeated the Mexicans after a fierce two-day battle in which his own personal courage was again a significant factor.

Campaign of 1848. Polk blamed Taylor for an unnecessary battle, while Taylor argued that he had "saved the honor of the country & our glorious flag from trailing in the dust." The public agreed with Taylor. In December 1847 a group of young Whig congressmen that included both Alexander H. Stephens and Abraham Lincoln organized a Taylor-for-President club, and the movement quickly spread. Taylor's heroic victories and his informal dress and style of command had earned him the sobriquet Old

Rough and Ready and made him seem like a natural successor to Andrew Jackson.

Waiting in northern Mexico for Scott to take Mexico City and besieged with questions, Taylor wrote several highly revealing letters. He did not like political parties, he would spend no money, and if he were to become President it must be "by the spontaneous move of the people." Slavery had already been abolished in Mexico and it could never be revived in any of the new territories. Reminding JEFFERSON DAVIS of Taylor's own great financial stake in slavery, Taylor added that he would "respect the opinions and feelings of the non-slaveholding states on that subject" and would never interfere with "their legal rights as regards the same." Unfortunately, he wrote, "The intemperate zeal of the fanatics of the North and the intemperate zeal of a few politicians of the South" were making reasonable discussions impossible. The timeworn economic issues of the BANK OF THE UNITED STATES, tariffs, and internal improvements were dead, but the dangerous and unnecessary WILMOT PROVISO against slavery in the territories would shake the country. He was hopeful, however, that a compromise could be reached. Congress was responsible for legislation, and a President should veto laws only if they were clearly unconstitutional.

Taylor's insistence that he would run only as a national rather than a party candidate almost cost him the nomination, but despite this and his ownership of some 140 slaves, he was nominated on the fourth ballot at the WHIG PARTY convention in 1848. The Whig leaders waited several weeks for his acceptance because he had refused to pay the postage on the many letters he was receiving and his official notification had been returned to the dead-letter office. Assisted by the candidacy of Martin Van Buren on the FREE-SOIL PARTY ticket, Taylor was elected over his hated enemy LEWIS CASS.

Presidency. As he had promised, Taylor chose for his Cabinet three moderate southerners, three northerners, and one man from Delaware, nominally a slave state but not involved in the slavery quarrel. Because the Whigs had never really had an administration before, thousands of the party faithful lined up for jobs and handling this problem took many hours of valuable time and energy and caused great dissatisfaction within the party. Much of the New York PATRONAGE was given to Senator WILLIAM H. SEWARD, the highly vocal antislavery New Yorker who had won Taylor's personal friendship despite his position on slavery. The mere fact that the hated Seward was welcome at the White House at all immediately roused southern suspicions that they had chosen a traitor to their interests.

Domestic affairs. Facing a Congress bitterly divided over the question of territorial slavery, Taylor acted promptly. Northerners and southerners alike agreed that a new state could make its own decision regarding slavery. Taylor believed, therefore, that the best way to avoid a dangerous congressional debate would be to make California and New Mexico into states as soon as possible and he planned accordingly. In April 1849 he sent a slaveholding Congressman, Thomas Butler King, to midwife California into statehood but to take no stand on slavery. The Californians quickly wrote a constitution barring slavery and asked for statehood. The process was more complicated in New Mexico because Texas was claiming all of New Mexico's settled area—about two-thirds of the present state—and New Mexico was daring Texas to take it. Was the area to be part of the slave state of Texas or to remain free, as it had been under Mexican rule? Taylor had written to Jefferson Davis saying that he would defend southern slavery with the sword if it should come under military attack but that he did not consider status of California and New Mexico as a threat to slavery. When New Mexico had surrendered peacefully to the U.S. Army it had been promised territorial status and eventual statehood. Taylor always kept his and his country's promises, and he would defend New Mexico personally if necessary. He deplored the Wilmot Proviso as both useless and dangerous, but it was constitutional. He assured angry southerners that he would not veto it if Congress passed it and that he would hang anyone who threatened the American Union. The proviso was never passed, but its very consideration was a red flag to most southerners.

With Congress at a standstill, Henry Clay introduced a set of compromise resolutions in the Senate. California should enter the Union with no federal action on slavery. The boundary between Texas and New Mexico should be compromised, and Texas should be rewarded by federal assumption of the Texas debt. New Mexico should establish a territorial government with no action on slavery and settle the question later. The South should receive a more effective fugitive slave law. The slave trade in the District of Columbia should be abolished. These measures might have passed fairly quickly, but a group of southerners persuaded Clay to combine them into a single bill, which could not pass because neither side would accept the concessions made to the other.

President Taylor has usually been blamed for helping block the compromise, but this is unjustified. Taylor preferred his own plan (to grant quick statehood for California and New Mexico), but he opposed Clay's Omnibus Bill only because he knew it could not pass without significant amendments and he believed the southerners were using it to hold California as a hostage for the cession of most of New Mexico to Texas. Indeed, since every day for five long, hot months brought new efforts by both sides to amend the bill, no one really knew what the bill would contain if it ever reached a final vote. (After Taylor's death, the Omnibus Bill was defeated and broken into separate bills that passed one at a time. California became a free state. New Mexico preserved its territorial integrity with self-determination on slavery. Texas bondholders got $10 million. The Fugitive Slave Act was passed, and the District of Columbia slave trade was moved to Virginia. While Taylor opposed the Omnibus Bill, there is no reason to believe that, had he lived, he would have vetoed any of the measures that actually passed.)

By late June 1850 Texas had made serious preparations to invade New Mexico, and several southern governors were offering their support to Texas if the federal government should intervene. It is entirely possible that only Taylor's resolute announcement that the U.S. Army would defend New Mexico if necessary prevented a Texas invasion that could have triggered a civil war.

Meanwhile, a well-publicized scandal was causing Taylor even greater pain. For years Secretary of War George W. Crawford had argued a claim against the government that dated back to the revolutionary war, but he had left the case when appointed to the Cabinet. The Polk administration had paid the principal but not the interest, which was now five times the principal. When a new attorney asked for the total interest, Attorney General Reverdy Johnson ruled that it should be paid, and Treasury Secretary Meredith paid the sum in full. As the original attorney, Crawford received more than $115,000. It was all legal, but excessively greedy, and political opponents easily turned it into a major scandal.

Foreign affairs. In foreign affairs Taylor performed very creditably. He won minor claims disputes with the French and the Portuguese and upheld the NEUTRALITY laws by refusing to allow a German warship to sail from an American port without pledges that it would not be used in the German war against Denmark. When various American newspapers and groups supported revolutionary activities in Canada, he warned that he would send an army to prevent any American violence against Canada. He also offered to help the British find the lost Arctic expedition of Sir John Franklin, but Congress denied him the money. His good personal relations with the British helped him cope successfully with British activities in Central America. He

concluded treaties with Nicaragua, Costa Rica, and Honduras and negotiated a contract for an American company to dig a canal across Nicaragua. The British, however, had established a Mosquito Indian kingdom under their protection at San Juan del Norte, Nicaragua, which controlled the eastern end of the proposed canal, and were threatening to expand further. A serious confrontation ensued, but Taylor insisted that he would not abandon the alliance with Nicaragua unless the British gave up their Mosquito protectorate. Ultimately, the CLAYTON-BULWER TREATY, which Taylor signed on his deathbed, provided that neither government would have exclusive control of a future canal or fortify or attempt to colonize any part of Central America.

Taylor's fellow slaveholders expected him to remain neutral or perhaps even assist the Cuban Narciso Lopez's efforts to conquer CUBA with the help of southern volunteers from the U.S. Taylor, however, announced that he would prevent aggression from America against friendly nations and that those who violated American laws or treaty obligations would be severely punished. He stopped one expedition, but another escaped and invaded Cuba with the capture of fifty-two Americans and the loss of seventy American lives. Taylor ignored southern pressures for action against Spain and ordered the surviving leaders prosecuted in New Orleans. They were acquitted by southern juries, but Taylor's efforts strengthened his hand when he successfully persuaded Spain to release its American prisoners.

Death. The possibility of a Texas invasion of New Mexico and the scandal involving Secretary Crawford had put Taylor under great stress. On 4 July 1850, he ate green apples in the morning, sat through an interminable speech under a hot sun at the Washington Monument, and gorged on cherries and iced milk back at the White House. He developed gastroenteritis, and his weakened condition combined with the treatments given him by his doctors killed him. He died on 9 July. Vice President Millard Fillmore succeeded him. Taylor received a magnificent funeral, and for a brief time at least northerners and southerners were united in their grief and in his praise.

As President, Taylor invariably put the national interest first, usually made wise decisions, and always acted decisively. Had he lived, he would probably have been reelected. He has been a grossly underrated president.

BIBLIOGRAPHY

Bauer, K. Jack. *Zachary Taylor*. 1985.
Benton, Thomas Hart. *Thirty Years View*. Vol. 2. 1856.

Dyer, Brainerd, *Zachary Taylor*. 1946.
Hamilton, Holman. *Prologue to Conflict, The Crisis and Compromise of 1850*. 1964.
Hamilton, Holman. *Zachary Taylor, Soldier in the White House*. 1951.
Hamiton, Holman. *Zachary Taylor, Soldier of the Republic*. 1941.
Nevins, Allan. *Ordeal of the Union*. 2 vols. 1947.
Samson, William H. *Letters of Zachary Taylor from the Battlefields of the Mexican War*. 1908.
Smith, Elbert B. *The Presidencies of Zachary Taylor and Millard Fillmore*. 1988.

ELBERT B. SMITH

TEAPOT DOME SCANDAL. The Teapot Dome scandal involved the bribery of a CABINET officer by two developers who received leases for private development of oil reserves previously sequestered for use by the United States Navy. It featured a great debate over federal conservation policy and resulted in the first imprisonment of a Cabinet member for malfeasance of office.

President Warren G. Harding appointed Senator Albert Fall as Secretary of the Interior in 1921. Although a westerner and advocate of national parks, Fall was not a conservationist. He believed that natural resources, including oil, on public lands should be available for private development. In 1920 the navy had taken control of two large reserves that had been secured during the administration of William Howard Taft and a third, at Teapot Dome in Wyoming, added by President Woodrow Wilson. Fall convinced Harding to transfer the three naval oil reserves from the Navy Department to the Department of Interior by EXECUTIVE ORDER on 31 May 1921. Fall argued that Interior could better control drainage of the reserves to adjacent private property. Secretary of the Navy Edwin Denby did not oppose the action, viewing it as protection of the navy's oil rather than an opening to private exploitation.

Without holding public bids, Secretary Fall leased Elk Hills in California to Edward L. Doheny, president of Pan-American Oil Company, and awarded a twenty-year lease on Teapot Dome to Harry Sinclair, head of the Sinclair Consolidated Oil Corporation, in exchange for a 16 percent royalty. Both firms were obligated to construct pipelines and storage tanks, including a facility at Pearl Harbor; in addition, Doheny had to build a refinery.

Conservationists, learning of the deals, opposed the action and convinced Senator ROBERT M. LA FOLLETTE of Wisconsin to look into the matter. In April 1922 the United States Senate passed a resolution to investigate the leases. Senator Thomas J. Walsh, Democrat from Montana, headed the inquiry but did not press the matter immediately; his philosophy was closer to Fall's than to La Follette's.

Albert Fall left the Harding Cabinet in March 1923, because he was disappointed that Herbert Hoover, Charles Evans Hughes, and Henry C. Wallace exerted more influence on the President than he did. Fall's successor, Hubert Work, moved over from the Post Office. A moderate conservationist, Work stabilized the department during the subsequent scandal, modernized its operations by applying efficient business methods, and revised Fall's anticonservation policies. He helped to establish a Federal Oil Conservation Board consisting of the secretaries of Commerce, the Interior, War, and the Navy. Work continued as secretary for five years, staying on in Calvin Coolidge's administration after Harding's death on 2 August 1923.

In the autumn of 1923, Senator Walsh began hearings. Early testimony was not very revealing, but in late November, there were rumors that Fall's finances had improved significantly at about the time of the leases. While Doheny and Sinclair denied any transfer of funds to Fall, the latter refused to testify because of illness. He claimed, instead, that Edward B. McLean, publisher of the *Washington Post*, had loaned him $100,000 for improvements on his New Mexico ranch. McLean tried to avoid testifying but eventually confessed that he had not loaned the money to Fall.

The $100,000 had come from Doheny, who volunteered the information on 24 January 1924, but insisted that there was no connection between the loan and the oil leases. Subsequent investigation revealed that Sinclair had given Fall more than $300,000 in bonds. It is likely that Fall would have granted the leases irrespective of receiving the money, which came in the form of loans rather than an outright gift. But he was found guilty of malfeasance of office, was charged with a $100,000 fine (which he never paid), and served nine months of a one-year sentence. He thus became the first Cabinet member to go to jail for activities in office. On the day Fall entered prison, Doheny secured the mortgage on Fall's ranch at a sheriff's sale; he foreclosed three years later and evicted the ex-Secretary. Doheny and Sinclair lost the oil leases but were not convicted of bribing a public official. Sinclair, however, was found guilty of jury tampering and served a brief sentence. Although not guilty of any wrongdoing, Secretary of the Navy Edwin Denby was forced to resign from the Coolidge Cabinet on 18 February 1924.

While the Teapot Dome scandal as well as corruption in the Veterans' Administration hurt Harding's reputation, the President's death allowed the Republican Party to focus blame on him and his appointees. The party also claimed credit for 1920s prosperity, an argument that contributed markedly to Coolidge's 1924 election victory.

BIBLIOGRAPHY

Bates, J. Leonard. *The Origins of Teapot Dome: Progressives, Parties, and Petroleum, 1909–1921.* 1963.

Noggle, Burl. *Teapot Dome: Oil and Politics in the 1920s.* 1962.

Stratton, David H. "Behind Teapot Dome: Some Personal Insights." *Business History Review* 31 (1957): 385–402.

Trani, Eugene P. *The Secretaries of the Department of the Interior, 1849-1969.* 1975.

Trani, Eugene P., and David Wilson. *The Presidency of Warren G. Harding.* 3d prt. 1989.

EUGENE P. TRANI

TEHERAN CONFERENCE. From 28 November to 1 December 1943 the first meeting of the Big Three wartime leaders, Franklin D. Roosevelt, Winston Churchill, and Joseph Stalin took place in Teheran, Iran. The conference proved cordial since recent Allied military successes heralded eventual victory over Germany in WORLD WAR II, and the leaders postponed issues on which they could not agree. Roosevelt strived to establish the same warm rapport with Stalin that he enjoyed with Churchill.

The American and British leaders satisfied Stalin's insistence on their opening a second front in Europe by revealing plans for a cross-channel invasion of Europe to take place in 1944. The leaders discussed important political questions about the shape of the postwar world. Roosevelt requested Soviet support for a new international organization in which the United States, the Soviet Union, Great Britain, and China would guarantee collective security. Stalin doubted that the four powers could contain Germany or Japan and wanted more tangible assurances of their future physical security. Roosevelt approached Stalin with plans for international trusteeship for the Baltic states, but the Soviet leader expressed reservations. Roosevelt agreed that the Soviets had "historic ties" to Lithuania, Latvia, and Estonia. Roosevelt also tried unsuccessfully to reconcile Soviet demands to control Poland with American and British commitments to restore self-determination to the Poles. The conferees eventually acknowledged that the Soviet view would predominate in postwar Poland. The Big Three reaffirmed their commitment to demand Germany's unconditional surrender, but they left vague its future borders. They turned the future of Germany over to the Allied European Advisory Council. Roosevelt returned from Teheran optimistic about his personal ties to Stalin and hopeful that the Soviet Union would cooperate with the United States in the postwar world. Churchill, on the other hand, doubted that Stalin was interested in cooperating with the Western powers after the defeat of Germany and Japan.

BIBLIOGRAPHY

Dallek, Robert. *Franklin D. Roosevelt and American Foreign Policy, 1932–1945.* 1979.

Gaddis, John Lewis. *The United States and the Origins of the Cold War, 1943–1947.* 1972.

ROBERT D. SCHULZINGER

TELEVISION AND PRESIDENTIAL POLITICS. The formal powers of the presidency are rather modest; they include taking care that the laws are faithfully executed, giving information to Congress, and recommending that certain "necessary and expedient" actions be taken. In addition, there are specific formal powers of appointment, pardon, and military command associated with the office. By contrast, the informal powers of the President are quite imposing; and it is television that has made them so. Television marries substance and symbol in the presidential office and enables its occupant to become the personal ideal of national government. Americans see the President as more than the CHIEF EXECUTIVE or head of state, he is also the embodiment of a national values. In times of crisis Americans look to the President for symbolic reassurance and comfort.

In 1970, Senator J. William Fulbright observed that "television has done as much to expand the powers of the president as would a constitutional amendment formally abolishing the [other] branches of government." A society dominated by the television media emphasizes perceptions more than reality, and pictures not policies make the lasting impressions on viewers, who are also voters. Television is the most popular and trusted form of communication. Most homes in America have a television set, and the average set is turned on more than seven hours a day. The typical American viewer spends over three hours a day watching television, and the most believable news events are those that are televised.

In such a media milieu, the President is an actor with exceptional symbolic authority. There is a story on the daily activities of the President during the evening news shows virtually every night. The power of the office stems from its visibility, which has a dramatic impact on the nation. The television President can frame the issues, determine their content, and decide the timing of policy announcements. Americans have great reverence for the office of the President and are willing to listen to what their leader has to say on most any subject at any time. A presidential address is a unifying experience, what George Gerbner has called "a centralized system of storytelling." No wonder, then, that the manipulation of symbols, words, television pictures and expressions are the focus of much planned White House activity, all designed to influence the viewing audience.

Television is mass communication, in the sense that it reaches nearly everyone and the viewer must either see the political event as it is broadcast, or else change the channel or turn off the set. Visual television images communicate feelings as well as words. In American democracy great power is derived from the influence that television exerts over its audience. As political journalist Theodore White observed, the press, especially television, sets the agenda of public discussion and determines what people will talk about and think about. The potential consequences of press power will be discussed following a brief history of television's influence on presidential politics.

History. Television became a fixture in American politics in the early 1950s. In 1952 Richard M. Nixon chose the television medium to make his famous Checkers speech in a successful attempt to remain on the Republican presidential ticket. The 1960 televised PRESIDENTIAL DEBATES between John F. Kennedy and Nixon were said by some analysts to have been crucial to the outcome of the race in November. Broadcasts of the living room war in Vietnam enervated Lyndon B. Johnson's popularity and led to his decision not to seek reelection. Network coverage of the protests surrounding the Democratic national convention in 1968 scarred the party election effort. In 1973 the television coverage of hearing on the WATERGATE AFFAIR had diminished Nixon's standing from his landslide election of the year before.

Lasting memories of Presidents are often remarkable television moments. Voters remember ads from political campaigns, one-sentence gaffes from presidential debates, and dramatic footage from presidential trips years after the President has left office. The effect of the failed rescue mission during the IRANIAN HOSTAGE CRISIS and the picture of Islamic mullahs pawing through the wreckage of American military aircraft had much to do with the perception that Jimmy Carter was a weak leader in 1980. Conversely the mastery Ronald Reagan, the "Great Communicator," showed over the media did much to defuse the IRAN-CONTRA AFFAIR in his second administration and further his image as an effective leader. Television stories, and the filmed images that accompany them, shape the impressions voters have of the President as weak or strong, confident or vascillating, electable or unelectable. To analyze the power the electronic press has over viewers, this discussion turns first to political elections and then to governing in the presidential office itself.

Presidential Elections. Political power in the American democracy comes from winning elections, and nothing has changed the nature of those elections since the 1960s more than television. In the 1990s candidates for the nation's highest office recognize that voters have become consumers, who function as an audience by observing the presidential contest on the television screen and by changing their opinions with events. Presidential candidates vie with one another trying to improve their appeal and convince voters of their ability to win. A large portion of the candidates' strategy involves trying to attract coverage, and an equally large amount of the media time involves trying to project winners and losers against a backdrop of expectations created by earlier news stories.

What matters in political elections is the personality and image, the gut impressions a viewer receives from a thirty-second campaign spot or a ragtag interview on the airport tarmac. Presidential campaigns are superficial and the links between candidate and party loyalist are tenuous because television is so occupied with the immediate and the visual. When the press examines a politician's performance in detail, few voters bother to read even the abstract of the critique; but everyone notices the visual misstatement of a television interview. The art of political campaigning has been handed to professional media specialists who work with pollsters to give the best spin on an issue for the candidate.

In sum, television has changed the campaigning for President in four significant ways. First, it has altered the process of NOMINATING PRESIDENTIAL CANDIDATES. Candidates compete through a series of presidential preference primaries and come to the convention with enough delegates to win nomination on the first ballot. The party convention serves no purpose other than to give the nominee an opportunity to showcase his vice presidential candidate and address the American people without editing by television. Second, it has altered campaigning to the point where the television sound bite is the focus of the day's activities. The planning and execution of a campaign is now largely in the hands of media experts and public relations specialists who script events for visual consumption. Third, television has weakened the role political parties play in the selection process. The development of computerized, direct-mail fund-raising techniques, aided by televised appeals, make the party organization less important than it once was. Finally, the advent of television has led to packaged candidates, in the sense that they are marketed through the strategic selection of issues with effective television commercials to shape their images and properties. Such is the "new politics" of television political campaigning.

Political Leadership. Governing is also a function of media perceptions. One goal of the White House is to manage the press agenda by framing the pictures and stories in such a way as to increase the appeal of the President. David Gergen, Ronald Reagan's first White House communications director, recalls a rule in the Nixon White House that required "before any public event was put on [the President's] schedule, you had to know what the headline out of that event was going to be, what the picture was going to be, and what the lead paragraph would be." The presence of television has made the White House conscientiously try to manage every move in the presidential schedule for maximum media impact.

For example, there was a planned public relations strategy built into the story-of-the-day approach employed by the Reagan White House. Each morning the staff would meet to select which messages would be given to the press that day. PRESS CONFERENCES were scheduled early in the morning to give television journalists plenty of time to complete their stories. To ensure that television cameras recorded just what was wanted, statements before the press corps were limited to just a few sentences to restrict editorial discretion. Schedule constraints allowed for only a few select questions, all supervised by administration officials after the briefing. To guard the image of the President further, fewer and fewer news conferences were scheduled by the White House, and those that were called were well rehearsed for media consumption. Although George Bush frequently talked informally with the press, the Reagan pattern of fewer news conferences has become the norm for occupants in the Oval Office.

To govern effectively a President must not only have the formal powers of the office but also be perceived as powerful by friends and foes alike. Both substance and symbol combine to make the presidential office what it is. Much presidential behavior is "posturing for the media," for viewing on the evening news. Statements are often made for mass appeal, then evaluated for their effect on the audience and Washington elites. No other Western democracy has brought the press into such close physical proximity to the head of its government. The result is that politics by the President is personalized to a degree not seen in other governmental systems.

It can be reasonably argued that virtually all coverage of national government is a drama surrounding the President. Energy programs, defense announcements, budget cuts, and anti-inflation actions are all given the angle of involving the White House is some way. The President gets a lot of coverage, and most of it is favorable. But the media management strategies are not always successful. The increased autonomy of the press means that when bad news does come it invariably descends on the White House first. The relationship between the press and the President is one of a struggle, meaning that each is at the same time somewhat dependent on the other, and yet autonomous.

Reality and Image. From Plato's parable of the shadows in the cave to the riddle of the tree falling out of earshot of the forest, human beings have wondered whether there is a reality out there that truly exists apart from their flawed perceptions of it. Today the answer about shadows and trees is solved if there is videotape on the nightly news confirming the event. Television is reality, and regardless of what really happened, what matters is the perception of that reality by the audience. Never was Machiavelli's adage more appropriate for the presidential office than today. "It is not necessary for a prince to have all the above-named qualities, but it is very necessary to seem to have them."

Television has made the President a star, and he uses his office to give the appearance of being able to make a difference in the world. The White House works to create an image of the President that is a reservoir of political capital for use in battles with Congress and gaining support for the administration's programs. The creation of public good will is invisible, it is a power nowhere enumerated in the Constitution and exists wholly as a legacy of the way we communicate in the electronic age. Yet of all the powers of the presidency, the ability to set the national agenda through command of the press environment on television may be the greatest one of all.

[*See also* MEDIA, PRESIDENT AND THE; PRESS AND THE PRESIDENCY, HISTORY OF; PRESS RELATIONS.]

BIBLIOGRAPHY

Alger, Dean E. *Media and Politics.* 1989.

Gerbner, George, et al. "Charting the Mainstream: Television's Contributions to Political Orientations." *Journal of Communication* 32 (1982).

Mendelsohn, Harold, and Irving Crespi. *Polls, Television, and the New Politics.* 1970.

Patterson, Thomas. *The Mass Media Election.* 1980.
Ranney, Austin. *Channels of Power.* 1983.
Smith, Hedrick. *The Power Game.* 1988.
White, Theodore. *The Making of the President, 1972.* 1972.

J. DAVID WOODARD

TENNESSEE VALLEY AUTHORITY ACT.

The Tennessee Valley Authority (TVA) Act, signed into law by President Franklin D. Roosevelt in 1933, was a bold attempt to transform the Tennessee River basin by "regional development," an idea that ignored state boundaries and promoted public development of natural resources. Running through the South's most depressed areas, and a source of destructive floods, the Tennessee River first drew public scrutiny because of navigational problems at an area known as Muscle Shoals, but the river's potential for hydroelectric power garnered the most attention. When the need for nitrates during WORLD WAR I produced a dam at the Shoals, there ensued a debate over private versus public development of natural resources, especially water and timber, that culminated under Roosevelt in an audacious experiment.

The President, TVA's congressional sponsor Senator George Norris (R-Neb.), and Arthur E. Morgan, an engineer, envisioned a transformed Tennessee Valley. Such a plan, Roosevelt said, "transcends mere power development: it enters the wide fields of flood control, soil erosion, afforestation, elimination from agricultural use of marginal land, and distribution and diversification of industry." The TVA's first chairman (of a board of three directors), Arthur E. Morgan, was a utopian thinker, hoping to launch TVA on a broad agenda of social change. He shared Roosevelt's vision of broad regional planning, but unfortunately he lacked Roosevelt's political skills, and his mishandling of the agency did much to shape the TVA's future.

David Lilienthal, Morgan's nemesis on the board, believed in cheap and abundant electricity as a counterweight to corporate utilities. The resulting competition would drive down private utility rates, increasing consumption. Lilienthal adapted the idea of a "grass roots democracy," implying decentralized (local) control over a centralized (federal) agency, to advance increased power production as the chief local need. While Morgan failed to gain local support, Lilienthal shrewdly built grass-roots backing among the politically influential local farmers and merchants by supplying cheap electricity with tangible and immediate benefits.

The rift between the TVA directors proved to be more than even the diplomatic Roosevelt could mend.

In March of 1938 the President was forced to remove Morgan from the board, since he was publicly accusing (without substantiation) Lilienthal of corruption. Under Lilienthal's subsequent leadership, TVA's power potential grew, but the planning ideals of Roosevelt, Norris, and Morgan were mostly lost. As REXFORD G. TUGWELL later commented, from that point on TVA should have been called the "Tennessee Valley Power Production and Flood Control Corporation."

The TVA has been criticized by environmentalists for promoting strip-mining, and by the valley's inhabitants for displacing thousands from their homes and farms. Regardless of the criticisms, however, the TVA did spur a new way of life. It provided thousands of badly needed jobs, improved river navigation, brought electricity to millions, and built twenty-one dams that saved the area from further flood-related devastation. Farmers learned much about soil conservation and land-use management. Recreational facilities enhanced leisure time and promoted tourism.

Roosevelt talked of seven or eight more TVAs that would divide the continental United States into regional resource management units, but opposition from Congress and the private sector halted all such plans. The TVA remains unique.

BIBLIOGRAPHY

Chandler, William U. *The Myth of TVA.* 1984.
Lilienthal, David. *Democracy on the March.* 1953.
Morgan, Arthur E. *The Making of the TVA.* 1974.
Selznick, Philip. *TVA and the Grass Roots: A Study in the Sociology of Formal Organization.* 1950.

OTIS L. GRAHAM, JR., and ELIZABETH KOED

TENURE OF OFFICE ACT.

The length of the term of public officials is specified by a tenure of office act. Such an act may also set forth the grounds on which the officials may be removed and may require the approval of the Senate for removals. By the Tenure of Office Act of 1820 (3 Stat. 582) Congress provided that certain officers involved with the collection or disbursement of funds, including district attorneys, collectors and surveyors of customs, and officials of public land offices, be appointed for terms of four years. It also specified that they served "at pleasure," implying that the President could remove such officers. President James Monroe signed the bill without objection, but former President James Madison warned that if Congress could displace officers every four years, "it can do so at the end of every year" and "the tenure will be at the pleasure of the Senate." Although Monroe and John Quincy Adams reappointed all such officials to new terms and resisted party pressure to put in new people, President Andrew Jackson subscribed to the principle of "rotation of office" and used the law to provide his congressional followers with PATRONAGE appointments and to build up the new DEMOCRATIC PARTY.

The term *Tenure of Office Act* usually refers to the Tenure of Office Act (14 Stat. 430) passed by Congress over President Andrew Johnson's veto on 2 March 1867. It provided that any person holding a civil office to which he had been appointed with the ADVICE AND CONSENT of the Senate was to hold that office until a successor was in like manner appointed. An additional clause stating that the secretaries of State, Treasury, War, Navy, and Interior, as well as the Postmaster General and Attorney General, "shall hold their offices . . . during the term of the President by whom they may have been appointed, and for one month thereafter, subject to removal by and with the advice and consent of the Senate." When any officer (except a judge) thus appointed should be shown guilty of misconduct in office or of a criminal offense or incapable of performing his duties, the President might suspend him and designate another person to perform his duties until the next meeting of the Senate. At that time the President would have twenty days to report to the Senate, which would act on the suspension by concurring or refusing. In the latter case the suspended person could immediately resume the functions of the office.

The Tenure of Office Act of 1867 was intended by RADICAL REPUBLICANS to curb Johnson's patronage power, to eliminate his influence in Congress, and to ensure that the President could not remove Secretary of War EDWIN M. STANTON, who was in overall charge of RECONSTRUCTION. Congress also passed the Army Appropriations Bill of 1867, which effectively removed Johnson's control over General of the Army Ulysses S. Grant—a provision strongly backed both by Grant and by the Secretary of War. On 21 February 1868, Johnson removed Stanton and replaced him with Adjutant General Lorenzo Thomas. Stanton remained in the War Department and posted armed guards. He arranged to have Thomas arrested for violating the Tenure of Office Act but then had the charges dropped to avoid a court case that might have invalidated the law. In fighting his removal, Stanton had shifted grounds about the law, for during a CABINET discussion after Congress had passed the bill he had denounced it as unconstitutional, and he had even participated in drafting Johnson's veto message.

On 24 February the House of Representatives voted for the IMPEACHMENT OF ANDREW JOHNSON on the grounds that he had violated the Tenure of Office Act. Johnson argued at his trial in the Senate that removals were his constitutional prerogative and that the act was unconstitutional. He also claimed that his removal of Stanton was not covered by the law since Stanton had been appointed by Abraham Lincoln, an argument Stanton himself had made in the cabinet. Johnson insisted that the law could not prevent the President from removing an official appointed by his predecessor but could only cover appointments he himself had made. Finally, Johnson argued that a President should not be impeached for taking an action that would result in a court test to determine the constitutionality of a statute that he believed infringed upon his prerogatives. After his acquittal by a one-vote margin Johnson compromised with Congress and named a general favored by Radical Republicans to be Secretary of War.

Near the end of Johnson's presidency the House voted to repeal the Tenure of Office Act, but the Senate took no action. President Grant called for its repeal in his first annual message in 1869, letting it be known that so long as it remained in force he would nominate no one for office. The Republicans in the House, eager for presidential patronage, quickly repealed the law. The Senate resisted but, in a compromise with the House (16 Stat. 6), dropped the requirements that the President report his reasons for removal to the Senate and that the Senate consent to the removal. The compromise did, however, retain the provision that an official who had been suspended retained office until the Senate consented to his successor. Grant agreed to the compromise and lost an opportunity to use his public prestige to restore presidential power.

Grant's failure to act decisively cost his successor dearly. Rutherford B. Hayes spent eighteen months trying to fire Chester A. Arthur, Collector of Customs for the Port of New York, and two other officials. Senator Roscoe Conkling of New York used the provisions of the Tenure of Office Act to keep Arthur and his colleagues in their posts. Eventually, when the Senate went out of session, Hayes suspended them and made new recess appointments, but the lengthy struggle demonstrated to the nation that the President had not yet gained mastery over civil administration.

When President Grover Cleveland assumed office (with Democratic control of the House) the Senate Republicans used the Tenure of Office Act to protect Republican appointees. Cleveland suspended 634 officials between his INAUGURATION and the opening session of Congress, sending his recess nominations to the Senate when Congress convened. Cleveland refused to honor Senate requests for information about the suspensions. Although the Senate passed a resolution condemning the refusal and indicating that it would refuse to consent to new nominations when such requests for information were denied, public opinion swung behind the President and the Senate capitulated. Soon thereafter the Senate repealed the Tenure of Office Act, with only one Republican voting in opposition (24 Stat. 500).

BIBLIOGRAPHY

Benedict, Michael. *The Impeachment and Trial of Andrew Johnson.* 1973.

Cleveland, Grover. *Presidential Problems.* 1904.

Fisher, Louis, "Grover Cleveland against the Senate." *Congressional Studies* 7 (1979): 11–25.

White, Leonard D. *The Jeffersonians: A Study in Administrative History, 1801–1829.* 1951.

White, Leonard D. *The Republican Era: A Study in Administrative History, 1869–1901.* 1958.

RICHARD M. PIOUS

TERM AND TENURE. Issues concerning the President's term and tenure have vexed the nation since the first week of the CONSTITUTIONAL CONVENTION of 1787. Among the longstanding and recurring debates are: How long should the President's term be? How many terms should the President serve? When should the President's term begin and end?

The convention was consumed by questions of presidential term and tenure. Afterward, dissatisfied with the delegates' decision to allow the President unlimited eligibility for reelection, President Thomas Jefferson managed to establish a two-term limit as a matter of tradition. In the twentieth century, two of the four constitutional amendments that have modified the presidency (the Twentieth and Twenty-second) deal with issues of term and tenure. Other possible amendments, such as a single six-year term for the President, have been proposed throughout American history.

The Constitutional Convention. Delegates to the Constitutional Convention began their labors in May 1787 by making one set of decisions about the President's term and tenure and, after numerous twists and turns, ended in September by making an entirely different set.

The delegates initially proposed to establish congressional election of the President to a seven-year term with no possibility of reelection. In the minds of most delegates, these three conditions were carefully connected. For example, if Congress was to choose the President, then the President should only serve one term. The reason, as George Mason of Virginia stated, was that if legislative reelection were permitted, there

would exist a constant "temptation on the part of the Executive to intrigue with the Legislature for a re-appointment," using political patronage and illegitimate favors in effect to buy votes.

As the convention wore on, the advantages delegates saw in eligibility for reelection became steadily more numerous. Not only would the country have a way to keep a good President in office, but reeligibility would give the President what GOUVERNEUR MORRIS of Pennsylvania called "the great motive to good behavior, the hope of being rewarded with a re-appointment." Morris also noted the dangers of not allowing the President to stand for reelection: "Shut the Civil road to Glory & he may be compelled to seek it by the sword."

To complicate their task further, the delegates' need to choose between election by Congress and presidential reeligibility implied a related choice between a longer term and a shorter one, seven years or four years. If the President was to be chosen by Congress for a single term only, the delegates believed, the term should be long. If the President was eligible for reelection, a shorter term was preferable.

In September, the convention resolved its dilemma by creating the ELECTORAL COLLEGE. Having taken presidential selection out of the hands of Congress, the delegates felt free to remove all restrictions on the President's right to run for an unlimited number of four-year terms.

The Constitutional Convention did not establish a starting date for the President's term. Instead, after the Constitution was ratified in 1788, the "old Congress" of the Articles of Confederation declared 4 March 1789 as the date "for commencing proceedings under the said Constitution." Congress passed a law in 1792 that codified the 4 March after each presidential election as the date on which the President's term would begin and end.

The Two-term Tradition. Thomas Jefferson, who was minister to France at the time of the Constitution Convention, had always opposed unrestricted presidential reeligibility. In 1807, as the end of Jefferson's second term as President drew near, the legislatures of eight states petitioned him to run for a third term. Jefferson refused in a letter to the Vermont legislature:

If some termination to the services of the Chief Magistrate be not fixed by the Constitution, or supplied by practice, his office, nominally four years, will in fact become for life, and history shows how easily that degenerates into inheritance. . . . I should unwillingly be the person who, disregarding the sound precedent set by an illustrious predecessor [George Washington] should furnish the first example of prolongation beyond the second term of office.

Although Jefferson's invocation of Washington was not altogether accurate (Washington retired from the presidency after two terms, he wrote in his FAREWELL ADDRESS, because he longed for "the shade of retirement"), the two-term limit quickly and securely took root in the American political tradition. Each of the first nine Presidents sought two terms but no more.

In 1840, the WHIG PARTY took Jefferson's precedent one step further, arguing that one four-year term was all that a President should serve. Most voters, including many Democrats, seem to have agreed: from 1840 to 1860 no President was even nominated to run for a second term. Although Abraham Lincoln restored the TWO-TERM TRADITION to respectability by winning reelection in 1864, he was more the exception than the rule. Of the first thirty-one Presidents (Washington to Herbert Hoover), twenty served one term or less and none served more than two terms. Even so, congressional discontent with the Constitution's provision for unlimited reeligibility simmered steadily on the legislative back burner. More than two hundred resolutions to limit the President's tenure were introduced between 1789 and 1928.

The two-term tradition was broken by the thirty-second President, Franklin D. Roosevelt. Elected in 1932 and reelected in 1936, Roosevelt became steadily more frustrated as his second term wore on with congressional resistance to his programs and policies. In 1939, WORLD WAR II broke out in Europe and Asia, posing a variety of risks to American security that made the argument for keeping a steady hand at the tiller of the ship of state uniquely persuasive. Waiting until the Democratic convention in July 1940 to signal his intention, Roosevelt finally agreed to be nominated for a third term. The delegates overwhelmingly approved his decision.

Roosevelt's Republican opponents emblazoned "No Third Term!" on their campaign banners, and public opinion polls found that the voters were deeply divided over the propriety of Roosevelt's candidacy. Wartime insecurity won him reelection against the Republican nominee, business leader WENDELL WILLKIE, but by a much narrower margin than in 1936—5 million popular votes, compared with 11 million. In 1944, with the United States and its allies nearing victory in the war, Roosevelt won a fourth term, by 3 million votes. He died on 12 April 1945 less than three months after his inauguration.

The Twenty-second Amendment. Republicans and conservative southern Democrats had chafed under Roosevelt's twelve-year reign as President; in the midterm elections of 1946, the REPUBLICAN PARTY took control of Congress for the first time since 1930. On 6 February 1947, less than five weeks after the opening of the Eightieth Congress, the House of Representatives passed a strict two-term-limit amendment to the Constitution by a vote of 285 to 121. Republicans supported the amendment unanimously (238–0); Democrats opposed it by 121 to 47, with most of the yea votes coming from southerners.

Five weeks later, on 12 March, the Senate passed a slightly different version of the amendment by a vote of 59 to 23. (The Senate version allowed a President who had served one full term and, because of succession, less than half of another, to run for reelection one time.) Again, the Republicans were unanimous (46–0); Democrats opposed the amendment by a vote of 23 to 13. On March 24, after the differences between the two houses' versions were ironed out in favor of the Senate, Congress officially sent the amendment to the states for ratification. The TWENTY-SECOND AMENDMENT became part of the Constitution three years and eleven months later, in February 1951—the longest time any constitutional amendment has taken to be ratified. Harry S. Truman, the incumbent President at the time, was exempted from the term limit.

Although the voting in Congress on the Twenty-second Amendment was partisan, the public debate was framed in philosophical terms. Supporters contended that the limit would protect Americans against the threat of an overly personalized presidency; opponents rejoined that if the people though the President had been in office too long, they could simply vote the incumbent out. Virtually no attention was given to the careful and thoughtful debates at the Constitutional Convention that underlay the original Constitution's lack of a restriction on presidential reeligibility. Nor did Congress foresee the effects of the two-term limit on the vice presidency. With second-term Presidents barred from seeking reelection, their VICE PRESIDENTS were free to campaign openly for the party's presidential nomination virtually from the start of the President's second term, as Richard M. Nixon and George Bush successfully did in 1960 and 1988, respectively.

So few Presidents have served two full terms since the Twenty-second Amendment was enacted that its effects on the presidency are hard to measure. One President was assassinated (John F. Kennedy), one resigned (Richard Nixon), one declined to run (Lyndon B. Johnson), and three were defeated in their bids for reelection (Gerald R. Ford, Jimmy Carter, and George Bush). The constraints of the constitutional two-term limit, then, have been felt by only two Presidents, both of them Republicans: Dwight D. Eisenhower in 1960 and Ronald Reagan in 1988.

Eisenhower publicly expressed "deep reservations" about the Twenty-second Amendment while in office; according to John Eisenhower, his son and deputy chief of staff, the President would have liked to run for a third term. During Reagan's second term, he unsuccessfully campaigned for a constitutional amendment that would repeal the two-term limit. Public opinion polls have consistently shown that although Americans thought at the time that Eisenhower and Reagan were good Presidents, they have consistently wanted to preserve the Twenty-second Amendment.

The Twentieth Amendment. The inauguration date that was instituted by Congress in 1792 left a four-month interregnum between the presidential election on the first Tuesday after the first Monday in November and the President's inauguration on the following 4 March. In the 1920s, Sen. George W. Norris of Nebraska, arguing that the March date was an artifact of the horse-and-buggy days of travel and communication and that four months was too long a time to have, in effect, two Presidents, campaigned for a constitutional amendment that would advance the start of the term.

Congress passed the TWENTIETH AMENDMENT on 2 March 1932. One section of the amendment provided that the President's term would begin at noon on the January 20 following the election. It was ratified without controversy and became part of the Constitution in 1933.

Proposed Reforms. Issues of presidential term and tenure, which were the subject of extensive deliberation at the Constitutional Convention and have already prompted two amendments to the Constitution, remain unresolved in American political discussion. As noted earlier, a campaign was launched by Republicans in the late 1980s to repeal the Twenty-second Amendment and restore the original Constitution's provision for unlimited reeligibility. A different, more longstanding and widely discussed idea is to limit the President to a single SIX-YEAR PRESIDENTIAL TERM. Advocates, including Presidents Andrew Jackson, Woodrow Wilson, Eisenhower, Johnson, and Carter, traditionally have claimed that awarding the President one long term would free him from the unwelcome pressures of reelection and grant the administration more time to accomplish its long-term objectives. Critics point out that under a single six-year term, an unpopular President would serve two years longer than under the current system and a popular President would be forced out two years sooner. In any event,

despite the ongoing discussion, no proposed amendment affecting the President's term and tenure has gained widespread public support.

BIBLIOGRAPHY

Milkis, Sidney M., and Michael Nelson. *The American Presidency: Origins and Development, 1776–1990.* 1990.

Sundquist, James L. *Constitutional Reform and Effective Government.* 1982.

Willis, Paul G., and George L. Willis. "The Politics of the Twenty-second Amendment." *Western Political Quarterly* 5 (September 1952): 469–482.

MICHAEL NELSON

TEXAS, ANNEXATION OF. American interest in the acquisition of Texas began in 1803 when American and Spanish authorities disagreed on whether the Spanish province of Texas was a part of the LOUISIANA PURCHASE. Partly because the American claim was weak and chiefly to secure a boundary between Spanish and American territories across the continent, the United States conceded all American claims to Texas in the Adams-Ónis Treaty with Spain in 1821.

American interest in Texas continued, however. Although Presidents John Quincy Adams and Andrew Jackson tried and failed to purchase Texas from the newly independent Mexico between 1821 and 1835, American settlers emigrated both legally and illegally into the area. By 1835, they outnumbered the Mexicans and demanded more and more local rule. In 1836 these Texans rose in revolution and established the beleaguered Republic of Texas.

President Andrew Jackson recognized the Republic of Texas on 3 March 1837, his last day in office. He had hoped to annex the territory, but considerable opposition among antislavery northerners who opposed the admission of any new slave territory to the Union forced Jackson to move slowly. Jackson's handpicked successor, Martin Van Buren of New York, was considerably less interested in annexation than Jackson. The combination of antislavery opposition to annexation, a severe economic depression, and concern that annexation could lead to war with Mexico led him to reject a formal Texan request for annexation.

The Texas question lay dormant until President John Tyler revived interest in annexation in 1843. Tyler, a Virginian who was committed to annexation and concerned that Britain was promoting the abolition of SLAVERY in the republic, orchestrated a propaganda effort aimed at winning popular support for annexation. In January 1844, he initiated covert negotiations for a treaty of annexation and promised Texas military protection should Mexico attack Texas when the treaty became known.

When Secretary of State Abel Upshur was killed in an accident, Tyler appointed JOHN C. CALHOUN, the powerful former Senator from South Carolina, as Upshur's successor to complete the negotiations for the United States. Calhoun's explicit defense of slavery, expressed in a letter to Britain included in the diplomatic papers that he sent to the Senate, outraged northerners, who came to regard annexation as a plot by an "aggressive slavocracy" to extend and perpetuate slavery in North America. The Senate rejected the treaty by a partisan and sectional vote of 35 to 16 on 8 June 1844.

Far from disappearing as an issue, the Texas question had already become a vital part of the campaign of 1844. The Whig candidate, HENRY CLAY, had made an agreement with the likely Democratic contender, Martin Van Buren, to avoid the issue, but the Democrats ignored Van Buren at their convention and nominated a DARK HORSE, James K. Polk of Tennessee, on a platform that called for the immediate annexation of Texas. During the campaign, Clay equivocated on annexation. Polk won the election in a close contest.

President Tyler chose to interpret Polk's election as a mandate for annexation, and realizing that annexationists did not have enough Senate votes to approve the Texas treaty, he called for ANNEXATION BY JOINT RESOLUTION of both houses of Congress. After considerable debate, the House passed the resolution 120 to 98, and the Senate followed suit 27 to 25. Tyler signed the measure on 1 March 1845. The Texas Congress unanimously voted to enter the United States on 16 June 1845, and a Texan constitutional convention agreed and approved a new constitution on 4 July. A bill for the admission of Texas to the Union as the twenty-eighth state passed the House of Representatives on 16 December and the Senate on 22 December, and President Polk signed the measure on 29 December.

The annexation of Texas inflamed sectional hostility, contributed to the creation of the FREE-SOIL PARTY, and set in motion events that led directly to the MEXICAN WAR in 1846.

BIBLIOGRAPHY

Morgan, Robert J. *A Whig Embattled: The Presidency under John Tyler.* 1954.

Peterson, Norma Lois. *The Presidencies of William Henry Harrison and John Tyler.* 1989.

Pletcher, David M. *The Diplomacy of Annexation: Texas, Oregon, and the Mexican War.* 1973.

Sellers, Charles G. *James K. Polk: Continentalist, 1843–1846.* 1966.

KINLEY BRAUER

TEXTBOOK PRESIDENCY. The term *textbook presidency* was coined by Thomas Cronin and developed in his book *The State of the Presidency* (1975). It refers to the idealized view of the presidency presented in introductory high school and college textbooks, which cast the President as "the central instrument of democracy." According to this idealized view, the President is the primary policy-maker in the American political system; only the President can effect positive change in American government and policy; the President should be the nation's personal and moral leader; and only the right person can fulfill the role of President—and the American electoral system will find him.

The image of the textbook president developed in the post–WORLD WAR II environment, when the United States became a world power and television was beginning to bring the world into every living room. The image of the President as a wise, powerful, and benevolent leader fulfilled the hopes of the nation as it emerged from a period of economic depression and war.

The national mood in the 1950s and 1960s contributed to the growth of this ideal. In an era that believed in heroes, the President came to be seen as a national hero and symbol of strength. For example, almost consistently from 1953 to 1972, the incumbent President was judged the "most admired man" in the annual Gallup poll (with the exception of 1967 and 1968, when President Lyndon B. Johnson was edged out by former President Dwight D. Eisenhower.) The national stature of the President was fostered by the belief that, regardless of the partisan battle waged for election, once a President had taken the oath of office, it was the duty of all Americans to unite behind him. During this period, the government also experienced unprecedented growth in size as well as in extent of involvement in Americans' lives. The President emerged as the most visible leader—marshalling extensive resources of information and power. Proponents of the textbook presidency believe that strong presidential leadership—leadership that is informed and responsive to the demands of the electorate—is vital to push policies through the complex maze of modern government and politics. Even critics writing during this period did not question the need for a strong President to provide direction on major policy issues.

The model of the textbook presidency was subject to reconsideration in the era after the VIETNAM WAR and the WATERGATE AFFAIR. The IMPERIAL PRESIDENCIES of Johnson and Richard M. Nixon prompted disillusionment in the ideal of the textbook presidency. Nonetheless, the textbook presidency image has persevered in introductory textbooks and, in some cases, been rekindled outside the classroom, as voters look for "textbook" presidential candidates who can recapture the idealized image of the office.

[*See also* COMMENTATORS ON THE PRESIDENCY.]

BIBLIOGRAPHY

Cronin, Thomas. *The State of the Presidency*. 1975.

MARGARET JANE WYSZOMIRSKI

THANKSGIVING PROCLAMATIONS.

The custom of proclaiming public days of thanksgiving, prayer, and fasting dates back to the earliest days of the colonies, and the practice was embraced by the federal government from its inception. Responding to a call from Congress, President George Washington declared the first day of thanksgiving under the new Constitution on Thursday, 26 November 1789. John Adams similarly proclaimed two days of prayer and fasting while President. Thomas Jefferson abandoned the practice, arguing that no constitutional power existed for him to declare days of religious obligation. When Andrew Jackson embraced the same doctrine during a worldwide outbreak of Asiatic cholera in 1832, he provoked an angry debate on the subject in Congress. Subsequent Presidents proclaimed days of thanksgiving and prayer on an irregular basis until the administration of Abraham Lincoln. Lincoln adopted the suggestion of reformer Sarah Hale and turned Thanksgiving Day into an annual event, reserving the last Thursday in November for this purpose in 1863. The festival has been observed annually ever since. Following his predecessors, Lincoln also appointed periodic days of fasting and prayer during the CIVIL WAR, a practice that some later Presidents also adopted during times of crisis. In 1952, Congress regularized such days by establishing a yearly day of national prayer.

The dominant theme articulated by most Presidents in their Thanksgiving Day and prayer day proclamations is that God is the author of every good and, hence, citizens are urged to ask God for continued blessings and to render thanks for those blessings already bestowed. Other themes have also been enunciated, depending on the President. Proclamations up through the Civil War often stressed the need for citizens to ask God for forgiveness for national sins, exhorted citizens to virtuous behavior, and even acknowledged the justice of God's judgments on national transgressions. Lincoln especially emphasized the last point, declaring in an 1861 proclamation that the Civil War constituted God's "punishment . . . most richly deserved" for "our . . . faults and crimes as a nation and as individuals." This thought anticipated Lincoln's later argument in his profound Second Inaugural Address of 1865.

After the Civil War, the high moral tone of thanksgiving and prayer proclamations temporarily diminished, and they primarily became vehicles for touting national prosperity. Sin, self-sacrifice, and judgment generally disappeared as themes. These sterner ideas resurfaced at the end of the century, however, in proclamations issued by Grover Cleveland, and they have appeared intermittently in proclamations ever since. When WORLD WAR II ended, for example, President Harry S. Truman used a thanksgiving proclamation to urge civic self-sacrifice by calling on Americans to "aid . . . sufferers in war-devastated lands."

Although thanksgiving and prayer proclamations are chiefly a rhetorical responsibility of the presidency, they fulfill an important theoretical function in America's constitutional system. Unlike the Roman Caesars or the totalitarian regimes of more recent times, the government of the United States does not claim the prerogatives of God. Thanksgiving and prayer proclamations remind Americans of this fact by acknowledging that in America, worship and absolute obedience are reserved for the Almighty alone.

BIBLIOGRAPHY

Richardson, James D., ed. *A Compilation of the Messages and Papers of the Presidents*. 1911.
Stokes, Anson Phelps. "Government Religious Observance of Special Days and Occasions." In *Church and State in the United States*. 3 vols. 1950. Vol. 3, pp. 176–200.

JOHN G. WEST, JR.

THEORIES OF THE PRESIDENCY.

The President is arguably the most closely watched, highly scrutinized, and frequently chronicled individual in the United States. Yet the office of the President is said by many to be the most difficult aspect of American government to comprehend. A great deal may be documented and understood about the men who have held the office of the presidency, but far less is known about the institution and how it operates within the larger political system.

Various theories have developed to explain the

office of the presidency. Some describe the functions of the office and the constraints under which it operates, while others develop prescriptions for effective PRESIDENTIAL LEADERSHIP or categorize presidential behavior and leadership in terms of personality characteristics or psychological development.

A successful unified theory of the presidency requires a balance between both personal and historical characteristics. It should not only describe the President as a human being but also evaluate presidential performance and the viability of the institution of the presidency within the political system. Many theories fall short in developing both aspects equally.

Certain theories of the presidency are normative, but most echo the empirical emphasis of social science research. Although the empirical theories are wide-ranging, they fall into four broad categories, focusing on the person in the office, the political presidency, the office (or institution) of the presidency, or the presidency in the context of the larger political system.

The Person in the Office. Theories that focus on the person in the office start with the assumption that the person occupying the office of President is the most important variable in determining the performance of the entire administration. In presidential biographies, for example, the author generally discusses the presidency in terms of a particular person and his political philosophy.

Psychological studies of the presidency, first seen in the 1970s, have been among the most interesting and popular pieces of scholarship to have emerged. James David Barber's *The Presidential Character: Predicting Performance in the White House* (1972) identifies various personality and character traits and then generalizes them to allow correlations with presidential leadership.

Barber's theory rests on understanding the extent to which the personality of a President influences that President's approach to the office. The "presidential personality," according to Barber, is determined chiefly by three factors: character, worldview, and style.

Barber places four personality traits (active, passive, positive, negative) on a two-by-two grid, producing four combinations (active/positive, active/negative, passive/positive, passive/negative), that can be used to define PRESIDENTIAL CHARACTER. Barber concludes that a President with an active/positive personality type makes the strongest and most effective leader because such a person views productivity as essential to the job and displays confidence in his ability to suceed. Barber presents his theory as a predictive model, suggesting that the electorate should select the right personality for a President to function effectively in office.

Barber's theory and others like it have their drawbacks, however. Because these psychological approaches concentrate solely on personality, they exclude or ignore many significant outside influences. As a result, they convey very little substantial information about the office of the presidency or the institutional variables that have an impact on a President's behavior. In fact, their psychological projections cannot even be supported because of a lack of adequate data. It is questionable whether the complex individuals who become American Presidents can be pigeonholed so neatly into four simple types, despite the scheme's elegance.

The Political Presidency. Some theorists define the presidency as the outcome of a host of political forces. Their theories envision the President as one actor in an environment containing varied and independent power bases, including governmental actors (Congress, the courts, and the bureaucracy) and outside forces such as the press, organized interests, and the public. In order to be persuasive, Presidents must be able to exert influence over each of these areas.

Richard Neustadt's *Presidential Power: the Politics of Leadership* (1960) is a prime example of this approach. In Neustadt's view, an effective President harnesses his power, uses all the resources at his disposal, and takes an activist role in every aspect of his job. Presidential power comes through an ability to persuade the other actors in the political system.

The imperative of political persuasion requires Presidents to use several important tools at their disposal, including prestige and popularity. Presidents have prestige when there is a sense among those in Washington that the public will back presidential decisions. As Neustadt points out, it is much harder to say no to a President whose record the public supports. This relates to presidential popularity. Popular Presidents can often invoke voter pressure to help sway colleagues.

Samuel Kernell, in *Going Public: New Strategies of Presidential Leadership* (1986), focuses on the role of the public. In one sense, Kernell tries to extend and refine Neustadt's framework, explaining presidential leadership strategies in the post-Neustadt, media age. Kernell argues that presidential power is gained through manipulating and responding to public opinion. Using this strategy, Presidents can go over the heads of Congress and the other traditional players in the political process to appeal directly to the public and garner support for their policy agenda.

Kernell argues that his theory takes account of the changes in society and in technology since the emergence of Neustadt's theory on presidential power. In the contemporary era, Presidents place greater emphasis on achieving public support than on mastering the arts of political bargaining and negotiation. He argues that the President's knowledge of the Washington community has dwindled in part because the system of PRESIDENTIAL PRIMARIES has evolved so that non–Washington insiders are able to win the presidency. In addition, he notes the decline of "institutional pluralism," which has contributed to the lack of a closely knit political community that values honor and commitment. If independent political actors, like members of Congress have few institutional loyalties and if Washington becomes individualized (as opposed to institutionalized), directly appealing to the public will remain, according to Kernell, a viable political option.

Going to the public, however, is a steep political gamble that can damage a President's long-run chances for success. Kernell points out that even when appealing to the public is an option, negotiation and political bargaining should not be entirely bypassed.

Edward Tufte's *Political Control of the Economy* (1978) explores how presidential power is exercised through control of the nation's economy and how the health of the economy affects the electoral fate of the President. Jeff Fishel's *Presidents and Promises* (1985) describes how Presidents gain political power—and ultimately reelection—by living up to the promises they make to the American public or how they lose clout by failing to meet expectations. Some critics of these power-based theories argue that, by concentrating on the personal politics and actions of the President, they ignore the goals and methods of the administration as well as the many factors that influence presidential behavior, such as political ideology. Other critics find that these theories exaggerate the confrontational nature of the political system by suggesting that Presidents are engaged in a constant battle to overcome the conflicting interests and forces around them.

The Office and the Person. This is the institutional approach to understanding the presidency. Ever since Franklin D. Roosevelt's BROWNLOW COMMITTEE proposed the creation of the EXECUTIVE OFFICE OF THE PRESIDENT (EOP), the presidency has become increasingly institutionalized. Staff and resources have constantly expanded to create the huge EOP that exists today. Unsurprisingly, a number of recent theories have focused on the institutionalized presidency.

Richard Nathan's *The Administrative Presidency* (1983) focuses on the relationship between elected officials and career bureaucrats and poses the central question, "To what extent and in what way should politicians manage the bureaucracy?" He argues that to achieve domestic policy goals in the modern era of big government, the President must attempt to penetrate and manage the bureaucracy.

Nathan uses examples from the presidencies of Richard M. Nixon and Ronald Reagan to identify elements of the ADMINISTRATIVE PRESIDENCY strategy. According to Nathan, Nixon in his first term took a legislative-strategy approach to policy-making, focusing on the Congress and virtually excluding the domestic departments. Toward the end of his first term, Nixon shifted to an administrative approach. He reduced the legislative agenda, cut the WHITE HOUSE STAFF, and brought in a new breed of CABINET secretaries—people who were considered loyal to the President's policy goals. In addition, drastic changes were made at the sub-Cabinet level. Nathan believes that Nixon was probably on the right track with the administrative approach he adopted for his second term. Unfortunately, because his second term was cut short by the WATERGATE AFFAIR, he was never able to carry out many of his domestic initiatives.

Reagan, according to Nathan, also employed the administrative presidency strategy. Reagan's agenda included a strong commitment to reducing the size and scope of the federal government in domestic affairs. Using a dual strategy, he pushed his domestic program through the budget process in the legislature while at the same time attempting to control the federal bureaucracy.

Reagan attempted to structure the domestic agencies in such a way that they were united by the common goals of his administration. He penetrated the operations of the bureaucracy and implemented his policies by appointing loyal and committed policy officials. Nathan concludes that, to succeed, future Presidents must adopt an administrative presidency strategy. He argues that "in a complex, technologically advanced society in which the role of government is pervasive, much of what we would define as policy making is done through the execution of laws in the management process."

James Pfiffner's *The Strategic Presidency: Hitting the Ground Running* (1988) attempts to set out a strategy for a successful transition to the presidency that centers on a mastery of the internal structures of the office of the President [see STRATEGIC PRESIDENCY]. A modern President must seize executive power at the outset, not take it for granted. Pfiffner argues that the postelection window of opportunity has grown so narrow that a contemporary President must claim his victory as a mandate for immediate action and make sure that his staff, Cabinet, and legislative agenda are firmly in place when he takes office.

According to Pfiffner's plan, recruiting a White House staff and Cabinet must be a presidential candidate's first priority. Some key posts should be filled well ahead of election day. A President should choose a WHITE HOUSE CHIEF OF STAFF who will act as an "honest broker," negotiating with Cabinet secretaries on budgets and personnel and allowing them access to the President. Cabinet members should be independent but loyal, agreeing to operate within budget constraints and to clear major policy decisions with the White House.

Pfiffner details several successful strategies used by new Presidents: Lyndon B. Johnson's courting of Congress, Ronald Reagan's skillful use of the media, and Gerald Ford's Economic Policy Board. He also highlights some administrations' blunders and missteps, maintaining that the transition process is best served by studying past mistakes.

Another genre of the institutionally focused presidential theory examines the decision-making process. A classic example is Graham Allison's *Essence of Decision: Explaining the Cuban Missile Crisis* (1971), which attempts to explain why Presidents choose a certain course of action and what factors influence their decision. Using the CUBAN MISSILE CRISIS as a case study, Allison develops three models of presidential decision making.

The first model, based on the so-called rational actor, is commonly assumed to be the dominant mode of presidential decision making. Government behavior is action "chosen by a unitary, rational decision-maker: centrally controlled, completely informed, and value maximizing." Allison admits that this model does no account for the intricacies of decision making in the modern era. A second model emphasizes the processes and procedures of government organizations that operate largely independently of the President. The third model explains how politics affects the decision-making process, with decisions seen as resulting from various bargaining games among many governmental actors. These factors limit the President's ability to make executive decisions.

Other authors have offered institutionally based theories of the presidency: Aaron Wildavsky's work on the budgetary process, Stephen Wayne's analysis of the legislative process, and Hugh Heclo's studies on the OFFICE OF MANAGEMENT AND BUDGET (OMB) are notable examples. These theories regard the presidency first and foremost as an institution, concentrating more on the structures, functions, and operations of the presidency than on the person who occupies the office.

Some critics have argued that institutional theories tend to be overly descriptive, offering insight into how the presidency works but providing little if any analysis of policy outcomes. Another common criticism is that by emphasizing structure and process, these theories ignore the importance of ideology, personality, and political skill in determining a President's success.

The Office in the Political System. Another group of theories looks at the presidency as it functions in the larger political system. In a 1966 article, Wildavsky argued that, although the United States has one President, "it has two presidencies." One presidency focuses on domestic policy, the other on FOREIGN AFFAIRS. Almost invariably the latter has the greater success. In domestic policy, the President faces resistance from Congress, special interest groups, and the public, but he encounters considerably less resistance in mapping out a strategy for foreign policy [*see* TWO PRESIDENCIES].

Steven Skowronek's article "Presidential Leadership in Political Time" (1984) takes issue with studies that characterize the presidency as a constant struggle between the man and the system, emphasizing political skill and personal character. He argues that these accounts obscure crucial changes in the political system over time. Skowronek refers to "political time" rather than historical time, viewing the history of the presidency as episodic rather than evolutionary.

To support his theory, Skowronek identifies patterns of political leadership that transcend historical and personal differences. He draws parallels between the presidencies of Andrew Jackson and Franklin D. Roosevelt (both of whom he characterizes as regime builders); James K. Polk and John F. Kennedy (managers in established regimes); and Franklin Pierce and Jimmy Carter (both of whom faced the challenge of establishing credibility in an enervated regime).

Theories about the office in the political system often start with the premise that the political system has undermined the office of the presidency. Congress has become too decentralized, the bureaucracy too powerful, political parties too weak, and the media too adversarial. While the President's capacity to lead has been diminished, public expectations of the presidency have increased. As Michael Nelson points out, these theories highlight the growing gap between what Presidents are capable of doing and what they are expected to do.

One example of this approach is Theodore Lowi's *The End of Liberalism* (1969), which describes the decline of organized parties and the rise of what he calls "interest group liberalism." According to Lowi, government attempted to respond to the needs for organized interests by assuming responsibility for their programs. As a result, many sources of power acted independently and the public interest became merely an amalgam of various claims and interests. The rise of interest groups might have made the American political system more representative, but Lowi concludes that this development actually made democratic institutions less responsive and unable to function capably. In 1979, Lowi argued that throughout the 1960s and 1970s the President amassed a great deal of power but that because the political system evolved as it did he was unable to exercise that power for the good of the nation.

Another scholar who touches on these themes is Godfrey Hodgson. In *All Things to All Men* (1980), he argues that as the demands placed on the President have grown in both volume and complexity, his ability to meet those demands has declined. While the President still has vast powers (including the power to start a nuclear war or to invade another country), he is paralyzed when it comes to dealing with many domestic policy issues (such as the federal budget, education, and various social programs). Drawing on the work of Wildavsky, Hodgson argues that the gridlock that the President faces stems from "institutional competitors": the bureaucracy, special interests (which have taken over the role of political parties), and a growing and changing media that is more and more difficult to master and control.

Many of these theories about the "imperiled" or "fettered" presidency appears after the weak (and what some perceived to be ineffectual) presidencies of Ford and Carter. These theories sought systemic explanations for the failures of presidential leadership, but Reagan's successes in 1981 quickly called into question many of their most basic assumptions and conclusions. The problems encountered by Reagan, however, especially in his second term, revived more skeptical theories. A series of works in the late 1980s and early 1990s from a different group of activists (conservatives such as Gordon Crovitz and Terry Eastland) concluded that the presidency had been hobbled to the extent that serious constitutional change was required to restore energy to the executive.

Normative Theories. Several theories are explicitly normative, that is, based on what the presidency *should* be. Sometimes normative theorists assume that the executive should be the most powerful branch of government: a STRONG PRESIDENT will be a good President. As Michael Nelson puts it, "strength and goodness go hand in hand." Nelson groups these theories together under the heading of the savior model. The model's underlying rationale, as Nelson describes it, makes the President "the chief guardian of the na-

tional interest, not only in foreign policy because no one else can speak and act for the nation, but also in domestic affairs because of the pluralistic structure of government and society."

In a 1970 article entitled "Superman: Our Textbook President," Thomas Cronin described how studies in the 1950s and 1960s characterized the President as "benevolent" and "omnipotent" [*see* TEXTBOOK PRESIDENCY]. To some extent Richard Neustadt's work falls into this category, as does the early work of James MacGregor Burns. Some authors, such as Clinton Rossiter and Herman Finer, showed reverence for the institution. For many of these proponents of a strong presidency, their advocacy was closely connected with their liberal policy preferences. It is easy to understand why the tide quickly turned when presidential power was misused and even abused in the late 1960s and early 1970s.

Arthur Schlesinger's *The Imperial Presidency* (1973) illustrates the kind of negative assessments of presidential power that began to emerge in the 1970s [*see* IMPERIAL PRESIDENCY]. According to Schlesinger, the potential for the abuse of presidential power is inherent in our constitutional system of SEPARATION OF POWERS. Faced with a legislature that is large and slow-moving, a President may try to circumvent the Congress by building an independent power base.

Schlesinger sees the greatest potential for the abuse of power in the area of WAR POWERS. He points out, however, that the President cannot reach imperial heights without some acquiescence by Congress: "The assumption of power by the [imperial] president was gradual. . . . It was as much a matter of congressional abdication as of presidential usurpation." Congress has a responsibility, therefore, to prevent abuses of presidential power. Schlesinger does not advocate a weak presidency but, rather, seeks a middle ground: "The answer to the runaway presidency is not the messenger-boy presidency. . . . We need a strong presidency—but a strong presidency within the Constitution."

BIBLIOGRAPHY

Burns, James MacGregor. *Presidential Government*. 1965.
Finer, Herman. *The Presidency: Crisis and Regeneration*. 1960.
Nelson, Michael, ed. *The Presidency and the Political System*. 1984.
Rossiter, Clinton. *The American Presidency*. 1956.
Skowronek, Stephen. "Presidential Leadership in Political Time." In *The Presidency and the Political System*. Edited by Michael Nelson. 1984. Pp. 87–132.
Wildavsky, Aaron. "The Two Presidencies." *Trans-Action* 4 (December 1966): 7–14.

NORMAN ORNSTEIN

THIRD PARTIES. Given the nature of the American electoral process—the election of a single chief executive, the election of representatives to Congress within single-member districts, state-level election laws, and two-hundred years of tradition—presidential contests are dominated by two-party competition. Although numerous small parties and independent candidates have appeared on the ballot, they receive only a minute share of the popular votes. When third-party candidates manage to garner appreciable popular votes—more than 5 or 6 percent—they are inevitably met with surprise and hostility not just from their major-party opponents but the general public as well. Third parties are usually seen as inappropriate, even harmful, to the integrity of the American political process.

They are said to be only spoilers; by drawing away votes from the major parties a third party can prevent the election of a President by a true majority, not to mention the mischief it may cause in the ELECTORAL COLLEGE in a close presidential contest. This is often stated (and indeed theoretically possible), despite the fact that seldom have third parties denied the most popular of the two major parties the presidency. Yet the fear of disruption remains. It is also argued that third parties introduce foreign ideas, receive undue publicity, and influence the course of public policy in far greater proportion than their numbers can justify. Viewed from the conventional standards of their day, most of the significant third parties have called for radical changes in American society—from anti-slavery in the mid nineteenth century, to socialism in the early twentieth century, to segregation in the late 1960s—and this can be disquieting to public sensibilities.

Nonetheless, contemporary scholars view the role of third parties on the whole as a healthy one. They serve as a safety valve for discontent within a democratic framework, venting minority views that cannot find a home in the consensus-and-compromise oriented two major parties. In times of major political transitions in society, third parties have also served as "stepping-stones" as voters shift from one to the other of the major parties. As a matter of principle, third parties reflect the basic right of all citizens to organize freely within the electoral arena.

Policy Impacts. While few third-party candidates expect to win a presidential election, most believe that by raising issues and demonstrating support at the polls, they will affect the course of public policy. In this they have had mixed success. Immigration was not halted in the 1850s in response to the demands of the nativist KNOW-NOTHING (AMERICAN) PARTY, nor were railroads, telegraph, and telephone industries nationalized following the strong showing of the Populist Party in 1892. The Coolidge and Hoover administrations did not make the sweeping reforms in the industrial system called for by the 1924 PROGRESSIVE PARTY. After decades of campaigning, the Socialist Party failed to achieve its objective of nationalizing major industries.

Although third parties' programs may not be implemented directly or immediately, many of their ideas have been adopted by the major parties and enacted into public policy. The SLAVERY restriction and INTERNAL IMPROVEMENTS themes of the FREE-SOIL PARTY of 1848 and 1852 were seized by the REPUBLICAN PARTY of 1856, and both became public policy under the Republican administrations of the 1860s. Progressive taxation, regulation of railroads, child labor laws, and social insurance were ideas introduced into the political dialogue by Socialists, Farmer-Laborites, Progressives and Populists. The major portion of the NEW DEAL programs of Franklin D. Roosevelt can be traced to the Progressive platforms of the preceding decades. More contemporarily, following the election of Richard M. Nixon in the three-way race of 1968, the administration took steps to placate the constituency of GEORGE WALLACE's American Independence Party by postponing school desegregation deadlines, curtailing civil rights activities of the Justice Department, and appointing racially conservative judges to the federal courts.

Third parties have been especially prominent in battles over suffrage and election reform. The Populists, Progressives, and Socialists were advocating the direct election of United States senators, women's suffrage, the recall and referendum, primary elections, and corrupt practices legislation long before the major parties. On these as on most issues, however, the connection between third-party activity and their adoption was neither direct nor pervasive.

Explaining Third-Party Voting. What makes third parties so intriguing is that by the logic of the two-party system they should not appear, let alone garner any significant number of popular votes. Their candidates never win the presidency, their programs cannot be at all assured of success, and they must overcome the strong cultural antipathy and electoral rules designed to thwart them. Yet third parties have emerged as significant in one out of five presidential elections; receiving from the 8 percent of the popular presidential vote for the Anti-Mason Party in 1832, to 10 percent for the Free-Soilers in 1848, 21 percent for the American party in 1856, 13 percent for the Constitutional Union's and 18 percent for the Breckinridge

(Southern) Democrats in 1860, 8.5 percent for the Populists in 1892, 27 percent for Theodore Roosevelt's PROGRESSIVE (BULL MOOSE) PARTY and 6 percent for the Socialists in 1912, 16.5 percent for the Progressives of 1924, 13.5 percent for the American Independent Party in 1968, and 6.5 percent for John Anderson in 1980.

One of the more general explanations of third-party voting is that they are the product of the thwarted ambitions of major-party politicians. Indeed, third parties receiving numerous votes have been led by major party politicians prominent at the state or national level prior to their third-party bid. The 1924 Progressive candidate, Senator ROBERT M. LA FOLLETTE was the leader of the reformist wing of the Republican Party in Wisconsin and nationally for two decades before his third-party campaign. Similarly, George Wallace served as the Democratic governor of Alabama before and after his third-party candidacy in 1968. More recently, John Anderson was a Republican congressman from Illinois for two decades before leading the independent National Unity campaign in 1980. Three of the most prominent third-party contenders—Martin Van Buren in 1848, Millard Fillmore in 1856, and Theodore Roosevelt in 1912—formerly had been President of the United States under the banner of one of the major parties. There is a clear relationship between having a nationally prestigious candidate at the head of the ticket and a significant third-party vote. To find that third parties do best with nationally known political figures at the head of the ticket, however, only begs the questions of when and why such figures bolt from the major parties.

The explanation appears to be that there are three necessary conditions for a significant third party to emerge. Most important, there must be a departure from the normal bell-shaped or evenly spread distribution of opinion found on most major issues, with some views to the left and the right but the bulk of Americans in the middle. The absence of the "normal" distribution of views usually occurs in a period of intense social and political controversy which results in an estranged minority separated from the much larger majority opinion, such as in 1832, 1848, 1892, 1912 (especially with respect to the Socialist vote), 1924, and 1968. In an extremely rare case of bipolar distribution, the way is open for a centrist third party such as with the Constitutional Unionists of 1860 or possibly even the vote for John Anderson in 1980. Second, the minority position on the leading issues of the day must be either rejected or shunned by both major parties, alienating the minority. Finally, a politician or political group willing to exploit the situation by initiating a new party must step forward.

Also, the conditions appear to be cumulative; each is necessary for the next to operate. Except in a period of social and political crisis or the turmoil that can occur during a realignment of the major parties, politically active minorities are usually absorbed by the major parties. And, if the major parties take opposite positions on controversial issues, little leeway remains for a third party. Lastly, lacking an intense minority abandoned by both of the major parties, few politicians of repute will venture out to lead a third-party effort. It has taken the coincidence of all three conditions before Americans have flocked to third parties in any significant numbers.

The Withering of Third Parties. Even more predictable than the emergence of significant third parties is their demise. While parties such as the PROHIBITIONIST PARTY, Socialist Labor Party, and Libertarian Party have had long histories, no third party garnering a significant popular vote in a presidential election has returned to better its initial success. The consistent decline is principally due to two factors: the major parties' efforts to adopt their rhetoric if not their position on issues following the strong showing of a third party, and the inevitable lesson learned by the third-party candidates of the insurmountable obstacles they face competing within a system designed to foster only two parties. Consequently, by the following election the third-party constituency has a choice between an already defeated "extremist" third party with little hope of victory and a major party more sympathetic to its cause.

Once the major parties begin to undermine its position on one or two divisive issues, the third party is at a distinct disadvantage. The majors have the organizational resources, deep-rooted party attachments, moderate and reasonable image, and access to policy-making needed to deliver on campaign promises. They offer the hope of patronage and other rewards to the party activists. And the fervor aroused by the third party when it initially entered the two-party system is difficult to sustain.

Third parties also lose ground because of shifts in public concern. As a political crisis runs its course and its intensity subsides, the prospects for maintaining voter support for the third party diminishes. Thus a third party that in one election gains attention with a highly visible and divisive issue may find itself irrelevant and ignored by most voters four years hence as the system returns to its conventional two-party configuration.

BIBLIOGRAPHY

Mazmanian, Daniel A. *Third Parties in Presidential Elections.* 1974.

Rae, Douglas W. *The Political Consequences of Electoral Laws.* 1967.

Rosenstone, Steven J., Roy L. Behr, and Edward H. Lazarus. *Third Parties in America: Citizen Response to Major Party Failure.* 1984.

Smallwood, Frank. *The Other Candidates: Third Parties in Presidential Elections.* 1984.

Spitzer, Robert J. *The Right to Life Movement and Third Party Politics.* 1987.

Steadman, Murray S., and Susan W. Steadman. *Discontent at the Polls.* 1950.

DANIEL A. MAZMANIAN

THIRD-PARTY CANDIDATES. Third-party or insurgent candidates have contested all twentieth-century presidential elections. No nonmajor-party candidate has won the presidency, and, since, 1824, a major party candidate has won an outright ELECTORAL COLLEGE majority. Voting levels for nonmajor-party candidates have ranged from the minuscule to Theodore Roosevelt's 27.4 percent in 1912. Yet insurgent candidates continue to contest the presidency. What obstacles face an insurgent candidate, why do candidates choose to forgo the two-party system, and what is their overall political influence?

Barriers to Third Parties. Electoral laws and other institutional barriers present perhaps insuperable difficulties for alternative candidates; access to the ballot, fund-raising and federal financing, and the electoral system all impose obstacles. Alternative candidates first must ensure their names are on the presidential ballot, a difficult, costly, and time-consuming task requiring state by state organizational campaigns. Ballot requirements differ by state, and deadlines for ballot petitions are often early in the election year.

Campaign funding is a second barrier. No alternative candidate in this century (with the possible exception of H. ROSS PEROT) has had access to funding equal to major party presidential candidates. The Federal Election Campaign Act of 1974 exacerbates this division. This act, which guarantees set sums to the major-party campaigns, grants insurgent candidates funds retroactively, only after the candidate has received more than 5 percent of the national vote. Much of an alternative candidate's campaign is therefore devoted to fund-raising; the 5 percent minimum thus tends to eliminate potential candidates.

Perhaps the greatest institutional difficulty facing the insurgent presidential candidate is the electoral system itself. Political scientists argue that the single–member-district plurality system discourages third-party activity. In contrast to a proportional representation system, the single-member district does not reward the second- or third (or more) place finisher in any particular district. At first glance, however, the Electoral College for choosing the President appears to be an exception to this rule: the successful presidential candidate must have a majority (not just a plurality) of Electoral College votes; otherwise choice of the President goes to the House of Representatives, which widens the possible range of election outcomes. In the 1992 campaign, much speculation centered on whether Perot's candidacy would be sufficient to forestall an outright winner in the Electoral College. The majority provisions for Electoral College victory, however, appear to create a far greater political fluidity than has historically existed. The electoral votes for each state are winner-take-all; no system of proportional representation protects the second- or third-place finisher at the state level. Insurgent presidential candidates are therefore little better off than their counterparts at the congressional or state level: the electoral system does not reward partial success within particular states.

Just as problematic for outside presidential candidates is the widespread acceptance among politicians, political activists, theorists, and the voting public that America possesses a two-party system. With the exceptions of the 1815–1832, 1852–1856, and perhaps the 1892–1900 periods, two highly organized and competitive parties have functioned in the United States. The major parties are loosely organized, state-centered, permanent institutions whose purpose is winning electoral office. Theorists note that the party systems have been remarkably adept at altering policy positions and voter constituencies to match changing political realities. What distinguishes the American two-party system is not so much the major parties' ability to offer programmic or ideological alternatives as much as its ability to incorporate new political adaptations within the party framework. The Jeffersonian Democratic-Republicans (the first national opposition party) argued for their own existence by suggesting that they must restrain the FEDERALIST PARTY in power for the nation's sake. After attaining power in 1800, however, the Democratic-Republicans did not dismantle their party organization, nor did they outlaw outright opposition Federalists (though they prosecuted several of the Federalist press). The major parties have changed, but their functions have not fundamentally: they provide program apparatuses for attaining political office, combining numerous social and economic interests to widen overall electoral appeal.

The extension of PRESIDENTIAL PRIMARIES in 1968 has increased the efficacy of two-party dominance in presidential campaigns. The primaries focus media attention on the major parties far in advance of the election date and allow voters to vent frustrations with particular candidates within the structure of the major parties. Some analysts, however, have argued that the recent party system has proved less flexible in this adaptive function. Indeed, Ross Perot's candidacy can be understood as a reaction against the party system itself. As trust in the parties remains low, indicated in continued low voter turnouts, the possibility of Perot-like insurgency remains high. Perot insisted that both parties are too bound to their respective constituencies (or special interest groups) to manage government efficiently. Party government itself, Perot's candidacy implied, limits the possibilities for effective change.

Given the overall strength of the two-party system and the existence of institutional and electoral barriers, outside candidates and their potential voters face numerous questions. Third-party or outside candidates tend not to possess backgrounds in significant office holding (although important exceptions exist to this rule), nor do they receive equal media attention. Alternative candidates must tear voters from their customary party allegiances, or convince nonvoters that their participation matters. The predominance of the two-party system poses a basic strategic problem for alternatives candidates: they must provide a compelling case that a vote for them will not be a waste. Potential voters for the Populists in 1896, the Socialists in 1912 and 1916, the PROGRESSIVE PARTY of 1924 and 1948, segregationists in 1968, and centrist reformers in 1980 confronted the same dilemma in voting: by voting for the third-party candidate (who admittedly may have the best program), is my vote wasted, and do I not indirectly aid the party I least support by not voting for the major party closest to my political inclinations? The rational voter must answer no to such calculations before choosing the alternative candidate.

Reasons for Running. Candidates choose to run for President outside the major parties for several reasons: they may be eliminated from consideration by the major parties and hope to attract support for a later major-party candidacy; they may campaign for a particular issue or set of issues excluded by the major parties; they may represent a social movement or political party that stands outside the political mainstream, or, for ideological reasons, resist incorporation into the major parties; or, finally, they may head coalitions, parties, or movements that they hope will replace one or other of the major parties in the future.

Many examples exist of seasoned politicians leaving their party commitments to run as alternative presidential candidates: Martin Van Buren, JOHN BELL, Theodore Roosevelt, ROBERT M. LA FOLLETTE, STROM THURMOND, HENRY P. WALLACE, GEORGE C. WALLACE, John Anderson. Although all these individuals were prominent politicians, none won the presidency as an independent. Several interrelated reasons account for their abandonment of their old party: the party's commitment to another candidate; intraparty struggle; adherence to a new program that the party was unwilling to accept; attempts to find more viable electoral alternatives; or influencing party nominations in the future. The politicians who formed or joined an alternative coalition to run for President may have done so because he believed his popularity and the new coalition's machinery was sufficient to win, that the issue or issues he campaigned needed independent and visible representation, or the new coalition's present and future electoral viability was stronger than the old party.

Alternative candidates also emerge to represent interests ignored by the major parties. James Birney's LIBERTY PARTY campaigns of 1840 and 1844, and George Wallace's American Party 1968 campaigns revolved around single issues; Birney ran on an abolitionist platform and Wallace on a segregationist one. In each case, because they wished to remain within the broadly defined political mainstream and because they could not antagonize their bisectional core constituencies, the major parties largely ignored the Birney and Wallace positions on race. Single issues, such as abortion or the environment, have shown similar signs of being inimical to major-party compromise and assimilation.

A third category of candidate is one who stands for a social movement or alternative third party. Typically such candidates represent the movement's or party's viewpoint but are not necessarily the focal point or originator of the cause. For example, Populist JAMES B. WEAVER (1892) was a compromise candidate; populism as a movement predated Weaver, and indeed Weaver played only a small role in the movement. EUGENE V. DEBS was the standardbearer of the Socialist Party not its founder. Moderate social movements or third parties (those who believe in the efficacy of American electoral politics) often aspire to becoming a legitimate third voice in national politics. The Socialist Party of America, the Progressives under La Follette, and the Libertarians all hoped to create such a third voice.

Candidates have led coalitions that they hoped would replace existing national parties. Indeed the REPUBLICAN PARTY in a sense can be understood as a successful example of such a strategy. Social crisis or political discontinuity (a critical election or series of critical elections) creates the preconditions for a new party system. WILLIAM WIRT, under the ANTI-MASONIC PARTY, Martin Van Buren, under the FREE-SOIL PARTY, Millard Fillmore, under the KNOW-NOTHING (AMERICAN) PARTY, and perhaps La Follette and Henry Wallace under the Progressives follow this pattern. The Anti-Masonic, Free-Soil, and American parties emerged during moments of crisis or weakness for the reigning two-party system. La Follette and Henry Wallace attempted to substitute an American labor party for either the Republicans and Democrats. With the possible exception of the Libertarians, few examples of substituting for existing major parties has occurred, possibly because of changes in the electoral laws or the hegemony of two-party conceptualization. Increasingly activists appear convinced that the dominant party system of the Republicans and Democrats is here to stay; and increasingly, too, political dissent from the left and the right has centered on party government itself. Widespread doubts exist over whether the institution of the political party can be an engine for social progress (of whatever description). Hence, perhaps, fewer attempts are made to form new parties.

Significance of Third-party Candidates. Candidates outside the major parties serve to register dissent from existing choices. If the major parties offer poor candidates or platforms, voters may choose to voice their opposition through third-party voting, yet such a tactic minimizes the value of their vote in a close election.

Alternative candidates serve to introduce ideas or policy positions excluded or minimized by the major parties. The articulation of an alternative ideology or policy position carries with it, however, the possibility that one or more of the major parties may coalesce against that position. Progressive-era reforms and many of the pillars of the welfare state came from movements outside the mainstream political parties. Indeed the emergence of modern liberalism cannot be understood without examination of political dissent in the late nineteenth century and early twentieth and how political institutions responded to such dissent.

[See also THIRD PARTIES.]

BIBLIOGRAPHY

Fresia, Gerald. *There Comes a Time: A Challenge to the Two Party System.* 1986.

Goodman, William. *The Party System in America.* 1980.

Rae, Douglas. *The Political Consequences of the Electoral Laws.* 1967.

Rosenstone, Steven, Roy Behr, and Edward Lazarus. *Third Parties in America.* 1984.

Smallwood, Frank. *The Other Candidates: Third Parties in Presidential Elections.* 1983.

Sorauf, Frank. *Party Politics in America.* 3d ed. 1976.

JOHN F. WALSH

THOMAS, NORMAN (1884–1968), Socialist Party presidential candidate. A pastor, civil libertarian, intellectual, and pacificist, Norman M. Thomas was a strong voice of conscience in twentieth-century America. Though never successful in electoral politics, Thomas's non-Marxist, Christian socialism influenced several generations of American intellectuals and social activists.

Thomas was born in Marion, Ohio, in 1884. His father, grandfather, and great-grandfather were all Presbyterian ministers. Thomas attended Princeton University, studying with Woodrow Wilson and the Social Gospel economist Walter Wyckoff. After graduating Princeton in 1905 he worked in a settlement house in New York and later entered Union Theological Seminary, from which he graduated in 1911. Thomas combined social activism with his duties in the ministry.

Thomas supported Wilson in 1912 and 1916, although he became suspicious of Wilson's intentions regarding the European war. In 1916, Thomas announced his commitment to pacifism, and, in *The Church and the City*, his belief in non-Marxian socialism. He decried the gap between rich and poor in industrial America and argued that business practice violated Christian ethics. During WORLD WAR I, Thomas defended the rights of conscientious objectors and helped found the National Civil Liberties Bureau, the forerunner of the American Civil Liberties Union.

By the war's end, Thomas joined the Socialist Party of America (SPA), which was falling apart. Left-wing agitators sought to remake the SPA into a party advocating revolution. Thomas rejected revolutionary violence and argued that the Russian revolution was no model for America to follow.

In the 1920s, Thomas turned to journalism, labor activism, and politics. He was arrested in 1926 for organizing a mass meeting in support of striking mill workers in Passaic, New Jersey. Entering politics Thomas ran for governor of New York in 1924, polling 100,000 votes; he supported the Progressive ROBERT LA FOLLETTE nationally in the same year. In his 1925 and 1927 New York mayoral campaigns, he gained widespread notoriety and support from intellectuals and students.

Thomas first ran for President on the Socialist ticket in 1928; he ran consecutively through the election of

1948. Although he polled nearly 900,000 votes in 1932, his greatest total, Thomas's electoral support never matched EUGENE V. DEBS's. Part of Thomas's difficulty rested with his opponent, Franklin Roosevelt, whose NEW DEAL program appropriated many of the SPA's policies. In the election of 1936 particularly, Roosevelt's left rhetoric took much away from the SPA's appeal. Thomas himself at times praised the New Deal, notably the Tennessee Valley Authority program.

Another difficulty Thomas faced was the seemingly constant sectarian battles within the party itself. Thomas rested at the conservative pole of American socialism. Against him stood the increasingly vocal communists and Trotskyites. Throughout the 1930s, the SPA continually debated what relationship it should have with the Soviet Union. Thomas remained critical of communism, and after a visit to the Soviet Union in 1937 declared that nation an oppressive failure. He was also willing to support nonsocialist leaders, such as Fiorello LaGuardia, the New York Congressman, if their positions approximated the Socialist one. In 1935, Thomas advocated the idea of an all-inclusive party, one hospitable even to the revolutionary left. Trotskyites sabotaged this effort in 1936, forcing Thomas to abandon this approach.

From 1938 to 1941, Thomas delicately positioned himself with respect to the coming war. Although anti-Hitler and anti-fascist (he tried unsuccessfully to organize a Debs Column to support the Spanish Loyalists), he nonetheless wished to keep America out of a European war. In 1942, however, he announced his support for America's entrance into WORLD WAR II. At the same time, he staunchly defended CIVIL LIBERTIES (speaking out even for jailed communist rival Earl Browder and interned Japanese Americans), organized for southern tenant farmers, and worked to save German Jews.

In the postwar ear, Thomas backed the UNITED NATIONS and supported the PROGRESSIVE PARTY, although he disliked HENRY A. WALLACE. In the 1950s, he supported ADLAI E. STEVENSON. Thomas was one of the founders of the antinuclear organization SANE and criticized the VIETNAM WAR in 1965. He died on Long Island, New York, in 1968 at the age of eighty-four.

BIBLIOGRAPHY

Duram, James C. *Norman Thomas.* 1974

Johnpoll, Bernard K. *Pacificist's Progress: Norman Thomas and the Decline of American Socialism.* 1970.

Seidler, Murray B. *Norman Thomas: Respectable Rebel.* 1961.

JOHN F. WALSH

THURMOND, STROM (b. 1902), governor of South Carolina, Senator, presidential candidate in 1948. The career of James Strom Thurmond, which defies the conventional rules of survival in American politics, is an example of a southern politician who has learned to change with the times. A lifetime of public service has brought notable accomplishments. The senior Senator from South Carolina has run for President on a third-party ticket; won a statewide election on a write-in ballot; established the Senate filibuster record; changed his political party affiliation and won reelection to office; been a confidant or opponent of nine Presidents; and married two beauty queens. He has a reputation among some people of being a right-wing nay-sayer and among others of being an honest politician of down-home sincerity. Whatever else is said of Strom Thurmond, he is the supreme politician, so far managing to outlive or neutralize his opponents.

Born the son of a politician, Thurmond spent his years after graduation from Clemson College as a school superintendent, state senator, and circuit judge. He served in WORLD WAR II as a soldier who saw action in the D-Day invasion, eventually winning twelve military medals for service. After returning home he ran for governor, and in 1947 moved into the state mansion as the first bachelor chief executive since 1897.

Thurmond was thrust into the national spotlight by his staunch opposition to federally mandated integration. In 1948 his contempt of the Truman civil rights platform inspired a run for President on the STATES' RIGHTS (Dixiecrat) ticket. He garnered thirty-nine electoral votes in that contest and earned the allegiance of white South Carolinians opposed to federal intervention in society. Buoyed by his newfound national reputation, Thurmond chose to challenge Olin D. Johnston in the Democratic primary for the United States Senate in 1950. Johnston circulated a postcard to registered voters of Thurmond standing on his head, with the inscription, "We need a man who can stand on his feet and not his head." In that race Johnston defeated Thurmond by more than 24,000 votes.

In 1951 Thurmond left the governor's mansion and opened a law practice in Aiken, South Carolina. To all outward appearances he seemed to be settling into political exile, but the unexpected death of Burnet Rhett Maybank in 1954 left a vacancy for the United States Senate seat that had eluded him earlier. In a surprise move the Democratic executive committee picked a popular state senator to fill the remaining six-year term. An angry Strom Thurmond made the Democratic committee decision the main issue of a write-in campaign. Backed by editorial endorsements of leading newspapers in the state and supported of prominent politicians, Thurmond won by a large margin.

In Washington, Thurmond's politics were described by one writer as "full of vinegar," but his career is a combination of firmness and flexibility. He talked for twenty-four hours and eighteen minutes against Lyndon Johnson's civil rights bill in 1957 [see CIVIL RIGHTS ACT OF 1957], then later reacted to the enfranchisement of South Carolina's blacks by working doggedly for their appointment to federal positions. His political gospel is a textbook of traditional conservatism: anticommunist, against gun control, in favor of voluntary prayer in schools, against government welfare programs, and in favor of state solutions to problems. Fed up with liberal Democratic social programs, Thurmond decided to change parties in 1964. In the REPUBLICAN PARTY his influence grew; he traveled around the South helping Richard Nixon win southern states in 1968. In the Reagan administration he served as pro tempore of the Senate, fourth in the line of succession to the presidency.

In January 1960 Thurmond's wife, Jean, died from a brain tumor. After her death he cultivated a reputation as a southern eccentric, attending receptions with five or six women on his arm and challenging his opponents to a wrestling match to settle an issue. In the Nixon White House years, Thurmond announced that at age sixty-six he was taking a new bride, a twenty-two-year-old Miss South Carolina named Nancy Moore. Though the two separated in 1991, their union produced four children.

At different times in his career, Thurmond's political demise was forecast by enemies and friends alike. But he consistently adapted to new political currents despite the liabilities associated with a change. He is remembered by older voters as a feisty populist who fought against government intrusion, and by younger voters as the champion of Ronald Reagan's conservatism. He courted black voters over the years, and while they never voted for him in large numbers, at least they did not come out to vote against him. Strom Thurmond is a survivor, a maverick, and a relic.

BIBLIOGRAPHY

Bruck, David. "Strom Thurmond's Roots." *New Republic* (3 March 1982).

Germond, Jack W., and Jules Whitcover. "Strom Thurmond." *Conservative Digest* (May 1978).

Lowe, Stephen. "Party vs. Politics: The 1954 Senate Campaign in South Carolina." Master's thesis, Clemson University, 1990.

J. DAVID WOODARD

TILDEN, SAMUEL J. (1814–1886), governor of New York, Democratic presidential nominee in 1876. Samuel Jones Tilden's father was a prominent merchant in New Lebanon, New York, with connections to leading state Democrats such as Martin Van Buren and Silas Wright. The young Tilden was frail and developed a lifelong concern for his physical well-being. This concern fortified a natural shyness and a scholarly demeanor that made him seem overly mature at a young age. He was studious and became a vigorous proponent of laissez-faire economics and strict construction of the Constitution. After a legal education he began practicing law in New York City in 1841. He developed a special expertise in complex problems concerning railroad organization, which made him wealthy.

Tilden opposed the CIVIL WAR and saw the REPUBLICAN PARTY under Abraham Lincoln as an agent of centralization. He had no interest in racial or social justice. In the immediate postwar era, he became concerned over political corruption, which he saw as unethical, inefficient, and a kind of favoritism that undermined competition. As chairman of the state Democratic committee, he first worked with William Marcy "Boss" Tweed of New York City, then broke the Tweed Ring. He was also important in purifying the state judiciary. These activities brought Tilden national stature as a reformer and took him to the governorship of New York in 1874. In that office he attacked the Canal Ring, which profited from corruption in the awarding of state contracts.

By 1876, he was the DEMOCRATIC PARTY's leading presidential contender and won its nomination on the second ballot. The Republicans named Governor Rutherford B. Hayes of Ohio, and a bitter contest followed. Republicans charged Tilden with being an old-fashioned representative of limited, indifferent government, which favored the South. Democrats charged that a Hayes victory would mean more divisive RECONSTRUCTION legislation and centralism. Both parties employed unethical tactics in the South.

The first tally gave Tilden about 250,000 more popular votes than Hayes and 184 electoral votes, one short of a majority. But the Republicans refused to concede and sought the electoral votes of Oregon, South Carolina, Florida, and Louisiana. Congress finally established a special ELECTORAL COMMISSION, which awarded the disputed votes and a majority of one electoral vote to Hayes. The facts of the contest seem beyond recovery. More popular votes probably were reported for Tilden than for Hayes, but the Democrats had intimidated many southern black Republicans. If everyone who wished to vote had done so, and had those votes been counted fairly, Hayes probably would have won.

Tilden later faced an investigation of his income tax returns and other troubles. He retired to his estate, Greystone, in Yonkers, New York, where he pursued his passion for books. Faithful Democrats depicted him as a martyr and mentioned him for nomination in 1880 and even in 1884, but he declined. He died in 1886, and after a contest over his will, a large portion of his estate went to what became the New York Public Library.

Tilden's attractions as a presidential candidate reflected some basic political and social changes. He was an apparent ascetic at a time when many politicians seemed self-serving. He favored efficiency and minimal government when demands on government, and thus taxes, were rising. He seemed in many ways an upright throwback to a previous era of small-scale enterprise and individual responsibility, which many found attractive as industrialism was transforming the country. And he dominated New York, the major northern state, which Democrats had to carry both to win an election and to avoid seeming a mainly southern party.

BIBLIOGRAPHY

Flick, Alexander Clarence. *Samuel J. Tilden.* 1939.
Haworth, Paul. *The Hayes-Tilden Disputed Election of 1876.* 1906.
Kelley, Robert. *The Trans-Atlantic Persuasion.* 1969.
Polakoff, Keith Ian. *The Politics of Inertia.* 1973.

H. WAYNE MORGAN

TOMPKINS, DANIEL D. (1774–1825), sixth Vice President of the United States (1817–1825). Tompkins was born in Scarsdale, New York, the son of Jonathan G. Tompkins, a prosperous farmer and local official, and Sarah Hyatt Tompkins. He graduated from Columbia College in 1795, studied law and then practiced in New York City. In 1797 he married Hannah Minthorne with whom he had seven children. His wife came from a prominent Jeffersonian Democratic-Republican family, and, probably with their support, Tompkins entered the tangled, faction-ridden Democratic-Republican politics in New York City as a loyal supporter of AARON BURR and his Tammany Hall organization. He was a member of the state constitutional convention in 1801 and was elected to the state assembly in 1803.

In 1804, Tompkins began his national career by being elected to the House of Representatives of the Ninth Congress but he resigned before he took his seat to accept an appointment as associate justice of the New York State Supreme Court, sitting there until 1807. Later that year he ran for governor as a member of the Clintonian Republican faction against the incumbent Morgan Lewis. Identified as the "farmer's son," opposed to the great manorial lords who had long controlled the state, Tompkins won the first of four successive victories. Reelected in 1810, 1813, and 1816, he served ten years as governor. In office he proved to be something of a popular reformer, leading the fight to end slavery in the state, to widen public educational opportunities, and to promote fairer tax policies. In national affairs, he was a loyal supporter of Thomas Jefferson, including the latter's often unpopular foreign policies such as the embargo that hurt New York trading interests. During his governorship, Tompkins fell out with DE WITT CLINTON and became part of Martin Van Buren's emerging Republican faction, the Bucktails.

Tompkins came to national prominence in 1812 as a very effective war governor. Loyally supporting the Madison administration during the WAR OF 1812, he organized the state for defense, built up the state militia, and took command of the Third Military District, encompassing southern New York and parts of New Jersey, and energetically prepared to resist a threatened British invasion. As commander, he personally underwrote or borrowed a great deal of money to buy supplies and munitions and to pay his troops. After the war ended he had difficulty accounting for all of his expenditures and was accused of an unaccounted shortage of $120,000. He spent several very difficult years defending himself in and out of court, an experience which severely affected him emotionally and physically.

President James Madison offered to appoint him Secretary of State in 1814 but he turned it down to remain as governor. In 1816, he was pushed as a potential presidential nominee as part of brief challenge by northern Democratic-Republicans to the Virginia Dynasty's dominance of the presidency. He accepted the vice presidential nomination on the ticket with James Monroe, winning an easy victory. By the time he became Vice President, however, Tompkins had lost a great deal of his drive and spirit. He had begun to drink heavily in response to his financial problems (only resolved at the end of his life when Congress voted an appropriation to repay him for the money he had laid out during the war). One historian refers to him as "a pathetic figure" in those years. "Rarely sober," he was only occasionally in Washington during his term and played little direct part in most Monroe administration policies. Nevertheless, he was renominated for the vice presidency in 1820 and, in the less institutionalized political structure of that period, he also ran in that year, once more, for the governorship of New York. His old enemy, Clinton defeated him for the latter position but the Democratic-Republican electors loyally reelected him as Vice President. Briefly in Washington, he returned to his home on Staten Island in 1822 and never returned to the national capitol. His last prominent political act was to preside over the New York State constitutional convention of 1821. He died just after his term as Vice President formally ended.

BIBLIOGRAPHY

Ammon, Harry. *James Monroe: The Quest for National Identity.* 1971.
Irwin, Ray W. *Daniel D. Tompkins: Governor of New York and Vice President of the United States.* 1968.
Kass, Alvin. *Politics in New York State, 1800–1830.* 1965.

JOEL H. SILBEY

TOWER COMMISSION. In November 1986, the public learned that staff of the NATIONAL SECURITY COUNCIL (NSC) had secretly sold arms to Iran in an effort to secure the release of American hostages in Lebanon and had diverted the profits to the contras, Nicaraguan military forces seeking to overthrow the communist Sandinista government in Nicaragua. In December 1986, President Ronald Reagan appointed the Tower Commission, a blue-ribbon special review board consisting of Senator John Tower, former Secretary of State Edmund Muskie, and once and future national security adviser Brent Scowcroft, to investigate the IRAN-CONTRA AFFAIR. Reagan directed the commission not to make judgments regarding criminal culpability but to review the National Security Council staff's "proper role in operational activities" and to study its "future role and procedures . . . in the development, coordination, oversight, and conduct of foreign and national security policy."

Three months after its appointment, the commission issued a report that was long on facts and short on policy or legislative recommendations. Factual gaps dot the final report. Thinly staffed and lacking the power to subpoena witnesses, to take sworn testimony, or to grant witnesses immunity against prosecution, the commission could not demand documents from nongovernmental agencies or compel testimony from key figures in the affair. Consequently, both the FEDERAL BUREAU OF INVESTIGATION and independent counsel Lawrence Walsh rejected the commission's information requests, and three of the affair's key protagonists—national security adviser John Poindexter, Lieutenant Colonel Oliver North, and Richard Secord—simply refused to appear before it.

The commission concluded that the affair was an aberration, strongly criticizing President Reagan's lax "management style." But at the same time, the commissioners rejected the need for legislative reform, finding existing congressional oversight of the INTELLIGENCE COMMUNITY to be adequate and rejecting proposals that the NSC be statutorily barred from implementing policy or that the national security adviser be subject to Senate confirmation. Nor did the commission "recommend barring limited use of private individuals to assist in United States diplomatic initiatives or in covert activities" so long as "implementation and policy oversight [are not] dominated by [private] intermediaries."

Although the Tower Commission served the valuable function of quickly bringing important information about the Iran-contra affair to light, its report served mainly to insulate the President from criticism for inaction and to present an early consensus regarding relatively restrained reforms. The few structural reforms actually offered by the commission yielded little long-term effect. President Reagan subsequently ignored the commission's suggestion that NSC actions be subjected to interagency legal review by the JUSTICE DEPARTMENT or the legal adviser to the DEPARTMENT OF STATE, and Congress rejected the commission's proposal that the existing House and Senate intelligence committees be merged into a smaller joint committee. The commission's main legacy was its recommendation that the national security assistant should have greater access to legal counsel. Ironically, in the subsequent administration of George Bush, the role of the NSC in national security decision making was if anything, enhanced under the direction of Tower Commission member Brent Scowcroft.

BIBLIOGRAPHY

Koh, Harold. *The National Security Constitution: Sharing Power after the Iran-Contra Affair.* 1990.
President's Special Review Board. *The Tower Commission Report.* 1987.

HAROLD HONGJU KOH

TRADE EXPANSION ACT (1962). A major legislative achievement of the administration of John F. Kennedy, the 1962 Trade Expansion Act authorized the President to make broad reductions in U.S. tariffs on imports in exchange for reciprocal reductions by other nations. The act also codified escape-clause procedures offering temporary relief from injurious imports, established a program of Trade Adjustment Assistance for workers, and mandated the appointment of a Special Representative for Trade Negotiations. Proposed in Kennedy's special presidential message of 25 January 1962, the bill passed the House of Representatives, 298 to 125, in June and the Senate, 78 to 8, in September. It was signed into law on 11 October 1962.

The law was an ambitious response to altered international circumstances. The European Economic Community (EEC), established in 1958, was eliminating tariffs among its members, provoking fears it might become a protectionist trade block. Through reciprocal tariff reductions across the board (rather than item by item, as under previous trade laws), Kennedy offered the alternative of trans-Atlantic economic interdependence. The law was drafted so as to authorize even deeper cuts on products where the EEC and United States dominated world trade. The number of such products would multiply if the United Kingdom entered the EEC, and in fact the bill was designed to encourage this outcome. In this Kennedy failed, as French president Charles de Gaulle vetoed British entry. But the multilateral negotiations were nonetheless a success. In the so-called Kennedy Round agreements of 1967, U.S. tariffs were cut by 35 percent, and the EEC and other U.S. trading partners made comparable reductions.

During the late 1950s, resistance to trade liberalization had grown, particularly in depressed industries such as textiles. Kennedy won that industry's support by negotiating, outside the act, a special international arrangement limiting quantities of cotton textile imports from low-cost producers. The act itself contained escape clauses granting industries temporary import protection—subject to presidential approval—if they were suffering serious economic injury, the major cause of which was an increase of imports due to U.S. trade concessions. The act also established a new program of Trade Adjustment Assistance (TAA) under which workers could obtain funds for subsistence and retraining if imports cost them their jobs. (Few industries or workers proved able to qualify for escape-clause or TAA relief under this statute, however, and the criteria were relaxed in the Trade Act of 1974.)

Finally, the Trade Expansion Act of 1962 directed the President to appoint a special representative, responsible directly to him, to lead the U.S. delegation in trade negotiations [see OFFICE OF THE U.S. TRADE REPRESENTATIVE].

BIBLIOGRAPHY

Preeg, Ernest H. *Traders and Diplomats.* 1970.
Evans, John W. *The Kennedy Round in American Trade Policy.* 1971.

I. M. DESTLER

TRADE POLICY. Product-specific governmental measures that affect the movement of goods and services across national boundaries constitute trade policy. Aimed at influencing imports and exports of particular types of goods, trade policy is distinguished from macroeconomic (fiscal and monetary) policies, which influence the balance of trade through their impact on overall supply and demand.

Measures regulating imports include tariffs, taxes levied on goods as they enter a country. More restrictive are quotas, which place ceilings on the volumes of particular imports. Both reduce the level of imports. Actions affecting exports include subsidies, which tend to increase the volume of exports and allow the sale of products abroad at prices lower than those that prevail in the home country. Export controls, on the other hand, prevent or limit sales of specific products abroad—for NATIONAL SECURITY reasons or to ameliorate shortages of goods in the home country.

Policies or measures that limit imports are called *protectionist*. By contrast, a *free trade* policy imposes no barriers to imports. A *liberal trade* policy aims at reduction of trade barriers at home and abroad. Generally accepted economic analysis holds that free trade aids a nation's welfare by allowing maximum scope for comparative advantage: each nation can concentrate on producing the goods that it is relatively more efficient at producing and can exchange these for goods produced more efficiently elsewhere. Free trade is difficult to achieve politically, however, because of its cost to less-efficient domestic producers, who lobby government for relief.

From Tariffs to Fast-Track. In the United States, debate over trade policy was particularly fierce in the nineteenth and early twentieth century. Northern manufacturing interests sought protection for their emerging industries, while southern agricultural producers favored maximum trade and maximum exports. Over time, policy became more protectionist, reaching a climax in 1930, when Congress enacted and President Herbert Hoover signed the SMOOT-HAWLEY TARIFF ACT. This raised tariff levels to an average of 60 percent of the price of dutiable imports.

Smoot-Hawley provoked broad foreign retaliation and helped worsen the Great Depression. The administration of Franklin D. Roosevelt responded by winning passage of legislation in 1934 authorizing the President to reduce tariffs in exchange for reductions by foreign governments [see RECIPROCAL TRADE AGREEMENTS. These reduced tariffs were made available to all nations with which the United States had normal trade relations through the most-favored-nation (MFN) principle.

Roosevelt's successors continued this policy. After WORLD WAR II, the major negotiations were multilateral, as the United States led a series of trade "rounds" through which a growing number of nations committed themselves to barrier-reducing measures [see GATT (GENERAL AGREEMENT ON TARIFFS AND TRADE)]. By the time of the Uruguay Round, inaugurated in 1986, U.S. tariffs had become insignificant (averaging below 5 percent), and the main focus of negotiations had become nontariff barriers (NTBs): quotas, product standards, and other measures with trade-restricting effects. To facilitate negotiations on these, Congress, beginning in 1975, established fast-track procedures through which the House and Senate pledged to vote expeditiously, without amendment, on legislation proposed by the President to implement certain NTB agreements [see FAST-TRACK AUTHORITY].

Congress Delegates Trade Power. This shift in policy was made possible by a shift in the locus of power: from Congress and U.S. producers hurt by imports to the executive branch and producers helped by exports. Members of Congress became less protectionist and more willing to delegate power to the executive. Congress insisted that all important interests get a fair hearing but generally avoided direct legislation imposing trade barriers—in total contrast to earlier years. From the 1930s through the 1950s, the prime locus of executive trade policy responsibility was the DEPARTMENT OF STATE. In 1962, however, Congress insisted on creation of a trade representative in the EXECUTIVE OFFICE OF THE PRESIDENT (EOP) to balance U.S. interests at home and to represent them abroad [see TRADE EXPANSION ACT (1962) and OFFICE OF THE U.S. TRADE REPRESENTATIVE].

From the 1930s through the 1960s, trade policy receded as a national issue. Since the 1960s it has regained most of its former prominence. One reason is the internationalization of the economy: the value of merchandise imports jumped from 8.7 percent of U.S. goods production in 1970 to above 20 percent after 1980. A second reason is the deterioration in the trade balance: from surpluses in every twentieth-century year through 1970 to consistent deficits after 1975. From 1984 through 1990, the U.S. trade deficit exceeded the previously unheard-of level of $100 billion.

Congress responded neither by reclaiming detailed control nor by turning protectionist. Support for trade restrictions increased somewhat, but legislators' mainly demanded that the executive branch be tougher in getting other nations to open their markets. The main target was Japan, whose goods had been phenomenally successful in U.S. markets but whose own markets were difficult for non-Japanese goods to penetrate. But emerging industrial economies such as Korea, Taiwan, and Brazil felt greater American pressure also. So did the European Community, particularly with respect to its highly protected agricultural markets.

The second administration of Ronald Reagan responded by pressing a number of cases under section 301 of the Trade Act of 1974, charging that foreign markets imposed "unjustifiable" or "unreasonable" barriers to U.S. exporters. Congress also insisted on passing a new, comprehensive trade law: the Omnibus Trade and Competitiveness Act of 1988. The bill began as a partisan and somewhat protectionist move, as Democrats exploited the Republican President's vulnerability as defender of U.S. economic interests. As finally enacted, however, it was not so much protectionist toward imports as it was aggressively unilateralist on exports—toughening the language of Section 301, for example.

Limited Trade Protection. To contain political and limit trade's disruptive effects, the United States has developed two forms of limited trade protection. First, trade remedy measures provide import relief to petitioning firms and workers who meet statutory criteria: proof that imports are "a substantial cause of serious injury" can bring temporary protection under the GATT escape clause. Proof of dumping (generally sales of imported goods at prices below those in the exporter's home market) or foreign government subsidies leads to antidumping or countervailing duties that offset the price advantage imports gain from such practices, which U.S. law labels "unfair." Another trade remedy is assistance for adjustment: workers can qualify for income support and retraining if they lose their jobs to import competition.

A second means of limited protection has been negotiation of so-called voluntary export restraints (VERs), under which the source country agrees to limit the quantity of goods it sells to a particular trading partner. Japan, for example, has imposed ceilings on passenger car sales to the United States since 1981. The most comprehensive system of VERs applies to trade in textiles and apparel: the Multi-Fiber Arrangement (MFA) negotiated in 1973 and renewed thereafter established a framework for bilateral quota agreements between importing and exporting countries.

When the administration of George Bush came to power in 1989, import growth was ebbing and an export boom was underway. It responded by giving priority to completing the multilateral Uruguay Round negotiations, the most comprehensive and difficult the world had yet undertaken. European resistance to agricultural concessions caused a breakdown in these talks in 1990. That same year, Mexico's president asked Bush to open negotiations for a bilateral free-trade agreement, and Canada—which had signed such an agreement with the United States in 1988—asked to join. The projected North American Free Trade Area (NAFTA) became the most controversial U.S. trade proposal in decades, attacked by labor groups fearing low-wage competition and environmental groups concerned that NAFTA would undercut their goals. It also generated fears overseas, particularly in Asia, that the U.S. was retreating from multilateralism and forming a regional trading bloc.

By extending the deadline for fast-track procedures in May 1991, Congress gave the administration two more years to complete both negotiations. The Uruguay Round talks were resumed, but a tentative U.S.–European Community agricultural deal was not reached until late 1992, and it proved impossible to resolve other issues during the transition from Bush to President Bill Clinton. The NAFTA agreement was completed and signed by Bush in December 1992. Clinton endorsed the pact generally but conditioned final action on negotiation of supplemental agreements dealing with labor and the environment. He also inherited the mostly completed Uruguay Round under domestic and international circumstances that made its success anything but automatic.

BIBLIOGRAPHY

Bauer, Raymond A., Ithiel de Sola Pool, and Lewis Anthony Dexter. *American Business and Public Policy: The Politics of Foreign Trade*. 2d ed. 1972.

Bhagwati, Jagdish. *Protectionism*. 1988.

Destler, I. M. *American Trade Politics*. 2d ed. 1992.

Jackson, John H. *The World Trading System: Law and Policy of International Economic Relations*. 1989.

I. M. DESTLER

TRANSITIONS, PRESIDENTIAL. Perhaps the most trying crisis, aside from war, that a polity can face is the problem of governmental succession, that is, the transfer of power from one ruler to another. In the United States the head of government, the President, is elected in a four-year cycle, with no Chief Executive being eligible for election more than twice (since the TWENTY-SECOND AMENDMENT was adopted in 1951).

From the time of George Washington until Franklin D. Roosevelt, the INAUGURATION of the new President took place on 4 March of the year after the election. This interregnum of about four months was useful during the early years of the republic. But, with the development of modern technologies of communica-

tion and transportation, such a long period became unnecessary and the delay in implementing the choice of the electorate became less understandable. In 1933, the TWENTIETH AMENDMENT was adopted, mandating that the new President be inaugurated at noon on 20 January of the year after a presidential election. The sixteen-week transition period was reduced to about eleven weeks.

Continuity versus Change. The two main, conflicting challenges of presidential transitions for the U.S. political and constitutional system are the need for continuity in the modern nation-state and the need for change in response to a democratic election. The process must ensure continuity of purpose so that foreign enemies are convinced of the steadfastness of U.S. intentions and will not attempt to take advantage of the shift in power by initiating hostile actions. The nation's allies must be reassured that the broad outlines of U.S. interests—and alliances—will remain in place. Internally, the public must be confident that the commitments of the government reflected in public law will be respected.

But the major requirement of party-turnover transitions in a democratic polity is the need to change to reflect the wishes of the electorate. For this change to occur, the administrative apparatus of the executive branch must be at the service of, though not at the complete disposal of, the new administration. The permanent bureaucracy must possess the merit-system value of *neutral* competence so that the incoming administration will have confidence that the permanent government will be responsive to new policy direction. But there must also be enough continuity in the bureaucracies of the executive branch to ensure the public that ongoing programs will be competently administered and that public law will be faithfully executed.

In the political system of the United States, there are several types of presidential transitions. Each presents its own challenges. From a democratic perspective, the most challenging and important type is the party-turnover transition, in which the former opposition party comes to office. This party usually intends to make significant changes in public policy.

A second type of transition occurs when a President dies in office or resigns and the Vice President succeeds to the office of President. This type of transition offers its own challenges, depending on the circumstances. For instance, in 1963, Lyndon Baines Johnson emphasized the theme of continuity with the agenda of the assassinated John F. Kennedy. In 1974 Gerald Ford took the opposite approach, distinguishing himself from the discredited administration of Richard M. Nixon.

A third type of transition is a same-party transition, when a new President belonging to the outgoing President's political party is elected, as happened in 1928 and 1988. Presidents elected in these circumstances are faced with a delicate task. They must emphasize party and policy continuity, which is presumably what the citizens voted for, but they must also establish their own political identity so that they are not seen as mere shadows of their immediate predecessors. They may also choose to replace the political appointees of the previous administration with their own people, a traumatic process in the 1988–1989 transition.

President Dwight D. Eisenhower insisted that there is really no *transition* of the presidency but rather a *transfer* of power at noon on 20 January. Eisenhower was correct in a legal sense, and all Presidents have jealously guarded their constitutional prerogatives while still in office. The legal and symbolic transfer of power does indeed occur at noon on Inauguration Day. But in a practical sense political power begins to slip away immediately after an election in which the incumbent was not a candidate or was defeated. The President in office then becomes a LAME-DUCK PRESIDENT, and foreign leaders, domestic political leaders, and even career public servants begin to look to the person who soon will take office and who will control the government for the next four years.

The full power of the presidency is not transferred to the new President immediately on taking office. Only the authority of the office is automatically transferred. The actual power of the presidency—that is, control of the policy agenda and the apparatus of government—is something that a President must consciously grasp. The real transition therefore extends forward in time from the inauguration as well as backward. In the modern presidency, given the many political appointments that must be made, along with an extensive WHITE HOUSE STAFF and institutionalized EXECUTIVE OFFICE OF THE PRESIDENT to organize, the full transition into office cannot be considered complete until at least several months into the new administration.

For the incoming administration the major problem of transition lies in having to cram so many important tasks into the eleven-week period between election and inauguration. The core of a White House staff must be selected as the entourage moves from campaigning to governing. Immediate attention must be given to designating CABINET nominees and recruiting hundreds of other presidential appointees. The new President's stamp must be put on the budget proposal that will soon be sent to Congress. And the administration must establish an office of legislative liaison to conduct congressional relations.

Before 1963, presidential transitions had been conducted according to custom and precedent. In 1944, Roosevelt began the tradition of the President briefing his opponent on NATIONAL SECURITY and foreign policy matters. Eisenhower met personally with President-elect Kennedy in 1960 and established the precedent of designating presidential liaisons between the incoming and outgoing administrations. Johnson broke new ground by inviting before the election HUBERT HUMPHREY'S opponents, Richard Nixon and GEORGE WALLACE, to the White House for personal briefings and inviting personal representatives to coordinate transition matters.

After the 1960 election Kennedy spent some of his own money for office space and expenses for his agency-head designates before they could occupy government offices on 20 January. As a result of the recommendations of a special commission Kennedy established, Congress passed the Presidential Transition Act of 1963 (P.L. 88-277, 78 Stat. 153) to provide for the transition expenses of the outgoing president and to provide the President-elect with office space, staff, travel, communication, and printing expenses. The act authorized $900,000 to be spent for a presidential transition, an amount that was increased in the 1970s and again in 1980s.

Transition Planning. Until 1976 most presidential candidates had taken the need to prepare for office quite casually, not wanting to appear overly confident before the election. Kennedy did ask Richard Neustadt and CLARK CLIFFORD to prepare memos for him as plans for what his first steps should be as President in case he won the election. Nixon, Kennedy's opponent in the 1960 race, felt that his experience as Vice President made any elaborate preparation unnecessary. Both Kennedy (in 1960) and Nixon (in 1968) established task forces after their elections to brief them on various policy issues and to screen potential members of the new administrations. The first systematic preelection preparation for the transition to the presidency was undertaken by Jimmy Carter's staff in the summer of 1976. Carter, who was running as an outsider, decided to divert $150,000 from his campaign to set up a planning project in Atlanta, Georgia. The group of staffers conducted a series of budget and policy studies and set up a "talent inventory program" of potential nominees for political appointments.

The next outsider to gain his party's nomination was Ronald Reagan, who initiated a transition planning operation in the spring of 1980. The operation was much more elaborate than the Carter effort, with hundreds of people organized into working groups. After the election more than one hundred transition teams were formed for the various federal agencies. The teams were like an occupying army, establishing themselves in agency-provided offices so that they could be briefed on ongoing operations and programs. The teams submitted reports to transition headquarters, a large office building on M Street in Washington, D.C. The transition bureaucracy was so large that its leaders had a difficult time controlling its members' activities and establishing who was actually speaking for the incoming administration.

George Bush had the distinction of being the first Vice President to succeed to the presidency by election since 1837. On the surface the transition was smooth. It was, after all, an election of continuity, with Bush promising to carry on the policies of the Reagan administration. With no major policy changes expected and loyal Republicans in political positions throughout the government, the transition promised to be tranquil. But underlying friction marked the relationship between the Reagan appointees in office and the incoming Bush administration. Political personnel turnover ended up being about 70 percent, much higher than expected.

Opportunities and Dangers. The task facing a newly elected President is formidable. After the long and tiring year (or years) of campaigning, attention must now be turned to the process of governance. Campaign promises and platforms must be translated into coherent policies, policies must be transformed into program proposals, bills must be shepherded through Congress, and legislation must be implemented by the executive branch.

The consensus of scholars and politicians is that, for a new President to have the best chance of accomplishing an agenda, the administration must move quickly. A President's opportunities are most open at the beginning of an administration. Public approval ratings are characteristically high in the early months. The President can claim a mandate from the voters to move on the agenda. The new beginning is a hopeful period when few enemies have been made by the tough policy choices that will necessarily follow. During this HONEYMOON PERIOD, Congress is disposed at least to listen sympathetically to new policy proposals, even though it will not give any President a blank check. In recent decades legislative proposals introduced in the early months of an administration have been more likely to be enacted into law than later initiatives. The closer the midterm election year grows, the more difficult it will be for a President to succeed in pushing legislation through Congress.

New presidents must also move quickly in personnel selection. In the late twentieth century the task of staffing a new administration grew steadily more complex, taking ever-longer periods of time. The complexity came with the increasing scope of federal activities and the greater degree of professionalism essential to leadership of the executive branch. The number of presidential appointees also increased, with the OFFICE OF PRESIDENTIAL PERSONNEL responsible for about one thousand full-time appointments in the executive branch and about two thousand part-time appointments to boards and commissions, all requiring confirmation by the Senate.

The screening process for political personnel has taken longer for two reasons: to make sure that all factions within the President's party are pleased but also to ensure that appointees will not cause the new administration any ethical embarrassment. The Senate confirmation process has also been taking longer. As a result of all of these factors the time it has taken to get top administration officials in office increased from 2.4 months in the Kennedy administration to more than eight months for President Bush.

Modern presidential transitions have in general been run smoothly and professionally. The 1953 transition from Harry S. Truman to Eisenhower, however, was marked by bitterness. The 1961 transition to Kennedy was cordial but strained, with Eisenhower having some doubts about Kennedy's maturity. The 1969 transition from Johnson to Nixon went very well, in part because Johnson did not seek reelection and prepared for a transition regardless of the election's outcome.

A major internal danger an incoming President can face is the new administration's tendency toward arrogance, especially after capturing the presidency from the other party. Having won the election against a presumably discredited administration, members of the new administration may feel that they know best how to run the government and that they have nothing to learn from the outgoing administration. Ironically, at the point of transition most officials of the outgoing administration do not feel partisan hostility but want to pass on the hard-won accumulated wisdom of their experience in the White House. Kennedy came to regret his administration's early optimism, which was in part responsible for the ill-fated BAY OF PIGS INVASION of CUBA. Kennedy's administration has been faulted for the wholesale jettisoning of the administrative apparatus built over the previous eight years of the Eisenhower administration, especially the national-security policy machinery. Kennedy wanted to run his administration from the White House, but his disposal of the Cabinet-coordinating mechanisms developed by Eisenhower went further than necessary.

Nixon began his administration with the intention of letting his Cabinet secretaries run domestic policy, but he ended up overcentralizing power in his White House staff. Reacting against Nixon's powerful White House staff, Carter delegated too much authority to his Cabinet secretaries and tried, unsuccessfully, to be his own CHIEF OF STAFF. The new Reagan administration, in turn, reacted against what it thought was Carter's too-delegated approach to the Cabinet by centralizing policy making, budget decisions, and especially personnel selection in the White House. The personnel centralization went so far as to require White House approval of all political appointees, whether presidential or agency-head appointments.

One attitude that consistently marks incoming administrations is a distrust of the career CIVIL SERVICE. There is almost always the suspicion that the bureaucracy is too cumbersome to change quickly or that it will resist policy change in order to defend the status quo. This attitude eventually dissipates when new political appointees learn to work with rather than against the permanent bureaucracy. But transitions can be speeded up by a more positive attitude toward the career executives who will be carrying out the policies of the new administration, whatever they are.

Presidential transitions thus present several challenges to the American polity. They must be accomplished with a delicate mix of continuity and change. The incoming administration must shift gears from campaigning to governing and move quickly on its policy agenda and personnel selection. New Presidents should be aware that their early actions may set the tone for their administrations and that their greatest opportunities for policy initiatives will most likely come in the early months of their administrations. Transitions have become more institutionalized since 1960, and preelection planning for a new administration has been partially legitimized. Personnel recruitment remains in need of advance preparation, but legislative proposals to provide public money for preelection personnel planning have been defeated.

BIBLIOGRAPHY

Brauer, Carl M. *Presidential Transitions: Eisenhower through Reagan.* 1986.
Henry, Laurin L. *Presidential Transitions.* 1960.
Mosher, Frederick C., W. David Clinton, and Daniel G. Lang. *Presidential Transitions and Foreign Affairs.* 1987.
Neustadt, Richard E. *Presidential Power and the Modern Presidents.* 1990.
Pfiffner, James P. *The Strategic Presidency.* 1988.
Pfiffner, James P., and R. Gordon Hoxie, eds. *The Presidency in Transition.* 1989.
Stanley, David T. *Changing Administrations.* 1965.

JAMES P. PFIFFNER

TRANSPORTATION, DEPARTMENT OF. After several efforts to rationalize federal transportation policy, President Lyndon B. Johnson submitted legislation to Congress on 6 March 1966, to establish a CABINET-level department of transportation. Johnson's administration designed the department to provide guidance in resolving transportation problems and to develop national transportation policies. Johnson's aim was to solve the following dilemma: while the United States had one of the best-developed transportation systems in the world, the system lacked the coordination that would let travelers and goods move conveniently and efficiently from one mode of transport to another, using the best characteristics of each. Johnson maintained that a modern transportation system was critical to the national economic health and well-being, including high employment, a high standard of living, and national defense.

The Johnson administration was not alone in seeking a Cabinet-level Department of Transportation. This new Department was the result of a combination of factors, ranging from suggestions that had long been made by government reorganization teams such as the HOOVER COMMISSION to the realization by the administrator of the Federal Aviation Agency that he needed representation at the Cabinet table.

The Enabling Legislation. The White House framed the legislation to combine agencies involved in transportation enterprises scattered throughout the federal government. The bill, however, avoided matters of transportation policy.

Johnson signed the Department of Transportation Enabling Act on 15 October 1966. By this act, thirty-eight agencies or functions and ninety thousand employees came under the control of the department. Various congressional compromises had made the final version of the bill less than what the White House had wanted. Even in its watered-down form, however, the act produced the most sweeping reorganization of the federal government since the NATIONAL SECURITY ACT of 1947, which, among other things, set up the DEPARTMENT OF DEFENSE. Johnson endorsed the compromise measure as the most acceptable piece of legislation that could be pushed through Congress, the first step toward bringing efficiency and rationality to federal transportation policy.

The new department would do more than simply set in motion aviation policies, or say, surface transporta-

Secretaries of Transportation

President	Secretary of Transportation
36 L. B. Johnson	Alan S. Boyd, 1967–1969
37 Nixon	John A. Volpe, 1969–1973
	Claude S. Brinegar, 1973–1974
38 Ford	Claude S. Brinegar, 1974–1975
	William T. Coleman, Jr., 1975–1977
39 Carter	Brock Adams, 1977–1979
	Neil Goldschmidt, 1979–1981
40 Reagan	Andrew L. Lewis, 1981–1983
	Elizabeth H. Dole, 1983–1987
	James H. Burnley, IV, 1987–1989
41 Bush	Samuel K. Skinner, 1989–1992
	Andrew H. Card, 1992–1993
42 Clinton	Federico F. Pena, 1993–

tion policies. Rather, it would develop coordinated transportation policies to meet the continuing needs of the nation. For instance, Secretary-designate Alan Boyd maintained that, with the Department of Transportation (DOT) in place, specific bills such as the National Traffic and Motor Vehicle Safety Act of 1966 would in some manner have an impact on other modes of transportation besides the automobile. The National Transportation Safety Board (established by the 1966 DOT act) would investigate many kinds of transportation-related accidents, whatever the mode of transportation, and use the gathered data to start what Boyd claimed would be a national approach to transportation safety. In his message to Congress on 2 March 1966, President Johnson claimed that no function of the new department and no responsibility of its secretary would be more important than safety.

Planners designed the department with a view to combining the experience of the various agencies regulating different modes of transportation with the general skill of the Office of the Secretary of Transportation to devise long-range plans and policies. A diverse group of agencies were to be brought under the new department's umbrella, including the Maritime Administration (made part of the department in 1981), the Car Service Division, the SAINT LAWRENCE SEAWAY, the Federal Aviation Agency, and the Bureau of Public Roads. Because these agencies' operating characteristics had so little in common in terms of skills required, clients served, problems faced, and general system character, planners called for decentralized operations with DOT staff control limited to testing the effectiveness of the various systems. From the start, the department functioned with as much of a sense of purpose as the planners could have expected. Five and a half months after Johnson signed the

enabling legislation, the Department of Transportation—the twelfth Cabinet department and suddenly the fourth-largest department—had a combined annual budget of nearly $5 billion.

Post-1967 Organization. Conceding the link between transportation needs and the needs of urban areas—where more than 70 percent of the U.S. population lived—the White House transferred most urban mass-transportation functions to the Department of Transportation from the DEPARTMENT OF HOUSING AND URBAN DEVELOPMENT, effective 1 July 1968. Responsibility for these was placed in the newly established Urban Mass Transportation Administration (now the Federal Transit Administration).

By the end of the Johnson administration, the Department of Transportation embraced the U.S. Coast Guard, the Federal Aviation Administration, the Federal Highway Administration, the Federal Railroad Administration, the Saint Lawrence Seaway Development Corporation, the Urban Mass Transportation Administration, and, tangentially, the National Transportation Safety Board.

In 1970, Boyd's successor, John Volpe, proposed to separate functions involving the safety of highway construction (under the Bureau of Public Roads) from those of the National Highway Safety Bureau (NHSB), which was responsible for enforcing the National Traffic and Motor Vehicle Safety Act. Volpe approved the transfer of the NHSB to the Office of the Secretary. To emphasize the high-level commitment to preventing traffic fatalities, Volpe separated the NHSB from the Federal Highway Administration completely. The Highway Safety Act formally separated the safety bureau from the highway administration and created a new administration, the National Highway Traffic Safety Administration.

In moves to limit the President's powers, Congress gave the NTSB full autonomy in the early 1980s, having begun to move toward this in 1976. Congress now feared that the loose autonomy that the Department of Transportation Enabling Act had given the NTSB made it too vulnerable to executive pressure.

On 23 September 1977, Jimmy Carter's first Transportation Secretary, Brock Adams, established the Research and Special Programs Administration (RSPA), an institutional development of major import. When Adams created RSPA, he combined the Transportation Systems Center, the hazardous materials program, and diverse activities that did not readily fit under any of the existing operating administrations. RSPA moved cross-cutting research and development pursuits from the Office of the Secretary to an autonomous operating administration.

The Inspector General Act of 1978, created an inspector general for the Department of Transportation as well as for other executive agencies. The mission of this officer, appointed by the President and confirmed by the Senate, was to help the secretary cope with waste, fraud, and abuse. Though housed in the department and given the rank of Assistant Secretary, the inspector general was autonomous.

President Carter's second Secretary of Transportation, Neil Goldschmidt, established the Office of Small and Disadvantaged Business Utilization in the Office of the Secretary. OSDBU was responsible for implementing procedures, consistent with federal laws, to provide policy guidance for minority-owned, woman-owned, and disadvantaged businesses that joined the department's procurement and federal financial assistance activities.

President Ronald Reagan's first Transportation Secretary, Drew Lewis, succeeded in moving the Maritime Administration from the DEPARTMENT OF COMMERCE to Transportation, providing the department with the maritime element it needed to frame national transportation policy. While Elizabeth Dole, Reagan's second secretary, held the post, the Commercial Space Launch Act of 1984 gave the department a new mission: the promotion and regulation commercial satellite launches. As none of the department's existing operating administrations had a mission compatible with this, Dole housed the Office of Commercial Space Transportation in the Office of the Secretary.

BIBLIOGRAPHY

Burby, John. *The Great American Motion Sickness: Or Why You Can't Get from There to Here.* 1971.

Davis, Grant Miller. *The Department of Transportation.* 1970.

Dean, Alan L. "The Organization and Management of the Department of Transportation." Paper. National Academy of Public Administration. 1991.

Hazard, John L. "The Institutionalization of Transportation Policy: Two Decades of DOT." *Transportation Journal* 26 (Fall 1986): 17–31.

R. DALE GRINDER

TRAVEL, RIGHT TO. Article 13 of the Universal Declaration of Human Rights, adopted by the UNITED NATIONS in 1948, recognizes the right to travel both inside one's country and internationally. In the United States, the history of the right to travel provides a case study of the issues concerning presidential power to limit individual liberty in order to further NATIONAL SECURITY or foreign policy goals as well as of the different approaches taken by the Supreme Court to protect individual liberty against government actions taken in the name of national security.

Since WORLD WAR II, there has been little controversy over the right of interstate travel within the United States. Although the Supreme Court approved the detention and internment of citizens of Japanese ancestry during World War II [*see* JAPANESE AMERICANS, TREATMENT OF], it is now settled law that the right to travel across state lines is a fundamental freedom that cannot be abridged except for the most compelling reasons. Thus, for example, the Supreme Court in *Shapiro v. Thompson* (1969) struck down state laws that gave residents who had lived in a state for less than a year fewer welfare benefits than those who had been resident longer on the grounds that the laws unconstitutionally burdened the right to interstate travel.

Restrictive Legislation. United States citizens' right to travel abroad is, however, subject to several significant restrictions. According to the MCCARRAN-WALTER ACT of 1952, it is illegal for U.S. citizens to leave or enter the United States without a valid passport. The Passport Act of 1926 gave the President authority to impose certain restrictions on the use of passports, including denying passports on the grounds of national security, although he may not deny passports based on activities protected by the First Amendment. The law also prohibits the President from barring the use of American passports in a particular country unless the United States is at war with that country or there are imminent hostilities or danger to U.S. travelers in the country. At the same time however, the Supreme Court in REGAN V. WALD (1984) upheld the President's authority under the trade embargo statutes to make it a crime to spend money to travel in embargoed countries. In 1992, President had declared travel to Libya and Lebanon off-limits under the Passport Act because of dangerous conditions in those countries and had embargoed the spending of money to travel to CUBA and Iraq. (The trade embargo restrictions applicable to Cuba permitted travel by journalists, professional researchers, and persons traveling to see close relatives in Cuba.)

The President's authority to restrict Americans' rights to travel abroad and the constitutionality of such restrictions have long been the subject of controversy. That history discloses that the efforts of Chief Executives to increase the presidency's power and authority have at times been opposed by the Congress and the Supreme Court and at other times supported by one or the other branches.

Congress passed the first Passport Act in 1856 and reenacted it in 1926. That act, with some amendments, is still in effect today. It provides that only the Secretary of State may issue passports and that he shall do so under such rules as the President may prescribe. The act was originally passed in 1856 to eliminate the confusion that then existed because many state and local officials issued passports, that is, requests for safe passage addressed to foreign sovereigns. This centralization of passport authority in the President did not at first, however, include authority to restrict travel. Not until 1918 did Congress make it illegal to travel without a passport. The 1918 statute delegated to the President the right during time of war to impose by PROCLAMATION a requirement that U.S. citizens use a passport when entering or leaving the country. In 1918 and again in 1941, the President issued such proclamations.

In 1952, as part of the McCarren-Walter Act, Congress again delegated power to the President to proclaim national emergencies during which use of a passport would be required. In 1953, President Harry S. Truman issued such a proclamation, finding that communist aggression in North Korea was part of a worldwide conspiracy aimed at communist domination that constituted a national emergency.

In 1952, the Secretary of State declared, pursuant to the delegation provision in the 1926 Passport Act, that, for reasons of national security, passports were not to be issued to members of the Communist Party. This prohibition was challenged as unconstitutional and unauthorized, and in *Kent v. Dulles* (1958) the Supreme Court struck down the regulation on the ground that Congress had not authorized it.

Court Interpretations. In doing so, the Court took a narrow view of presidential authority, which has since been disavowed by a more conservative Court. In *Kent* the Court held that the freedom to travel abroad was part of the liberty protected by the due process clause of the Constitution and that all delegated powers that would curtail or dilute such liberty must be narrowly construed. The Court reasoned that it should not find congressional authorization for the President to restrict fundamental liberties unless there was a clear statement by the Congress that such restrictions were necessary. The Court specifically noted that *Kent* did not arise under the constitutional WAR POWERS, and it stated that liberty could only be regulated by law—the province of Congress, not of the President. If power to make law was to be delegated, there had to be standards for such delegation. The Court noted that in the case of the internment of Japanese Americans during World War II, Congress and the President had acted together.

Six years later, in *Aptheker v. Secretary of State* (1964), the Court again considered the issue of revocation of passports of Communists and held that the Subversive Activities Control Act, which authorized such revocation, was unconstitutional. That act specifically provided that members of the Communist Party should have their passports revoked. Because there was no question in this case concerning whether the executive had authority to revoke the passports, the Court was forced to rule on the constitutional issue, and it struck down the law as overly broad and indiscriminate. Justice William O. Douglas declared that in the absence of war, the government had no power to keep a citizen from traveling unless the government would be justified in detaining him or her. The decisions in *Kent* and *Aptheker* find an implicit premise in Justice Hugo Black's observation that Congress has broad passport powers under the foreign commerce provision of the Constitution.

The power of these rulings, however, has been diminished in later cases in which the Court has upheld government restrictions on travel abroad, though *Kent* and *Aptheker* have never been explicitly overruled. New members of the Court held a more expansive view of presidential power in FOREIGN AFFAIRS and deemed that power relevant to the travel issue.

In *Zemel v. Rusk* (1965) the Court decided that the language of the 1926 Passport Act which had been held not to authorize the President to refuse passports to communists, did authorize the President to refuse to validate passports for travel to specific countries—in this case Cuba. The Court went on to find that the restriction on travel to Cuba was constitutional. The Court distinguished *Kent* by finding that there had been a substantial and consistent executive practice of imposing restrictions on the use of passports to travel to specific areas. It upheld the constitutionality of the travel ban by downplaying the significance of the constitutional right at stake and finding that the restriction was supported by the "weightiest considerations of national security." In *Aptheker*, the government had likewise argued that the passport restrictions were required in the interests of national security, but the *Zemel* Court, unlike the majorities in *Kent* and *Aptheker*, treated the President's assertion of national security deferentially and viewed the President's foreign affairs powers as broad enough to encompass restrictions on passports. The dissenters disagreed that the President, rather than Congress, had any inherent power over the issuance of passports.

Two years later, however, in *United States v. Laub* (1967), the Court refused to go any further, rejecting the government's position that a violation of the area restrictions constituted a crime under section 215 of the McCarren-Walter Act.

Zemel was followed in 1981 and in 1984 by two rulings upholding the Secretary of State's authority to revoke passports on the ground that the holder's activities were likely to cause serious damage to the national security and finding presidential authority to prohibit all currency transactions in connection with travel to embargoed countries. In HAIG v. AGEE (1981) the Court explicitly stated that regulation of passports is a matter within the executive's authority. Instead of analyzing the Passport Act as a delegation of congressional authority, the Court described the 1856 Passport Act as a recognition of executive authority in the area. In the 1984 *Regan* decision, the Court no longer treated the right to travel abroad as a fundamental liberty, to be limited only in the most compelling circumstances, but instead as subject to limitation by the President in the name of national security or foreign policy.

Congress Protects the Right. Even as the Supreme Court retreated from the position that the Constitution directly protects international travel and deferred to the executive concerning passport and other travel controls, Congress was increasingly active in protecting travel rights against executive limitation.

For example, in the *Haig* case the SOLICITOR GENERAL told the Supreme Court that the President's foreign policy powers include the right to revoke an American's passport in order to prevent him or her from denouncing U.S. policy abroad. In response, in 1991, Congress amended the Passport Act to prohibit revocation of passports on the basis of activities protected by the First Amendment.

Similarly, in 1978, after the ruling in *Zemel*, Congress had explicitly limited executive authority under the Passport Act to impose geographic restrictions on the use of passports. In 1982, however, President Reagan found a way around that limitation by using the trade embargo statutes to impose currency restrictions on travel to embargoed countries. Although the Supreme Court subsequently found (in the *Regan* case) that those restrictions had been authorized by Congress, it did not explain how its conclusion could be reconciled with Congress's explicit prohibition on imposing geographic restrictions on the right to travel. As of late 1992 this controversy was not settled. In 1992, Congress considered the Free Trade in Ideas bill, which would limit all travel bans to situations, already covered in the Passport Act, involving war or imminent danger to travelers, by prohibiting the use of currency restrictions imposed under trade embargoes to ban travel.

Finally, the courts have not recognized any right of foreigners to travel to the United States. [*For discussion of the rights of persons seeking to immigrate to the United States and the rights of aliens to remain in the United States, see* IMMIGRATION POLICY.] Suits such as *Kleindienst v. Mandel* (1972) and *Abourezk v. Reagan* (1986), that have challenged the exclusion of foreign visitors have been brought by Americans claiming that their First Amendment rights to meet with and hear the foreigners were being abridged.

Executive authority to exclude foreign visitors is limited by statute, most notably the McCarren-Walter Act and the Immigration Act of 1990. Those statutes set forth categories of aliens who may not be admitted into the United States, for example, persons who have committed certain kinds of crimes or terrorist activities. In addition, the statutes delegate to the President the power to bar by proclamation persons whose entry "would be detrimental to the interests of the United States." Although the law explicitly authorizes exclusions based on foreign policy reasons, it limits the executive's discretion to make such exclusions, especially when such reasons are based on the visitor's beliefs, statements, or associations. In certain cases the statute requires a personal determination of harm by the Secretary of State and that Congress be notified of such a determination.

BIBLIOGRAPHY

Chafee, Zechariah. *Three Human Rights in the Constitution of 1787.* 1956. Chap. 3.

Dorsen, Norman, Paul Bender, and Burt Neuborne. *Political and Civil Rights in the United States.* 1976. Chap. 11.

Koh, Harold Hongju. *The National Security Constitution.* 1990.

KATE MARTIN

TREASURY, DEPARTMENT OF THE. The second-oldest of the current CABINET departments (after the STATE DEPARTMENT), the Department of the Treasury is the branch of the federal government charged with the management and supervision of the nation's finances. Because most governmental functions overlap with financial and economic issues, the Treasury, with its broad responsibilities, is among the most important of the executive departments, and the Secretary of the Treasury is necessarily a key adviser to the President in the formation and execution of economic policy.

Origins. The Department of the Treasury was created by an act of Congress on 2 September 1789 as the third of the original Cabinet departments, following the departments of State and War. Treasury became the second-ranking department in the Cabinet when the Department of War was eliminated in 1948 and its

Secretaries of the Treasury

President	Secretary of the Treasury
1 Washington	Alexander Hamilton, 1789–1795 Oliver Wolcott, Jr., 1795–1797
2 J. Adams	Oliver Wolcott, Jr., 1797–1800 Samuel Dexter, 1801
3 Jefferson	Samuel Dexter, 1801 Albert Gallatin, 1801–1809
4 Madison	Albert Gallatin, 1809–1814 George W. Campbell, 1814 Alexander J. Dallas, 1814–1816 William H. Crawford, 1816–1817
5 Monroe	William H. Crawford, 1817–1825
6 J. Q. Adams	Richard Rush, 1825–1829
7 Jackson	Samuel D. Ingham, 1829–1831 Louis McLane, 1831–1833 William J. Duane, 1833 Roger B. Taney, 1833–1834 Levi Woodbury, 1834–1837
8 Van Buren	Levi Woodbury, 1837–1841
9 W. H. Harrison	Thomas Ewing, 1841
10 Tyler	Thomas Ewing, 1841 Walter Forward, 1841–1843 John C. Spencer, 1843–1844 George M. Bibb, 1844–1845

President	Secretary of the Treasury
11 Polk	Robert J. Walker, 1845–1849
12 Taylor	William M. Meredith, 1849–1850
13 Fillmore	William M. Meredith, 1850 Thomas Corwin, 1850–1853
14 Pierce	James Guthrie, 1853–1857
15 Buchanan	Howell Cobb, 1857–1860 Philip F. Thomas, 1860–1861 John A. Dix, 1861
16 Lincoln	Salmon P. Chase, 1861–1864 William P. Fessenden, 1864–1865 Hugh McCulloch, 1865
17 A. Johnson	Hugh McCulloch, 1865–1869
18 Grant	George S. Boutwell, 1869–1873 William A. Richardson, 1873–1874 Benjamin H. Bristow, 1874–1876 Lot M. Morrill, 1876–1877
19 Hayes	John Sherman, 1877–1881
20 Garfield	William Windom, 1881
21 Arthur	William Windom, 1881 Charles J. Folger, 1881–1884 Walter Q. Gresham, 1884 Hugh McCulloch, 1884–1885

functions subsumed under the DEPARTMENT OF DEFENSE. In creating the Treasury in the first session after the ratification of the Constitution, Congress recognized the critical importance of national finance to the success of the new government.

The Department of the Treasury grew out of the old Treasury Office of Accounts, which was created by the Continental Congress in 1775 to raise and manage funds necessary to finance the then-impending War of Independence. In this capacity, the Office of Accounts issued bills of credit for sale to the public with the promise that they would be redeemed at some point in the future.

The new department was given far broader powers by the Congress than had been held by the Office of Accounts. The Treasury, in the original legislation, was charged with the following responsibilities: preparing plans for the improvement and management of the nation's revenue and support for the public credit, supervising the collection of government revenue, preparing and reporting estimates of the public revenue and expenditures, enforcing tariff and maritime laws, overseeing the sale of public lands, making reports on all matters pertaining to the Treasury, and receiving, keeping, and distributing the moneys of the United States. These broad financial powers have

remained with the Treasury down to the present day, with appropriate adjustments and additions in response to changing circumstances in the nation.

Treasury, though created in conjunction with the State and War departments, was given a unique and ambiguous status by Congress. State and War were clearly identified as EXECUTIVE DEPARTMENTS in the original legislations, but Treasury was not so clearly identified. The Secretary of the Treasury was required by the statute to provide periodic reports on finance to Congress and to respond in writing and in person on any matter referred to him by Congress. No similar requirements were imposed on the other DEPARTMENTAL SECRETARIES.

The statute suggested that Congress intended Treasury to be affiliated with it in some way, either as the agent of Congress or as the agent jointly of Congress and the President. Congress, jealous of its own powers in the area of finance, may have expected to exercise influence over the Treasury that it did not seek in relation either to State or War with their responsibilities in FOREIGN AFFAIRS. However, the first Treasury Secretary, ALEXANDER HAMILTON, immediately acted as the agent of the executive branch, exactly as did the secretaries of the other departments. The status of the Treasury remained controversial until 1833, when

Secretaries of the Treasury

President	Secretary of the Treasury
22 Cleveland	Daniel Manning, 1885–1887 Charles S. Fairchild, 1887–1889
23 B. Harrison	William Windom, 1889–1891 Charles Foster, 1891–1893
24 Cleveland	John G. Carlisle, 1893–1897
25 McKinley	Lyman J. Gage, 1897–1901
26 T. Roosevelt	Lyman J. Gage, 1901–1902 Leslie M. Shaw, 1902–1907 George B. Cortelyou, 1907–1909
27 Taft	Franklin MacVeagh, 1909–1913
28 Wilson	William G. McAdoo, 1913–1918 Carter Glass, 1918–1920 David F. Houston, 1920–1921
29 Harding	Andrew W. Mellon, 1921–1923
30 Coolidge	Andrew W. Mellon, 1923–1929
31 Hoover	Andrew W. Mellon, 1929–1932 Ogden L. Mills, 1932–1933
32 F. D. Roosevelt	W. H. Woodin, 1933–1934 Henry Morgenthau, Jr., 1934–1945

President	Secretary of the Treasury
33 Truman	Henry Morgenthau, Jr., 1945 Fred M. Vinson, 1945–1946 John W. Snyder, 1946–1953
34 Eisenhower	George M. Humphrey, 1953–1957 Robert B. Anderson, 1957–1961
35 Kennedy	C. Douglas Dillon, 1961–1963
36 L. B. Johnson	C. Douglas Dillon, 1963–1965 Henry H. Fowler, 1965–1968 Joseph W. Barr, 1968–1969
37 Nixon	David M. Kennedy, 1969–1971 John B. Connally, Jr., 1971–1972 George P. Shultz, 1972–1974 William E. Simon, 1974
38 Ford	William E. Simon, 1974–1977
39 Carter	W. Michael Blumenthal, 1977–1979 G. William Miller, 1979–1981
40 Reagan	Donald T. Regan, 1981–1985 James A. Baker, III, 1985–1988 Nicholas F. Brady, 1988–1989
41 Bush	Nicholas F. Brady, 1989–1993
42 Clinton	Lloyd M. Bentsen, 1993–

President Andrew Jackson succeeded, despite initial opposition from the Senate, in removing a Treasury Secretary who defied his orders concerning the BANK OF THE UNITED STATES. Jackson's successes in this confrontation with the Congress thus solidified executive control over the Treasury and ended this controversy.

Functions. The principal functions of the Treasury are to manage the financial and economic affairs of the United States government. Within this mandate, the Treasury has a unique package of responsibilities that cut across both domestic policy and foreign affairs. On the domestic side, the Treasury collects revenue for the government, disburses funds for approved purposes, manages the public debt, keeps government accounts, oversees national banks and insures the soundness of the national banking system, and manufactures coins and currency. On the international side, the Treasury works on dollar exchange, trade, Group of Seven meetings, the International Monetary Fund (IMF), the World Bank, and many other issues dealing with international finance and economic policy.

Both on the domestic and international fronts, Treasury also carries out important law enforcement functions, including the enforcement of tax and tariff laws, interdicting illegal narcotics traffic into the United States, and conducting antifraud and anti-

counterfeiting operations. Following the assassination of President William McKinley in 1901, the SECRET SERVICE, a bureau within Treasury that had earlier been established to stop counterfeiting of U.S. currency, began to provide protection for the President. Its functions were later expanded to include the protection of the President-elect, the President's immediate family, the Vice President, former Presidents, presidential candidates, and other high-ranking officials and foreign diplomats. The Department of the Treasury is thus not only the chief financial institution of the U.S. government but also one of its most important law enforcement agencies.

Congress has seen fit over the years to broaden the scope of the Treasury's responsibilities to keep pace with the expansion of the country and the ever-growing size and complexity of the nation's financial system. Despite these growing responsibilities, there is a fundamental continuity in the history of the department from Hamilton's time to the present; indeed, when I first assumed the office of Secretary of the Treasury in 1974, I was struck by how similar the problems confronting me were to those facing Hamilton when he took his post as the first Treasury Secretary in 1789.

While most government departments are preoccupied with spending funds on programs assigned to them, Treasury has a broader mandate. It must concern itself with raising needed revenue, keeping the government's accounts, financing deficits, and assessing the effects of federal policy on the economy as a whole. These responsibilities have been faced by all secretaries since Hamilton, and though the department itself has grown, it has done so out of the basic structure and functions assigned to it more than two hundred years ago.

Office of the Secretary. Appointed by the President with the consent of the Senate, the Secretary of the Treasury is the chief financial officer of the federal government, responsible for the smooth functioning of revenue collection and disbursement of federal funds, management of the public debt, and the operation of the various Treasury bureaus. The Secretary is also the President's chief economic spokesman and the chief architect to the administration's economic policy. As the second-ranking Cabinet official, the secretary is the key adviser to the President on a range of issues involving government finance.

As the chief financial officer and economic spokesman, the Secretary of the Treasury represents the U.S. government in trade, monetary policy, and economic policy negotiations with foreign governments. He represents the United States as a governor of the International Bank for Reconstruction and Development, the Inter-American Development Bank, and the International Monetary Fund. The Secretary is an ex officio member of various governmental boards concerned with domestic and international financial issues. The Secretary also has chief fiduciary responsibility for the SOCIAL SECURITY trust funds.

The Treasury was once solely responsible for most of the President's economic forecasts, budgets, and economic proposals. Today, however, the Department works with the COUNCIL OF ECONOMIC ADVISERS (CEA), the OFFICE OF MANAGEMENT AND BUDGET (OMB), and the Bureau of Economic Analysis in the DEPARTMENT OF COMMERCE to develop the forecasts that serve as a basis for the administration's budget projections. The Secretary also chairs the "troika" meetings to establish such economic forecasts. These meetings are attended by the Chairman of the CEA, the Director of the OMB and, informally, by the Chairman of the FEDERAL RESERVE BOARD.

The Secretary of the Treasury frequently consults with the Chairman of the Federal Reserve Board on a host of financial questions that concern both institutions. The Federal Reserve is an independent agency charged with regulating the money supply, with powers delegated to it by the Congress. Coordination

between the Treasury and the Federal Reserve is critical, because the Treasury issues and manages the federal debt, and the Federal Reserve regulates the money supply through its open market operations and the sale of federal debt instruments. The Treasury no longer dictates policy to the Federal Reserve, but the Secretary meets often on an informal basis with the Chairman of the Federal Reserve Board to exchange views on the economy and on regulatory issues concerning the financial industry and credit markets.

Organization. The Treasury in 1991 had an annual operating budget of approximately $11 billion and employed more than 160,000 people, making its workforce third in size among Cabinet departments (behind the departments of Defense and VETERANS AFFAIRS) and meaning that, in sheer size, it is the largest law enforcement agency in the U.S. government. The department has its headquarters in Washington, D.C., but maintains field organizations in every state and offices in nearly every major city.

The government's financial activities were at one time concentrated exclusively within the Treasury, but in the last fifty years, several other institutions and agencies have been created to perform functions that had previously been reserved for the Treasury alone. These institutions include, most notably, the Bureau of the Budget (which later became the Office of Management and Budget), the Council of Economic Advisers, and the Federal Reserve Board.

Treasury itself has also experienced much internal diversification in the postwar years. It is currently organized into thirteen departmental offices, which are responsible for making policy and managing the department, and thirteen bureaus, which perform the specific operating functions of the department. The Secretary is aided by a Deputy Secretary, two Undersecretaries, and thirteen Assistant Secretaries who head the various departmental offices. The key assistant secretaries manage the offices for Economic Policy, Tax Policy, International Affairs, and Domestic Finance.

Each of the bureaus is managed by a director who reports to the Secretary through one of the assistant secretaries. Many of the operating bureaus within the Treasury are well known in their own right, independent of their relationship to the Treasury. The thirteen existing operating bureaus are the Bureau of Alcohol, Tobacco, and Firearms; the Internal Revenue Service; the Mint; the Secret Service; the Customs Service; the Comptroller of the Currency; the Bureau of the Public Debt; the U.S. Savings Bond Division; the Financial Management Service; the Federal Law Enforcement Training Center; the Bureau of Government Financial Operations; the Bureau of Engraving and Printing; and the Office of Thrift Supervision.

Treasury Building. Completed in 1842, the Treasury Building is an imposing, five-story, Neoclassical structure, located immediately east of the WHITE HOUSE. In addition to the main building, three wings were constructed between 1860 and 1869 to accommodate the growing department.

The existing building was constructed after the building that had previously housed the department was destroyed by fire in 1833 (arson was suspected). Construction of the new building was to have begun in 1836, but work was delayed when builders and architects could not agree on a location for the cornerstone. Legend has it that President Jackson, frustrated by the haggling, walked over to the site one day, planted his cane in the ground, and declared, "Right here is where I want the cornerstone." Thus was established the location of the building, which, because of Jackson's haste, blocks the view of the Capitol Building from the White House.

The proximity of the Treasury Building to the White House is a clear sign of the importance of the Treasury to the President, and because of its location the building has been the scene of many important historical events. Indeed, President Andrew Johnson even had to keep his offices in the Treasury Building for a time after Abraham Lincoln's death when MARY TODD LINCOLN refused to leave the White House.

Treasury's Changing Role. Since the department's beginnings, the scope and magnitude of the Treasury's functions and responsibilities have grown enormously. In large part, this growth has resulted from the continuing expansion of the federal government's presence in nearly every aspect of the nation's life. Government expenditures in the early days of the Republic represented a very small fraction of the total income produced in the country. These expenditures now amount to one-quarter of the nation's gross domestic product. Taxes have grown along with expenditures, though at a somewhat slower rate, and they now represent about one-fifth of gross domestic product. The accumulated difference between the growth in expenditures and taxes is the national debt, which in 1992 totaled $3.9 trillion, of which $2.7 trillion was held by the public. These facts and figures significantly understate the pervasive role of the federal government, however. Government regulations and mandates apply to virtually every type of economic activity and exert a major and, not infrequently, harmful influence on the conduct of all aspects of the daily economic affairs of every household and business in the country.

This imposing array of government activities must be financed. As the scope of government activities has increased, so too has the federal government's claim on the income of the American people. The federal tax system, especially the income tax, has become ever more complex and demanding; the Internal Revenue Code now consists of hundreds of sections and thousands of pages, defying comprehension by even the most skillful and experienced tax experts.

We need to remind ourselves that our government has no power except that granted to it by the American people. As I maintained throughout my tenure as Treasury Secretary and in my 1978 book *A Time for Truth*, much of the cynicism and negativism in late twentieth-century America is the result of the demonstrated failure of collectivist approaches to national problems that have promised so much and delivered so little. In the process, a mood of dependence on government has increased, feeding on itself and creating still more demands for benefits without recognizing that the bills must be paid—either directly in higher taxes and growing debt burdens or indirectly through accelerating inflation and economic disruption.

We ignore at our peril the fundamental truth that our personal, political, and economic freedoms are inextricably linked and that loss of economic freedom invariably leads to loss of political and personal freedoms. Our basic challenge, then, is to determine how much personal freedom, if any, we are willing to give up in seeking security through government. It is not easy to live with the uncertainties of a free society, but the real personal benefits it creates are far superior to those created in any other system. In short, it is America's faith in a free economy, more than anything else, that is in need of revitalization if we are going to remain the freest and most prosperous nation into the twenty-first century.

BIBLIOGRAPHY

Simon, William E. *A Time for Action.* 1980.

Simon, William E. *A Time for Truth.* 1978.

U.S. Treasury Department. *The Treasury Story.* 1966.

Walston, Mark. *The Department of the Treasury.* 1989.

White, Leonard D. *The Federalists: A Study in Administrative History.* 1948.

White, Leonard D. *The Jacksonians: A Study in Administrative History, 1829–1861.* 1954.

White, Leonard D. *The Jeffersonians: A Study in Administrative History, 1801–1829.* 1951.

White, Leonard D. *The Republican Era: A Study in Administrative History, 1869–1901.* 1958.

WILLIAM E. SIMON

TREATIES, MUTUAL SECURITY. In the years following WORLD WAR II, the United States entered into several mutual security treaties that bound it militarily to a number of foreign countries. The more prominent of these treaties are the ANZUS (Australia, New Zealand, and the United States) TREATY, the NATO (North Atlantic Treaty Organization) TREATY, the RIO TREATY (the Inter-American Treaty of Reciprocal Assistance), and the SEATO (Southeast Asia Collective Defense) TREATY.

There is a broad misunderstanding that these treaty obligations constitute ironclad guarantees that the United States will automatically come to the defense of a treaty partner subject to armed attack. Similar confusion exists about the effect of these treaties on the allocation of WAR POWERS within the federal government. On various occasions Presidents have interpreted the security treaties as sources of authority to introduce U.S. armed forces into hostilities. The Lyndon B. Johnson administration claimed that the SEATO Treaty committed the United States to defend South Vietnam and authorized the President to undertake independent military action toward that end. President Richard M. Nixon, in vetoing the WAR POWERS RESOLUTION of 1973 objected that it contained prohibitions "against fulfilling our obligations under the NATO treaty as ratified by the Senate."

These views are seriously mistaken. Mutual security treaties generally provide that they will be carried out by the United States in accordance with its "constitutional processes." The procedure to be used by the United States in discharging its treaty obligations is left undecided. Under the Constitution the decision to go to war does not reside in a single branch but rather is lodged in both Congress and the President. Article VI provides that the Constitution, the federal laws, and all treaties shall be the "supreme Law of the Land," binding all judges in the states. The fact that treaties are supreme law does not mean that a mutual security treaty can amend or alter the Constitution, however. As the Supreme Court noted in *Geofroy v. Riggs* (1890), the TREATY-MAKING POWER does not "authorize what the Constitution forbids, or [effect] a change in the character of the government." The President and the Senate may not enter into a treaty that takes constitutional prerogatives over foreign commerce, the power of the purse, or the power to go to war away from the House of Representatives. The war-making power was intended to reside jointly in the House of Representatives and the Senate.

A 1979 report of the Senate Foreign Relations Committee (S. Rept. No. 7) correctly sums up the legal and constitutional status of treaties: no mutual security treaty to which the United States is a party "authorizes the President to introduce the armed forces into hostilities or requires the United States to do so, automatically, if another party to any such treaty is attacked." By including language that treaties will be carried out by the United States in accordance with its "constitutional processes," or by adopting similar qualifications, "the distribution of power within the United States Government is precisely what it would have been in the absence of the treaty, and . . . the United States reserves the right to determine for itself what military action, if any, is appropriate."

The meaning of the phrase "constitutional processes" remains a complex legal issue. It is less difficult, however, to analyze whether U.S. mutual security treaties serve as a supplementary source of authority enabling the President to introduce U.S. armed forces into hostilities. Part of the confusion has derived from a focus on the word *constitutional* to the virtual exclusion of the word *processes*. "Process" suggests deliberation; it implies procedure leading to choice. In certain circumstances, the question of whether Congress should choose to act is academic. The President clearly possesses independent constitutional authority to introduce armed forces into some hostilities, such as taking defensive measures in response to an armed attack. In such situations the language in a mutual security treaty is irrelevant because the U.S. Constitution provides all the authority the President requires.

On the other hand, the issue is far from academic in circumstances where no source of authority exists other than a mutual security treaty. In debates on the mutual security treaties, members of the Senate often repeated that the United States was committing itself to do only what it deemed appropriate. The terms of the treaties say nothing about what the United States must do if another party is attacked. The treaties leave the war-making powers of each branch precisely where those powers would have been in the treaties' absence. None of the treaties confers any additional war-making power on the President. The negotiators wrote into the treaties the fullest measure of commitment that their domestic legal and political systems would allow—which was, in fact, none at all.

BIBLIOGRAPHY

Glennon, Michael J. *Constitutional Diplomacy.* 1990.

Glennon, Michael J. "United States Mutual Security Treaties: The Commitment Myth." *Columbia Journal of Transnational Law* 24 (1986): 509–552.

MICHAEL J. GLENNON

TREATY-MAKING POWER. Article II of the Constitution gives the President the "Power, by and with the Advice and Consent of the Senate, to make Treaties, provided two thirds of the Senators present concur." The President serves as the nation's DIPLOMAT IN CHIEF and the authority to make treaties is one of the President's most significant foreign affairs powers. This presidential power includes making the United States' bilateral and multilateral treaties with other countries on a variety of topics (for example, treaties on tariffs, economic relations, nuclear arms, mutual defense, human rights, and terrorism). Through his treaty-making capacity, the President or his designees conduct communications and negotiations with other foreign leaders. The President's treaty-making authority, however, is subject to the Senate's ADVICE AND CONSENT; this requirement often has led to disputes between the executive branch and the Senate over treaties that the President has negotiated with another country. Such disputes are part of a broader SEPARATION OF POWERS controversy between the political branches over the treaty power.

In the Constitution. Framers of the Constitution established the treaty power so that it would be centralized in the new national government, rather than dispersed among the several separate states of the Union. Indeed, a major impetus for forging the Constitution was to avoid the individual states' embarrassing international forays under the weak Confederacy following the War for Independence. James Madison wrote that the Confederacy's main defect was its inability to "cause infractions of treaties, or of the law of nations to be punished," and thus "particular states might by their conduct provoke war without control." The Articles of Confederation conferred upon Congress "the sole and exclusive right and power of . . . entering into treaties and alliances," although the states could still enter into a treaty with another nation with the Congress's consent. The Articles of Confederation, moreover, created neither an executive nor a judiciary of which to speak; the Confederacy lacked an effective enforcement mechanism to stop the individual states from rambunctiously entering into treaties and from conducting foreign affairs on their own. It was important for the United States to coordinate successful foreign relations, particularly given the wary existence of a country in its infancy. As a result of these concerns, the new Constitution placed the treaty power in the new national government and expressly says that "No State shall enter into any Treaty, Alliance or Confederation." This and other constitutional prescriptions helped to ensure that the treaty power is centralized, and more generally that foreign relations are federal relations.

The Framers, however, still had to decide how to distribute the treaty-making power (and other FOREIGN AFFAIRS powers) among the three branches of the new federal government. In July 1787, the CONSTITUTIONAL CONVENTION appointed a Committee of Detail to create a draft constitution, pursuant to the Convention's prior resolutions. That committee's draft placed the treaty-making power exclusively in the Senate; it did not provide any presidential involvement in the treaty-making process. The draft clause simply read: "The Senate of the United States shall have power to make treaties, and to appoint Ambassadors." The Committee of Detail's delegation of the treaty power to the legislative branch was reminiscent of the Articles of Confederation, which, as noted, also had conferred the treaty power exclusively upon Congress. The committee's draft proposal stirred controversy at the Convention, although the initial negative reaction had little to do with the President's absence from the treaty-making process. Instead, the controversy stemmed from the fact that the House of Representatives would not participate in making treaties; that debate involved the more general issue of how the states should be represented (equally or proportionate to their populations) when regulating various federal powers. Relatedly, the committee draft also engendered discussion about the fact that a simple majority of Senators could make a treaty, since the proposal did not contain any special voting requirement for a treaty's passage (e.g., a two-thirds or other "super majority" rule).

Of course, the Constitutional Convention adopted a treaty clause markedly different from the Committee of Detail's version. The treaty clause does still preclude the "fluctuating" and "multitudinous" House of Representatives from making treaties (FEDERALIST 75). As ALEXANDER HAMILTON reasoned in that essay: "Accurate and comprehensive knowledge of foreign politics; . . . a nice and uniform sensibility to national character; decision, secrecy, and dispatch, are incompatible with the genius of a body so variable and numerous." Unlike the committee version, however, the Constitution's treaty clause requires not just a simple majority, but a two-thirds majority of the Senators voting to adopt a treaty. And the most significant difference between the proposed and adopted treaty clauses is that the Framers gave the treaty-making power to the President. Why did they empower the President to make treaties, while the committee had given him absolutely no role in treaty making? Unfortunately, the records from the Constitutional Convention inadequately illuminate this dramatic shift in the treaty power. According to James Madison's notes, one speaker, John Francis Mercer of Maryland, strongly favored presidential domination of treaty making, following the British model: Mr. Mercer "contended . . . that the Senate ought not have the power of treaties. This power belonged to the Executive department" (2 M. Farrand, *The Records of the Federal Convention of 1787*, at 297). This was the case of treaties in Great Britain. But it should be noted that Mercer was not one of the most influential or significant convention delegates.

Interpreting the Constitution. Certain essays in *The Federalist* (published to support the Constitution's ratification) argue for the President's authority over foreign affairs, including the treaty-making power. For example, in *Federalist* 75, Alexander Hamilton asserts that if the President played only a "ministerial" role in treaty making, he "could not be expected to enjoy the confidence and respect of foreign powers in the same degree with the constitutional representative of the nation, and, of course, would not be able to act with an equal degree of weight or efficacy." Those who argue for executive supremacy over treaty making cite to such passages, as they do to John Marshall's later, much-quoted remark: "The President is the sole organ of the nation in its external relations, and its sole representative with foreign nations" (10 *Annals of Cong.* 613 [1800]). But the significance of Marshall's stanza should not be exaggerated or taken out of context; he actually uttered it in a speech before the House of Representatives on an extradition matter. Moreover, those who argue for a greater sharing of the treaty power between the President and the Senate can also cite *The Federalist*. In fact, also in *Federalist* 75, Hamilton himself writes that the treaty-making power "does not seem strictly to fall within the definition of either" the executive or legislative authority. And "the history of human conduct does not warrant the exalted opinion of human virtue which would make it wise . . . to commit interests of so delicate and momentous a kind, as those which concern its intercourse with the rest of the world, to the sole disposal of . . . [the] President." Given the fact that Article II subjects presidential treaty making to the Senate's advice and consent—and given the lack of historical evidence for trivializing the senatorial role in treaty making—it is reasonable to conclude that the Framers simply intended for some balancing of the treaty power between the President and the Senate.

The Role of the Senate. The President and the Senate, however, have not balanced the treaty power easily. In 1789, President George Washington initiated a meeting with the Senate to seek its advice on the terms of a treaty that he wanted to negotiate with southern Indians. The President was displeased when the Senate then referred the matter to a committee, causing him to return to the Senate for a second meeting on the treaty. No President (including Washington) has ever again so personally sought the Senate's advice on a treaty before its negotiation. Thereafter, during the early 1790s, Washington dealt with the Senate on such matters only in writing. But in 1794, Washington did not at all seek (even in writing) the Senate's advice on JAY's TREATY before concluding negotiations with Great Britain. Not having had the opportunity previously to give advice on Jay's Treaty, the Senate retaliated by revising one article of the treaty as part of its decision to consent to the treaty; Washington was then forced to seek Great Britain's agreement to the revised article. This reduction or postponement of the Senate's advice function was not limited to Jay's Treaty. Only rarely over the next two hundred years have Presidents solicited the Senate's advice prior to concluding treaty negotiations. Since the Senate does not usually participate in treaty making until its consent to ratification is solicited, the Senate is more likely to reject a treaty than might otherwise be the case. At a minimum, the Senate is more likely to seek treaty amendments or reservations, causing the President either to reopen negotiations with the other sovereign, or to decide himself to shelve a treaty if the Senate's amendments are too substantial. In short, the treaty-making process is inefficient, controversial, and potentially embarrassing and adverse to the President's dealings with foreign sovereigns. Without its more timely advice on treaties, the Senate has indeed become the graveyard of treaties.

Despite these significant problems, the executive branch has not tried to improve the Senate's advice function. A President apparently would rather risk the rejection of his treaty than to give the Senate a more meaningful role in treaty making—which might be taken as a concession that he is not the sole organ of foreign affairs but a copartner with the Senate in shaping the nation's international commitments. Presidents occasionally have appointed a few key Senators to a treaty's negotiating team, ostensibly seeking their advice during a treaty's formulation. But such a practice may violate the Constitution's prohibition in Article I against a Senator being "appointed to any civil office under the authority of the United States, which shall have been created, or the emoluments whereof shall have been increased during such time." A cynic, moreover, might suggest that the executive branch has appointed Senators as treaty negotiators not really to gain their wise advice but to make them feel superficially that they are part of the treaty-making process, so that they will later work to gain the Senate's consent to a treaty. That practice does not meaningfully enhance the advice function of the Senate as a whole. Presidents, however, might contend that most Senators lack the foreign affairs expertise to provide helpful advice during a treaty's negotiation. In addition, soliciting the Senate's advice throughout the treaty-making process might itself be inefficient, time-consuming, and counterproductive. It is arguable that the United States should speak in one, unified voice (the President's) when negotiating with another nation's executive branch; this argument recommends postponing the Senate's input until the President has concluded his treaty negotiations.

Executive Agreements. It is thus not surprising that Presidents have tried to circumvent the treaty-making process. Presidents historically have established certain international agreements without following the treaty clause's procedures. Such instruments are called EXECUTIVE AGREEMENTS and are classified by three categories: a treaty-authorized executive agreement, which is an agreement that the President establishes with another nation pursuant to a treaty to which the Senate earlier consented; a congressional-executive agreement, to which the President procures a majority of both Houses' consent (rather than two-thirds of the Senate's consent) before or after making the agreement with the other nation; and a sole-executive agreement, which the President establishes with another nation without any senatorial or congressional consent.

The first category, the treaty-authorized executive agreement, has not been problematical because the President originally received the Senate's consent when the initial compact (the treaty) was created; so the Senate essentially preapproved the subsequent compact (the executive agreement) by which the President executes the initial compact (the treaty). However, the second and third categories, the congressional-executive agreement and the sole-executive agreement, have been very controversial. Since Article II of the Constitution mentions only treaties and not other international compacts, it is arguable that all compacts must be made pursuant to the treaty clause's procedures or are otherwise unconstitutional. Apart from this textual argument that all nontreaty agreements are invalid, sole-executive agreements raise more difficult separation-of-powers issues than do congressional-executive agreements.

Although they can be approved by a simple majority (not a two-thirds majority), congressional-executive agreements do involve the Congress in checking and balancing presidential power. The Framers may have intended for just the Senate and not the House of Representatives to participate in making international compacts, but actually democracy might be better served when the entire Congress plays a representational role in ratifying congressional-executive agreements, as compared with the more elite Senate representing the people in ratifying treaties. Sole-executive agreements, however, are particularly problematical because they are made exclusively by the President and without any congressional input or oversight. The President's creation of sole-executive agreements is inconsistent with the Framers' view that the Senate and President should share the treaty-making power.

In the final analysis, congressional-executive agreements are probably too entrenched in the political system for them to be discarded as an alternative to treaties; but sole-executive agreements should not be created unless they concern either mundane matters or substantive topics clearly within the President's exclusive Article II powers. Furthermore, the executive and legislative branches should try to find mutually acceptable criteria for determining when an accord may be cast as an executive agreement and when it must be cast as a treaty. Until the political branches (or the courts) establish such criteria, executive agreements will continue to be a controversial alternative to the treaty-making process.

The Treaty Process. Within the executive branch, the President (or usually his designees in the White House or the State Department) decides whether and how to negotiate both treaties and executive agreements with other nations. The President or his designee identifies and instructs the individuals who will negotiate the accord. The nature and significance of a particular agreement dictates both who will represent the United States in the negotiations and how long the negotiations will take. The treaty negotiations are regulated by diplomatic protocol and international law (not constitutional law). Once the executive branch is satisfied with the agreement, it will transmit the agreement to the Senate in the case of treaties—which is where the dispute begins about the Senate's advice and consent. Presidents later decide, one last time, whether the United States should sign the formal documents obligating the country to follow treaties to which the Senate has consented.

But even if the President signs such documents and the United States becomes a party to the treaty, the executive and legislative branches may argue further about the President's interpretation of the treaty, and whether that interpretation is consistent with the Senate's original understanding of the treaty. For example, the Senate disagreed with the SOFAER DOCTRINE, which President Ronald Reagan invoked to reinterpret nuclear arms agreements with the Soviet Union to allow for the deployment of new technology. And the political branches may also argue about whether the President alone can terminate a treaty without any congressional consent, as they did when President Jimmy Carter unilaterally terminated the Mutual Defense Treaty with Taiwan. Such controversies about interpreting and terminating international agreements are linked with the historic controversy about treaty making; all of these debates essentially concern balancing the power to shape the nation's treaty obligations. The Framers committed that power to two branches of government, so that they could oversee each other. Although such oversight has advantages, it certainly has caused treaty making to be disputatious.

[See also INTERNATIONAL LAW, PRESIDENT AND.]

BIBLIOGRAPHY

Bestor, Arthur. "Respective Roles of Senate and President in the Making and Abrogation of Treaties—The Original Intent of the Framers of the Constitution Historically Examined." *Washington Law Review* 55 (1979): 1–135.

Franck, Thomas M., and Michael J. Glennon. *Foreign Affairs and National Security Law.* 1987. Chapter 3.

Franck, Thomas M., and Edward Weisband. *Foreign Policy by Congress.* 1979. Chapter 6.

Henkin, Louis. *Foreign Affairs and the Constitution.* 1972.

Randall, Kenneth C. "The Treaty Power." *Ohio State Law Journal* 51 (1990): 1089–1126.

KENNETH C. RANDALL

TREATY OF GHENT. Although President James Madison did not manage the WAR OF 1812 very well, he did much better with the peace negotiations that resulted in the Treaty of Ghent. Within a week after the declaration of war in June 1812, Madison sent out peace feelers, apparently hoping that the decision for war itself would induce the British to make concessions on the two leading issues—the orders in council regulating American trade with Europe and impressment (forcing sailors from American ships into British naval service). By this time the British had repealed the orders in council but refused to give up impressment. Hence the negotiations of 1812 ended in failure even though both sides were interested in peace.

In early 1813 Madison eagerly accepted a Russian offer to mediate an end to the war, but the British declined to take part. Later that year, however, the British offered direct negotiations, and again Madison, who was increasingly anxious to liquidate a war that was going badly, eagerly accepted. To represent the United States in the negotiations, the President chose an excellent commission that included ALBERT GALLATIN, John Quincy Adams, and HENRY CLAY. The British, on the other hand, appointed an undistinguished commission.

When the negotiations began in Ghent (in present-day Belgium) in August 1814, the British demanded as the price for peace that the United States create an INDIAN reservation in the Northwest Territory, surrender territory in northern Maine and Minnesota, withdraw its warships and destroy its fortifications on the Great Lakes, and surrender fishing privileges in Canadian waters. The American envoys rejected these terms, and in a deft move Madison publicized the British demands, thereby increasing support for the war at home and undermining support in England.

The British gradually retreated from their initial position and ultimately dropped all their demands. The Treaty of Ghent, which was signed on 24 December 1814 (and thus is known as the Peace of Christmas Eve), provided for returning to the status quo ante bellum. When this agreement reached the United States in February 1815, Madison promptly submitted it to the Senate, where it was unanimously approved.

In announcing the restoration of peace, the President proclaimed the war a success. Even though the United States had failed to achieve its war aims, Democratic-Republican orators and editors echoed the President's cry and made much political capital out of the war. Madison may not have managed the war effort efficiently, but his envoys had outmaneuvered the British in the peace negotiations, and as a result the nation was able to escape from the war with its honor and territory intact.

BIBLIOGRAPHY

Engelman, Fred L. *The Peace of Christmas Eve.* 1962.

Perkins, Bradford. *Castlereagh and Adams: England and the United States, 1812–1823.* 1964.

Updyke, Frank A. *The Diplomacy of the War of 1812.* 1915.

DONALD R. HICKEY

TREATY OF GUADALUPE HIDALGO (1848). In the Treaty of Guadalupe Hidalgo, which ended the Mexican War, Mexico relinquished all claims to Texas north of the Rio Grande and ceded New Mexico and California to the United States. Ten months earlier President James K. Polk had moved to capitalize on a succession of American military victories in Mexico by sending Nicholas P. Trist, chief clerk in the Department of State, to join General WINFIELD SCOTT's army outside Vera Cruz and negotiate a peace with Mexican officials at his first opportunity. Trist's instructions of 15 April 1847, favored a boundary that included the Rio Grande, the southern line of New Mexico, and the Gila and Colorado rivers "to a point directly opposite the division line between Upper and Lower California; thence, due west, along the said line which runs north of the parallel of 32 degrees and south of San Miguel to the Pacific Ocean." New England merchants had convinced Polk that San Diego Bay was as essential as San Francisco in providing ample frontage on the Pacific. The proposed boundary was designed to acquire San Diego as the sine qua non of any treaty. Although the President claimed New Mexico and California as war indemnity, he agreed to compensate Mexico as much as $25 million for the two north Mexican provinces.

After months of futile efforts Trist, in August 1847, managed to negotiate an armistice; in the interest of peace he accepted the Mexican offer of the Nueces in Texas and San Francisco along the Pacific, an agreement that soon filtered across the United States through the New Orleans press. When the Mexicans broke the truce, Scott's army advanced on Mexico City and occupied the capital in September. Upon his discovery that Trist had ignored his instructions the President recalled his agent without naming a successor. In his December message to Congress, Polk denied the possibility of peace and urged Congress to support him in increasing the tempo of the war against an already defeated enemy. While the President searched futilely for some means to negotiate an end to the war, Mexican officials promised Trist a suitable treaty if he would disregard his orders and remain in Mexico. Encouraged by General Scott and the British legation, Trist informed Washington in December that he intended to negotiate a treaty, leaving the administration at liberty to disavow his proceeding if it chose.

Negotiations began on 2 January 1848, in the village of Guadalupe Hidalgo outside Mexico City. The Mexican negotiators accepted the Rio Grande line to the southern boundary of New Mexico readily enough. For Trist, however, the primary challenge was the negotiation of a boundary that secured San Diego Bay. Secretary of State James Buchanan had reminded Trist in October that the administration regarded San Diego almost as important commercially as San Francisco and that his instructions had been phrased to assure its acquisition. The negotiators agreed to the Gila River line between New Mexico and the Colorado. The short segment between the Colorado and the Pacific presented a greater difficulty because the Mexicans were determined to hold San Diego. They ar-

gued that San Diego lay south of the historic line separating Upper from Lower California. Trist, having agreed to accept the historic boundary, proceeded to prove through an examination of old maps and other evidence that San Diego lay historically in Upper California. Trist now constructed a boundary that joined the mouth of the Gila at the Colorado with a point on the Pacific one league south of the southern tip of San Diego Bay. That boundary completed the American quest for frontage on the Pacific. The Treaty of Guadalupe Hidalgo, with its transfer of California and New Mexico, as well as portions of Arizona, Utah, Nevada, Colorado, and Texas, ceded about 1.2 million square miles of Mexican territory to the United States. In exchange the United States agreed to pay Mexico $15 million and assume the claims of U.S. citizens against that country, totaling $3,250,000.

Although the treaty, signed 2 February 1848, achieved all of his territorial objectives, Polk hesitated to submit it to the Senate for approval. The treaty was unauthorized and faced heavy opposition from those who demanded the annexation of all Mexico and those who opposed all territorial acquisitions, fearful that New Mexico and California would raise the divisive issue of SLAVERY in the territories. Finally on 23 February the President forwarded the treaty to the Senate, which approved it on 10 March by a vote of 38 to 14. In the majority were twenty-six Democrats and twelve Whigs; opposed were seven Democrats and seven Whigs. On 25 May the Mexican congress ratified the treaty; five days later the treaties were formally exchanged. Polk proclaimed the treaty in effect on 4 July 1848.

BIBLIOGRAPHY

Bauer, K. Jack. *The Mexican War, 1846–1848.* 1974.

Graebner, Norman A. *Empire on the Pacific: A Study in American Continental Expansion.* 1955.

Klein, Julius. *The Making of the Treaty of Guadaloupe Hidalgo on February 2, 1848.* 1905.

Pletcher, David M. *The Diplomacy of Annexation: Texas, Oregon, and the Mexican War.* 1973.

Smith, Justin H. *The War with Mexico.* 2 vols. 1919.

NORMAN A. GRAEBNER

TREATY OF VERSAILLES. At the end of WORLD WAR I, President Woodrow Wilson attended the Paris Peace Conference of 1919 to prepare the conditions of peace for Germany. Before the armistice, the United States and the Allies had promised to base the settlement on Wilson's FOURTEEN POINTS. After several months of negotiations, the delegates completed the peace treaty and presented it to the Germans at Versailles. This treaty shaped the context for international politics until WORLD WAR II.

The Paris meeting, reflected the global character of world politics as the United States and Japan joined Great Britain, France, and Italy to make up the five great powers. New states, such as Poland and Czechoslovakia, that had emerged from the collapse of the Russian, Austro-Hungarian, and German empires were also represented. Delegates from every continent attended. But Russia, following the Bolshevik revolution of 1917, did not participate. The Weimar Republic, which had replaced the Imperial German government of Kaiser Wilhelm II, sent its delegation to Versailles only after Allied and U.S. leaders had prepared the treaty.

Wilson had reiterated the redemptive theme of his foreign policy at the beginning of the peace conference. He urged the Allies to join the United States in a new world order of democracy and capitalism that his Fourteen Points had promised. Emphasizing the principle of national self-determination, he viewed the LEAGUE OF NATIONS as the most important feature of his peace program. His first priority in Paris was the drafting of the Covenant for this new international organization to preserve postwar peace. For him, the Covenant would become an essential and integral part of the Treaty of Versailles.

Because the Allies did not share Wilson's concept of global interdependence, he needed to accommodate their interests to win their approval for his League of Nations. British delegates usually cooperated with the United States in drafting the Covenant, but Prime Minister David Lloyd George still forced Wilson to accept a system of mandates and a naval agreement that would protect British imperial interests. The British also convinced him to obligate Germany to pay unspecified sums for reparations to the Allies, including some indirect war costs as well as compensation for damage in the war zone and on the high seas. To exclude even larger claims, Wilson approved the assertion of Germany's moral responsibility for the war, or war guilt, in the treaty.

Rather than rely on a weak League, the French wanted to restore the European balance of power by establishing alliances and strategic frontiers around Germany. Wilson and the Allies agreed to disarm Germany and restrict the size of its future armed forces and transferred German territory to France and Poland. They also rejected Germany's right to annex Austria or any other part of the former Austro-Hungarian empire. In his definition of national self-determination, the President showed more sympathy for the Allies and the new nations of Poland and Czechoslovakia than for the defeated enemy.

Other Allies also extracted some concessions from Wilson. Italy claimed Fiume and other territory that had been in the Austro-Hungarian empire, and Japan demanded control over China's Shantung province. By accommodating various Allied interests, Wilson succeeded in drafting the Covenant for the postwar League.

The Germans strenuously objected to the Treaty of Versailles as a violation of the Fourteen Points. It fell far short of what they had expected. They interpreted Wilson's principles to their own advantage, in contrast to the Allies and the United States. Protesting against Germany's exclusion from the League of Nations, the Germans denounced the treaty for requiring their nation to disarm unilaterally, to surrender territory to France and Poland, to pay unspecified reparations, and to admit war guilt. Only under duress did the Weimar Republic, with a new coalition government and different delegates, finally sign the Versailles Treaty on 28 June 1919. The U.S. Senate, though, rejected the treaty. Unable to reconcile the deep conflicts among nations after World War I, the treaty did not inaugurate a new era of peace as Wilson had hoped.

[See LEAGUE OF NATIONS *for discussion of the American ratification controversy.*]

BIBLIOGRAPHY

Ambrosius, Lloyd E. *Woodrow Wilson and the American Diplomatic Tradition: The Treaty Fight in Perspective.* 1987.

Floto, Inga. *Colonel House in Paris: A Study of American Policy at the Paris Peace Conference, 1919.* 1980.

Levin, N. Gordon, Jr. *Woodrow Wilson and World Politics: America's Response to War and Revolution.* 1968.

Schwabe, Klaus. *Woodrow Wilson, Revolutionary Germany, and Peacemaking, 1918–1919: Missionary Diplomacy and the Realities of Power.* 1985.

Walworth, Arthur. *Wilson and His Peacemakers: American Diplomacy at the Paris Peace Conference, 1919.* 1986.

LLOYD E. AMBROSIUS

TREATY OF WASHINGTON (1871). During the CIVIL WAR the Lincoln administration warned the British government repeatedly that it would demand full compensation for damage done to Northern shipping by British-built Confederate cruisers. After the war the U.S. government pressed London for a settlement of the so-called *Alabama* claims, but without success. British spokesman readily acknowledged Britain's responsibility. Despite such admissions of liability, however, the London government insisted that British behavior during the war was justified by law. Meanwhile Senator Charles Sumner of Massachusetts, chairman of the Foreign Relations Committee, argued that Britain pay not only $125 million for direct Union losses at sea but also an additional $2 billion for indirect costs resulting from Britain's encouragement of Southern resistance.

Early in 1871 the Anglo-Russian crisis over the Black Sea question created a war scare, prompting the Russians to scatter rumors of possible United States–Russian cooperation. Convinced that such rumors frightened the British, President Ulysses S. Grant's Secretary of State HAMILTON FISH informed London that they were possibly valid. The British agreed to settle the *Alabama* claims, but insisted on arbitration. To this Fish agreed. The Joint High Commission met in Washington on 27 February 1871. It required two months of deliberation to produce an agreement. The two countries signed the Treaty of Washington on 8 May 1871; the Senate approved it against little opposition. Unfortunately, the agreement provided only for arbitration of claims. In the preliminary American case Fish presented the indirect claims; the British insisted that he withdraw them. When the tribunal convened at Geneva in June 1872, the two sides again clashed over indirect claims. Only when the U.S. representatives withdrew them did the British submit their arguments and enable the tribunal to hear testimony. In August the tribunal found the British guilty of negligence and awarded the United States $15.5 million.

BIBLIOGRAPHY

Cook, Adrian. *The Alabama Claims: American Politics and Anglo-American Relations, 1865–1872.* 1975.
Smith, Goldwin. *The Treaty of Washington, 1871: A Study of Imperial History.* 1941.

NORMAN A. GRAEBNER

TREATY OF WASHINGTON (1921–1922).

Meeting from 12 November 1921 to 6 February 1922, the Washington Armament Conference produced three major and several lesser treaties. The most important, the Five-Power Naval Treaty or simply the Washington Treaty, called for a ten-year moratorium on capital ship (over 10,000 tons) construction; for scrapping sixty-six capital ships, leaving the United States with 525,850 tons, Britain 558,950, Japan 303,320, France 221,170, and Italy 182,800; for replacement ratios of 5:5:3:1.75:1.75; and for maintaining the status quo on naval fortifications in the western

Pacific. Also negotiated were the Four-Power Treaty, committing the United States, Britain, Japan, and France to respect one another's Pacific possessions and consult if peace in the area was threatened, and the Nine-Power Treaty, committing its signatories (the five naval powers plus Portugal, Belgium, the Netherlands, and China) to the OPEN DOOR principle in China.

The impetus for such action came from combined concerns about high naval expenditures, renewal of the Anglo-Japanese alliance, and international rivalry in the Far East. In response, Secretary of State CHARLES EVANS HUGHES took the lead in convening the conference, electrifying it by specifying the ships to be scrapped, and shaping the subsequent negotiations. President Warren G. Harding, however, strongly backed Hughes and played an important role in getting Senate approval of the outcome. Some historians still consider the conference's success in alleviating international tensions as a major diplomatic achievement of which the Harding presidency could be rightfully proud. But others have criticized the treaties for giving Japan effective control of the western Pacific, and still others have seen them as part of the period's naive and misguided effort to build an American peacekeeping system outside the LEAGUE OF NATIONS structure. The naval treaty expired following Japanese denunciation of it in 1934.

BIBLIOGRAPHY

Buckley, Thomas H. *The United States and the Washington Conference, 1921–1922.* 1970.
Dingman, Roger. *Power in the Pacific: The Origins of Naval Arms Limitation, 1914–1922.* 1976.
Vinson, John Chalmers. *The Parchment Peace: The United States Senate and the Washington Conference, 1921–1922.* 1955.

ELLIS W. HAWLEY

TREATY REINTERPRETATION.

During the 1980s, the executive branch and the Senate debated the President's authority to reinterpret a treaty. Article II of the Constitution empowers the President to make treaties, subject to the ADVICE AND CONSENT of two-thirds of the Senators present. The President must administer treaties, just as he executes all other federal laws. Every time the executive administers the law, he obviously interprets it and must be given some reasonable leeway in doing so. It is arguable that the President needs particular discretion when executing treaties, since he is the nation's DIPLOMAT IN CHIEF. The TREATY-MAKING POWER, however, is subject to senatorial oversight. And the treaty-reinterpretation debate concerns whether the President must implement a treaty pursuant to the Senate's original understanding of that compact, or whether he may revise the executive branch's interpretation of the treaty contrary to the Senate's view of the treaty. This debate has had serious constitutional and political implications.

The Sofaer Doctrine. When President Reagan inaugurated SDI (STRATEGIC DEFENSE INITIATIVE) in 1983, many Senators claimed that the SDI's development and deployment would illegally contravene the Senate's understanding of the ABM (ANTIBALLISTIC MISSILE SYSTEM) TREATY when it consented to that treaty in 1972. President Ronald Reagan initially agreed with this position; he conceded that if the SDI ever moved from the "research" phase to the "development" and "deployment" phases, the United States would have to renegotiate the ABM Treaty with the Soviet Union. Two years later, however, the Reagan administration announced its reinterpretation of the ABM Treaty, under which at least the SDI's development is permissible. Although inconsistent with the Senate's original understanding of the treaty, the reinterpretation involved an innovative reading of one Treaty provision; it also drew upon an agreed statement that was appended to the treaty but had been kept secret from the Senate during the advice-and-consent process. The State Department legal adviser, Abraham Sofaer, claimed that when the Senate "gives its advice and consent to a treaty, it is to the treaty that was made, irrespective of the explanations it is provided" by the executive branch; this interpretation was called the SOFAER DOCTRINE. Unless the Senate expressly confirms its particular understanding of a treaty by itself appending a condition or reservation to the accord, the executive branch has the exclusive authority to interpret a treaty and even to reinterpret it to meet its goals. The Senate claimed that such a treaty reinterpretation demeaned its constitutional participation in the treaty-making process; by reinterpreting a treaty, the President was essentially remaking a treaty without the Senate's consent to the revised treaty. Senator Joseph Biden urged his colleagues to adopt a resolution against the ABM Treaty reinterpretation: "First and foremost, this resolution is about the Constitution. For never before has a President sought to revise unilaterally and fundamentally the meaning of a treaty." The constitutional and political controversy over that position was momentarily quieted only when President Reagan later said that he would voluntarily adhere to the ABM Treaty's original interpretation.

The Biden Condition. The treaty-reinterpretation controversy, however, again reared its head in 1987 when President Reagan transmitted for Senate ratifi-

cation the INF (INTERMEDIATE RANGE NUCLEAR FORCES) TREATY. The Senate consented to the INF Treaty with the Soviet Union but was concerned that a President one day might reinterpret the INF Treaty, just as President Reagan had tried to do with the ABM Treaty. According to the Senate Committee on Foreign Relations, the one legacy of the ABM Treaty debate was that the Senate could not overlook "the Administration's constitutional assertion of a clearly delineated and unprecedented doctrine under which the President has wide latitude for treaty 'reinterpretation,' notwithstanding what the Senate may have been told in the course of granting consent to ratification." The Senate sought to reclaim its constitutional "share" of the treaty power. It was not satisfied with executive branch assurances that "the Reagan Administration will in no way depart from the INF Treaty as we are presenting it to the Senate." Accordingly, the Senate adopted the Biden Condition in its resolution ratifying the INF Treaty. Originally drafted by Senator Biden, the condition reads: "The United States shall interpret the Treaty in accordance with the common understanding of the Treaty shared by the President and the Senate at the time the Senate gave its advice and consent to ratification." The "common understanding" should draw upon the text of the INF Treaty; the Senate's ratification resolution; and the executive branch's representations to the Senate during the ratification process. The Biden Condition further provides that the United States "shall not agree to or adopt an interpretation different from that common understanding except pursuant to Senate advice and consent to a subsequent treaty or protocol, or the enactment of a statute."

The Reagan administration criticized the Biden Condition because it would "grant the Senate a role in interpreting treaties not contemplated by the Constitution"; requiring the Senate's approval of treaty reinterpretation "interferes with the President's constitutional responsibility to interpret and implement treaties and also constitutes an unprecedented arrogation of treaty power by the Senate." President Reagan nevertheless exchanged instruments with the Soviet Union ratifying the INF Treaty and containing the Biden Condition. Shortly thereafter, however, the President disavowed the Biden Condition as an unconstitutional "diminution" of his responsibilities and powers. The Senate vehemently disagreed with President Reagan and claimed that the Biden Condition was binding because it had been attached to the INF Treaty's ratification documents.

The Senate and the President. It is uncertain whether future controversies will surround the President's interpretation of treaties. But it is likely that the Senate will scrutinize future treaties and create a more explicit record of its understanding of particular treaty terms; the Senate may even express those understandings in conditions that it attaches to the treaty. Despite President Reagan's protest, the Biden Condition is probably constitutional. The Biden Condition simply requires the President to follow the executive branch's and the Senate's original understanding of a treaty. The President and the Senate share the treaty-making power, with the President making treaties, and the Senate providing advice and consent on those treaties. Accordingly, the President should be bound to follow the treaty to which the Senate thought it had consented. Of course, the President should have some reasonable discretion to interpret and enforce treaties, and it would not be sensible to tie the President's hands every time he administers a treaty. It is untenable for the executive to claim an omnibus authority to reinterpret treaties, however, since Article II requires the Senate's participation in treaty-making; the Senate is correct to complain that the President bypasses the Senate when he essentially remakes a treaty or fundamentally reinterprets significant provisions in a treaty. Unilateral executive branch reinterpretation is anathema to the CHECKS AND BALANCES that the Framers of the Constitution envisioned when drafting the treaty clause; it leaves no one but the President to supervise the nation's treaty commitments and arguably is undemocratic without the Senate's participation.

Granted, it is usually optimal for a nation to speak with one voice on important foreign affairs issues, and the executive branch normally should serve as the department that conveys the United States' position on such matters. The United States' dealings with other nations might be damaged by presidential and senatorial disagreement over the executive branch's stance on a particular treaty. Nevertheless, it is probably politically and constitutionally wrong for a President to try to change a well-accepted interpretation of a treaty that is already in force. Furthermore, if a treaty reinterpretation is significant, international law may require the President to contact the other countries that are also a party to the treaty. The President may even have to renegotiate the treaty with a foreign sovereign to avoid the allegation that the President's new interpretation violates the treaty or the customary practices that have surrounded the treaty's operation. In such cases, the Constitution would seem to require the Senate's advice and consent concerning the renegotiated instrument.

BIBLIOGRAPHY

Biden, Joseph R., Jr., and John B. Ritch III. "The Treaty Power: Upholding a Constitutional Partnership." *University of Pennsylvania Law Review* 137 (1989): 1529–1557.

Chayes, Abram, and Antonia Handler Chayes. "Testing and Development of 'Exotic' Systems under the ABM Treaty: The Great Reinterpretation Caper." *Harvard Law Review* 99 1986):1956–1971.

Koplow, David A. "Constitutional Bait and Switch: Executive Reinterpretation of Arms Control Treaties." *University of Pennsylvania Law Review* 137 (1989): 1353–1435.

Randall, Kenneth C. "The Treaty Power." *Ohio State Law Journal* 51 (1990): 1089–1126.

Sofaer, Abraham D. "The ABM Treaty and the Strategic Defense Initiative." *Harvard Law Review* 99 (1986): 1972–1985.

KENNETH C. RANDALL

TREATY TERMINATION. The question of whether the President is constitutionally empowered to terminate treaties is the subject of a long-standing debate. The uncertainty, which stems from the fact that the Constitution is silent on the repository of the power to denounce treaties, has engendered doctrinal confusion on the point and variety in practice. The Supreme Court bypassed an opportunity to resolve the controversy in GOLDWATER V. CARTER (1979), when it dismissed as nonjusticiable a challenge to President Jimmy Carter's termination of the 1954 Mutual Defense Treaty with Taiwan. While the decision, technically, did not establish a precedent, it left Carter's act undisturbed, and it was invoked in 1986 as authority for President Ronald Reagan's termination of a treaty of commerce and friendship with Nicaragua.

The locus of authority to terminate treaties presents serious ramifications for constitutional doctrine and the course of American foreign policy, as measured by the MUTUAL SECURITY TREATIES, treaty alliances, and NUCLEAR WEAPONS agreements that expressly govern United States security matters, and other international arrangements that have an important affect on economic, environmental, and commercial interests. Apparently, the CONSTITUTIONAL CONVENTION did not address the issue of treaty termination. It seems likely, however, that the Framers' fear for unilateral executive power in FOREIGN AFFAIRS, their commitment to collective decision making, and the policy concerns that impelled them to create a treaty power shared by the President and Senate would have precluded the possibility of a unilateral presidential power to terminate treaties. This shared power regarding the treaty power satisfied the southern states, which feared that their regional, economic, and security interests would be ignored by northern states. It was made clear at the convention that without these accommodations, including Senate approval of a treaty by a two-thirds vote, the treaty power would not have been accepted. Manifestly, the termination of a treaty could do as much harm to the jealously guarded sectional and state interests as the negotiation of a treaty, and its denunciation by one person could hardly maintain the delicate balance of this carefully crafted system. In fact, writings at the time suggest that the Framers assumed that the power to make treaties implied the power to terminate them. This principle of symmetrical construction was endorsed by JOHN JAY who wrote in FEDERALIST 64 that "they who make treaties may alter or cancel them," and by James Madison, who stated: "That the contracting parties can annul a treaty cannot, I presume, be questioned, the same authority, *precisely*, being exercised in annulling as in making a treaty" [emphasis added].

Nevertheless, a unilateral presidential power to terminate treaties has been adduced on constitutional, historical, and policy grounds. Various commentators and Presidents, including Franklin D. Roosevelt and Jimmy Carter, have invoked the sole-organ doctrine advanced by Justice George Sutherland's bizarre opinion in UNITED STATES v. CURTISS-WRIGHT EXPORT CORP. (1936), as a foundation for a unilateral presidential power to terminate treaties. In dicta, Sutherland stated that the external sovereignty of the nation is vested in the presidency and is neither derived from nor restrained by the Constitution. Foreign affairs powers were essentially executive, which Sutherland explained as "the very delicate, plenary, and exclusive power of the President as the sole organ" of American foreign policy. Sutherland's theory of inherent presidential power rests on the premise that domestic and foreign affairs are different. Domestic affairs are confined by the Constitution, but authority over foreign affairs is not dependent upon a grant from the Constitution since the powers of external sovereignty were somehow transferred directly from the Crown to the Continental Congress and then to the federal government in a way that bypassed the Articles of Confederation and the Constitutional Convention.

Sutherland's historical thesis is untenable. Under the Articles of Confederation, states were sovereign entities that delegated foreign affairs powers to Congress. Moreover, the Supreme Court has consistently held that foreign affairs powers are derived from and limited by the Constitution. Sutherland's sole-organ doctrine, moreover, rests on a distortion of Representative John Marshall's statement in 1800 that the President was solely responsible for communicating with foreign nations. Sutherland infused this purely communicative role with a substantive policy-making power, an assumption that finds no foundation in the text or architecture of the Constitution. Indeed, the constitutional design for foreign policy rests on the premise of shared powers and responsibilities, but the Framers clearly vested the bulk of foreign-affairs powers in Congress. At bottom, the sole-organ argument cannot be reconciled with the policy concerns that determined the nature of the treaty-making power.

Other commentators have attempted to forge an exclusive presidential termination power through analogy to the removal of executive officers. Since Article II of the Constitution vests the President with the power to make treaties and appointments, with the ADVICE AND CONSENT of the Senate, treaty termination and the removal power, neither of which is mentioned in the text of the Constitution, are analogous powers. Because the President may remove a subordinate executive officer without the consent of the Senate, and in defiance of an act of Congress, it is argued that he may likewise terminate treaties without the consent of the Senate. The argument is fragile and the analogy is weak. The REMOVAL POWER is derived from the President's obligation to see that the laws are faithfully executed. By contrast, the treaty power is not executive in character, but legislative, as ALEXANDER HAMILTON and James Madison explained, and treaty termination is a contradiction rather than a corollary of the President's enforcement obligation. A third argument for exclusive presidential termination is grounded in the claim that the Framers were concerned only to check the President from "entangling" the United States with foreign powers. "Disentangling" is less risky and may have to be done quickly by various means or acts, and Senate approval, therefore, should not be required. This view ignores the Framers' paramount concerns surrounding the treaty power, which included a commitment to collective decision making and, as Hamilton noted in *Federalist* 22, the rehabilitation of the United States' reputation abroad as an unreliable treaty partner, a reputation attributable to the states' frequent violations of the nation's international obligations under the Articles of Confederation. These concerns hardly could have been satisfied by placing an unchecked termination power in the hands of a single officer.

The United States has terminated approximately two dozen treaties, either by the President acting alone, by Senate directive, or by joint resolution. The

Constitution provides no role for the House of Representatives in the treaty-making process [see TREATY-MAKING POWER]. It would seem incongruous then to suppose that the Framers intended the House to participate in the termination of treaties. The case for a congressional role is rooted in the supremacy clause of the Constitution. Since treaties are the supreme law of the land, it should take a legislative act to repeal a law. That argument ignores the fact that the provision in Article VI that treaties "are the supreme Law of the Land" is addressed principally to the courts and is designed to assure the supremacy of treaties over state laws. The first treaty termination effectuated at international law occurred in 1856 as a result of a directive from the Senate to President Franklin Pierce to provide notice of termination of a commercial treaty with Denmark. William Howard Taft was the first President to invoke a unilateral executive power of termination when he denounced in 1911 a commercial treaty with Russia. While Taft acted alone, he exhibited concern for constitutional procedure by seeking, and obtaining, Senate ratification of his action. The trend toward unilateral presidential authority to terminate treaties probably began in 1927 when President Calvin Coolidge denounced an antismuggling treaty with Mexico in the mist of badly strained relations. President Franklin D. Roosevelt independently terminated several commercial treaties, some of which were dictated by the circumstances of WORLD WAR II. In 1939, for the first time, Roosevelt invoked the sole-organ doctrine as a basis for a unilateral power to terminate treaties, in this case a commerce and navigation agreement with Japan. Presidents Dwight D. Eisenhower, John F. Kennedy, and Ronald Reagan also asserted an independent termination power. Historically, Presidents have complied with Senate instructions and joint resolutions that have directed them to denounce treaties in accordance with their provisions, but in the past half-century Presidents have captured the termination authority, much as they have aggrandized other foreign-policy powers.

BIBLIOGRAPHY

Adler, David Gray. *The Constitution and the Termination of Treaties.* 1986.

Berger, Raoul. "The President's Unilateral Termination of the Taiwan Treaty." *Northwestern University Law Review* 75 (1980): 577–634.

Bestor, Arthur. "Respective Roles of Senate and President in the Making and Abrogation of Treaties—The Original Intent of the Framers of the Constitution Historically Examined." *University of Washington Law Review* 55 (1979): 1–135.

Emerson, J. Terry. "The Legislative Role in Treaty Abrogation." *Journal of Legislation* 5 (1978): 46–80.

Glennon, Michael J. *Constitutional Diplomacy.* 1990.

Henkin, Louis. "Litigating the President's Power to Terminate Treaties." *American Journal of International Law* 73 (1979): 647–654.

DAVID GRAY ADLER

TRUMAN, BESS (1885–1982), First Lady, wife of Harry S. Truman. Elizabeth Virginia (Bess) Wallace of Independence, Missouri, married Harry Truman on 28 June 1919. Born and brought up in Independence, daughter of David W. and Madge Gates Wallace, she was the granddaughter of a wealthy flour maker (the brand was Queen of the Pantry flour, whose advertising slogan was "the finest biscuit and cake flour in the world"). Mrs. Truman's relationship with her husband was close, but she disliked politics. Truman adored her and often spoke of having met her in Sunday school in 1890 and having fallen in love at that time. They graduated from the same high school in 1901. Truman tried to write to Bess whenever he was away from home, and almost thirteen hundred of his letters to her have survived. He always asserted that his wife helped him with politics, but there is little evidence she did. He also liked to say that he put women on pedestals, where seemingly they were supposed to stay. Bess did not want her husband nominated for the vice presidency in 1944. Because of President Franklin D. Roosevelt's ill health, she believed that his nomination meant he would one day assume the presidency. During Truman's nearly eight years as the nation's Chief Executive she often was in Independence and was happy to return there permanently in 1953.

BIBLIOGRAPHY

Truman, Harry S. *Dear Bess: The Letters from Harry to Bess Truman, 1910–1959.* Edited by Robert H. Ferrell. 1983.

ROBERT H. FERRELL

TRUMAN, HARRY S. (1884–1972), thirty-second President of the United States (1945–1953). A skilled party leader, an effective campaigner, and a possessor of common touch that appealed to many ordinary Americans, he ended WORLD WAR II, contained Soviet political ambitions, and devised plans for reconstructing the postwar world.

When Truman became President on the death of Franklin D. Roosevelt, 12 April 1945, he reached the apex of a career that had included farming (1906–1919), several failed business ventures (1916–1928), active military duty as a captain of artillery in France during WORLD WAR I, and a subsequent rise to the rank of colonel in the Reserve Officers Corps. He was a leader in the Masonic Order. As a local politician, he had been a county executive (1923–1924; 1927–1934) who combined a reputation for honesty and efficiency with a loyal allegiance to Kansas City's notorious Pendergast machine.

Elected to the U.S. Senate in 1934, he quickly became a popular and effective legislator, heavily involved in important transportation legislation (Civil Aeronautics Act of 1938; Transportation Act of 1940). A reliable supporter of President Roosevelt, he could be characterized as a neopopulist "insurgent" liberal in the mold of such senatorial colleagues as George Norris, Burton K. Wheeler, and Robert M. La Follette, Jr. During World War II, he chaired a special Senate committee to investigate problems of defense production. Acting as a lightning rod for public discontent, the Truman Committee made Americans feel that it represented the ordinary person against the excesses of profiteers, big business, and the military.

Widely considered among the most able of Senators and acceptable to all wings of the DEMOCRATIC PARTY, Truman was the compromise choice for Vice President in 1944. Elected along with Roosevelt, he served for less than three months before Roosevelt's death.

Management of the Presidency. In contrast to his predecessor, Truman believed in neat, well-defined lines of authority and deplored conflict among his subordinates. While willing to delegate responsibility freely, he jealously guarded his ultimate authority. He told British Foreign Secretary Anthony Eden in May 1945: "I am here to make decisions, and whether they prove right or wrong I am going to make them." In practice, this generally meant giving Cabinet members and presidential aides wide latitude for policy formulation as long as the President was asked for final approval.

During the Truman years, the WHITE HOUSE STAFF consisted of no more than a dozen immediate aides supplemented by the heads and professional staff of several agencies that operated as part of the EXECUTIVE OFFICE OF THE PRESIDENT, including the Bureau of the Budget (later the OFFICE OF MANAGEMENT AND BUDGET) and the COUNCIL OF ECONOMIC ADVISERS. In all, this assistance was inadequate for the responsibilities the modern presidency had taken on by 1945. It rarely provided much White House input into important policy decisions and was never able to handle congressional liaison on a sophisticated and continuing basis.

Truman, like Roosevelt before him, acted as his own CHIEF OF STAFF, meeting on an almost daily basis with his key aides, and largely saw to congressional relations himself. On numerous details that did not require

presidential attention, the Special Counsel to the President (SAMUEL ROSENMAN, 1945–1946; CLARK CLIFFORD, 1946–1950; and Charles Murphy, 1950–1953) might act as a de facto chief of staff.

In his dealings with the press and the wider public, Truman at his best could appear crisp and decisive, at his worst impetuous and not in control of events. Handicapped by myopic eyesight, he had trouble reading a typescript and was a poor speaker. He carried a lot of latent, unfocused anger within himself as a result of the bitterness of his business failures and the many attacks subsequently made on him for his alliance with a corrupt machine. Throughout his life, he was distrustful of the press, especially large publishers and opinionated columnists, who he felt had vilified him for their own interests.

As had been his practice throughout his career, he worked very hard, often to the point of exhaustion. Stress was a frequent problem during his years in the White House, despite regular exercise and frequent weekend relaxation. Consequently, he often was snappish with journalists, politicians, or others who annoyed him at bad moments; during such episodes, he could appear unpresidential and petty.

All the same, he was in many respects a powerful President. For all his determination to be decisive, he did not make crucial decisions lightly. On such matters as the atomic bomb, the decision to intervene in Korea, and the dismissal of General Douglas MacArthur, he engaged in wide and time-consuming consultations before acting. Priding himself on mastery of detail, he knew the structure of the federal budget as well as any twentieth-century President. As an experienced professional politician, he was an above average party leader ultimately successful in holding the Democratic coalition together despite intense centrifugal forces. For all his difficulties as a speaker, he could be a startlingly effective campaigner who channeled his anger into attacks on the opposition. Having spent years in the practice of grassroots politics, he possessed a common touch that had considerable charm and effectiveness for many ordinary Americans who instinctively identified with him.

At various times, he might be anxious to please, shrewd and aggressive in contests for power, direct and decisive, capable of disinterested statesmanship, or a no-holds-barred political street fighter. His success in the presidency at any given time depended on which of these personas he displayed to the public.

The End of World War II and the Origins of the Cold War. When Truman became President, World War II in Europe was nearly over. On 8 May (his sixty-first birthday), Germany surrendered, leaving as his major challenge on the Continent the devising of a satisfactory postwar order in cooperation with Great Britain, France, and the Soviet Union. In the Pacific, however, the war had reached a bloody peak in the battle of Okinawa (1 April–21 June 1945), where fierce Japanese resistance resulted in forty-five thousand American casualties. The Pacific endgame thus appeared likely to be long and painful.

Shortly after becoming President, Truman learned about the top-secret development of the atomic bomb. Neither he nor any other policymaker was capable of fully understanding the ramifications of NUCLEAR WEAPONS at that point, but he and his chief advisers never doubted that, if developed, they would be used to end the war. [See ATOMIC BOMB, USE OF.]

In the meantime, Truman faced deteriorating relations with the Soviet Union. By mid-April, the two countries were at odds over Soviet behavior in Eastern Europe, which in the minds of American policymakers violated the YALTA AGREEMENT. The establishment of the UNITED NATIONS organization, an enterprise for which the Soviets had little enthusiasm, was at the same time a major personal priority for Truman and a critical objective of American diplomacy.

In order to obtain Soviet consent for a workable United Nations, Truman, in a series of negotiations in the spring of 1945, agreed to Soviet hegemony in Poland. Privately, he was willing to concede a Soviet sphere of influence in Eastern Europe, so long as the U.S.S.R. behaved with some circumspection. The Soviet decision to move for total dominance and the exclusion of all Western influences made such a solution impossible.

In July, Truman met with Joseph Stalin and Winston Churchill (who was succeeded by Clement Atlee in the midst of the meeting) at the POTSDAM CONFERENCE, to discuss a wide range of European issues and to pin down Soviet participation in the war against Japan. Shortly after his arrival, he got word that the first atomic bomb had been successfully tested in the New Mexico desert. Even then, unable fully to grasp the importance of the event, he sought and received pledges of Soviet entry into the Pacific war by mid-August. The meeting lasted for more than two weeks but accomplished very little. Truman nonetheless went home feeling that he had achieved a good personal relationship with Stalin, who reminded him of tough American political bosses he long had been able to deal with. Actually, Potsdam was the high point of American-Soviet relations during the Truman presidency; the downhill slide would be very long and the bottom very low.

At Potsdam, the United States and British governments had issued an ultimatum to Japan calling for unconditional surrender and threatening absolute destruction if the Japanese continued the war. Neither the ultimatum nor other demands mentioned an atomic bomb, nor did they state that unconditional surrender would not mean removal of the Japanese emperor, Hirohito. It is unclear whether more explicitness on these points would have made a difference. The Japanese government, deadlocked between peace and war parties, responded with a curt dismissal. On 6 August, an atomic bomb destroyed Hiroshima; on 9 August, another destroyed Nagasaki. At the behest of the emperor, Japan offered peace terms, and Truman withheld shipment of another atomic bomb to the Pacific. (As HENRY A. WALLACE recorded it: "He said the thought of wiping out another one hundred thousand people was too horrible. He didn't like the idea of killing, as he said, 'all those kids.'") On 14 August, he announced the surrender of Japan.

The postwar world soon was characterized by growing tension between the United States and the Soviet Union. Truman's administration, much in line with broad American opinion, opposed Soviet ambitions to dominate Eastern Europe, gain effective control of the Turkish straits, and establish a friendly separatist state in northwestern Iran. Strong diplomatic representations (Truman later, with some exaggeration, used the word *ultimatum*) contributed to a Soviet decision to withdraw troops from Iran. Steady support of Turkey kept the Soviets out of the straits. In Eastern Europe, however, the administration was essentially helpless; the U.S.S.R., employing the leverage given it by occupying armies, established "friendly" governments that excluded noncommunists from any real power.

The atomic bomb became another divisive issue. There is no significant evidence that Truman had employed it against Japan not just to end the war but also to demonstrate American power to the Soviet Union; still, he and his new Secretary of State, JAMES F. BYRNES, clearly believed it would enhance their bargaining position. Instead, shrewd Soviet diplomacy made it a liability. The Soviets, correctly perceiving that the bomb could be used only in an extreme situation, discounted it as a meaningful threat and scored diplomatic points by accusing the United States of practicing nuclear intimidation.

International opinion, Soviet complaints, and the urgings of the articulate foreign-policy elite in the United States forced the administration to offer a plan drawn up by BERNARD BARUCH for international control of atomic energy. The proposal was hedged with restrictions and safeguards that the U.S.S.R. refused to accept. Although frequently criticized then and later as insufficiently forthcoming toward the Soviets, the Baruch Plan was at the outer limits of what the U.S. Senate was likely to accept. Truman, feeling that the United States needed ironclad security guarantees, was in full agreement with it. Those who continue to dissent must assume that so important an international agreement could have been concluded and maintained on a basis of mutual trust with Joseph Stalin's Soviet Union, without the safeguards.

Truman still intermittently felt that one could deal with Stalin, but he also had rather quickly concluded that the Soviet system, as exemplified by Foreign Minister Vyacheslav Molotov, was hopelessly intransigent. "I'm tired babying the Soviets," he declared in a handwritten memorandum at the beginning of 1946. Increasingly, American diplomacy concentrated on the containment of Soviet power, an objective supported by a majority of Americans but not by the left wing of the Democratic Party. In September 1946, after an embarrassing public controversy, Truman dismissed from his Cabinet Henry A. Wallace, the leader of the Democratic left and the last foreign-policy dissenter in the administration.

Reconversion and the Election of 1946. With the end of the war, Truman had to turn much of his attention to domestic problems. In the fall of 1945, he presented to Congress a broad reform program squarely in the tradition of Roosevelt's NEW DEAL. He was granted little of it. Perhaps the most notable legislation was the EMPLOYMENT ACT of 1946, which committed the federal government to a policy of maintaining maximum employment and established the Council of Economic Advisers to help the President manage economic policy.

Truman's biggest challenge was managing the economic transition from war to peace. Although the assignment was much more compatible with his experience and expertise than was foreign policy, it proved politically much more damaging. The goal—a smooth changeover to civilian production while avoiding both a return to the Great Depression and a dangerous inflationary boom—was practically impossible to achieve, given the administration's close relationship to organized labor and its decision to continue wartime controls, especially on prices.

From the end of the war through the first half of 1946, the economy was plagued by shortages of many consumer goods. Total abandonment of controls was probably not feasible, but neither in retrospect was the effort to maintain them at wartime levels. In the course of protecting the consumer against price increases, controls tended to dry up supply and force many transactions onto the black market, where a buyer paid

high prices anyway. Even the government found itself unable to obtain sufficient supplies of grain for European relief until it raised price ceilings.

Truman himself, pulled between his inner liberalism and his experience as a businessman, had an ambivalent attitude toward price controls. After some wavering, he endorsed a one-year extension, vetoed legislation he thought was too weak, then signed another bill that was about equally flawed. The result was simply to make himself the focus of discontent over the inflationary surge that came in from the black market and registered in the on-the-books economy.

Labor unions, capitalizing on Truman's decision to allow them to seek wage increases that would not require compensating price raises, called one strike after another, making demands that business would not accept without price concessions, tying up key segments of American industry and thus adding to consumer frustration. The administration found its hopes dashed at every turn. In order to settle major strikes, it invariably had to drive "bulges in the price line."

Attempting to get production moving full tilt by reining in union propensity to walk out, Truman suggested compulsory mediation and arbitration as an interim solution, thereby infuriating labor leaders. In May 1946, when the railroad unions called a national strike, the President forced a settlement by asking Congress to give him temporary power to draft strikers into the army. The ploy further damaged his standing with labor, although he vetoed the Case bill, which placed onerous permanent restrictions on unions. That November, after the midterm elections, he ordered a prosecution of the United Mine Workers (UMW) and its leader, John L. Lewis, for their defiance of government orders. The action resulted in a victory for the government and substantial fines for Lewis and the UMW.

By the fall of 1946, Truman's approval rating had fallen from 87 percent (in June 1945) to 32 percent (in September 1946). The public in general perceived him as unable to handle his domestic responsibilities. The dominant labor-liberal wing of the Democratic Party was alienated from him. The firing of Wallace, after Truman had personally approved a controversial Wallace speech, both split the Democratic Party and allowed some critics to argue that the President did not understand his own foreign policy.

Although Truman was not up for election in 1946, he was in a very real sense the issue, and by then so obviously a losing issue that the Democratic National Committee asked him to refrain from campaigning. Moreover, meat, one of the few commodities still subjected to tight price controls, disappeared from butcher shops and grocery stores, providing an irritation that spotlighted public anger. With no feasible way to get beef and pork back into the stores, Truman lifted controls on 14 October. The move worked, but it also seemed a demonstration of weakness.

Three weeks later, the Republicans swept the congressional elections. It seemed unlikely that in the next two years, the President could rebuild his shattered reputation.

Rebuilding a Democratic Majority. In a sense, the election provided Truman a new opportunity by giving him a Congress controlled by the opposition in place of one that was Democratic but cool to his initiatives. The worst disruptions of economic reconversion were over, and Truman's postelection decision to end economic controls ensured that he would no longer be a target for all who were discontented with them.

It remained, however, for the President to establish himself as a forceful leader and build a platform on which to campaign for reelection. Above all, he had to rally behind him a Democratic core constituency that included the labor movement, ethnic-religious minorities in urban areas, blacks, and liberal activists—and to do so while forging and maintaining an appeal to the larger public.

His stand during the railroad strike and his decision to prosecute the UMW had demonstrated that he would stand up to labor's excesses, even though in both instances the unions were outside the mainstream of organized labor. In June 1947, Truman made a symbolic demonstration of even-handedness and sympathy for labor's legitimate objectives by vetoing the restrictive TAFT-HARTLEY ACT. Although Congress overrode the veto, Truman made his point and brought most of organized labor behind him.

The minorities responded to different issues, but all found something to like. Truman's alignment with labor and backing of social welfare programs had natural appeal to groups that were predominantly working class. Catholics in general, and those of Eastern European descent in particular, liked his anticommunist foreign policies. Many Jews approved of his liberalism and his decision, late and blatantly political though it was, to recognize the new state of Israel.

Feeling that civil rights legislation had no chance for passage in Congress and somewhat ambivalent in his personal attitudes, Truman had done little for blacks during his first two years in office. Near the end of 1947, however, in response to the recommendations of a special committee he had appointed, he endorsed

the most sweeping civil rights program ever espoused by any President.

The liberal activists tended to respond positively to Truman's domestic program, but a substantial minority opposed his COLD WAR policies and aligned themselves with Henry Wallace. By and large, however, the liberals were won over by the MARSHALL PLAN, which they conceived as a badly needed program for European reconstruction. More worrisome and exemplifying the continuing appeal of Franklin D. Roosevelt, even those who supported all or most of Truman's policies continued to doubt that he possessed the personal qualities needed to be a successful President. In the end, the administration's program—and the lack of a viable alternative to Truman—won them over.

By mid 1948, Truman had committed himself to a program that included repeal of the Taft-Hartley Act for labor, civil rights, housing subsidies for the middle class, public housing for the poor, price supports for the farmer, tax relief for the common man but not the upper brackets, federal aid to education, and national health insurance. He had developed a new speaking style that relied more on extemporaneous delivery than following a prepared text. And, most importantly, he was prepared to engage in an all-out rhetorical offensive against the Republican Eightieth Congress.

The Crystallization of the Cold War. In early 1947, Truman, responding to notification that Britain no longer had the resources to protect Greece from a pro-Soviet insurgency, decided that American interests required assumption of the old British imperial position in the eastern Mediterranean as part of an effort to contain Soviet expansion. Speaking to a joint session of Congress, he proposed $250 million in aid to Greece and $150 million to Turkey, still under Soviet diplomatic pressure to relinquish the straits.

In a declaration that would become known as the TRUMAN DOCTRINE, he asserted: "I believe that it must be the policy of the United States to support free peoples who are resisting attempted subjugation by armed minorities or by outside pressures." The implicit universalism of these words privately horrified some administration foreign-policy officials and elicited criticism from a few commentators with impeccable anti-Soviet credentials. The decision against intervention in the Chinese civil war makes it clear, however, that Truman never intended to distribute blank checks to every nation threatened by a communist insurgency. He did believe that it was important to state a principle without hedging.

The proposal drew vocal opposition from right-wing isolationists and from liberals more appalled by the reactionary character of the Greek government than by Soviet ambitions. Truman, nonetheless, was successful in appealing to the broad center of the political spectrum. The Greek-Turkish aid program passed Congress by large majorities.

The administration quickly followed with the Marshall Plan (named for GEORGE C. MARSHALL, Secretary of State, 1947–1949). Designed as a comprehensive plan for European reconstruction that included Soviet participation, it won over many of Truman's liberal critics. Soviet rejection of it in June 1947, the pro-Soviet coup in Czechoslovakia in February 1948, and the Berlin blockade (June 1948–May 1949) assured its passage by Congress and reduced both the open isolationists and the pro-Soviet left to insignificant splinter groups in American politics.

The same events caused the Western European democracies to propose an outright military alliance with the United States. Completed in early 1949, the North Atlantic Treaty (NATO TREATY) would be ratified by an overwhelming margin in the U.S. Senate and then followed by military aid that rearmed Western Europe under the aegis of the North Atlantic Treaty Organization (NATO). For the United States, the new commitment meant a formal end to the traditional policy of no entangling alliances and the assumption of what amounted to imperial responsibilities thousands of miles distant.

The Election of 1948. By mid 1948, it already was manifest that Truman's foreign policy was historic in its implications and likely to be successful. In his handling of domestic problems, he had moved far toward rebuilding the Democratic presidential coalition and was in a position to make inaction on his program by the Republican-controlled Congress a campaign issue.

Still, few observers thought he could win. Henry Wallace had declared his candidacy on the PROGRESSIVE PARTY ticket. He was expected to poll millions of votes—and might well have done so had Soviet foreign policy not been so belligerent. Liberal Democrats attempted to draft General Dwight D. Eisenhower, but he turned them down. After the Democratic convention adopted a strong civil rights plank, southern conservatives walked out. They formed the States Rights ("Dixiecrat") Party with J. STROM THURMOND as its candidate and seemed a good bet to carry much of the normally Democratic South. Truman responded with a long-sought objective of civil rights groups: an EXECUTIVE ORDER mandating a policy of equal opportunity in the U.S. armed forces. Over the next several years, the military would become the most integrated institution in American life.

Truman's major opponent was the Republican governor of New York, THOMAS E. DEWEY. Popular and widely respected, he had in 1944 run strongly against Roosevelt. Truman's strategy was less to attack him than to paint the Republican Congress as more representative of the party, determined to repeal the New Deal, and likely to do so with Dewey's acquiescence. To dramatize the alleged danger, he called Congress into special session and presented it with his entire legislative program, secure in the knowledge that it would do nothing.

That fall, he crisscrossed the country in his campaign train, displaying both a folksy, ordinary fellow personality and the belligerence of a bareknuckled fighter. Targeting his talks toward the dominant interests at any given stop, he reminded his audiences of specific benefits they had received from the Democrats under Roosevelt, then expressed his determination to defend these from the Republicans. In the meantime, the Wallace campaign, which had once seemed a major force in key urban states, wilted in the inhospitable atmosphere that Soviet foreign policy had created for it.

Dewey might have countered Truman's charges by proclaiming his commitment to the New Deal status quo—and perhaps also by pointing out that the Republicans in Congress had provided the votes and leadership to pass the administration's epochal foreign-policy initiatives. Instead, persuaded that he had the election won, unwilling to risk a party split, and wanting a free hand, he confined himself to bland generalizations about cleaning up the mess in Washington.

On election day, Truman surprised the country, defeating Dewey by a margin of 49.4 percent to 45.0 percent with Wallace and Thurmond each receiving a meager 2.4 percent. He also carried with him substantial Democratic majorities in both houses of Congress, raising again the question of whether he could put his program through a legislative branch in which Democratic control did not necessarily mean executive mastery.

Fair Deal Politics. Truman called his ambitious domestic program—civil rights legislation, repeal of Taft-Hartley, the Brannan Plan for farmers, federal aid to education, an omnibus housing bill, and national health insurance—the FAIR DEAL. It ran into one roadblock after another in a Congress still run by ideological conservatives. In the end, only the housing bill passed, although the administration was successful in enlarging many established New Deal programs; the Social Security Act of 1950, for example, was a major step in the program's development.

Truman and his advisers had misread the mandate of the election as one for an increased social welfare state rather than for consolidation and protection of the status quo against possible Republican attempts to turn back the clock. A sharp economic recession in 1949 was also politically damaging. Still, with the economy moving back up by the beginning of 1950, the President hoped to build a liberal majority.

He and Leon Keyserling, the new chairman of his Council of Economic Advisers, stressed economic growth, not just social welfare programs, as a goal of liberalism. He also hoped to build a farmer-labor coalition around Secretary of Agriculture Charles Brannan's agricultural program that proposed to pay direct income subsidies to family farms while letting the price of agricultural commodities drop to market levels. Superficially impressive, the political strategy failed to take into account the vast cultural gap between blue-collar laborers (employees paid by the hour) and farmers (small producer-businessmen). Finally, by mid 1950, American politics had become focused not on domestic reform but on reverses in the cold war, which had given birth to a virulent politics of anti-Communism.

The Changing Cold War and McCarthyism. By mid 1949, the structure of containment had been successfully put into place in Western Europe. Yet this accomplishment, among the most impressive in the history of American statecraft, was beginning to be overshadowed by communist gains elsewhere. In the summer of 1949, mainland China fell to the communist insurgency of Mao Zedong. Several weeks later, U.S. government intelligence analysts concluded that the U.S.S.R. had exploded its first atomic device. Both developments led to attacks on Truman's policies.

The collapse of the Chinese Nationalist government of Chiang Kai-shek shocked an American public told since the 1930s that Chiang was a revered democratic leader rather than an ineffectual dictator. The administration, with Truman's emphatic approval, had decided that Chiang was a failure, China a quagmire, and Europe a much higher priority. Hence, it had cut off aid to the Nationalists and had been prepared to deal with Mao, hoping that he would be an independent national leader.

Mao's announcement that he would lean toward the U.S.S.R. and his vocal anti-Americanism made such a policy impossible in the short run, no matter how plausible it remained for the long haul. The continuance of Chiang's regime on the island of Taiwan provided a rallying point for Truman's critics and made the debacle a continuing embarrassment. Republicans combined genuine indignation with political

calculation as again and again they raised the question: Who lost China?

The Soviet atomic bomb called into question Truman's entire defense policy, which had been based on deep cuts in the military. Truman had reasoned that so long as the United States had an atomic monopoly, the U.S.S.R., even with its huge army, would refrain from seriously threatening the West. The NATIONAL SECURITY COUNCIL in the spring of 1950 produced an important working paper, NSC-68, which advocated a major rearmament program; the President remained reluctant but would feel compelled to implement it after the beginning of the KOREAN WAR. He also gave approval to another deferred project, the production of a thermonuclear super bomb, because analysts agreed that the U.S.S.R. would soon be able to produce one of its own.

The political dialogue, however, came to focus on internal communist activities. In January 1950, Alger Hiss, a former Assistant Secretary of State identified with the liberal wing of the Democratic Party, was convicted of perjury for denying under oath that he had once passed classified information to the U.S.S.R. At about the same time, Dr. Klaus Fuchs, an atomic scientist with British citizenship who had worked on the World War II nuclear project (the Manhattan project), was arrested in England, charged, and sentenced to prison for having passed atomic secrets to the U.S.S.R. That summer some American Communists, including Julius and Ethel Rosenberg, were arrested for having been couriers for Fuchs's spy ring. These episodes, as well as some others of lesser significance, provided fodder for Republicans who charged that the Democrats—at least Truman and the liberals who dominated the administration—were soft on communism and insufficiently vigilant against domestic subversion.

Such accusations had long been a staple of partisan Republican rhetoric but had been more in the nature of throwaway lines than serious, sustained charges. In February 1950, a hitherto obscure freshman Republican Senator, Joseph R. McCarthy of Wisconsin, showed how the climate had changed. He gained enormous national attention with a declaration that more than two hundred "card-carrying" communists worked for the State Department. McCarthy made one attention-grabbing accusation after another, mostly against prominent targets. Although taken seriously by much of the press and public, none of his charges was ever proved. By June the focus of Truman's domestic agenda was to contain and discredit McCarthy, despite Truman's opinion that McCARTHYISM was a brief aberration. The North Korean invasion of South Korea, on 25 June 1950, put an end to such thinking.

The Korean Stalemate. Ten years later, Truman remarked that when informed of the North Korean attack by Secretary of State DEAN ACHESON, he said: "Dean, we have to stop the sons of bitches no matter what." No doubt he recalled his impulse accurately, but in fact only after several days of meetings and consultations did Truman decide to make an irrevocable commitment to the defense of South Korea. This delay reflected in part his practice of making big decisions carefully rather than impulsively, but it also was a consequence of the way in which the unexpected Korean conflict had laid bare the strategic inadequacies of the administration's diplomatic and defense policies for Asia.

Throughout the twentieth century Asia had been an afterthought for American policymakers intensely concerned with Europe. Truman's State Department continued that tradition. Acheson had deliberately or otherwise excluded South Korea when he made a speech defining the American defense perimeter in East Asia. American troops had been withdrawn from the Korean peninsula; the United States had left the South Korean army lightly armed. No one appears to have expected an isolated attack from the North, the assumption being that war, if it came, would involve a Soviet offensive concentrating on Europe. Finally, Truman's policy of rigid limits on defense spending had left the U.S. armed forces overextended and hard pressed to engage even the North Korean army.

Still, the administration decided that aggression had to be challenged. It obtained a United Nations resolution calling for the defense of South Korea and threw ill-prepared U.S. occupation troops from Japan into the fight. Under the command of General Douglas MacArthur, the Americans and the South Koreans (both operating under the U.N. flag) managed to hold the southeastern port of Pusan. In mid September, MacArthur, employing the last division of ready reserves in the U.S. Army, staged a successful landing far behind the lines at Inchon and coordinated it with an offensive from Pusan. Caught in a trap, the North Koreans were soon routed.

With total victory apparently in sight, Truman approved a general advance north, the anticipated outcome being the unification of Korea under an anticommunist government. On 15 October, he met with MacArthur at Wake Island; the general discounted fears that China might intervene in the war, which he asserted was nearly over. Three weeks later, American forces fought their first engagement with Chinese troops. By the end of November, China had intervened massively and the once triumphant U.N. army was in full retreat.

Rejecting a full-scale war with China, worried about the possibility of a Soviet attack against Western Europe, militarily stretched to the limit, the administration redefined its objective as restoration of the status quo ante. In practice, this meant stabilizing the fighting front in the vicinity of the old boundary, the thirty-eighth parallel, then negotiating peace with the Chinese. Reasserting traditional priorities, the administration concentrated on strengthening European defenses.

MacArthur vehemently dissented, requesting authorization instead to extend the war to China, involve Chiang's troops on Taiwan, and possibly employ atomic bombs. Such options were unacceptable to the United Nations, to the Europeans, and to Truman. On 11 April 1951, after MacArthur had openly and insubordinately conveyed his views to Republican leaders, Truman relieved him of all his commands. The action created a firestorm of criticism, much of it irrational. The Chinese military situation in the spring of 1951 was shaky, and the general's recommendations may have possessed more merit than historians customarily give them. Nonetheless, his means of advocacy left Truman with no choice but to dismiss him.

MacArthur's command passed to General Matthew B. Ridgway, who already as local commander in Korea had achieved the administration's military objectives. Yet the war continued for the remainder of Truman's presidency as truce talks stalled largely because China demanded forced repatriation of its prisoners of war, whether they wished to return or not. In a rather thoughtless moment, Truman had called the Korean conflict a police action; instead it had become a bloody stalemate that would dominate and ultimately ruin his last two years in office.

Farewell to Reform: The Politics of the Korean War. The most immediate impact of the fighting in Korea was to give free rein to the politics of anticommunism, not simply in the actions of Senator McCarthy himself but in the behavior and rhetoric of much of the opposition to the administration. The most important immediate consequence was the passage in September 1950 of an omnibus Internal Security Act sponsored by Senator Pat McCarran of Nevada, a Democrat but long a foe of Truman. The President vetoed the bill, characterizing it as an attack on CIVIL LIBERTIES akin to the ALIEN AND SEDITION ACTS, but Congress overrode his action easily and it became the McCARRAN INTERNAL SECURITY ACT. (Two years later, Truman would veto the McCARRAN-WALTER ACT, an immigration bill, on the same grounds and with the same result.)

In the short run, the war diverted attention from Truman's Fair Deal agenda, leaving him unable to campaign for it and thus insuring that he would not be able to obtain the congressional majorities required for its passage. Democratic losses in the 1950 elections (held just as the first signs of Chinese intervention appeared) were relatively small, but the administration had needed gains. After the MacArthur dismissal, Truman could do little more than circle the wagons, concentrate on uniting the Democratic Party, and fight for his foreign policy against increasing neo-isolationist and Asia First attacks.

At home, the war also brought with it inflation, then economic controls differing in degree but not in kind from those during World War II. The sacrifices required of civilians were small but irritating all the same—especially after the conflict degenerated into what appeared to be a no-win, no-end situation. Revelations of corruption in some executive agencies were also damaging. On 3 April 1952, Truman fired his Attorney General, J. Howard McGrath, for failure to move vigorously against it.

Less than a week earlier, Truman had announced that he would not be a candidate for the presidency in 1952. He opposed a third term as a matter of principle, but he doubtless also realized that he probably could not be reelected. According to the Gallup poll, his public approval rating fell to 23 percent after the MacArthur firing and rebounded no higher than 32 percent for the remainder of his presidency.

Truman originally had offered to support Dwight Eisenhower as the Democratic candidate. When Eisenhower opted to pursue the Republican nomination instead, the President turned to Governor ADLAI E. STEVENSON of Illinois, who after some hesitation accepted a draft. Although personal tension developed between the two, Truman campaigned intensively for Stevenson that fall. At that low point of his public standing, he may have been less an asset than a liability, but nothing could have stopped the Eisenhower landslide.

Evaluation. Truman returned to Independence, Missouri, where he produced his memoirs and spoke out on public issues. Although he had no real power, he retained considerable moral influence within the Democratic Party. Many scholars, influenced by the upsurge of intellectual radicalism in the 1960s and 1970s, criticized him as the instigator of the cold war, a bogus liberal, and an incompetent unfit for the presidency. But among the general public, his standing as an effective, plain-speaking, straightforward leader grew steadily.

Truman liked to think of himself as a common man in the presidency and successfully retailed that image to the public. His career does indeed tell us much about the nature of democracy and democratic politics in twentieth-century America. But it is equally true that beneath this surface commonness lay unusual character and resolve. Drawing on these resources, Harry Truman did almost as much as Franklin Roosevelt to lead America into the second half of the twentieth century.

BIBLIOGRAPHY

Donovan, Robert J. *Conflict and Crisis: The Presidency of Harry S. Truman, 1945–48.* 1977.

Donovan, Robert J. *Tumultuous Years: The Presidency of Harry S. Truman, 1949–1953.* 1982.

Ferrell, Robert H., ed. *Off the Record: The Private Papers of Harry S. Truman.* 1980.

Gosnell, Harold F. *Truman's Crises: A Political Biography of Harry S. Truman.* 1980.

Hamby, Alonzo L. *Beyond the New Deal: Harry S. Truman and American Liberalism.* 1973.

Hamby, Alonzo L., ed. *Harry S. Truman and the Fair Deal.* 1974.

Lacey, Michael, ed. *The Truman Presidency.* 1989.

McCoy, Donald R. *The Presidency of Harry S. Truman.* 1984.

McCullough, David. *Truman.* 1992.

Miller, Merle. *Plain Speaking: An Oral Biography of Harry S. Truman.* 1974.

Truman, Harry S. *Memoirs.* Vol. 1: *Year of Decisions.* 1955. Vol. 2: *Years of Trial and Hope.* 1956.

Truman, Margaret. *Harry S. Truman.* 1973.

ALONZO L. HAMBY

TRUMAN DOCTRINE. The Truman Doctrine of 1947 provided military and economic aid for Greece and Turkey in an effort to contain communism. According to President Harry S. Truman, both countries were in danger of falling to totalitarianism and needed massive infusions of American aid to survive. Civil war had broken out in Greece between communist-led guerrillas and the royalist regime. In Turkey, widespread fear had developed of a Russian invasion. The British government, hurt by two world wars, gave up its longtime commitment to Greece and Turkey and urged the United States to accept the responsibility. The President, informing Congress of the twin crises along the northern tier of the Mediterranean, asked for $400 million in military and economic aid. Congress approved the appropriation after a long, bitter battle.

Although Russian pressure on Turkey had eased, the situation in Greece had become desperate as American aid and advisers began to arrive in 1947.

The guerrillas received assistance from surrounding communist countries, leading the Truman administration to debate whether to send combat troops. The President, however, approved sending only operational advisers, hoping that continued American training of the Greek army would eventually lead to victory.

Truman's restraint paid off, for in 1949 the royalists won the war. U.S. military advisers and aid were important to this outcome, but only in combination with several other factors—particularly the rift between Yugoslavia's Josip Tito and Russia's Joseph Stalin that had led to a closing of the Yugoslav sanctuary for the guerrillas. With no place of escape left, they collapsed before a massive bombardment of U.S. and Greek firepower.

Though critics have accused Truman of establishing an interventionist policy that ultimately led to the VIETNAM WAR, the truth is that he worked with his advisers to create a policy characterized by flexibility and restraint. The Truman Doctrine did not signify an automatic global commitment: assistance would go only to those countries about to yield to totalitarianism; the countries also had to be vital to American interests and capable of being saved. Used within presidential guidelines, the Truman Doctrine offered the potential for preserving national self-determination.

BIBLIOGRAPHY

Jones, Howard. "A New Kind of War": America's Global Strategy and the Truman Doctrine in Greece. 1989.
Kuniholm, Bruce R. The Origins of the Cold War in the Near East: Great Power Conflict and Diplomacy in Iran, Turkey, and Greece. 1980.
Woods, Randall B., and Howard Jones. Dawning of the Cold War: The United States' Quest for Order. 1991.

HOWARD JONES

TUGWELL, REXFORD G. (1891–1979), presidential adviser. A prominent economist at Columbia University, Rexford Guy Tugwell was recruited by RAYMOND MOLEY into Franklin D. Roosevelt's BRAIN TRUST in 1932. During the presidential campaign, Tugwell assisted Roosevelt by writing speeches, preparing memoranda, and explaining the economic crisis and possible solutions for it. Tugwell was especially concerned with the farm problem. Once Roosevelt was elected, Tugwell helped in the preparations for the London Economic Conference in June 1933, the banking crisis, and legislation for implementing the Agricultural Adjustment Administration (AAA). After the inauguration, Tugwell served in an official capacity as Assistant and Under Secretary of Agriculture and as director of the Resettlement Administration. He was also involved in reorganizing the Department of Agriculture, revising the Pure Food and Drug Law of 1906, and creating the CIVILIAN CONSERVATION CORPS. Unofficially, Roosevelt used Tugwell in other capacities, such as a trouble-shooter in the National Recovery Administration, liaison with congressional progressives such as ROBERT M. LA FOLLETTE, and a public apologist for the NEW DEAL. By 1935, Tugwell's own position within the New Deal was, however, seriously undermined by the "purge" of the AAA, which Secretary of Agriculture HENRY A. WALLACE and AAA director Chester Davis engineered. By 1936, Tugwell's reputation as a radical, moreover, was so entrenched that JAMES A. FARLEY convinced the President to keep Tugwell out of the reelection campaign. Realizing that his influence as an adviser was over, Tugwell resigned in December 1936. Unlike many of his colleagues from the early days of the New Deal, he always remained a loyal supporter of Roosevelt and his program.

BIBLIOGRAPHY

Namorato, Michael V. Rexford G. Tugwell: A Biography. 1988.
Namorato, Michael V., ed. The Diary of Rexford G. Tugwell: The New Deal, 1932–1935. 1992.

MICHAEL V. NAMORATO

TWELFTH AMENDMENT. The Twelfth Amendment to the United States Constitution changed the manner of electing the President and Vice President from that which the Framers had devised. Ratified on 25 September 1804 the amendment provided for separate ballots for President and Vice President, thereby superseding Article II, Section 1, clause 3, of the Constitution.

Prior to 1804, electors voted in one presidential election for two persons. The person with the most electoral votes, if a majority, became President; the runner-up was Vice President. Since electors had to cast at least one vote for someone from a state not their own, the Framers expected the system to overcome regional loyalties to produce a national consensus President. And, since the runner-up became Vice President, he, too, would be presidential caliber.

The system worked initially, selecting George Washington and John Adams as the first President and Vice President. The development of political parties revealed flaws in the design. In 1796, the electoral scheme produced Adams, a Federalist President, and Thomas Jefferson, a Democratic-Republican Vice President who were politically incompatible.

Four years later, the election disclosed a second

defect. Democratic-Republican electors were to support Jefferson for President and AARON BURR for Vice President. When all did so, Jefferson and Burr inadvertently tied for the Presidency, throwing the election to the House of Representatives to prevent a result—Burr's election—which had not been intended.

Finally, the system allowed a minority party, too weak to win the Presidency, to divert its votes to the majority party's vice presidential candidate to elect him as President. To combat this tactic, the majority party could withhold votes from its vice presidential candidate, thereby allowing the opposition to win that position. The initial system, which the Framers designed to produce a consensus President of excellence, had degenerated into a competition in strategic voting.

These defects prompted calls for reform. Not all favored abandoning the original system. Small states feared the change would diminish their power by reducing the likelihood of tie votes, thereby lowering the chance of the House of Representatives electing the President. Federalists feared the change would reduce their chance of electing at least a Vice President. Still, the amendment received the necessary two-thirds vote (22 to 10 in the Senate and 84 to 42 in the House).

The Twelfth Amendment provided for distinct ballots for President and Vice President with a majority electoral vote required in each election. If no presidential candidate received a majority, the House of Representatives, with each state receiving one vote, would choose a President from the three leading candidates. If no Vice President were elected, the Senate would choose from the top two vice presidential candidates.

The Twelfth Amendment solved the problems the Framers targeted but created others. It diminished the vice presidency. No longer was its occupant the presidential runner-up. Instead, the office frequently attracted lesser persons. Some foresaw the diminution of the vice presidency and proposed its abolition.

The new system also potentially lent itself to some odd results. It provided that if the ELECTORAL COLLEGE failed to provide any candidate with a majority, the outgoing Congress would convene to elect a President and Vice President, an anomalous procedure especially if many of its members had lost at the polls. The amendment required that the House "shall choose immediately" a President, suggesting an imperative. Election required a majority of the total number of states. If three candidates commanded support or if some states were divided so no candidate had a majority of their delegations, the House might be unable to comply with its constitutional command. Under the

Twelfth Amendment, the person elected Vice President by the Senate would then "act as President."

The Twelfth Amendment did not make clear whether the Vice President would act for the remainder of the term or only until a President was chosen, or who would act as President if neither a President nor Vice President were chosen, ambiguities the TWENTIETH AMENDMENT subsequently addressed. Under the Twelfth Amendment, the House and Senate could elect persons from different parties to the two top positions, replicating the result of 1796. Moreover, since all states count equally in the voting, states with a minority of the population could elect the Chief Executive.

Since the adoption of the Twelfth Amendment, the House has only elected the President on one occasion, in 1825, when it chose John Quincy Adams over Andrew Jackson notwithstanding the fact that Jackson won more popular and electoral votes. The prospect of serious THIRD-PARTY CANDIDATES for the presidency—ROBERT M. LA FOLLETTE (1924), STROM THURMOND (1948), GEORGE WALLACE (1968), John Anderson (1976), and ROSS PEROT (1992)—has raised the possibility of the House again being called upon to decide an election. Yet, in each of these cases the THIRD PARTY lost support and a major-party candidate obtained an electoral vote majority.

The Twelfth Amendment also changed original law by requiring a majority electoral vote for Vice President. Under the initial system, the runner-up for President became Vice President whether he received a majority or not. The Senate has elected the Vice President only in 1837 when it chose RICHARD M. JOHNSON after he failed to achieve an electoral vote majority.

The Twelfth Amendment also provides that the eligibility requirements for President also apply to the Vice President. The original Constitution did not contain such a provision since it was implicit in the electoral arrangement, which made the presidential runner-up Vice President.

Parts of the Twelfth Amendment have been modified or superseded by the Twentieth Amendment.

BIBLIOGRAPHY

Feerick, John D. *From Failing Hands.* 1965.
Peirce, Neal R. *The People's President.* 1968.
Wilmerding, Lucius, Jr. *The Electoral College.* 1958.

JOEL K. GOLDSTEIN

TWENTIETH AMENDMENT. The Twentieth Amendment to the United States Constitution, which was ratified in 1933, addressed several topics—the dates upon which presidential and congressional terms begin and end (Section I), when Congress convenes (Section II), what happens if the President-elect dies before his term begins or if no President or Vice President has qualified (Section III), and what happens if a presidential or vice presidential candidate dies under certain contingencies (Section IV). The amendment corrected some defects in the constitutional design. Its net result was probably to strengthen the presidency and to improve the provisions for filling presidential vacancies in certain contingencies.

Section I provides that the terms of President and Vice President begin and end at noon on 20 January, and that those of Senators and Representatives begin and end at noon on 3 January. Previously all terms started and finished on 4 March. Section II requires Congress to assemble on 3 January each year.

The changes improved the operations of the federal government and coordinated better the activities of the executive and legislative branches. Previously, approximately four months passed between the popular vote for President and Vice President and Inauguration Day. This interlude created a lengthy lame-duck period when the White House changed hands [*see* LAME-DUCK PRESIDENTS]. Section I reduced that period by six weeks, thereby leaving an incoming President reasonable opportunity to form an administration without deferring the transition so long.

The change in congressional terms remedied some outdated practices. Before the Twentieth Amendment, a new Congress did not regularly convene until December, thirteen months after representatives were elected. That practice developed when travel was slow, communications difficult, and Senators were elected by state legislatures. Technological advances and the adoption of the Seventeenth Amendment (direct election of Senators) made the practice obsolete.

The previous system diluted the impact of elections by deferring for more than a year installation of Representatives and Senators. It made it difficult to assess the performances of a legislator; he began running for reelection shortly after beginning his duties.

The new schedule also meant that the President and Congress would begin work together soon after their elections. It enhanced the President's ability to offer a legislative program since it provided an assembled Congress at the outset of his term elected by the same electorate.

Moreover, the changes addressed the remote contingency of the House and Senate electing the President and Vice President respectively if the ELECTORAL COLLEGE did not produce a majority for any candidate. Prior to the Twentieth Amendment, the Congress elected two years earlier would have had to choose the President and Vice President if no candidate won an electoral majority since the new Congress did not take office until 4 March, the same date the President and Vice President did. Oddly, legislators who had been defeated could decide who would be President or Vice President for the next four years. By beginning the new Congress's term on 3 January the Twentieth Amendment effectively gave the new Congress that task and gave it seventeen days to act before the presidential term.

The amendment also addressed some gaps in provisions regarding presidential vacancies. Although the Constitution provided for succession after the death, resignation, removal, or disability of the President, it made no provisions if those contingencies visited a President-elect. The Twentieth Amendment provides that if the President-elect dies, the Vice President–elect becomes President; if he fails to qualify or if no President is elected, the Vice President–elect acts as President until the President-elect qualifies. "Failure to qualify" is a somewhat ambiguous term that probably refers to a range of contingencies, including disability, failure to take the oath of office, constitutional disqualification, and perhaps even death.

The amendment also empowered Congress to provide who shall act as President if neither a President-elect nor Vice President–elect have qualified. Under the PRESIDENTIAL SUCCESSION ACT of 1947 the Speaker of the House acts as President in this eventuality. Interestingly, the Twentieth Amendment does not explicitly authorize Congress to designate an Acting President if both President-elect and Vice President–elect die before Inauguration Day but presumably "failure to qualify" is sufficiently broad to cover that situation.

The amendment also authorized Congress to provide for the case of the death of one of the three persons from whom the House may choose a President or one of the two persons from whom the Senate may choose a Vice President if no one receives an electoral vote majority. Congress has not yet done so. Accordingly, the House could be limited to choosing between minority party and THIRD-PARTY CANDIDATES while the Senate might have no alternative.

Although the Twentieth Amendment improved upon the provisions of the TWELFTH AMENDMENT, it left gaps and ambiguities. It does not allow Congress to provide for the disability or resignation of persons from whom the House or Senate may choose. It does not dictate procedures if a candidate dies before the electoral votes are counted. John D. Feerick, a leading authority on presidential succession, has suggested persuasively that under the Twelfth Amendment, the electoral votes cast for a person who subsequently died should be counted; and if he (and his running mate) were elected, the latter would become President under the Twentieth Amendment. It does not make clear how long the House or Senate need continue to try to elect a President or Vice President. Can the House suspend voting and allow the Vice President–elect or Speaker to act as President? Could the House, having suspended voting, later elect a President well into the term, thereby displacing the Acting President and his administration? And, under the TWENTY-FIFTH AMENDMENT, can an acting President appoint a Vice President pending action by the House or Senate?

BIBLIOGRAPHY

Abrams, Herbert L. *"The President Has Been Shot": Confusion, Disability, and the 25th Amendment in the Aftermath of the Attempted Assassination of Ronald Reagan.* 1992.

Feerick, John D. *From Failing Hands.* 1965. Pp. 270–275.

Peirce, Neal R. *The People's President.* 1968. Pp. 71–74, 132–136, 196–197.

U.S. House of Representatives. *Fixing Commencement of Terms of President, Vice President, and Members of Congress* 72d Cong., 1st sess. 27 February 1932. Conference Report.

U.S. Senate. Committee on the Judiciary. *Fixing the Commencement of the Terms of the President and Vice President and Members of Congress.* 72d Cong. 1st sess. 4 January 1932.

JOEL K. GOLDSTEIN

TWENTY-FIFTH AMENDMENT. The Twenty-fifth Amendment makes provisions for dealing with vacancies in the vice presidency and with PRESIDENTIAL DISABILITY. The need for the kind of provisions contained in the Twenty-fifth Amendment was demonstrated long before its adoption in 1967. On several occasions in American history, Presidents suffered temporary disabilities that affected their capacity to discharge the powers and duties of office. In these instances, no transfer of power to their Vice Presidents occurred because of the Constitution's silence on the subject of presidential disability.

Article II, Section 1, clause 6, simply provided that in case of the President's "inability" (also known as disability) to discharge the powers and duties of his office, "the Same shall devolve on the Vice President." No guidance was provided on such issues as the meaning of the term *inability*, the status of a VICE PRESIDENT in such a case, and who had the power to determine the beginning and ending of an inability. The Constitution also prescribed no procedure for filling a vacancy in the vice presidency when a Vice President either

succeeded to the presidency, died in office, or resigned. Sixteen times between 1841 and 1967 there was a vacancy in the vice presidency caused by such events, leaving the office unoccupied for more than thirty-seven years in the aggregate.

The assassination of President John F. Kennedy in 1963 led Congress to deal with these problems once and for all. His death and the succession of Lyndon B. Johnson to the presidency not only left a vacancy in the vice presidency but vividly focused the nation on the unanswered questions surrounding presidential disability, since there was a possibility that the fallen President might have lingered between life and death for a period of time. At congressional hearings held in 1964 and 1965 numerous proposals for dealing with these issues were considered. A consensus developed and, on 6 July 1965 Congress proposed the Twenty-fifth Amendment to the Constitution, which was quickly ratified by the necessary thirty-eight state legislatures.

The Vice Presidency. The amendment that was ultimately adopted sets forth a procedure for filling a vacancy in the vice presidency and a mechanism for handling instances of presidential disability. Section 1 makes clear that a Vice President becomes President when there is a vacancy in the presidential office because of the President's death. It confirms the precedent that was originally established by Vice President John Tyler in 1841, when President William Henry Harrison died of pneumonia. The TYLER PRECEDENT was subsequently followed by seven other Vice Presidents (Millard Fillmore, Andrew Johnson, Chester A. Arthur, Theodore Roosevelt, Calvin Coolidge, Harry S. Truman, and Lyndon B. Johnson), upon the deaths of their Presidents. The amendment also extends the precedent to cover vacancies in the presidency caused by resignation and removal from office after IMPEACHMENT. In any of these situations, the Vice President takes the PRESIDENTIAL OATH OF OFFICE and serves as President for the remainder of the term.

Section 2 of the amendment provides a procedure for filling a vacancy in the vice presidency upon the death, resignation, or removal of the President or Vice President. In such a situation, the President is empowered to nominate a successor who becomes the new Vice President once confirmed by a majority of both houses of Congress. This section is intended to keep the vice presidency filled at all times and, in authorizing the President to initiate the nomination, it follows the historical practice whereby Presidents have chosen their Vice Presidents.

Disability. Sections 3 and 4 deal with presidential disability. They provide that in such a situation, the

Vice President discharges the powers and duties of the presidency, without assuming either the office or title of President. The Vice President exercises presidential power under the title of Acting President. Section 3 involves situations where the President recognizes his own disability and wishes to suspend temporarily the powers and duties of the office. The President can declare himself disabled under section 3, for either an indefinite or specific period of time, and can resume the powers and duties of office simply upon his own declaration of recovery.

Section 4 deals with the more troublesome situation of a President who is either unable or unwilling to declare his own disability. It empowers the Vice President and a majority of the principal officers of the executive departments (commonly known as the CABINET) to declare the President disabled. The Vice President and Cabinet were chosen because of their close relationship to the President. It was thought that they would be in command of the facts and always would act fairly toward the President in a case of disability.

Upon a declaration of presidential disability, the Vice President becomes Acting President until such time as the President announces his recovery. If the President challenges the declaration of disability or the Vice President and Cabinet challenge the President's declaration of recovery, section 4 provides for Congress to decide the disagreement within twenty-one days. If Congress is not in session at the time, it is required to assemble within forty-eight hours. Under the section, a two-thirds vote of each house of Congress is required in order to prevent the President from resuming his powers and duties. As Congress decides the issue, the Vice President continues to serve as Acting President. If Congress does not act within the twenty-one-day period, however, the President immediately resumes his powers and duties. Section 4 also contains a clause authorizing Congress to substitute a body other than the Cabinet to function with the Vice President in deciding cases of presidential disability. This clause was intended to cover the possibility that the Cabinet might prove to be an unworkable body under section 4.

In order to assure public notice and public confidence in the process, sections 3 and 4 of the amendment prescribe that all declarations of inability and restoration to capacity are to be transmitted to the Speaker of the House of Representatives and the President pro tempore of the Senate before they can become effective.

The term *inability* is not defined in the amendment. Situations involving physical or mental illness, temporary or permanent, were the most frequently mentioned contingencies in the congressional hearings and debates that preceded the amendment. It was deemed unwise to include in the Constitution a precise definition of the inability because it could take various forms not neatly fitting into any such definition.

The Amendment in Practice. Since the amendment's adoption, it has been invoked on two occasions, both involving vacancies in the vice presidency. Section 2 was first used in 1973, upon the resignation of Vice President SPIRO T. AGNEW, to select Gerald R. Ford as Vice President. It was implemented again in 1974, upon the resignation of President Richard M. Nixon and Ford's succession to the presidency, to designate NELSON A. ROCKEFELLER as Vice President. Section 2 of the amendment operated smoothly during the scandals of the Nixon administration to give the nation continuity of leadership.

The amendment has never been formally invoked in a case of presidential disability. When President Ronald Reagan became temporarily incapacitated while in office, he chose not to invoke section 3, although he took all the steps required by the section at the time he underwent surgery in July 1985. His failure to implement the amendment prompted criticisms and may have set the stage for Presidents to invoke section 3 in the future.

Complementing the Twenty-fifth Amendment is the PRESIDENTIAL SUCCESSION ACT of 1947, which provides that if a President should die, resign, or be removed when there is a vacancy in the vice presidency, the Speaker of the House of Representatives would fill out the presidential term. In the absence of a Speaker, the President pro tempore would be next in the line of succession, followed by the members of the Cabinet in the order that their respective departments were created. The 1947 act is a successor to laws passed in 1792 and 1886. None of these laws has ever been implemented. The Twenty-fifth Amendment closes loopholes in the Constitution and in so doing makes resort to the line of succession even more unlikely.

BIBLIOGRAPHY

Abrams, Herbert L. *The President Has Been Shot: Confusion, Disability, and the 25th Amendment in the Aftermath of the Attempted Assassination of Ronald Reagan.* 1992.

Bayh, Birch. *One Heartbeat Away: Presidential Disability and Succession.* 1968.

Feerick, John D. *The Twenty-Fifth Amendment: Its Complete History and Earliest Application.* 1976.

Thomas, Kenneth W., ed. *Papers on Presidential Disability and the Twenty-Fifth Amendment By Six Medical, Legal, and Political Authorities.* 1988.

JOHN D. FEERICK

TWENTY-FOURTH AMENDMENT. In 1964, at a time of heightened civil rights awareness, the Twenty-fourth Amendment expressly prohibited the imposition of a poll tax or other tax requirement as a prerequisite for voting in federal elections. Only five states (Arkansas, Alabama, Mississippi, Texas, and Virginia) actually imposed this type of voting requirement at the time; however, the amendment nevertheless eliminated a mechanism that had been widely used throughout the history of the United States to limit the ability of certain classes of people to vote in both federal and state elections. Although the Twenty-fourth Amendment only covered a citizen's ability to vote in federal elections, the Supreme Court later declared, in *Harper v. Virginia Board of Elections* (1966), that the use of a poll tax requirement in state elections was unconstitutional as well.

Since the framing of the Constitution, states had imposed certain qualifications on their inhabitants as a prerequisite to voting. Some of the most common types of voting requirements included property ownership, literacy tests, and the payment of poll taxes and other forms of taxes. Such requirements presumably promoted civic responsibility, limiting voting to those with a stake in the community. Following the CIVIL WAR, the use of poll taxes increased, as many southern states found that they could be used to limit black suffrage since blacks as a group were among the poorest members of society.

In order to protect the voting rights of the newly emancipated slaves, the Fifteenth Amendment to the Constitution provided that the right to vote shall not be abridged on account of race, color, or previous condition of servitude. Many southern states, however, took the position that Article I, Section 2, reserved the state's right to establish qualifications for its voters and argued that the poll tax was a neutral qualification within the meaning of this section. In practice, however, the poll tax became a mechanism for reducing black participation in voting, although it also disenfranchised poor whites.

The first legal attack on the poll tax was unsuccessful; several courts ruled that the imposition of a poll tax as a voting prerequisite was within the bounds of the Constitution, and in 1937 the Supreme Court affirmed this view. In its decision, the Court declared that the "privilege of voting is not derived from the United States but is conferred by the State and, save as restrained by the Fifteenth and Nineteenth Amendments and other provisions of the Federal Constitution, the State may condition suffrage as it deems appropriate."

Given this view by the courts, the anti–poll tax movement moved to the legislative arena. As early as 1939, Congress began considering legislative initiatives that would ban the poll tax. It was not until the early 1960s, when civil rights issues began to make significant progress, and the John F. Kennedy administration lent its support to the anti–poll tax effort, that the movement gained enough momentum for the proposed amendment to obtain congressional approval and to be ratified by the requisite thirty-eight states.

BIBLIOGRAPHY

Lawson, Steven. *Black Ballots: Voting Rights in the South, 1944–1969.* 1976.

Christensen, Jan E. "The Constitutionality of the National Anti-Poll Tax Bills." *Minnesota Law Review* 33 (1949): 217.

U.S. House of Representatives. Committee on the Judiciary. *Outlawing Payment of Poll or Other Tax as Qualification for Voting in Federal Elections.* S. Rept No. 1821. 87th Cong., 2d sess., 1962.

U.S. Senate. Committee on the Judiciary. *Poll Tax and Enfranchisement of District of Columbia.* Hearings, 86th Cong., 1st sess., 1959.

JOHN D. FEERICK

TWENTY-SECOND AMENDMENT. The Twenty-second Amendment is short and to the point. It provides that "no person shall be elected to the office of the President more than twice" or more than once if that person has held the office for more than two years of a term to which someone else was elected (but could not serve because of death or disability).

An informal TWO-TERM TRADITION for American Presidents started by President George Washington and reinforced by President Thomas Jefferson continued for about 150 years. In 1940, however, President Franklin D. Roosevelt ran for and was elected to a third term, and in 1944 he won a fourth term.

Adopting the Amendment. Roosevelt's breaking tradition prompted, soon after his death, a successful campaign to place a limit of two terms for Presidents in the U.S. Constitution. This was hardly a new idea. Term limits and even the notion of a single term had been proposed at the CONSTITUTIONAL CONVENTION of 1787. And at least 270 resolutions in favor of term limits for President had been introduced in Congress by 1947.

In 1947 such a resolution, unanimously supported by Republicans in Congress, passed easily. The House of Representatives voted 285 to 121 in favor of it and the Senate approved it 59 to 23. Thus it readily obtained the necessary two-thirds support in both chambers. Forty-one states ratified it within four years of submission, and thus in 1951 the Twenty-second Amendment was incorporated into the Constitution.

Its terms did not apply to Harry S. Truman but only to his successors.

A Source of Dispute. TERM AND TENURE for Presidents were the sources of prolonged dispute and deliberation in Philadelphia in 1787. The Framers settled the matter temporarily. In 1951 Americans fundamentally altered the Framer's decision.

Seldom are procedural constitutional reforms such as term limits for elected officials neutral in terms of their policy and power consequences. Certain partisan or political interests are plainly affected. Certainly this has been the case with the two-term limit on Presidents. The post-Roosevelt crusade to enact the Twenty-second Amendment was clearly an exercise in retroactive partisan vengeance. Having failed to defeat Roosevelt when he was alive, the Republican leadership punished him and sought to limit the influence of his party after his death. A minor boomlet in 1972 and 1973 to repeal the two-term limit was an effort by Richard M. Nixon's friends to pave the way for his possible reelection to a third term. A 1986 boomlet to repeal this amendment was yet another transparent partisan ploy to retain the White House for yet another four years and to reap the political advantages of PATRONAGE, APPOINTMENT OF JUDGES, and Ronald Reagan's once-magical partisan fund-raising talents. These last two repeal efforts died with the revelations of the WATERGATE AFFAIR and the IRAN-CONTRA AFFAIR. Predictably, however, there will be similar drives to repeal the two-term limit, and almost always they will be motivated by anticipated short-term policy and political advantages.

Presidents Harry S. Truman, Dwight D. Eisenhower, and Ronald Reagan have urged that this amendment be repealed. Many noted historians such as Arthur M. Schlesinger, Jr., and political scientists such as James MacGregor Burns have also supported repeal.

Arguments for Repeal. Advocates of repeal say this limit violates the people's democratic rights: the people ought to decide who their leaders will be. If the people want to vote for someone, especially an experienced veteran in the office, there should not be any rule telling them they do not have that choice. Constitutional historians like to note that this limitation upon the electorate is the first change since the Constitution was adopted that has restricted rather than expanded the voter's suffrage.

The Framers of the Constitution, repeal advocates note, considered and debated the idea of limiting the number of terms but rejected it. Reeligibility, they also contend, makes Presidents more attentive to popular concerns. Also, echoing ALEXANDER HAMILTON's reason-ing in FEDERALIST 72, they point out that the United States may someday desperately need an experienced veteran of public and world affairs during a time of crisis—for example, a Roosevelt to continue in office in the 1940s during WORLD WAR II or an Abraham Lincoln to stay in office in the 1860s to stay the course in the CIVIL WAR.

Advocates of repeal believe Roosevelt's reelection in the 1940s proves that a multiterm presidency can happen without impairing the Republic. After all, they say, there are plenty of safeguards against the power of the presidency that would prevent Presidents from becoming tyrants. Indeed those who would repeal the Twenty-second Amendment often believe that the American presidency is too weak an institution, given voters' expectations of leadership. They say, too, that the system of multiple CHECKS AND BALANCES can only work if there is a strong President in a strong presidency. Thus the country needs Hamiltonian energy in the presidency to make its Madisonian system of dispersed powers and checks and balances work in such a way as to allow it to achieve its Jeffersonian ends of liberty and justice.

Those who favor repeal raise some good points. Clearly, the amendment does diminish the choices of a voter, and it is true that voters in the 2040s will be in a better position than those who supported the Twenty-second Amendment in the 1940s to decide who should be their President.

Arguments for Retention. But the case of retaining this amendment is strong. Eight years strikes most people as long enough. Americans do not like the idea of a permanent President nor do they view the presidency as a career job. Presidents such as Thomas Jefferson, Andrew Jackson, and John F. Kennedy have praised the notion of rotation in office as healthy and desirable. Jefferson warned that history shows how easily unlimited tenure might degenerate into an inheritance.

Most Americans, polls show, favor retaining the Twenty-second Amendment. The public supports it as an additional check against the ultimate type of abuse of power, the arrogant view that a particular President is indispensable. Other constitutional democracies from Germany to Chile to the Philippines have all suffered when there would-be savior became in fact their enslaver.

Eight years, most people believe, is ample time for a President and a party to introduce and bring about major changes in policy. And if these changes are valued and effective, they will be continued and honored by succeeding Presidents of whatever party.

The two-term limit is healthy for the two-party

system. It helps prevent political stagnation. The two parties benefit and are rejuvenated by the challenge at least every eight years of nurturing, recruiting, and nominating a new team of national leaders. In this sense, the very structure of this amendment prevents the hardening of the political arteries.

Americans reject the idea that any political leader is indispensable. The nation is seventy to seventy-five times larger than in 1789. There are plenty of talented leaders and would-be effective Presidents. Moreover, if a President of the ability of a Washington, a Lincoln, or a Roosevelt were available and if the nation were facing an exacting emergency, the services and leadership of such a person would not need to be thrown out and ignored merely because a successor President would come to office at the end of eight years. Common sense would usually suggest that these exceptional public servants be retained as counselors, roving ambassadors, or Cabinet members with specialized portfolios—precisely in order to take advantage of their expertise and experience.

Also, a President who stays on for twelve or sixteen years would very likely be able to pack the Supreme Court and fundamentally alter the partisan leanings of the entire federal judiciary.

The formal constraints of the two-term limit have, ironically, only been felt by two Republican Presidents, Eisenhower and Reagan. It is thus too soon fully to evaluate the effect of the amendment. But it is clear that there is widespread acceptance of the idea that Presidents should serve just two terms lest one person or one party be allowed to become too powerful.

Although the Twenty-second Amendment has its drawbacks, its virtues will be appreciated by future generations. Americans want an effective presidency, yet they fear the arbitrary abuse of power and the potential of Presidents who someday may delude themselves into believing they are indispensable. The two-term limit allows a citizen to serve eight years in one of the world's most powerful positions, while it protects the country from the potential excesses of power that could come with prolonged tenure. On balance, therefore, the Twenty-second Amendment is an acceptable, if imperfect, compromise.

BIBLIOGRAPHY

Cronin, Thomas E. "Two Cheers for the 22nd Amendment." *The Christian Science Monitor* (23 February 1987): 16.
Cronin, Thomas E., ed. *Inventing the American Presidency*. 1989.
Petracca, Mark. *Rotation in Office: The History of an Idea*. 1992.
Schlesinger, Arthur M., Jr., ed. *Critical Presidential Elections in American History*. 1971.
Stathis, Stephen W. "The Twenty-Second Amendment: A Practical Remedy or Partisan Maneuver?" *Constitutional Commentary* 7 (Winter 1990): 61–88.
Stein, Charles W. *The Third Term Tradition: Its Rise and Collapse in American Politics*. 1943.

THOMAS E. CRONIN

TWENTY-THIRD AMENDMENT. The Twenty-third Amendment grants voting rights in presidential elections to residents of the District of Columbia. It was proposed by Congress on 16 June 1960 and ratified by the necessary thirty-eight states on 4 April 1961. Prior to the passage of the amendment, residents of the district had been denied the right to vote in presidential elections on the basis of Article II, Section 1, of the Constitution, which provides that "each state shall appoint in such manner as the Legislature thereof may direct, a number of electors, equal to the whole number of Senators and Representatives to which the State may be entitled in Congress." Since the federal district was not a state, there was no basis for District residents to vote for President and Vice President.

The District's unique status is derived from the difficulties that originally arose when the national government was located in a state. In the early history of the country, eight cities had served as the meeting place for Congress. Therefore, in drafting the Constitution, the Framers granted Congress in Article I, Section 8, clause 17, "exclusive legislation in all cases whatsoever, over such district as may by cession of particular states and the acceptance of Congress become the seat of the government of the United States." The creation of such a district was complicated by the issue of SLAVERY. Through compromise, the District was formed by the cession of land by a nonslaveholding state (Maryland) in 1788 and by a slaveholding state (Virginia) in 1789. The Framers sought to protect the functioning of the federal government from interference by any one state by granting Congress exclusive jurisdiction over the District.

Denying the right to vote to residents of the federal capital, of course, contradicted some of the most important ideals expressed in the Constitution. The residents of the District bore the responsibility of citizenship in their service in the United States military and in their payment of federal taxes. Yet they had no voice in choosing the government of their country by voting in presidential and congressional elections.

The resolution that resulted in the Twenty-third Amendment reflected a political compromise in the sense that it provided the District with "a number of electors of President and Vice President equal to the whole number of Senators and Representatives in Congress to which the District would be entitled if it were a state, but in no event more than the least populous state." The latter clause was included as a means of protecting the states from the District's wielding more power than intended by the Constitution. Without the clause, the District would have more weight in presidential elections than a quarter of the states because of its population. The proposed amendment received strong support from the Republican platform of 1956 and from President Dwight D. Eisenhower. A number of earlier Presidents (especially James Monroe, Andrew Jackson, and William Henry Harrison) also had favored the idea of greater representation in the national government by residents of the District.

In 1978 Congress submitted another proposed amendment to the Constitution concerning the District. It would have repealed the Twenty-third Amendment and eradicated the "least populous state" clause by granting the District representation in the electoral college as though it were a state. In addition, this proposal would have accorded the District representation in Congress. The amendment, however, did not receive ratification by the necessary three-fourths of the states.

The District therefore continues as an anomaly, participating somewhat in presidential elections and not at all in congressional elections. It also remains a stronghold for the DEMOCRATIC PARTY, never failing to produce an overwhelming popular vote for its candidates in presidential elections.

BIBLIOGRAPHY

Schmeckebier, Laurence F. *The District of Columbia, Its Government and Administration*. 1928.

U.S. House of Representatives. Committee on the Judiciary. *National Representation and Suffrage for the Residents of the District of Columbia*. Hearings, 75th Cong., 3d sess., 1938.

U.S. Senate. Committee on the District of Columbia. *Legislative History of District of Columbia Self-Government and Governmental Reorganization Act, S. 1435 (P.L. 93-198)*. 93d Cong., 2d Sess., 1974.

U.S. Senate. Committee on the Judiciary. Subcommittee on Constitutional Amendments. *Enfranchisement of the District of Columbia*. Hearings. 86th Cong., 1st sess., 1959.

JOHN D. FEERICK

TWO PRESIDENCIES. In 1966 the political scientist Aaron Wildavsky declared that presidential influence with Congress differs so much in foreign and domestic policy that there are, in effect, "two presidencies." Wildavsky advanced the idea of using the content of policy to distinguish among Presidents' powers in dealing with Congress. Since then scholars have made numerous theoretical and empirical arguments and interpretations about the two-presidencies thesis. In 1991 Steven Shull compiled a quarter-century assessment of this literature. Such research has guided much of our understanding of PRESIDENTIAL-CONGRESSIONAL RELATIONS in the post-WORLD WAR II era.

Wildavsky's classic article argued that EXECUTIVE POWER in foreign policy is vastly superior to what it is in domestic policy. In a study of Presidents from 1948 to 1964 Wildavsky discovered that Congress supported a President's foreign-policy initiatives 70 percent of the time compared with about 40 percent of domestic-policy initiatives. In this first quantitative study, he stated that determined Presidents, although often frustrated in the domestic sphere, do not fail on any major foreign-policy issues. That assertion may have been true at the time, but an examination of the presidency since the 1960s shows that Congress has thwarted Presidents on such issues: Lyndon Baines Johnson on foreign aid and military assistance, Richard M. Nixon on arms sales and his Vietnam policies, Gerald R. Ford on aid to Southeast Asia and African development, Jimmy Carter on the SALT II Treaty, Ronald Reagan on the Strategic Defense Initiative (SDI) and aid to the contras, and George Bush on his Secretary of Defense nominee.

In 1979, Lance LeLoup and Steven Shull updated Wildavsky's study from 1953 through 1975 finding that the gap in presidential success between the two areas had narrowed to 55 percent congressional support in foreign policy and 46 percent approval of domestic initiatives. Wildavsky is probably correct that foreign policy usually overshadows domestic policy, but when LeLoup and Shull looked at specific domestic issues, they found considerable variation from these percentages (ranging from 50 percent success in social welfare and agriculture to just 26 percent success in civil liberties).

Jeffrey Cohen found Presidents more successful in foreign policy since 1861 and, thus, the two-presidencies phenomenon is not just a post-World War II occurrence. This finding adds longevity and credibility to the two-presidencies thesis. In the 1970s, Congress undertook numerous initiatives to limit the presidency. Besides greater constraints, a blending of foreign and domestic policy issues occurred. For example, such issues as immigration, trade, and military sales increasingly involve foreign, economic, and domestic concerns. Has this blending and the increased importance of international economics reduced the usefulness of the two-presidencies thesis? Subsequent research did show that Presidents received less foreign policy support in the 1970s than in the 1950s.

The *Congressional Quarterly*'s data on presidential initiatives to Congress were the statistical basis for these early studies. Because the *Congressional Quarterly* stopped collecting these data after 1975, scholars since then have sought to measure the two-presidencies thesis differently, by studying presidential positions on congressional votes rather than presidential initiatives. Lee Sigelman and Harvey Zeidenstein used only the key votes in criticizing the PRESIDENTIAL BOXSCORE for including inconsequential and noncontroversial matters. The emphasis shifted therefore from presidential actions to presidential reactions. The boxscore is the President's legislative agenda; key votes are his positions on Congress's agenda. Clearly, scholars make different assumptions when using different measures. The results also differ.

Subsequent studies of the two-presidencies thesis have considered political party, member status, chamber, and ideology. For example, senior and more ideological legislators more often support a President of their party. Zeidenstein found chamber important, with greater policy differences in the Senate. For George Edwards, party rather than chamber or even policy was the explanation for the observed differences. Richard Fleisher and Jon Bond found that the two-presidencies thesis depends on party and applies to Republican Presidents only.

Terry Sullivan argued that the two-presidencies thesis is more about winning (success) than about the President's ability to influence individual legislator's voting. His analysis uses new data composed of presidential head counts (compiled by the White House itself rather then by the *Congressional Quarterly*). These data provide a source of information related to but different from the data commonly used for testing the two-presidencies thesis. Head counts offer a different and possibly more detailed picture of the process leading up to votes in each chamber. Using these data, Sullivan discovered statistically significant differences in domestic and foreign issues similar to those uncovered by Bond and Fleisher.

Ronald Reagan's tenure with its divided congressional majorities from 1981 to 1986 revealed some aspects of the two-presidencies thesis, thereby questioning Edward's assertion that it is time-bound. Meanwhile, Bond and Fleisher reconfirmed the two-presidencies thesis for Republican Presidents. However, the dramatic party difference they observed occurred on domestic policy but not on foreign policy.

Russell Renka and Bradford Jones suggested that the two-presidencies thesis in the Reagan administration and in George Bush's first year resulted from presidential minority-party status. The authors concluded that in a minority-party situation presidential influence is found more wanting in domestic than in foreign policy. Thus, differences by chamber, party, member status, and philosophy are important factors in the two-presidencies thesis.

Many years after proposing the two-presidencies thesis, Wildavsky contended that several changes had diminished the President's influence in foreign policy: ironically as foreign policy increasingly dominates the President's agenda, it has become more partisan and ideological and, most importantly, it has become more complex. Despite mixed empirical evidence, Wildavsky and his colleague Duane Oldfield claimed that the two-presidencies thesis may no longer be valid—if indeed it ever had been—because foreign policy has become more similar to domestic policy. Foreign policy is now more conflictual on both partisan and ideological grounds. Thus differences between the policy areas today are more muted.

Criticisms of the thesis exist on both methodological and conceptual grounds. Steven Shull and James Vanderleeuw acknowledged that different types of legislative votes exist and suggested conceptual and measurement problems with key votes, especially relating to small number of cases. They questioned how *CQ* operationalize "a matter of major controversy, a test of presidential power, and a decision of potentially great impact in the lives of Americans." Also, the small number of cases complicates measurement. Fleisher and Bond claimed that their expanded data set (close votes plus key votes) create a set of issues more important to Presidents than the key votes themselves. But such closely contested roll calls are biased against the thesis since closer votes naturally are less consistent winners or losers for the White House. Also, such aggregations of votes may be less reliable than key votes.

Perhaps scholars have concentrated too much on the congressional literature in studying the two-presidencies thesis. Orfield and Wildavsky pointed the need to go beyond the confines of Congress. The two-presidencies thesis should be considered during elections, when the incumbent has the advantage to manipulate foreign policy. Scholars should analyze such nonlegislative features as EXECUTIVE ORDERS and EXECUTIVE AGREEMENTS and consider subdividing foreign policy into specific issues. Resurrecting the presidential boxscore as Mark Peterson has done would also provide useful data for more definitive tests.

Although a blending of foreign and domestic policy has taken place, a complete merger will never happen.

Congress has increased its checks but a true balance cannot exist because Congress has been unable to put forth its own in foreign policy. Moreover, inherent differences in domestic and foreign policy are tempered by growing economic influences. All research suggests that variables discussed here have conditioned and limited the two-presidencies thesis. A continuing question is whether party is more important than policy in determining presidential-congressional relations. This question requires further study.

As yet, no one has challenged Wildavsky's original notion that developments in the rise of the modern presidency and the changing international leadership role of the United States have altered foreign-policy decision making in the President's favor. The increased blending of foreign, economic, and domestic policies does not mean differences in the roles of Congress and the President have disappeared. The increased incidence of divided government has exacerbated such differences.

Conceptual and empirical differences in domestic and foreign policy are still evidence as seen in the latest data by Renka and Jones and by Sullivan. So are differences in objectives, organization, personnel, decision making, group support, perceptions, stakes, and ease of implementation. Since such distinctions exist, real differences in the President's impact in the two policy areas will persist. Some research challenges the explanatory power of policy content in studying presidential-congressional relations, but the most recent studies reveal the reemergence of the two presidencies in the 1980s and into the 1990s.

Further development of the two-presidencies thesis requires consideration of the legislative history of bills in Congress and ascertaining whether bills are part of the President's legislative program. Better data on the President's ability to shift votes in Congress are needed along with improved ways of measuring presidential success and failure with Congress. Multivariate, nonlinear, analysis is called for.

The two-presidencies thesis does, nevertheless, enhance our ability to compare Presidents and to understand their relations. It shows the utility of a policy approach for studying the presidency. The two-presidencies thesis has endured because it is one of the few attempts in presidential studies to avoid "stylized" facts and instead to examine actual behavior. Although not a fully developed theory, the two-presidencies thesis provides a useful basis for empirical analysis on presidential-congressional relations.

BIBLIOGRAPHY

Peterson, Mark A. *Legislating Together*. 1990.

Shull, Steven A., ed. *The Two Presidencies: A Quarter Century Assessment*. 1991.

Shull, Steven A., and James Vanderleeuw. "What Do Key Votes Measure?" *Legislative Studies Quarterly* 12 (1987): 573–582.

Wildavsky, Aaron. "The Two Presidencies." *Transaction* 4 (1966): 7–14.

STEVEN A. SHULL

TWO-TERM TRADITION. Delegates to the CONSTITUTIONAL CONVENTION considered both four-year and six-year terms for the office of the President. When they decided on a four-year term, reeligibility was assumed. At the close of his second term, President George Washington declined a third term, which he undoubtedly could have had. His refusal was based primarily on reasons of personal convenience. But when President Thomas Jefferson announced in 1807 that he would withdraw after two terms, he stressed Washington's example and raised the issue to a principle, arguing that indefinite reeligibility might undermine the elective system and turn the presidency into a life-tenure post. The subsequent two-term administrations of James Madison, James Monroe, and Andrew Jackson gave the tradition almost unassailable validity.

The first concerted attack on the two-term tradition came in 1876 from a group of Republicans who wanted Ulysses S. Grant to run for a third term, but the resistance was overwhelming. In 1908 Theodore Roosevelt, having served three and one-half years of William McKinley's term and one term in his own right, stated that "the wise custom which limits the President to two terms regards the substance and not the form" and announced flatly that "under no circumstances will I be a candidate for or accept another nomination." By 1912, however, he had changed his mind, and he unsuccessfully sought a third term. Calvin Coolidge found himself in somewhat the same situation in 1928, but he never definitely stated his view on the application of the two-term tradition in his case, merely announcing that he did not "choose to run for President in 1928."

It was left for Franklin D. Roosevelt definitely to breach the tradition in 1940, when the electorate concluded that maintenance of the two-term limit was less important than retaining his experienced leadership in a world at war. Roosevelt's election to a precedent-shattering fourth term in 1944 was quickly followed by his death on 12 April 1945. The tragic denouement of this experience with unlimited reeligibility, combined with pent-up Republican frustration over four successive defeats by the same candidate, quickly resulted in a campaign to write the two-term limit into the Constitution. When the Republicans won control of the Eightieth Congress, they immediately pushed through such an amendment, which was ratified in 1951.

The TWENTY-SECOND AMENDMENT provides that no person shall be elected to the office of President more than twice and that no person who has held the office of President, or acted as President, for more than two years of a term to which another person was elected President shall be elected more than once. The terms of the Twenty-second Amendment would have made Theodore Roosevelt ineligible in 1912 and Coolidge ineligible in 1928 but would not have prevented Lyndon Baines Johnson from seeking reelection in 1968, since he had served for less than two years after the assassination of John F. Kennedy. It is ironic that the Republican-sponsored two-term limitation eliminated potential third terms for two Republicans, Dwight D. Eisenhower and Ronald Reagan.

It has been argued against the two-term limit, that the electorate should not be foreclosed from complete freedom of choice in selecting the President. ALEXANDER HAMILTON wrote, "How unwise must be every . . . self-denying ordinance as serves to prohibit a nation from making use of its own citizens, in the manner best suited to its exigencies and circumstances." A second objection is that the two-term limitation creates the possibility of LAME-DUCK PRESIDENTS, since a President's constitutional inability to seek reelection could conceivably handicap him as he tries to maintain party support during the second term.

The idea of a single SIX-YEAR PRESIDENTIAL TERM, though rejected by the Constitutional Convention, has occasionally been revived. President Jackson in each of his annual addresses invited consideration of a single-term amendment. The Progressive movement of the late nineteenth and early twentieth century alleged that Presidents manipulated second-term elections and supported the single term, as did the Democratic national convention of 1912. But its nominee, Woodrow Wilson, promptly rejected the idea and served two terms.

[*See also* TERM AND TENURE.]

BIBLIOGRAPHY

Corwin, Edward S. *The President: Office and Powers, 1787–1957.* 1957.

C. HERMAN PRITCHETT

TYLER, JOHN (1790–1862), tenth President of the United States (1841–1845). A Virginian, Tyler was the Whig candidate for Vice President, running with William Henry Harrison ("Old Tippecanoe") on the famous 1840 campaign slogan, "Tippecanoe and Tyler Too." On 4 April 1841, a month after taking office, Harrison died and Tyler became America's first accidental President as well as the youngest man to become President to that time. Tyler served out Harrison's term but failed to be nominated for the 1844 election. As a peace commissioner he represented Virginia during the SECESSION crisis, but when his state left the Union Tyler became the only ex-President to serve in the government of another nation (and take up arms against the United States), when in November 1861 he won a seat in the Confederate Congress, where he served until his death in January 1862.

Tyler's presidential administration was one of chaos, confusion, and constant wars with Congress, his party, and his Cabinet. Although his administration had some notable successes—especially in FOREIGN AFFAIRS—Tyler's presidency was generally a failure, which was rooted in his political isolation.

Tyler was stubborn, impolitic, inconsistent, and unpredictable. These traits, his political philosophy, and his lack of any clear party affiliation undermined his administration. In the mid 1830s his opposition to Andrew Jackson led him to leave the DEMOCRATIC PARTY and become a Whig. His nomination as Vice President provided ideological and sectional balance to the WHIG PARTY ticket, the STATES' RIGHTS former Democrat running with Harrison, a nationalist mainstream Whig. Although elected as a Whig, Tyler was at heart a states' rights southern agrarian who was most comfortable in the conservative, proslavery, states' rights wing of the Democratic Party. Tyler was ideologically closer to JOHN C. CALHOUN than to any other major politician.

When Harrison died, Whigs found the presidency in the hands of a man who rejected most Whig policies and who resisted almost all compromises. This "Whig" President opposed the key banking and tariff programs of the mainstream of his party. Four months into his administration five of his six CABINET officers resigned and congressional Whigs rightly read him out of the party for his obstinate refusal to sign critical banking legislation passed by the Whig majority in Congress. Democrats, on the other hand, mistrusted the President who had abandoned them in the 1830s. He was thus a President without a party.

Illustrative of Tyler's impolitic stubbornness was his appointment of CALEB CUSHING as Secretary of the Treasury. When the Senate refused to confirm Cushing, Tyler immediately renominated him, and hours after the second rejection, Tyler sent Cushing's name forward again. Thus, three times in one day the Senate refused to confirm Cushing for the Cabinet. Indicative of Tyler's slide to states' rights extremism is the make-up of his Cabinet. His initial Cabinet, which he inherited from Harrison, had three southerners and three northerners, and was led by the staunch Whig nationalist, Secretary of State DANIEL WEBSTER. When Tyler left office, his Cabinet had five southerners and was led by the embodiment of Democratic, states' rights, proslavery zealotry, Secretary of State John C. Calhoun.

Early Career. Tyler grew up in Tidewater Virginia on a twelve-hundred-acre plantation with forty slaves. His father, John Tyler, was a member of the Virginia House of Delegates (1785–1786), an ardent ANTI-FEDERALIST at the Virginia ratifying convention in 1788, a governor of Virginia (1809–1811), and a United States district judge from 1811 until his death in 1813.

The younger Tyler graduated from the College of William and Mary in 1807 and read law under EDMUND RANDOLPH, the former Attorney General of the United States. At age twenty-one, Tyler began practicing law and won a seat in the Virginia House of Delegates. He served in the Virginia house until 1816, when he was elected to the United States Congress—the first year he was old enough for the office. There he was a strict constructionist advocate of states' rights, SLAVERY, limited government, and a weak President. He opposed chartering the Second BANK OF THE UNITED STATES, the Bonus Bill, protective tariffs, and the MISSOURI COMPROMISE. Tyler left Congress in 1821 because of poor health but by 1823 he was back in the Virginia House of Delegates. He served two terms as governor of Virginia (1825–1826), and in 1827 he entered the United States Senate, where he once again took a strict-constructionist stand.

Ostensibly a Democrat, Tyler was an inconsistent ally of Andrew Jackson. He supported Jackson's vetoes of the Maysville road bill and the recharter of the Second Bank of the United States, but opposed his removal of deposits from the bank. Tyler backed Old Hickory for reelection in 1832 but opposed Jackson on numerous appointments (including Secretary of the Treasury ROGER B. TANEY) and the NULLIFICATION proclamation. Tyler was the only Senator to vote against the FORCE BILL, which he believed unconstitutionally threatened states' rights. Tyler, a Tidewater aristocrat, was uncomfortable with the rough-hewn quality of Jacksonian democracy. He was socially more at home with Whigs, even though he rarely agreed with their programs. Most of all, Tyler disliked Jackson's somewhat imperial presidency. By 1834 Tyler was aligned with HENRY CLAY in his opposition to Jackson. In 1836 the Virginia legislature instructed Tyler to rescind his vote to censure Jackson for the removal of the federal deposits from the Second Bank of the United States. Tyler refused to do so, but consistent with his states' rights views, he resigned from the Senate rather than disregard his state legislature's instructions.

In 1836 the Whig Party was hardly more than a loose coalition of politicians who agreed on only one thing: their opposition to Andrew Jackson and his heir apparent, Martin Van Buren. Most Whigs also supported the Bank of the United States and high tariffs, although some, like Tyler, did not. To avoid facing these contradictions within the party, the Whigs held no convention in 1836 and did not field a single candidate. Instead, three Whigs—William Henry Harrison, Daniel Webster, and Hugh L. White—and Willie P. Mangum, an anti-Jackson independent, opposed Van Buren. The Whigs hoped to prevent any candidate from getting a majority of the electoral vote, thus throwing the election to the House of Representatives. John Tyler was on the ballot as Harrison's running mate in Maryland, as White's running mate in Tennessee, North Carolina, and Georgia, and as Mangum's running mate in South Carolina. In Virginia both Harrison and White were on the ballot with Tyler as their running mate. In this confused race with five presidential candidates and three vice presidential candidates, Tyler ran third for Vice President with forty-seven electoral votes.

After the election, Tyler sought, and failed, to regain his Senate seat. He returned to his law practice in Williamsburg. In April 1838, running as a Whig, Tyler won a seat in the Virginia House of Delegates. In 1839 he became the speaker of that body. Throughout that year Tyler actively supported Henry Clay for the 1840 Whig presidential nomination. In December 1839 he attended the Democratic Whig national convention in Harrisburg, Pennsylvania, as a Virginia delegate unalterably committed to Clay. Initially Clay had the most votes in a three-way race, but eventually Harrison won the nomination.

For Harrison's running mate the party needed a southerner (and preferably an easterner) who could balance the ticket headed by the candidate from the Northwest. Also useful would be someone who might placate the disappointed Clay, or at least his followers. Few prominent Whigs fit the bill, and they declined to run. Tyler gained the nomination almost by default. None of Harrison's supporters asked him any questions, secured any promises from him, or attempted to discover his views. Had they done so, it is doubtful the Whigs would have nominated Tyler.

Although Tyler was supposed to be part of the Clay faction of the Whig Party, in truth, he and Clay agreed on very little. Clay hoped to revive the Bank of the

United States; Tyler opposed the bank on both constitutional and policy grounds. Both men agreed that Jackson and Van Buren had abused the power of their office, but their solution differed. Clay believed in a weak President who would carry out the wishes of Congress; Tyler favored a moderately strong executive who would preserve states' rights from incursions by a nationalist Congress. Tyler was a proslavery Virginian who deeply mistrusted the nationalizing tendencies of the bank, Clay's AMERICAN SYSTEM, and most other Whig policies. Tyler represented the small states' rights wing of the party, not the nationalist wing of Clay.

The Accidental President. During the 1840 campaign Tyler spoke rarely, and under orders from Harrison, he avoided discussing controversial issues, especially the bank. This was just as well, because most voters considered Tyler's views generally irrelevant to the campaign. After a half century under the Constitution, the vice presidency had, by and large, become a dead-end position. Since 1800 only one Vice President, Martin Van Buren, had succeeded to the presidency, and the Whigs were certain they could end his career after one term. Although if elected Harrison would be the oldest President ever inaugurated, the hardy general appeared in good health. When Tyler was nominated, no one imagined he would be anything more than the presiding officer of the Senate. But, to the nation's shock and the chagrin of Whigs who declined the vice presidential spot, Harrison died exactly one month after his inauguration. The United States had its first accidental president.

Harrison's death immediately raised questions about Tyler's powers, title, and role. Initially the Cabinet called Tyler the "Vice President, acting as President." Chief Justice Roger B. Taney, when asked about Tyler's status, declined to respond, deeming it improper for one branch of government to intrude on the other. Tyler believed that he had become President the moment Harrison had expired and did not even need to take the oath of office. However, the Cabinet insisted on this, and on 6 April District of Columbia Judge William Cranch administered the oath of office to Tyler. Cranch provided a written certification of Tyler's oath taking, but noted that before taking the oath Tyler "deem[ed] himself qualified to perform the duties and exercise the powers and office of President on the death of William Henry Harrison . . . without any other oath than that which he has taken as Vice President." Even while taking the oath of office, Tyler revealed his obstinacy and his often foolish proclivity to elevate even minor matters to issues of constitutional or political principle. These traits would undermine his presidency in the next four years.

In May the House adopted a resolution that referred to Tyler as President, thus recognizing he was not the "acting president." A day later the Senate joined the House in this position by a vote of 38 to 8. Nevertheless, some critics continued to call Tyler "His Accidency" or referred to him as the "vice president, acting as president."

Tyler's succession set two precedents: first, that the Vice President must take the oath of office to assume the presidency; and second, that once the oath has been taken the former Vice President becomes the President, with all the powers and responsibilities of that office, and is not an acting president. [See TYLER PRECEDENT.]

Economic Policy. Once in office Tyler turned to the nation's economic problems. Before he died, Harrison had called for a special session of Congress for the end of May. This special session, which lasted the entire summer of 1841, was superficially productive, leading to a repeal of the INDEPENDENT TREASURY, the adoption of the nation's first federal bankruptcy law, and a law strengthening the navy. But the main agenda of congressional Whigs was to create something with which to replace Van Buren's Independent Treasury system. On this point, the most crucial issue facing the nation, Congress and Tyler failed miserably.

After vetoing the bill to recharter the bank of the United States, President Jackson had removed federal deposits from that bank, placing them in state banks. The unreliability of state banks led President Van Buren to propose that the federal government be its own bank through an Independent Treasury system. This system kept federal funds safe from incompetent state banks, but also kept a vast amount of money out of circulation, thus prolonging the depression that followed the Panic of 1837. In the summer of 1841 Congress demolished the nascent Independent Treasury. But Congress and Tyler could never agree on a replacement system.

Tyler's solution to the financial crisis was the creation of a bank in Washington, D.C., where Congress clearly had the power to charter a financial institution. The United States government would own stock in the new bank—as it did in the old Bank of the United States—as would states and private individuals. But, underscoring Tyler's strong states' rights views, the bank would not operate in the states without their consent. Under this scheme the federal bank would not compete with local and state banks without state permission, but could otherwise function as a bank, collecting money for the federal government and at the same time keeping some of that money in circulation through loans.

Tyler's proposal had strong support in much of the South, among state bankers, and with some Democrats. Sen. Henry Clay, still smarting over his loss of the Whig nomination in 1840, adamantly opposed Tyler's plan. Like Tyler, Clay had wanted to abolish the Independent Treasury. But Clay wanted to replace it with a new Bank of the United States, authorized to do business in every state. Clay eventually compromised on a bill that would allow state legislatures to reject branch banks, but if they failed to do so at their first session after the creation of the new national bank, the bank would be free to open branches in their states. To the dismay of Whigs, on 16 August 1841 Tyler vetoed this compromise bill. Clay and others had been led to believe Tyler would accept the compromise. But, if Tyler had once agreed to the bill, he no longer did. Tyler believed the provision allowing for branch banks was unconstitutional. He also objected to allowing the national bank to give loans because it would then compete with local banks. Clay and other Whigs believed the power to make loans was essential if the bank was to regulate currency and help create economic stability.

After Tyler's bank veto, Congress passed the FISCAL CORPORATION BILL, which would have created a bank in Washington with agencies in the states. This was an attempt to get around Tyler's objections and at the same time provide for some centralized control of the economy. Ignoring the pleas of his Cabinet, on 9 September Tyler vetoed the bill with "great pain" and "extreme regret." He felt it was an unconstitutional attempt to create a national bank, rather than a local bank in the District of Columbia for the purpose of accepting federal deposits. In his veto message, Tyler reminded Congress that he had signed every bill Congress sent him during the special session except the two dealing with banking.

In his annual message in December 1841, Tyler proposed the exchequer plan, yet another solution to the problem of where to store the government's money. This plan would have created a government entity (rather than a private corporation like the Bank of the United States) located in Washington with branches throughout the country. The exchequer would issue bank notes and accept deposits, but not make loans, and thus not compete with state banks.

Although a plausible answer to the problem of currency and federal deposits, Tyler's proposal was ignored by the Whig majority in Congress. Senator Clay, already considered the Whig presidential candidate for 1844, would not allow any of Tyler's proposals to pass. Even after Clay resigned from the Senate in early 1842, the impasse continued. By the summer the national government was teetering on bankruptcy. In late June Tyler vetoed an interim tariff bill. Tyler, who had always opposed high tariffs, vetoed the interim bill because it did not raise tariffs enough to continue funding the government. Because of the economic crisis—and his own refusal to compromise—Tyler, a conservative, antitariff southerner, was now forced to argue for higher taxes. In August Tyler vetoed yet another tariff bill. At the end of the month a new tariff bill passed by one vote in each house and Tyler signed it. This law alienated Tyler's southern, states' rights, Democratic base because it was too protective, while it alienated northern Whigs because it was not protective enough.

Tyler's inability to compromise on financial issues nearly bankrupted the nation while destroying his effectiveness and undermining his administration. After his two bank vetoes in 1841 and the two tariff vetoes in 1842 the treasury was empty and federal employees were going without pay. This led to the higher tariff of 1842, which Congress grudgingly passed and Tyler unhappily signed. Oddly, by the end of his presidency the nation had a budget surplus, as a result of improved economic conditions and the tariff of 1842.

Cabinet and Party Relations. Tyler's vetoes of the two bank bills in the summer of 1841 set the stage for a civil war within the Whig Party. After the first veto of the modified bank bill, Henry Clay denounced Tyler in an hour-and-a-half speech, suggesting Tyler should have resigned his office if he could not sign a constitutionally valid bill passed by Congress. Other Whigs also attacked Tyler, who in turn, felt betrayed by his own party. Secretary of State Daniel Webster was the only prominent Whig to defend Tyler. Webster argued that except for their differences over the bank, Tyler was a mainstream Whig. In some ways, Webster was correct. Tyler had resisted the overtures of extreme states' rights southerners, as when he had appointed Edward Everett, a moderate northern Whig, to be ambassador to Great Britain.

The day Tyler vetoed the Fiscal Corporation bill all the Cabinet but Webster secretly met with Henry Clay, and within a few days, Attorney General John J. Crittenden, Thomas Ewing (Treasury), Badger (Navy), and JOHN BELL (War) resigned. Two days later Postmaster General Francis Granger left the Cabinet. Never before had a President's Cabinet resigned en masse.

To the surprise of Clay and the nationalist Whigs, on the day Granger resigned, the last day of the special session of Congress, Tyler presented the Senate with a list of new Cabinet members: Hugh S. Legaré (Attorney General); Walter Forward (Treasury); Abel P. Upshur (Navy); John C. Spencer (War); and Charles A. Wickliffe (Postmaster General). All the appointees were Whigs; all but Spencer had previously been Democrats. Spencer and Forward were northerners (joining Webster, who remained in the Cabinet), while the rest were from the South. The Senate confirmed these nominations and then adjourned. Meanwhile, a group of Whig leaders formally read Tyler out of the party. The party was not unanimous in this position, and in Congress pro- and anti-Tyler members came to blows.

The September 1841 resignations set the stage for the most disrupted Cabinet in presidential history. In his four years in office Tyler's six Cabinet positions had twenty-two occupants. The Senate refused to confirm two interim and three regular Cabinet appointments. Congress also twice refused to confirm John C. Spencer (who served as Secretary of War and Secretary of the Treasury) to the Supreme Court. Three Cabinet officers died, including two (Abel Upshur and Thomas Gilmer) who were killed when a naval gun exploded during a demonstration of the Navy's newest vessel, the *Princeton.* Tension within the administration almost always ran high, and on one occasion Tyler personally broke up a fistfight between his secretaries of the Navy and War.

The early Cabinet resignations reflected the huge chasm in ideology and policy between Tyler and the Whigs. Within four months of Tyler's having taken office, Whig leaders read him out of the party. The immediate cause of this rift was Tyler's veto of the Fiscal Corporation bill, but the root of the problem went much deeper. As a states' rights Democrat for most of his career, Tyler opposed high tariffs, the Bank of the United States, Clay's American System, and most other programs that came to be the backbone of the Whig program. Like Calhoun, who served in his Cabinet, Tyler became a Whig because it was the only credible vehicle for opposing "King Andrew" and his successor, Martin Van Buren, and not because he agreed with the goals and programs of the Whigs. Philosophically, Tyler was always closer to southern states' rights Democrats than to the mainstream of the Whig Party.

Tyler exacerbated his relations with Congress and the Whig Party by his inconsistent policies, his refusal to compromise bank and tariff policy, his appointing Cabinet members on the basis of their political allegiance, rather than any skills or expertise, and his penchant for nepotism, appointing relatives to at least eight different government positions.

Tyler's Accomplishments. Despite his political failures and inability to find a sound basis for regulation of the economy, Tyler had some successes and left a small but useful legacy of accomplishments. Tyler or his Cabinet officers reorganized the navy, which began building its first steam-powered ships, set up a Depot of Charts and Instruments, and constructed the United States Naval Observatory. In intervening on behalf of Commander Uriah P. Levy (who was court-martialed for refusing to flog a teenage sailor), Tyler helped end flogging in the navy. Tyler initially resisted requests for federal intervention in the DORR WAR in Rhode Island. When he later threatened to bring in federalized militia from other New England states, the Dorrites dispersed. The Dorr War, which might have led to a bloodbath, ended without violence. He also helped negotiate an end to the Second Seminole War. Tyler encouraged exploration of the West just as he had encouraged exploration of the heavens through the Naval Observatory. On his last day in office Tyler signed the Postal Reform Act, which reduced rates and set the stage for modern postal and telegraphic communications.

Tyler was even more successful in foreign affairs. The Senate ratified thirteen of the fifteen treaties he submitted to that body, including some that aided American trade in Asia. More importantly, the WEBSTER-ASHBURTON TREATY probably prevented a war between Great Britain and the United States. This treaty also led to some Anglo-American cooperation on the suppression of the African slave trade.

The treaty was not, however, a reflection of antislavery sentiment. Tyler's administration was generally proslavery. His administration was filled with southern nationalists and proslavery ideologues like Abel Upshur. Tyler attempted to pack the diplomatic corps with slaveowners or their northern doughface allies. As a southern nationalist, Tyler's favored the expansion of slavery to the west. This culminated in the ANNEXATION OF TEXAS, which has been aptly described as an empire for slavery. However, this triumph virtually guaranteed a war with Mexico and a reopening of the question of slavery in the West.

Tyler was the first President to be widowed in office, when Letitia Tyler died in September 1842. A year and a half later Tyler became the first sitting President to marry. His bride, Julia Gardiner, was thirty years his junior.

After leaving the White House, Tyler practiced law and served on the board of visitors of the College of William and Mary in the 1850s and in 1860 became its chancellor, an honorary post previously held only by George Washington. In 1861 he served as a delegate to the Washington peace conference. He was subsequently a secessionist delegate to the Virginia convention, which brought the state out of the Union. He then served as a member of the provisional Congress of the Confederacy, but died before he could take his seat in the Confederate House of Representatives. These last public acts underscore Tyler's southern nationalist, proslavery sympathies.

BIBLIOGRAPHY

Chitwood, Oliver Perry. *John Tyler: Champion of the Old South.* 1939.

Jones, Howard. *To the Webster-Ashburton Treaty: A Study in Anglo-American Relations, 1783–1843.* 1977.

Lambert, Oscar D. *Presidential Politics in the United States, 1841–1844.* 1936.

McCormick, Richard P. *The Second American Party System.* 1966.

Morgan, Robert. *A Whig Embattled: The Presidency under John Tyler.* 1954.

Peterson, Norma Lois. *The Presidencies of William Henry Harrison and John Tyler.* 1989.

Seager, Robert, II. *And Tyler Too: A Biography of John and Julia Gardiner Tyler.* 1963.

PAUL FINKELMAN

TYLER PRECEDENT. On 4 April 1841, William Henry Harrison became the first President of the United States to die in office. The "influence of this event upon the condition and history of the country," John Quincy Adams wrote later the same day, "can scarcely be foreseen." Not only was this the "first instance of a VICE PRESIDENT being called to act as President of the United States," it also tested "that provision of the Constitution which places in the Executive chair a man never thought of for it by anyone."

When Tyler was selected as Harrison's running mate in 1839, neither his opinion nor his loyalties were considered important. He received the Whig vice presidential nomination without ever actually embracing the party he represented. All that really mattered was his ability to garner the southern vote.

At his home in Williamsburg, Virginia, Tyler learned of President Harrison's death on the morning of 5 April. Shortly thereafter, he departed for the nation's capital, arriving in Washington the following morning. By the time Tyler arrived, Washington was already alive with rumors and speculation regarding his succession. Because of the vagueness of the Constitution, it was unclear whether he was President or would act as such until a special election could be held.

He immediately met with the Cabinet at Brown's Hotel, where he learned from them that he had not fully become the President; hence, all administration matters were to be approved by them. Tyler responded sternly, saying he would not consent to their opinion, and if they could not cooperate, their resignations would be accepted. Considering the temperament of the Cabinet, and to remove all doubt, Tyler subsequently decided to take the PRESIDENTIAL OATH OF OFFICE under the direction of William Cranch, chief judge of the Circuit Court of the District of Columbia. Tyler's independence and courage assured him enduring significance as the author of the PRESIDENTIAL SUCCESSION precedent, which ensures a legitimate and orderly transfer of power at the highest level of American government.

BIBLIOGRAPHY

Dinnerstein, Leonard. "The Accession of John Tyler to the Presidency." *Virginia Magazine of History and Biography* 70 (October 1962): 447–458.

Stathis, Stephen W. "John Tyler's Presidential Succession." *Prologue* 8 (Winter 1976): 223–236.

STEPHEN W. STATHIS

U

UDALL, STEWART (b. 1920), Secretary of the Interior. Stewart Lee Udall became one of the most prominent and respected secretaries of the Interior. A Mormon upbringing, a rugged Western environment, and the spirit of Franklin D. Roosevelt's conservation New Deal of the 1930s all left their imprint on the youthful Udall, who in 1954 was elected to the first of three successive terms as a member of the U.S. House of Representatives. In the House, he distinguished himself as a member of the so-called conservation bloc on the Committee on Interior and Insular Affairs.

Seeking a young and imaginative CABINET, in 1961 President John F. Kennedy appointed Udall as Secretary of the Interior. Legislative successes came slowly. Then Kennedy's assassination on 22 November 1963 propelled Lyndon B. Johnson into the White House. Johnson asked Udall to stay on, promising prompt attention to the needs of America's public lands, especially the national parks.

Udall's initial support for two dams that would have flooded portions of Grand Canyon National Park and Monument, as well as neighboring Marble Canyon, was the only major blemish on an otherwise notable record of additions to the national park system, including 3.6 million acres of new parks under the Johnson administration alone. The creation of Redwood National Park and North Cascades National Park and the passage of the Wild and Scenic Rivers Act, all approved by Congress in 1968, were but a few of the major achievements linked directly to Udall's personal interest and support. Indeed, according to President Johnson, "the person mainly responsible for it all is Secretary Udall."

With the exception of the Alaska lands legislation sponsored during the late 1970s by Secretary of the Interior Cecil D. Andrus, no American conservation program has equaled Udall's in breadth, sophistication, and overall significance. Two books, *The Quiet Crisis* (1963) and *1976: Agenda for Tomorrow* (1968), further distinguish Stewart Udall as one of the nation's most dedicated and informed secretaries of the Interior.

BIBLIOGRAPHY

Frome, Michael. *Regreening the National Parks.* 1992.
Unes, Barbara Le. "The Conservation Philosophy of Stewart L. Udall, 1961–1968." Ph.D. diss., Texas A & M University. 1977.

ALFRED RUNTE

UNDERWOOD TARIFF ACT (1913). Elected in 1912 on a Democratic platform calling for a revenue-only tariff (a position he had embraced as early as 1882), Woodrow Wilson attacked the protective tariff as an engine fostering special privilege and trust formation. He advocated sharply lower tariffs, providing protection only for legitimate enterprise, opening all home markets to some measure of foreign competition, and eliminating duties entirely on goods subject to domestic monopolies and on goods that, by reason of foreign comparative advantage, ought not to be produced domestically at all.

Wilson's tariff efforts redefined presidential leadership in the legislative arena. Calling Congress into special session, Wilson appeared personally before Congress to initiate tariff reform (the first President to so appear since John Adams) and worked intimately with the chairperson of the House Ways and Means Committee, Oscar Underwood (D-Ky.), in drafting the bill. Confident that the measure would secure quick

House passage, Wilson broke tradition again by meeting with Democratic members of the Senate Finance Committee. As the bill stalled in the Senate—threatened by Democrats from Louisiana and from the West who opposed free sugar and free wool—Wilson pressured Senate Democrats publicly by denouncing the influence of lobbyists and special interests and privately by threatening to withhold patronage.

Unlike the reform measures sought by Cleveland and Taft, so brutalized by the Senate in 1894 (*see* WILSON-GORMAN TARIFF ACT) and 1909 (*see* PAYNE-ALDRICH TARIFF ACT), Wilson's bill survived the Senate gauntlet and emerged even less protectionist than when passed by the House. The act imposed the lowest tariffs since the TARIFF ACT OF 1857, substituting ad valorem duties for most specific duties, reducing average rates from approximately 40 percent to less than 30 percent, and adding numerous goods to the free list. It made up revenue shortfalls by imposing the first personal income tax under the newly ratified Sixteenth Amendment, entirely abandoned the Republican concept of international reciprocity, and eliminated the Tariff Board.

BIBLIOGRAPHY

Clements, Kendrick A. *The Presidency of Woodrow Wilson.* 1992.
Link, Arthur S. *Woodrow Wilson and the Progressive Era, 1910–1917.* 1954.
Taussig, F. W. *The Tariff History of the United States.* 8th ed. 1931.

RALPH MITZENMACHER

UNITED NATIONS. The United Nations is an international organization designed to foster world peace. Nearly a creation of the American presidency, it was an outcome of the widespread belief during WORLD WAR II that the LEAGUE OF NATIONS had failed to preserve peace because of American nonparticipation. Thus establishment of a new international organization became an important objective of American diplomacy, much more than for the other two great powers, the Soviet Union and Great Britain. The United States achieved wide agreement on the character of the United Nations at the Dumbarton Oaks Conference (August to October 1944). Significant details, however, remained to be worked out at the YALTA CONFERENCE (February 1945) in discussions between Franklin D. Roosevelt, Winston Churchill, and Joseph Stalin.

Shortly after Harry S. Truman succeeded Roosevelt, these issues resurfaced at the San Francisco conference (April to June 1945), which drew up the charter for the organization. Truman in effect secured Soviet acquiescence to the establishment of the organization by ceding control of Poland to the U.S.S.R., a decision that showed how central the establishment of the United Nations had become to American diplomacy. Truman himself, more so than Roosevelt, was a strong believer in the Wilsonian tradition and hoped that an effective United Nations could underwrite world peace. During the KOREAN WAR, its sanction for the U.S.–South Korean struggle was vitally important to him.

None of Truman's successors possessed his devotion to the organization, but all considered it an important tool of American diplomacy. The American delegation was headed by an ambassador, who was a presidential appointee, not a Department of State functionary; in numerous administrations, he or she received CABINET status. From Truman through Lyndon Baines Johnson, the ambassador was a high-profile individual chosen on the basis of prior prominence and oratorical proficiency. From the beginning, however, he or she was only marginally involved in the making of foreign policy, a process that remained in the control of Presidents and their Secretaries of State or NATIONAL SECURITY ADVISERS.

During the period when the Western democracies wielded effective control of the United Nations, American administrations saw the organization as an important sounding board and an effective provider of symbolic legitimacy for their policies, including the Baruch plan for the control of atomic energy, the decision to fight in Korea, and the ultimatum to the Soviet Union during the CUBAN MISSILE CRISIS.

By the end of the 1960s, however, a majority of the membership was from developing countries, neutralist, and pointedly indifferent to Western liberal democratic values, making the United Nations at worst a diplomatic liability, at best a constant nuisance to American policy. During the presidencies of Richard M. Nixon and Gerald Ford, American policy toward the organization was predominantly adversarial, perhaps most effectively so in the ambassadorship of Daniel P. Moynihan (January 1975 to April 1976).

The administration of Jimmy Carter attempted a reconciliation under the ambassadorships of Andrew Young, a former civil rights leader, and Donald McHenry, a foreign service officer. Both were African Americans who placed a high premium on conciliation with developing countries. Few disinterested observers, however, could judge the effort a conspicuous success.

The administration of Ronald Reagan was at least as adversarial as those of Nixon and Ford. Under Ambassador Jeane Kirkpatrick (January 1981 to April 1985), the United States stopped paying its full assessment of financial support. During the Reagan presidency, the relationship reached a rhetorical low when one U.S. delegate sarcastically declared that anti-American nations that did not want the organization in New York might take it with them and "sail off into the sunset."

The presidency of George Bush, a former ambassador to the United Nations and an individual who had matured politically during the hopeful days of World War II, saw an attempt to reestablish the organization as a legitimator of American diplomacy, most notably in the conflict with Iraq, and as one of the bases for a "new world order."

BIBLIOGRAPHY

Fasulo, Linda M., ed. *Representing America: Experiences of U.S. Diplomats at the U.N.* Foreword by Elliot L. Richardson. 1985.

Moynihan, Daniel P. *A Dangerous Place.* 1978.

Riggs, Robert E. *US/UN: Foreign Policy and International Organization.* 1971.

Weiler, Lawrence D., and Anne Patricia Simons. *The United States and the United Nations: The Search for International Peace and Security.* 1967.

ALONZO L. HAMBY

UNITED NATIONS DECLARATION. Initiated by President Franklin D. Roosevelt and embodying the objectives he enumerated two days after the Japanese attack at PEARL HARBOR, the United Nations Declaration was drafted by the United States and then negotiated with our allies and signed on 1 January 1942. It was the principal item on the agenda during the second Roosevelt-Churchill summit conference—code-named Arcadia—in December 1941. The initial draft was produced by Secretary of State CORDELL HULL, and presented to the President before Churchill's arrival. It was coordinated with the governments of the United Kingdom, China, the Soviet Union, and other allied countries, and a final text was agreed upon by Roosevelt and Churchill on 29 December. The declaration is unique in several respects. It was negotiated with Britain and the other signatories within only one week. Containing merely fifty-two words, it specified that its signatories were pledged "to employ" their full resources to defeat the Axis powers, "to cooperate" with one another, and "not to make a separate armistice or peace with the enemies." In the declaration's preface the signatories also subscribed to the "common program of purposes and principles" embodied in the ATLANTIC CHARTER of 14 August 1941, which specified eight sets of objectives to apply during and after the war. This differed from WORLD WAR I, when there was no comparable binding international commitment on war and peace aims.

The declaration was personally signed at the White House by Roosevelt, Churchill, Soviet Ambassador Maksim Litvinov, and Foreign Minister Tzu-wen Soong of China and at the Department of State by the representatives of twenty-two other nations. This process distinguished the Big Four as the leaders of the anti-Axis alliance. From 1942 to 1945 it was acceded to by twenty-one additional nations. In early drafts the signatory nations were identified as Associated Powers; Roosevelt changed this to the UNITED NATIONS. Initially applied to wartime allies, the name was ultimately given to the postwar international organization.

Unlike the secret alliances and alignments of World War I, the text of the declaration was published immediately. Although not formally a treaty and designated a joint declaration, it constituted a solemn and binding covenant in the nature of an EXECUTIVE AGREEMENT, and it continues to be listed in the Department of State *Treaties in Force.*

As a military alliance, the declaration bound the signatories to a set of principles that provided for unity and purpose during the war and, together with the Atlantic Charter, for postwar integration. In this sense the United Nations, as a wartime alliance, marked a departure from traditional U.S. noninvolvement and presaged the postwar United Nations organization. (With a few exceptions, only those states that signed the declaration—and therefore subscribed to the Atlantic Charter—were invited to participate in the San Francisco Conference in 1945 and became original members of the United Nations organization.) Identified with Franklin Roosevelt, the United Nations Declaration was of critical importance in the development of U.S. foreign policy and the forging of post–World War II affairs.

BIBLIOGRAPHY

Hull, Cordell. *The Memoirs of Cordell Hull.* Vol. 2. 1948.

Russell, Ruth B. *A History of the United Nations Charter: The Role of the United States.* 1958.

Sherwood, Robert E. *Roosevelt and Hopkins: An Intimate History.* 1948.

ELMER PLISCHKE

UNITED NATIONS PARTICIPATION ACT. The basic legislation by which the United States participates in the UNITED NATIONS and implements the U.N. Charter is the United Nations Participation Act (UNPA). The U.S. decision to join the United Nations in 1945 posed important questions concerning the American constitutional system, including questions of the respective powers of the President and the

Congress. The main questions were the following. Who shall determine for the United States the policies to be pursued in the United Nations, including the casting of votes in U.N. organs? By what means shall the mandatory decisions of the U.N. Security Council be carried out (for example, with respect to economic sanctions or similar measures)? Which branch of the U.S. government shall have authority to decide to participate in military actions sponsored by the United Nations?

Policies, Voting, and Appropriations. U.S. representatives to the United Nations are executive officers appointed by the President with the confirmation of the Senate pursuant to Article II of the Constitution; they act on the instructions of the President and the Secretary of State. In speaking or voting within the international organization, U.S. delegates are expected to reflect policies consistent with the U.S. Constitution and with any legislation relevant to the subject matter. The President (or his delegate) determines whether to exercise the prerogative of veto accorded to permanent members of the Security Council under the U.N. Charter. Congress, however, must appropriate any funds with respect to budgetary assessments or other financial commitments. Frequently Congress has either failed to act in timely fashion on presidential requests for appropriation of funds or has imposed conditions and limitations that Presidents would have preferred to avoid.

Economic Sanctions. The UNPA confers authority on the President to implement economic sanctions or similar measures mandated by the U.N. Security Council. Because such sanctions involve the constitutional power of Congress over foreign commerce, the UNPA serves as an advance DELEGATION OF LEGISLATIVE POWER from Congress to the President and enables him to put the measures into effect without applying to Congress for specific approval. Uses of this authority during the early 1990s included sanctions imposed pursuant to Security Council resolutions with respect to Iraq (1990–), Yugoslavia (1991–), and Libya (1992–).

Congress, in the exercise of its plenary power over foreign commerce, may withdraw or change the terms of the general authority granted by the UNPA, even if such action would place the United States in violation of an obligation imposed by the Security Council. Thus in 1971 Congress passed the Byrd Amendment, which instructed the President not to restrict imports of Rhodesian chromium despite a binding embargo on such imports passed by the Security Council with U.S. support.

Military Action. The U.N. Charter establishes a system of collective security under which the Security Council may authorize military responses to threats to the peace, breaches of the peace, or acts of aggression. Pursuant to Article 42 of the charter, the Security Council may authorize "demonstrations, blockade, and other operations by air, sea, or land forces of Members of the United Nations." Article 43 contemplates a system of agreements—to be ratified by member states "in accordance with their respective constitutional processes"—pursuant to which member nations would make available to the Security Council contingents of military forces to serve under the council's command.

The intersection of this U.N. system with the U.S. constitutional system for WAR POWERS has given rise to important issues that were anticipated in 1945, largely ignored in the KOREAN WAR, and eventually addressed through joint action of the President and Congress in the Persian Gulf crisis of 1990–1991. The U.S. Senate, in giving advice and consent to ratification of the U.N. Charter, and both houses of Congress in enacting the UNPA, considered the relationship of the U.N. Charter's provisions to the constitutional distribution of war powers between Congress, which has the power to declare war and establish the armed forces under Article I, Section 8, and the President, who is the COMMANDER IN CHIEF under Article II. Congress wanted to ensure that the United States would be able to participate effectively in the new institution of collective security while remaining true to the constitutional principle of shared responsibility for decisions regarding war and peace.

The solution embodied in the UNPA focused on the agreements contemplated under Article 43 of the U.N. Charter: the President was authorized to negotiate such agreements, while Congress reserved to itself the authority to approve them. (Congress endorsed the position that approval should be granted by Congress as a whole, rather than by the Senate under its treaty powers, in view of Congress's constitutional prerogatives with respect to war powers.) Once Congress had approved such an agreement, the President could make forces available to the Security Council according to the agreement's terms: it would not be necessary to return to Congress for further approval of use of troops pursuant to the agreement. Congress specifically denied the President the authority to make troops available beyond those approved by Congress. A 1949 amendment to the UNPA authorized the President to make available no more than one thousand military personnel to serve in a noncombatant capacity as observers or guards.

The system of Article 43 agreements fell victim to COLD WAR tensions, and through the early 1990s Congress had never been called on to approve any such agreement. Nonetheless, in the Korean War and in at least the early stages of the GULF WAR, U.S. Presidents claimed that they had authority to send U.S. troops to fight in U.N.-endorsed military actions, whether or not Congress had specifically authorized involvement in such actions. Regarding Korea, President Harry S. Truman obtained a U.N. Security Council resolution in favor of the dispatch of national contingents to defend South Korea from the North Korea's attack, but he did not seek either a formal declaration of war from Congress or any explicit legislative authorization, nor did he bring any Article 43 agreement to Congress for approval pursuant to the UNPA. Rather, he maintained that his own constitutional powers as Commander in Chief were sufficient for the purpose. Congress did not press a constitutional confrontation over the issue and indeed lent implicit support through measures such as extending the draft and appropriating funds to sustain the war effort.

When Iraq invaded Kuwait in August 1990, President George Bush embarked on political and military initiatives within the framework of the United Nations on authority that he claimed to derive from the Constitution, without in the first instance seeking congressional imprimatur. Asserting that his powers as Commander in Chief were sufficient authority, he called up troops and mobilized them to the Persian Gulf region, increasing the troop strength to approximately a half-million by the end of 1990. Over the same period he obtained a series of U.N. Security Council resolutions, including Resolution 678, of 29 November 1990, which authorized states cooperating with Kuwait to use "all necessary means"—implicitly including armed force—to remove Iraqi forces from Kuwaiti territory should Iraq not do so by 15 January 1991. As military confrontation loomed, members of Congress insisted that even if the troop deployments fell within the Commander in Chief power, the President could not initiate conflict against Iraq on his own authority, and that the approval of the U.N. Security Council could on no account substitute for the constitutionally required involvement of the Congress in the decision to go to war. Members also claimed that involvement of U.S. troops in hostilities would violate the WAR POWERS RESOLUTION of 1973 unless Congress either declared war or granted specific statutory authorization. A group of members sought judicial clarification of the President's constitutional powers, but the case was dismissed on the threshold ground that Congress as a whole had not acted to confront the President. Passages in the opinion criticized the President's position on the question of constitutional interpretation (*Dellums v. Bush* [1990]).

Ultimately President Bush asked Congress to lend its formal approval to the anticipated military action. Accordingly, the Authorization for Use of Military Force against Iraq Resolution was adopted by both houses of Congress and signed by the President on the eve of the 15 January deadline set by the Security Council resolution. That resolution authorized the President to use force against Iraq to enforce the resolutions of the United Nations. President Bush continued to maintain that he requested congressional approval for political rather than legal reasons and that his constitutional powers would have sufficed to enable him to implement the Security Council resolutions even without this explicit congressional authorization.

Defenders of the contentions of Presidents Truman and Bush have suggested that a U.N.-authorized "police action" is not "war" in the constitutional sense. On the opposite side it is argued that neither this semantic shift nor the fact that "declarations" of war have essentially disappeared from international practice since WORLD WAR II should be allowed to obscure the fundamental constitutional preference that Congress be the primary decision-maker, or at least an equal partner, where war in the functional sense is at stake.

BIBLIOGRAPHY

Franck, Thomas M., and Faiza Patel. "UN Police Action in Lieu of War: 'The Old Order Changeth.' " *American Journal of International Law* 85 (1991): 63–74.

Glennon, Michael J. "The Constitution and Chapter VII of the United Nations Charter." *American Journal of International Law* 85 (1991): 74–88.

Glennon, Michael J. *Constitutional Diplomacy.* 1990.

Glennon, Michael J. "War and the Constitution." *Foreign Affairs* 70 (Spring 1991): 84–101.

Stromseth, Jane. "Rethinking War Powers: Congress, the President, and the United Nations." *Georgetown Law Journal* 81 (1993): 597–673.

LORI FISLER DAMROSCH

UNITED STATES POSTAL SERVICE. After considering bills that proposed scrapping the POST OFFICE DEPARTMENT and creating a "government-owned postal system," an "independent Postal Service wholly owned by the Federal Government," "a public authority," or a "body corporate and an instrumentality of the United States," the Ninety-first Congress in 1970 opted for "an independent establishment of the executive branch of the Government of the United States, the United States Postal Service." It was to be operated as a "basic and fundamental service provided to the people by the Government of the United States . . . and supported by the people." People, in this case, referred to postal customers, not taxpayers.

Symbolized by a post rider on a galloping horse, the old Post Office Department might better have been represented by a great, broad-backed horse spurred by many riders headed in different directions. Postage rates, pay rates, postal facilities and, to a large degree, use of transportation were determined outside the organization. That the department carried the mail in spite of these crippling conditions pays tribute to its strength and determination.

But, in 1966, post rider and horse stumbled to a halt in the country's largest postal facility, the Chicago Post Office. Postal management could no longer push mail through a decrepit physical plant.

The President and the Congress agreed on the need for postal reform and in 12 August 1970, President Richard M. Nixon signed the Postal Reorganization Act into law. On 1 July 1971, the United States Postal Service began to function—an organization that could be managed, not merely administered.

The changes were dramatic. First, authority to determine policy and rates was vested in nine governors, appointed by the President and approved by the Senate, with no more than five of any one political party. The governors select the POSTMASTER GENERAL, the Postal Service's chief executive, who serves at their pleasure.

The President no longer directly appoints the Postmaster General and, in turn, the Postmaster General no longer serves in the President's Cabinet. By moving the Postmaster General away from the political arena, the President and the Congress hoped to stabilize postal management and establish a career service based on performance, not partisanship.

Second, the Postal Reorganization Act authorized collective bargaining on wages and working conditions. Strikes remain outlawed, but binding arbitration ends impasses between postal management and unions.

Third, the Postal Service received authority to issue public bonds to finance postal buildings and equipment. In the past, when the Post Office Department had to compete with other national interests for building funds, it usually came in last. Not knowing whether funding would be granted made planning impossible.

Once it could operate in a more businesslike manner, the United States Postal Service needed less of a tax subsidy and, in 1983, announced it no longer needed any subsidy. Postal operations are financed solely by the sale of stamps and postal services, and the United States Postal Service is symbolized by the stylized profile of the bald eagle, a more independent, nationally recognized image.

BIBLIOGRAPHY

Towards Postal Excellence: The Report of the President's Commission on Postal Organization. 1968.

MEGAERA HARRIS

UNITED STATES v. BELMONT 301 U.S. 324 (1937). In this case, the Supreme Court confirmed presidential power to conclude certain binding international agreements, even without Senate ADVICE AND CONSENT. The decision arose in the course of litigation against the estate of a private banker with whom a Russian corporation had deposited funds prior to 1918. In 1918 the new Soviet government nationalized the firm through a decree that also purported to appropriate all its property, wherever located. Because the United States declined to recognize the new regime, U.S. courts refused to acknowledge the decree's legitimacy, leaving the Soviet Union unable to recover debts owed its nationalized firms when those debts were held in the United States.

In November 1933, President Franklin D. Roosevelt concluded several agreements with Maksim Litvinov, the Soviet commissar for foreign affairs, that resulted in U.S. diplomatic recognition of the U.S.S.R. One impediment to recognition had been the need to provide for the resolution of claims against the United States or the U.S.S.R. by one another's nationals. The U.S.S.R. assigned to the U.S. government all claims it had against U.S. nationals, recovery of which would provide funds to satisfy U.S. claims against the Soviets. The United States relied on this so-called Litvinov assignment in a New York court, seeking to recover the funds held on behalf of the nationalized firm. New York at first refused to honor the U.S. claim. The state court said that to give effect to the 1918 decree would be to honor a confiscatory act in violation of both New York State and U.S. public policy.

The Supreme Court held, however, that states may not impose state-law barriers against U.S. claims rooted in lawful international agreements. The 1918 decree encompassed the Russian firm's U.S. deposits, and the President's recognition of the Soviet Union validated all acts of the latter government from its inception.

The agreements on which the *Belmont* litigation was based were neither the consequence of statutory authorization nor the subject of Senate advice and consent. Nonetheless, the Court treated the agreements as having constitutional status equivalent to treaties. Moreover, the Court indicated that the agreements—rooted in the national government's exclusive foreign relations powers—would have preempted state law even if the Constitution had made no express provision for federal law's supremacy. Of key importance was the Court's assertion that the "negotiations, acceptance of the assignment and agreements and understandings in respect thereof" were within the authority of the President, who the Court said "had sole authority to speak as the sole organ of national government."

Presidents since 1933 have relied increasingly on EXECUTIVE AGREEMENTS for the formalization of international commitments, citing *Belmont* as authority for broad executive power to conclude such agreements. It is unclear, however, whether *Belmont* applies fully to agreements not integrally related to establishing diplomatic relations. That process, since Thomas Jefferson's time, has been recognized as an exclusive presidential function, signaled by the constitutional authority for the President to receive ambassadors.

BIBLIOGRAPHY

Henkin, Louis. *Foreign Affairs and the Constitution.* 1972.
Margolis, Lawrence. *Executive Agreements and Presidential Power in Foreign Policy.* 1986.
Millett, Stephen M. *The Constitutionality of Executive Agreements: An Analysis of United States v. Belmont.* 1990.

PETER M. SHANE

UNITED STATES v. CURTISS-WRIGHT EXPORT CORP. 229 U.S. 304 (1936).

In an extravagant opinion by Justice George Sutherland for a 7 to 1 majority, the Supreme Court fundamentally altered American FOREIGN AFFAIRS jurisprudence with its unprecedented concept of plenary presidential power in the field. For all its infirmities, *Curtiss-Wright* has provided a wellspring of alleged authority for presidential domination of foreign policy, including unilateral acts of war making, COVERT OPERATIONS, suppression of travel abroad [see TRAVEL, RIGHT TO], TREATY TERMINATION, and EXECUTIVE AGREEMENTS, and it is the most widely cited judicial decision regarding the allocation of foreign affairs powers. It possesses uncommon significance in spite of the fact that it raised merely the narrow question of the constitutionality of a joint resolution that authorized President Franklin D. Roosevelt to halt the sale of arms to Bolivia and Paraguay, then at war in the Chaco, if he found that it would contribute to the reestablishment of peace between those countries.

Inherent Presidential Power. Curtiss-Wright Export Corp. was convicted for violation of the embargo resolution and Roosevelt's proclamation, and on appeal it challenged the constitutionality of the law on the ground that it violated the delegation doctrine. Justice Sutherland wrote for the Court that the law was not "vulnerable to attack under the rule that forbids a delegation of the law-making power." If in his opinion Sutherland had confined himself to the delegation issue, *Curtiss-Wright* would have been lost in the shadow of PANAMA REFINING CO. v. RYAN (1935) and SCHECHTER POULTRY CO. v. UNITED STATES (1935). But Sutherland strayed from the issue before the Court and in some ill-considered dicta imparted an unhappy legacy, the chimerical idea that the external sovereignty of the nation is vested in the presidency and is neither derived from nor restrained by the Constitution. Foreign affairs powers, moreover, were essentially executive, which Sutherland explained "as the very delicate, plenary, and exclusive power of the President as the sole organ of the federal government in the field of international relations—a power which does not require as a basis for its exercise an act of Congress." Justice James C. McReynolds dissented but filed no opinion. Justice Harlan Fiske Stone was ill and did not participate in the case, but subsequently criticized the opinion in UNITED STATES v. PINK (1942) and in private correspondence.

Sutherland's theory of inherent presidential power stems from his bizarre reading of Anglo-American legal history. For Sutherland, domestic and foreign affairs are different, "both in respect of their origin and nature." The "domestic or internal affairs" are confined by the reach of the Constitution. But authority over foreign affairs is not dependent upon a grant from the Constitution since the powers of external sovereignty "passed from the Crown not to the colonies severally, but to the colonies in their collective and corporate capacity of the United States of America." Sutherland's historical excursion is without factual foundation. Scholars have demolished his thesis by demonstrating that in 1776 states were sovereign entities. Proof is found in Article II of the Articles of Confederation, which stated: "Each State retains its sovereignty, freedom and independence, and every power . . . which is not . . . expressly delegated to the United States, in Congress assembled." The states, in turn, grudgingly delegated powers to the Continental Congress including those, per Article IX, of making war and peace and entering into treaties.

Even if it were assumed that the power of external sovereignty had been by some method transferred directly from the Crown to the Union, there is nothing in Sutherland's theory that would explain why that power would be granted to the President. As Justice Felix Frankfurter stated in YOUNGSTOWN SHEET & TUBE CO. v. SAWYER (1952), "the fact that power exists in the Government does not vest it in the President." In fact, the Court has ruled on several occasions that the sovereign power in foreign affairs is held by Congress.

Sutherland's contention that the Constitution does not govern the conduct of foreign policy is indefensible. In FEDERALIST 45, James Madison put the question beyond doubt: "the powers delegated by the Constitution are few and defined . . . [they] will be exercised principally on external objects, as war, peace, negotiation, and foreign commerce." There is no evidence from the records of the CONSTITUTIONAL CONVENTION to suggest even the slightest flirtation with the concept of an undefined reservoir of presidential power. Moreover, since *Curtiss-Wright* the Court consistently has held that powers are tethered to the Constitution, as illustrated by Justice Hugo Black's opinion for the Court in REID v. COVERT (1957): "The United States is entirely a creature of the Constitution. Its powers and authority have no other source. It can only act in accordance with all the limitations imposed by the Constitution."

The Sole-Organ Doctrine. Justice Sutherland's invocation of the sole-organ doctrine has been excoriated by scholars. Sutherland expanded on Congressman John Marshall's speech in 1800 in which he remarked: "The President is sole organ of the nation in its external relations. . . . Of consequence, the demand of a foreign nation can only be made on him." Marshall was defending the decision of President John Adams to surrender to British officials a British deserter, Jonathan Robbins, in accordance with JAY'S TREATY. The Robbins affair involved a demand upon the United States, according to Marshall, and it required a response from the President on behalf of the American people. At no point in his speech did Marshall argue that the President's exclusive authority to communicate with a foreign nation included the power to formulate or develop policy. All Marshall had in mind was the President's role as an instrument of communication with other governments, a point of procedure that had been acknowledged in 1793 by Thomas Jefferson, who remarked that the President was "the only channel of communication between this country and foreign nations." That understanding had not been challenged until Sutherland infused the purely communicative role with a substantive policy-making function and thereby manufactured a great power out of the Marshallian sole-organ doctrine.

The claim that the President is the sole organ in making foreign policy cannot survive close scrutiny. As Article II of the Constitution indicates, the President shares the TREATY-MAKING POWER and the power to appoint ambassadors [*see* AMBASSADORS, RECEIVING AND APPOINTING] with the Senate. In fact, the Framers assumed that the treaty power would constitute the primary mechanism by which American foreign policy relations would be conducted. Congress has complete power over foreign commerce and, of course, it alone is the repository of the power to authorize war. Only two powers in foreign relations are assigned exclusively to the President. He is COMMANDER IN CHIEF (but he acts in this capacity by and under the authority of Congress) and he has the power to receive ambassadors. ALEXANDER HAMILTON, Madison, and Jefferson agreed that his clerklike function was purely ceremonial in character. While it has come to entail recognition of states at international law, which carries with it certain legal implications, the Framers declined to make it a discretionary policy-making instrument. As Hamilton explained it in *Federalist* 69, the duty of recognizing states was more conveniently placed in the hands of the executive than the legislature. The constitutional blueprint for the conduct of foreign policy thus rests on the premise of shared powers and responsibilities, but the Framers clearly granted the bulk of foreign relations powers to Congress.

Curtiss-Wright was a radical, path-breaking case. Despite the fact that the opinion is grounded in flawed history and that its rhetoric was dismissed as dictum by Justice Robert H. Jackson in *Youngstown,* it has enjoyed vitality and longevity because it has provided the principal source of, and justification for, presidential hegemony in foreign affairs during the COLD WAR period.

BIBLIOGRAPHY

Adler, David Gray. "The Constitution and Presidential Warmaking: The Enduring Debate." *Political Science Quarterly* 103 (1988): 1–36.

Berger, Raoul. *Executive Privilege: A Constitutional Myth.* 1974.

Fisher, Louis. *Constitutional Conflicts Between Congress and the President.* 3d rev. ed. 1991.

Glennon, Michael J. *Constitutional Diplomacy.* 1990.

Keynes, Edward. *Undeclared War: Twilight Zone of Constitutional Power.* 1991.

Koh, Harold Hongju. *The National Security Constitutional: Sharing Power After the Iran-Contra Affair.* 1990.

Lofgren, Charles. "*United States v. Curtiss-Wright Export Corporation:* An Historical Reassessment." *Yale Law Journal* 83 (1973): 1–32.

Wormuth, Francis D., and Edwin Firmage. *To Chain the Dog of War: The War Power of Congress in History and Law.* 1986.

DAVID GRAY ADLER

UNITED STATES v. GUY W. CAPPS, INC.

UNITED STATES v. GUY W. CAPPS, INC. 348 U.S. 296 (1955). In the AGRICULTURAL ADJUSTMENT ACT of 1948, the United States government tried to prop up the price of potatoes by agreeing to purchase unsold potatoes at 90 percent parity. The statute also authorized the President to protect American producers and the parity program from cheaper Canadian potatoes by setting import quotas or raising import duties, but only after a hearing before the Tariff Commission. Instead of following that procedure, however, the Truman administration entered into an EXECUTIVE AGREEMENT with Canada in which Canada agreed not to allow the export of potatoes to the United States except for use as seed. Subsequently, the government filed suit against the Guy W. Capps company, charging that it had purchased fifty thousand bags of Canadian potatoes, which it had then resold to a subsidiary of the A & P Company.

The federal district court ruled in favor of the Capps company in 1951, holding that there was no evidence that Capps had sold the potatoes for purposes other than seed. In 1953, the Fourth Circuit Court of Appeals upheld the lower court's decision, but on very different grounds. The appeals court ruled unanimously that the executive agreement with Canada was unconstitutional and, therefore, unenforceable, because the Constitution gave Congress, not the President, the power to regulate foreign commerce and because the legislature had not authorized or approved this agreement, which was contrary to the Tariff Commission hearings procedures specified in the statute.

The Eisenhower administration asked the Supreme Court to overturn the appeals court's decision voiding the executive agreement, arguing that the Agricultural Act of 1948 had clearly contemplated the use of such agreements, since it stipulated that the procedures set forth in the statute were not to be enforced "in contravention of any treaty or other international agreement to which the United States is or hereafter becomes a party."

Executive agreements were at the center of a number of controversies in the early 1950s. Many legislators still resented Franklin D. Roosevelt's use of an executive agreement to transfer American destroyers to Great Britain in 1940 [*see* DESTROYERS FOR BASES] and conservatives continued to denounce the wartime agreements Roosevelt had entered into with Winston Churchill and Joseph Stalin at the YALTA CONFERENCE. The *Capps* case also occurred right in the middle of the fight over the BRICKER AMENDMENT—Senator John Bricker's attempt to amend the Constitution to limit the use and effects of treaties and executive agree-

ments. Among other things, the Bricker Amendment would have given Congress the power to regulate executive agreements and would have required implementing legislation before such agreements went into effect as internal law within the United States. The amendment's proponents cited the Eisenhower administration's decision to appeal the *Capps* case as proof that the Bricker Amendment was needed to prevent Presidents from using executive agreements to supersede state, local, and even federal statutes. The amendment's opponents, however, saw nothing wrong with the administration's desire to obtain a definitive ruling from the Supreme Court. In the meantime, they emphasized, people should be reassured by the appeals court's holding that the President could not use executive agreements to deal with matters that were under the jurisdiction of Congress.

When the Supreme Court decided the *Capps* case in 1955, it ignored the question of the validity of the executive agreement. The justices ruled that the government had not proved that the Capps company had sold the potatoes for purposes other than seed, so they dismissed the case without commenting on the constitutionality of the executive agreement with Canada. Thus, the Supreme Court's decision in the *Capps* case did nothing to clarify the status and reach of executive agreements.

BIBLIOGRAPHY

Roche, Clayton. "Constitutional Law: Executive Agreements: Effect When in Conflict with Constitutional Rights." *California Law Review* 43 (1955): 525–530.

Sutherland, Arthur. "The Bricker Amendment, Executive Agreements, and Imported Potatoes." *Harvard Law Review* 67 (1953): 281–292.

Sutherland, Arthur. "The Flag, the Constitution, and International Agreements." *Harvard Law Review* 68 (1955): 1374–1381.

DUANE TANANBAUM

UNITED STATES v. LOVETT

UNITED STATES v. LOVETT 328 U.S. 303 (1946). The *Lovett* case established the principle that in spite of Congress's considerable authority over federal personnel, it cannot effectively fire or bar specific persons from government service short of impeaching them. The case grew out of hearings held by the House Committee on Un-American Activities, also known as the Dies Committee after its chairman, Martin Dies (D-Tex.). Dies attacked thirty-nine government employees as "irresponsible, unrepresentative, crackpot, radical bureaucrats" affiliated with "Communist front organizations." After investigation, he convinced the House to include in section 304 of the Urgent Deficiency Appropriations Act of 1943 a provision prohibiting the payment of compensation to three federal employees, Robert Lovett, Goodwin Watson, and William Dodd, Jr., except for being jurors or members of the armed services, unless they were reappointed by the President with the ADVICE AND CONSENT of the Senate. Although the Senate and the President were opposed to the provision, they eventually capitulated in the interests of funding the war effort.

The three employees remained in their jobs but received no compensation. They brought suit in the Court of Claims to recover their pay. That court ruled in their favor. The Supreme Court granted certiorari and affirmed the decision.

Speaking for the Supreme Court, Justice Hugo Black reasoned that the intent of section 304 was not merely to deprive the three employees of compensation "but permanently to bar them from government service." Consequently, the issue was not the extent of Congress's appropriations powers regarding the federal service but rather whether the legislature could punish specific employees by statute. According to the Court, such action is squarely prohibited by Article I, Section 9, clause 3, which reads, "No Bill of Attainder or ex post facto Law shall be passed." Although technically a bill of attainder inflicts death, whereas bills of pains and penalties inflict lesser punishment, the Court relied on post-CIVIL WAR precedents holding that the bill of attainder clause in the Constitution prohibits all punishment by legislative act. In the Court's view, section 304 was unconstitutional because it "clearly accomplishes the punishment of the named individuals without a judicial trial." In a concurring opinion, Justice Felix Frankfurter, joined by Justice Stanley Reed, argued that although section 304 was not a bill of attainder, it was an invalid way of negating the government's obligation to pay employees for their services.

Constitutionally speaking, *Lovett* is important for three main reasons. First, it establishes the principle that even though Congress has considerable powers over federal personnel administration, it cannot effectively fire or bar specific individuals from government service short of impeaching them. Theoretically, Congress could refuse to fund an entire agency or bureau, but it cannot prevent the employees therein from obtaining other jobs with the government. Second, the decision prevented other employees and applicants from being barred from federal employment for fixed periods on grounds of disloyalty (as in *Bailey v. Richardson* [1951]). Third, the case was of some significance in eroding the constitutional doctrine of privilege, which held that because federal employees and applicants have no right to civil-service jobs, they can be dismissed for almost any reason, however arbitrary, capricious, or invasive of the constitutional rights they have as ordinary citizens. By the early 1970s, the Supreme Court had completely rejected this doctrine in *Board of Regents v. Roth* (1972).

BIBLIOGRAPHY

Ely, John Hart. "*United States v. Lovett*: Litigating the Separation of Powers." *Harvard Civil Rights–Civil Liberties Law Review* 10 (1975): 1.

Schuman, Frederick. "Bill of Attainder in the Seventy-eighth Congress." *American Political Science Review* 37 (October 1943): 819–829.

DAVID H. ROSENBLOOM

UNITED STATES v. NIXON 418 U.S. 683 (1974). Prior to and during the two-year period between the 1972 break-in at the National Democratic Party headquarters and the Supreme Court decision of 1974, President Richard M. Nixon had secretly taped all conversations in his office and those conducted over the telephone. The Senate committee investigating the WATERGATE AFFAIR immediately requested transcripts of the tapes from the Special Prosecutor, Archibald Cox.

While Cox was, technically, a member of the executive branch, the guidelines printed in the *Federal Register* underscored Cox's virtual independence. Cox's office had the power to prosecute as well as the power "to determine whether or not to contest the assertion of 'executive privilege' or any other testimonial privilege." Finally, the guidelines noted that the prosecutor could not be removed "from his duties except for extraordinary improprieties on his part."

These guidelines and the subsequent actions of the special prosecutor led directly to *United States v. Nixon.* A number of issues arose: Was the Special Prosecutor truly independent or was the person a subordinate of the President without independent authority? Could the Special Prosecutor subpoena information, including transcripts and tapes, from the President, in order to develop the criminal case against the defendants involved in the Watergate cover-up? Could EXECUTIVE PRIVILEGE be used to prevent the documents and tapes from being given to the Special Prosecutor?

Cox wanted to review certain tapes because his staff was preparing the criminal case, to be presented to a grand jury, against seven Nixon appointees. The tapes were, claimed Cox, essential evidence that would shed light on criminal behavior of those charged in the cover-up.

The President categorically refused to turn over the tapes. Claiming executive privilege, Nixon wrote that he could not and would not "consent to giving any investigating body private presidential papers."

Cox asked Judge John Sirica of the U.S. District Court, District of Columbia, to issue an order, using rule 17c of the Federal Rules of Criminal Procedure, compelling the President to produce the requested documents because no one, not even the President, can "withhold material evidence from a grand jury. . . . The public, in the pursuit of justice, has a right to every man's evidence." The President's lawyers countered that federal courts were without power and authority to serve a sitting President with a subpoena.

On 29 August 1973, Judge Sirica ordered President Nixon to turn over the nine tapes for an in camera inspection. Nixon appealed the Sirica order to the Court of Appeals but the Court of Appeals, by a 5 to 2 vote announced on 12 October, upheld the Sirica order. The court majority ruled that the tapes held "evidence critical to the grand jury's decisions as to whether and whom to indict." In such a situation, a federal court had the jurisdiction to examine the matter and that the claim of executive privilege was not absolute.

Events moved dramatically. An effort by the President to circumvent the order was quickly rejected by Cox, and then on 20 October 1973, the President ordered Attorney General Elliot Richardson and his deputy, William Ruckelshaus, to fire Cox, and when they refused and resigned, asked acting Attorney General Robert Bork to do so. Although Cox was fired, within days Nixon agreed to turn over the tapes (two were missing and a third had eighteen minutes erased) and to appoint a second Special Prosecutor, Leon Jaworski.

In March 1974 a grand jury, after reviewing portions of the six tapes given by Nixon to the court, indicted seven persons including John Mitchell, former Attorney General, H. R. Haldeman, and John Ehrlichman, and secretly named Nixon as an unindicted coconspirator. Jaworski now had the task of presenting the prosecution's case, in *United States v. Mitchell, et al.*, to a trial jury. In April 1974, he went to federal district court to ask Judge Sirica to order President Nixon to turn over another sixty-four tapes. Nixon, claiming executive privilege and maintaining that the federal courts had no jurisdiction in an intrabranch dispute between the President and a subordinate, Jaworksi, again refused to submit the tapes to an in camera inspection.

In late May 1974, Sirica ordered Nixon to turn over the tapes. Nixon appealed to the Court of Appeals. On 24 May 1974, however, Jaworski took a surprising and risky step. He bypassed the Court of Appeals and

asked the Supreme Court to grant certiorari under expedited review as permitted in rule 20 of the Supreme Court's rules.

The Court could have declined the request (granted only five previous times in the nation's history). However, the Justices, after initially deciding 6 to 2 not to grant expedited certiorari, ultimately took the case. Justice William J. Brennan helped persuade a 6 to 2 Court to hear the case on an expedited appeal (Justices Harry Blackmun and Byron White disagreed). Said Brennan: "[We] had to act lest the nation lose all confidence in the criminal justice system." Justice William Rehnquist, until the fall of 1971 a member of the Justice Department, recused himself and did not participate in the deliberations. Oral argument was set for 8 July 1974.

For the Supreme Court, the litigation revolved around the concept of SEPARATION OF POWERS and came down to three questions: Did Jaworski have standing to sue or was it, as Nixon argued, an intrabranch conflict immune from court review? Did the Supreme Court have jurisdiction to hear the case and was it a justiciable controversy, that is, could a federal court provide a remedy? Could a prosecutor, using rule 17c, issue a subpoena to a sitting President for documents and tapes relevant to a criminal proceeding or did the President have an absolute immunity from the compulsory processes of law because of the existence of presidential confidentiality?

On 24 July 1974, after almost two months of intense discussion and numerous drafts written by most of the eight participating Justices, the Court unanimously (8 to 0) concluded that the Court had jurisdiction to hear the case, the matters raised in the litigation were justiciable, Special Prosecutor Jaworski satisfied the requirements in rule 17c that govern the issuance of subpoenas, even to the President of the United States, and, finally, while there is a constitutionally derived executive privilege, "absent a claim of need to protect military, diplomatic or sensitive national security secrets," the claim of privilege had to fall in light of a prosecutorial need for information for a pending criminal trial.

The Court ordered Sirica to review the tapes that would be submitted to his federal court by President Nixon, affording presidential confidentiality "that high degree of deference . . . and the highest protection consistent with the fair administration of justice." After reviewing the opinion for a full day, Nixon complied with the Supreme Court opinion and turned over the tapes. One of them contained the "smoking pistol" implicating Nixon in the cover-up and, on 8 August 1974, the President resigned.

BIBLIOGRAPHY

Ball, Howard. *"We Have a Duty": The Supreme Court and the Watergate Tapes Litigation.* 1992.
Congressional Quarterly. *Watergate: Chronology of a Crisis.* 1975.
D'Ovidio, Jean. "Executive Privilege." *University of Richmond Law Review* 18 (1983): 12–79.
Jaworski, Leon. *The Power and the Right: The Prosecution of Watergate.* 1976.
Sirica, John. *To Set the Record Straight.* 1979.
White, Theodore. *Breach of Faith: The Fall of Richard Nixon.* 1975.

HOWARD BALL

UNITED STATES v. PINK 315 U.S. 203 (1942). In this case, the Supreme Court granted the federal government rights under an EXECUTIVE AGREEMENT in a way that helped ensure the future attractiveness of such presidential agreements for facilitating international claims settlements. The federal government filed *Pink* to recover assets of a Russian insurance company. Although nationalized by Soviet decrees that also seized its property, the company's New York branch remained open until 1925. A New York court then placed the company in receivership, directing that its assets be distributed first to U.S. creditors, then to foreign creditors, and finally to the board of directors. After all U.S. creditors were paid but before further disbursements were made, the United States claimed the surplus. The government relied on President Franklin D. Roosevelt's 1933 agreements with Maksim Litvinov, the Soviet foreign affairs commissar, which had resulted in diplomatic recognition of the Soviet government. These included the so-called Litvinov assignment, which assigned to the U.S. government all Soviet government claims against U.S. nationals, including claims to nationalized property.

The Supreme Court in UNITED STATES v. BELMONT (1937) had already upheld the Litvinov assignment and determined that states could not impose barriers to U.S. claims rooted in such international agreements. The Court upheld the assignment even though it had neither been authorized by statute nor subject to Senate ADVICE AND CONSENT. In *Pink,* the Court reaffirmed *Belmont,* holding further that U.S. government claims could not be subordinated to those of the corporation or of foreign creditors. Insofar as the U.S. action prevented the Russian directors from recovering sums due them, their only remedy lay with their own government.

The Court determined that the United States could constitutionally insist on the priority of its claims over those of foreign creditors. The Litvinov assignment was intended to provide the U.S. government with funds to satisfy the claims of U.S. nationals against the U.S.S.R. or its nationals, the nonpayment of which had frustrated diplomatic recognition of the Soviet regime. Foreign nationals were not entitled to have their claims given priority over such domestic claims.

Pink is a critical authority in support of presidential power to conduct FOREIGN AFFAIRS, including the RECOGNITION POWER; President Jimmy Carter's recognition of the People's Republic of China is but the most recent instance of diplomatic recognition facilitated by claims settlement through executive agreement. Yet the scope of *Pink* is uncertain. The Court reserved the question whether executive agreements could deprive U.S. creditors of the priority of their claims against foreign governments. Further, in upholding the President, the Court explicitly relied on the relationship between his disputed claims-settlement power and his ability to implement his more firmly established power to recognize other governments. Finally, although Roosevelt had not relied on statutory authority to conclude the Litvinov agreements, the Court noted that Congress had tacitly ratified the negotiation by authorizing the appointment of a commissioner to determine the claims of U.S. nationals against the Soviet government, which were to be paid from funds realized through the Litvinov assignment.

BIBLIOGRAPHY

Henkin, Louis. *Foreign Affairs and the Constitution.* 1972.
Lillich, Richard B., and Burns H. Weston. *International Claims: Their Settlement by Lump-Sum Agreements.* 1975.
Margolis, Lawrence. *Executive Agreements and Presidential Power in Foreign Policy.* 1986.

PETER M. SHANE

UNITED STATES v. RICHARDSON 418 U.S. 166 (1974). This Supreme Court case grew out of a challenge from a Pennsylvania citizen, William B. Richardson, who was upset about the covert nature of budgeting for the CENTRAL INTELLIGENCE AGENCY (CIA), the most important of the United States' clandestine services. In Richardson's opinion, the Central Intelligence Act of 1949 (an amendment to the NATIONAL SECURITY ACT of 1947, which had created the CIA) was in direct violation of the STATEMENT AND ACCOUNT CLAUSE of the Constitution (Article I, Section 9, clause 7), which states, "A regular Statement and Account of the Receipts and Expenditures of all public Money shall be published from time to time."

Despite this injunction, the budget of the CIA remains a tightly kept secret. In 1967 Richardson wrote to the Government Printing Office requesting an explanation that would clarify the apparent contradiction between the statement and account clause and the special dispensation given to the CIA. No satisfying response was forthcoming; nor did Richardson's inspection of publicly available Treasury Department documents settle the matter in his mind. He then turned to the courts for assistance.

His first step down the judicial path led immediately to a roadblock: in 1968 a U.S. district court in Pennsylvania concluded that Richardson lacked standing to raise a justiciable controversy. Within a few weeks, however, the Supreme Court coincidentally broadened the grounds on which citizens could establish standing (in *Flast v. Cohen* [1968], a church-state case). Nevertheless, the U.S. Court of Appeals for the Third Circuit declined to overturn the district court holding against Richardson. Further, the Supreme Court refused to grant certiorari to review his case (with only Justice William O. Douglas in support of the motion for review).

Not easily dissuaded, Richardson initiated a new suit in 1970, requesting that a three-judge court be convened to judge the constitutionality of the CIA law. Again, the district court decided that Richardson—however irrepressible—continued to lack standing, adding that the whole issue raised "political questions in a governmental sense . . . not open to a United States District Court for adjudication in any manner." The court had rejected Richardson's case on three powerful grounds—standing, jurisdiction, and justiciability—but Richardson was not yet ready to give up.

On 20 July 1972, the Court of Appeals heard Richardson's plea once more and this time, by a vote of 6 to 3, vacated the district court ruling, agreeing that a three-judge court should be established by statute to weigh the merits of his argument and adjudicate the issue of covert financing. Writing the opinion, Judge Max Rosenn pointed to the importance of the statement and account clause in the controversy:

> A responsible and intelligent taxpayer and citizen, of course, wants to know how his tax money is being spent. Without this information he cannot intelligently follow the actions of the Congress or of the Executive. Nor can he properly fulfill his obligation as a member of the electorate. The framers of the Constitution deemed fiscal information essential if the electorate was to exercise any control over its representatives and meet their new responsibilities as citizens of the Republic.

The Supreme Court consented to review the procedural aspects of the case—namely, the merits of Richardson's claim to have standing. A separate writ of certiorari introduced by Richardson to seek the Court's substantive judgment on the issue was denied. On 25 June 1974, the Court decided by a vote of 6 to 3

that Richardson lacked standing. Writing for the majority, Chief Justice Warren Burger stated that relief could be found through the electoral process. If he wished, Richardson and others could vote for legislators who would support the publication of the CIA's budget. In dissent, Justice Douglas concluded that it was "astounding" that a majority on the Court was prepared to allow Congress the right to keep the CIA budget secret; he viewed this as tantamount to excising the statement and account clause from the Constitution.

BIBLIOGRAPHY

Fisher, Louis. *Presidential Spending Power*. 1975.
Schick, Allen. *Congress and Money: Budgeting, Spending, and Taxing*. 1980.
U.S. Senate. Select Committee on Intelligence. "Whether Disclosure of Funds Authorized for Intelligence Activities Is in the Public Interest," *Hearings*. 95th Cong., 1st sess., 1977.

LOCH K. JOHNSON

UNITED STATES v. UNITED STATES DISTRICT COURT 407 U.S. 297 (1972). In KATZ v. UNITED STATES (1967), the Supreme Court decided that a prior court order is required for law-enforcement use of ELECTRONIC SURVEILLANCE. It reserved judgment, however, concerning whether different standards apply to surveillance conducted for NATIONAL-SECURITY purposes.

Congress enacted the Omnibus Crime Control and Safe Streets Act in 1968 to authorize federal courts to issue orders for law-enforcement electronic surveillance, but it also avoided restricting national security surveillance and specifically disclaimed any intent to limit the President's constitutional power to obtain essential foreign intelligence, protect national security information, prevent unlawful overthrow of the government, and protect against "any other clear and present danger." Information acquired under such circumstances could be used as evidence in any proceeding so long as the interception was "reasonable."

The scope of the issue deferred in *Katz* and avoided by Congress in 1968 was explored in 1972, when the Supreme Court decided *United States v. United States District Court*, also known as the *Keith* decision after District Court Judge Damon Keith, whose decision was being appealed. The Court held that the Constitution bars warrantless electronic surveillance of domestic organizations to maintain internal security (also called domestic security), but reserved judgment again as to cases involving foreign intelligence regarding foreign powers or their agents.

Several individuals had been charged with bombing government offices . One defendant had been overheard on warrantless wiretaps authorized by Attorney General JOHN MITCHELL to obtain information about domestic organizations that were attacking the government. Keith ruled the surveillance unlawful and ordered the government to disclose information to the defendant. The government appealed the decision. The Sixth Circuit Court of Appeals agreed with the district judge's ruling and an appeal was filed with the Supreme Court.

The Supreme Court noted the balance between the government's right to protect itself and the individual's right to privacy. The basic question was whether the executive had authority to conduct electronic surveillance without a court order.

The 1968 law referring to the power of the President to protect the nation was interpreted by the Court as neither authorizing warrantless national security surveillance nor recognizing any presidential power to authorize such activities. Instead, the Court viewed Congress's purposes as merely to preserve whatever power the President might have in this regard. Thus it was necessary to examine the President's constitutional power.

The Court made clear it was not addressing whether prior judicial review is required for electronic surveillance of foreign powers or their agents within or outside the United States. But this case concerned an internal security matter, not one of national security, since it involved domestic organizations with no ties to foreign powers.

Warrantless electronic surveillance had been presidentially authorized in internal security investigations since 1946. Nonetheless, the Court recognized that Fourth Amendment principles applied to such surveillance. Special attention was required concerning the limits of government conduct in such matters because of the political nature of the activities being investigated.

A two-part test determined whether government or individual interests would prevail in such circumstances: would individual privacy and free speech be better protected by a prior warrant or would a warrant "unduly frustrate" government efforts against subversion? The Court ruled that allowing law enforcement officials to determine reasonableness was not sufficient protection for individual interests and that the Fourth Amendment required prior judicial review.

The temptation to use law-enforcement powers to monitor political dissent argued in favor of a prior warrant. The government's argument that courts were not skilled nor secretive enough to review such matters

was not persuasive. Any inconvenience to the government was justified by the need to protect constitutional values and reassure the public.

The Court emphasized that it was not ruling in any way on surveillance of foreign powers or their agents. Furthermore, the Court invited Congress to consider procedures for internal, or domestic, security surveillances that differed from those that governed law-enforcement surveillances. The Court even offered examples, such as different probable-cause standards, a specially designated court, and less stringent time and reporting limitations.

These observations paved the way for the 1978 enactment of the FOREIGN INTELLIGENCE SURVEILLANCE ACT (FISA), which created a special court and probable-cause and notice requirements for foreign intelligence–related surveillance that differ substantially from those required for law-enforcement surveillance. However, the Congress has never devised surveillance standards for internal security surveillances that differ from the law-enforcement provisions.

AMERICO R. CINQUEGRANA

UNVOUCHERED EXPENSES. With precedents dating back to 1790, Congress provides the President with small amounts of appropriations that allow the use of "certificates" instead of vouchers. A certificate, when signed by an authorized official, becomes a sufficient voucher that the funds have been spent as authorized. Detailed vouchers, including receipts and documents that show accounting officers how the funds were spent, are not required. The use of certificates prevents the GENERAL ACCOUNTING OFFICE (GAO) from performing a full-scale audit.

Legislation in 1790 provided the President with a $40,000 account "for the support of such persons as he shall commission to serve the United States in foreign parts" (1 Stat. 128–129). The President could account for expenditures "as in his judgment may be made public, and also for the amount of such expenditures as he may think it advisable not to specify, and cause a regular statement and account thereof to be laid before Congress annually." Part of the reason Congress gave the President this discretion was to avoid publicizing different salaries for American ministers and making invidious distinctions among various nations. Congress extended the statute in 1793, authorizing the President to use certificates in lieu of vouchers.

Confidential funding by the President precipitated two controversies in the nineteenth century. The first arose in 1846, when the House of Representatives asked President James K. Polk to furnish an account of all payments made on presidential certificates for the contingent expenses of foreign intercourse, covering the period from 4 March 1841 to the retirement of DANIEL WEBSTER as Secretary of State on 8 May 1843. Polk refused to release the information on the ground that Congress had given the President statutory authority to decide whether such expenditures should be made public. He advised Congress that President John Tyler had signed certificates after determining that the objects and items of those expenditures should remain confidential. It would be inadvisable, Polk said, for a President to criticize the act of a predecessor without fully comprehending the circumstances operating at that time. Lacking such information, a President would be unable to judge whether an earlier President had exercised his discretion wisely.

A second dispute arose after the CIVIL WAR and involved the use of confidential funds by President Abraham Lincoln, who justified the expenditure not on statutory authority but on the basis of executive prerogative. The heirs of William A. Lloyd, who served as a spy for the Lincoln administration, tried to recover compensation in the courts for Lloyd's services. The Supreme Court decided in *Totten v. United States* (1875) that Lincoln, as COMMANDER IN CHIEF, could properly employ secret agents to cross Confederate lines and obtain reconnaissance information. The Court held that the contract between Lincoln and Lloyd had to remain forever confidential, because disclosure could compromise or embarrass the government or endanger the life or injure the character of the agent. Furthermore, successful litigation in the courts by Lloyd's heirs could expose the very details that were supposed to be kept secret. The Court therefore denied the heirs' claim.

In 1899, Congress authorized a second confidential account, this time appropriating $63,000 for emergencies arising in the diplomatic and consular service, to be expended with certificates in lieu of vouchers (30 Stat. 826). In 1906 Congress created a confidential travel account for the President (34 Stat. 454) and in 1916 authorized a confidential fund for the Secretary of the Navy (39 Stat. 557). In 1935 the FEDERAL BUREAU OF INVESTIGATION received authority to make unvouchered expenditures (49 Stat. 78).

In subsequent years, Congress authorized a number of unvouchered accounts for the President: the President's Special Authority in the foreign assistance act; entertainment expenses for the Executive Residence; Compensation of the President; and a separate account to pay staff assistants for special projects. In 1978, Congress authorized two confidential funds for the VICE PRESIDENT. Justifications for these funds included deference to the President under the SEPARATION OF POWERS doctrine, the need to escape statutory restrictions on travel allowances, and a perceived need to conceal entertainment expenses to avoid possible embarrassments.

During the 1970s, Congress adopted a number of restrictions on these accounts, converting some to regular vouchered expenditures. In other cases Congress authorized the GAO to perform audits, allowing the COMPTROLLER GENERAL to inspect all necessary documents and records to assure that the funds are properly spent. Confidential funds place strains on the constitutional principle embedded in the STATEMENT AND ACCOUNT CLAUSE of the Constitution, which requires that federal expenditures be published "from time to time."

Congress also created confidential funds for the DEFENSE DEPARTMENT, the ATOMIC ENERGY COMMISSION, the District of Columbia, the ATTORNEY GENERAL, U.S. Coast Guard, and the TREASURY DEPARTMENT, and the Food and Drug Administration. These unvouchered accounts were justified in large part to support investigative efforts that depend on informers. Revealing the identity of an informer could jeopardize the person's life and dry up similar sources of intelligence. Reforms during the 1970s also eliminated or restricted a number of these confidential funds.

BIBLIOGRAPHY

Fisher, Louis. "Confidential Spending and Governmental Accountability." *George Washington Law Review* 47 (1979): 347–385.

LOUIS FISHER

URBAN POLICY. See HOUSING POLICY.

U-2 INCIDENT. On 1 May 1960 an unarmed U-2 CENTRAL INTELLIGENCE AGENCY espionage plane, piloted by Francis Gary Powers, was shot down by a Soviet missile near Sverdlovsk, approximately 1,250 miles within Soviet territory. The incident quickly escalated into a major crisis in U.S.-Soviet relations that reversed a promising trend toward DETENTE.

The United States had been conducting such photographic reconnaissance flights for four years and CIA officials were surprised that the Soviets had finally succeeded in shooting down a U-2. At first CIA officials advised President Dwight D. Eisenhower that the episode could easily be denied, since they expected that Powers had committed suicide to avoid capture. Instead of swallowing the cyanide capsule provided by the CIA, he had parachuted from the plane and been captured alive. As the Soviet leader Nikita Khrushchev gradually revealed the details, Eisenhower became embroiled in a series of evasions and outright lies. At first he denied that the United States had conducted overflights of Soviet territory and insisted only that a weather surveillance plane had strayed a few miles off course. Khrushchev then sprung a trap by announcing first that Soviet authorities recovered the wreckage of the plane and then, a few days later, that they had custody of a healthy Powers. The Soviet leader expected that Eisenhower would deny personal knowledge of the overflights and try to smooth relations on the eve of a four-power (Great Britain, France, the United States, and the Soviet Union) summit conference, scheduled to open in Paris on 16 May. Eisenhower, however, considered the U-2 program enormously valuable and resented wildly inaccurate criticism that he did not know what happened within his administration. He took personal responsibility for the overflights, explained that he considered them vital for U.S. military security, and refused to apologize for violating Soviet airspace. He suspended U-2 flights but did not promise not to engage in future surveillance of Soviet missile development. Khrushchev was surprised and angry that Eisenhower did not offer more conciliatory gestures and the Soviet leader broke up the summit meeting one day after it began. Progress stopped on disarmament and a resolution of the dispute over Berlin. The U-2 incident foreshadowed the chill in U.S.-Soviet relations of the first years of the Kennedy administration.

BIBLIOGRAPHY

Ambrose, Stephen. *Eisenhower*. Vol. 2. 1983.
Beschloss, Michael. *Mayday: Eisenhower, Khrushchev, and the U-2 Affair*. 1986.

ROBERT D. SCHULZINGER

V

VACANCIES ACT. Article II, Section 2, of the Constitution provides that the President shall appoint with the ADVICE AND CONSENT of the Senate all officers of the United States established by law. By statute Congress later recognized that the President needed authority to make temporary appointments, without Senate action, in case of the death, absence, or sickness of the heads of executive departments. Congress granted that authority in 1792 and then in 1795 restricted the length of a temporary appointment to six months (1 Stat. 281, Sec. 8; 1 Stat. 415).

Congress sought to control the use of temporary appointments by the enactment over time of a series of vacancies acts. Legislation in the 1860s limited the President's ability to bypass the Senate by requiring that the person receiving a temporary appointment be someone who had previously been appointed with the advice and consent of the Senate. The Vacancies Act of 1863 specified a maximum term of six months for temporary appointments, at the end of which time such appointees would have to step down if not confirmed by the Senate (12 Stat. 656). In 1868, the Vacancies Act became part of the conflict between President Andrew Johnson and the Congress. In a speech on the Senate floor, Sen. Lyman Trumbull (R-Ill.) described the intent of the Congress in reducing the tenure of a temporary appointee to thirty days:

> The intention of the bill was to limit the time within which the President might supply a vacancy temporarily in the case of the death or resignation of the head of any of the Departments or of any officer appointed by him and with the advice and consent of the Senate in any of the Departments. As the law now stands, he is authorized to supply those vacancies for six months without submitting the name of a person for that purpose to the Senate;

and it was thought by the committee to be an unreasonable length of time, and hence they have limited it by this bill to thirty days."

The 1868 statute (15 Stat. 168) was amended again in 1891 (26 Stat. 733). It is clear from Trumbull's comment and from earlier legislative history that the Congress intended the Vacancies Act to place limitations on the President's ability to have vacancies filled temporarily for long periods of time.

From time to time, Presidents have kept temporary appointees in place for lengthy periods of time exceeding thirty days without submitting a nomination to the Senate. Sometimes this was done to allow a questionable appointee to demonstrate his or her skills in office before undergoing confirmation review in the Senate. In May 1972, for example, President Richard M. Nixon named L. Patrick Gray to be acting director of the FEDERAL BUREAU OF INVESTIGATION (FBI). Though the Senate was in session for most of the remainder of 1972 and the early months of 1973, it was not until February 1973 that Gray was nominated to be the director of the FBI. Gray withdrew his nomination when it became the focus of intense controversy related to the WATERGATE AFFAIR during confirmation hearings. He resigned as acting FBI director in April 1973. Thus Gray served as head of the FBI for almost a year without his appointment ever having been confirmed by the Senate.

At other times, lengthy acting or temporary appointments have occurred at the beginning of a new administration while the White House processed the backlog of hundreds of appointments that are common at the outset of a new presidency. In 1989 and into 1990, for example, the administration of President George Bush moved slowly through its appointment selections, and many federal agencies were led by acting or temporary directors until an official leader was nominated and confirmed. Recently, as well, Presidents in the final year of their term have found it difficult to recruit highly qualified appointees and have relied on temporary agency and department heads, avoiding the confirmation process entirely until after the election. When the presidency and the Senate are controlled by different parties, Presidents have little choice in this regard during the last few months of their terms. A Senate dominated by the opposition party is often reluctant to confirm any appointment—especially judges and term appointments in the regulatory commissions—in the months immediately preceding an election, usually in the hope that the majority party's nominee will win the election and make his own nomination after inauguration day.

Enforcement of the Act. Temporary appointees, like Patrick Gray, have served beyond the time specified by the act without suffering any limits on their ability to act. In the twentieth century, legal counsel in several executive departments, including the DEPARTMENT OF ENERGY and the DEPARTMENT OF HEALTH AND HUMAN SERVICES argued that the Vacancies Act does not apply to positions that fall under the ambit of the basic authorizing statutes for those departments. Hence there has continued to be legal and political dispute about the applicability of the Vacancies Act.

In 1988, the Congress sought to clarify once again the meaning of the Vacancies Act. A provision of the Presidential Transitions Effectiveness Act of 1988 (102 Stat. 988, Sec. 7) amended the Vacancies Act to provide that a vacancy "caused by death or resignation may be filled temporarily . . . for not more than 120 days, except that . . . if a first or second nomination to fill such vacancy has been submitted to the Senate, the position may be filled temporarily . . . until the Senate confirms the nomination; or . . . until 120 days after the date on which the Senate rejects the nomination or the nomination is withdrawn; or if the vacancy occurs during an adjournment of the Congress sine die, the position may be filled temporarily until 120 days after the Congress next convenes . . . . Any person filling a vacancy temporarily . . . whose nomination to fill such vacancy has been submitted to the Senate may not serve after the end of the 120-day period . . . if the nomination of such person is rejected by the Senate or is withdrawn."

By its action in 1988, the Congress sought to make it clear that the Vacancies Act is the exclusive authority for the temporary appointment, designation, or assignment of one officer to perform the duties of another whose appointment requires Senate confir-

mation. That exclusive authority can only be superseded by the enactment of specific statutory language providing some other means for filling vacancies.

BIBLIOGRAPHY

Fisher, Louis. *Constitutional Conflicts between Congress and the President.* 3d ed. 1991.

G. CALVIN MACKENZIE

VACATION SPOTS, PRESIDENTIAL. Anyone who has spent a summer in Washington, D.C., can easily understand why Presidents have sought a location far removed from the heat and humidity. Most Presidents were, however, limited by transportation and communication considerations.

With improved communications and transportation, Presidents of the twentieth century have been more flexible in their choice of location. President Theodore Roosevelt moved most of the White House operations to his home on Sagamore Hill overlooking Oyster Bay Harbor in Long Island Sound. This family home served as the "Summer White House" from 1901 to 1908. President Herbert Hoover established a federally owned camp at the headwaters of Virginia's Rapidan River. Camp Rapidan was a 164-acre retreat, which is now known as Camp Hoover. It was at this camp that President Hoover negotiated a naval treaty with Great Britain's Prime Minister Ramsay MacDonald.

President Franklin D. Roosevelt took a liking to a camp built in Catoctin Mountain Park by the Civilian Conservation Corps and the Works Progress Administration in 1939. Roosevelt named the camp Shangri-la after the mythical utopia in James Hilton's novel *Lost Horizons.* Roosevelt was also a frequent visitor to the soothing waters of Warm Springs, Georgia. In addition to these two locales, the family home in HYDE PARK was often used as a "Summer White House."

Shangri-la was renamed by President Dwight D. Eisenhower as CAMP DAVID after his grandson. Eisenhower added to the main house and renamed it Aspen. Among the additions were the large flagstone terrace and a putting green. Eisenhower received Soviet leader Nikita Khrushchev at Camp David.

President John F. Kennedy was an infrequent visitor of Camp David, preferring a hideaway, named Akota, in Middleburg, Virginia, in the heart of horse country. Additionally, Kennedy would use the family compound at Hyannis Port, Cape Cod, as a retreat. President Richard M. Nixon was perhaps the most frequent user of Camp David. He made over 100 trips to it in his five and one-half years as President. Nixon upgraded the camp into a luxury resort. He often spent weeks at a time there. This was in addition to the home the President frequented in Florida. President Jimmy Carter also spent a lot of time at Camp David. Carter used the site as a place to negotiate a peace treaty between Israel and Egypt. President Anwar Sadat of Egypt and Prime Minister Menachem Begin of Israel agreed to a historic peace, which was dubbed the CAMP DAVID ACCORDS.

President and Mrs. Ronald Reagan's use of Camp David was solely as a weekend get-away. For longer periods, they preferred their 638-acre ranch called Rancho del Cielo in Santa Barbara, California. As the official Western White House, the property was equipped with the necessary security and communications systems.

President George Bush shunned Camp David for the family home in Kennebunk Port, Maine. He used this retreat as Presidents have always used their get-aways, as places to avoid both the heat of the Washington weather and the heat of the Washington press corps.

BIBLIOGRAPHY

Ferris, Robert G. *The Presidents*. 1977.

Kern, Ellyn R. *Where the American Presidents Lived*. 1982.

JEFFREY D. SCHULTZ

VAN BUREN, MARTIN (1782–1862), eighth President of the United States (1837–1841). Van Buren was born in Kinderhook, New York, on 5 December 1782. During his boyhood, the bitter rivalry between the Jeffersonian (Democratic-)Republicans and the Federalists dominated the political scene. Though Kinderhook was staunchly Federalist, the elder Van Buren and his older stepsons supported Thomas Jefferson.

Van Buren attended the village school and completed legal studies under the tutelage of William P. Van Ness, an established lawyer and politician in New York City.

Early Career. Van Ness introduced Van Buren to Aaron Burr, whose techniques of strict political organization Van Buren studied. Sensing Burr's decline in power and influence, Van Buren associated himself with DEWITT CLINTON, who had succeeded Burr as the Democratic-Republican Party leader. Van Buren slowly advanced in the Clinton machine. In 1812 he became a state senator, and his political and legal career advanced rapidly. His alliance with the pro-war Federalists headed by RUFUS KING gave Van Buren the opportunity he needed to consolidate his hold on what

was now the majority party in New York State politics. He headed the so-called Albany Regency, a group of gifted lawyers and publicists who not only governed the state for lengthy periods but consolidated the Democratic-Republican Party and its successor, the DEMOCRATIC PARTY.

National Politician. After serving in a series of state offices, Van Buren was elected in 1819 to the United States Senate, where he sought to cement an alliance between northern farmers and southern planters and also promoted the continuation of the political coalition in the congressional caucuses of Virginia and New York, the two most populous states, which had provided all the Presidents and Vice Presidents except one since 1801.

Impressed by Andrew Jackson's popularity, Van Buren took the lead in bringing JOHN C. CALHOUN's and WILLIAM H. CRAWFORD's supporters behind the frontier commander and politician for the campaign and election of 1828. A major issue—with sectional overtones—that arose from the mid 1820s on was the tariff. Van Buren had an influential role in the enactment of the tariff bill of 1828. President John Quincy Adams approved it to the consternation of southern planters, who saw themselves as consumers taxed unfairly to support northern industry. Under the leadership of Calhoun, the act was denounced as the TARIFF OF ABOMINATIONS and almost instantly became a divisive issue in South Carolina.

Meanwhile, Van Buren managed to hold the emerging Jacksonian coalition together despite the divisive aspects of the tariff. When Jackson was elected President over Adams in 1828, Van Buren was elected governor of New York. He had served almost eight years in the U.S. Senate.

Cabinet Officer and Vice President. Van Buren's tenure as governor was brief. Jackson appointed him Secretary of State. Calhoun, who had again been elected Vice President, saw Van Buren as his principal rival to succeed Jackson, and he sought to make himself a dominating influence in the selection of the new Cabinet.

Van Buren and John H. Eaton, the Secretary of War and a Jackson crony, were Calhoun's only obstacles in the new administration. Van Buren soon gained Jackson's confidence. One of his major successes was his reinforcement of hallowed Jeffersonian policies on INTERNAL IMPROVEMENTS while at the same time scoring political points against HENRY CLAY, Jackson's major opponent in Congress. Van Buren made a distinction between government funded internal improvements for intra- and interstate projects. Clay had championed a bill for federal support of a turnpike that began and ended in the state of Kentucky. Van Buren drafted, and the President signed, the so-called Maysville veto, which for many years set policy on federal government public works. Further, on information supplied by Crawford, Van Buren reinforced his position by reminding the President that Calhoun, as Secretary of War during James Monroe's administration, had censured Jackson's conduct as a military commander in Florida. Calhoun had not improved his position with Jackson by being the supposed author of the South Carolina Exposition and Protest that threatened to nullify the tariff of 1828 [*see* NULLIFICATION].

But the event that destroyed Calhoun's influence in the administration was the refusal of his wife—along with the wives of the Attorney General and the secretaries of the Treasury, and Navy—to receive Peggy Eaton, the wife of the Secretary of War, socially. Mrs. Eaton had a questionable background involving possible adultery, but there was little factual evidence to back up the rumors. Van Buren, a widower, was able to socialize with the Eatons, but when Jackson demanded that his other Cabinet officers do likewise or offer proof of the allegations against Mrs. Eaton, they all refused. Sensing an opportunity to resolve the social impasse and to eliminate Calhoun's influence, Van Buren proposed to Jackson that he ask the entire Cabinet to resign and then reconstruct it, leaving out himself, Eaton, and the Calhoun contingent. Jackson accepted this solution. Nor was he concerned when the new Cabinet, composed primarily of Van Buren's selections, tended to reflect Van Buren's opinions in political and even policy matters.

Van Buren himself was given a RECESS APPOINTMENT as minister to Great Britain. When Congress convened in regular session on 5 December 1831, the Senate rejected Van Buren's nomination by the tie-breaking vote of Vice President Calhoun. Jackson had already wanted Van Buren to be his running mate in the election of 1832, but Calhoun's shortsighted action converted Van Buren into a political martyr and virtually assured his nomination for Vice President at the Baltimore convention of what was now being styled the Democratic Party.

Jackson's battle against the Second BANK OF THE UNITED STATES and against its president, Nicholas Biddle, came to a head when Jackson vetoed the bill that would have rechartered the bank for another twenty years. The Jackson–Van Buren ticket was triumphantly elected in 1832 partly because of Jackson's veto message concerning the bank-rechartering bill and partly because of his great popularity as a vigorous Chief Executive. After the election Van Buren sought to moderate Jackson's continuing assault on the bank, but he was eventually brought into line on the issue of removal of the federal deposits in the Bank.

As Vice President, Van Buren presided over a Senate that was dominated by the three great personalities in antebellum politics and statecraft—Calhoun, Clay, and DANIEL WEBSTER, all of whom were his political enemies. Clay and Webster were soon the leading figures in the emerging WHIG PARTY, and Calhoun moved from party to party as he deemed the occasion warranted. The four years of Van Buren's vice presidency witnessed momentous changes in the new republic: territorial expansion, removal of the INDIANS to the west, abolitionist agitation for terminating SLAVERY, a vigorous assertion of nationalism at home and abroad, the threatened SECESSION of a state over a federal policy in the tariff of 1828 and its resolution in the compromise TARIFF ACT OF 1833, and, finally (after a brief recession in 1834), an unparalleled boom in land values and in state- and privately supported enterprises such as turnpikes, canals, and railroads.

Van Buren's principal role in these events was to cast himself as a moderate voice in national affairs. He threw his political weight behind measures to regularize the payment of government deposits into selected banks under the Deposit Banking Act of 1836. He counseled moderation in dealing with South Carolina's nullification and backed the easing of the protective tariff. He followed the Jacksonian hard-money line and its policy of Indian removal and resettlement. Acting with other members of the Cabinet, he managed to restrain Jackson's impetuous diplomacy and improve international relations, especially with Britain and France. When the slavery issue flared up as a result of John Quincy Adams's campaign to present abolitionist petitions in the House of Representatives, Van Buren had his lieutenants in both chambers pass the so-called gag rule. Adams and other antislavery Congressmen and Senators were prevented from reading the petitions, which were automatically tabled.

Van Buren was one of the first American statesmen to recognize that the slavery issue threatened the intersectional political coalition he had put together. But, far more seriously, if agitation proceeded unchecked and evolved into a sectional antislavery movement in the North and its opposite in the South, the issue would threaten the very existence of the Union. Van Buren's future course in public life would be dedicated to holding his party to this concept. When it failed, as it inevitably would given the basic differences in culture, attitudes, and economy between the two sections, Van Buren would be stigmatized in his own region as a "dough face."

Presidency. With Jackson's wholehearted support, the Democratic convention in Baltimore nominated Van Buren for the presidency in May 1835 and selected RICHARD M. JOHNSON, a Kentucky politician and an old Indian-fighter, for Vice President. The Whigs—in the throes of national organization and divided by the individual pretensions of its leaders—were unable to mount an effective campaign. Van Buren and Johnson were elected with a majority of the electoral and popular votes over William Henry Harrison, the principal Whig contender (there were three).

Not two weeks after Van Buren's inauguration on 17 March 1837, a disastrous panic in New York's commercial and financial community broke the speculative bubble that had been expanding over the previous two years. The panic quickly spread to other cities, endangering the government's supply of bullion (and hence its credit) as the deposit banks suspended specie payments and hundreds of other banks and financial institutions throughout the nation failed. A widespread depression ensued, affecting all elements of society and all economic interests.

Ever cautious and deliberative when it came to important policy moves with significant political consequences, Van Buren solicited recommendations from party leaders throughout the Union on how to deal with the crisis. Of the responses he received, one in particular commanded his support: a recommendation that the federal government separate itself completely from the deposit banks and store its specie in vaults or subtreasuries throughout the country. After consulting with his Cabinet, almost all of whose members were holdovers from the previous administration, Van Buren decided to call for a special session of Congress that would meet on 4 September 1837.

During the summer, as the depression worsened and the government's credit became increasingly endangered, Van Buren and his advisers developed a program that they hoped would deal with the grave financial and fiscal problems that beset the nation and still not violate Jeffersonian precepts.

Despite pressure from business and financial groups, Van Buren refused to repeal the SPECIE CIRCULAR of the previous administration, which had demanded hard currency in payment for public lands. In order to rescue government credit from potential default, he recommended to the Congress that the Deposit Banking Act be repealed, to be replaced by an INDEPENDENT TREASURY or subtreasury system. With the Treasury bare and its funds temporarily locked up in the deposit banks, Van Buren called for an issue of treasury notes and short-term rather than long-term bonds to meet the government's obligations and, incidentally, to improve the money supply, which had been badly depleted by suspension, hoarding, and the flight of specie to Europe.

After considerable wrangling in the Senate, spearheaded by Calhoun's amendments to the government's program, the subtreasury- and Treasury-note bills passed. But when the legislation reached the House, the subtreasury bill was defeated by a combination of conservative banking interests allied with those in favor of looser credit and monetary policies, which the Whigs had always liked. A splinter group of recusant Democrats existed briefly as a third party but then cast off its independent status to join the Whigs.

The division that the subtreasury measure had created within the Democratic Party had far deeper ramifications than merely the secession of few malcontent partisans. Commercial manufacturing and banking interests, especially in New York but also in other middle Atlantic and New England states, formed the nucleus of a wide-scale rebellion against the administration. The New York Democrats who opposed the subtreasury came to be called the Hunkers and were led by Van Buren's former Albany Regency lieutenant, William L. Marcy. Those who supported the administration's laissez-faire financial policy were labeled the Barnburners. Such differences over financial policies became questions of personal prestige and ultimately came to reflect opposing views on slavery when that issue came to the forefront of political debate. The administration's issue of Treasury notes did ease the monetary stringency, and by 1838 there were signs that the economy was improving. Deposit banks began paying specie again, and the government's credit was rescued from default. But the worldwide depression that then began pulled the fragile American economy down with it. Congress finally passed the subtreasury bill during the last year of Van Buren's administration, only to have it repealed by the Harrison-Tyler administration in 1841.

Apart from the financial perplexities suffered by the Van Buren administration, it was also saddled with executing the policy of Cherokee Indian removal that it inherited from the Jackson administration. This unfortunate episode resulted in the deaths of several thousand Cherokees on the long trek west. Nor did Van Buren's reaction to the slave takeover of a Spanish vessel, the *Amistad*, which strayed into American waters, partake of humanitarian zeal. Despite the administration's efforts to return the *Amistad*'s blacks to Spain, the federal district court for Connecticut disposed of the matter by freeing them and ordering their return to their homeland.

Relations with Great Britain were disturbed when William Lyon MacKenzie headed a short-lived rebellion in Canada. MacKenzie and his followers were defeated, but fled to New York where they hoped to regroup and renew their efforts to gain Canadian independence. A British force crossed over to the American side, seized and burned a small rebel-owned steamer, the *Caroline*. Complicating the diplomatic problem was the emergence of what were known as Hunter's Lodges or Patriot Societies of American adventurers all along the border whose aims were the seizure of lands to the north and west in Canada. Such groups welcomed and supported MacKenzie rebels.

During this violation of American sovereignty some American supporters of MacKenzie were killed while resisting the attack. Van Buren sent General WINFIELD SCOTT to the border between New York and Canada to pacify the region, a move that was successful. At the same time he had the State Department lodge a formal protest to Great Britain and a request for indemnity.

But before the British government could reply, a far more serious incident occurred on the Maine border with New Brunswick, which very nearly caused war between the two nations. The incident stemmed from a quarrel over timberlands between Maine loggers and those of New Brunswick. Militia troops under Maine Governor John Fairfield prepared to engage the New Brunswick forces, under the equally bellicose Sir John Harvey. With troops mobilized on each side, Van Buren reacted quickly to the danger and again sent General Scott to the region, where he managed to defuse tensions.

Although Van Buren maintained a warlike stance by seeking and receiving a $10 million grant from Congress to strengthen the nation's military and naval forces, he had the Secretary of State, John Forsyth, join with the British minister in Washington, Henry Fox, to urge Maine and New Brunswick to withdraw from the disputed territory. These efforts ended the so-called Aroostook war without a shot being fired.

Postpresidential Career. Although Calhoun and his adherents became reconciled to Van Buren, the continued hard times and the Whigs' use of dramatic new electioneering techniques brought about his defeat in 1840. In 1842, Van Buren made a tour of the south and west, an obvious move to gain support for his being nominated for the presidency again. By then the Whig Party was in deep trouble. John Tyler, who had become President after Harrison's sudden death, had refused to accept his party's key platform, the reestablishment of central banking in a third Bank of the United States. Then, to the consternation and active opposition of a majority of Whigs, Tyler, with the

covert assistance of Calhoun, brought the issue of the ANNEXATION OF TEXAS to the forefront of political discussion.

The United States had recognized Texas as an independent republic in 1837. Slavery, however, was a recognized institution in Texas. Foreseeing a political and sectional quagmire, Van Buren had resisted the efforts for annexation by Texas and its U.S. allies. The annexation of such a huge territory that could become not just one state but several would in Van Buren's opinion unleash dire sectional forces that might place the Union at extreme jeopardy. Thus the administration pursued a policy of calculated delay reinforced by astute political logrolling in Congress that postponed this potentially divisive question. But if anything, slavery had become an even more pressing matter in 1843, when Tyler again raised the issue. Public opinion was favorable in the South and Southwest, less so in the Northwest and Northeast. Sensing its divisive aspects, Van Buren and Clay, the leading Whig candidate, both wrote public letters that opposed immediate annexation.

The issue was sure to be brought up at the Democratic nominating convention in Baltimore in 1844. In this yeasty atmosphere, Van Buren was the front-running Democratic candidate. He received a majority of the delegate votes on the first ballot, but he was unable to win two-thirds of the vote, a requirement that had been imposed at the 1840 convention and that was approved again by a close vote in 1844.

Van Buren's letter on annexation had severely hurt his standing with many of the delegates. After the first roll call, Van Buren steadily lost strength, until by the eighth ballot his managers conceded defeat and reluctantly cast their vote for James K. Polk of Tennessee, a Jacksonian Democrat, a former Speaker of the House, and a moderate on the slavery issue, but a known Texas-annexationist. Polk was nominated on the ninth ballot. Clay had already received the Whig nomination. Despite his disappointment at not being renominated, Van Buren and his Barnburners joined the Hunkers in supporting the ticket. Silas Wright, Van Buren's chief lieutenant, refused the vice presidential nomination at Baltimore and ran for governor of New York. He won the election and helped to carry the state for Polk, who would otherwise have lost to Clay.

Van Buren and Wright sought to influence the selection of the principal members in the Cabinet and to direct PATRONAGE in New York. But Polk not only rejected their recommendations, but he also appointed William L. Marcy, a prominent Hunker, as Secretary of War. The split in the New York Democratic Party widened. The MEXICAN WAR hastened this process, as the question of slavery in the new western territories gained from Mexico again made the expansion of slavery a matter of burning public concern.

The WILMOT PROVISO, which would have made all these lands free, was defeated in the U.S. Senate, but it became a rallying cry for the New York Barnburners. In early 1848, Van Buren gave a lengthy address on the matter that allied him firmly on the side of free soil for the territories. He had always been privately opposed to slavery, but he recognized its constitutional protection in the states where the institution was established and the divisive aspects of political agitation on the subject. Thus, he had sought to muffle public controversy and to control any policy that would threaten the integrity of the Union.

By embracing free soil, Van Buren moved to a more advanced antislavery position, hoping that his moral influence would regain the initiative for his Democratic Party organization in New York state and perhaps begin the process of extinguishing slavery throughout the nation. At the same time, he believed that it was time to rally party opinion on an issue that would isolate southern extremists and defuse a possibly explosive situation. Van Buren had no desire to head a THIRD PARTY movement that he knew would be doomed to failure.

But he was unable to resist the demand of his own party organization and cooperating antislavery groups. Under the slogan "Free Soil Free Labor Freemen," Van Buren became the presidential nominee of the FREE-SOIL PARTY at Buffalo in August 1848. Charles Francis Adams, who was known as a conscience Whig and who was the grandson and son of Presidents, was nominated for Vice President. The Whigs nominated Zachary Taylor, a Mexican War hero, a southerner, and a slaveowner, for President. The Democrats named LEWIS CASS, an old Jacksonian from Michigan. Cass owed his nomination to his support of what he called "popular sovereignty," in which the people of a given territory would decide for themselves when they petitioned for admission to the Union whether their proposed state would come in free or slave.

Van Buren received 290,000 popular votes, most of them in New York and New England, but no electoral votes. His candidacy, however, cost Cass the election. Though Van Buren took no active role in politics for the rest of his life, his counsel as an elder statesmen was often sought.

Van Buren was distressed at the effect that his championing of free soil had had on the national party apparatus. He had hoped the shock treatment of the Free-Soil campaign would bring Democratic leaders to their senses and set the stage for the extension of

freedom into the vast territories acquired from Mexico. Unfortunately, it had the reverse outcome. The secession of the slave states became more than a remote possibility when California demanded admission as a free state. Van Buren began to retreat from his former opinion and supported the COMPROMISE OF 1850, which averted secession and a probable conflict. He supported Franklin Pierce for President in 1852 on an orthodox Democratic ticket that embraced the Compromise, and he deplored the sectional aspects of the KANSAS-NEBRASKA ACT in 1854.

Reluctantly, Van Buren backed party regular James Buchanan for the presidency in 1856, fearing that the election of JOHN C. FREMONT, the candidate of the new REPUBLICAN PARTY, would destroy the Union. "Now for the first time in our history," he wrote, "one side and that the one in which we reside has undertaken to carry an election including control of the Federal government against the united wishes of another." In 1860, his opinion had not changed. With Abraham Lincoln's election he prepared for the worst. When the CIVIL WAR came, however, he loyally supported the Union cause.

As a spectator of the political scene rather than activist, Van Buren occupied his leisure time at Kinderhook with the writing of his autobiography and a history of American political parties. The autobiography contains much valuable material on his early political career, but unfortunately it was never completed. His history of political parties explored the American experience as seen from a Jacksonian Democrat point of view. Van Buren lived long enough to witness his nation torn apart by the advent of the Civil War but not long enough to see the restoration of the Union on northern terms or the changes that followed, which he would have deplored because of his reverence for the concept of STATES' RIGHTS and other Jeffersonian and Jacksonian principles. He died at his home in Kinderhook on 24 July 1862.

BIBLIOGRAPHY

Cole, Donald B. *Martin Van Buren.* 1984.
Curtis, James C. *The Fox at Bay: Martin Van Buren and the Presidency.* 1970.
Niven, John. *Martin Van Buren: The Romantic Age of American Politics.* 1983.
Remini, Robert V. *Martin Van Buren and the Making of the Democratic Party.* 1959.
Wilson, Major. *The Presidency of Martin Van Buren.* 1984.

JOHN NIVEN

VANDENBERG RESOLUTION (1948). The resolution, sponsored by Senator Arthur H. Vandenberg (R-Mich.), Chairman of the Foreign Relations Committee, in the spring of 1948, committed the United States to regional collective security within the framework of the UNITED NATIONS Charter, pointed the way to American participation in the North Atlantic Treaty Organization, and reflected unprecedented cooperation between the President and Congress in foreign affairs—crucial to the success of the postwar CONTAINMENT policy.

As the COLD WAR deepened in 1948, President Harry S. Truman and his advisers sought to establish a collective security pact for the North Atlantic community. But they doubted Congress would be politically willing to consider American membership in the proposed alliance in an election year. Truman thus pursued a preliminary step instead: a "sense of the Senate" resolution endorsing U.S. participation in regional security treaties. The Truman administration wanted a Republican Senator to introduce the resolution in order to smooth its passage through the shoals of partisanship. It wisely chose Arthur H. Vandenberg, an influential and powerful isolationist-turned-internationalist whose stature as chairman of the Foreign Relations Committee almost assured the resolution's success. Vandenberg agreed and, with Under Secretary of State Robert A. Lovett, drafted Senate Resolution 239. It passed the Senate after little debate in June 1948 by the lopsided vote of 64 to 4.

With this green light—an extraordinary manifestation of cooperation between a Republican-controlled Senate and a Democratic-controlled White House in an election year—the State Department accelerated talks to include the United States in a Western European defense alliance. Nine months later, on 4 April 1949, delegates from twelve nations met in Washington to sign the North Atlantic Treaty [see NATO TREATY].

BIBLIOGRAPHY

Donovan, Robert J. *Conflict and Crisis: The Presidency of Harry S. Truman, 1945-1948.* 1977.

Tompkins, C. David. *Senator Arthur H. Vandenberg: The Evolution of a Modern Republican, 1884-1945.* 1970.

Vandenberg, Arthur H., Jr., ed. *The Private Papers of Senator Vandenberg.* 1952.

BRIAN VANDEMARK

VERSAILLES, TREATY OF. See TREATY OF VERSAILLES.

VETERANS AFFAIRS, DEPARTMENT OF. Two-thirds of American Presidents—twenty-five of the forty-one through George Bush—had some prior military service, ranging from high command (George Washington, Ulysses S. Grant, Dwight D. Eisenhower), to wounded or decorated heroism in combat (James Monroe, Rutherford B. Hayes, John F. Kennedy, George Bush), to three months of volunteer service in 1832 in the INDIAN Wars (Abraham Lincoln).

The compassion of the pledge in Lincoln's second inaugural address in 1865—"to care for him who shall have borne the battle, and for his widow and his orphan"—is cast in metal plaques at both sides of the entrance to the massive headquarters of the Department of Veterans Affairs (DVA) in Washington, D.C. Lincoln's aspiring words, turned into sprawling bureaucracy by the demands of five subsequent wars and influenced by partisan politics, set the stage for more than a century of enormous government growth.

In 1992, thirty-six children of CIVIL WAR veterans were still receiving benefits from the DVA. They were among nearly 3.5 million others cared for under veteran's expenditures that totaled $16 billion a year in tax-free monthly benefit checks. Separately, to run the world's largest medical care network, the DVA spent another $14 billion a year.

About 10 percent of the 26.6 million living U.S. veterans and 820,000 of their widows, children, and dependents received ongoing veterans' benefits. At a time when the U.S. Census counted about 248.7 million Americans, the 3.5 million beneficiaries were between 1 and 2 percent of the total population. But serving them involved a DVA staff approaching a quarter million.

In 1989 the DVA was set on a course to further growth by its elevation from an independent agency, the Veterans Administration (VA) to a CABINET-rank department. The VA had been created in 1930, midway through the administration of President Herbert Hoover, by the consolidation of various small veterans' bureaus, until then established on a war-by-war basis. In the aftermath of WORLD WAR II, the KOREAN WAR, and VIETNAM WAR, the low-profile agency grew to such massive proportions that its $32 billion annual budget exceeds all but that of the DEFENSE DEPARTMENT.

In 1944 the Roosevelt administration greatly broadened veterans' benefits by creating what is widely believed to have been the most enlightened and successful veterans' compensation program ever enacted, the Serviceman's Readjustment Act of 1944 or "GI Bill of Rights." In a program which created a new middle-class, nearly 2 million veterans of World War II were supported while enrolled in colleges and universities.

President Ronald Reagan personally arranged the elevation of the VA to the Department of Veterans' Affairs. At a time when the veteran population was

Secretaries of Veterans Affairs

	President	Secretary of Veterans Affairs
41	Bush	Edward J. Derwinski, 1989–1992
42	Clinton	Jesse Brown, 1993–

declining because aging veterans were expiring at nearly twice the rate of discharge from the armed forces, Reagan proposed, on Veterans' Day 1987, elevating the VA to the Cabinet. (In practical terms, giving a Secretary of Veterans Affairs the fourteenth seat at the Cabinet table was an elevation already effectively granted de facto by President Jimmy Carter's 1977 EXECUTIVE ORDER appointing the VA Administrator, then Max Cleland, a wheelchair-bound amputee, as a regular participant in Cabinet meetings.) The House of Representatives approved the VA's Cabinet status within a week. The Senate approved departmental status despite the advice of a negative report prepared for it by a panel of management experts at the National Academy of Public Administration. The panel warned that the grant of Cabinet status imposed no requirements for reform of the VA's seemingly unremediable administrative mismanagement and programmatic failures.

At the time, the agency's reputation was in decline because thousands of Vietnam veterans, disenchanted and alienated from civilian society in the 1960s and 1970s, felt estranged and rejected. Their problems were not then widely reported by the press, an abdication that helped perpetuate the broad array of bureaucratic abuses disclosed later in congressional investigations and by the DVA's strengthened in-house Inspector General.

In 1988 a new U.S. Court of Veterans' Appeals was created. Judicial review of denials of claims gives DVA applicants for the first time the due process afforded all other citizens. Veterans have standing to sue to rectify the mistakes of a historically paternalistic, assertedly nonadversarial bureaucracy.

Given the choice of the first Secretary of Veterans Affairs in 1989, President Bush chose Edward J. Derwinski, until 1982 an unchallengable twelve-term Republican member of the House of Representatives. Derwinski proved to be a surprisingly apolitical incumbent, gaining from Congress added billions of dollars for deteriorating DVA hospitals, and suggesting limited access to them for the nonveteran poor in Appalachia and elsewhere. In proposing that opening, Derwinski so deeply offended the Veterans of Foreign Wars that President Bush, by then fearing a reelection defeat, sacrificed him to VFW demands by summarily dismissing him six weeks before election day.

In 1992, the DVA's quarter-million employees dispensed $16 billion a year in monthly checks—no longer "charity," but firmly established as "entitlements," which are periodically increased based on the cost-of-living index.

To run its 58 regional offices; 171 veterans' hospitals and 350 out-patient, community, and outreach clinics; 128 nursing homes and old soldiers' domiciliaries, 196 storefront veterans' outreach centers, and 114 national cemeteries in thirty-eight states and PUERTO RICO, the new Secretary of Veterans Affairs has more moderately to well-paid employees in the fifty states than the UNITED STATES POSTAL SERVICE.

[*See also* VETERANS POLICY.]

BIBLIOGRAPHY

Department of Veterans Affairs. *Survey of Disabled Veterans.* 1989.

National Academy of Public Administration. *Evaluation of Proposals to Establish a Department of Veterans Affairs.* 1988.

Severo, Richard, and Lewis Milford. *The Wages of War: When America's Soldiers Came Home—From Valley Forge to Vietnam.* 1989.

Stewart, Anne C. *Proposals in the 100th Congress to Make the Veterans Administration a Cabinet-Level Department: Background Information and Analysis of Issues.* 1987.

U.S. House of Representatives. Committee on Government Operations. *Investigation of Disability Compensation Programs of the Veterans' Administration.* 100th Cong., 2d Sess. 1988. H. Rept. 100-886.

BEN A. FRANKLIN

VETERANS POLICY. The American colonists were the first to institutionalize military pensions by obligating all taxpayers to finance them. The Pilgrims' system was strategically motivated to deter reluctance to volunteer for military service by a new generation of young men who had observed the postcombat hardships of armless and legless veterans under primitive medical care. This pension plan was incorporated into law when Plymouth merged with the Massachusetts Bay Colony in 1691. The New England colonists thus adopted the first system anywhere that charged the cost of veterans' benefits to the general treasury. Little did they know that they were setting the precedent for what has become a $32 billion a year obligation of the United States government.

Other colonial governments followed, but sometimes with elitist distinctions. In Maryland and Virginia, the disabled veteran—or, in case he was dead, his widow and family—were declared to be "objects of charity" who would receive a stipend "according to his place and quality."

The first national act granting pensions to officers and enlisted men of the United States "disabled in the line of duty" was passed by the post-revolutionary war Continental Congress in 1789. As the United States government matured and other wars ensued, the administration of veterans' grants led to the establishment of coexisting small offices, including one called the War Risk Insurance Bureau, to maintain veterans on a war-by-war basis.

The Veterans Administration (VA), designed to consolidate the existing programs for veterans of the War of Independence, the WAR OF 1812, the CIVIL WAR, the INDIAN Wars, the MEXICAN WAR, and WORLD WAR I, was not established by Congress until 1930, midway through the Hoover administration. It was regarded as a streamlining stroke of government reorganization, but it came as public sympathy for veterans vanished.

The new agency appeared something less than a success. This reputation persists despite the agency's avowal that it is "nonadversarial" and gives veteran claimants "every benefit of the doubt" and despite the historic success of the Roosevelt administration's Serviceman's Readjustment Act of 1944, or the GI Bill, the post-WORLD WAR II program that sent nearly 2 million American veterans to college and produced a generation of well-educated, middle-class professionals and homeowners.

In 1989, some three hundred years after the Pilgrims' first obligation of all taxpayers to pay the cost of veterans' programs, the VA was elevated to CABINET-rank as the DEPARTMENT OF VETERANS AFFAIRS (DVA). The DVA stands second only to the DEFENSE DEPARTMENT both in its bureaucratic payroll, with 252,000 employees, and in its annual appropriations, at $32 billion and growing.

In the United States, the majority of wartime draftees and volunteers since World War II have emerged from military service to civilian life with little or no participation in any veterans' program, or at most the arm's length contact of low-cost life insurance or GI home loans. A less generous KOREAN WAR GI Bill went relatively unused.

All told, veterans comprise only a little over 10 percent of the population of the United States. Of these 26.6 million men and women, about 10 percent (2.7 million) receive benefits for service-connected disabilities or old-age pensions for unemployability at age 65, whether service-connected or not. Another 820,000 spouses and children receive survivors' benefits.

Public questioning of large-scale government aid to veterans is virtually nonexistent, even among the fiercest ideological opponents of "welfare programs."

Veterans' programs that fill hundred of pages of federal statute books are insulated from review by the public by their complexity, a cover enhanced by lack of attention by the press and by congressional indifference to legislative details. Although the Veterans Affairs committees of the Senate and the House of Representatives are so powerful in their narrow oversight of the DVA and its programs that veterans policy legislation is often adopted on their say so, without even token floor debate, membership on these committees is regarded by most as a dull and undesirable assignment, to be avoided.

Under this legislative shroud, it took more than a century for reformists in Congress to end, in 1989, one of the most flagrant legacies of the government's "nonadversarial" but autocratically paternalistic view of veterans.

At the end of the Civil War, veterans and their widows were denied by law the services of lawyers—suspected carpetbaggers—in pressing claims and appealing denials, no matter how capriciously in error.

At each of the few attempts over the years to end this unique denial of due process—a right-of-attorney representation granted even to illegal immigrants—it was perpetuated with the support of most of the 8-million-member national veterans' organizations. Only when the grant of Cabinet-rank status became a reality in 1988 did the veterans' groups relent enough to permit passage of the Veterans' Judicial Review Act. It was a trade off that allowed lawyers for the first time to represent veteran claimants under a controlled but reasonable schedule of fees. The long resistance of the veterans' organizations to judicial review reflected both a reluctance to end decades of paralegal aid to VA claimants by their own cadres of advisers—a service they sometimes used to recruit members—and the parochially fraternal separatism of veterans for veterans. Civilian lawyers and judges were regarded as intrusive and unwelcome.

By allowing lawyers to practice before a new and separate U.S. Court of Veterans Appeals, the Judicial Review Act also began to end decades of occasional but sometimes corrupt neglect and favoritism in the administrative echelons of veterans' claims processing. The new court has found repeatedly that the DVA has ignored or punishingly misinterpreted the law and its own rules and regulations to the detriment of veterans.

Congress also strengthened the DVA's in-house self-investigation staff under the departmental Office of Inspector General, or IG. The IG's discoveries include high numbers of unreported patient deaths at some troubled DVA hospitals and a 76 percent error rate—$669 million in the lenders' favor—in calculating the amounts payable to mortgage lenders when veterans defaulted under DVA-guaranteed home loans.

One reason the DVA has been less well monitored and less critiqued by Congress than other bureaucracies is an inherent congressional conflict of interest.

In Congress, the DVA's large and nationally dispersed payroll creates two constituencies—the veterans receiving government benefits, and the recipients' bureaucratic benefactors, the clerks and managers who process veterans' claims in regional and local offices in their congressional districts. As vote-getting participants in income centers back home, DVA employees hold jobs uniquely manipulated by members of Congress.

Thus, the DVA has become not only a $16 billion a year income-maintenance system for the 3.5 million Americans receiving tax-free monthly benefit checks—they range from a low of $83 for a 10 percent disability rating to the neighborhood of $4,800 a month for care of the totally incapacitated—it also is an agreeably inconspicuous pork barrel.

Guarding that, although it encumbers the DVA's struggles toward efficiency, Congress has forbidden the agency to reduce local office staffs without first having its approval. Although members of Congress would not admit it, the headcount of DVA employees on the departmental payroll in their home districts sometimes seems quietly as important to them as their more noisily celebrated constituencies of veterans.

BIBLIOGRAPHY

Department of Veterans Affairs. *Survey of Disabled Veterans.* 1989.
National Academy of Public Administration. *Evaluation of Proposals to Establish a Department of Veterans Affairs.* 1988.
Severo, Richard, and Lewis Milford. *The Wages of War: When America's Soldiers Came Home—From Valley Forge to Vietnam.* 1989.
Stewart, Anne C. *Proposals in the 100th Congress to Make the Veterans Administration a Cabinet-Level Department: Background Information and Analysis of Issues.* 1987.
U.S. House of Representatives. Committee on Government Operations. *Investigation of Disability Compensation Programs of the Veterans' Administration.* 100th Cong., 2d Sess. 1988. H. Rept. 100–886.

BEN A. FRANKLIN

VETO. The following three articles discuss presidential vetoes. The first, VETO, ITEM, discusses proposals to give the President the ability to veto single items within bills passed by Congress. The other two articles—VETO, POCKET, and VETO, REGULAR—deal with the veto power as set out in the Constitution. See also LEGISLATIVE VETO.

VETO, ITEM. The power of an executive to veto, delete, or send back to the legislature some section or part of a bill is called an item veto. Depending on how the power is defined, an item veto might apply only to appropriations bills or to all legislation. It might also be defined as an item reduction power allowing the executive to reduce appropriations levels. An amendatory veto, possessed by some state governors, amounts to a conditional approval of a bill pending adoption by the legislature of changes suggested by the governor. Forty-three of fifty state governors possess some kind of item-veto power. The President does not possess an item veto, but many have argued that such power should be granted. Most of these proposals have advocated granting the President the power to disapprove items in appropriations bills.

Despite the occasional suggestion that the Constitution already provides for an item veto (if one considers a piece of legislation incorporating several provisions dealing with different matters as several bills instead of one) or that the Framers would have approved of the power in the modern legislative setting, no evidence supports either claim. No debate on item-veto powers appears in the transcripts of the CONSTITUTIONAL CONVENTION, although the practice of attaching unrelated amendments to legislation—a practice giving rise to calls for a presidential item veto—was a matter of debate and controversy in the British Parliament, as it was during the earliest days of the U.S. Congress. George Washington, who presided over the Constitutional Convention, noted, "From the nature of the Constitution, I must approve all parts of a Bill, or reject it in toto."

Suggestions that the President be granted item-veto powers were first made in the 1840s. The first codification of the item veto appeared in the CONFEDERATE CONSTITUTION of 1861, in which the Confederate president was given the power to veto parts of appropriations bills. Although JEFFERSON DAVIS used the regular veto thirty-eight times, he never exercised the item veto. After the CIVIL WAR, the item veto was adopted by Georgia (1865) and Texas (1866). The idea then spread rapidly, so that by 1920 thirty-seven states had adopted the item veto. The rapid spread of this power is largely attributable to the widespread corruption and irresponsibility of many state legislatures during this period.

At the federal level, Ulysses S. Grant became the first President to call for an item veto, which he did in his fifth STATE OF THE UNION MESSAGE to Congress, 1 December 1873. Grant justified the request as a means for the President to stem the abuse and waste of government funds. Three years later, the first such proposal was formally introduced into Congress. Since then, many Presidents, including Rutherford B. Hayes, Chester A. Arthur, Grover Cleveland, Franklin

D. Roosevelt, Ronald Reagan, and George Bush, have urged adoption of the power. Presidents who have spoken against the item veto include Benjamin Harrison, William Howard Taft, and Jimmy Carter. From the time of Grant to the 1980s, more than 150 item-veto proposals have been introduced into Congress. One such proposal was reported out of a Senate committee in 1884. In 1938, the House passed a bill that gave the President the power to reduce or eliminate appropriations subject to congressional disapproval within sixty days. In 1992, the Senate defeated a asure that would have given the President enhanced rescission power (the equivalent of an item veto).

Arguments For. The debate over granting the President an item veto revolves around several issues that have maintained a considerable degree of constancy over the last century. Those who advocate this power argue, first, that the President's existing veto powers are, or have become, inadequate to tackle Congress's penchant for attaching riders and other nongermane amendments to legislation. This practice unfairly forces the President to make an all-or-nothing choice regarding the veto decision, sometimes precipitating a veto of an otherwise desirable piece of legislation in order to block a single provision. So-called Christmas tree legislation, composed of diverse special-interest provisions, has long fanned antagonism toward Congress, and both within and outside Congress there is agreement that this technique is used to win enactment of measures that could not otherwise stand on their own. Concern over congressional attachment of riders to bills has probably been the most important spur to the call for an item veto.

Second, proponents argue that the President needs this power to weed out excessive and unwise spending provisions found in appropriations and other omnibus bills. Congress has long been accused of enacting pork barrel legislation to win voter loyalty even when such legislation may represent poor public policy. According to proponents, the President is in the best position to rein in such congressional budgetary excess. The need for fiscal frugality took on even greater urgency with the federal government's spiraling deficits of the 1980s and 1990s, and many looked to an item veto as a means for paring down aggregate government spending.

Third, item-veto advocates point to the fact that so many state governors possess the power, arguing that this shows that the idea is practical, workable, and reasonable. Ronald Reagan possessed the power when he served as governor of California, for example, and he relied in part on that experience to advocate its extension to the presidency.

Arguments Against. Opponents of the item veto argue, first, that the President's existing veto powers have if anything grown more formidable over time. The use of the veto expanded dramatically in the mid-nineteenth century, and about 93 percent of all regular vetoes have been upheld. While Presidents may be reluctant to veto a bill because of one offending provision within it, the all-or-nothing quality of the veto has not prevented them from doing just that on many occasions. The attachment of riders may be politically objectionable, but the practice is endemic to the legislative process and as old as the country itself. And the definition of a bill has always incorporated the idea that provisions within a piece of legislation may involve diverse subjects. Both sides agree that an item veto would enhance the President's power over the legislative process, but item-veto opponents argue that proponents underestimate or ignore the vast increase of presidential powers that has occurred in the twentieth century, suggesting that the addition of an item veto would tip the balance scales too far toward the President.

Second, opponents point out that the actual impact of an item veto on overall spending levels would be marginal, since most federal spending is mandated by contract, law, or other obligations, and federal appropriations bills are not itemized—that is, Presidents would literally be unable to weed out specific offending provisions. Opponents also observe that the presumption that Congress alone cares about enacting pork barrel legislation is fallacious; Presidents are no less interested in the enactment of such legislation. Indeed, Presidents have vigorously assisted political allies in enacting pork-barrel programs.

Third, according to opponents, the fact that forty-three governors possess the power provides no basis for assuming that the power would be appropriate for the President. State governments are more executive centered than the federal government by design, since state legislatures are normally part-time governing bodies. This necessitates stronger executives to run state governments during the many months legislatures are not in session. In addition, several studies of the political effects of the gubernatorial item veto conclude that the power has not had an appreciable impact on overall spending levels but rather has been used mostly as a partisan tool to provide greater political advantage for governors and their political allies.

Later Debate. The item-veto debate was reinvigorated in the 1980s when President Reagan called for a presidential item veto in his 1984 state of the union message. That plea renewed legislative efforts to create the power by both constitutional and statutory means, although some argued that the latter approach was unconstitutional. A 1985 Gallup poll revealed that 71 percent of Americans supported the idea. But like other proposed structural reforms, such as proposals to alter or abolish the ELECTORAL COLLEGE, this move has engendered little deep feeling among the American public. The debate over the item veto is important as part of the larger debate over competing conceptions of EXECUTIVE POWER. Questions concerning how executive powers are or should be defined bear directly on this debate.

BIBLIOGRAPHY

Fisher, Louis, and Neal Devins. "How Successfully Can the States' Item Veto Be Transferred to the President?" *Georgetown Law Journal* 75 (1986): 159–197.

Spitzer, Robert J. *The Presidential Veto: Touchstone of the American Presidency.* 1988.

"Symposium on the Line-Item Veto." *Notre Dame Journal of Law, Ethics & Public Policy* 1 (1985): 157–283.

U.S. House of Representatives. Committee on the Budget. "The Line-Item Veto: An Appraisal." Report no. CP-4A. 98th Cong., 2d sess.

U.S. House of Representatives. Committee on the Judiciary. Subcommittee No. 3. "Item Veto." Hearings, 85th Cong., 1st sess.

ROBERT J. SPITZER

VETO, POCKET. Provided for in Article I, Section 7, of the Constitution, the pocket-veto power allows the President to withhold approval of a bill sent to the CHIEF EXECUTIVE for signature after Congress has adjourned. The Constitution's wording is deceptively simple: "If any Bill shall not be returned by the President within ten Days (Sundays excepted) after it shall have been presented to him, the Same shall be a Law, in like manner as if he had signed it, unless Congress by their Adjournment prevent its Return, in which case it shall not be a Law." A regular, or return, veto is exercised when the President vetoes a bill by returning it to the house of origin. The pocket-veto power was inserted to guard against the possibility that Congress could pass a bill but then, as a way of avoiding a veto, quickly adjourn before the President had a chance to return the bill. Since pocket-vetoed bills cannot be returned to Congress, they are in effect absolute-vetoed—that is, Congress has no opportunity to override a pocket veto. Congress's only alternatives are to stay in session for at least ten days after the passage of a bill that may be subject to veto or to start from scratch and repass the bill when Congress reconvenes.

During the CONSTITUTIONAL CONVENTION of 1787, no debate was recorded concerning the pocket veto. But the Framers did discuss and emphatically reject efforts to give the President an absolute veto—that is, one not subject to override. That the pocket veto operates as an absolute veto is explainable by the Framers' concern that the President needed this power to defend against any congressional effort to duck the regular veto. Unlike the regular veto, the pocket veto is carefully circumscribed by the fact that it may only be used when "Congress by their Adjournment prevent [a bill's] Return."

The first two pocket vetoes were exercised by President James Madison; they aroused little attention. The next President to use the power, Andrew Jackson, aroused considerable controversy by exercising the power seven times (out of a total of twelve bills vetoed in his two terms), although his opponents' objections were founded mostly in their general dissatisfaction with his aggressive political style. The term "pocket veto" was apparently coined during Jackson's term.

Early concern about use of the pocket veto centered on two principles. First, the Framers wanted to ensure that Presidents would have adequate time to consider legislation sent to them. The pocket veto would come into play at the end of a congressional session, when Congress would be likely to present the President with a rush of last-minute bills, and would ensure that Presidents would not be forced into signing what they considered to be imprudent legislation. The second principle was to ensure that Congress would have time to consider and, if it chose, override the President's objections. Since the pocket veto does not allow for any reconsideration or override, the return veto is the preferred option, if such return can occur.

Persisting ambiguities have surrounded the pocket-veto power. For example, the Constitution allows for the pocket veto when congressional adjournment prevents a bill's return, but what constitutes adjournment? When does adjournment prevent bill return? May proxies for Congress or the President serve as legal stand-ins to receive veto messages or enrolled bills (bills passed by Congress but not yet signed by the President)? Some of these questions have been addressed in court cases.

In the *Pocket Veto Case* (1929), the Supreme Court ruled on a challenge to a pocket veto by President Calvin Coolidge that occurred between sessions at the start of a six-month congressional break in 1926. In grappling with the key question of the meaning of adjournment, the Court noted that "the determinative question . . . is not whether it is a final adjournment of Congress or an interim adjournment . . . but whether it is one that 'prevents' the President from returning the bill to the House in which it originated within the time allowed." The Court rejected the idea that a bill could be returned to a designated agent when Congress was not in session, both because Congress had never actually done this and because the Court feared that this might cause bills to hang in limbo for many months.

In *Wright v. United States* (1938), the Court considered a challenge to a regular veto of a bill returned to the Secretary of the Senate during a three-day Senate recess. The court said that it did not consider the three-day period an adjournment, but it also contradicted its previous conclusion in the *Pocket Veto Case* by saying that Congress could indeed designate agents on its behalf, rejecting what it now considered in the earlier ruling "artificial formality" by saying that the "Constitution does not define what shall constitute a return of a bill or deny the use of appropriate agencies in effecting the return." The Court also dismissed the potential delay problem mentioned in the *Pocket Veto Case* as "illusory."

In 1974, the U.S. Court of Appeals upheld a lower court ruling that struck down a 1970 pocket veto by Richard M. Nixon that occurred during a six-day Christmas recess (*Kennedy v. Sampson* [1974]); in this case, the tenth day had lapsed during the six-day break. The Court noted that bill return could have been effected, consistent with *Wright,* and cast doubt on pocket vetoes applied during any intra- or intersession adjournment as long as appropriate arrangements were made for bill receipt, suggesting that a pocket veto was now only possible after Congress adjourned *sine die* (literally, "without a day") at the end of a two-year Congress. The Court also noted that congressional practices had changed dramatically since the 1920s, in that Congress was now in session nearly year-round. The Nixon administration declined to appeal the ruling to the Supreme Court.

During the 1970s, Presidents Gerald Ford and Jimmy Carter abided by the principle of avoiding pocket vetoes during intra- and intersession adjournments, and Congress formalized procedures for receiving presidential messages during adjournments, just as Presidents have long delegated to agents the authority to receive enrolled bills on their behalf. Ronald Reagan backtracked on this arrangement, however, when he pocket-vetoed a bill between the first and second sessions of the Ninety-eighth Congress in 1983. Members of Congress took the President to court, but the Supreme Court refused to hear the case on its merits, vacating it as moot in *Burke v. Barnes* (1987).

George Bush went even farther than Reagan, arguing that a pocket veto may be used whenever Congress recesses for longer than three days. Critics have taken issue with this interpretation, citing the weight of court precedent, the workability of bill-receipt procedures during adjournments, the fact that this interpretation would allow pocket vetoes even during long weekends in the middle of a session, and the desirability of interbranch comity. Presidents' temptations to use pocket vetoes will continue to be great, as pocket-vetoed bills avoid any override fight. In 1990, the House Judiciary and Rules committees reported legislation to restrict pocket vetoes to the end of a Congress.

One other constitutional ambiguity surrounds the pocket veto. While the Constitution mandates that the President include written objections to vetoed bills returned to Congress, it says nothing about the necessity of written messages for pocket vetoes. Presidents from Madison to Andrew Johnson did prepare written messages for pocket vetoes, but the practice lapsed with Ulysses S. Grant, probably because of the vast increase in pocket vetoes. The practice of issuing no public message (the so-called silent pocket) persisted until 1934, when Franklin D. Roosevelt announced that he would resume preparing written messages—something all Presidents have done since. In this instance, constitutional ambiguity was resolved amicably.

BIBLIOGRAPHY

Antieau, Chester J. *The Executive Veto.* 1988.

Dumbrell, John W., and John D. Lees. "Presidential Pocket-Veto Power: A Constitutional Anachronism?" *Political Studies* 28 (1980): 109–116.

Spitzer, Robert J. *The Presidential Veto: Touchstone of the American Presidency.* 1988.

Spitzer, Robert J. "Presidential Prerogative Power." *PS: Political Science and Politics* 24 (1991): 38–42.

U.S. House of Representatives. Rules Committee. Subcommittee on the Legislative Process. *Hearings on H.R. 849, A Bill to Clarify the Law Surrounding the President's Use of the Pocket Veto.* 101st Congress, 1st sess., 1989.

Zinn, Charles J. *The Veto Power of the President.* 1951.

ROBERT J. SPITZER

VETO, REGULAR. The power to veto legislation is one of the few explicit powers granted to the President that formally involves the Chief Executive in legislative affairs. Described in Article I, Section 7, of the Constitution, the veto is a capstone decision, the final leg of the legislative gauntlet before a bill becomes a law.

When presented with a bill by Congress, the President faces four possible choices: the executive may approve the bill by signing it into law; the executive may exercise the regular, or return, veto by refusing to sign the bill and returning it to the house of origin, including a statement of objections; the President may do nothing, in which case the bill automatically becomes law after ten days (Sundays excepted); and, lastly, if Congress adjourns within ten days of having presented a bill to the President, the President may choose to do nothing, in which case the bill is killed by POCKET VETO if, according to the Constitution, "Congress by their Adjournment prevent its Return." A return veto is subject to override by a two-thirds vote of both houses of Congress; a pocket veto is not.

The veto power is indisputably a presidential power, yet its location in Article I, the article otherwise devoted to the legislative branch, reflects the fact, first, that it is a legislative power possessed by the executive and, second, that the Constitution's system of CHECKS AND BALANCES permits some sharing of powers between the branches of government.

The Framers' Purposes. Fears of the baneful consequences of strong executives motivated the new nation's leaders to create a governing system without an independent executive branch under the Articles of Confederation. But by the time the CONSTITUTIONAL CONVENTION met in 1787, the prevailing sentiment favored an independent executive. Even though many still remembered the oppressive veto practices that the British king and his appointed colonial governors had exercised before the Revolution, there was little disagreement that the new President should have a qualified veto power. The Framers were adamant, however, that the President's veto not be absolute, as was that of the British monarch.

A central reason for granting the President this power was the Framers' realization that the executive would need such a power to protect the executive branch against legislative encroachments on executive power —a tendency observed in many state governments during the time the nation was governed by the Articles of Confederation. The Framers expected that the veto would be used to block legislation that was hastily conceived, unjust, or of dubious constitutionality. The power was not considered to be a purely negative action. Often called the revisionary power, the veto was conceived as a creative, positive device whereby the President could bring a bill back to Congress for a final round of debate and consideration. This constructive purpose of the veto has mostly been lost in the intervening years.

Early Presidents used the veto power cautiously and sparingly, giving rise to claims that the Constitution somehow countenanced restrictions on the numbers

Vetoes, 1789–1993

President	Vetoes			Vetoes Overridden
	Regular	Pocket	Total	
Washington	2	0	2	0
J. Adams	0	0	0	0
Jefferson	0	0	0	0
Madison	5	2	7	0
Monroe	1	0	1	0
J. Q. Adams	0	0	0	0
Jackson	5	7	12	0
Van Buren	0	1	1	0
W. Harrison	0	0	0	0
Tyler	6	4	10	1
Polk	2	1	3	0
Taylor	0	0	0	0
Fillmore	0	0	0	0
Pierce	9	0	9	5
Buchanan	4	3	7	0
Lincoln	2	5	7	0
A. Johnson	21	8	29	15
Grant	45	48[a]	93	4
Hayes	12	1	13	1
Garfield	0	0	0	0
Arthur	4	8	12	1
Cleveland	304	110	414	2
B. Harrison	19	25	44	1
Cleveland	42	128	170	5
McKinley	6	36	42	0
T. Roosevelt	42	40	82	1
Taft	30	9	39	1
Wilson	33	11	44	6
Harding	5	1	6	0
Coolidge	20	30	50	4
Hoover	21	16	37	3
F. Roosevelt	372	263	635	9
Truman	180	70	250	12
Eisenhower	73	108	181	2
Kennedy	12	9	21	0
L. Johnson	16	14	30	0
Nixon[b]	26	17	43	7
Ford	48	18	66	12
Carter	13	18	31	2
Reagan	39	39	78	9
Bush[c]	29	17	46	1
Clinton				

[a] The total of pocket vetoes by Grant does not include one bill that was not placed before the President for signature.

[b] Two of Nixon's "pocket vetoes," overruled in the courts, are counted here as regular vetoes.

[c] Bush claimed to pocket veto two bills (H.R. 2712 in 1989 and H.R. 2699 in 1991), but actually returned them to Congress, which attempted to override the veto on the first bill; these vetoes are counted here as regular vetoes because they were returned to Congress. Congress argued that two other pocket vetoes by Bush (of H.J. Res. 390 in 1989 and S. 1176 in 1991) were invalid and that the bills became law. Because the National Archives did not recognize those bills as enacted law, they are counted here as pocket vetoes.

SOURCE: U.S. Senate, Office of the Secretary. *Presidential Vetoes, 1989–1991* (1992), pp. viii-ix.

or kinds of bills vetoed. Neither claim is substantiated by the Constitution itself or the debates of the time. George Washington, who had presided over the Constitutional Convention, used the veto twice in his two terms as President—once for constitutional reasons and once for policy reasons. Andrew Jackson aroused deep antipathy by invoking the veto twelve times. His veto of a bank bill in 1832 infuriated his foes and was the pivotal issue for that year's presidential election. Jackson's sweeping reelection victory was viewed, at least in part, as a referendum on the bank veto. Some of Jackson's vetoes also focused attention on another major issue of the time—government involvement in public works and other internal improvement projects.

Among early Presidents seeking to use the veto, the greatest difficulties were faced by John Tyler. During Tyler's term of office (1841–1845), he vetoed a total of ten bills. While his political problems sprang primarily from his maladroit political leadership, controversy surrounding his use of the veto contributed directly to the effort to impeach him in 1843. Indeed, the two central IMPEACHMENT charges brought against him centered on his alleged improper use of the veto. Tyler also bears the distinction of being the first President to have a veto successfully overridden by Congress (in 1845).

From the 1820s to the 1840s, Congress frequently entertained proposals to modify or to strip the President of the veto power. Yet, after Tyler's term, complaints over the terms and conditions of the veto subsided. For example, despite the many problems faced by Andrew Johnson, none of his opponents charged him with improper use of the veto, even though he vetoed twenty-nine bills from 1865 to 1869, a record number up to that time. Use of the veto exploded after the CIVIL WAR. From the first veto to 1868, Presidents vetoed eighty-eight bills. From that time to 1990, more than two thousand bills were vetoed.

Franklin D. Roosevelt holds the record for the most vetoes, blocking a total of 635 bills in his four terms. On a per-year basis, Roosevelt comes in second behind Grover Cleveland, who averaged seventy-three vetoes per year (584 total). Most of these two Presidents' vetoes involved private bills sponsored by members of Congress trying to obtain relief for specific individuals seeking pensions and other private benefits that only Congress could authorize.

As use of the veto increased, its importance seemed to recede as Presidents acquired a wide array of political powers that enabled them to influence virtually every aspect of the legislative process. Yet the veto power provided a key means by which Presidents inserted themselves into the legislative process. Early in the nineteenth century, many in Congress considered it improper for Presidents to express public opinions about legislation pending before Congress, based on the fear that such expressions might taint or alter the congressional deliberations. As the veto was used more often, however, Senators and Representatives began openly to solicit Presidents' opinions as to whether they might be planning to veto legislation. These informal inquiries opened the door to more formal requests that Presidents submit statements of their legislative preferences to Congress—a process that now takes the form of extensive legislative agendas presented to Congress annually by the President.

Consequences of the Veto. Although use of the veto has expanded the power of the presidency, the delicate politics of that power are demonstrated by the fact that vigorous use of the veto has usually been politically detrimental to the Presidents involved. Americans tend to view the veto as a negative, reactive move and to reward Presidents for assertive, positive leadership. Cleveland's prolific vetoes certainly contributed to his defeat in his first bid for reelection in 1888. Franklin Roosevelt, who used a large number of vetoes, seems to be an exception to this rule. His repeated use of the veto was symptomatic of a powerful President who felt free to use all the tools at his disposal. Moreover, most of Roosevelt's vetoes involved bills of little importance. Cleveland was compelled to rely heavily on the veto; Roosevelt could influence legislation in a variety of ways before legislation reached his desk.

In more recent times, Gerald Ford found reliance on a veto strategy to be both necessary and damaging to his presidency. Appointed Vice President by Richard M. Nixon after the resignation of SPIRO T. AGNEW in 1973, Ford suddenly found himself sitting in the OVAL OFFICE when Nixon resigned the following year. Ford had neither won an electoral mandate nor had time to develop a legislative program of his own. As a result, Republican Ford and his aides felt compelled to rely heavily on the veto to try to control the actions of a headstrong post–WATERGATE AFFAIR Democratic Congress. In his two and one half years in office, Ford vetoed sixty-six bills. Taken together, these vetoes helped encourage the attitude that Ford was unable to engage in affirmative governance and the kind of positive leadership the country had come to expect—an attitude that contributed to his defeat in 1976.

George Bush was also criticized by some for overreliance on the veto and an apparent failure to produce positive policy alternatives, but Bush was careful in his use of the veto. (In his first three years in office, for example, he vetoed twenty-five bills; all the vetoes were sustained.)

For Presidents, one appealing trait of the veto is its effectiveness. Of the 1,436 regular vetoes applied by Presidents from 1789 to 1991, only 103 have been overridden by Congress. When that figure is broken down between public and private bills, the record is somewhat less impressive: public bills have been overridden 19.3 percent of the time, private bills 0.8 percent. Still, a presidential success rate of more than 80 percent for important legislation poses a daunting challenge to anyone seeking to overturn a veto.

Various studies of the veto have helped to delineate conditions of its use. Presidents are more likely to use a veto when the executive and legislative branches are controlled by different parties, when the President lacks congressional experience, when the President's public standing is low, and during the second and fourth years of a presidential term. Congress is more likely to override a veto when party control is split between the two branches, when the President's popular support is low, after a midterm election, and in times of economic crisis. In short, a veto is most potent when it is least needed by a President—that is, at the beginning of a term.

A related tool stemming from the veto power is the veto threat. Discussed by ALEXANDER HAMILTON in *Federalist* 73, the veto threat has been an important, if underrecognized, attribute of the veto power. As early as 1789, Washington's expression of displeasure over the passage of a tonnage bill prompted Congress to pass a second bill more to the President's liking. A veto threat forces congressional proponents of a bill to contemplate the task of having to rouse an extraordinary two-thirds majority to ensure the bill's eventual passage—even before the bill has arrived on the President's desk. Such threats may alone be sufficient to modify or deter legislation the President opposes. Threats can also have the effect of an ITEM VETO, in that the President may (and indeed often does) threaten to veto a bill because of an offensive provision. Such occurred frequently in the latter part of the nineteenth century. Rutherford B. Hayes, for example, complained loudly and often about Congress's penchant for attaching objectionable riders to appropriations bills. Congress ignored Hayes's objections on most occasions; nevertheless, Hayes vetoed several bills because of riders and successfully fought override attempts.

Both Ronald Reagan and George Bush were prolific and relatively successful users of the veto threat. For example, of twenty-nine veto threats issued by Reagan from 1981 to 1986, Congress either backed down or modified the legislation in question nineteen times.

Yet the veto threat is not without costs. A threat applied too often is likely to lose credibility, and if threats are followed by too many actual vetoes, Presidents risk being criticized for being too negative and reactive. Resort to frequent veto threats may also be viewed as a sign of presidential weakness, since such threats probably reflect the President's failure to influence the course of legislation in other, more subtle or substantive ways.

Deciding When to Veto. Presidents rarely act alone in making important decisions, and since Washington they have sought advice on whether to veto bills. Washington often solicited opinions from CABINET members such as Hamilton and Thomas Jefferson and from members of Congress such as James Madison.

As the presidency became more institutionalized in the twentieth century, so did the handling of veto decisions. The drive to institutionalize the process stemmed from the volume of legislation and the constitutionally mandated ten-day period within which the veto decision must be made. In typical nineteenth-century practice, when an enrolled bill (passed by Congress but not yet signed into law) reached the White House, a presidential aide would guess which agency or agencies would be affected, have the bill delivered to them, and then wait for a reply. This process yielded inadequate, ill-considered veto decisions.

The effort to deal more systematically with enrolled bills began with the 1921 creation of the Bureau of the Budget (known after 1970 as the OFFICE OF MANAGEMENT AND BUDGET [OMB]). The Budget Bureau was asked to render its views of enrolled appropriations bills as part of the larger effort to enhance executive authority over the budget process. This led naturally to occasional veto recommendations from the bureau. The examination of enrolled bills was expanded by Roosevelt in 1934 to include private bills. By 1938, the Budget Bureau was assessing all enrolled bills, a procedure that included contacting affected departments and compiling views on the bills under scrutiny. Since the 1930s, these procedures have varied little, except that ever greater attention has been focused on the President's priorities as distinct from the independent opinions of affected agencies. Indeed, one of the first actions of the OMB after receiving an enrolled bill is to draft a memorandum summarizing the background, purposes, and relation of the bill to the President's program. This information, along with any agency reactions, is sent to the White House, usually by the fifth day of the ten-day period. There, presidential aides add their own recommendations to assist the President in the final decision. Since the 1960s, the number of WHITE HOUSE STAFF devoted to the consideration of enrolled bills has increased. Still, the OMB continues to exert decisive influence over the veto-versus-sign decision. Although an OMB recommendation to veto does not assure a veto, the President rarely vetoes a bill when OMB does not make such a recommendation.

BIBLIOGRAPHY

Antieau, Chester J. *The Executive Veto.* 1988.
Jackson, Carleton. *Presidential Vetoes, 1792–1945.* 1967.
Mason, Edward C. *The Veto Power.* 1890.
Presidential Vetoes, 1789–1976. U.S. Senate Library. 1978.
Spitzer, Robert J. *The Presidential Veto: Touchstone of the American Presidency.* 1988.
Zinn, Charles J. *The Veto Power of the President.* 1951.

ROBERT J. SPITZER

VICE PRESIDENT. The American vice presidency has always been a somewhat anomalous office. Its awkward nature has provided rich stores for satirists and a source of lingering concern for students of American political institutions. Unlike other major offices, the legitimacy of the vice presidency has always been controversial; whereas other offices undergo attack at the margins, the questions about the vice presidency are more basic and address the very character of, and need for, the office.

The Vice President's Situation. During the twentieth century, particularly since the 1940s, the vice presidency was transformed into a position of greater importance. The development of the office has followed changes in American politics and government, particularly the growth of the presidency since the NEW DEAL. These changes have drawn the vice presidency into the executive branch and made it attractive to competent people with presidential ambitions. Yet this progress has not resolved all problems inherent in the office or eliminated skepticism regarding its ultimate merit.

The doubts about the vice presidency have related to three characteristics that have, to varying degrees, defined the office during its history. First, there is a huge discrepancy between what the Vice President is and what he may become. "I am nothing," recognized John Adams, the first Vice President. "But I may be everything." In eight words Adams expressed a dilemma that has persisted for two hundred years. The office, Adams recognized, was a modest position. Yet as the designated successor in case of the death, resignation, disability, or removal of the President, he may be "everything." Indeed, Vice Presidents become everything with unhappy frequency. Nine have become President following the death or resignation of the CHIEF EXECUTIVE; they have served as President for twenty-six years during terms to which someone else was elected. Put differently, up to 1992, 20 percent of Vice Presidents have been Presidents by succession for 13 percent of the history of the presidency.

If the most evident rationale for the vice presidency is to provide a competent successor ready to assume the presidency following an unscheduled vacancy, the vice presidency must be structured to attract able persons and to prepare them to be President. Yet that plausible purpose falls victim to the huge disparity between the power of the presidency and the power of the vice presidency. For how can a "nothing" office routinely attract persons of presidential caliber? How can a sinecure engage its occupant sufficiently to prepare him to assume the presidency?

The vice presidency seems to deviate from basic premises of American government in a second important respect. Certainly the belief that decision makers should be elected by or accountable to the populace remains a fundamental tenet of American democracy. Notwithstanding the survival of the ELECTORAL COLLEGE, most Americans would no doubt apply that principle most rigorously to the presidency. Yet the Vice President is not separately elected, and has not been since 1804. He comes as part of a package under circumstances that limit greatly the ability of the electorate to vote based upon the relative merits of the vice presidential candidates. Nonetheless Vice Presidents may serve as President following the premature departure of the elected Chief Executive for as much as four years without being elected directly. Indeed, on seven occasions presidential successions have occurred with more than half of the four-year term remaining; in five instances more than three years and five months lay ahead.

Finally, the constitutional scheme places the vice presidency in an ambiguous position. By design it is something of a hybrid between the executive and legislative branches. The Vice President is elected with the President, becomes President or Acting President upon the death, resignation, removal, or disability of the President and has acquired some prerogatives within the executive branch such as membership in the CABINET by custom and in the NATIONAL SECURITY COUNCIL by statute. Yet his sole constitutional function of an ongoing nature is to preside over the Senate, a role that, though seldom performed, allows him to break

Vice Presidents of the United States

President	Vice President
1 Washington	John Adams, 1789–1797
2 J. Adams	Thomas Jefferson, 1797–1801
3 Jefferson	Aaron Burr, 1801–1805
	George Clinton, 1805–1809
4 Madison	George Clinton, 1809–1813
	Elbridge Gerry, 1813–1814
5 Monroe	Daniel D. Tompkins, 1817–1825
6 J. Q. Adams	John C. Calhoun, 1825–1829
7 Jackson	John C. Calhoun, 1829–1832
	Martin Van Buren, 1833–1837
8 Van Buren	Richard M. Johnson, 1837–1841
9 W. H. Harrison	John Tyler, 1841
10 Tyler	None
11 Polk	George M. Dallas, 1845–1849
12 Taylor	Millard Fillmore, 1849–1850
13 Fillmore	None
14 Pierce	William R.D. King, 1853
15 Buchanan	John C. Breckinridge, 1857–1861
16 Lincoln	Hannibal Hamlin, 1861–1865
	Andrew Johnson, 1865
17 A. Johnson	None
18 Grant	Schuyler Colfax, 1869–1873
	Henry Wilson, 1873–1875
19 Hayes	William A. Wheeler, 1877–1881
20 Garfield	Chester A. Arthur, 1881
21 Arthur	None

President	Vice President
22 Cleveland	Thomas A. Hendricks, 1885
23 B. Harrison	Levi P. Morton, 1889–1893
24 Cleveland	Adlai E. Stevenson, 1893–1897
25 McKinley	Garret T. Hobart, 1897–1899
	Theodore Roosevelt, 1901
26 T. Roosevelt	Charles W. Fairbanks, 1905–1909
27 Taft	James Schoolcraft Sherman, 1909–1912
28 Wilson	Thomas R. Marshall, 1913–1921
29 Harding	Calvin Coolidge, 1921–1923
30 Coolidge	Charles D. Dawes, 1925–1929
31 Hoover	Charles Curtis, 1929–1933
32 F. D. Roosevelt	John Nance Garner, 1933–1941
	Henry A. Wallace, 1941–1945
	Harry S. Truman, 1945
33 Truman	Alben W. Barkley, 1949–1953
34 Eisenhower	Richard M. Nixon, 1953–1961
35 Kennedy	Lyndon B. Johnson, 1961–1963
36 L. B. Johnson	Hubert Humphrey, 1965–1969
37 Nixon	Spiro Agnew, 1969–1973
	Gerald R. Ford, 1973–1974
38 Ford	Nelson A. Rockefeller, 1974–1977
39 Carter	Walter F. Mondale, 1977–1981
40 Reagan	George Bush, 1981–1989
41 Bush	Dan Quayle, 1989–1993
42 Clinton	Al Gore, 1993–

tie votes and to make parliamentary rulings. Over time the vice presidency has migrated between the two branches in search of a home. Yet the manner in which Vice Presidents have been selected and the security of their tenure have complicated their quest to find a place where they are welcomed. Until recently presidential candidates played little or no role in the selection of their running mate; once in office, the President could not remove the second man until the end of the term. Accordingly, Presidents historically have been reticent to entrust executive powers to their Vice President. Similarly, unlike other legislative officers the Vice President is not chosen by the body over which he presides; the Senate can remove him only if the House of Representatives first goes to the extraordinary means of impeaching him. Not surprisingly, the Senate has not assigned much power to an officer not responsible to it.

The Constitutional Design. The reasoning that inspired the creation of the office is somewhat obscure. The position was an afterthought conceived in the closing days of the CONSTITUTIONAL CONVENTION and devised despite the misgivings of prominent members including ALEXANDER HAMILTON who observed that "the appointment of an extraordinary person, as Vice-President, has been objected to as superfluous, if not mischievous." Although much discussion addressed the need for a presiding officer who was not a Senator (otherwise the Senate might deadlock and some state would be underrepresented if one of its two delegates relinquished his vote to chair the sessions), this consideration did not lead to the invention of the office. These difficulties were susceptible to other solutions. Moreover, some observed that the Vice President "would be without employment" unless he presided over the Senate, an argument that suggests that the role was an expedient to occupy the Vice President.

The Founders spent little time discussing presidential succession, making that factor an unlikely explanation for the office. More likely, the office was invented to facilitate the election of a national President. Fearing that electors would favor citizens from their home state for President, the Founders gave electors two votes but required that they cast at least one for a citizen of a different state. They expected the electors' second-choice votes to identify a national consensus President; the second office, the Founders apparently reasoned, would ensure that electors voted seriously. The office, said delegate Hugh Williamson, "was introduced only for the sake of a valuable mode of election which required two to be chosen at the same time."

Inasmuch as the electoral scheme offered electors the opportunity to vote for two persons of presidential caliber, it seemed destined to produce Vice Presidents of real stature. Indeed, the first two Vice Presidents—John Adams and Thomas Jefferson—were men of unquestioned ability who brought impeccable credentials to the office. Adams established cordial relations with President George Washington and acted as one of his chief advisers. He occasionally met with the Cabinet, though apparently Jefferson, as Secretary of State, not Adams, presided in Washington's absence. Yet Adams was essentially a legislative officer who regularly presided over the Senate and indeed broke twenty-nine deadlocks, the most by any Vice President.

The office was not unduly taxing; Adams found it "too inactive and insignificant" and, during his first term, wrote that "[m]y country has in its wisdom contrived for me the most insignificant office that ever the invention of man contrived or his imagination conceived; . . . I can do neither good nor evil." Adams hoped Jefferson would follow him "for . . . if he could do no good, he could do no harm." Jefferson viewed the office as "honorable and easy" and admitted to some ambivalence regarding whether he would rather be Vice President or not. Jefferson insisted that the Vice President was a legislative officer and accordingly refused proffered assignments from Adams.

The initial system, then, provided for a truly elected Vice President and filled the office with eminent figures. Separate election raised the specter of a Vice President at odds with the Chief Executive on fundamental issues of policy. The office was essentially a creature of the legislative branch particularly when President and Vice President represented different parties.

The Nineteenth-century Vice Presidency. The office underwent fundamental change in 1804. Parties had begun to form and to designate a ticket; electors would cast their votes for the two men their party had designated. In 1800 the Republican-Democratic presidential nominee, Thomas Jefferson, and the vice presidential nominee, AARON BURR, received an equal number of votes. Although Jefferson was clearly intended for the presidency, the election was thrown into the House of Representatives, which held thirty-six ballots before Jefferson prevailed. The traumatic events caused dissatisfaction with the electoral system. Accordingly, the TWELFTH AMENDMENT to the Constitution was ratified in 1804; it provided that electors would vote separately for President and Vice President.

The amendment worked a dramatic change in the vice presidency. Some legislators anticipated that the new electoral procedure would jeopardize the ability of the office to provide high caliber successors. Their fears were prophetic.

The remainder of the nineteenth century witnessed a sharp decline in the vice presidency. Inasmuch as the Vice President was no longer the runner-up for President the quality of Vice Presidents suffered. The running mate was chosen based on partisan considerations rather than merit. Occasionally, the office still attracted someone of presidential stature, JOHN C. CALHOUN and Martin Van Buren being two examples. Most occupants fell far short of that standard. GEORGE CLINTON (1805–1812), ELBRIDGE GERRY (1813–1814), WILLIAM R. KING (1853), and THOMAS A. HENDRICKS (1885) had served in important positions but were in failing health when they became Vice President. Others brought lackluster credentials to the office. Chester A. Arthur's prior public service consisted of seven years as collector of customs for the port of New York; GARRET A. HOBART had served as presiding officer of the New Jersey assembly and state senate but had never held statewide or national office. Millard Fillmore had served in the House of Representatives but had not been considered presidential timber before becoming Zachary Taylor's running mate. LEVI P. MORTON (1889–1893) served in the House and as minister to France but had generally been unsuccessful when he ran for office. His successor, ADLAI E. STEVENSON (1893–1897), was Assistant Postmaster General in President Grover Cleveland's first term before becoming Vice President in his second.

The conduct of nineteenth-century Vice Presidents often fell below the deportment that would have been expected. DANIEL D. TOMPKINS spent most of his term responding to charges that he had improperly used public funds as governor of New York. RICHARD M. JOHNSON kept a series of slave mistresses and preferred presiding over his tavern to the Senate. Andrew Johnson appeared intoxicated at his inauguration. SCHUYLER COLFAX was nearly impeached for questionable financial transactions.

Election as a ticket promoted, but did not ensure, compatibility. Party leaders, not the presidential candidate, typically filled the second spot. Accordingly, the Vice President was not beholden to the Chief Executive for his position. Moreover, the vice presidential nomination was often used to unify the party by selecting a candidate who disagreed with the standard-bearer on important issues to placate a faction not enchanted with the head of the ticket. Occasionally, harmonious relations did exist, most notably between James Madison and Gerry, Andrew Jackson and Van Buren, James Polk and GEORGE DALLAS, and William McKinley and Hobart. More often, acrimony characterized dealings between the occupants of the two positions. Clinton refused to attend Madison's inauguration and was contemptuous of him. Calhoun openly opposed Jackson on important matters. Arthur denounced President James Garfield in a newspaper article.

The nineteenth-century vice presidency was a legislative office. Although an occasional President involved his running mate in business of the executive branch—Polk consulted Dallas and McKinley conferred with Hobart—they were exceptions. Rarely did Presidents enlist the assistance of their Vice President. The second man was not included in Cabinet meetings or sent on international missions. His sole governmental function was to chair sessions of the Senate. Although some—Dallas, Morton, and Hobart for instance—discharged that task with skill, others were indifferent to that role. Tompkins frequently absented himself, Richard Johnson preferred his tavern, HENRY WILSON spent his term writing a three-volume history of slavery in America.

On four occasions, nineteenth-century Vice Presidents succeeded to the presidency upon the death of the Chief Executive. When President William Henry Harrison died in 1841, John Tyler became the first Vice President to confront questions relating to presidential succession. The Constitution provided that in case of the President's death, resignation, removal, or inability "to discharge the powers and duties of the said office, the same shall devolve on the Vice President." The clause was ambiguous as to whether what devolved was the "office" or merely its "powers and duties." The issue had more than academic significance. If the "powers and duties" only passed to the Vice President, a disabled President could, upon termination of the inability, resume his position. If, on the other hand, the office itself was transferred, the elected Chief Executive would apparently be displaced permanently even if temporarily disabled. Although informed opinion was divided, Tyler insisted that he became President, not merely a Vice President acting as President. Tyler probably mistook the Framers' intent; records of the Constitutional Convention sug-

gest that they intended that the powers, but not the office, pass to the Vice President. Nonetheless, the TYLER PRECEDENT prevailed and when Fillmore, Andrew Johnson, and Arthur were faced with an unscheduled presidential vacancy they each claimed that they became, and they were accepted as, President.

Several features characterized the four instances of presidential succession in the nineteenth century. On each occasion the Vice President came either from a different party or faction than his predecessor. Major upheavals in policy and personnel ensued. All but one member of the Cabinet that Tyler inherited resigned within five months. Arthur replaced six of seven Cabinet members in five months; Fillmore discharged Taylor's entire Cabinet in approximately two months. Each President by succession occupied a position of weakness for the remainder of his term. None won a term of his own.

Finally, the nineteenth-century vice presidency became a poor stepping stone to the presidency. Of the twenty-one Vice Presidents in the nineteenth century after the Twelfth Amendment only one (Van Buren) was elected Chief Executive. Six were not nominated for a second term with the Chief Executive. The four who became President by succession were not re-elected. Of the twenty-one Vice Presidents from 1805 to 1899, only three (Clinton, Calhoun, and Hendricks) had been plausible presidential candidates before seeking at lest one term as Vice President; only Van Buren and JOHN C. BRECKINRIDGE of those who did not succeed to the presidency subsequently became a serious candidate.

In short, the nineteenth-century vice presidency was a hollow shell. The office and the quality of its occupants declined precipitously after 1804. In *Congressional Government*, first published in 1885, Woodrow Wilson devoted less than a page to the vice presidency because "the chief embarrassment in discussing his office is, that in explaining how little there is to be said about it one has evidently said all there is to say."

The Twentieth-century Office. The new century began a slow, but discernible rise in the office. McKinley's Vice Presidents, in different ways, revealed long latent possibilities in the office. Owing to his rapport with the Chief Executive, Hobart gained real influence beyond what would have been anticipated for someone whose résumé was so modest. Conversely, Theodore Roosevelt lacked a close relationship with McKinley but elevated the office by his prominence, his energy, and by becoming the first President by succession to win his own term.

To be sure, the office did not suddenly become robust. From 1900 until 1940, party leaders, not the presidential candidate, filled the second spot on the ticket. Accordingly, the running mate was not beholden to the Chief Executive. The two generally came from different wings of their party; often they were not personally or politically compatible. Presidents Theodore Roosevelt, William Howard Taft, and Herbert Hoover opposed the selections of Vice Presidents CHARLES W. FAIRBANKS (1905–1909), JAMES S. SHERMAN (1909–1913), and CHARLES CURTIS (1929–1933) respectively; once in office, the second man was ignored. THOMAS MARSHALL (1913–1921) was more involved but he, too, found himself often excluded.

Yet the office underwent some change during the first half century. First, the quality of Vice Presidents improved. From the anonymous figures of the nineteenth century, the office began to attract persons of stature. Roosevelt, Fairbanks, Curtis, JOHN NANCE GARNER (1933–1941), and ALBEN W. BARKLEY (1949–1953) were leaders in their parties before becoming Vice President; CHARLES G. DAWES (1925–1929) had received the Nobel Peace Prize; HENRY A. WALLACE (1941–1945) had served in the Cabinet.

Second, the office handled presidential succession more efficiently. Whereas nineteenth-century Vice Presidents quickly jettisoned the Cabinets they inherited, Roosevelt and Calvin Coolidge essentially retained top administration officials, thereby lending stability to government. Whereas those who became President in the nineteenth century following the death of their predecessor failed to be reelected or even renominated, Roosevelt, Coolidge, and Harry S. Truman won terms.

Moreover, the vice presidency was no longer a dead end for the ambitious. In addition to the three Vice Presidents who succeeded to the presidency and won election in their own right, others made credible, though unsuccessful attempts. Fairbanks campaigned to follow Roosevelt but failed largely due to the President's active opposition. Marshall and Dawes enjoyed some support for the presidential nomination. Garner was the most popular Democrat in preference polls from 1937 to 1940, excluding Franklin D. Roosevelt; his ambitions fell victim to Roosevelt's desire for a third term.

Finally, the duties of the vice presidency underwent subtle change. Whereas nineteenth-century Vice Presidents presided over the Senate and did little else, some Vice Presidents assumed duties in the executive branch. The change began with Hobart, who became a close adviser to President McKinley, and continued during the tenure of some of his successors. Roosevelt, Fairbanks, and Curtis, for instance, had little, if any, discernible involvement and Dawes refused to meet with the Cabinet before he was invited to do so. Yet during Wilson's absence from the country Marshall became the first Vice President to preside over Cabinet meetings, a task he undertook diffidently and surrendered eagerly. Coolidge attended Cabinet meetings, as did Garner, Wallace, and Barkley. Garner advised Roosevelt on legislative and other matters; Wallace chaired the Economic Defense Board, an entity that included seven Cabinet members. By statute, Vice Presidents from Barkley on became members of the NATIONAL SECURITY COUNCIL.

The Modern American Vice Presidency. The real growth in the vice presidency began during the NEW DEAL and continued at an accelerated rate in the following decades. The New Deal and WORLD WAR II worked fundamental changes in government. In essence, those events drew power to the federal government generally and to the presidency in particular, increasing the influence of its occupant with respect to Congress and political parties.

These changes transformed the vice presidency. First, the office was in effect pulled into the executive branch. No longer did Vice Presidents define themselves, as had Jefferson and Dawes, as legislative officers precluded from participating in the executive branch. Rather, they began to receive presidential assignments. As the President became responsible for offering a legislative agenda, Vice Presidents, especially those with congressional experience, became active as a liaison to Capitol Hill. Garner, for instance, advised Roosevelt on legislative strategy and lobbied for the New Deal. Richard M. Nixon brought legislative background to the Eisenhower administration. Even after Presidents developed their own professional legislative staffs, a Vice President like WALTER F. MONDALE could help with Congress.

As the presidency became the fulcrum of government and its occupant became expected to address a range of issues, Presidents often appointed Vice Presidents to head executive commissions. Nixon chaired the President's Committee on Government Contracts and Lyndon B. Johnson headed the President's Committee on Equal Employment Opportunity, both of which had some responsibilities in combatting racial discrimination. NELSON A. ROCKEFELLER chaired the Domestic Council and an investigation into the CENTRAL INTELLIGENCE AGENCY.

Although many Vice Presidents embraced such "line" assignments, and some had significance, they also posed real dangers. The direct responsibilities Vice Presidents accepted normally invaded the province of some other player. Accordingly, each such assignment risked antagonizing other administration officials, often for little real power. Vice Presidents had to move cautiously to avoid an embarrassing reversal by the Chief Executive. Many assignments were so trivial they demeaned the vice presidency; HUBERT H. HUMPHREY, for instance chaired presidential committees on marine resources, Indian opportunity, and domestic travel, issues not high on the nation's agenda in the 1960s, or since. Yet Vice Presidents typically lacked sufficient staff support to handle true administrative tasks. Moreover, line assignments took time that could better have been spent on more urgent issues.

Vice Presidents also assumed some role in international affairs. From Barkley on, they were members of the National Security Council, which, depending on the extent to which the President used that body, afforded some opportunity to learn about and participate in foreign and strategic policy. Vice Presidents also began to make frequent trips abroad. Trips served a variety of purposes including fact finding, building goodwill, and discharging ceremonial functions the President or Secretary of State were too busy to perform. They gave Vice Presidents exposure and the semblance of participation.

Vice Presidents also became active as administration spokespersons, able to exploit the podium their office guaranteed to raise issues that shaped the nation's political discourse. Nixon, for instance, spoke widely on the threat of communism. Johnson delivered a series of addresses on civil rights. Humphrey became a leading salesperson of the VIETNAM WAR. SPIRO T. AGNEW and DAN QUAYLE accused diverse elites of corrupting societal values.

Moreover, Vice Presidents devoted time to partisan work—raising funds, appearing for administration allies, campaigning for the President's renomination—particularly under Presidents who cultivated a nonpolitical image. Nixon, for instance, performed especially well in this task for the Eisenhower administration. As presidential primaries proliferated and the President suddenly became subject to challenge for renomination, Vice Presidents like Mondale and Quayle undertook much of the campaign role for Presidents Jimmy Carter and George Bush respectively.

Finally, Vice Presidents became presidential advisers. Attendance at Cabinet meetings symbolized the office's migration toward the executive branch where some achieved some influence. Garner advised Roosevelt during their first term before their relationship deteriorated. Rockefeller persuaded Ford to undertake some initiatives early in his tenure before his position eroded as the term continued.

Mondale, more than any other Vice President, achieved real influence in that role. He lunched alone with Carter once a week during which he could raise any topic. He was granted access to the same documents Carter received and was given the right to attend any meeting Carter held. The Vice President's staff, which had been relatively small during the 1960s, exceeded sixty persons during Mondale's tenure. Mondale was given an office in the White House close to the OVAL OFFICE and Carter's other top advisers; physical proximity encouraged involvement. Mondale was able to place associates in important administration positions and formed alliances with key members of Carter's staff. He participated in virtually all significant decisions during the Carter years and his counsel was valued.

Bush and Quayle retained many of these amenities—the lunch, the staff, the office. Bush's experience in foreign policy and in Washington, D.C., were important assets in the Reagan White House populated as it initially was with outsiders. Quayle participated actively in debates in the Bush White House though it is not clear that he had the clout Mondale and, to some extent, Bush had had. Vice President AL GORE played a prominent role as presidential adviser in choosing personnel for the Clinton administration.

Selecting Vice Presidents. The rise of the presidency also changed the manner of selecting vice presidential candidates. Beginning in 1940, the presidential nominee, not party leaders, filled the second spot on the ticket. In that year, Roosevelt forced the convention to accept Wallace despite its misgivings. To be sure, presidential candidates continued, in most cases, to solicit advice from other party leaders and rarely ignored strong sentiment. Still, presidential candidates began to submit a nominee who invariably was selected with little or no opposition. Presidential candidates followed many of the same strategies conventions had long employed in selecting vice presidential candidates. They sought to balance the ticket geographically (e.g., Dewey-Warren, Dukakis-Bentsen) or ideologically (e.g., Carter-Mondale) or to placate a defeated wing of the party (e.g., Kennedy-Johnson, Reagan-Bush). They chose running mates to appeal to an important state (e.g., Earl Warren, Johnson), to emphasize a particular issue (e.g., Nixon) or to place an effective campaigner on the ticket. Yet these strategies were rarely pursued to the extremes common in the nineteenth and early twentieth centuries. The exigencies of a national campaign with many competitive states made it impractical to pick a running mate with one state's electoral votes in mind. The need to preserve national credibility made it difficult for presidential candidates to select running mates whose views on important issues diametrically opposed their own. The ideological balance that occurs tends to be much more subtle. Finally, the scrutiny vice presidential candidates receive provided some incentive to select a running mate of presidential quality. On rare occasions, presidential candidates ignored ticket-balancing criteria and selected a running mate with similar characteristics to the standard-bearer in order to emphasize particular issues or themes. The most successful examples of this strategy were the Truman-Barkley ticket of 1948 and the Clinton-Gore ticket of 1992. With few exceptions, vice presidential candidates on winning tickets have generally brought imposing credentials to the office.

The increased presidential role in vice presidential selection has had implications for the vice presidency. First, the President has become responsible for the selection of his running mate. Accordingly he has some incentive to involve the second man at least to some degree to deter speculation that he regretted his choice. Moreover, the new method has increased the likelihood that the two top officers would be compatible politically and personally. Theoretically the candidate for the top spot could make certain that his running mate shared similar views. Although some Presidents and Vice Presidents have disliked each other—Nixon and Agnew, for instance—other relationships have been harmonious (Carter and Mondale, Reagan and Bush come to mind).

The succession of Vice Presidents to the presidency has changed also. The Truman, Johnson, and Ford successions operated relatively smoothly under quite different circumstances; Truman and Johnson won terms of their own and Ford lost but narrowly even while inheriting the baggage of the WATERGATE AFFAIR. Owing to the vast responsibilities of the President, it has become far more difficult to select a running mate totally unsuited to office. With rare exceptions modern Vice Presidents have brought to office impressive credentials. Since 1952 every Vice President except Agnew and Quayle had either been considered presidential timber prior to his selection or else subsequently won his party's nomination. Presidents particularly since Carter have taken steps to ensure that the second man would be knowledgeable regarding administration programs and pressing issues. Sections 3 and 4 of the TWENTY-FIFTH AMENDMENT, which provide relatively clear guidelines for handling situations of presidential disability, enhanced the ability of the Vice President to act temporarily to avoid a hiatus in the exercise of presidential power.

Finally, during the latter half of the twentieth cen-

tury the vice presidency has become the best springboard to a presidential nomination. Virtually every Vice President since Nixon has either become President, been nominated by his party, or been a serious contender for the nomination. Ratification of the Twenty-fifth Amendment, which includes a mechanism for filling vice presidential vacancies, reflected the new respectability of the job. Presidential candidates with a serious chance of winning have found that virtually all leading figures in their party will make themselves available for the ticket.

Although the vice presidency has achieved new stature its growth has not resolved all of the problems that historically afflicted it. The office remains devoid of any ongoing function other than to inquire regularly regarding the President's health. The Vice President depends on the President for the assignments that give his service meaning and make his office something. But, as Hubert Humphrey observed, "He who giveth can taketh away and often does."

Accordingly, the success of a vice presidency depends on the relationship between the President and Vice President, the relationship between the Vice President and the WHITE HOUSE STAFF, and the ability of the second man to offer resources the administration needs. All factors become important in determining a Vice President's success. Rockefeller clearly had skills and experience that the Ford administration needed and enjoyed cordial relations with the President. Yet, the animosity that developed between Rockefeller and the White House staff, particularly Chief of Staff Donald Rumsfeld, undermined his effectiveness. Agnew's standing with the Republican right wing provided an asset for the Nixon administration but Nixon excluded his running mate due to his low regard for him. Certainly the most successful vice presidency was Mondale's; he developed a close rapport with the President and his staff that enabled him to be a player in all significant decisions. His experience in Washington and ties to traditional Democratic groups with which the administration was weak enhanced his position as did the manner in which he and Carter shaped his role and their sensitivities to each other.

The rise of the vice presidency has neither satisfied the skeptics nor muted the calls for reform. Professor Arthur M. Schlesinger, Jr., has forcefully advocated abolition of the vice presidency. He argues that the office is a "maiming" rather than a "making" job whose incumbent devotes his time to insignificant makework. He objects that the Vice President is not truly elected; he would favor having a caretaker succeed temporarily following a presidential vacancy with a special election to follow. Others favor expanding the office to assign its occupant meaningful roles in the executive branch, such as requiring him to hold a Cabinet position, or giving him a vote or powers in the Senate. Finally, a third reform impulse focuses on the selection of the Vice President. The preferred solutions range from having tickets run together in PRESIDENTIAL PRIMARIES to voting separately for the two offices to voting not at all for the Vice President but instead allowing the President o nominate him after the election subject to approval by each house of Congress as is done under the Twenty-fifth Amendment.

It seems unlikely that any of these reforms will be enacted or that they would improve the overall performance of government. The changes that have enhanced the office in recent decades seem likely to continue. Further growth in the vice presidency will follow larger changes in American politics and government and will depend upon the relation between future Presidents and Vice Presidents.

BIBLIOGRAPHY

Feerick, John D. *From Failing Hands*. 1965.

Goldstein, Joel K. *The Modern American Vice Presidency: The Transformation of a Political Institution*. 1982.

A Heartbeat Away. Report of the Twentieth Century Fund Task Force on the Vice Presidency. 1988.

Light, Paul C. *Vice-Presidential Power: Advice and Influence in the White House*. 1984.

Milkis, Sidney M., and Michael Nelson. *The American Presidency: Origins and Development, 1776–1990*. 1990. Chapter 14, "The Vice Presidency."

Pika, Joseph A. "Bush, Quayle and the New Vice Presidency." In *The Presidency and the Political System*. Edited by Michael Nelson. 3d ed. 1990.

Schlesinger, Arthur M., Jr. "On the Presidential Succession." *Political Science Quarterly* 89 (1974): 475–505.

"Symposium on the Vice-Presidency." *Fordham Law Review* 45 (1977): 707–799.

Williams, Irving G. *The Rise of the Vice Presidency*. 1956.

Witcover, Jules. *Crapshoot: Rolling the Dice on the Vice Presidency*. 1992.

Young, Donald. *American Roulette: The History and Dilemma of the Vice Presidency*. Rev. ed. 1972.

JOEL K. GOLDSTEIN

VICE PRESIDENT'S RESIDENCE. The Official Residence of the Vice President is a white-painted three-story brick Victorian house located on the grounds of the U.S. Naval Observatory. The Residence and its immediate grounds, at Massachusetts Avenue and 34th Street in northwest Washington, D.C., occupy twelve of the Naval Observatory's seventy-three acres. Built in 1893 for the superintendent of the Naval Observatory, the structure served from 1929 until 1974 as the official residence of the Chief of Naval Operations. In 1974 the premises were designated as the temporary Official Residence of the Vice President (P.L. 93-346).

The main floor of the Residence includes a dining room, a living room, a combination garden and sun room, a small pantry, an office for the administrator of the Residence, and bathrooms. Between the first and second floors is an enclosed patio. The second and third floors comprise the family living quarters. The second floor contains two bedrooms, a sitting room, an office for the Vice President, and bathrooms. The third floor includes four bedrooms, a sitting room, an office, and bathrooms. A kitchen, laundry room, mess stewards' room, and Secret Service room are located in the basement.

Leisure facilities on the grounds include a swimming pool, a golf putting green, and a tennis court. A helicopter landing pad for the Vice President's helicopter is also located on the grounds.

The Residence carries a temporary designation because the Navy Department still owns the property. Navy personnel staff the entrance to the Naval Observatory grounds and provide security for the area, but the Secret Service is responsible for the security of the Vice President and of the Residence.

The Navy is also responsible for the custody, maintenance, and renovation of the Residence and its surroundings. A handful of Navy personnel are assigned to the Residence for day-to-day maintenance and monitoring functions. Personnel assigned to the Naval Observatory tend the gardens and provide other services as needed. In addition, several Navy mess stewards assigned to the Residence prepare and serve meals, take care of the laundry, and perform other general housekeeping functions. Additional stewards are provided as needed, mostly when the Vice President is hosting official functions.

The Navy pays for all the operations and personnel involved. In addition, a small line-item appropriation in the annual budget of the Executive Office of the President provides for an administrator and for the daily operation of the Residence.

The need for an official residence for the Vice President had been obvious for some time before one was designated. The cost of safeguarding the Vice President and his family had risen sharply, because each time a new Vice President took office completely new security arrangements had to be created. Moreover, few Vice Presidents had the financial means necessary to occupy a residence compatible with the office and with the official entertainment requirements associated with it.

Vice President Walter Mondale was the first Vice President to live in the Residence, moving in with his family in 1977. Since then, every Vice President has lived in the Residence.

BIBLIOGRAPHY

Cleere, S. Gail. *The House on Observatory Hill: Home of the Vice President of the United States.* 1989.

ROGELIO GARCIA

VIETNAM WAR. The Vietnam War was a presidential war. Long before President Lyndon Johnson deployed over half a million U.S. troops in Vietnam without first seeking a congressional DECLARATION OF WAR, he and his predecessors in the Oval Office had dominated and controlled the policy process that brought the United States to that action.

Although Franklin Roosevelt exercised enormous freedom as COMMANDER IN CHIEF during WORLD WAR II and had on occasion criticized French colonial rule in Indochina, he left no clearly defined policy in Vietnam. With Roosevelt's death in 1945, it fell to Harry Truman to define postwar presidential leadership in foreign policy and to articulate a U.S. approach to Southeast Asia. Drawing on a small group of advisers more experienced than he in foreign affairs, notably DEAN ACHESON from the State Department, Truman waged a campaign aimed at securing congressional support for his tough line against the Soviet Union. With his TRUMAN DOCTRINE speech, he used the presidency to proclaim the global danger of communist totalitarianism. His rhetoric led Congress and the public to accept major commitments, like the MARSHALL PLAN and NATO, and seemingly minor steps, like providing military assistance to French forces fighting a communist-led independence movement in Vietnam. When Truman sent American troops to fight in Korea in 1950 without a congressional declaration of war [see KOREAN WAR] and, at the same time and with little notice, expanded aid to the French in Indochina, presidential preeminence in conducting the COLD WAR in Asia was established.

When Dwight Eisenhower took office in 1953, the French prospects for success in Vietnam appeared dim, and the new President and his staunchly anticommunist Secretary of State, JOHN FOSTER DULLES, faced a pivotal decision. Should they continue support of their NATO ally, France, in the struggle against global communism, or should they separate the United States from France's failing effort to reassert its colonial authority? Drawing on his army command experience from World War II, Eisenhower felt confident involving himself in this military-strategic decision. He made the determination not to launch a U.S. air attack to rescue besieged French forces during the decisive battle at Dienbienphu in 1954. Like Truman, however, he used the BULLY PULPIT of his office to proclaim the strategic importance of Vietnam. He compared the country and its neighbors to "falling dominoes" and claimed that the collapse of one would topple the others. After France agreed to a cease-fire at the Geneva Conference of 1954, Eisenhower directed the creation of the Southeast Asia Treaty Organization and began a U.S. assistance program to build a new nation in the southern remnant of Vietnam that was temporarily beyond the military control of the Vietnamese communists. Eisenhower had managed the public and political dimensions of the Vietnam issue masterfully. He appeared cautious but firm. The fatal flaw, however was that his new creation, South Vietnam, was totally dependent on the United States for survival.

John Kennedy entered the White House pledging progress, even victory, in the stalemated cold war that ranged from the nuclear standoff with the Soviet Union to the frustrating local conflict in Vietnam. Like Truman and Eisenhower, he shunned public debate on Indochina and relied only on a small group of executive advisers. He decided to escalate U.S. aid to the floundering government of President Ngo Dinh Diem in South Vietnam. Unlike the confident Eisenhower, Kennedy felt compelled to prove that he could produce results, especially after his administration began with a bungled invasion of CUBA [see BAY OF PIGS INVASION] and an indecisive confrontation with the Soviet Union over Berlin [see BERLIN CRISIS]. Kennedy doubled U.S. financial assistance to Saigon, placed 16,500 military advisers in South Vietnam, and gave his approval to U.S. complicity in a coup that produced Diem's murder.

Lyndon Johnson inherited from Kennedy a situation out of control in Vietnam. Although some Kennedy advisers later claimed that their chief would have gotten out of Vietnam if he had lived, Johnson believed that Kennedy's commitment to South Vietnam, as well as those of Eisenhower and Truman, required the United States to stand firm. No stronger without Diem than with him, the Saigon regime remained completely dependent on U.S. backing. Acutely aware that his own skills and interests were in his domestic reform program [see GREAT SOCIETY], Johnson allowed himself to be convinced by aides like Secretary of State DEAN RUSK and Secretary of Defense ROBERT S. McNAMARA, holdovers from the Kennedy administration, that military escalation was the answer in Vietnam. As had become the presidential pattern, this decision was reached behind closed doors. An accomplished politician, Johnson calculated that he had to expand the war gradually and with a minimum of discussion to prevent conservatives in Congress from using the war to postpone his domestic agenda. He took the political precaution of using a minor naval incident, however, to obtain from Congress the GULF OF TONKIN RESOLUTION in 1964 that allowed him to use armed force to protect Americans in the region. He then proceeded under this authority and his powers as Commander in Chief to place over 500,000 U.S. troops in Vietnam and to conduct a sustained bombing assault against enemy targets in North and South Vietnam [see PRESIDENTIAL STRATEGIES (VIETNAM)].

Johnson achieved his desired result—passage of the Great Society and the continued survival of South Vietnam—but he did not realize success. The escalation of the fighting only increased South Vietnam's dependency. The mounting violence and the administration's secretive methods produced suspicion, cynicism, and a growing antiwar protest movement that condemned "Johnson's War." The President's combined pursuit of ambitious domestic and foreign programs also increased government expenditure and fueled inflation. After U.S. and South Vietnamese forces suffered brief but stunning reverses during the enemy's Tet Offensive of January 1968, Johnson realized that he was not producing a victory and that Americans other than the vocal protestors were now questioning the costs and purposes of the war. Thus, Johnson announced that he was willing to negotiate and that he would not seek reelection as President.

Although Johnson's post-Tet actions seemed to set the stage for a U.S. withdrawal from Vietnam, Richard Nixon continued American combat for four more years. He and his principal aide, HENRY A. KISSINGER, maintained the practice of keeping the decision making confined to a small group. Indeed, Nixon was more secretive and manipulative than his predecessors. He surreptitiously bombed new areas, like Cambodia, while diverting public attention with a reduction of U.S. ground combat forces. Public outcry erupted in 1970, however, when U.S. troops crossed into Cambodia. National guardsmen killed four students at Kent State University (Ohio) during a protest; it was clear that the war was tearing the United States apart. Nixon appealed to what he called the "silent majority" to support his Vietnam policies, but his critics christened the continued fighting "Nixon's War." The President used wiretapping, tax audits, and other harassment to try to silence his opponents. Some of these abuses of executive power later became part of

the Watergate-related charges against Nixon [see WATERGATE AFFAIR]. Finally, after secret negotiations by Kissinger and more heavy bombing of North Vietnam, Nixon arranged a withdrawal of all remaining U.S. forces in January 1973—an outcome he called "peace with honor" but one that left the internal war raging in Vietnam and Cambodia.

Several facts about presidential conduct of the Vietnam War are apparent. From Truman through Nixon, presidents shared the belief that Vietnam was strategically important to the United States, and each feared that, if South Vietnam was lost as a U.S. cold-war outpost, he would suffer personal political defeat for this outcome. The Presidents displayed differing styles of leadership: Truman was tough, Eisenhower was self-confident, Kennedy was eager, Johnson was misleading, and Nixon was manipulative. Each was determined in his own way, however, to keep Vietnam decision making in his own hands and not share it, especially with Congress. This fact finally led law makers to pass the WAR POWERS RESOLUTION over Nixon's veto in 1973 and to enact other legislation specifically prohibiting further U.S. military action in Indochina.

The last presidential decisions of the Vietnam War fell to Gerald Ford. When the final North Vietnamese assault on the South began in March 1975, Ford's hands were legally tied. He could not respond militarily to the attack or even use U.S. military units to evacuate endangered American diplomats and their Vietnamese staffs. Ford's impotence contrasted sharply with the presidential preeminence that had led the United States into Vietnam. When he finally ordered a desperate helicopter rescue of personnel from the U.S. embassy in Saigon as enemy forces closed in on it, the image of both the presidency and the American nation had reached a low point. Only three weeks later, however, Ford claimed his constitutional authority as Commander in Chief to send U.S. Marines to rescue merchant sailors taken from the U.S. ship *Mayaquez* by Cambodian forces [see MAYAGUEZ INCIDENT]. A majority in Congress and the public applauded his action. Congress and the people had come to oppose the Vietnam War, but the possibility of presidential war remained.

BIBLIOGRAPHY

Anderson, David L., ed. *Shadow on the White House: Presidents and the Vietnam War, 1945–1975*. 1993.

Anderson, David L. *Trapped by Success: The Eisenhower Administration and Vietnam, 1953–1961*. 1991.

Burke, John P., and Fred I. Greenstein. *How Presidents Test Reality: Decisions on Vietnam, 1954 and 1965*. 1989.

Gibbons, William Conrad. *The U.S. Government and the Vietnam War: Executive and Legislative Roles and Relationships.* 3 parts. 1986–1989.

Goodman, Allen E. *The Lost Peace: America's Search for a Negotiated Settlement of the Vietnam War.* 1978.

Kattenburg, Paul M. *The Vietnam Trauma in American Foreign Policy, 1945–75.* 1980.

Small, Melvin. *Johnson, Nixon, and the Doves.* 1988.

VanDeMark, Brian. *Into the Quagmire: Lyndon Johnson and the Escalation of the Vietnam War.* 1991.

DAVID L. ANDERSON

VOTING RIGHTS. Prior to the 1950s, the American presidency had little direct involvement with voting rights policy. The American political tradition and constitutional structure had reserved decisions on voter qualifications and electoral arrangements to state and local governments. Furthermore, the Constitution gave control over the amending process to Congress and the state legislatures, leaving no formal role to the executive branch. Congress dominated construction of the two great enfranchising amendments—the Fifteenth (1870), which prohibited voting discrimination by race, and the Nineteenth (1920), which prohibited voting discrimination by sex—and the federal courts defined their constitutional reach. Although conflict over female suffrage was resolved by the Nineteenth Amendment, conflict over voting by African Americans ultimately drew the presidency into the center of the policy process.

In 1940, 77 percent of the nation's 12.8 million African Americans lived in the South, but only 3.1 percent of the region's voting-age blacks were registered to vote. The postwar attack on racial segregation began in 1944, when the U.S. Supreme Court in *Smith v. Allwright* ruled white-only primaries unconstitutional, and accelerated with the school desegregation decision, *Brown v. Board of Education*, in 1954. By 1956, 25 percent of the South's 5 million voting-age blacks were registered. In 1957 the President and Congress, responding to the rising civil rights movement in the South, enacted the CIVIL RIGHTS ACT OF 1957. Essentially a voting-rights law, it required individuals claiming racial discrimination in voter registration to sue local governments in federal court. By 1964 the percentage of voting-age blacks registered in the South had risen to 41.9 percent, and Congress passed the CIVIL RIGHTS ACT OF 1964, which concentrated on ending job discrimination and desegregating restaurants, hotels, and stores throughout the South.

In the fall 1964 elections, however, black disfranchisement had helped swing five Deep South states to the conservative Republican nominee, BARRY M. GOLD-WATER, while black votes in upper South states had provided slim margins for President Lyndon B. Johnson. Early in 1965 Dr. Martin Luther King, Jr., led voting-rights demonstrations in Selma, Alabama, and in August President Johnson, enjoying huge Democratic majorities in Congress from his landslide victory over Goldwater, signed a Voting Rights Act that lodged enforcement power in the DEPARTMENT OF JUSTICE.

The 1965 statute, by shifting the burden of enforcement from individuals to the ATTORNEY GENERAL, made voting-rights policy a responsibility of the presidency. Without using racial categories, Congress established a simple statistical formula in section 4 of the law that identified seven southern states (Alabama, Georgia, Louisiana, Mississippi, South Carolina, Virginia, and twenty-seven counties in North Carolina) where literacy tests had been used and where fewer than half of the voting-age residents were registered to vote in the 1964 elections. Section 4 then authorized the Justice Department to send federal examiners to these "triggered" jurisdictions and, if necessary, require federally supervised registration. A supplementary preclearance provision (section 5) required these jurisdictions to obtain prior permission from the Attorney General or from a federal district court in Washington for any proposed electoral changes. The Johnson administration and Congress designed the teeth of the Voting Rights Act (sections 4 and 5) as five-year emergency provisions that would force enfranchisement and return electoral authority to state and local jurisdictions in 1970.

The radical new approach of 1965 was remarkably successful. By 1970 more than 930,000 African Americans had been added to the voter rolls in the South. During the 1970s blacks enjoyed free access to the polls, white racist demagogues became largely a relic of the past, and a new type of southern politician began to win statewide office in the South by appealing to blacks and working-class whites alike—most notably governors like Jimmy Carter of Georgia, James B. Hunt of North Carolina, Richard W. Riley of South Carolina, and Bill Clinton of Arkansas.

In 1970 Republican President Richard Nixon proposed a nationwide ban on literacy tests to replace sections 4 and 5 and end the Justice Department's special enforcement powers in the South. The Democratic-controlled Congress, however, renewed the 1965 law for five more years. The key to demands for renewal was section 5, the "insurance" provision designed to prevent sabotage against black electoral chances by racist election officials (through such tactics as converting elective office to appointive offices, increasing candidate filing fees and bond requirements, and manipulating district boundaries to minimize the success of black candidates). Although the Justice Department between 1965 and 1970 had rejected only ten of 345 preclearance requests from covered jurisdictions, section 5 provided important leverage for expanding intervention by the federal courts. In 1969 Chief Justice Earl Warren, in *Allen v. State Board of Elections* (of Mississippi), ruled that the Voting Rights Act not only guaranteed free access to the ballot box but also protected minority voters from the dilution of their potential voting power. Under this ruling, civil rights organizations during the 1970s filed increasingly successful section 5 challenges against electoral arrangements, such as large voting districts and at-large representation, that favored white over minority candidates.

During the 1970s voter-dilution complaints and lawsuits nourished a rapidly growing field in the legal and policy community—the voting-rights bar. It included career attorneys in the Voting Rights Section of the Justice Department, legal staff for civil rights organizations (such as the National Association for the Advancement of Colored People, the Mexican-American Legal Defense and Education Fund, and the American Civil Liberties Union) and private foundations, social science professionals in universities and Washington think tanks, counsel for the Senate and House judiciary committees, and the staff of the Leadership Conference on Civil Rights, which coordinated Washington lobbying for the civil rights coalition. These powerful forces encouraged a receptive Democratic Congress to expand the voting-rights responsibilities of the Justice Department and the federal courts.

In 1975, Congress responded to growing demands from Hispanic rights organizations by amending the Voting Rights Act to create minority-language rights. The 1975 amendments added a language-based trigger (Spanish-speaking, Asian, Alaskan Native, and American Indian) that added Texas, Alaska, Arizona, and scattered counties in the rest of the country to the Justice Department's list of covered jurisdictions and required them to provide bilingual election materials. In 1982, Congress extended section 5 for twenty-five years and expanded the review authority of the Justice Department and federal courts to cover nine states and portions of a dozen others, including large metropolitan areas of California, Massachusetts, Michigan,

and New York. Also in 1982, Congress by large majorities declared in section 2 that citizens bringing a voting-rights lawsuit need show only discriminatory *effects* rather than *intent*—thus reversing a Supreme Court ruling of 1980, *Mobile v. Bolden*, that the 1965 law prohibited only intentional discrimination. So powerful was the civil rights coalition on voting-rights issues that conservatives in the Reagan administration and in the Republican-controlled Senate were unable to make significant changes in the legislation.

In the decade following the 1982 amendments, the Justice Department under Presidents Reagan and George Bush found it advantageous to Republicans to enforce the Voting Rights Act vigorously. Especially following the 1990 census, redistricting requirements that concentrated black and Hispanic voters in minority-majority districts (usually Democratic) tended to elect more Republicans from surrounding districts and in the process threatened to end the careers of senior (white) urban Democrats. By the 1990s there appeared to be little disagreement over voting-rights policy between Bush Republicans and Clinton Democrats. Congress and the presidency shared the consensus of the civil rights coalition and the voting-rights bar that the Justice Department and the federal courts should monitor the electoral arrangements under which a majority of Americans voted, and should require voting districts, however irregular their shapes, that maximized the election of minorities. Opinion polls in the 1990s showed little public understanding of the complexities of vote-dilution issues, and white voters, while strongly opposing affirmative-action preferences for minorities in jobs and education, expressed little opposition to federally required preferences for minorities in electoral outcomes.

BIBLIOGRAPHY

Garrow, David J. *Protest at Selma: Martin Luther King, Jr., and the Voting Rights Act of 1965.* 1978.

Grofman, Bernard, and Chandler Davidson, eds. *Controversies in Minority Voting: The Voting Rights Act in Perspective.* 1992.

Lawson, Steven F. *In Pursuit of Power: Southern Blacks and Electoral Politics, 1965–1982.* 1985.

Parker, Frank R. *Black Votes Count: Political Empowerment in Mississippi after 1965.* 1990.

Thernstrom, Abigail M. *Whose Votes Count? Affirmative Action and Minority Voting Rights.* 1987.

HUGH DAVIS GRAHAM

W

WAGNER ACT (1935). In an effort to foster peaceful industrial relations and revive the American economy during the Great Depression, Congress passed the Wagner (National Labor Relations) Act in 1935. Sponsored by Senator Robert F. Wagner, Democrat of New York, the legislation established an equality of bargaining power between employers and wage earners by protecting the right of workers to unionize free from employer intimidation, thereby, it was hoped, leading to stable collective bargaining and increasing wage levels. Though regarded as one of the NEW DEAL's most important lasting reforms of American economic life, the bill did not have the public backing of President Franklin D. Roosevelt, a Democrat, until shortly before its final passage, but afterwards the act assumed critical political importance to the President.

Roosevelt's ambivalence toward Wagner's bill resulted from feared competition with the centerpiece of his own economic reform program, the NATIONAL INDUSTRIAL RECOVERY ACT (NIRA) of 1933, a law that promoted recovery by encouraging business cooperation. In fact, the Wagner Act itself had stemmed from Senator Wagner's difficult experiences as chairman of the National Labor Board (NLB) of the NIRA, an agency that the President had established to oversee the implementation of Section 7a of the 1933 law, a provision also protecting collective organization. The NLB, however, had no enforcement powers and was too easily ignored. Thus Senator Wagner saw the need for a separate law with the power to determine majority union representation and adjudicate unfair labor practices hampering employee free choice. More importantly, a new National Labor Relations Board (NLRB) with federal court-based enforcement powers would administer the act.

By 1935 the NIRA was increasingly seen as a law that had not worked. Moreover, a conservative Supreme Court was debating the law's constitutionality. President Roosevelt, aware of the NIRA's administrative difficulties and fearing the outcome of the court challenge, finally backed the bill's objectives only shortly before the Court decided the NIRA was unconstitutional in late May 1935. The Wagner Act then assumed critical political importance for Roosevelt as the only existing symbol of the New Deal's commitment to social and economic reform. Afterwards, it played an important role in marshaling labor support for Roosevelt's 1936 landslide reelection. In 1937, a somewhat chastened Supreme Court read the election returns and ruled the law constitutional. The Wagner Act thereafter remained unchanged until the TAFT-HARTLEY ACT revisions of 1947.

BIBLIOGRAPHY

Gross, James A. *The Reshaping of the National Labor Relations Board: National Labor Policy in Transititon, 1937–1947.* 1981.

Vittoz, Stanley. *New Deal Labor Policy and the American Industrial Economy.* 1987.

GILBERT J. GALL

WALKER TARIFF ACT (1846). The period 1833 through 1860 was one of tariff moderation and reduction. The mildly protective Tariff Act of 1842, adopted by a Whig-controlled Congress, had been an exception to such pattern.

James K. Polk, Jacksonian to the core and a consistent opponent of high tariffs and other attributes of HENRY CLAY'S AMERICAN SYSTEM during his congressional career, assumed the presidency in 1845 committed to a program of lower tariffs, lower spending, and the INDEPENDENT TREASURY. Nevertheless, during the election campaign of 1844, Polk had signalled to Pennsylvania's manufacturers that he was not opposed to a revenue tariff providing incidental protection to home industries. Polk's leanings became more apparent when he appointed Senator Robert J. Walker of Mississippi, a free trader, as Secretary of Treasury.

Polk and Walker, in their separate annual messages of 1845 to Congress, delivered vigorous calls for tariff reduction. Walker, engaging in constitutional argument, asserted that the Constitution permits tariff increases for revenue purposes only, and then only to the point that still higher tariff rates would reduce total revenue collections. Both men approved of the possibility that revenue tariffs might provide incidental protective effects, but they argued that protection should be fairly allocated among all sectors of the national economy, not just manufacturing. The administration's program for tariff revision included elimination of specific duties, minimum valuation formulas, and most ad valorem rates (rates calculated on an item's value) exceeding 20 percent.

The Tariff Act of 1846 did not effect as large a reduction as had been proposed and retained many protective features of the prior law. Nevertheless, Congress eliminated most specific duties and minimum valuations and reduced the average ad valorem rate below 30 percent. The tariff, as so modified, remained in effect without substantial further change until 1857.

BIBLIOGRAPHY

Bergeron, Paul H. *The Presidency of James K. Polk*. 1987.

McCormac, Eugene Irving. *James K. Polk, A Political Biography*. Repr. 1965.

Stanwood, Edward. *American Tariff Controversies in the Nineteenth Century*. Vol. 2. Repr. 1967.

RALPH MITZENMACHER

WALLACE, GEORGE (b. 1919), governor of Alabama, presidential candidate in 1968, 1972, and 1976. Wallace is the last of a group of southern leaders who represent the Solid South NEW DEAL legacy of the DEMOCRATIC PARTY. In 1968 he received nearly ten million votes in a third-party campaign for the presidency. Four years later he was the leading Democratic vote-getter, until an assassination attempt left him handicapped for life. Wallace mounted serious campaigns in three presidential contests, and won the Alabama governorship four times. Though he was called a demagogue and racist, his antigovernment

theme of "getting government off the backs of the people" became accepted conservative fare in the administration of Ronald Reagan.

George Corley Wallace was born in the southeastern Alabama town of Clio in 1919. He entered the University of Alabama in 1937 and immediately became involved in campus politics, defeating a more-established fraternity candidate for president of the student body. He worked his way through law school, and upon graduation he joined the Army Air Corps and served in the Pacific theater during WORLD WAR II. Wallace married Lurleen Brown while on a fifteen-day furlough, and after the war they returned to his hometown; there he received a gubernatorial appointment as state assistant attorney general.

In 1946 Wallace campaigned throughout Barbour County in southeastern Alabama for the state legislature, an office he won convincingly. This area has been the breeding ground of many Alabama politicians. While in Montgomery, Wallace worked to increase the welfare of his rural constituents. He was early influenced by the populist antics of James E. "Big Jim" Folsom, the "Little Man's Big Friend," who dominated Alabama politics from 1946 to 1958. After the death of his first wife in 1968, Wallace married Folsom's niece. Folsom was the ultimate friends-and-neighbors candidate who promised to pave rural roads, provide relief to the elderly, and improve the education in the public schools. Wallace became part of the Folsom crowd and was pegged as a "radical" and "do-gooder" by the legislative establishment opposed to the new governor. By 1954 the grim realities of Alabama's economic situation and the alcoholism of Jim Folsom precipitated a break between the two, and Wallace returned home to Barbour County to be elected circuit judge.

On the bench of the third judicial circuit, Wallace became known as the "Fighting Judge" owing to his defiance of the U.S. Commission on Civil Rights investigation of discrimination in black voting rights. In 1958 he mounted a "Win with Wallace" campaign for governor, a race he lost by more than 64,000 votes because he was perceived as being soft on the race issue. When Wallace ran again for governor in 1962, he emphasized the actions of the Supreme Court in desegregation and the threat the Kennedy administration posed to Alabama's way of life. With his victory, he used the inauguration to declare from "the great Anglo-Saxon Southland . . . Segregation now! Segregation tomorrow! Segregation forever!"

Aside from this racial aberration, the Wallace administrations have all the trappings of populism reminiscent of the Folsom regime. He built junior colleges and trade schools, initiated multimillion dollar school-construction programs and a free textbook policy, and launched numerous road-building projects. But these programs were overshadowed by his racial resistance, for example, blocking enrollment of black students at the University of Alabama in June 1963, and his opposition in the presidential campaign of 1972 to school busing. In the 1960s Wallace's confrontations with the federal authorities of Tuskegee, Birmingham, Huntsville, and Mobile made him the nationwide symbol of intransigence toward racial integration.

Because Wallace was legally ineligible to succeed himself as governor in 1966, his wife Lurleen was elected as his surrogate. When she died in 1968, Wallace ran again and was reelected in 1970 and 1974. The assassination attempt on 15 May 1972 at Laurel, Maryland, left Wallace permanently paralyzed, but he campaigned again for the Democratic nomination in 1976. His 1982 election as governor depended on substantial support from black voters, who supported him after he recanted his segregationist past. Widowed once and divorced twice, Wallace retired from politics in 1987 due to ill health.

For many people Wallace will be remembered as a racist southern governor who fought integration, as did many others during the violent 1960s in the South. But in the 1970s his message changed, and the influence he had on American politics was apparent in the years of the Reagan presidency. Wallace was the first national politician to capitalize on the anti-Washington mood that influenced the presidential elections of 1976 and 1980. His message was for the working, middle-class, white voter who later abandoned the Democratic Party for the conservative policies favored by Ronald Reagan and George Bush.

BIBLIOGRAPHY

Carlson, Jody. *George C. Wallace and the Politics of Powerlessness.* 1981.
Frady, Marshall. *Wallace.* 1970.
Wallace, George C. *Stand Up for America.* 1976.

J. DAVID WOODARD

WALLACE, HENRY A. (1888–1965), thirty-third Vice President of the United States (1941–1945), Progressive Party presidential nominee in 1948. Wallace was the major architect of the controversial NEW DEAL farm policy but lost popularity because of his conciliatory policy toward the Soviet Union after WORLD WAR II. Henry Agard Wallace was born into an Iowa farm family known for its rural leadership. He gained renown as a corn geneticist, agricultural economist, and editor of the *Wallace's Farmer*. Active in politics, he left the REPUBLICAN PARTY to support Franklin D. Roosevelt for President and became Roosevelt's Secretary of Agriculture.

The main pillar of the massive farm program, which Wallace designed as part of Roosevelt's attempts to overcome the Great Depression, was the AGRICULTURAL ADJUSTMENT ACT of 1933. This first of several agricultural statutes initiated the concept of federal management of agriculture. Overall farm production was reduced via acreage allotments and marketing controls to raise the prices of agricultural commodities. Federal price supports were paid to farmers to insure compliance and to place a floor under farm income. The 1933 act was supplanted by the Agricultural Adjustment Act of 1938. It utilized the Commodity Credit Corporation (a federal agency) to store surplus agricultural commodities to maintain market stability and fair farm prices. New Deal farm programs resulted in a huge increase in the federal bureaucracy, involved the government in what previously had been considered a private sector of the economy, operated on a plan of deficit spending, and sought to create scarcity while millions were unemployed; accordingly, Wallace was often the center of political controversy.

Loyal to Roosevelt in all areas, Wallace supported his unpopular COURT-PACKING PLAN, his attempt to purge conservatives from the Democratic Party, and his endeavor to move the nation away from its traditional isolationism. Wallace helped build popular support for all facets of the New Deal through political speeches and books. He advocated the creation of a welfare state, reciprocal trade, regulation of business, and Roosevelt's internationalistic foreign policy. Roosevelt rewarded Wallace by selecting him as his 1940 vice presidential running mate despite the strong opposition of conservative Democrats.

In 1941 Wallace became the thirty-third Vice President of the United States. During his one term in office he was given administrative duties by Roosevelt far exceeding those held by any previous Vice President. In addition to presiding over the Senate, Wallace was made chairperson of the Board of Economic Warfare in 1942 and a year later also headed the Supply Priorities and Allocation Board. He vigorously prosecuted the war effort and strove to lay the basis for amicable Soviet-American relations following the conclusion of World War II.

Besides heading two wartime agencies Wallace served as a PRESIDENTIAL PRIVATE ENVOY for Roosevelt and went on goodwill missions abroad. He visited Latin America, China, and the Soviet Union. Envisioning a peaceful postwar world based on the mutual cooperation of all nations within the framework of the United Nations, Wallace championed free trade, disarmament, and an end to imperialism. To promote his ideas, Wallace wrote *The Price of Free World Victory* (1942) and the *Christian Bases of World Order* (1943). He was again criticized for his globalistic vision and for trying to keep New Deal liberalism alive even though Roosevelt ceased to push for domestic reforms. Wallace also advocated government protection of civil rights for minorities.

When Wallace got into a public dispute with Secretary of Commerce Jesse Jones (a staunch conservative who also headed the RECONSTRUCTION FINANCE CORPORATION), Roosevelt dropped Wallace from the 1944 presidential ticket. In 1945 Harry S. Truman became Vice President while Wallace took over as Secretary of Commerce at the outset of Roosevelt's fourth term. After Roosevelt died, Wallace remained in Truman's CABINET, but he opposed Truman's get-tough policy with the Soviets and publicly criticized the MARSHALL PLAN, the TRUMAN DOCTRINE, and increased military spending. When Wallace refused to remain silent on foreign policy issues, Truman dismissed him from the Cabinet in 1946.

In 1947 Wallace became editor of the liberal *New Republic* magazine and helped found the PROGRESSIVE PARTY to oppose Truman's 1948 bid for the presidency. In his *Toward World Peace* (1948) Wallace opposed U.S. participation in the North Atlantic Treaty Organization (NATO) and proposed a conciliatory policy toward the Soviet Union and a reliance on the United Nations as an international peacekeeper. Wallace was attacked by Democrats and Republicans alike for his stance, which seemingly belied the belligerence of the Soviet Union as reflected in the Communist coup d'état in Czechoslovakia and the Berlin blockade.

At the 1948 nominating convention in Philadelphia Wallace was chosen to be the Progressive Party's presidential nominee. During the 1948 campaign Truman and the Democrats charged Wallace with being soft on communism and dovishly naive regarding Joseph Stalin's COLD WAR objectives. The infiltration of American Communists within the Progressive Party gave Wallace's crusade for peace a bad image. The third party's platform always castigated the United States for its role in the cold war while failing to criticize any actions of the Soviet Union. Actually, Wallace did not subscribe to communism and believed the Soviets would become truly democratic over time if they felt secure and were given economic assistance. This view, obviously, ran counter to public opinion in that era.

After making a very poor showing in the 1948 presidential election, Wallace retired to a New York farm. He withdrew from politics and resumed his genetic experiments with plants. He attempted to create a hybrid corn suited for the climate of Latin America. When the KOREAN WAR broke out in 1950, he backed Truman's intervention. Wallace quit the Progressive Party, which died soon thereafter. Wallace was a much pilloried political figure during the era of MCCARTHYISM and was not welcome at White House ceremonies until 1960, when he was invited to John F. Kennedy's inauguration. In 1965 he received a Distinguished Achievement Citation from the Iowa State University Alumni Association (his alma mater) and died later that year of amytropic lateral sclerosis (Lou Gehrig's disease). In 1985 Iowa State University honored his memory by establishing the Henry A. Wallace Chair of Rural Studies.

BIBLIOGRAPHY

Blum, John Morton, ed. *The Price of Vision: Diary of Henry A. Wallace, 1942–1946.* 1973.
Lord, Russel. *The Wallaces of Iowa.* 1947.
Markowitz, Norman. *Henry A. Wallace and American Liberalism.* 1973.
Schmidt, Carl T. *Henry A. Wallace: Quixotic Crusade.* 1960.
Schapsmeier, Edward L., and Frederick H. Schapsmeier. *Henry A. Wallace: The Agrarian Years, 1910–1940.* 1968.
Schapsmeier, Edward L., and Frederick H. Schapsmeier. *Prophet in Politics: Henry A. Wallace and the War Years, 1940–1965.* 1970.

EDWARD L. SCHAPSMEIER

WAR, DECLARATION OF. The Constitution explicitly places the President in command of all military forces belonging to the United States. Article II, Section 2, states that "The President shall be Commander in Chief of the Army and Navy of the United States, and of the Militia of the several States, when called into the actual Service of the United States." The President's power to initiate military action, however, is limited by Article I, Section 8, which states that "Congress shall have Power . . . to declare War, grant Letters of Marque and Reprisal, and make Rules concerning Captures on Land and Water." Therefore, the Constitution places the decision to engage in hostilities with other nations in the hands of Congress.

Constitutional Context. These limitations may best be understood in historical context. In the eighteenth century the United States had no standing army. With no ability to wage war, a President would clearly have no recourse but to turn to Congress. The President may initiate hostilities only when swift action is necessary to repel a sudden attack. Otherwise, Congress is granted the sole authority to "raise and support Armies," "provide and maintain a Navy," "make Rules for the Governance and Regulation of" the armed forces, and "provide for calling forth the Militia to execute the Laws of the Union, suppress Insurrections and repel Invasions." In short, the armed forces may be used only to pursue legislatively authorized goals. As Attorney General CALEB CUSHING stated in an 1853 legal opinion, the President is like a "commander in command of a squadron or a general in the field." Any orders issued by the President "must be within the range of purely executive or administrative action."

Those who drafted the Constitution considered the war clause to be a comprehensive ban against presidential warmaking. From the outset of the debate on the Constitution's structure, the Framers expressed the fear that executive WAR POWER would lead to the "evils of elected Monarchies." Subsequent debate on the precise phrasing of the war clause itself shows that the drafters of the clause originally sought to bar the President from "making" any war but drafted the clause to bar the President from "declaring" war so that the President could legally respond to a surprise attack on the United States without congressional approval.

The Framers' interpretation of their own document as a comprehensive check on executive war power is reflected in a statement made by Thomas Jefferson regarding the war clause: "We have already given . . . one effectual check to the dog of war by transferring the power of letting him loose, from the executive to the legislative body." The Framers consciously repudiated the European concept of monarchical war power. The U.S. Constitution is a product of the Enlightenment, and the Framers, aspiring to achieve the Enlightenment ideal of republican government, drafted a Constitution that allowed only Congress to loose the military forces of the United States on other nations.

The war clause's injunction against executive warmaking was respected by Presidents Jefferson and James Madison, both of whom participated in framing the Constitution, though Jefferson was not at the CONSTITUTIONAL CONVENTION. Moreover, the U.S. Supreme Court also recognized and affirmed the war clause's exclusive grant of war power to the Congress in such early cases as *Bas v. Tingy* (1800), *Talbot v. Seeman* (1801), and LITTLE V. BARREME (1804). Those decisions recognized that Congress must either declare war or explicitly authorize it, as it did with the QUASI-WAR WITH FRANCE.

Under the constitutional model of war power, there is no question that the COMMANDER IN CHIEF clause allows the President to engage U.S. military forces after war is declared. Full declarations of war have occurred at five points in United States history: the WAR OF 1812, the MEXICAN WAR of 1846, the SPANISH-AMERICAN WAR of 1898, WORLD WAR I, and WORLD WAR

II. In each instance, Congress declared by joint resolution that the United States was at war with other nations, thus empowering the President to wage war against those nations named. Congress can also empower the President by issuing a conditional declaration of war, consisting of an ultimatum to another nation. Interestingly, while conditional declarations of war have been issued several times in U.S. history, only the 1898 ultimatum that Spain relinquish its claim to CUBA actually led to violence.

Congressional Authorization. Short of a declaration of total war, the President can obtain limited war power where Congress by statute authorizes the President to use military force limited to certain means or objectives. Statutory authorization to wage limited war was one of the earliest exercises of constitutional war power. The Congressional authorizations for naval actions against the Barbary states of North Africa from 1794 to 1815 [*see* BARBARY WAR] are examples of constitutional delegation of limited war power to the President. Presidential war power only exists within the limits established by the authorization.

Congressional grants of limited war power have routinely been abused in the modern era. The GULF OF TONKIN RESOLUTION of 1964 (originally referred to as the Southeast Asia Resolution) authorized the President to repel North Vietnamese attacks on U.S. armed forces and allowed the President to provide military support for any nations that were signatories of the SEATO TREATY. The Tonkin Gulf Resolution's ambiguous phrasing and nearly limitless delegation of war power frustrated the constitutional constraints on executive warmaking and resulted in the escalation of the VIETNAM WAR, a war that in many ways resembled the long, bloody, and inclusive wars of Europe that the Framers had sought to avoid.

More recently, the 1991 resolution authorizing the President to use armed forces in the GULF WAR came only after President George Bush had massed troops and equipment for the offensive against Iraqi forces. To be in accordance with the constitutional model of war-power delegation, congressional resolutions for limited warfare must be carefully tailored, narrowly construed, and made a prerequisite before the commitment of any U.S. forces to a conflict.

With the advent of nuclear war strategies, defense against nuclear attack included the President's authority to launch America's entire arsenal of NUCLEAR WEAPONS without congressional approval. The events surrounding the CUBAN MISSILE CRISIS, when the united States moved dangerously close to nuclear confrontation without full congressional approval, demonstrated the extent of presidential war power in the COLD

WAR era. Nevertheless, many commentators believe that any FIRST USE OF NUCLEAR WEAPONS demands congressional authorization.

Despite the Constitution's injunction against executive war power, the executive branch now seems to possess the ability to initiate military action without congressional approval or even congressional consultation. The expansion of presidential war power paralleled the perception that the United States was threatened with imminent attack from communist forces in virtually every corner of the world. This fear led to increasing judicial deference to aggressive executive foreign policy.

The Courts Defer. The creation of the so-called fluctuating powers doctrine bolstered judicial deference toward executive foreign policy decisions. In his concurrence in YOUNGSTOWN SHEET & TUBE CO. v. SAWYER (1952), Justice Robert Jackson said that "presidential powers are not fixed but fluctuate, depending on their disjunction or conjunction with those of Congress." In other words, if Congress has not clearly expressed its will on a matter relating to foreign policy, the courts will allow the President successfully to exercise a certain degree of power, including war power. Both the KOREAN WAR and the Vietnam War demonstrated the executive branch's newfound ability to wage undeclared war under the rubric of containing communism.

The confusion over where foreign policy power ends and war power begins was exacerbated by the judiciary's refusal to adjudicate war power disputes. The tendency of the courts to avoid war power issues emerged during the Vietnam era, when several suits were brought by members of Congress and other citizens to halt the undeclared war in Indochina. Despite the Supreme Court's ruling in *Baker v. Carr* (1962) that "it is error to suppose that every case or controversy which touches foreign relations lies beyond judicial cognizance," the federal courts consistently invoked the political question doctrine to avoid addressing the constitutionality of the Vietnam War.

The judiciary's refusal to address war power issues continues to frustrate attempts by Congress to restore the constitutional delegation of war powers. In 1990, several members of Congress sought to reestablish congressional control over the decision whether to attack Iraqi forces in the Persian Gulf. Their suit, *Dellums v. Bush*, was dismissed as not ripe for adjudication by a federal district judge.

Covert Warmaking. After Vietnam, the executive branch resorted to large-scale covert military actions in order to free military activity from the constraints of the war clause of the Constitution and the WAR POWERS RESOLUTION of 1973. The executive branch contended that covert activity was constitutionally authorized, but that argument is flawed. The Constitution does require congressional approval for covert military actions. The war clause gives Congress the exclusive power to grant "Letters of Marque and Reprisal"—the eighteenth-century equivalents of authorization for private acts of war and covert military activities. Nonetheless, examples of COVERT OPERATIONS engineered by agencies in the executive branch abound. U.S. sponsorship of the Nicaraguan contra rebels during the 1980s is an example of presidential sponsored covert warfare that clearly violates constitutional war power [*see* IRAN-CONTRA AFFAIR].

The executive branch also resorted to warfare that was covert only in the sense that the decision to engage U.S. forces was made without informing Congress. This practice reached its height during the 1980s; the tactic that emerged was a quick and decisive use of military force without congressional approval. By adopting blitzkrieg-type tactics, the executive branch could complete a military campaign before Congress could assert constitutional constraints. Military operations such as the invasion of GRENADA in 1983 and the invasion of PANAMA in 1989 involved commitments of military force. The war clause surely applied. Nonetheless, the executive branch was able to evade a constitutional challenge because the rapid conclusion of the activity rendered the question moot. So, while it is true that large-scale, decisive use of armed force represents a trend in executive use of war power, the practice nonetheless violates constitutional SEPARATION OF POWERS.

Perhaps in a period when the specter of communism no longer haunts foreign policy makers, American foreign policy will retreat from the perpetual state of emergency that existed for more than forty years. If this occurs, the power to engage U.S. forces in warfare may return to the constitutional model and a congressional declaration or authorization of war will again be a prerequisite to the use of armed force by the President. While it remains to be seen what practical war powers will remain with the presidency after the cold war, the constitutional constraints on executive warmaking cannot be denied. According to the war clause of the Constitution, a congressional declaration of war or its equivalent is required before the President may engage U.S. military force.

BIBLIOGRAPHY

Firmage, E. B. "Rogue Presidents and the War Power of Congress." *George Mason Law Review* 11 (1988): 79.

Firmage, E. B., and J. E. Wrona. "The War Power." *George Washington Law Review* 59 (1991): 1684.

Glennon, M. J. *Constitutional Diplomacy.* 1990.

Keynes, E. *Undeclared War.* 1982.

Lobel, J. "Emergency Power and the Decline of Liberalism." *Yale Law Journal* 98 (1989):1385.

Wormuth, F.D., and E.B. Firmage. *To Chain the Dog of War.* 2d ed. 1989.

EDWIN B. FIRMAGE

WAR, DEPARTMENT OF. The Department of War was established in 1789 to maintain and direct the nation's armed forces, including the navy until it became a separate department in 1798. General Henry Knox, the first Secretary of War, headed a small establishment that initially consisted of himself and one clerk. Even though the United States faced significant challenges in the 1790s, including a QUASI-WAR WITH FRANCE, the department remained small. The public's traditional disdain for standing armies diminished support. Throughout Thomas Jefferson's presidency (1801–1809), the army averaged 3,300 officers and men.

The Nineteenth Century. The War Department performed poorly during the WAR OF 1812. There were few competent army leaders, the supply system failed, and confusion reigned supreme. In 1813 the War Department adopted a general staff system, including an adjutant and inspector general, a quartermaster general, a commissary general of ordinance, a paymaster, and a topographical engineer, but these officials were housekeepers and did not serve as a general staff as the term was later understood. In this way the War Department bureaus came into being.

JOHN C. CALHOUN (1817–1825), under President James Monroe, was the best Secretary of War in the nineteenth century. An excellent leader, Calhoun concentrated authority in the center and lodged responsibility all over the organization. He chose qualified managers, improved the supply system, located army agency heads in Washington, D.C., and appointed the first commanding general. He rejuvenated the U.S. Military Academy at West Point, which had struggled since its founding in 1803.

Between 1829 and 1861, the War Department and the army suffered through lean years, with the exception of the successful military effort in the MEXICAN WAR (1846–1848). The heads of the War Department bureaus operated independently of the Secretary of War and the commanding general. Traditional distrust of standing military forces combined with con-

gressional stinginess kept the army at minimum strength—about ten thousand after the Mexican War and sixteen thousand on the eve of the Civil War.

When the CIVIL WAR began in 1861, the War Department was still small, consisting of only the Secretary, the bureau chiefs, and a few clerks and assistants. By December 1861 the Union army had over 660,000 men, most of them raised by the states. Then the War Department took over recruiting, eventually resorting to conscription.

President Abraham Lincoln was an active COMMANDER IN CHIEF, especially until early 1864 when he found a capable military leader in General Ulysses S. Grant. After this Secretary of War EDWIN M. STANTON (1861–1867) spent most of his time administering the War Department and Lincoln permitted Grant a relatively free hand. The War Department's civilian staff expanded greatly during the war, with the bureaus increasing in number and size.

The victorious Union army of over 1 million men demobilized rapidly after April 1865; by 1874, the army's authorized size was slightly over twenty-seven thousand, but actual strength up to 1898 was less. During the RECONSTRUCTION period, army troops helped to maintain order in the South and assisted with land redistribution, elections, and electoral reforms. Otherwise the army's duty was to fight the INDIANS, maintain coastal forts, and run West Point.

War Department organization between 1865 and 1898 remained in a confused state, mainly because of a lack of clarity in relations among the Secretary of War, the commanding general, and the bureaus. The bureaus operated with a considerable degree of autonomy, and there was a gulf between the bureau staffs in Washington and the field line organizations. By the 1890s the principal bureaus were the Judge Advocate General's Department, the Inspector General's Department, the Adjutant General's Department, the Quartermaster's Department, the Subsistence Department, the Pay Department, the Medical Department, the Corps of Engineers, the Ordinance Department, and the Signal Corps.

Reform and Reorganization. All of the problems with War Department and army leadership and organization came to the fore during the SPANISH-AMERICAN WAR. President William McKinley took seriously his role as Commander in Chief and proved to be the only person capable of containing the divisive rivalry between the army and the navy. Symbolizing the problem, Admiral William Sampson and General William Shafter refused to collaborate in the Santiago, CUBA, area until they received a direct order from McKinley. The Quartermaster's Department proved incapable of

Secretaries of War

President	Secretary of War	President	Secretary of War
1 Washington	Henry Knox, 1798–1795 Timothy Pickering, 1795–1796 James McHenry, 1796–1797	11 Polk	William L. Marcy, 1845–1849
		12 Taylor	George W. Crawford, 1849–1850
2 J. Adams	James McHenry, 1797–1800 Samuel Dexter, 1800–1801 Roger Griswold, 1801	13 Fillmore	George W. Crawford, 1850 Charles M. Conrad, 1850–1853
		14 Pierce	Jefferson Davis, 1853–1857
3 Jefferson	Henry Dearborn, 1801–1809	15 Buchanan	John B. Floyd, 1857–1861 Joseph Holt, 1861
4 Madison	William Eustis, 1809 John Armstrong, 1813–1814 James Monroe, 1814–1815 William H. Crawford, 1815–1816	16 Lincoln	Simon Cameron, 1861–1862 Edwin M. Stanton, 1862–1865
		17 A. Johnson	Edwin M. Stanton, 1865–1867 Ulysses S. Grant, 1867–1868 Lorenzo Thomas, 1868 John M. Schofield, 1868–1869
5 Monroe	George Graham, 1817 John C. Calhoun, 1817–1825		
6 J. Q. Adams	James Barbour, 1825–1828 Peter B. Porter, 1828–1829	18 Grant	John A. Rawlins, 1869 William T. Sherman, 1869 William W. Belknap, 1869–1876 Alphonso Taft, 1876 James D. Cameron, 1876–1877
7 Jackson	John H. Eaton, 1829–1831 Lewis Cass, 1831–1836		
8 Van Buren	Joel R. Poinsett, 1837–1841	19 Hayes	George W. McCrary, 1877–1879 Alexander Ramsey, 1879–1881
9 W. H. Harrison	John Bell, 1841	20 Garfield	Robert T. Lincoln, 1881
10 Tyler	John Bell, 1841 John McLean, 1841 John C. Spencer, 1841–1843 James M. Porter, 1843–1844 William Wilkins, 1844–1845	21 Arthur	Robert T. Lincoln, 1881–1885
		22 Cleveland	William C. Endicott, 1885–1889

coping with the war, and the Medical Department was not up to the job. The United States emerged from the Spanish-American War as a colonial power as well as a world power, making the need for reform in the War Department and the army obvious.

Reform began in President Theodore Roosevelt's administration. Under the guidance of his Secretary of War, ELIHU ROOT (1899–1904), Congress approved legislation in 1903 creating a general staff, with a chief of staff and forty-four officers, whose duties included preparing defense plans, investigating army efficiency, providing professional advice to the Secretary of War, and coordinating the branches of the army. The chief of staff was responsible for supervision of line troops and the bureaus, which became subordinate to him and the Secretary of War. Root also founded the Army War College, located in Washington, D.C., to train officers in strategy and command.

The Root reforms did not stick after William Howard Taft succeeded him as Secretary of War in 1904. Taft confined the general staff to military matters and allowed the bureau heads to report to him. Later, when Taft was President, Secretary of War HENRY L. STIMSON curbed the powers of the bureaus, but opposition to his reforms in Congress, where the

bureau heads still had influence, limited their success. The National Defense Act of 1916, which defined the roles and mission of the army, national guard, and reserves, limited the general staff to war planning, excluded the War College from general staff functions, and forbade the general staff from interfering with the bureaus.

During WORLD WAR I, Secretary of War NEWTON BAKER struggled with organizational matters. Administrative efficiency was difficult to accomplish, given the obstinancy of the bureaus. Forced by a major distribution crisis, Baker centralized the supply system in the general staff. Reorganization of the general staff gave it direct supervision over most War Department activities, and later the bureaus were consolidated along functional lines.

Baker and President Woodrow Wilson re-created the position of commanding general by giving broad powers to General John J. Pershing, who headed the American Expeditionary Forces (AEF) in Europe. Pershing organized his staff on the French model, with G-1 handling administration, G-2 intelligence, G-3 operations, G-4 supply, and G-5 training. Despite jurisdictional problems, the War Department tightened its organization during the war, strengthening

President	Secretary of War
23 B. Harrison	Redfield Proctor, 1889–1891
	Stephen B. Elkins, 1891–1893
24 Cleveland	Daniel S. Lamont, 1893–1897
25 McKinley	Russel A. Alger, 1897–1899
	Elihu Root, 1899–1901
26 T. Roosevelt	Elihu Root, 1901–1904
	William H. Taft, 1904–1908
	Luke E. Wright, 1908–1909
27 Taft	Jacob M. Dickinson, 1909–1911
	Henry L. Stimson, 1911–1913
28 Wilson	Lindley M. Garrison, 1913–1916
	Newton D. Baker, 1916–1921
29 Harding	John W. Weeks, 1921–1923
30 Coolidge	John W. Weeks, 1923–1925
	Dwight F. Davis, 1925–1929
31 Hoover	James W. Good, 1929
	Patrick J. Hurley, 1929–1933
32 F. D. Roosevelt	George H. Dren, 1933–1936
	Harry H. Woodring, 1936–1940
	Henry L. Stimson, 1940–1945
33 Truman	Henry L. Stimson, 1945
	Robert P. Patterson, 1945–1947
	Kenneth C. Royall, 1947

the general staff and cutting the power of the bureaus. The department successfully expanded the army, which made a substantial contribution to the victory in Europe. After the war, while the bureau again operated autonomously, the general staff continued to be a planning and coordinating agency, and the War Plans Division became the center of a general headquarters staff. This organization prevailed between the two world wars.

In 1926, Congress created a separate army air corps, providing a separate air corps commander, an air section in the general staff and an assistant secretary of war for air in the War Department. The army itself was small between the wars, typically less than 150,000. Budget cuts, exacerbated by the economic collapse after 1929, and lack of public support for the army, made it difficult for the War Department to carry on.

World War II. General GEORGE C. MARSHALL, who became chief of staff in 1939, recognized the need for reorganization of the army and the War Department, and he and Secretary of War Henry Stimson (appointed by President Franklin D. Roosevelt in 1940) collaborated to accomplish it. Between 1939 and 1941 the War Department grew rapidly, causing Marshall's management responsibilities to interfere with his duty as military adviser to Roosevelt. And he met resistance

to modernization from some old-line army leaders, for example the head of the cavalry, who fought against the development of armored forces, preferring to stick with the horse.

In March 1942, three months after PEARL HARBOR, Marshall reorganized the army, replacing the many agencies reporting to him with the army ground forces, the army air forces, and the army service forces. The War Plans Division, later the Operations Division, became Marshall's command post, assisting with strategy and the conduct of military operations. A smaller general staff, excluded from operations, was to concentrate on policy planning and coordination. Marshall also ordered staff procedures that resulted in quicker decisions and more effective action.

Roosevelt, an active Commander in Chief, worked directly with Marshall on military matters. Stimson dealt with nonmilitary issues, such as manpower, civil affairs, and scientific matters such as atomic energy, and Marshall concentrated on strategy and operations. The War Department and the army, needing to collaborate with the navy, the White House, the Congress, and many allies, equipped themselves through the Marshall reorganization to meet the demands of total war.

Marshall's successor as chief of staff, General Dwight D. Eisenhower, reorganized the army in June 1946, returning to a decentralized system. Eisenhower relied more on teamwork and cooperation than the close executive control that had characterized Marshall's organization. The War Department in 1946, under Secretary of War Robert Patterson, included a general staff with six directorates, ten special staff units (such as the Public Relations Division and the Manpower Board), and a larger number of administrative and technical staffs and services, some of which resembled the old bureaus. The army organization included the army ground forces, the army air forces, army areas within the United States, and overseas departments and commands.

During the war Marshall gave thought to postwar unification of the armed forces. His plan envisioned integrating the military services into a single department headed by a secretary charged with the civilian administration and a chief of staff who would direct operating commands for the army, navy, air forces, and a common supply and hospitalization service. A joint chiefs of staff, including the three service chiefs and a chief of staff to the President, would be responsible for top-level planning and coordinating. Marshall's postwar scheme also included universal military training.

Opposition to Marshall's plan centered in the navy,

which opposed a separate air force because it feared loss of its air arm, especially its land-based air forces. The navy also opposed unification in general, fearing army domination, and its proposals provided for separate but equal military departments. President Harry S. Truman eventually ordered the War and Navy Departments to agree on a plan. Their subsequent compromise provided the basis for the NATIONAL SECURITY ACT of 1947, which created the National Military Establishment (renamed the DEPARTMENT OF DEFENSE in 1949), with separate departments for the army, navy, and air force. The Department of the Army replaced the War Department, thus ending the 158-year history of one of the earliest CABINET-level departments in the United States.

BIBLIOGRAPHY

Cosmas, Graham A. *An Army for Empire: The United States Army in the Spanish-American War.* 1971.

Hewes, James E., Jr. *From Root to McNamara: Army Organization and Administration, 1900–1963.* 1975.

Huntington, Samuel. *The Soldier and the State.* 1959.

White, Leonard D. *The Federalists: A Study in Administrative History, 1789–1801.* 1948.

White, Leonard D. *The Jacksonians: A Study in Administrative History, 1829–1861.* 1954.

White, Leonard D. *The Jeffersonians: A Study in Administrative History, 1801–1829.* 1961.

White, Leonard D. *The Republican Era: A Study in Administrative History, 1869–1901.* 1958.

ROGER R. TRASK

WAR, UNDECLARED. During the last two centuries the United States has been involved in approximately two hundred military engagements without formally declaring war. In many cases Congress adopted legislation either authorizing or subsequently supporting the President's conduct. These military engagements vary in scope and magnitude from troop deployments for humanitarian purposes, hostage rescue operations, brief naval engagements, occupations of other countries to restore peace and protect U.S. interests, to full-scale military hostilities. Only on five occasions has the United States fought formally declared wars: the WAR OF 1812, the MEXICAN WAR (1846), the SPANISH-AMERICAN WAR (1898), WORLD WAR I (1914–1918), and WORLD WAR II (1939–1945). Since World War II, the United States has fought the KOREAN WAR (1950–1953) the VIETNAM WAR (1965–1973), the longest war in the nation's history, without formally declaring war. The United States also conducted military hostilities in PANAMA (1989) and in the GULF WAR (1990–1991) without a DECLARATION OF WAR.

The frequency and intensity of recent undeclared wars reflects the tendency to employ the military as an instrument of American foreign policy. Generally, the United States has deployed armed forces to unstable countries and regions (Southeast Asia, the Middle East, and Latin America) to further its economic, political, and security interests or those of its regional allies. In 1989, President George Bush ordered U.S. armed forces to invade Panama in order to oust General Manuel Noriega. Responding to the Iraqi invasion of Kuwait in August 1990, President Bush dispatched army, navy, air force, and marine corps forces to the Persian Gulf. Acting under a United Nations resolution and a congressional statute, on 16 January 1991, President Bush ordered the 430,000 U.S. troops in the region to liberate Kuwait.

A second important reason for the increasing frequency of undeclared wars is that the UNITED NATIONS Charter (Article II, Section 4) prohibits member states from using force to threaten the political independence or territorial integrity of other nations. Since the charter condemns aggressive or offensive wars to resolve political and territorial disputes, declarations of war are obsolete. While the charter condemns offensive war, it permits regional security arrangements such as the North Atlantic Treaty Organization (NATO) for purposes of regional self-defense. Thus virtually all military hostilities (undeclared wars) are defensive measures. While the charter encourages the peaceful resolution of disputes, it has blurred the distinction between offensive and defensive warfare by permitting regional security arrangements, while failing to define offensive war.

Since the World War II, guerrilla wars, insurgency warfare, and wars of national liberation also have undermined the distinction between offensive and defensive war. To the Soviet Union and its allies, the Palestine Liberation Organization (PLO) appeared as a legitimate instrument of national liberation defending the rights of the Palestinian people. For the United States, the PLO was an aggressive, terrorist organization that threatened peace in the Middle East, the security interests of U.S. allies, and, ultimately, U.S. regional security interests. In addition, many modern weapons systems are neither exclusively defensive nor offensive. While the Soviet Union regarded U.S. intermediate range missiles in Turkey as an offensive threat, American policymakers characterized these missiles as defensive weapons. Similarly, the United States and the Soviet Union perceived the introduction of Soviet intermediate range missiles in Cuba in 1962 in diametrically opposite ways [*see* CUBAN MISSILE CRISIS].

The dominance of the United States as a superpower, the collapse of the Soviet Union, and the U.N.'s reliance on the industrial democracies to maintain order in unstable regions imply the continuing use of U.S. armed forces in undeclared wars and military hostilities. As of the 1990s, Americans faced recurrent political conflict over the constitutional allocation of the WAR POWERS between Congress and the President. While Congress asserted its constitutional authority to initiate war and military hostilities, the President claimed authority as COMMANDER IN CHIEF to deploy the nation's armed forces and commit them to combat. These conflicts resulted from the constitutional separation of the war powers from the office of Commander in Chief as well as an unstable international environment.

The Constitutional Context. In 1789, the Framers of the Constitution allocated all war powers to Congress. They granted Congress the power to declare war. They also gave Congress the power to authorize limited military hostilities below the threshold of a declared war. In *Bas v. Tingy* (1800) and *Talbot v. Seeman* (1801), the Supreme Court recognized Congress's power to authorize undeclared wars. Furthermore, the Framers vested all of the auxiliary war powers in Congress. Congress has the power to appropriate funds, raise and support armies, make rules for captures on land and water, provide and maintain a navy, make rules for the land and naval forces, and to provide for a militia (the National Guard). If Congress chooses, it can use these auxiliary war powers to limit the scope and duration of military hostilities that the President initiates on his own. Finally, the Constitution gives Congress the power to grant letters of MARQUE AND REPRISAL, which is the power to initiate and control the scope of military hostilities short of a declaration of war.

Although the Framers did not allocate any of the war powers to the President, they conferred on him the office of Commander in Chief. By conferring this office on the CHIEF EXECUTIVE, they hoped to make the military accountable to a civilian Commander in Chief who, in turn, would be responsible to the people. As Commander in Chief, the President has responsibility for superintending the armed forces in time of peace and directing their overall operation in time of war. However, the Commander in Chief clause of the Constitution is not an independent grant of power to the President to initiate offensive military hostilities. As the records of the CONSTITUTIONAL CONVENTION imply, the Framers recognized that the President might have to respond to sudden attacks. By implication, they granted the President authority to repel sudden attacks on United States territory, citizens, property, and armed forces.

The Framers' allocation of the war powers to Congress and defensive powers to the Commander in Chief rests on the eighteenth-century distinction between offensive and defensive war, a distinction that twentieth-century conditions have virtually annihilated. From the Framer's perspective, as long as the President's action can be characterized as "defensive," he is operating within his constitutional zone of authority. Once his actions become "offensive," he requires congressional approval to continue military hostilities. By 1801, however, Presidents began testing the boundaries between executive and legislative power. In the BARBARY WAR (1801–1805), Thomas Jefferson publicly acknowledged the limits of presidential power but nevertheless initiated naval maneuvers nine months before requesting and receiving congressional authority. Jefferson began the now familiar pattern of presenting Congress with a military fait accompli and, then, seeking post hoc congressional approval for his actions. Then, as now, Congress responded pliantly to the President's requests, providing the necessary resources for American troops in harm's way.

Presidential Interpretation and Expansion. By the beginning of the twentieth century it had become customary for Presidents to claim authority to commit the nation's armed forces to combat without prior congressional authorization. Since World War II, Presidents have dispatched the U.S. military around the globe, under mutual-security agreements, for extended periods and in large numbers, to protect NATIONAL SECURITY interests. Under such defense treaties as NATO, SEATO (Southeast Asia Treaty Organization), and ANZUS (Austrailia, New Zealand, and United States) various Presidents have sent troops to Europe, Asia, and the Pacific. Despite presidential claims, these treaties do not authorize the President to decide unilaterally to commit the United States to military hostilities. The NATO Treaty, for example, provides that an attack on any of the partners shall be considered as an attack on all. However, Article 11 of the treaty reserves the right of each member to decide how it will respond in accordance with its own constitutional processes. This reserve clause implies that Congress retains authority to declare war or authorize limited military hostilities. The NATO alliance expanded presidential power to include protecting the territorial integrity of U.S. allies. The treaty also transformed the President's defensive power into an indeterminate power to protect the diverse security of NATO's European members.

The War Powers Resolution. In response to the erosion of legislative power over war making, Congress passed the WAR POWERS RESOLUTION of 1973, over President Richard Nixon's veto. Adopted in response to the VIETNAM WAR, the War Powers Resolution attempted to redress the balance of power between Congress and the President to initiate undeclared wars and military hostilities. The resolution encourages the President to consult with Congress before committing combat forces to hostilities or to regions where hostilities are imminent. In the absence of a declaration of war, other authorization, or a sudden attack, the resolution requires the President to report to Congress, within forty-eight hours, the introduction of U.S. combat forces into regions where hostilities are present or imminent. Unless Congress authorizes his decision, the President has between sixty and ninety days to repatriate U.S. armed forces. Of course, Congress can require the Commander in Chief to bring the troops home earlier by passing legislation, which would be subject to the President's veto.

As a technique of accountability, the War Powers Resolution suffers from several defects. First, the Constitution vests the power to declare war and authorize military hostilities exclusively in Congress. Congress can not delegate discretion to the President to choose the time, the place, and the enemy, even for a limited period of time. Second, it is unlikely that Congress will refuse to support U.S. armed forces committed to combat. Third, the act telescopes the time frame for making important national-security decisions, which increases pressure on Congress to support the President's decisions as Commander in Chief. Finally, virtually every American President since 1973 has found ways to circumvent the resolution. During the ill-fated attempt to rescue hostages during the IRANIAN HOSTAGE CRISIS, President Jimmy Carter argued that the War Powers Resolution did not apply since his action was defensive. Similarly, Ronald Reagan argued that the resolution did not apply to the dispatch of marines to Beirut, Lebanon, in 1982, since hostilities were not imminent.

As long as the United States remains a major global power, it will face domestic and international pressures to use armed force to protect the nation's security interests as well as those of its allies. Following the disintegration of the Soviet Union, the projection of American military power into unstable regions will create conflict between Congress and the President concerning the initiation of military hostilities and undeclared wars. Both Congress and the President should reexamine the suitability of the War Powers Resolution as a methodology for promoting military decisions that are constitutionally palatable and politically responsible.

BIBLIOGRAPHY

Adler, David Gray. "The Constitution and Presidential Warmaking: The Enduring Debate." *Political Science Quarterly* 103 (Spring 1988): 1–36.

Emerson J. Terry. "Making War without a Declaration." *Journal of Legislation* 17 (1990): 23–63.

Ely, John Hart. "Suppose Congress Wanted a War Powers Act that Worked." *Columbia University Law Review* 88 (1988): 1379–1431.

Fisher, Louis. *Constitutional Conflicts between Congress and the President.* 3d ed. 1991.

Keynes, Edward. *Undeclared War: Twilight Zone of Constitutional Power.* 1991.

Reveley, W. Taylor, III. *War Powers of the President and Congress: Who Holds the Arrows and Olive Branch.* 1981.

Sofaer, Abraham D. *War, Foreign Affairs, and Constitutional Power: The Origins.* 1976.

Wormuth, E. D., and Edwin Firmage. *To Chain the Dog of War: The War Power of Congress in History and Law.* 1986.

EDWARD KEYNES

WAR OF 1812. The War of 1812 (1812–1815) is one of America's least memorable wars. President James Madison was unable to provide the leadership that the nation needed to conquer Canada or to force the British to stop encroaching upon America's neutral rights on the high seas. As a result, instead of bringing the British to their knees, the United States was lucky to escape from the conflict without having to make major concessions.

The war grew out of British encroachments on American rights during the Napoleonic Wars (1803–1815). When diplomatic negotiations and trade restrictions failed to win greater respect from the British, Madison decided to seek stronger measures. Hence when the Twelfth, or War, Congress convened in November 1811, the President asked it to put the nation "into an armor and an attitude demanded by the crisis." Congress responded by adopting war preparations.

In the hope of stimulating the war spirit further, Madison in early 1812 authorized the purchase and publication of the papers of John Henry, a British spy who had visited New England several years before. The following April Madison endorsed a ninety-day embargo to protect American trade and to prepare the American people for war. When the British still refused to make concessions on the two leading issues—the orders in council (by which the British regulated American trade with Europe) and impressment (the British practice of taking seamen from American merchant ships)—the President on 1 June recommended that Congress consider a DECLARATION OF WAR.

Many Democratic-Republicans and Federalists did not accept the president's logic on the wisdom of war, and the congressional vote on the war bill—seventy-nine to forty-nine in the House and nineteen to thirteen in the Senate—was the closest vote on any declaration of war in American history. Some members of Madison's cabinet, most notably Secretary of State James Monroe and Secretary of the Treasury ALBERT GALLATIN, favored a limited naval war, and the Senate very nearly adopted an amended war bill that would have limited hostilities to the high seas. What Madison's own preference was is unknown.

Within a week of the declaration of war, Madison sent out peace feelers, evidently hoping that the news of America's decision would be enough to shock the British into concessions. By this time, the British had repealed the orders in council but still refused to give up impressment. Hence nothing came of this initial round of negotiations even though both sides were interested in peace.

The decision for war had been made precipitously—without adequate military preparation and (judging by the vote in Congress) against the express wishes of move than a third of the American people. Madison and other Democratic-Republicans were willing to take this risk not only because they hoped that the declaration itself would lead to British concessions but also because they assumed that the conquest of Canada would be (in the words of Thomas Jefferson) "a mere matter of marching."

But such was not to be. A decade of retrenchment under the Democratic-Republicans had taken a heavy toll on the American military establishment. The War Department was in disarray, and Madison was slow to replace its head, William Eustis, even though his incompetence was plain to almost everyone. In addition, most of the senior army officers owed their appointment to politics and were superannuated and incompetent.

To compound the nation's problems, the strategy devised for conquering Canada, which divided American forces among three fronts and focused on the politically important West rather than the strategically important East, was doomed to failure. Although the United States launched major campaigns in 1812 and again in 1813, Canada remained in British hands. Thereafter, the British were able to take the offensive because the defeat and abdication of Napoleon enabled them to shift men and material to the American theater. Thus by 1814 the United States was strictly on the defensive.

Throughout the war Madison had trouble persuading Congress to support many measures that he considered essential. Federalists opposed all war measures (except those connected to the navy or coastal defense), and they were often joined by dissident Democratic-Republicans, particularly in the Senate, which was especially hostile to the President. Not only did the Senate reject several of Madison's diplomatic appointments, but Congress was slow to adopt a comprehensive tax program, and it voted down administration schemes for raising military personnel (including a conscription plan), establishing a national bank, and adopting additional trade restrictions.

The nadir for the administration came in August 1814 when a British army swept aside a hapless American force composed mostly of militia and occupied and burned the nation's capital, compelling government officials to flee. During his flight Madison was reportedly subjected to various insults for mismanaging the war, and when he returned to the charred capital, rumors circulated that his life was in danger. Graffiti appeared on the walls of the capitol that read: "George Washington founded this city after a seven years' war with England—James Madison lost it after a two years' war."

Madison proved much more adept at managing the peace negotiations. He appointed a first-rate commission that included Albert Gallatin, John Quincy Adams, and HENRY CLAY, and in August 1814, when the British demanded concessions from the United States in the first round of negotiations, he published the terms, thereby increasing support for the war at home and undermining support in England. It was a tribute to Madison's choice of ministers that in the TREATY OF GHENT (which ended the war) the United States sacrificed neither territory nor honor but simply agreed to return to the status quo ante bellum.

In February 1815 when news of the treaty reached Washington on the heels of Andrew Jackson's lopsided victory at New Orleans, Madison proclaimed the war a success, and Democratic-Republican orators and editors across the country echoed his cry. Thus the war passed into history not as a futile and costly struggle in which the nation had barely escaped dismemberment and disgrace but as a glorious triumph in the which the young republic had single-handedly defeated the conqueror of Napoleon and the mistress of the seas.

Although his enemies called it "Mr. Madison's War," the conflict never bore the fourth President's stamp. Cautious and shy, Madison was unable to supply the leadership the nation needed. In some ways, to be sure, his caution served the republic well. He showed a remarkable respect for the civil rights of his domestic opponents and refused to heed the call of other Democratic-Republicans—most notably Attorney General William Pinckney and Judge Joseph Story— for a sedition law. His circumspect policy toward New England disaffection was also well judged.

In other ways, however, Madison's cautious brand of leadership undermined the war effort. He tolerated incompetence, backbiting, and political disloyalty in his CABINET; he was slow to remove incompetent men from important civilian and military positions; he lacked a commanding influence in Congress; and he was unable to inspire the American people to open their hearts and purses in support of the war.

Contemporaries, including many loyal Republicans, acknowledged Madison's shortcomings as a war leader. "Mr. Madison is wholly unfit for the storms of War," Henry Clay said in 1812. "Nature has cast him in too benevolent a mould." "His spirit and capacity for a crisis of war," added Pennsylvania Congressman Charles J. Ingersoll in 1814, "are very generally called in question." The best that could be said of this gentle and thoughtful leader is that he embraced war reluctantly, that he eagerly sought to liquidate the conflict as quickly as possible, and that (unlike other war Presidents) he never used his power to harass or silence his domestic foes.

BIBLIOGRAPHY

Brant, Irving. *James Madison*. 6 vols. 1941–1961.
Hickey, Donald R. *The War of 1812: A Forgotten Conflict*. 1989.
Ketcham, Ralph. *James Madison: A Biography*. 1971.
Perkins, Bradford. *Prologue to War: England and the United States, 1805–1812*. 1961.
Rutland, Robert Allen. *The Presidency of James Madison*. 1990.
Stagg, J. C. A. *Mr. Madison's War: Politics, Diplomacy, and Warfare in the Early American Republic, 1783–1830*. 1983.

DONALD R. HICKEY

WAR POWERS. The term *war powers*, which is not mentioned in the Constitution, refers to the panoply of powers granted principally to Congress, but also to the President, to preserve and safeguard the existence of the nation. War powers embrace every aspect of NATIONAL SECURITY, including the authority to maintain peace, to declare NEUTRALITY, and to wage war successfully.

In EX PARTE MILLIGAN (1866), the Supreme Court affirmed that "The government, within the Constitution, has all the powers granted to it which are necessary to preserve its existence." The war clause of the Constitution (Article I, section 8) says, "The Congress shall have power . . . to declare war [and] grant Letters of Marque and Reprisal." By virtue of this clause, Congress possesses all war-making powers. Thus, the courts have held that it is the sole and exclusive province of Congress to change a state of peace into a state of war. This grant of authority gives to Congress, as James Madison explained, the decision to "commence, continue, or conclude" a war. In order to exercise that judgment, the Constitution vests Congress with a number of specific powers to control war and military affairs: to raise and support armies and provide and maintain a navy, to make the regulations of the land and naval forces, to call forth the militia, and to provide for organizing, arming, and disciplining the militia. The President's war powers are derived from the COMMANDER IN CHIEF clause, and they are quite narrow. In FEDERALIST 69, ALEXANDER HAMILTON, an exponent of broad presidential power, explained that the President is empowered to repel sudden attacks against the United States. As Commander in Chief, moreover, he is "first General and admiral" of the military forces, and he is to conduct war when "authorized" by Congress. The President has no constitutional authority to initiate hostilities.

The Constitutional Convention. An illuminating debate on the proper repository of the authority to make war occurred at the outset of the CONSTITUTIONAL CONVENTION. On 29 May 1787, EDMUND RANDOLPH of Virginia proposed a constitution that included a provision "that a national Executive be instituted." The seventh paragraph stated that the executive "ought to enjoy the Executive rights vested in the Congress of the Confederation." The Randolph Plan was taken up by the convention on 1 June. In considering the proposal to give to the national executive the executive powers of the Continental Congress, Charles Pinckney objected that "the Executive powers of [the existing Congress] might extend to peace and war which would render the Executive a Monarchy, of the worst kind, to wit an elective one." Fellow South Carolinian John Rutledge "was for vesting the Executive power in a single person, tho' he was not for giving him the power of war and peace." JAMES WILSON sought to reassure them, pointing out that "making peace and war are generally determined by writers on the Laws of Nations to be legislative powers." Wilson added that "the Prerogatives of the British Monarchy" are not "a proper guide in defining the executive powers. Some of the prerogatives were of a legislative nature. Among others that of war & peace." James Madison agreed that the war power was legislative in character. RUFUS KING noted, "Mad: agrees with Wilson in his definition of executive powers—executive powers . . . do not include the Rights of war & peace and c. but the powers should be confined and defined—if large we shall have the Evils of elective Monarchies." Randolph did not defend his proposal but pressed for a plural executive: "A unity of the Executive he observed would savor too much of a monarchy. We had he said no motive to be governed by the British Governmt. as our prototype." There was no vote on Randolph's resolution, but the discussion reflects an understanding that the power of war and peace—that is, the power to initiate war—did not belong to the executive but to the legislature.

On 6 August, the Committee of Detail circulated a draft constitution that provided, "The Legislature of the United States shall have the power . . . to make war." This bore sharp resemblance to the position of the Articles of Confederation, which vested the Continental Congress with "sole and exclusive right and power of determining on peace and war." When the war clause was considered in debate on 17 August, Pinckney opposed placing the power in Congress: "Its proceedings were too slow. . . . The Senate would be the best depository, being more acquainted with foreign affairs, and most capable of proper resolutions." Pierce Butler "was for vesting the power in the President, who will have all the requisite qualities, and will not make war but when the nation will support it." Butler's opinion shocked ELBRIDGE GERRY, who said that he "never expected to hear in a republic a motion to empower the Executive alone to declare war." Butler stood alone in the Convention: there was no support for his opinion and no second to his motion.

The proposal of the Committee of Detail to vest the legislature with the power to make war proved unsatisfactory to Madison and Gerry, and they persuaded the convention to substitute "declare" for "make," thus "leaving to the Executive the power to repel sudden attacks." The meaning of the motion is unmistakable. Congress was granted the power to make—that is, initiate—war; the President, for obvious reasons, could act immediately to repel sudden attacks without authorization from Congress. There was no quarrel whatever with respect to the sudden-attack provision, but there was some question as to whether the substitution of "declare" for "make" would effectuate the intention of Madison and Gerry. Roger Sherman of Connecticut thought that the joint motion "stood very well. The Executive shd. be able to repel and not to commence war. 'Make' better than 'declare' the latter narrowing the power [of the legislature] too much." Virginia's George Mason "was agst. giving the power of war to the Executive, because [he was] not [safely] to be trusted with it; or to the Senate, because [it was] not so constructed as to be entitled to it. He was for

clogging rather than facilitating war; but for facilitating peace. He preferred 'declare' to 'make.' " The Madison-Gerry proposal was adopted by a vote of 7 to 2. When Rufus King explained that the word "make" might be understood as authorizing Congress to initiate as well as conduct war, Connecticut changed its vote so that the word "declare" was approved, eight states to one.

The debates and the vote on the war clause make it clear that Congress alone possesses the authority to initiate war. The war-making authority was specifically withheld from the President, who was only given the authority to repel sudden attacks. Confirmation of this understanding was provided by ratifiers in various state conventions. For example, Wilson, whose role as an architect of the Constitution was only slightly less important than Madison's, told the Pennsylvania ratifying convention, "This system will not hurry us into war; it is calculated to guard against it. It will not be in the power of a single man, or a single body of men, to involve us in such distress; for the important power of declaring war is vested in the legislature at large."

Questions of Terminology. It is worth noting that, at the time the Constitution was being framed, the word "declare" enjoyed a settled understanding and an established usage. Simply stated, as early as 1552, the verb "declare" had become synonymous with the verb "commence"; they both denoted the initiation of hostilities. This was the established usage in international law as well as in England, where the terms *declare war* and *make war* were used interchangeably. This practice was familiar to the Framers. As Chancellor James Kent of New York, one of the leading jurists of the founding period, stated, "As war cannot lawfully be commenced on the part of the United States without an act of Congress, such an act is, of course, a formal notice to all the world, and equivalent to the most solemn declaration." While Kent interpreted "declare" to mean "commence," he did not assert that the Constitution requires a congressional declaration of war before hostilities could be lawfully commenced, but merely that it must be initiated by Congress.

Given the equivalence of "commence" and "declare," it is clear that a congressional declaration of war would institute military hostilities. According to international-law commentators, a DECLARATION OF WAR was desirable because it announced the institution of a state of war and the legal consequences it entailed—to the adversary, to neutral nations, and to citizens of the sovereign initiating the war. Indeed, this is the essence of a declaration of war: notice by the proper authority of its intent to convert a state of peace into a state of war. But all that is required under American law is a joint resolution or an explicit congressional authorization of the use of the military force against a named adversary. This can come in the form either of a declaration "pure and simple" or of a conditional declaration of war. There are also two kinds of war: those that U.S. courts have termed "perfect," or general, and those labeled "imperfect," or limited. Three early Supreme Court cases decided that the power of determining whether a war is perfect or imperfect lay with Congress.

The Constitution, then, locates all the offensive powers of the nation in Congress. Consistent with this constitutional theory, the Framers gave Congress the power to issue "letters of marque and reprisal." Dating back to the Middle Ages, when sovereigns employed private forces to retaliate for injuries caused by the sovereign of another state or his subjects, the practice of issuing reprisals gradually evolved into the use of public armies. By the time of the Constitutional Convention, the power to issue letters of marque and reprisal was considered sufficient to authorize a broad spectrum of armed hostilities short of declared war. In other words, it was regarded as a species of imperfect war and thus within the province of Congress.

The Framers' Decision. The Constitutional Convention's decision to withhold the power to commence war from the President signaled a marked departure from existing models of government, which placed the war power, indeed, virtually all FOREIGN AFFAIRS powers, in the hands of the executive. The Framers' rejection of the prevailing models is primarily attributable to two factors. First, the Framers were attached to republican ideology, the core principle of which was collective decision making in domestic as well as foreign affairs. Second, the founding generation, influenced by its own experience under King George III and by its understanding of history, lived in fear of a powerful executive and was adamantly opposed to the idea that a President would unilaterally control foreign policy. History had its claims. In *Federalist* 75 Hamilton stated that "the history of human conduct does not warrant that exalted opinion of human virtue which would make it wise in a nation to commit interests of so delicate and momentous a kind, as those which concern its intercourse with the rest of the world, to the sole disposal of . . . a President." In 1798 Madison wrote to Thomas Jefferson, "The constitution supposes, what the History of all Govts demonstrates, that the Ex. is the branch of power most interested in war, & most prone to it. It has accordingly with studied care, vested the question of war in the Legsl." The Framers' decision to create a new blueprint for foreign affairs justified Wilson's observation that the "prerog-

atives of the British Monarch" could not be used as a guide to define the executive powers since some, including the power of war and peace, were legislative in nature.

When the Framers granted Congress the power to declare war, they were vesting that body with the sole and exclusive prerogative to initiate military hostilities on behalf of the American people. The record reveals that no member of the Philadelphia convention and no member of any state ratifying convention held a different understanding of the meaning of the war clause. That this was the settled understanding of the war power is evidenced by statements of the founding generation, views of eminent treatise writers, and early judicial decisions as well as by nineteenth-century practice.

In 1793 war broke out between Great Britain and France. President George Washington declared that the treaty of alliance of 1778 did not obligate the United States to defend French territory in America, and he issued a PROCLAMATION OF NEUTRALITY. Whether this power belonged to the President or Congress was debated by Hamilton and Madison. Hamilton sought to defend the proclamation: "If the legislature have the right to make war on the one hand—it is on the other the duty of the Executive to preserve Peace till war is declared." For Hamilton, that duty carried with it the authority to determine the extent of the nation's treaty obligations. In response, Madison contended that if the proclamation was valid it meant that the President had usurped congressional power to decide between a state of peace and a state of war. Despite this difference, both agreed that the power to commence war is vested in Congress. Moreover, throughout their lives both Hamilton and Madison maintained the doctrine that it is Congress's responsibility alone to initiate hostilities.

In 1798 France repeatedly raided and seized American vessels. When asked whether a new law that increased the size of the navy authorized the President to initiate hostilities, Hamilton stated that he had not seen the law and that, if it did not grant the President any new authority but left him at the foot of the Constitution," then the President had only the power to "employ the ships as convoys, with authority to *repel* force by *force* (but not to capture) and to repress hostilities within our waters, including a marine league from our coasts. Anything beyond this must fall under the idea of *reprisals*, and requires the sanctions of that department which is to declare *or make war*" [emphasis in original].

Contrary to the claim that President John Adams engaged in an exercise of unilateral war-making in the

QUASI-WAR WITH FRANCE (1798–1800), the facts demonstrate that the war was clearly authorized by Congress. Congress debated the prospect of war and passed some twenty statutes permitting it to be waged. Moreover, Adams took absolutely no independent action. In *Bas v. Tingy* (1800), the Supreme Court held that the body of statutes enacted by Congress had authorized imperfect, or limited, war. In *Talbot v. Seeman* (1801), a case that arose from issues in the quasi-war, Chief Justice JOHN MARSHALL wrote for the Court, "The whole powers of war being, by the Constitution of the United States, vested in Congress, the acts of that body can alone be resorted to as our guides in this inquiry." In LITTLE V. BARREME (1804), Marshall emphasized the control that Congress can wield over the President as Commander in Chief. One of the statutes passed by Congress during the Quasi-War with France authorized the President to seize vessels sailing *to* French ports. President Adams issued an order directing American ships to capture vessels sailing *to or from* French ports, but in the opinion for the Court, Marshall held that Adams's order had exceeded his authority since congressional policy set forth in the statute was superior to presidential orders inconsistent with the statute. Subsequent judicial holdings have reiterated the fact that the Commander in Chief may be controlled by statute.

As President, Thomas Jefferson acknowledged that his powers of war were limited to defensive actions. In his first annual message to Congress in 1801, he reported the arrogant demands made by Joseph Caramanly, the pasha of Tripoli. Unless the United States paid tribute, the pasha threatened to seize American ships and citizens. Jefferson responded by sending a small squadron to the Mediterranean to protect against the threatened attack. He then asked Congress for further guidance, stating he was "unauthorized by the Constitution, without the sanction of Congress, to go beyond the line of defense." It was left to Congress to authorize "measures of offense also." Jefferson's understanding of the war clause underwent no revision. In 1805, he informed Congress of the dispute with Spain over the boundaries of Louisiana and Florida. Jefferson warned that Spain evidenced an "intention to advance on our possessions until they shall be repressed by an opposing force. Considering that Congress alone is constitutionally invested with the power of changing our condition from peace to war, I have thought it my duty to await their authority for using force."

Other early Presidents, including Washington, Madison, James Monroe, and Andrew Jackson, also refused to exercise offensive military powers without

authorization from Congress, which they understood to be the sole repository of the power to initiate war. There was no departure from this understanding of the war clause throughout the nineteenth century. In 1846, President James K. Polk ordered an army into a disputed border area between Texas and Mexico; it defeated the Mexican forces [*see* MEXICAN WAR]. In a message to Congress, Polk offered the rationale that Mexico had invaded the United States, which prompted Congress to declare war. If Polk's rationale was correct, then his action could not be challenged on constitutional grounds, for it was well established that the President had the authority to repel sudden attacks. If, however, he was disingenuous—if he had in fact initiated military hostilities—then he had clearly usurped the war-making power of Congress. It is worth noticing that he made no claim to constitutional power to make war. Although Congress declared war, the House of Representatives censured Polk for his actions because the war had been "unnecessarily and unconstitutionally begun by the President of the United States." Representative Abraham Lincoln voted with the majority against Polk. As President, Lincoln maintained that only Congress could authorize the initiation of hostilities. None of his actions in the CIVIL WAR, including the SUSPENSION OF HABEAS CORPUS, the appropriation of funds from the U.S. treasury, or his decision to call forth regiments from state militias, each of which was eventually retroactively authorized by Congress, constituted a precedent for presidential initiation of war. Moreover, in the PRIZE CASES (1863), the Supreme Court upheld Lincoln's blockade against the rebellious Confederacy as a constitutional response to sudden invasion, which began with the attack on Fort Sumter. The Court stated that the President, as Commander in Chief, "has no power to initiate or declare war either against a foreign nation or a domestic state." Nevertheless, in the event of invasion by a foreign nation or a state, the President was not only authorized "but bound to resist force by force. He does not initiate the war, but is bound to accept the challenge without waiting for any special legislative authority." According to the Court, the President had to meet the crisis in the shape it presented itself "without waiting for Congress to baptise it with a name; and no name given to it by him or them could change the fact."

Presidential War-making. Until 1950, no President, no judge, no legislator, and no commentator ever contended that the President has legal authority to initiate war. Since then, however, a steady pattern of presidential war-making has developed, from the KOREAN WAR and the VIETNAM WAR to U.S. incursions in

GRENADA and PANAMA, and revisionists have defended its legality on various grounds.

The Commander in Chief clause has been invoked as the principal pillar supporting presidential claims to the constitutional power of war and peace. The title of Commander in Chief, however, confers no war-making power whatever; it only vests the President with the authority to repel sudden attacks on the United States, and to direct war, as Hamilton explained, "when authorized or begun." In this capacity, the President can direct those forces placed at his command by an act of Congress. The Framers adopted the titled of Commander in Chief and its historical usage from England, where it was introduced in 1639 by King Charles I. The title was used as a generic term referring to the highest-ranking officer in a particular chain of command or theater of action. But the ranking commander in chief was always subordinate to a political superior, whether a king, Parliament, or, with the development of the cabinet system in England, a secretary of war. The practice of giving the officer at the apex of the military the title of commander in chief and of making him subject to instructions from a political superior was embraced by the Continental Congress and by most of the states in their early constitutions. This usage had been established for a century and a half and was thoroughly familiar to the Framers when they met in Philadelphia. There was no effort at the Constitutional Convention or at any state ratifying convention to redefine the office of Commander in Chief. Moreover, no court has ever held that the Commander in Chief clause is a source of presidential war-making power.

The executive power clause has also been adduced as a source of unilateral presidential war-making power, but this claim is of no moment. In fact, the claim that the grant of executive power includes the authority to initiate hostilities was considered and rejected in the Constitutional Convention; indeed, it caused much alarm. Delegates were concerned that, if the President inherited the executive powers vested in Congress by the Articles of Confederation, that grant of authority might include the power of war and peace. But Madison and Wilson allayed those fears when they explained that, according to "the Law of Nations," the war power is "legislative" in nature: "executive powers," he said "do not include the Rights of war and peace." Neither does the revisionist argument find any support in judicial precedents.

Other legal arguments have been contrived to defend presidential war-making. Some commentators have invoked Justice George Sutherland's dictum in his bizzare opinion in UNITED STATES v. CURTISS-WRIGHT EXPORT CORP. (1936). But even Sutherland disavowed any claim to a presidential war power. Others have claimed that, while Congress may "declare" war, the President may initiate hostilities that fall short of outright war. The Supreme Court, however, has held that Congress possesses exclusive authority to initiate total as well as limited war. Moreover, the President's possession of such authority would eviscerate the Constitution's placement of the war power in Congress.

Finally, it has been argued that executive war-making, if repeated often enough, acquires legal validity. This argument rests on the premise that Presidents have in fact frequently exercised the war power without congressional authorization. The actual number of such episodes varies according to who is doing the counting, but defenders usually list between one hundred and two hundred unilateral acts, each of which constitutes, for them, a legitimizing precedent for future executive wars. The argument is flawed in both detail and conception. In the first place, the revisionists' lists are inaccurately compiled. Most begin with the claim that President John Adams engaged in unilateral war-making with France in 1798. But that claim is false: Adams took absolutely no independent action. Moreover, many of the episodes recited on the revisionists' lists involved initiation of hostilities by a military commander, not authorization from a President. If practice establishes law, then this argument's inescapable conclusion is that every commander of every military unit has the power to initiate war. What is perhaps most revealing about presidential understanding of the constitutional locus of the war power is that in the one or two dozen instances in which Presidents have personally made the unconstitutional decision to initiate acts of war, they have *not* purported to rely on their authority as Commander in Chief or as CHIEF EXECUTIVE. Rather, they have made false claims of authorization—by statute, by treaty, or by international law. Moreover, it cannot be maintained that constitutional power, in this case the war power, can be acquired through practice. Justice FELIX FRANKFURTER echoed a centuries-old principle of Anglo-American jurisprudence when he stated, "Illegality cannot attain legitimacy through practice."

It has thus been in defiance of the intentions of the Framers, of the Constitutional Convention's debate and vote on the war clause, and of a wealth of executive, legislative, and judicial precedents of the nineteenth century that recent executives have invoked a presidential power to initiate military hostilities. The evidence against their case is overwhelming. Their claims ignore the text of the Constitution and find no authority in American legal history.

BIBLIOGRAPHY

Adler, David Gray. "The Constitution and Presidential Warmaking: The Enduring Debate." *Political Science Quarterly* 103 (1988):1–36.

Berger, Raoul. *Executive Privilege: A Constitutional Myth.* 1974.

Fisher, Louis. *Constitutional Conflicts between Congress and the President.* 3d rev. ed. 1991.

Glennon, Michael J. *Constitutional Diplomacy.* 1990.

Keynes, Edward. *Undeclared War: Twilight Zone of Constitutional Power.* 2d ed. 1991.

Koh, Harold. *The National Security Constitution: Sharing Power after the Iran-Contra Affair.* 1990.

Schlesinger, Arthur, Jr. *The Imperial Presidency.* 1973.

Sofaer, Abraham D. *War, Foreign Affairs, and Constitutional Power.* 1976.

Wormuth, Francis D., and Edwin B. Firmage. *To Chain the Dog of War: The War Power of Congress in History and Law.* 1986.

DAVID GRAY ADLER

WAR POWERS RESOLUTION (1973). Concerned that its role in making decisions to send military forces into combat had atrophied, Congress attempted to reassert itself in 1973 with the passage of the War Powers Resolution. The statute sought to curb presidential war-making and to require the "collective judgment" of the President and Congress before U.S. troops could be committed to hostilities. The resolution was passed within the immediate context of the white-hot debate surrounding American involvement in the VIETNAM WAR, but it can also be set within the larger context of legislative efforts to recapture the WAR POWER, which had been usurped by Presidents since Harry S. Truman's unilateral entry into the KOREAN WAR.

President Richard M. Nixon vetoed the War Powers Resolution. In his veto message, he stated that it was unwise, impractical, and dangerous to legislate the procedure by which the President and Congress would share the war power. Moreover, he argued that the measure infringed on the President's constitutional power as COMMANDER IN CHIEF. Nixon informed Congress that the "only way in which the constitutional powers of a branch of the Government can be altered is by amending the Constitution—and any attempt to make such alterations by legislation alone is clearly without force." But both houses of Congress summoned the requisite two-thirds majority to override the veto: the House by a narrow vote of 284 to 135 and the Senate by the wider margin of 75 to 18. The resolution thus became law on 7 November 1973 (P.L. 93-148).

Provisions. The War Powers Resolution consists of three main procedures to govern the deployment of U.S. military force abroad: presidential consultation with Congress, presidential reports to Congress, and congressional termination of military action. The purpose of the resolution, according to section 2(a), is "to insure that the collective judgment" of the President and Congress will apply to both the introduction of American troops into hostilities and the length of their involvement. Under section 3 of the resolution, the President is required "in every possible instance" to consult with Congress before he introduces troops into "hostilities" or into "situations where imminent involvement in hostilities is clearly indicated by the circumstances." This provision obviously vests the President with discretion to determine, at a minimum, whether consultation is "possible" and, perhaps somewhat more generously, whether it is desirable. Apparently, it also permits the President to determine when, how, and even whom to consult. Debate has arisen about the very meaning of "consultation." Presidents have tended to treat it as a synonym for notification, while Congress has viewed it as a joint deliberation on a pending issue or problem.

It has been contended that the statute does not require the President to consult with all members of Congress, but this claim raises a serious constitutional issue. The war clause of the Constitution (Article I, Section 8) requires a majority vote of both houses of Congress to authorize the initiation of hostilities against a foreign nation. It follows, therefore, that no smaller contingent in Congress may lay claim to the war power. And section 3 of the resolution also contains a greater, perhaps more fundamental, constitutional flaw. Since the provision empowers the President to introduce troops into combat without prior congressional authorization, it not only repudiates the resolution's stated aim of ensuring the "collective judgment" of both branches but also grants the President more power than he derives from the Constitution. The Constitution vests no power to initiate war in the President. Moreover, in his capacity as Commander in Chief he is only permitted to repel sudden attacks against the United States and to command military forces once war has been authorized by Congress. Bluntly stated, the resolution unconstitutionally delegates the power to make war to the President. This grant of authority also contradicts section 8(d) of the resolution, which states that the resolution is not intended to alter the constitutional authority of the President or Congress or to grant any authority to the President that "he would not have had in the absence" of the statute. Any attempt to vest the war power in the President, properly undertaken, would require a constitutional amendment since it involves a fundamental transfer of power from the legislature to the executive.

Section 4 of the Resolution imposes on the President important reporting requirements, which establish the foundation of congressional control over war making. When the President introduces forces into hostilities or into situations in which hostilities are imminent, he is required to submit a report to Congress within forty-eight hours. The submission of the report triggers the mechanisms of congressional control, but these are thwarted if the report is delayed. Section 5(b) provides that after a report "is submitted or is required to be submitted," the President must terminate the use of U.S. forces after sixty days unless Congress has declared war, authorized the action, or is physically unable to convene as a result of an attack on the United States. The President may extend the sixty-day period for an additional thirty days if he certifies that it is necessary to protect American forces and remove them from the conflict. Section 5 vests in Congress two mechanisms for controlling the involvement of U.S. forces in hostilities: Congress can decide to withhold authorization of presidential action during the sixty-to-ninety day period or it can pass a concurrent resolution at any time to order the President to remove forces involved in hostilities.

The instruments of congressional control may be frustrated, however, since the sixty-to-ninety-day clock does not begin to run until the President submits a report to Congress under section 4(a)(1). The clock has been triggered on only two occasions. In 1975, President Gerald Ford reported to Congress after the *Mayaguez* had been captured, but the issue of the time limit was moot because the military operation had been completed by the time the report was filed [*see* MAYAGUEZ INCIDENT]. In the second instance, Congress itself started the clock in October 1983 with the passage of the LEBANON RESOLUTION, which reflected its frustration with President Ronald Reagan's unwillingness to file a report under section 4(a)(1) after Marines he had sent to Lebanon became targets of hostile fire in August 1983. That measure permitted President Reagan to keep forces in Lebanon for a period of eighteen months, but he removed most of the troops in February 1984.

The resolution's most immediate and powerful congressional mechanism to control war making—the passage of a concurrent resolution to order the removal of U.S. troops engaged in hostilities—was gutted by the Supreme Court's decision in INS V. CHADHA (1983), which held the legislative veto unconstitutional. Although the case involved the use of a one-house legislative veto, the decision cast doubt on the

legality of any legislative veto that was not presented to the President for his signature.

Military Actions. Presidents filed approximately two dozen reports "consistent" with, but not under, the War Powers Resolution from 1973 to 1993. The record is checkered at best. On the whole, the experience has justified Arthur M. Schlesinger, Jr.'s characterization of the resolution as a "toy handcuff," for it has not effectuated the collective judgment of the two branches sought by Congress. While most of the military actions during these twenty years were short-lived, they were terminated solely by the President.

On three occasions in April 1975, President Ford reported to Congress the use of military force to help evacuate American citizens and refugees from Vietnam and Cambodia. But in these reports, Ford adduced the Commander in Chief clause, and not statutory sources, as authority for his actions. In May 1975, Ford ordered Marines to recapture a U.S. merchant vessel, the SS *Mayaguez*, which had been seized by the Cambodian navy. Ford's report on the *Mayaguez* incident was the first and only one to date that specifically cited section 4(a)(1). The time-limit issue was moot, however, because Ford's report was filed after the military operation had been completed. Controversy surrounded these early tests of the War Powers Resolution. The Ford administration contended that it had satisfied the consultation requirements because it had notified congressional leaders prior to the introduction of armed forces. Members of Congress argued that consultation requires solicitation of congressional opinion prior to a decision to commit U.S. forces and that the premise and promise of collective judgment had been violated.

In 1980, President Jimmy Carter filed a report with Congress on his unsuccessful effort to rescue American hostages in Iran [*see* IRANIAN HOSTAGE CRISIS; DESERT ONE]. Carter submitted the report "consistent" with the War Powers Resolution but like Ford claimed authority for his action as Commander in Chief and CHIEF EXECUTIVE. Carter defended his refusal to consult with Congress in advance on two grounds: the mission was a rescue attempt, not an act of aggression against Iran, and it depended on total surprise.

President Reagan's introduction of U.S. forces into Lebanon in 1982 and 1983 as part of a multinational force revealed the fragility of the resolution's mechanisms for legislative participation in war making. Military hostilities had actually broken out when Reagan deployed the Marines pursuant to the President's "constitutional authority" to conduct American foreign policy. Reagan filed three reports "consistent" with the War Powers Resolution, but he refused to report under section 4(a)(1), which would have limited the use of military forces to sixty to ninety days unless Congress authorized an extension. In reaction to Reagan's refusal to file under section 4(a)(1), Congress passed legislation to trigger the clock, but it authorized the continued participation of the marines in the multinational force for the lengthy period of eighteen months. The broad delegation of war-making authority reflected the assumption among members of Congress that Reagan's signature on the bill would represent a presidential acknowledgment of the legitimacy of the resolution. Reagan, however, made it clear that as President his authority could not be "infringed by statute" and that he might deploy troops beyond the eighteenth-month authorization period. The political compromise reflected a mutual concern to remove the issue of military action from the 1984 election-year calendar. By virtue of its action, Congress may have reaped short-term political benefit, but in the process it virtually surrendered its voice with respect to the continued use of military force and thereby undermined the resolution's premise of collective judgment in war making.

In April 1986, President Reagan announced that there was irrefutable evidence of Libyan involvement in recent terrorist acts, and in response he ordered bombing strikes on military installations and other facilities in Libya. Reagan engaged in no meaningful consultation prior to the air strikes, and while he reported to Congress, he did not cite section 4(a)(1). Reagan invoked the Commander in Chief clause as authority and justified the bombings as an act of "self defense" and a deterrent to further Libyan terrorism.

In the 1980s, members of Congress filed four lawsuits against President Reagan on grounds that he had violated the War Powers Resolution. In May 1981, several members of Congress went to court charging that Reagan had violated both the resolution and the Constitution when he sent U.S. military advisers to El Salvador. The State Department contended that the President was not required to submit a report since U.S. personnel were not being introduced into hostilities or situations of imminent hostilities. Eventually, twenty-nine members of the House joined the suit against Reagan. But an equal number of Senators and Representatives who supported the President intervened in the case and asked that it be dismissed. In *Crockett v. Reagan,* a federal district court refused to perform the fact-finding necessary to determine whether hostilities or imminent hostilities existed, holding that that was a question for Congress, not the court, to answer. The judge noted, moreover, that Congress as an institution had not acted to restrain Reagan.

In October 1983, President Reagan ordered an invasion of GRENADA. Reagan submitted a report to Congress "consistent" with the resolution, but he failed to cite section 4(a)(1). Eleven members of Congress brought a suit charging that Reagan had violated the power of Congress to declare war. But in *Conyers v. Reagan,* a federal court refused to exercise its jurisdiction since members of Congress had avenues of relief available to them through the regular legislative process. Guided by *Crockett,* the court made it clear that if Congress wished to restrain the President it could not rely on the courts but rather must exercise its own powers. In *Sanchez-Espinoza v. Reagan,* twelve members of Congress challenged President Reagan's actions in Nicaragua, but the court dismissed their suit on similar grounds.

In 1987, in *Lowry v. Reagan,* 110 members of Congress brought a lawsuit in which they contended that President Reagan had violated the resolution when he failed to report his use of military force in the Persian Gulf under section 4(a)(1). The suit was dismissed as a nonjusticiable political question. The federal court stated that the plaintiff's dispute was "primarily with fellow legislators" and it echoed a familiar refrain: if Congress chooses not to confront the President, it cannot expect the courts to undertake that task.

In December 1989, President George Bush ordered U.S. troops into PANAMA. A day later, he reported to Congress, but, like his predecessors, he refused to cite section 4(a)(1). He set forth several justifications for the invasion, including the duty to protect American citizens in Panama and the need to bring General Manuel Noriega, the Panamanian strongman, "to justice in the United States." Although Bush did not consult with congressional leaders in reaching his decision, there were few complaints in Congress, presumably because Americans embraced the military operation. In February 1990, the House passed a resolution that declared that the President had acted "decisively and appropriately in ordering United States forces to intervene in Panama."

In August 1990, Bush, in response to Iraq's invasion of Kuwait, sent U.S. military forces to Saudi Arabia and other countries in the region. Following the deployment, Bush reported to Congress "consistent" with the War Powers Resolution, but again he refrained from citing section 4(a)(1), declaring "I do not believe involvement in hostilities is imminent." Efforts to repel the Iraqi invasion led to the GULF WAR—the largest war in which the United States has been involved since the passage of the resolution. The Bush administration maintained that the President did not need congressional authorization for the use of force, but as an act of supererogation Bush did obtain permission from Congress.

On 13 December 1990, two federal district courts rejected legal challenges to President Bush's deployment of forces to Saudi Arabia. In *Ange v. Bush,* the court invoked the political question doctrine to dismiss a reservist's challenge to Bush's action. In *Dellums v. Bush,* fifty-four members of Congress sought an injunction against President Bush to bar him from "initiating an offensive attack" against Iraqi forces without explicit authorization from Congress. The court denied the injunction on grounds that the issue was not ripe for resolution, but it also dismissed the sweeping claims of a presidential war-making power. In a notable passage, the court stated that if a majority of Congress took action to assert its constitutional power to declare war and the president refused to comply, then such a constitutional impasse would be ripe for review.

The Constitution grants to Congress the sole and exclusive power to authorize or declare war. The War Powers Resolution violates that constitutional principle by granting the President power to commence war without congressional authorization. Some scholars contend that the Resolution, while flawed in theory, has succeeded in tempering unilateral presidential war-making. They hold that the executive branch believes that it must act precipitously, before the sixty-day clock expires. That issue is not settled, but experience under the resolution reaffirms that in the area of war making a great gulf separates constitutional principle and governmental practice.

BIBLIOGRAPHY

Ely, John Hart. "Suppose Congress Wanted a War Powers Act That Worked." *Columbia Law Review.* 88 (1988): 1379–1431.
Fisher, Louis. *Constitutional Conflicts between Congress and the President.* 3d rev. ed. 1991.
Glennon, Michael J. *Constitutional Diplomacy.* 1990.
Keynes, Edward. *Undeclared War: Twilight Zone of Constitutional Power.* 2d ed. 1991.
Koh, Harold. *The National Security Constitution: Sharing Power after the Iran-Contra Affair.* 1990.
Wormuth, Francis D., and Edwin B. Firmage. *To Chain the Dog of War: The War Power of Congress in History and Law.* 1986.

DAVID GRAY ADLER

WARREN COMMISSION (President's Commission on the Assassination of President Kennedy). The first urgent priority of Lyndon B. Johnson as thirty-sixth President of the United States was to come to terms with the assassination of his predecessor, John F. Kennedy. Johnson was sworn in at 2:38 on the after-

noon of 22 November 1963, aboard *Air Force One* just before the airplane returned to Washington from Dallas; and while the world was preoccupied with ceremonies for the fallen leader, the business of government proceeded with Johnson at the helm. A suspect named Lee Harvey Oswald had been arrested and charged with the murder of Kennedy; and while Oswald insisted he was innocent, the FEDERAL BUREAU OF INVESTIGATION was so confident of his guilt that evidence inconsistent with it was rejected out of hand. On 24 November, as the late President lay in state at the Capitol, the main concern of J. EDGAR HOOVER, the director of the FBI, was how to convince the public that Oswald was the actual assassin. Hoover proposed to Deputy Attorney General NICHOLAS DEB. KATZENBACH that the FBI submit a report on the assassination, which President Johnson could make public if he wished. It was Hoover's intention to obviate the necessity of a presidential commission, but his strategy depended upon public acceptance of the assassination as an isolated event with no rhyme or reason. Any hope of this was destroyed when at 11:21 that Sunday morning a Dallas nightclub operator, Jack Ruby, stepped from a crowd at police headquarters, as Oswald was being transferred to the county jail, and shot the suspect, wounding him fatally. The idea of two unrelated lone assassins striking within forty-eight hours was more than most people would accept easily. General Maxwell D. Taylor, chairman of the JOINT CHIEFS OF STAFF, expected there would be suspicion that Oswald had been killed "to suppress something"; and Johnson would write in his memoirs: "With that single shot a nation turned to skepticism and doubt. The atmosphere was poisonous and had to be cleared."

Establishing the Commission. On 25 November, the day of the Kennedy funeral, Hoover took credit for prevailing on the editors of the *Washington Post* to withdraw an editorial calling for a presidential commission by assuring them a full report would be made by President Johnson based on the FBI investigation; Katzenbach, though, was hedging his bets, trying to accommodate Hoover but also heeding public reaction, which seemed to be based on a fear that assassins were still at large. Katzenbach urged in a note to the White House assistant Bill Moyers that the prompt release of the FBI's report, maintaining the reputation of the bureau, would offset hints of a communist conspiracy by police officials in Dallas; the alternative, he noted, would be a presidential commission to review the evidence, which had "both advantages and disadvantages" and could "await publication of the FBI report and public reaction to it." Johnson was also ambivalent and responsive to the will of others: he directed the FBI to submit its report, but when influential members of the House and Senate issued calls for a congressional investigation, and a court of inquiry was established in Texas, the President informed Hoover that the only way to stop the "rash of investigations" was to appoint a blue-ribbon panel to evaluate the FBI report. Hoover accepted the decision, of course, though on the issue of Oswald's single-handed guilt he was in a position to direct a verdict. On 25 November he had sent two senior FBI officials to Dallas; Assistant to the Director Alan H. Belmont described their mission: "to set out the evidence showing that Oswald is responsible for the shooting that killed the President." Katzenbach in his note to Moyers also revealed a closed-case attitude in citing certain assassination facts he believed ought to be made public: "Oswald was the assassin . . . ; he did not have confederates . . . ; and the evidence was such that he would have been convicted."

On 29 November Johnson summoned Chief Justice Earl Warren to the White House, aware that Warren had already declined his request that he serve as chairman of the commission. A renowned manipulator, Johnson told the old soldier, a WORLD WAR I veteran, that rumors were afloat in the world that could lead to nuclear war, and he speculated that investigations by committees of Congress and in Texas would leave the American people frightened and bewildered. Then came the clincher, which Johnson described in retrospect: "When the country is confronted with a threatening division and suspicions, I said, and its foundation is being racked, and the President of the United States says you are the only man who can handle this matter, you won't say, 'no,' will you? [Warren] swallowed hard and said 'No, sir.' " (Johnson had chosen six distinguished members of the panel, whose names he read to Warren: Senator Richard B. Russell, Democrat of Georgia; Senator John Sherman Cooper, Republican of Kentucky; Representative Hale Boggs, Democrat of Louisiana; Representative Gerald R. Ford, Republican of Michigan; Allen W. Dulles, former director of the CIA; John J. McCloy, former U.S. high commissioner for Germany and president of the World Bank.) That evening Johnson signed the EXECUTIVE ORDER creating the President's Commission on the Assassination of President Kennedy, to be known as the Warren Commission, which would be charged with "the responsibility for finding the full facts of the case and reporting them, along with appropriate recommendations, to the American people."

The Commission's Report. Warren saw the role of the commission as more judicial than investigative or prosecutorial, that its purpose was to evaluate the case of the FBI and other agencies, rather than assemble new evidence. There would, therefore, be no need for an independent investigative staff, and the commission would make do with fourteen attorneys recruited by J. Lee Rankin, the general counsel, who was sworn in on 16 December. (Warren also believed it would not be necessary for the commission to seek subpoena power, though he was overruled, and it was granted by congressional resolution.) Warren's faith in the reliability of the FBI was severely shaken, however, by the poor quality of the bureau's report on the assassination, which was submitted on 9 December. According to reports of a commission meeting a week later, the report was received with disappointment: it was difficult to understand, much of its content had been leaked to the press, and it left "millions of questions" unanswered, in the words of Congressman Boggs. Rankin, who was instrumental in a decision to continue to rely on the resources of federal agencies, remarked that it did not seem as though the FBI was "looking for things that this Commission has to look for in order to get the answers that it wants and it's entitled to." The commission came to realize it faced in Director Hoover an active antagonist, who was defensive to the point of paranoia and concerned that the commission would discover relevant facts the FBI had missed, and his reputation would be ruined. As Katzenbach told the House Select Committee on Assassinations in 1978, Hoover would have been deeply troubled by evidence that contradicted the conclusion that Oswald was the lone assassin. (The CENTRAL INTELLIGENCE AGENCY was not as outwardly resistant as the FBI, but it took the position that the commission would only receive responses to specific inquiries, a policy that eventually would prove more damaging to the commission's credibility than Hoover's outright opposition.)

Hoover need not have worried; the Warren Commission found no important evidence that the FBI had overlooked. The testimony of 552 witnesses and the thousands of exhibits of analyzed evidence attest to a dedicated effort to extract truth from a massive accumulation of information. The performance of the commission staff was exceptional, even heroic, in light of an impossible 30 June 1964 deadline for the final report. President Johnson wanted the work of the commission completed in advance of the presidential nominating conventions that summer, for he feared the Kennedy assassination would become a political issue (he also worried lest his campaign be overshadowed by memories of Kennedy). When the 888-page report did appear on 24 September, it was a well-crafted and comprehensive document, and it was generally accepted as the truth. "No material question now remains unsolved," wrote journalist Anthony Lewis in an introduction to the *New York Times* edition of the report. The case against Oswald was such that Chief Justice Warren would reflect on it in his *Memoirs* from his position as a former California prosecutor: "I have no hesitation in saying that had it not been for the prominence of the victim, the case against Oswald would have been tried in two or three days with little likelihood of any but one result."

The commission concluded that three shots had been fired from a sixth-floor southeast corner window of the Texas School Book depository in Dallas: one a probably miss, one that wounded Kennedy and Governor John B. Connally of Texas, and one that hit Kennedy in the head, killing him. All the shots had been fired by Oswald, whose guilt was based on impressive evidence: he had owned the 6.5 millimeter Mannlicher-Carcano from which the shots were fired; he had carried the rifle into the book depository on the morning of 22 November; he had been at the window at the time the shots were fired; the rifle had been found shortly after the assassination on the sixth floor along with a paper bag in which he had carried the weapon into the building. The commission also concluded that Oswald had murdered a Dallas police officer, J. D. Tippit, and it considered this corroboration of his guilt in the assassination.

Questions about a Conspiracy. The commission found no evidence of conspiracy, and, while it left room for a reversal based on information not available in 1964, it went to great length to dismiss the possibility of a plot. It said that no limitations had been placed on the inquiry, that all government agencies had "fully discharged their responsibility to cooperate." The commission added a final comment: "if there is any evidence [of a plot], it has been beyond the reach of all the investigative agencies and resources of the United States." From its study of Oswald's background the commission proposed a number of possible motives: his deep-rooted resentment of authority, his inability to enter into meaningful relationships, his urge to find a place in history, his capacity of violence, his commitment to Marxism. While finding none of these satisfactory in itself, the commission theorized that taken together they may have been "the moving force of a man whose view of the world had been twisted."

The commission's conclusion that there was no conspiracy was the result of a systematic examination of the issue that was thorough and supposedly foolproof. Here the commission employed the same meticulous approach that established Oswald's guilt: first, a step-by-step analysis of the modus operandi of the assassination to see if there were indications that Oswald had been assisted; then, careful scrutiny of Oswald's life from when he was discharged from the Marine Corps in 1959 to learn if the seeds of conspiracy might have been sown during his defection to the Soviet Union or in his period of political activism on return to the United States in June 1962. Insinuations that Oswald had been a U.S. government agent were among the most troublesome for the commission, since it is always difficult "to prove a negative," that is, that a conspiracy did not occur, and the circumstantial evidence that Oswald had been some sort of intelligence agent was strong. The strategy used to refute the rumors was to dispense with lengthy analysis, issue an unequivocal denial, and hope the matter would be put to rest. The commission declared: "close scrutiny of the Federal agencies involved and the testimony of the responsible officials of the U.S. Government establish that there was absolutely no type of informant or undercover relationship between an agency of the U.S. Government and Lee Harvey Oswald at any time." (The innocence of the government's relationship with Oswald withstood the test of the 1979 House Select Committee on Assassinations, which went beyond taking affidavits of denial; however, the flat assertions of the commission raised understandable questions, since Oswald had come in contact with more than one federal agency, including the FBI; the committee, too, found that while the commission had conducted a thorough investigation of Oswald, it had failed to investigate adequately the possibility of a conspiracy (the committee found that it was likely that such a conspiracy existed), and although the commission acted in good faith, it presented its conclusions in a too definitive fashion.

In its evaluation of Jack Ruby the commission said it could discover no "sign of any conduct which suggests that he was involved in the assassination," and "his response to the assassination had been one of genuine shock and grief." But the key piece of evidence in the commission's case that Ruby had not participated in a plot was its finding that Ruby and Oswald had never been acquainted, though here again the commission was faced with the need to prove its negative—no conspiracy. It was able to do so, at least to its own satisfaction, by refuting all of the reported links between the two men. Ruby was described by the commission as an uncomplicated man with little mystery to his past: in 1963 he was fifty-two and unmarried; he ran a cheap Dallas nightclub not very successfully; his acquaintances included a number of Dallas police officers who frequented his club; he had broken the law several times in a minor way, but he was not connected to organized crime.

Doubts about the Commission's Findings. Early reviews of the Warren Commission's report were respectful of the diligent investigation on which it was based, and they generally accepted its interpretation of the assassination. There was, however, growing dissent as critics of the investigation—many of them politically motivated or with some ulterior motive—joined the chorus, and their influence was reflected in a Louis Harris poll in October 1964; 31 percent of the American people doubted that Oswald had acted alone, a figure that would double in a few years. There is little doubt the commission would have withstood the assault, which by the 1970s had been reduced to tedious nitpicking; however, in 1976 a Senate committee learned that the CIA had enlisted the Mafia in an effort to assassinate Fidel Castro of CUBA. The committee—the Senate Select Committee to Study Governmental Operations with Respect to Intelligence Activities—disclosed that government leaders, including President Kennedy, had not been fully briefed by CIA officers responsible for the plots.

If the Warren Commission, save one member who kept it to himself (Allen Dulles had been CIA director when these plots were conceived), knew about the CIA-Mafia connection, it left no record of it; therefore, it is not surprising that the revelation stirred new interest in the assassination of President Kennedy.

BIBLIOGRAPHY

Epstein, Edward Jay. *Inquest: The Warren Commission and the Establishment of Truth.* 1966.

Ford, Gerald R. *Portrait of the Assassin.* 1965.

Johnson, Lyndon B. *The Vantage Point: Perspective of the Presidency, 1903–1969.* 1971.

Lane, Mark. *Rush to Judgment.* 1966.

U.S. House of Representatives. Select Committee on Assassinations. *Final Report.* 1979. 95th Cong., 2d sess. H.R. 95-1828 (pts. 1 and 2).

U.S. House of Representatives. Select Committee on Assassinations. Vol 11. *Warren Commission.* 1979.

Warren Commission. *Report of the President's Commission on the Assassination of President Kennedy.* 1964.

Warren, Earl. *The Memoirs of Earl Warren.* 1977.

G. ROBERT BLAKEY

WASHINGTON, GEORGE (1732–1799), first President of the United States (1789–1797). George Washington was arguably the "Indispensable Man" of the founding epoch. His earliest aspiration was to be a Virginia country gentleman, and he did become a scientific farmer par excellence, and one of the richest men in America. He also aspired, however, to a public character that would win him fame. At the age of twenty-two he was entrusted with command of the Virginia troops sent to the backcountry in what became the French and Indian War. He took to warfare enthusiastically. Tall and powerfully built, he looked like a military hero, and he was a superb horseman. His appearance was complemented by an aura of invincibility. In one battle every other mounted officer was shot and killed—he was unscathed. Time and again his clothes were shredded and his horses shot, but he was never touched. He, almost alone among the officers, emerged from that war a hero destined for great things.

His first real opportunity for greatness came twenty years later in the War of Independence when he was chosen commander in chief by the Continental Congress (in which he was serving). By sheer force of character he created the Continental Army and held it together, under extremely adverse circumstances, for the eight years it took to win independence. Then in a dramatic fashion he faced down a mutiny of officers at Newburgh, New York, thus protecting the liberty that had just been won at Yorktown. And, like Cincinnatus, he himself relinquished power, said farewell to his troops, and returned to the life of a farmer.

The First President. In 1787 he was once again called to service, at the Constitutional Convention in Philadelphia. He presided over the convention, but his most vital contribution was his mere presence. His widely publicized participation gave legitimacy to the proceedings, and because he was universally trusted, the secrecy in which the convention operated did not undermine the result.

From the moment the Constitution was published, it was assumed that, should it be ratified, Washington would be the first President. In Europe as well as in America he was customarily described as the "Father of His Country," a designation more exalted than the "Father of His People" that was applied to kings. Mercy Otis Warren, in her 1805 history of the American Revolution, called Washington "the favorite of every class of people" and wrote that "Had any character of less popularity and celebrity been designated to this high trust, it might at this period have endangered, if not have proved fatal to the peace of the union. . . . The hearts of the whole continent were united, to give him their approbatory voice."

Warren also noted that "though some thought the executive vested with too great powers to be entrusted to the hand of any individual, Washington was an individual in whom they had the most unlimited confidence." Pierce Butler, a delegate from South Carolina to the Constitutional Convention and designer of the ELECTORAL COLLEGE system, commented that the President's powers "are full great" and added that he did not believe "they would have been so great had not many of the members cast their eyes toward General Washington as President; and shaped their Ideas of the Powers to be given to a President, by their opinions of his Virtue." Indeed, Americans were probably willing to try the experiment with a single, national republican chief executive only because of their unreserved trust in George Washington.

Washington, however, did nothing to seek the presidency or to promote himself as a candidate for it. Instead, he agreed to serve as President only with the greatest reluctance. He told his friend and former aide-de-camp, David Humphreys, "I have but one wish myself, which is to live & die on my own plantation. . . . I think there are a great many men in the U.S. much fitter for the office than I am. . . . I cannot pretend to be so well acquainted with civil matters, as I was with military affairs." His reluctance was expressed in terms of dread. So far from pursuing the office, when he began to receive word late in November of the outcomes of the voting for presidential electors, he told Humphreys, "I feel very much like a man who is condemned to death does when the time of his execution draws nigh."

Shortly after his inauguration, he once again voiced his misgivings in a letter to Edward Rutledge. "I greatly apprehend," he wrote, "that my Countrymen will expect too much from me. I fear, if the issue of public measures should not correspond [*sic*] with their sanguine expectations, they will turn the extravagant (and I may say undue) praises which they are heaping upon me at this moment, into equally extravagant (though I will fondly hope unmerited) censures."

For most of his first term, Washington's misgivings seemed unjustified. The EXECUTIVE DEPARTMENTS and the federal court system were put in place, the President was able to fill governmental offices with men of high quality, the public debts (which had been devastating and chaotic) had been brought into order in a way that increased the nation's prosperity, and the divisions over the ratification of the Constitution seemed to have been healed. Then, in 1792, the uncertainty of affairs in Europe, combined with the fact that the presidential experience so far had not been unpleasant, made it possible for other people to prevail upon Washington to serve a second term. His luster still untarnished, Washington was elected for the second time again by the unanimous vote of the Electoral College.

The second term, however, proved to be a nightmare. Washington saw his second administration imperiled by foreign wars and rent with violent political confrontations at home. The Father of His Country was indeed beset by "unmerited censures" of the vilest kind, and the psychic cost of the second term was more than any man could reasonably be expected to bear. But Washington, by the time he retired in 1797, had defined the presidency, established it on firm foundations, and made it central to the existence of the Republic. Not all the precedents he set would last, yet he made the office viable, an institution of flexibility and energy that could exert its will while still remaining under the ultimate control of organic law.

Establishing Precedents. The beginning of the office of President, nonetheless, got off to a slow start. Congress, scheduled by the old Confederation Congress to convene in New York on 4 March, did not have a quorum until 6 April, and it could not officially count the Electoral College votes until it had a quorum. Any other man than Washington would have been on the scene, ready to launch the ship of state, but to avoid seeming eager he remained at home awaiting official notification of his election as President. After Congress had counted the votes and sent a messenger to notify him, he made a leisurely trip northward, gratified but also somewhat distressed by the overwhelming popular acclaim shown him all along the way. He finally arrived in New York to be inaugurated—on 30 April.

During the week before he got to the city, and for two weeks afterward, the Senate was engaged in a debate over an appropriate form of address for the President. Vice President John Adams, having spent many years as American minister in the courts of Europe, had developed a taste for royal pomp and had convinced himself that some regal title would be necessary in America if people were to respect the new government. A goodly number of Senators, thinking of their body as an American House of Lords, seemed to agree. Senator Richard Henry Lee of Virginia, who had earlier been as ardent a radical republican as Adams, was among these. At one point Lee "read over a list of the Titles of all the Princes and Potentates of the Earth, marking where the Word Highness occurred." Senator Oliver Ellsworth of Connecticut observed that the "appellation of President" was too common for the chief executive of a nation, inasmuch as there were presidents "of Fire Companies & of a Cricket Club." Finally, the House of Representatives balked, refusing to accept anything but the simple constitutional formulation, "President of the United States."

President Washington was embarrassed by all this, because the debate suggested that the Senate viewed the presidency as a quasi-monarchical office. He himself was searching for rules of conduct that would suit a republican executive. He had scarcely taken up residence in a large rented house when throngs of visitors began to show up, some on business but most had come to gawk at him or to solicit jobs. All acted as if they had a constitutional right to be there. From breakfast to bedtime, Washington complained, it was impossible to be "relieved from the ceremony of one visit before I had to attend to another." Upon inquiring about the practice of the presidents of the Confederation Congress, he learned that they had been "considered in no better light than as a Maitre d'Hôtel . . . for the table was considered as a public one."

After consultation with John Adams, James Madison, JOHN JAY, and ALEXANDER HAMILTON, Washington devised rules of behavior that would strike a balance between "too free an intercourse and too much familiarity," which would reduce the dignity of the office, and "an ostentatious show" of monarchical aloofness, which would be improper in a republic. A "line of conduct" was worked out. Dinners were to be held every Thursday at four for government officials and their families on a regular system of rotation to avoid the appearance of favoritism. Two occasions a week were established for greeting the general public, a levee for men on Tuesdays from three to four and tea parties for men and women on Friday evenings. Anyone respectably dressed could attend either public function without invitation.

Three other matters of protocol were given careful attention. One concerned the President's salary. Washington had refused to accept a salary during the revolutionary war, and in his inaugural address he asked not to be compensated except by way of an expense account. Congress, however, took the position that the Constitution mandated a "fixed compensation" for the President and voted that the salary be $25,000 per year. (For Washington's eight years of service that should have amounted to $200,000, but he drew only $196,121, the difference being the salary for the fifty-six days his first administration fell short of being four full years. Such scrupulousness was characteristic of the man.)

A second concern was the INAUGURATION ceremony. Washington took the oath of office in the Senate chamber, where both houses of Congress had gathered, and then he delivered his address. This procedure was consciously patterned after the arrangements in England, where the king, at the beginning of each session of Parliament, addressed both houses in the chamber of the Lords. Each house of Congress completed the ritual by calling on the President later with a formal answer to his remarks, as the Lords and Commons customarily did. That pattern was repeated annually on the occasion of the STATE OF THE UNION MESSAGES. But Washington took some of the monarchical edge off the proceedings by wearing, for the occasion, a suit of brown broadcloth made in Connecticut.

A third matter involved federal-state relations. After the first session of the First Congress adjourned in the fall of 1789, Washington toured New England, avoiding Rhode Island, which had not yet ratified the Constitution, and Vermont, which was governing itself as an independent republic. As he approached Cambridge, Massachusetts, he was invited to review the local militia troops; he declined to do so "otherwise than as a private man," because they were under the jurisdiction of the state, not the federal government. Having deferred to STATES' RIGHTS in that regard, he similarly refused Governor John Hancock's invitation to stay in the governor's residence in Boston. He did agree to have dinner with Hancock—on the assumption that Hancock would acknowledge the subordinate position of governors by first paying a courtesy call upon the President. Hancock sent a message that he was crippled with gout and could not leave home, but Washington flatly refused to see him except in Washington's own lodgings. Next day the governor, heavily swathed in bandages, showed up at Washington's quarters, and the precedent was established.

Such matters can be regarded as trivial—some contemporaries thought them pretentious and even comical—but Washington did not so view them, and he was right. He wrote to James Madison (5 May 1789) that "As the first of everything, in our situation will serve to establish a precedent, it is devoutly wished on my part, that these precedents may be fixed on true principles." He clearly saw that the "founding" was a continuing process and that the President must take the lead in implementing the "true principles" of the Constitution, if the government were to perdure. Moreover, he understood that the presidency, if properly established, would be dual in nature: CHIEF EXECUTIVE but also ritualistic and ceremonial head of state; and the latter function was quite as vital as the administrative one. Furthermore, it was his task to enable the American people to make the transition from monarchy to republicanism by serving as the symbol of nationhood and to institutionalize that symbol by investing it in the office, not the man. To that end, he behaved as if his every move was being closely scrutinized—which to a considerable extent it was.

Washington was able to succeed, partly because of a

natural gravity and dignity combined with simplicity of tastes and manners, but more importantly because he was a consummate actor who had self-consciously been playing role all his adult life. In the eighteenth century it was conventional practice for those in polite society and public life to pick a role, like a part in a play, and act it consistently, which is to say always "be in character." If one chose a character that one could play comfortably, and if one played it long enough and well enough, by degrees it became a "second nature" that superseded one's primary base nature. One became, in other words, what one pretended to be. Washington differed from the ordinary by picking a progression of characters during his lifetime, each nobler and grander than the last, and playing each so well that he ultimately transformed himself into a man of almost extrahuman virtue.

Relations with Congress. The early preoccupation with ritual was appropriate for another reason: until Congress enacted the legislation, there were almost no laws to be executed, no executive departments to administer them, and no courts to adjudicate them. As it unfolded, the doings in the Congress amounted almost to a second constitutional convention, for they organically defined, shaped, and gave life to a government that the Constitution only authorized.

Washington had thought of actively directing the process, but then he decided it would be more prudent to let others lead. He had written a sixty-two-page statement of maxims, principles, and proposals but scrapped it and instead presented only a handful of legislative recommendations in his inaugural address. All concerned his duties in treaty making or as COMMANDER IN CHIEF: proposals for a law bringing the minuscule existing military establishment into conformity with the Constitution, one establishing a temporary commission to deal with southern INDIANS, and one authorizing the calling of the militia in the Ohio country if needed. All three proposals were acted upon. Perhaps it was Congress's apparent willingness to grant him blanket authority in such matters—most people in government seemed anxious to give the President adequate powers—that induced him to play a passive role in the definition of the executive power in 1789.

The extent to which Congress expected the executive branch to exercise discretionary powers is revealed by the process of making appropriations. The appropriations act of 1789, consisting of 125 words, allotted a "sum not exceeding" $216,000 for salaries and operations of the government, a limit of $137,000 for the War Department, a maximum of $190,000 for redeeming warrants issued by the former treasury board, and up to $96,000 for pensions to war invalids. From the outset, it was understood by all that executive officers could divert funds from the purposes for which they had been appropriated to meet special contingencies. For example, in 1793 both Thomas Jefferson and James Madison approved the advance of money to French refugees from Santo Domingo even though no funds had been appropriated for the purpose, and in 1794 Washington used unappropriated funds from the War Department to cover the cost of the militia troops that suppressed the WHISKEY REBELLION. From time to time Congress attempted to bring spending more fully under its control, but it was simply unable to micromanage the budget.

One of the most significant decisions regarding the EXECUTIVE POWER that was made early on arose in the House debates over the creation of the executive departments. Representative William Loughton Smith of South Carolina, citing Hamilton's FEDERALIST 77, contended that senatorial approval would be necessary for presidential removal of executive officeholders just as it was for appointment. As Madison summarized the arguments, four general positions on the subject were advanced: the matter was one for Congress to decide; "no removal can take place otherwise than by IMPEACHMENT"; "the power is incident to that of appointment, and therefore belongs to the President & Senate"; and the REMOVAL POWER is vested solely in the President. The last of these prevailed by a sizable majority.

That decision was not binding upon future Congresses or Presidents. The question would come up again on several pivotal occasions in American history, but the constitutional reasoning underlying the decision became established doctrine. The Constitution, Madison declared, vested the executive power in the President, with the exception that the Senate is to share the APPOINTMENT POWER and TREATY-MAKING POWER. Congress is not authorized to add other exceptions. Madison then asked, "Is the power of displacing an executive power? I conceive that if any power whatsoever is in its nature executive it is the power of appointing, overseeing, and controlling those who execute the laws." If the Constitution had not required senatorial approval of executive appointments, the President "would have the right by virtue of his executive power to make such appointment." In sum, the President has certain unspecified but real powers that he exercises by virtue of the vesting clause; the vesting clause was a positive grant, not an abstract generalization.

Some strain between President and Senate soon arose in regard to the advice portion of the appointment power. Congress had enacted the first revenue act, establishing duties on imported goods and providing for collectors. Washington sent to the Senate a list of nominees for collectorships. Among these was Benjamin Fishbourn, whom Washington had known as a good army officer during the war and who had been serving as the customs collector for Savannah under Georgia's import laws. The Senate approved all the other nominees but, without saying why, rejected Fishbourn, whereupon Washington promptly submitted another nominee. But the Senate also adopted a resolution that senatorial "advice, and consent to the appointment of Officers should be given in the presence of the President." Then it appointed a three-man committee to confer with Washington "on the mode of communication proper to be pursued between him and the Senate, in the formation of Treaties, and making appointments to offices." Washington told the committee that oral communications seemed necessary with regard to treaties and possibly for foreign ministers, though details of how to conduct such discussions would have to be worked out; but communications respecting other appointments should be in writing because of the awkwardness personal confrontations might entail. The Fishbourn episode is sometimes cited as the first example of the doctrine of senatorial courtesy, but a more likely candidate came two weeks later, when the two Georgia Senators objected to the appointment of one of the commissioners to negotiate with Indians in Georgia, and the Senate voted to postpone the confirmation.

Those ongoing Indian negotiations tested relations between President and Senate even further and established an important precedent. On 22 August 1789 the President called on the Senate for consultation together with Henry Knox, the acting superintendent of War. Knox handed a paper with seven points on which ADVICE AND CONSENT was being sought to Washington, who handed it to John Adams, who as Vice President was presiding over the Senate. Adams read it aloud, rapidly. Carriages outside made such a noise that no one understood "one Sentence of it." After the doorkeeper closed the windows, Adams reread the first point, which contained several references to the whole paper. Senator Robert Morris rose to say he had not been able to hear the paper and requested that it all be read again. It was. Then Adams asked the question on the first point, yes or no. An embarrassed silence followed; then Senator William Maclay of Pennsylvania rose to request that before an answer be given the relevant treaties be read, along with the instructions issued by the old Congress to the negotiators. The Senators then raised a cacophony of voices, speaking

of every manner of thing, at which Washington grew progressively angrier. Finally, he "started up in a Violent fret" and declared, *This defeats every purpose of my coming here.* Tempers gradually cooled, but after another fruitless session the following Monday, Washington resolved never to enter the Senate for a consultation again.

He kept that vow, and thus any idea that the Senate might serve as an advisory executive council was stillborn. In the future Washington consulted with Senators from time to time in his own office, individually or in small groups, and he received committees of the Senate; but by and large he consulted formally with the Senate only in writing, and he sought its consent after he had initiated and concluded negotiations with foreign powers.

Yet he continued to regard the Senate as constitutionally more important than the House because of its share in the executive power. That disposition led him to consider exercising the veto for the first time. Early in September he sent a letter asking James Madison for advice on a number of issues. One question read: "Being clearly of opinion that there ought to be a difference in the wages of the members of the two branches of the Legislature"—the appropriations bill had provided for equal pay—"would it be politic or prudent in the President when the Bill comes to him to send it back with his reasons for non-concurring?" Apparently Madison advised against the veto, for it was not exercised. Thereafter Washington grew extremely reluctant to veto any legislation and did not use the power until April of 1792—and then on a bill that was patently unconstitutional and only after Jefferson urged him to veto something lest the power fall into disuse, as it had in England. On the eve of his departure from office, he vetoed one more bill, not on constitutional grounds, but because he thought it poorly drafted, "inconvenient and injurious to the public," and "not consonant with economy." (His immediate successors, Adams and Jefferson, vetoed no bills.)

Setting Up the Government. By the end of summer of 1789, Congress had created all the executive departments: DEPARTMENT OF STATE, WAR DEPARTMENT, and DEPARTMENT OF THE TREASURY. Congress also established two additional executive agencies that had less than departmental status. The Post Office was simply carried over from the Confederation, though Washington replaced the old POSTMASTER GENERAL. The Judiciary Act of 1789 included the office of ATTORNEY GENERAL, consisting of a lawyer on retainer to advise the President as to constitutionality and law. Federal district attorneys to enforce the laws (except revenue laws, which were entrusted to Treasury) were subordinate to the SECRETARY OF STATE, not to the attorney general. The actual execution of the laws was the function of federal marshals, who were officers of the federal district courts.

As a result of this legislation, Washington found himself with nearly a thousand offices to fill. He was besieged with applications, but he shunned the opportunity to develop a PATRONAGE system. His appointments were nonpartisan in every sense but one; he refused to appoint anyone who was known to be an enemy of the Constitution. No job seeker was appointed unless Washington knew him personally, or his character was attested to by someone whom Washington trusted. For the major positions, the President consulted at length with several intimates, especially Madison (who had assumed a leadership role in the House of Representatives). For Secretary of State Washington preferred John Jay, but he bowed to Jay's wish to be Chief Justice of the Supreme Court and instead chose Thomas Jefferson, who was on his way to Virginia on leave from his post as minister to France. Henry Knox continued in the War Department, Alexander Hamilton was appointed Secretary of the Treasury after Robert Morris turned the job down, EDMUND RANDOLPH became Attorney General, and Samuel Osgood of Massachusetts became Postmaster General.

The chain of responsibility was curiously mixed. The statutes establishing the departments of State and War used identical language to describe the duties of the secretaries: "he shall perform and execute such duties as shall, from time to time, be enjoined on or entrusted to him by the president . . . agreeable to the constitution." The Post Office was different. Congress reserved to itself constitutional authority to "establish Post Offices and post Roads" instead of delegating the function to the executive branch, and since Washington was not particularly interested in the department, it operated without presidential direction. Timothy Pickering, who succeeded Osgood, went so far in the exercise of discretionary authority as to drop the customary practice of advertising for bids for mail contractors, until Congress made the practice mandatory in 1792.

The Treasury Department was put on a special footing. Despite recognition of the need for discretionary authority in spending, most Representatives were anxious to retain a general managerial control over the operations of the Treasury. Several Representatives feared that the Secretary of the Treasury might evolve into a British-style prime minister (as Hamilton privately intended he would). For these reasons, the secretary was required by law to report directly to the House as well as to the President. The secretary was empowered to appoint his assistants, superintend the collection of the revenues, decide upon the forms for keeping accounts, and prepare and report budgetary estimates. He was also "to digest and prepare plans for the improvement and management of the revenue, and for the support of public credit." He must make reports "and give information to either branch of the Legislature, in person or in writing (as he may be required) respecting all matters referred to him" or which shall concern his office. The aim of the statute was to keep the Treasury Department on a congressional leash; the effects were to endow Treasury with the authority to initiate legislation and to share the power of the purse between Congress and the executive branch.

In the ordinary course of things, Washington oversaw the work of his department heads closely, though he gave them a free hand in dealing with their subordinates. The essence of his administrative method was not so much to direct as to channel. He referred all letters he received to the department heads, and they referred all letters they received to him, along with drafts of proposed replies. Sometimes he suggested changes or called consultations. "By this means," Jefferson later recalled in a memorandum to his own department heads, Washington was "always in accurate possession of all facts and proceedings in every part of the Union, and to whatsoever department they related; he formed a central point for the different branches; preserved a unity of object and action among them"; and he assumed responsibility for whatever was done. This generated a huge amount of paperwork, but it kept Washington in charge.

There were, however, variations in the routine that stemmed from differences in temperaments and talents. Washington was an expert in foreign affairs and war, and thus he tended to be his own foreign secretary and war secretary. Jefferson, not fond of routine clerical work, tended to carry out his duties in a relaxed fashion. For example, in 1791 he wrote to the American chargé in Spain, William Carmichael, complaining mildly that Carmichael had sent no communications in two years; but Jefferson had written to Carmichael only once during that period. Knox adored Washington and happily did what he was told, but his competence was limited, and he devoted much of his energies to private land speculations.

Hamilton, by contrast, was brilliant in the field of finance, which was beyond Washington's ken or interest. That, and his special relationship with the House, gave Hamilton freer hand than the other secretaries had. Besides, Hamilton was a compulsive meddler; he often, when matters involving the other departments interested him, initiated action by submitting unsolicited proposals to Washington. At one point, when Knox was away for an extended period, Hamilton actually ran the War Department as well as Treasury. Furthermore, Hamilton was able to function as a prime minister because on a workday basis he and his department, with more than five hundred employees as compared to a total of twenty-two in the other departments, were the government during Washington's first term. Congress and the courts were normally in session only three or four months of the year; the President and the other secretaries were in the capital much of the year, but they had little to do. Only Treasury worked full-time the year around.

Perhaps it was because Washington sensed that his chief administrators were not fully compatible as a group that he did not consult them collectively during his first term. When his need for an advisory body increased, upon the outbreak of the French revolutionary wars, he began to consult them, but he also turned to the Supreme Court. In the summer of 1793 he submitted questions about international law and treaty obligations to the Court for its opinion. Chief Justice Jay had often advised him, and the other Justices would have been eager to become an ex officio advisory council—but for a fluke. Shortly before, Congress had assigned the Court the administrative duty of reviewing pension claims of war veterans. The Justices indignantly refused, saying that they were already overworked, that the function was not judicial, and that it violated the SEPARATION OF POWERS. Now, asked to assume an executive role, the Court could hardly reverse its stand. It accordingly refused. Thereafter, Washington regularly called the department heads together for meetings—and thus was born the presidential CABINET.

At first there had been accord among the department heads, even as to Hamilton's initial fiscal proposals. The funding and assumption features in his First Report on the Public Credit (9 January 1790) were enacted into law with only minor changes. When Madison proposed to discriminate between original and current holders of the public debt and when other southern Representatives objected to portions of the assumption plan, it was Jefferson who mediated. He arranged the deal involving the permanent location of the national capital that brought about passage of Hamilton's measures. It was not until after passage of the bill creating the national bank that the secretaries split irreconcilably.

When Jefferson and Madison arrived in Philadelphia for the December 1790 session of Congress in which the bank bill was to be considered, they were shocked to learn that the Pennsylvania legislature had appropriated money to build permanent federal buildings in Philadelphia. They feared that if the bank were also established there, it would be impossible to move the capital. Accordingly, Madison worked to limit the duration of the bank's charter to ten years, so that it would expire when the capital was schedule to be moved. When this effort failed, Madison took the position that Congress had no constitutional authority to incorporate a bank. And Jefferson echoed his constitutional doubts. The House rejected the argument by an almost two-to-one margin, but Washington was seriously upset by the raising of the constitutional issue, partly because he trusted Madison's judgment in matters of constitutional intent but also because he was concerned in a different way about the location of the capital.

The law providing for the site of the capital had required the President to appoint a three-man commission to consider and choose among various locations on the Potomac between two designated points. Instead Washington picked the area himself, three miles further downstream, nearer his estate at MOUNT VERNON. It was generally assumed that should a President find it expedient to act contrary to law, he should at the first opportunity ask Congress for indemnification—which Washington now proceeded to do. The House promptly passed the measure, but champions of the bank in the Senate held back, using indemnification as insurance against a veto of the bank bill. And so, while Randolph and Jefferson were giving their solicited strict constructionist opinions on the constitutionality of the bank and Hamilton was offering his loose constructionist argument, the question whether Washington would sign the bank bill into law hinged on an entirely different pivot. On the tenth day after the bill passed Congress (the constitutionally mandated last day for signing), Washington signed. Immediately the Senate approved the indemnification bill.

The Emergence of Parties. One by-product of the clash over the bank was a development that the Framers of the Constitution had not anticipated: the emergence of political parties. Parties were not unprecedented in America. Several colonies had had rudimentary court and country parties; Pennsylvania had a well-developed two-party system; and a powerful faction had gathered around Governor GEORGE CLINTON in New York. But these were local and transient affairs. It was almost universally believed that parties—or factions, as they were commonly called—posed a mortal threat to republics because they were by definition, as Madison put it, "a number of citizens, whether amounting to a majority or minority of the whole, who are united and actuated by some common impulse . . . adverse to the rights of other citizens, or to the permanent and aggregate interests of the community." Madison had argued persuasively in *Federalist* 10 that the structure of the government, together with the extent and diversity of the country, would prevent any faction from obtaining and holding a majority for a dangerous length of time.

Madison changed his mind in the spring of 1791 after Jefferson became convinced and then convinced him that Hamilton had organized a "money phalanx" through which he was dominating Congress and by which he intended to implement monocratic ends.

Jefferson set out to thwart Hamilton. First he appealed to Washington, but Washington, regarding Hamilton's establishment of public credit as virtually miraculous, could not be persuaded that Hamilton was the principal behind a nefarious plot. Inasmuch as Washington continued to serve as an aegis for Hamilton, Jefferson and Madison began to organize a party—not a narrow and self-interested one of the sort Madison had described, but a country party of the whole people. Such a party would gain control of government, throw the monocrats and moneymen out, restore the purity of the Constitution, and then wither away. Their immediate aim was to gain control of Congress in the 1792 elections and, if Washington should retire, the presidency itself.

Toward that end, they established contact with anti-Hamiltonian political leaders in New York, most notably George Clinton and AARON BURR. They established an opposition newspaper and subsidized it at government expense: Jefferson paid its editor, Philip Freneau, as a "translator" in the State Department; Madison pushed through Congress a cheap postal rate for newspapers. And they coordinated a series of attacks against Hamilton that continued throughout 1792. Washington was spared personal assault until his second term, but he took criticism of his administration as criticism of himself.

Hamilton and Washington were confused and angered by it all. Both were conscious of their rectitude and of the value of their services to the country; thus they could not imagine that anything other than the basest motives were behind the attacks. Furthermore, in the absence of a concept of a loyal opposition—which began to evolve in England only in the 1820s and in America a decade or so later—they tended to regard attacks upon the government's policy as attacks upon the government itself, which bordered on sedition.

From the first Washington had sought harmony in purpose and unity in support of the government. Toward those ends, in his first annual message to Congress (and in his eighth), he called for the creation of a national university. "The assimilation of the principles, opinions, and manners of our countrymen by the common education of a portion of our youth from every quarter well deserves attention. The more homogeneous our citizens can be made," he said, "the greater will be our prospect of permanent union." Recognizing the crucial role of education in a republic, he repeatedly proposed a course of study that would include "the science of *government*" whereby future leaders would "get fixed in the principles of the Constitution, understand the laws and the rue interests and policy of their country." By this means students from different regions would be freed from "those local prejudices and habitual jealousies which, when carried to excess, are never failing sources of disquietude." Congress never acted on his many calls for a national university, and during his second term factionalism became all consuming.

Foreign Affairs and the Whiskey Rebellion. The timing of the formation of an opposition party was especially unfortunate, for just then revolutionary France began intruding into American affairs. The United States was tied to France by bonds of gratitude for its help in winning independence and by the "perpetual" treaty of 1778. Most Americans cheered when the French Revolution began in 1789, for they regarded Louis XVI as a great champion of liberty. Most, except the more ardent republican ideologues, had stopped cheering by the time they learned of the king's execution in January 1793. Meanwhile, France declared war against Prussia and Austria, and shortly afterward it sent Citizen Edmond Genet as a special minister to enlist the United States in the cause of liberating the world. Genet was given three specific objectives: obtain American foodstuffs for France, open American ports as bases for privateering, and enlist Americans in expeditions to reconquer Canada, Florida, and Louisiana. Genet arrived in Charleston in April 1793 and began a tour northward, handing out privateering commissions along the way.

Washington, understanding that to incur the hostility of Great Britain could be catastrophic, asked his Cabinet for ideas about how to preserve NEUTRALITY. Jefferson, who usually took the position that foreign affairs was exclusively an executive province, now argued that since only Congress can declare war, it alone can declare neutrality, and thus a presidential proclamation of neutrality would be unconstitutional. Hamilton and Knox argued to the contrary and even induced Jay to draft a neutrality proclamation, separation of powers notwithstanding. Washington sided with them and issued the proclamation calling on Americans to act "with sincerity and good faith" in a "friendly and impartial manner" toward the belligerent powers. He also warned that "prosecutions" would be brought against those who "violate the law of nations with respect to the powers at war."

The neutrality issue was tangentially connected with another problem as well. Genet had promoted the organization of pro-French, "democratic-republican societies," political action clubs that formed the extreme left wing of the republican party. Three of the most radical societies were in the Pittsburgh area, a hotbed of resistance to the collection of the federal tax on whiskey. In the summer of 1794 the members and assorted hooligans burned the house of the tax inspector, robbed the mails, tarred and feathered tax collectors, defied court orders, and organized a march on Pittsburgh by a mob of five or six thousand armed men. County and state officials, when they did anything at all, supported the insurgents.

Washington determined to suppress the Whiskey Rebellion by force. Under the militia act of 1792, the President was authorized to call out the militia if a federal judge certified that the laws of the United States were being opposed "by combinations too powerful to be suppressed by the ordinary course of judicial proceedings." Justice JAMES WILSON so certified in August, and Washington issued a proclamation commanding the "insurgents to disperse and retire peaceably to their respective abodes." Knox, on the President's instructions, wrote to the governors of New Jersey, Pennsylvania, Maryland, and Virginia to mobilize a total of 12,950 militia men. In September the forces were assembled and began marching westward with Washington himself in command. He stayed with the troops for three weeks, then turned them over to Governor Henry (Light-Horse Harry) Lee. Resistance disappeared: two thousand men fled down the Ohio to Kentucky, a few score people were arrested, twenty were taken to Philadelphia and tried for treason, two were convicted, and Washington pardoned them.

Washington's handling of the episode was skillful and established important precedents. The guiding principle was, as Hamilton put it in another context, that "Whenever the Government appears in arms it ought to appear like a *Hercules*," for the respect it thus inspires is likely to prevent the necessity for bloodshed. Washington set another key precedent in the aftermath of the Whiskey Rebellion when, through General Lee, he granted a blanket AMNESTY to the insur-

gents—thereby simultaneously indicating that the President's pardoning power extends to a dispensation of the laws and showing a magnanimity that strengthened his administration in the eyes of the public. In his seventh annual message to Congress he explained that "though I shall always think it a sacred duty to exercise with firmness and energy the constitutional powers with which I am vested, yet it appears to me no less consistent with the public good than it is with my personal feelings to mingle in the operations of Government every degree of moderation and tenderness which the national justice, dignity, and safety may permit."

Other major issues regarding the executive that were addressed in Washington's second term arose from the diplomatic mission that was underway even as the Whiskey Rebellion was being suppressed. During the previous winter, Britain had invoked a questionable doctrine in international law to seize about three hundred American ships in the West Indies. Federalists as well as Republicans clamored for war, but Washington, heeding the advice of Hamilton and a handful of Senators, followed a policy of preparing for war but negotiating a peaceful settlement. He sent Chief Justice Jay to London as a minister plenipotentiary. The resulting treaty was not unflawed, but it preserved the peace, granted some commercial concessions, and pioneered the use of arbitration commissions to settle international disputes. Republicans organized protest rallies and petition drives against ratification. They had not actually seen the treaty, for its terms were kept secret until it was considered by the Senate, but they opposed any amicable agreement with Britain and tried to turn the treaty to their political advantage. Despite their efforts, the Senate ratified during the summer of 1795 by the narrowest constitutional margin, twenty to ten. The extent of the opposition, however, caused Washington to hesitate to sign the treaty, and Edmund Randolph (who had succeeded Jefferson at State) urged him not to sign. But then documents were intercepted that seemed to show that Randolph had sought French bribes to influence American policy. When they were shown to Washington, he became enraged and reacted by signing the treaty in a fury. And Randolph was forced to resign.

The matter did not end there. In March of 1796 Representative Edward Livingston of New York introduced a resolution requesting the President to provide the House will all the papers relevant to the negotiation of JAY'S TREATY. The partisan expectation was that the papers would reveal politically profitable information for use in the upcoming elections. The constitutional question, whether the House had a right to see the papers, turned on the point that the arbitration commissions would require appropriations—which could be initiated only in the House. The deeper issue, which has never been answered satisfactorily, was how much information the executive could properly withhold from Congress or the public in the interest of NATIONAL SECURITY. The House debated the resolution for three weeks, passing it on 24 March with the significant qualification, "excepting such of the said papers as any existing negotiation may render improper to be disclosed."

Washington responded with a thundering refusal. Placing his damaged but still great prestige on the line, he said that the papers were not "relative to any purpose under the cognizance of the House of Representatives, except that of an impeachment, which the resolution has not expressed." He went on to give Congress a lecture on the executive and the conduct of foreign affairs. Secrecy in the conduct of foreign relations was occasionally necessary, he said, and though that could be dangerous, the Constitution reduced the danger by making the Senate, not the House, privy to these matters. The Senate was employed in that way to protect the states; Senators represented states as states, and accordingly it had certain powers not shared with the House. Washington concluded by observing that the House had been implementing treaties for seven years without ever asserting a right to do otherwise, and that the Constitutional Convention had explicitly rejected a motion that treaties not be binding until they were ratified by a law. After a month of sometimes angry debate, the House voted by a narrow margin to appropriate the fund without seeing the requested papers.

Washington's Farewell. Washington's decision to retire at the end of his second term, setting a precedent for a two-term limit, had both positive and negative sources. On the one hand, he could take satisfaction in knowing that the government and the presidency had been firmly established as viable and stable institutions. On the other hand, the level of political discourse had degenerated so abysmally as to make continued service unacceptable to him. For more than three years he had been forced to endure calumnies that mounted steadily in shrillness and intensity. It was said that "gambling, reveling, horseracing and horse whipping" had been the essentials of his education, that he was "a most horrid swearer and blasphemer," even that he had taken British bribes when he commanded American troops during the revolutionary war. In public, Washington retained his poise, but in private, as Jefferson later recalled, he suffered "More than any person I ever yet met with."

In his FAREWELL ADDRESS he reflected this suffering by warning "in the most solemn manner against the baneful effects of the spirit of party generally." It "agitates the community with ill-founded jealousies and false alarms," stirs up animosities, and "foments occasionally riot and insurrection." In a popular government, moreover, the "constant danger of excess" demands that party spirit be checked. Washington, regarding "the unity of government" as a "main pillar in the edifice" of American independence, also warned against sectionalism and localism: "To the efficacy and permanency of your union a government for the whole is indispensable."

He stressed that the Constitution "is sacredly obligatory upon all" and that it is "the duty" of each to obey the constitutionally established government. He urged that "the spirit of innovation" be resisted, that all changed be by "amendment in the way which the Constitution designates," and that all branches of government "confine themselves within their respective constitutional spheres," not encroaching upon one another. And he made explicit what had been distinguishing features of his presidency (as well as his earlier military service): prudence and care for precedent. Otherwise his advice to the nation was to "cherish public credit," using it "as sparingly as possible," and to "observe good faith and justice toward all nations. Cultivate peace and harmony with all" and avoid "permanent alliances" with any foreign power.

Thus he concluded the "forty-five years of my life dedicated to [my country's] service with an upright zeal." Long after his death, Jefferson summed up his service as follows: "His was the singular destiny and merit of leading the armies of his country successfully through an arduous war for the establishment of its independence, of conducting its councils through the birth of a government, new in its forms and principles, until it settled down into a quiet and orderly train, and of scrupulously obeying the laws through the whole of his career, civil and military, of which the history of the world furnishes no other example." The most famous summation, of course, was that by Henry Lee, spoken before Congress two days after Washington died: "First in war, first in peace, first in the hearts of his countrymen."

BIBLIOGRAPHY

Cunliffe, Marcus. *George Washington: Man and Monument.* 1959.

DeConde, Alexander. *Entangling Alliance: Politics and Diplomacy under George Washington.* 1958.

Ferling, John E. *The First of Men: A Life of George Washington.* 1988.

Flexner, James Thomas. *George Washington and the New Nation, 1783–1793.* 1970.

Flexner, James Thomas. *George Washington: Anguish and Farewell, 1793–1799.* 1972.

Freeman, Douglas Southall. *George Washington: A Biography*. 7 vols. 1948–1957.

Marshall, John. *The Life of George Washington*. Vols. 4 and 5. 1926.

McDonald, Forrest. *The Presidency of George Washington*. 1974.

Miller, John C. *The Federalist Era, 1789–1801*. 1960.

White, Leonard D. *The Federalists: A Study in Administrative History*. 1948.

FORREST MCDONALD

WASHINGTON, MARTHA (1731–1802), First Lady, wife of George Washington. In her pathbreaking role, Martha Dandridge Custis Washington established patterns that her successors would follow and helped carve out a public role for presidential spouses, although no such role had been written into the Constitution. Her arrival in May 1789 in New York, the new nation's temporary capital, was greeted with fanfare, and newspaper articles debated what her title should be and how much public attention she deserved. President and Mrs. Washington decided that she would help in hosting gatherings that mixed social callers with political colleagues and she would oversee a residence that doubled as the Chief Executive's office, thus drawing the President's wife into the government process. Although Martha Washington refused to take sides in any partisan divisions or to speak up on public issues, she achieved a reputation for thoughtfulness and an even temper. She frequently wrote letters lamenting the public attention focused on her as the presidential spouse, but she did little to terminate or discourage it and earned popular acclaim as "Lady Washington."

BIBLIOGRAPHY

Decatur, Stephen, Jr. *Private Affairs of George Washington*. 1933.

Wharton, Anne Hollingsworth. *Martha Washington*. 1897.

BETTY BOYD CAROLI

WASHINGTON, TREATY OF. For discussion of the 1871 treaty, see TREATY OF WASHINGTON (1871). For discussion of the 1921–1922 treaty, see TREATY OF WASHINGTON (1921–1922).

WATERGATE AFFAIR. In 1973 and 1974, "Watergatitis" swept the United States as no scandal involving the highest officials of government had since the TEAPOT DOME SCANDAL of the 1920s. The cover-up by President Richard M. Nixon and his top aides of the break-ins and bugging of Democratic National Committee headquarters in Washington, D.C.'s Watergate office-apartment complex on 17 June 1972, and related corrupt or criminal political activities, ultimately resulted in the indictment, conviction, and sentencing of twenty men. These included John Ehrlichman and H. R. Haldeman, top White House aides; John W. Dean III, counsel to the President; Charles Colson, a special assistant to the President; former Attorney General JOHN MITCHELL; and others who worked for the Committee for the Re-election of the President (CRP, but derogatorily referred to as CREEP) and/or the White House Special Investigative Unit, more commonly known as the Plumbers. Initially established under Ehrlichman's direction to "plug" leaks to the press, the Plumbers had engaged in illegal break-ins and buggings before the Watergate crimes occurred.

Most of these men were REPUBLICAN PARTY officials or presidential advisers in whom public trust had been placed. A few Plumbers, including E. Howard Hunt, James McCord, and G. Gordon Liddy—all former CIA or FBI agents—were employed by the White House and paid with private funds specifically to carry out political espionage. They, in turn, hired the four Cubans actually arrested in the Watergate complex. All served time for their participation in the original crimes.

Despite the multitude of investigations, articles, and books on Watergate, many factual questions remain unanswered about the Watergate incident itself. Beyond those ambiguities, the historical significance of the entire Watergate affair is still disputed by scholars—and is likely to remain controversial for years to come.

Break-in and Cover-up. The arrest of James McCord, Bernard Baker, Virgilio Gonzalez, Eugenio Martinez, and Frank Sturgis after the night watchman at the Watergate twice discovered adhesive tape on basement doors of the complex set off a series of events and investigations unprecedented in U.S. history. These break-ins culminated a series of political DIRTY TRICKS authorized by CRP beginning in the fall of 1971, although it is still disputed whether the two Watergate break-ins were approved by Attorney General Mitchell and presidential counsel Dean. President Nixon learned of the burglars' connections with CRP and White House personnel on 20 June 1972. On 23 June he privately agreed with a recommendation (which he thought was from Mitchell and Haldeman but which probably originated with Dean) that the CENTRAL INTELLIGENCE AGENCY should prevent a FEDERAL BUREAU OF INVESTIGATION inquiry into the Watergate break-in on grounds of NATIONAL SECURITY. The CIA did not comply with this attempt by the President to obstruct justice in a criminal matter, and the investigation moved forward, though only after the 1972 presidential election had taken place.

The smoking-gun tape of 23 June 1972 (not released by the White House until 5 August 1974) revealed just how early Nixon had been involved in the cover-up. The Watergate Special Prosecution Task Force (WSPF) headed by Texas attorney Leon Jaworski concluded in February 1974 that

> beginning no later than March 21, 1973, the President joined an ongoing criminal conspiracy to obstruct justice, obstruct a criminal investigation, and commit perjury (which included payment of cash to Watergate defendants to influence their testimony, making and causing to be made false statements and declarations, making offers of clemency and leniency, and obtaining information from the Justice Department to thwart its investigation) and that the President is also liable for substantive violations of various criminal statutes.

All these actions had taken place in the space of two years—from the summer of 1972 to the summer of 1974. Early in 1973, federal judge John J. Sirica, using heavy-handed legal tactics, threatened the Watergate defendants with tough sentences unless they told the truth. As McCord and others began to talk about payoffs from the White House, evidence of illegal campaign contributions (not associated with the Watertate break-in) also began to emerge and was investigated by the WSPF. The WSPF ultimately set up five different task forces to investigate the variety of charges surfacing against the administration. These ranged from the Watergate cover-up itself, to illegal campaign contributions, to the IT&T antitrust suits, to the Plumbers' other break-ins, to Nixon's tax returns and his mistreatment of demonstrators. Nixon essentially fired Haldeman, Ehrlichman, Dean, and Mitchell by formally accepting their resignations on 30 April 1973, and on 22 May he announced that they had been involved in a White House cover-up without his knowledge. Dean then decided to testify before the Senate Select Committee on Presidential Campaign Activities, headed by conservative Democrat Samuel J. Ervin, Jr., on North Carolina and so known as the Ervin Committee. From 25 to 29 June, Dean in his testimony accused the President of being involved. Dean's and others' testimony before the committee also disclosed the existence of a White House enemies list of prominent politicians, journalists, academics, and entertainers, who had been singled out for various types of harassment, including unnecessary tax audits. In July 1973, former White House assistant Alexander Butterfield revealed in a suspiciously inadvertent way that Nixon had installed a voice-activated taping system in the OVAL OFFICE in 1971. Both Haldeman and Rose Mary Woods, Nixon's secretary, thought that Butterfield

was a CIA plant in the White House, but, as with similar charges made against Hunt and McCord, this claim has never been proved.

From this point forward, various attempts to obtain the tapes themselves or unedited transcripts from the White House failed until 24 July 1974, when the Supreme Court ruled in UNITED STATES V. NIXON that the President could not retain subpoenaed tapes by claiming EXECUTIVE PRIVILEGE. During this year-long legal struggle, Archibald Cox, the first special prosecutor appointed to investigate Watergate, also tried to gain access to the tapes. When Cox, who was acting on behalf of a federal grand jury, rejected a compromise proposed by Nixon, the President ordered, first, Attorney General Elliot Richardson and, then, Deputy Attorney General William D. Ruckelshaus to fire the special prosecutor. Refusing, they resigned. On 20 October 1973, Acting Attorney General Robert Bork (later unsuccessfully nominated by President Ronald Reagan to the Supreme Court) finally carried out Nixon's order. This so-called Saturday Night Massacre was subsequently ruled an illegal violation of Justice Department procedures in *Nader v. Bork*. The incident also created such negative public opinion that the President agreed to turn over nine subpoenaed tapes to Judge Sirica—only to announce, on 31 October, that two of the tapes did not exist and, on 26 November, that a third tape had an unexplained eighteen-and-a-half-minute gap. This erasure remains unexplained. Finally, on 30 October 1973, the House Judiciary Committee, headed by Democrat Peter W. Rodino, Jr., of New Jersey, began preliminary investigations; in April 1974 it launched a full-scale IMPEACHMENT inquiry. On 27 July 1974, even before the release of the smoking-gun tape, Rodino's committee recommended the impeachment of the President to the entire House of Representatives. Nixon resigned from office on 9 August rather than face almost certain conviction in an impeachment trial.

If it can be argued that Nixon's resignation thwarted the process of justice over Watergate, then Gerald Ford's pardon of him on 8 September 1974 also contributed to this miscarriage of justice. Nixon had appointed Ford Vice President after SPIRO AGNEW resigned in October 1973. Ford unconditionally pardoned the former President for all federal crimes he may have committed or been a party to, freeing Nixon from any federal criminal or civil liability in the Watergate affair. Questions about whether the pardon arose from a "deal" between Ford and Nixon before the latter resigned contributed to Ford's defeat by Democrat Jimmy Carter in the 1976 presidential election. Despite lingering suspicions among the public at large, no scholar or investigative reporter has found evidence of a pardon deal between Nixon and Ford.

A number of prestigious political figures agreed at the time that Nixon should be pardoned. While practical and moral reasons for the pardon varied, in retrospect they all disturbingly underestimated the ability of the American public to handle or understand difficult issues. Moreover, the haste with which the pardon was granted made it more difficult to select jurors for the seven original cover-up defendants. Last, Ford appeared to many to contradict his own confirmation testimony in November 1973 and a statement at his first press conference about letting justice take its course.

Ford's reasons for granting the pardon were: a trial would punish Nixon further (in addition to his resignation) and, in any case, could not take place for over a year, during which national divisiveness would continue; Nixon's health was in jeopardy; he and his family had suffered enough; and it was Christian to show mercy. In his autobiography Ford added an additional reason: he believed that Nixon's resignation from office was "an implicit admission of guilt." Ford never overcame the damage to his political credibility generated by his "full, free, and absolute pardon" of Richard Nixon and his action continues to symbolize a double standard of justice that seems to exist for Presidents and other high government officials.

Constitutional Issues. The reasons for the Watergate break-ins remained in dispute twenty years after the event. Despite these unknowns, the fact that the President and his closest aides had attempted to cover up criminal activities brought on a constitutional crisis. Potentially the most important legacy of Watergate is that it precipitated demands for accountability on the part of top officials and for greater public access to government information. Thus Watergate directly or indirectly produced a series of reforms of elections and the financing of political campaigns, as well as measures designed to ensure greater access to classified documents. These reforms included the establishment of the Federal Election Commission and the Congressional Budget Office and passage of the WAR POWERS RESOLUTION (1973), the Presidential Materials and Preservation Acts of 1974 and 1978, and the 1974 amendments to the FREEDOM OF INFORMATION ACT (FOIA). In addition, Congress agreed to open conference committees to public scrutiny and the DEMOCRATIC PARTY continued its efforts, begun before Watergate to reform the primary system (the Republican's followed suit). Unfortunately, most of these congressional acts and party reforms were ultimately violated, watered down, or contradicted by presidential actions, or they

created unforeseen additional problems, such as the uncontrolled financing of candidates by PACS (POLITICAL ACTION COMMITTEES), overly complicated ethical requirements, and the automatic triggering of INDEPENDENT COUNSEL investigations in response to trivial incidents.

Because these reforms failed to make government and the electoral process more accountable and democratic, the question remains whether Watergate was, in the final analysis, an example of how well the system works or of how intractable its problems are. Congress showed itself to be reluctant to act when it came to investigating the lawlessness of the Nixon presidency, and it was only after the Saturday Night Massacre—and a million letters demanding the impeachment of the President—that the Democrat-dominated House Judiciary Committee even began "an inquiry into *whether* to begin an inquiry into possible grounds for recommending impeachment to the House." Republicans legislators seemed to favor Nixon's resignation because, as Senator George Aiken (R-Vt.) noted, "Many prominent Americans, who ought to know better, find the task of holding a President accountable as just too difficult. . . . To ask the President now to resign and thus relieve Congress of its clear congressional duty amounts to a declaration of incompetence on the part of Congress."

In retrospect, it appears likely that, had those advising Nixon not prepared such an inept defense for him, Congress might never have acted. It took ten months of revelations of criminal acts, political misconduct, and presidential deceit before the House, on 6 February 1974, authorized the Judiciary Committee to investigate possible grounds for impeachment. Even the Special Prosecutor's Office under Jaworski seemed to move more cautiously than necessary when in February 1974 it recommended to the Watergate grand jury, which had been serving since 5 June 1972, that instead of indicting the President it simply give its report to the House Judiciary Committee. The grand jury, however, did secretly name Nixon as an unindicted coconspirator. Seven of Nixon's aides were publicly indicted by this same grand jury on 1 March 1974. But the wheels of justice ground exceeding slow.

Although post-Watergate reforms have proved to be more a placebo than a genuine cure for weaknesses in the American political system, it is important that the Watergate affair and its aftermath not be dismissed as an aberration nor, equally simplistically, blamed for all that has gone wrong in U.S. foreign and domestic policy since 1972. If, however, Watergate is ultimately viewed primarily as an isolated incident involving only a particular group of men around a particular President, then Watergate will have no more importance than the Teapot Dome scandal to future generations of Americans. The system worked poorly, both during and in the years immediately following Watergate, and again proved itself unworkable during the IRAN-CONTRA AFFAIR. Just as the NEW DEAL did not end the Great Depression, so the system could not put an end to problems that had plagued government long before Watergate. If anything, Nixon's resignation and his pardon by Gerald Ford (both of which were encouraged by the system), ended national agony Watergate caused without addressing its root causes or enhancing democratic accountability. Nixon should not be excused for obstructing justice and temporarily getting away with it. But if in the public mind he and Watergate remain primarily historical aberrations then little will have been learned from this painful period in the history of the U.S. presidency.

BIBLIOGRAPHY

Colodny, Len, and Robert Gettlin. *Silent Coup: The Removal of a President.* 1991.

Ervin, Sam J., Jr. *The Whole Truth: The Watergate Conspiracy.* 1980.

Jaworski, Leon. *The Right and The Power: The Prosecution of Watergate.* 1976.

Kutler, Stanley I. *The Wars of Watergate: The Last Crisis of Richard Nixon.* 1990.

Lukas, J. Anthony. *Nightmare: The Underside of the Nixon Years.* 1976.

Scudson, Michael. *Watergate in American Memory: How We Remember, Forget, and Reconstruct the Past.* 1992.

JOAN HOFF

WATT, JAMES G. (b. 1938), Secretary of the Interior. James Gaius Watt was born on 31 January 1938 in Lus, Wyoming. Before becoming President Ronald Reagan's first Secretary of the Interior, he was an aide to Senator Milward L. Simpson (R-Wyo.), Deputy Assistant Secretary of the Interior, director of the Bureau of Outdoor Recreation, and a federal power commissioner. Ironically, he led a Denver based public-interest law firm that specialized in opposing environmental groups.

The selection of Watt was perhaps the most controversial of the Reagan nominations. Conservation groups actively opposed his appointment as Secretary of the Interior. He testified during his confirmation hearings that he wanted to strike a balance between the use of federal lands for commercial projects and for environmental preservation.

Watt supported the leasing of federal oil and gas reserves off the coast of Alaska by private companies. He wanted to loosen the controls on federal lands in order to encourage multiple usages. He strongly favored the building of additional dams in the western part of the United States as both sources of energy and water for agricultural needs. Finally, Watt wanted Washington to repeal or amend many environmental regulations that impede the development of new energy sources.

Watt shifted scarce financial resources from the purchase of additional federal park lands to the restoration of the 333 already existing parks. Watt cited a GENERAL ACCOUNTING OFFICE report that identified 172 of the parks as not meeting federal health and safety regulations. Critics were more incensed by the reduction in purchase of new lands. Watt began to lease large portions of government land and offshore waters for mineral exploration. He wanted to reduce America's dependence on foreign sources. Critics claimed that Watt was underselling the land and that he was leasing it faster than companies could provide viable exploration impact statements.

Whatever James G. Watt did, he quickly became a lightening rod of controversy. He had a knack for offending almost everyone. Many White House advisers pushed the President to replace Watt because of the growing controversies. After Reagan's first term, Watt resigned.

BIBLIOGRAPHY

Arnold, Ron. *At the Eye of the Storm: James Watt and the Environmentalists.* 1982.

JEFFREY D. SCHULTZ

WEAVER, JAMES B. (1833–1912), monetary reformer, presidential candidate. James Baird Weaver's early life provided a range of experiences that were to make him an energetic participant in the monetary debates of the 1870s and 1880s, culminating in his presidential nomination by the Populist Party in 1892.

Son of a skilled mechanic, Weaver was born in Dayton, Ohio, in 1833. Two years later, the family moved to a farm in Michigan and, in 1843, to a frontier farm in Iowa, where Weaver grew to maturity. Lack of access to nonusurious credit plagued his family throughout his life and plagued Weaver himself when, in 1855, he borrowed $100 at 33 percent interest to enter Cincinnati Law School. He graduated the next year and established a law practice in Bloomfield, Iowa.

Though his political heritage was Democratic, he soon became a western free-soiler and an active participant in the emerging REPUBLICAN PARTY. He ardently supported Lincoln in 1860 and volunteered for military service in 1861, becoming a first lieutenant in the

Second Iowa Infantry. Courageous in western battles at Fort Donelson and Shiloh, he was advanced over senior captains to the rank of major and led his regiment during the battle of Corinth after the unit's senior commanders were killed. He served as a colonel in 1863–64, and was brevetted brigadier general upon his return to Iowa in 1865.

Active in Republican circles as a monetary reformer, Weaver was elected district attorney and later served until 1873 as federal assessor of internal revenue for the first district of Iowa. Despite his immense personal popularity, party regulars denied him a congressional nomination in 1874 and the gubernatorial nomination the following year because, as an outspoken anti-monopolist, he was not deemed trustworthy on "the money question." Weaver thereupon won election to the U.S. House of Representatives on the GREENBACK PARTY ticket in 1878 and received the party's presidential nomination in 1880. Though defeated both for President in 1880 and for Congress in 1882, he won back his congressional seat in 1884 and retained it in 1886.

Though Weaver's own monetary beliefs harmonized perfectly with those of the financial reformers who led the emerging National Farmers Alliance and Industrial Union, he did not participate in—and in pivotal ways did not understand—the grass-roots organizing methods that allowed the Alliance to spread across the South and the West in the period 1886–1892. He saw strategies of reform essentially from the perspective of a candidate, a view shaped in part by the fact that his victories in Iowa occurred because his basic Greenback Party constituency had been augmented by electoral fusion with the long moribund Iowa DEMOCRATIC PARTY. Compounding this situation was the fact that the Alliance organizing effort, grounded in local but far-flung agrarian cooperatives, came late to Iowa. A mass base of politicized farmers, such as the Alliance was able to fashion elsewhere in the plains states and the southern cotton belt, therefore did not come into existence in Iowa. Accordingly, Weaver saw fusion politics as an essential long-term political strategy for the People's (Populist) Party when it became a national institution in 1892.

This perspective became entrenched after Weaver, as the Populist presidential nominee in 1892, ran well in the West but poorly in the South, where unfounded but effective rumors were spread regarding his wartime treatment of Confederate refugees. The Populists's weak showing across the South fortified Weaver's affinity for Populist-Democratic cooperation. Though himself a sophisticated greenbacker with a fine grasp of the impact that currency contraction and Republican "hard-money" policies had upon the nation's farmers, Weaver came to believe that the growth of free silver sentiment in Democratic Party ranks offered a way for "uniting the reform forces" for a showdown battle with Republican goldbugs in 1896. A man of integrity in his commercial relations, Weaver nevertheless cooperated with a number of self-styled silver strategists, many in the pay of western silver mine owners, in a determined campaign to downplay greenback planks in the Populist platform. The object was to complete groundwork for a fusion campaign around the free silver issue, an intention realized with the 1896 nomination of WILLIAM JENNINGS BRYAN by the Democrats and, with Weaver's assiduous help, by the People's Party.

The resulting "Battle of the Standards" between the goldbug, William McKinley, and the silver advocate, Bryan, has become a landmark in American historical literature, endlessly debated and reinterpreted down to the present time. Less debatable was the effect of McKinley's victory on prospects for greenback reform of the monetary system. Fusion and defeat left the People's Party organization in ruins.

Interestingly, Weaver's book-length 1892 campaign document, *A Call to Action*, hurriedly stitched together from existing reform manifestos and campaign speeches, remains useful for that very reason—as a representative slice of agrarian radicalism.

BIBLIOGRAPHY

Allen, Emory. *The Life and Public Services of James B. Weaver.* 1892.

LAWRENCE C. GOODWYN

WEBSTER, DANIEL (1782–1852), Representative, Senator, Secretary of State. In 1852, after his final failure to gain the WHIG PARTY presidential nomination, Webster refused to quash independent efforts for him because that "would gratify . . . that great body of implacable enemies who have prevented me from being elected President of the United States." Webster's bitterness over this frustration shadowed his many achievements as lawyer, Representative, Senator, and Secretary of State and especially as the orator who most powerfully expressed his age's intense nationalism.

The much-loved, precocious youngest son in a large rural New Hampshire family, Webster as a youth displayed abilities that attracted sponsors who provided for his education at Dartmouth College and for his legal apprenticeship in Boston. He early developed the expensive tastes that were to keep him in debt all his life. Always wanting wealth, Webster had to settle throughout his life for "loans" or gifts from patrons that allowed him to live well while serving his, and their, vision of the public good. This practice darkened his career, lessened broad public support outside New England, and caused many who were awed by his abilities to doubt this character.

A Federalist, Webster represented New Hampshire in Congress from 1813 to 1817 and followed his party's policy of ambiguous opposition to the WAR OF 1812, at one point arguing that Republican policies might tragically cause national disintegration. After the war, Webster voted for INTERNAL IMPROVEMENTS but against both a national bank and the tariff in the forms presented.

Webster moved to Boston in 1816 and quickly built a lucrative law practice, highlighted by his appearances before the Supreme Court. JOHN MARSHALL enshrined parts of Webster's arguments in major decisions upholding the sanctity of contract and supporting broad power for the federal government derived from the "necessary and proper" and commerce clauses (especially *Dartmouth College v. Woodward* and *McCulloch v. Maryland* [both 1819] and *Gibbons v. Ogden* [1824]). Webster argued many other seminal Supreme Court cases throughout his life.

Webster again served in Congress from 1823 to 1827. His close ties to Boston's wealthiest textile magnates did not influence him to vote for a tariff. His position on this issue changed only after he entered the Senate in 1827; from this time he always fought strongly for protectionism. In 1830 he delivered his most famous speech, a reply to Thomas Hart Benton and Robert Hayne, who were supporting a western-southern coalition by arguing New England's hostility to the West, the common man, and the nation. Webster first forced Hayne to endorse NULLIFICATION and then replied with a full exposition of his own nationalism, ending with words that would be recited by American schoolchildren for generations: "Liberty and Union, now and forever, one and inseparable."

When in 1833 Andrew Jackson equally clearly denounced the doctrine of nullification, it seemed possible that Webster would be anointed Jackson's successor, but such thoughts vanished when Jackson continued his attack on the BANK OF THE UNITED STATES, an institution Webster strongly defended. Webster's only nomination for the presidency came in 1836 as part of the ill-fated Whig attempt to foil the Democrats by running several regional candidates. In other years, Whigs ran either HENRY CLAY or available military heroes. Webster tried to use his two stints as Secretary of State, under John Tyler and, later, Millard Fillmore, to win support for a presidential bid, but Whig hatred for Tyler and the competition between Webster and Fillmore truncated these efforts.

Webster influenced both the Tyler and the Fillmore administrations greatly. Under Tyler, the WEBSTER-ASHBURTON TREATY (1842) solved or shelved several problems with Great Britain, and Webster cleverly manipulated public opinion to present its compromises as a victory. Under Fillmore, Webster worked less effectively to soften tensions over SLAVERY by a verbal nationalism that stopped well short of the gestures of military adventurism of subsequent Democratic administrations.

Webster's fears for disunion led to his last great Senate speech, in which he endorsed sectional compromises that included acceptance of the Fugitive Slave Act. He had opposed slavery's extension from the time of the Missouri controversy through the aftermath of the MEXICAN WAR, but his central commitment to the Union led him to take in 1850 what many in Massachusetts believed was a position truckling to slavery.

During his long career, substantial consistency unified Webster's legal, political, and oratorical vision: a democracy safe because of broad property ownership and integrated social interests; a government empowered to promote the general freedom and welfare; and an indissoluble Union.

BIBLIOGRAPHY

Baxter, Maurice G. *One and Inseparable: Daniel Webster and the Union.* 1984.

Curtis, George Ticknor. *The Life of Daniel Webster.* 2 vols. 1870.

Erickson, Paul D. *The Poetry of Events: Daniel Webster's Rhetoric of the Constitution and Union.* 1986.

Shewmaker, Kenneth E., ed. *Daniel Webster: "The Completest Man."* 1990.

Wiltse, Charles M., et al. *The Papers of Daniel Webster.* 14 vols. in 4 series. 1974–1989. Wiltse also edited a complete microfilm edition of Webster papers with guide and index.

DAVID A. GRIMSTED

WEBSTER-ASHBURTON TREATY. The Webster-Ashburton Treaty of 1842, negotiated under the auspices of President John Tyler, resolved many longstanding problems between the United States and England that had fomented a crisis by the spring of that year. Shortly after Tyler took office in 1841, the ministry in London—led by Sir Robert Peel and his foreign secretary, Lord Aberdeen—confronted problems with America as well as France and decided to send Lord Ashburton (Alexander Baring) as special emissary to Washington to settle all problems between the Atlantic nations. He and Secretary of State DANIEL WEBSTER met numerous times during the summer of 1842, emerging with a treaty in August that finalized two major portions of the Canadian-American boundary in the northeast and that incorporated an extradition agreement and a clause providing for a joint squadron of American and British ships intended to suppress the African slave trade. The men resolved a host of other problems by exchanging notes attached to the treaty.

President Tyler deserves considerable credit for the treaty's success. He repeatedly eased the frustrations of the British envoy, who threatened to return home and remained only after delicate persuasions. In addition, Tyler authorized Webster to draw from the President's Secret-Service fund to facilitate the boundary negotiations. Four years later, in 1846, Webster stood accused of wrongdoing during the negotiations, and former President Tyler appeared before a congressional committee to defend Webster's behavior while Secretary of State, thereby helping to exonerate him of charges aimed at retroactive impeachment.

By the treaty, the United States received seven-twelfths of the area in dispute but four-fifths of its assessed value, a region encompassing an important military position at the top of Lake Champlain, and an area west of Lake Superior that later proved rich in iron ore. The Tyler administration had secured a pact that permitted United States attention to turn westward, while promoting a midcentury rapprochement that had major ramifications for both nations.

BIBLIOGRAPHY

Jones, Howard. "Daniel Webster: The Diplomatist." In *Daniel Webster: The Completest Man*. Edited by Kenneth E. Shewmaker. 1990.
Jones, Howard. *To the Webster-Ashburton Treaty: A Study in Anglo-American Relations, 1783–1843*. 1977.

HOWARD JONES

WEEKLY COMPILATION OF PRESIDENTIAL DOCUMENTS. Published every Monday, the *Weekly Compilation of Presidential Documents* contains the texts of presidential statements, messages, news conference transcripts, veto messages, and other such materials, including EXECUTIVE ORDERS, released by the White House up to 5:00 P.M. Friday of the previous week. Checklists of legislation approved by the President, nominations submitted to the Senate, White House press releases, and scheduled appointments and meetings of the President are also included. The documentary content of the *Weekly Compilation* overlaps with that of the annual PUBLIC PAPERS OF THE PRESIDENTS of the United States, but the former affords much quicker access to such materials and offers some items, such as the texts of executive orders, not contained in the *Public Papers*.

Inaugurated with the 2 August 1965 issue, the periodical is compiled and indexed by the Office of the Federal Register of the National Archives. The *Weekly Compilation* may be purchased on a subscription basis from the Government Printing Office and is also available in the collections of many federal depository, law, and major public libraries.

BIBLIOGRAPHY

Schmeckebier, Laurence F., and Roy B. Eastin. *Government Publications and Their Use*. 2d rev. ed. 1969.

HAROLD C. RELYEA

WEINBERGER, CASPAR (b. 1917), Chairman of the Federal Trade Commission, Deputy Director of the Office of Management and Budget; Director of the Office of Management and Budget; counselor to the President, Secretary of Health, Education, and Welfare; Secretary of Defense. A lawyer with a distinguished career in public service, Caspar W. Weinberger gained his first executive branch experience in California in the administration of Governor Ronald Reagan. There Weinberger earned the nickname "Cap the Knife" for his efforts to cut state expenditures. The nickname stuck as he moved through a succession of major posts in the Nixon administration.

As Nixon's head of the OFFICE OF MANAGEMENT AND BUDGET, Weinberger fought to reduce federal outlays and defended the administration's IMPOUNDMENT of congressionally appropriated funds. Weinberger argued that "until Congress gets its budget-making house in order, strong presidential leadership is the only weapon the people have to prevent higher taxes and ruinous inflation." His comments would prove prophetic as federal spending continued to spiral out of control in subsequent years.

In 1980, President-elect Reagan asked Weinberger to take over the DEFENSE DEPARTMENT in order to spearhead the administration's efforts to rebuild the nation's armed forces, which Reagan and Weinberger thought had dangerously deteriorated during the 1970s. Influenced by his formative experiences of reading Winston Churchill and serving in the infantry during WORLD WAR II, Weinberger set about this new task with the same determination that he had brought to his earlier efforts.

The fruits of Weinberger's labors at the Defense Department can be seen in the successful military actions waged in Grenada [see GRENADA INVASION], and after Weinberger retired, in PANAMA and the GULF WAR. Ironically, Weinberger himself was not keen on the extensive use of the military as an instrument of foreign policy. He opposed from the start the tragic stationing of American troops in Beirut; and in a major speech in 1984, he argued that any commitment of American forces should be made only as a last resort and tied to a very specific military objective.

In 1992, President Bush pardoned Weinberger, who was being prosecuted for withholding information related to the IRAN-CONTRA AFFAIR.

BIBLIOGRAPHY

Towell, Pat. "Caspar Weinberger: Secretary of Defense." *Congressional Quarterly Weekly Report* (20 December 1980): 3608–3111.
Weinberger, Caspar W. *Fighting for Peace: Seven Critical Years in the Pentagon.* 1990.

JOHN G. WEST, JR.

WELFARE POLICY. When President Franklin D. Roosevelt signed the Social Security Act on 14 August 1935, he initiated the modern welfare system. From that date, welfare, the provision of money or essentials to the needy, played a role on the President's domestic agenda. By 1967 welfare had become a major national concern.

Under Roosevelt. Before 1935, Presidents followed the general wisdom that welfare was a profoundly local concern, a responsibility of each community to provide for its permanent residents. Economic calamities, however, tended to overwhelm local efforts. Recognizing the inadequacy of local relief, Roosevelt had begun an emergency relief program, funded by the federal government, almost immediately on assuming office. As the title of the Federal Emergency Relief Agency implied, Roosevelt regarded this effort as temporary. In 1934 he expressed his preference for public works programs to provide relief for the able-bodied and for direct income assistance only to those excused from the labor force by virtue of their age or physical condition. He preferred contributory social insurance to noncontributory public assistance (the formal name for welfare) as the means of funding income-assistance programs. He accepted welfare only as a transitional device that would serve people already too old to contribute to SOCIAL SECURITY.

After 1935, the federal government provided permanent financial assistance to the states for the payment of pensions to dependent children (those deprived of paternal support due to the death or disability of their fathers), the blind, and the elderly.

The extent of cost sharing varied by category, but, for the elderly, the federal government agreed to match the first $15 per month per recipient contributed by the state. The President's original proposals had included only the elderly and dependent children on the list of eligible categories, but Congress insisted on adding a category for the blind. To receive these payments, recipients needed to prove to the satisfaction of local authorities that they fell into the eligible categories and, more importantly, that they lacked sufficient resources to provide for themselves (a "means test," in welfare jargon).

Between 1935 and 1950, the bulk of federal welfare funds were spent in aid of the elderly. In 1939, for example, 80 percent of the funds went to the elderly and only 16.9 percent went to dependent children (aid to families with dependent children, or AFDC). Roosevelt intervened little in the formation of welfare policy. His few executive actions reinforced the efforts of the Social Security Board to make sure that welfare was administered by professionally trained caseworkers and that money was awarded with strict regard to an applicant's financial need and without regard to an applicant's political preferences. When, for example, the Social Security Board withheld more than $1 million from Ohio in 1938 for awarding welfare without regard to an applicant's financial need, Congress passed a 1940 law restoring those funds. Roosevelt vetoed the law. Roosevelt said that states could not violate federal standards "with impunity and still get their money."

Under Truman. President Harry S. Truman also upheld the desires of the Social Security Board. In a message to Congress on 24 May 1948, he recommended the creation of a general-assistance category that would cover all needy persons, not just those who fell into the categories established by the 1935 law. He also pressed for federal grants to fund the medical care of welfare recipients and for new grant formulas that would permit the federal government to pay a greater share of welfare costs in poorer states than in richer states. Congress reacted with indifference, its chief concern being to raise the level of federal matching funds for the elderly. General assistance garnered little political support. Wilbur Mills (D-Ark.), an influential member of the House Ways and Means Committee, called it a "WPA for a Truman depression," a derogatory reference to President Roosevelt's WORKS PROGRESS ADMINISTRATION.

Congress did acquiesce in 1950 to the creation of a fourth welfare category, aid to the permanently and totally disabled, as well as to permitting states to spend welfare funds on "vendor payments" to doctors and hospitals that served the poor. Significantly, the 1950 Social Security Amendments, by raising social security benefit levels and expanding social security coverage, made it possible, beginning in 1951, for social security to replace welfare as the primary income maintenance program for the elderly.

In the 1950s and 1960s, attention shifted from welfare for the elderly to welfare for dependent children. In 1957, for the first time, more people received aid to dependent children than received aid to the elderly. Senator John F. Kennedy joined a growing number of liberal politicians who advocated a change in AFDC to include payments to families in which the father was unemployed, rather than dead or disabled. At the same time, interest grew among social welfare professionals in using federal money to fund special services designed to counsel welfare families on ways to escape welfare dependency and improve their ability to support themselves and raise well-adjusted children.

Under Kennedy. When Kennedy became President, he encouraged Abraham Ribicoff, the Secretary of Health, Education, and Welfare, and Wilbur Cohen, the Assistant Secretary of Legislation at HEW, to develop legislation to transform AFDC from an income-support system to a rehabilitation program. Cohen completed plans for this legislation in the fall of 1961. In February 1962, the President sent Congress the first presidential message devoted solely to welfare. Congress passed the Public Welfare Amendments of 1962 by the summer. These amendments encouraged the states to initiate service programs aimed at the rehabilitation of welfare recipients by providing three federal dollars for each dollar the state contributed. In addition, the law allowed states to establish work and training programs for welfare beneficiaries and to pay welfare benefits to families with unemployed parents.

Although every state established some sort of service program, only about half the states began programs for welfare families with unemployed parents (AFDC-UP). To help administer the law, Kennedy and Ribicoff created the Welfare Administration within the Department of Health, Education, and Welfare, separating the welfare and social security programs. The President appointed Ellen Winston, a dynamic program director from North Carolina, to head this new agency. The Welfare Administration was superseded by the Social and Rehabilitation Service in 1967, as Presidents continued to search for the proper bureaucratic framework in which to place welfare and improve its image.

Even by 1963, the image of welfare programs and welfare recipients already needed refurbishing. Welfare had begun to attract controversy, as typified by efforts in Louisiana in 1961 to remove illegitimate children from homes deemed to be unsuitable, by a 1961 controversy in Newburgh, New York, over the right of local authorities to refuse assistance to African Americans recently arrived from the South, and by controversy over welfare payments made to women who cohabitated with men (while claiming that no man lived in the house) in the District of Columbia. For all this controversy, Congress had passed the 1962 amendments with little partisan debate. Support for public assistance continued to be bipartisan, with Republicans often endorsing welfare as a locally based and fiscally prudent alternative to social security.

Under Johnson. Lyndon Baines Johnson accordingly saw little reason to reject the rehabilitation approach he inherited from Kennedy. Within four months of assuming office, Johnson approved a title in the 1964 Economic Opportunity Act that, in effect, funded rehabilitation services for welfare recipients under even more liberal terms than in the 1962 law.

Johnson also helped to establish Medicaid, a program run by state and local governments that funded medical care for welfare recipients and others deemed by local authorities to be medically indigent. Representative Mills, now Chairman of the House Ways and Means Committee, included the Medicaid proposal in the 1965 Social Security Amendments. When Mills decided early in March 1965 to incorporate Medicaid into omnibus legislation that also contained Medicare (hospital insurance for social security beneficiaries), Johnson gave his approval immediately and put his administration solidly behind the proposal. Medicaid ultimately became the most costly of the nation's welfare programs. Between 1966 and 1980 Medicaid costs doubled every four years. In 1980, Medicaid cost $30.4 billion at all levels of government, compared with $14.6 billion for AFDC.

As the 1960s advanced, urban riots, the continued growth in the welfare rolls, and the substantial increase in African American welfare recipients as a percentage of the total caseload all tended to increase public dissatisfaction with the welfare program and with the rehabilitation approach. During that decade, the unemployment rate was halved while AFDC recipients increased by almost two-thirds and AFDC money payments doubled. As early as 1962, many states, including New York and Pennsylvania, spent more for welfare than for highways.

Congress responded, over the objections of President Johnson, with legislation in 1967 that froze the level of federal expenditures for welfare grants to families with illegitimate children. The legislation also permitted states to discontinue welfare grants for people who refused to join work-training programs "without good cause." John Gardner, Johnson's Secretary of HEW, protested these actions, as did urban-based politicians such as New York City mayor John Lindsay and Senator ROBERT F. KENNEDY (D-N.Y.), all to no avail. A punitive approach to welfare, which emphasized the requirement that women on welfare should work, had begun to replace the more permissive rehabilitation approach.

Liberals tried to counter the growing emphasis on work requirements with work incentives. In 1967 the Johnson administration and Congress negotiated changes in the law, known as work disregards, that were designed to encourage welfare recipients to work by allowing them to keep some of their earnings without a reduction in their welfare payments. This law, part of the 1967 Social Security Amendments, established a new rule that permitted welfare recipients to keep the first $30 per month that they earned, as well as one third of the remainder. This rule signaled a change in welfare policy, away from psychologically oriented social services and toward more tangible economic incentives.

Under Nixon and Carter. Richard M. Nixon entered office with the view that welfare programs demanded immediate attention. Nixon referred to welfare as a "mess," a description that lingered over the course of the next two decades. He pointed with despair to the growing welfare caseload in urban areas. New York City had 500,000 people on the rolls in 1965 and 875,000 on the rolls in the middle of 1968. As Nixon began his presidency, that total reached 1 million. Resolving to encourage work among potential welfare recipients and to discourage illegitimacy and promiscuity, Nixon opted in August 1969 for comprehensive reform. He proposed to replace AFDC with a guaranteed income, payable to all families with children. His Family Assistance Plan promised to pay $1,600 annually to a family with four children, along with a $720 work disregard and a 50 percent marginal tax on earnings. That meant that someone could earn $720 and still receive the guarantee; for earnings above $720, the government reduced the family's payment by fifty cents for every dollar earned. Nixon accompanied this plan with rules to extend the food stamp program so that welfare recipients would not have to spend more than 30 percent of their income on food.

In making these recommendations, Nixon explicitly rejected the service approach to welfare with its emphasis on social work. "The best way to ameliorate the hardships of poverty is to provide the family with additional income—to be spent as that family sees fit," he said.

The Family Assistance Plan met with a hostile reaction in the Senate. Liberals such as Senator GEORGE MCGOVERN (D-S.D.) thought the guaranteed income contained in the plan was too low and that it was punitive to demand that mothers with children work; conservatives such as Senator John Williams (R-Del.) believed that a guaranteed income, even with work requirements, would be prohibitively costly and reduce the level of labor-force participation. Williams pointed to what the experts in the field, who were growing in number and in econometric sophistication, called notch effects. The existence of these effects, which phased out public housing and medical benefits at given levels of income, made it extremely difficult to design a welfare reform plan in which working mothers received more than nonworking mothers.

In October 1972, Nixon managed to salvage only a new program for the elderly, blind, and permanently and totally disabled from his proposals. (Congress left AFDC intact.) Supplemental Security Income (SSI), as the new program was called, allowed the federal government to take over the existing state programs in these categories and put the federal government behind an absolute guarantee of $210 a month for an elderly couple on welfare. Unlike the AFDC program, SSI was administered by the Social Security Administration, which enjoyed a wide reputation as a competent agency. SSI, in effect, separated the administration of welfare for the "worthy" poor from welfare for mothers with dependent children.

During the 1970s, welfare became a hotly debated topic, as experts debated the fine points of program design and the public questioned the utility of paying welfare mothers not to work. Both the deterioration of the national economy and changes in the African-American family influenced the discussion. As sociologist William Julius Wilson has reported, "In 1965 nearly 25 percent of all black families were headed by women and by 1980, 43 percent were."

President Jimmy Carter, in particular, highlighted welfare reform. He worked to pass a new version of a guaranteed income but achieved as little success as Nixon. Carter, whose Program for Better Jobs and Incomes appeared in 1977, hoped to guarantee a higher income for the disabled, blind, and elderly people who were not expected to work and a lower income for able-bodied adults. Able-bodied adults were expected to supplement their welfare grants with jobs that the government would guarantee them, either in the private sector or in public service. Skeptics inside and outside Congress doubted the ability of the federal government to provide sufficient jobs to those in need.

Under Reagan. Ronald Reagan had made welfare reform a priority of his tenure as governor of California, and his interest in the subject continued during his presidency. In 1981, he persuaded Congress, in the Omnibus Budget Reconciliation Act, to make substantial cuts in AFDC by changing the work-disregard formula and limiting welfare grants to 150 percent of a state's standard of need. Unlike Nixon and Carter, Reagan disapproved of a guaranteed income and instead stressed purifying the welfare rolls to remove ineligible recipients and requiring welfare recipients to perform public-service jobs as a means of paying off their grants. He favored state administration of welfare over federal administration.

In 1988 Reagan collaborated with congressional leaders such as Senator Daniel P. Moynihan (D-N.Y.) and with the National Association of Governors in sponsoring what became the Family Support Act of 1988. The law established comprehensive state education and training programs, transitional child care and medical assistance benefits, mandatory coverage for two-parent families for at least six months of each year, and strong child-support enforcement. With the passage of the Family Support Act, welfare receded as a priority item on the President's domestic agenda, with states expected to devise means of reducing welfare dependency while, at the same time, providing for those in need.

BIBLIOGRAPHY

Berkowitz, Edward D. *America's Welfare State: From Roosevelt to Reagan.* 1991.

Burke, Vincent J., and Vee Burke. *Nixon's Good Deed: Welfare Reform.* 1974.

Katz, Michael. *In the Shadow of the Poorhouse.* 1986.

Lynn, Laurence E., and David Whitman. *The President as Policymaker: Jimmy Carter and Welfare Reform.* 1981.

Patterson, James. *America's Struggle against Poverty, 1900–1980.* 1981.

Steiner, Gilbert. *Social Insecurity: The Politics of Welfare.* 1966.

Trattner, Walter. *From Poor Law to Welfare State.* 4th ed. 1990.

Wilson, William Julius. *The Truly Disadvantaged: The Inner City, the Underclass and Public Policy.* 1987.

EDWARD D. BERKOWITZ

WHEELER, WILLIAM ALMON (1819–1887), nineteenth Vice President of the United States (1877–1881). Born in Malone, New York, William Almon Wheeler attended the University of Vermont, where he was so poor that he existed for six weeks on bread and water. Financial difficulties and eye trouble forced him to return to Malone where he studied law. In 1845, Wheeler was admitted to the bar and married.

Wheeler was successful professionally and politically. A Whig, he was from 1846 to 1849 the district attorney of Franklin County and then served in the New York assembly from 1850 to 1851. He retired from politics temporarily to manage a bank and a railroad. Joining the REPUBLICAN PARTY in 1855, Wheeler returned to politics as a state senator in 1858 and was a member of Congress from 1861 to 1863. He presided over the New York State constitutional convention (1867–1868) and from 1869 to 1877 once again served in Congress.

Speaker of the House JAMES G. BLAINE called Wheeler an "admirable" legislator. He was an intelligent, conscientious worker, trustworthy and respected, but, not being a debater, he spoke rarely. In an age noted for corruption he was upright—refusing the gift of railroad stock—and frugal with public funds. His chief contribution as a congressman was working out the Wheeler "adjustment" or "compromise" that settled a disputed Louisiana election in 1874.

Although a moderate, Wheeler impressed General Philip Sheridan, the military commander in Louisiana. Looking toward the presidential election of 1876 he wrote his old comrade in arms Governor Rutherford B. Hayes of Ohio that "his ticket is *Hayes and Wheeler.*" Hayes, however, underscored Wheeler's obscurity when he admitted to his wife Lucy, "I am ashamed to say, Who is *Wheeler*?" When the Republicans nominated Hayes, Ohio's favorite son, they sought balance and looked to New York, which seemed essential for victory, for a vice presidential candidate. Thomas C. Platt of the Conkling machine nominated Stewart L. Woodford but antimachine people favored Wheeler. On the first ballot Wheeler opened up such a huge lead that the machine withdrew Woodford, and Wheeler triumphed unanimously. Wheeler's letter of acceptance upheld the civil, political, and public rights of all citizens from the "canebrakes of Louisiana" to "the banks of the St. Lawrence," called for federal aid to education in the South, which he hoped would reduce friction, but otherwise desired the "strictest economy in expenditures," and endorsed the projected 1879 return to the gold standard. Although both Hayes and Blaine asked him to campaign, Wheeler was convinced of his ill health and refused to do so.

Hayes and Wheeler triumphed in the disputed presidential election of 1876. The Hayes-Wheeler relationship was almost unique. They had few policy differences and were sincerely friendly. Hayes was unusually considerate and consulted Wheeler on his CABINET and major appointments. Wheeler was a shrewd judge of foes like Conkling, but also of friends like Secretary of State William M. Evarts ("not frank" and "equivocal"), James A. Garfield (not "firm"), and Hayes (whose "amiable obstinacy and independence" endeared him to Wheeler). Hayes wanted Wheeler to go to Louisiana in 1877 at the head of a commission to resolve another dispute between the Republicans and the Democrats over the control of that state, but Wheeler refused to take on that difficult task. He presided ably over the Senate but he would have preferred to be Speaker of the House had it been possible.

After retiring from the vice presidency Wheeler received considerable support for the Senate in 1881 but was not elected. The next year President Chester A. Arthur wanted him to chair the Tariff Commission, but Wheeler refused to serve. When he died on 4 June 1887 in Malone, Hayes called him "a New England man of ability and character, who by sheer force of perseverance, integrity, and good conduct, rose from poverty to independence and honorable place."

BIBLIOGRAPHY

Gillette, William. *Retreat from Reconstruction: 1869–1879.* 1979.

Hayes, Rutherford Birchard. *Diary and Letters of Rutherford Birchard Hayes: Nineteenth President of the United States.* Edited by Charles Richard Williams. 5 vols. 1922–1926.

Polakoff, Keith Ian. *The Politics of Inertia: The Election of 1876 and the End of Reconstruction.* 1973.

ARI HOOGENBOOM

WHIG PARTY. The Whigs emerged as a major political party during the presidency of Andrew Jackson (1829–1837). The President's unprecedented use of his office to shape national policy in particular ways, his dramatic use of the veto power in his battle with the BANK OF THE UNITED STATES, and his determination to take on South Carolina's claims to be able to nullify federal laws within its borders, appalled many. National Republicans and members of the ANTI-MASONIC PARTY, both long hostile to Jackson, now were joined by STATES' RIGHTS groups, national bank supporters, and conservatives outraged by what they considered to be Jackson's repeated challenges to good order. Behind the leadership of HENRY CLAY and DANIEL WEBSTER the sometimes confused factionalism of the late 1820s gave way to an increasingly well-organized political party with a clear center of gravity and significant electoral strength. Some Whigs originally resisted the organizational imperatives that were required of political parties in an electoral climate involving more voters than ever before, along with the submission of the individual to the discipline of the collective whole, but enough of them accepted such dictates that Whig Party coherence and organization forged ahead as an effective opposition to Jackson in Congress and state legislatures and in the elections contested throughout his tenure.

Reminding voters of the English Whigs' challenge to King George III, Whig resistance to the excesses of "King Andrew" gave them their name but only part of their appeal. Clay's AMERICAN SYSTEM of economic nationalism defined them, along with their persistent nativist Anglo-Saxon commitment, hostile to outsider threats to the nation's social stability. They fought to establish a new national bank, a protective tariff, federal financing of public works, and other measures designed to push forward an industrially driven market economy. At the state level, particularly in the northern states, the Whigs also were identified with legislation designed to shape and regulate people's personal behavior in the name of community order: placing limitations on liquor use, establishing particular school curricular measures, promoting antialien attitudes and sometimes antislavery as well.

While the Whigs successfully built up their strength, they could not break through to national power in the 1830s. Like the DEMOCRATIC PARTY, the Whig Party attracted a variety of supporters throughout the Union who cut across class and regional lines. They were particularly strong among old English population groups in New England, New York, and Ohio and in areas where religious revivalism had taken hold in these same states. They also did quite well in commercially vigorous and fast growing areas in northern port cities and in the South. Finally, they drew to them everywhere people, who for a myriad of local reasons, were hostile to others in their area who had become Democrats. The electoral geography of the United States indicated the existence of two national parties, competitive with each other in most states, particularly the largest, and drawing their strength from the support of different socioeconomic groups.

It was the presidential administration of another Democrat, Jackson's successor, Martin Van Buren, from 1837 onward that particularly pushed the Whigs toward national power. Van Buren's unwillingness to use government power to stimulate the economy during the panic of 1837 particularly heightened the differences between Democrats and Whigs on the creative use of federal authority to shape and direct the economy and promote the market revolution underway in the United States. The economic panic drove a significant group of Democrats into the Whig camp and also stimulated an unprecedented voter turnout at the polls in the presidential election of 1840, resulting in a Whig victory behind William Henry Harrison and John Tyler. While the Whigs were usually identified as the conservative balance to the more boisterous, antielite Democrats, in 1840 they adopted fully the egalitarian antielitism of the early Jacksonians and used it quite effectively in a noisy and rousing campaign. Whig organization was highly developed and vigorous, their party newspapers throughout the country provided a steady drumbeat of populist advocacy, denouncing an administration indifferent to the people's suffering. Whigs set a standard of popular campaigning that became the national norm for half a century thereafter.

Once in office, the congressional Whigs led by Clay pushed forward an extensive menu of federal legislation designed to promote Whig conceptions of federal power. They were frustrated, however. Harrison's sudden death propelled John Tyler, leader of the party's small and increasingly obsolete states' rights wing, into the presidency where he vetoed or hamstrung Clay's nationalist program at the only time it had a real chance of being enacted. At the same time, many states' righters left the Whigs as the nationalists came clearly to dominate the party. Throughout the 1840s the Whigs continued to do well at the state level in much of the Union, holding many governorships and controlling state legislatures in parts of New England, New York, Ohio, Kentucky, Tennessee, the border states, North Carolina, and Louisiana. But this did them little good nationally. In 1844, they lost a very close race to the Democrat James K. Polk and watched in anger, despite their powerful resistance, as the new President successfully pushed forward the traditional Democratic policy agenda.

Polk's missteps over territorial expansion and the MEXICAN WAR gave the Whigs a second chance at national power. Northern Whigs took the lead in trying to prevent the expansion of SLAVERY into new territories acquired as a result of the Mexican War. Southern Whigs were much exercised and many of them joined Southern Democrats in opposing any restriction on the growth of slavery. Both parties split and in 1848 a FREE-SOIL PARTY, consisting of some northern democrats and some northern Whigs, ran against slavery's extension. The Whig leadership chose a war hero, General Zachary Taylor, as their candidate, untrammeled by the political infighting of the past twenty years.

Taylor's victory over the divided Democrats pro-pelled the second Whig presidential administration into office. But Taylor's administration was largely preoccupied in working out the sectional crisis provoked by expansion that was accomplished largely on a nonpartisan basis by Clay and the Democrat STEPHEN A. DOUGLAS. Taylor's resistance to certain aspects of their efforts was overcome when he died in July 1850 and was succeeded by a traditional Whig, Vice President Millard Fillmore of New York. Unlike the situation ten years before, President Fillmore faced a Democratic Congress and was unable to push any aspects of the traditional Whig program through.

Through it all, in this era, the Whigs remained the minority party to the dominant Democrats. They elected only two Presidents in the seven races they contested and only controlled Congress once, briefly, in the 1840s. In an era distinguished by intense commitment to one's party, the Whigs could never win over to them in any sustained way more than their usual pockets of supporters. Whig leaders were quite conscious of this and in the presidential election of 1852, as in 1840 and 1848, they sought to broaden their base. With General WINFIELD SCOTT as their candidate, the Whigs in some parts of the North sought the support of traditionally Democratic Irish Catholics despite the Whigs' long identification as the party of the Anglo-Saxon establishment in the United States, quite hostile to Catholics.

Their tactic was unsuccessful and provoked a backlash against them in the mid 1850s. The rising tide of sectional confrontation and the threat of social chaos posed by increased Catholic immigration disrupted the Jacksonian party system and fatally weakened the Whigs. The emergence of the anti-Catholic KNOW NOTHING (AMERICAN) PARTY attracted many Whigs to it in 1853 and 1854. At the same time the renewal of the battle over slavery expansion into the territories in 1854 drove other northern Whigs into the emerging REPUBLICAN PARTY. Some Whig leaders tried to preserve the party. But others such as WILLIAM SEWARD and Thurlow Weed in New York worked to unite these people, along with new voters and former Democrats, into a movement that largely maintained the traditional Whig viewpoint in economic and social matters. The REPUBLICAN PARTY succeeded in his attempt but at the cost of the demise of the Whigs whose followers, perpetual losers and frustrated when they were in office, now found a home in a party that proved to be more successful than the Whigs had ever been.

BIBLIOGRAPHY

Ashworth, John. "Agrarians" and "Aristocrats": Party Political Ideology in the United States, 1837–1846. 1983.

Brown, Thomas. *Politics and Statesmanship: Essays on the American Whig Party.* 1985.
Gienapp, William. *Origins of the Republican Party, 1852–1856.* 1987.
Holt, Michael. *Political Parties and American Political Development from the Age of Jackson to the Age of Lincoln.* 1992.
Howe, Daniel Walker. *The Political Culture of the American Whigs.* 1979.
Van Deusen, Glynson. "The Whig Party." In vol. 1 of *History of U.S. Political Parties.* Edited by Arthur M. Schlesinger, Jr. 4 vols. 1973.

JOEL H. SILBEY

WHISKEY REBELLION. The Whiskey Rebellion of 1794 provoked the first occasion for a President to call out the militia to suppress an insurrection. Congress, under the Constitution, has the power to call forth the militia to execute national law and suppress insurrections. In 1792 Congress authorized the President to exercise that power, on condition that a federal judge should certify that the execution of law was obstructed by combinations too powerful to be suppressed by ordinary judicial proceedings or the power of federal marshals.

The federal excise tax on distilling whiskey, enacted by Congress in 1791 at the urging of Secretary of the Treasury ALEXANDER HAMILTON, was a means of financing federal assumption of state debts. But the incidence of the tax, a steep 25 percent of the net value of the product, fell heavily on grain farmers in western Pennsylvania who distilled their harvest so they could transport it; pack animals could not carry corn or wheat across the Alleghenies. Locally, whiskey was a medium of exchange and a valuable commodity. The farmers were indignant about the tax and about being served writs for nonpayment that required their presence in faraway Philadelphia, where they would be fined $250 each. They reacted not just by vehement remonstrances but by sabotaging collection of the tax by force and violence. Federal collectors were tarred and feathered. Federal officers who sought to serve the writs were also attacked. A mob assaulted the home of one and burned it to the ground. That was the Whiskey Rebellion.

Hamilton easily persuaded President George Washington that the integrity of the union was at stake because of the defiance of the whiskey rebels. According to Hamilton force had to be met with force. Washington, who had already issued a PROCLAMATION urging compliance with the laws, turned over to Justice JAMES WILSON the evidence of the rebellion and received his certification that ordinary legal means were insufficient to execute national law. Washington then proclaimed the existence of the rebellion and called forth the militias of four states, a total of nearly thirteen thousand men. For a month the armed force traveled into western Pennsylvania seeking rebels, but resistance melted away as the army approached. Washington personally accompanied the expedition for a while; Hamilton, Judge Richard Peters, and a federal prosecutor attended the whole time. Supposed rebels were apprehended and interrogated; about 150 arrests were made. Eventually twenty men were brought to trial. None was a leader. Two were convicted of treason and sentenced to death, but even Hamilton agreed that their execution would be needlessly cruel. Washington pardoned both. So ended the first inglorious instance of violent opposition to national law that required its vindication by presidential action.

BIBLIOGRAPHY

Baldwin, Leland D. *Whiskey Rebels.* 1939.
Slaughter, Thomas P. *The Whiskey Rebellion.* 1986.

LEONARD W. LEVY

WHISKEY RING. Of the several scandals that embarrassed the administration of Ulysses S. Grant, the Whiskey Ring was the one that led closest to the President himself. Whiskey distillers and distributors made it a routine habit to evade taxes by bribing tax agents. In the fall of 1874, Secretary of the Treasury Benjamin H. Bristow, working from evidence showing that since 1870 between twelve and fifteen million gallons had escaped the tax, launched an investigation. His operative, investigative reporter Myron Colony, accumulated massive evidence of a conspiracy that led directly to General John McDonald of St. Louis. In April 1875 McDonald confessed his guilt to Bristow, then sought protection from his friend President Grant.

Grant tolerated the investigation until its coils caught up his most trusted aide, Orville E. Babcock. Bristow sent General James H. Wilson (whose brother was a key investigator) to break the news to his old friend Grant; instead, the talk ruptured their friendship. Grant defended Babcock with a ferocity that betrayed his dark suspicion that he was Bristow's real target. Babcock encouraged Grant's fear and adroitly hid behind the President.

The investigation estranged Bristow from Grant and forced him out of the Cabinet in 1876. To defend his friend, Grant went to the extraordinary length of giving a deposition on his behalf (he offered to testify in person but was talked out of doing so). His support did much to gain Babcock's acquittal in February 1876. The evidence suggests that Grant knew Babcock was guilty but was willing to perjure himself to keep his aide out of jail.

The whole tawdry episode besmirched the final year of Grant's presidency and detracted his attention from more pressing issues. Although the CREDIT MOBILIER SCANDAL gained more public notoriety, it did not reach as close to the White House. The Whiskey Ring remained the worst scandal to blacken a presidential reputation until the TEAPOT DOME SCANDAL in the 1920s.

BIBLIOGRAPHY

McFeely, William S. *Grant: A Biography.* 1981.

MAURY KLEIN

WHISTLE-BLOWERS. Whistle-blowers are employees who expose—"blow the whistle on"—an action or condition that the employees believe is unlawful or constitutes mismanagement or abuse of authority. Whistle-blowing illuminates a tension between two precepts of American politics: hierarchy and unfettered discussion of public policy.

The President is the constitutionally designated manager of much of the federal bureaucracy. He, the White House staff, the Cabinet, and other presidential appointees have extraordinary power over the careers of federal employees. Whistle-blowing frequently represents a form of resistance to executive-branch leadership by communication to and alliance with those outside of its hierarchy. While some whistle-blowers communicate with the President or his appointees about misconduct by other policymakers, it is the whistle-blowers who expose behavior of their superiors within the executive branch who generally provoke employment reprisals. Communication may be with Congress, other employees, interest groups, professional associations, or the media. Whistle-blowers' allegations frequently expose ongoing policy feuds between the highest levels of the executive branch and other policymakers.

Until recently, federal employees have had little legal protection against retaliation for their infidelity. While communication about matters of public policy is at the core of free expression values represented in the First Amendment, the Supreme Court has been reluctant to inject the judiciary into the hierarchical arrangements of public employment. *Pickering v. Board of Education* (1968) extended limited First Amendment protection to public employees, conditioning protection upon a finding that the whistle-blower's communication "in [no] way either impeded . . . proper performance of his daily duties . . . or . . . interfered with the regular operation of [government]."

With the courts averse to developing broad First Amendment safeguards for whistle-blowers, the political branches responded with legislation. Reform of the CIVIL SERVICE was a campaign pledge of Jimmy Carter. Enactment of the CIVIL SERVICE REFORM ACT of 1978 (CSRA) was the fulfillment of that promise. The spectacle of a lengthy and notorious legal battle pitting Richard M. Nixon against defense analyst–whistle-blower Ernest Fitzgerald combined with frequent horror stories about government waste helped motivate Congress to include safeguards for whistle-blowers in CSRA.

The major thrust of CSRA was to reduce political patronage and expand merit hiring. One component of reform was a provision (5 U.S.C. 2302) prohibiting reprisals against employees who disclose illegal or improper government conduct. A second, which ultimately became much more controversial, was a set of procedures for implementing the protection. Eleven years later, the procedures were modified by the Whistleblower Protection Act of 1989.

The CSRA replaced the old Civil Service Commission with four entities, two of which affect whistle-blowers: the MERIT SYSTEM PROTECTION BOARD (MSPB) and Office of Special Counsel (OSC).

The MSPB is an independent, quasi-judicial agency with responsibility for protecting the integrity of the merit system. The OSC is an adjunct to the MSPB. It receives complaints of illegality and mismanagement, requires agencies to conduct investigations of the charges, and investigates and prosecutes (before the MSPB) complaints of retaliation against whistle-blowers. Anticipating that incompetent or unfit employees would use the whistle-blower provisions as a shield against adverse personnel actions, CSRA furnished OSC with discretion to choose which cases it took before the MSPB. The MSPB and OSC were fashioned to provide prompt, administrative resolution of whistle-blower disputes, to avoid protracted litigation in Article Three courts, and to preserve much of the hierarchy attendant to civil service.

Within four years of its creation, the principal congressional sponsor of the OSC introduced legislation to abolish it. Critics complained that it had become captive of executive branch policymakers who were using it selectively to persecute rather than protect whistle-blowers. Investigations were not being conducted, prosecutions of meritorious cases were suspended, and anonymous whistle-blowers were being identified to their superiors. OSC's ombudsman-like character meant that no attorney-client privilege was established between dissenters and OSC. Further, the head of OSC was a presidential appointee and staff consisted of political appointees. When one special counsel testified before Congress that most whistle-blowers were malcontents, momentum surged for revision of the system. In spite of presidential resistance to reform, including a veto by President Ronald Reagan, the Whistleblower Protection Act of 1989 emerged with the signature of President George Bush.

The Whistleblower Protection Act of 1989 modified the role of OSC, limiting its discretion and affirming that its basic function is to protect employees, particularly whistle-blowers, from prohibited personnel practices. The primary changes were to restrict the discretion of OSC to disclose the names of whistle-blowers to superiors and to authorize whistle-blowers to litigate their own claims before the MSPB. Three provisions attenuating presidential authority over the OSC provoked the threat of another veto and were deleted. These would have changed procedures for terminating the special counsel and OSC reporting to Congress and permitted the OSC to appeal adverse MSPB rulings to courts.

One ironic side effect of the CSRA was the dilution of First Amendment rights of federal employees. In the aforementioned dispute involving Richard Nixon and Ernest Fitzgerald, Fitzgerald sought to vindicate his First Amendment rights with *Bivens* suits against Nixon and his aides. *Bivens* suits—*Bivens v. Six Unknown Named Agents of the Federal Bureau of Narcotics* (1971)—are damage remedies for infringement of constitutional rights that courts create where statutory remedies are inadequate. With the enactment of the CSRA, federal employees had an alternative statutory remedy. Thus, in *Bush v. Lucas* (1983) the Supreme Court rejected the First Amendment *Bivens* claim of a federal employee. The *Bush* decision would have limited Ernest Fitzgerald's remedy to claims before the MSPB with representation by a hostile OSC. In *Nixon v. Fitzgerald* (1982) and *Harlow v. Fitzgerald* (1982) the Supreme Court granted absolute "presidential immunity" to Nixon, but only provided qualified immunity to his aides. The Whistleblower Protection Act of 1989 may resuscitate federal employee *Bivens* claims with a proviso that nothing in the Act is intended to limit remedies derived elsewhere.

BIBLIOGRAPHY

Fitzgerald, A. Ernest. *The Pentagonists: An Insider's View of Waste, Mismanagement, and Fraud in Defense Spending.* 1989.
Vaughn, Robert. *Merit Systems Protection Board: Rights Remedies.* 1984.
Westman, Daniel. *Whistleblowers: The Law of Retaliatory Discharge.* 1991.

PAUL PAVLICH

WHITE HOUSE (BUILDING). In the Residence Act of 1790, Congress designated that a capital city be established on the Potomac River and ordered that two official buildings be built there, a house for the Congress and a house for the President. President George Washington took great personal interest in the President's House, as it was then called, and took heed of the fact that the government was to move to the city ten years hence, in 1800. He approved the grand city plan we know today, and approved, at least in concept and dimensions, a "palace" for the chief of state. The White House, approximately one-fourth the size of the "palace," occupies a site nevertheless laid out to serve the larger, unrealized structure.

The Original Building. When the original program for putting the city and its buildings under one individual, Pierre Charles L'Enfant, did not materialize, it was determined to divide up the efforts. L'Enfant's plan was turned over to surveyors, and on the suggestion of Thomas Jefferson, the Secretary of State, a national competition was held for designs for the two principal public buildings. An impatient George Washington, through his own connections, brought to the competition James Hoban, with whom he had apparently come to agreements beforehand about the character of the proposed President's House. Hoban's design was for a Georgian country house, one he had known in his native Ireland, Leinster House, home of the Duke of Leinster in Dublin. His entry was the only one for a house of stone, which Washington wanted very much and which Jefferson had omitted from the competition specifications. The Hoban project won.

A building crew was assembled as best it could be, including Collen Williamson, an aging stonemason from the Scottish Highlands. Like Hoban, he had come to America shortly after the War of Independence and settled in the East. Work commenced in the vast cellars dug out for the house; George Washington himself came to the scene and drove the stakes siting the house. The cornerstone was laid on 13 October 1792. It was a brass plate proclaiming the event and listing the principal people involved. This was an important moment, the completion of a corner of the first building begun in the federal city.

Though not present for the cornerstone laying, Washington took a strong personal interest in the President's House. At the competition judging (where his opinion was the only one taken into account) he had ordered its size expanded and directed that it be greatly embellished with stone carving. In its departures from Leinster House, the plan shows Washington's ideas, notably in the East Room, which echoes the "new room" Washington had added to the end of

Mount Vernon for public events. On the south was a bow projection that, on the main floor, contained an oval saloon or drawing room. Washington had experimented with the oval idea in remodeling the presidential mansion in Philadelphia, adding a bow to his levee room to accommodate the oval lineup of his guests at formal weekly receptions. Washington was everpresent in the building of the President's House but was to be the only President not to live there.

Obtaining skilled labor proved a problem for the commissioners charged with the building of the federal city. Washington's insistence for stone kept them worrying and conflicts between Williamson and Hoban kept the building site in tension. At last, after inquiries in various foreign countries, they were able to persuade two lodges of Edinburgh stonemasons to journey to the United States. These fourteen experienced builders completed the house from about midway up the principal level of smooth ashlar walls to the fine, crisp modillions at the eaves.

The masons had worked on the restrained neoclassical buildings of New Town in Edinburgh and the preference of Washington for "old-fashioned" types of florid ornament must have surprised them. But they were able to produce it, and in so doing created the finest stonework in the United States up until that time. The stone itself was Aquia sandstone, quarried downriver on the Potomac at Aquia Creek in a quarry leased by the government for ten years.

After Williamson was fired by commissioners weary of his erratic conduct, Hoban remained as the respected superintendent of the work. He consulted with the master masons, who transferred his own drawings for carvings—roses, guilloches, pediments, swags, Ionic capitals, fish scaling, acanthus leaves—to full size renderings that would guide the carvers at their carving tables. Especially rich pieces, as the swag of roses and leaves over the north door, were roughed out on the work table from a large block, the block was set in the wall, then the carvings finished.

Washington lived to walk through a half-finished house in the brief years of his retirement. The first occupant of the White House moved in to the yet unfinished house on 1 November 1800, as specified in the law. John Adams did little to the place in his four months there. His successor, Jefferson, was the first two-term President to live in the President's House. Jefferson oversaw the completion of the interior and made changes as well—waterclosets were added even before he moved in (the privy at the side of the house was demolished). Jefferson devised plans for wings to the sides of the house; these were to connect to the public offices, which Washington had ordered built

on the grounds to the east and west. Jefferson overlooked Hoban and appointed a government architect, Benjamin Henry Latrobe, who saw to the erection of about half of his proposed wings, and these are today the east and west terraces or colonnades of the White House.

During the WAR OF 1812, the British burned the house on 24 August 1814, leaving only the stone walls, about half of which had to be demolished in the rebuilding. President James Madison, who with his wife, DOLLEY MADISON, had fled Washington, D.C., was emphatic that the resurrected house be as the old one had been and James Hoban was brought back to do the work, which was completed in January 1818 during the presidency of James Monroe. One alteration in the rebuilding plans was the addition of porticoes to the north and south. Latrobe and Hoban both claimed credit for these, although they are probably Hoban's.

President Monroe built the half-round south portico (so-called, but without a pediment it is actually a porch) in 1824, and the north portico, a deep porte-cochere, was built for Andrew Jackson in 1829–1830. Hoban directed both projects. The stone carvers were Scots and Italians, all of whom had worked on the reconstruction of the Capitol.

Uses of the White House. Thus, in 1830, the White House was complete. The grounds would change, but the architectural image was not to be altered, except in one particular, the Truman balcony of 1947. For the first seventy years of the nineteenth century the house was big enough to serve for state receptions as well as use as a residence and office. By 1825 the President's office was in the east end of the second floor, with the family apartments at the opposite end of the long transverse hall. This situation remained the same through the balance of the nineteenth century.

Monroe created the green of the Green Room in 1818; Martin Van Buren made the Blue Room blue in 1838. James K. Polk made the Red Room red in 1846. Jackson completed the East Room in 1829, giving it the trademark set of three giant glass chandeliers (those in place today are the third set, bought in 1902). The State Dining Room was expanded from the original—which could seat forty—in 1902 to a room that seats 104. It was Polk who began the entrance march to "Hail to the Chief" in 1846, but the Marine Band that plays it had originally been the "President's own." The President still eats on occasion on silver bought by the government for Monroe in 1818 and sits in chairs purchased at the same time. Many furnishings of the White House date back many years. They have been supplemented by antiques and memorabilia presented to the house through private funding or donation.

As for the physical house, conditions there became very crowded through the nineteenth century largely because it served so many functions. The office staff of two in 1861 rose to six in 1870 and to some thirty by 1900 (the numbers are difficult to ascertain, because most of these employees were "borrowed" from the various departments, which covered their salaries under concealed categories). Several projects were put forward for a new presidential residence, notably in 1867 and 1881, and for an expanded White House, in 1889, 1894, and 1900. In 1902 President Theodore Roosevelt settled the matter in calling for a restoration. Through pressures from the American Institute of Architects and personal persuasion on the part of Edith Wharton, he engaged the services of Charles McKim, of McKim, Mead & White. McKim rethought the use and functions of the house and achieved a revision of the White House that left it unchanged but renewed.

The West Wing was built to house the offices—only staff at first—and the East Wing, which had been demolished in 1868, was reconstructed as Jefferson had known it but revised to serve for a social entrance to the house. The basement, where dark storage rooms had once been, was restored as public space. On the interior, McKim replaced the simple, wood-floored Americanness of the house with the international chic of stone, and furnished the rooms in copies of European antiques, largely of the eighteenth-century type.

In 1927 the attic of the White House was removed and replaced with a heightened steel-structure roof, sheltering an entire third floor of guest rooms, baths, and domestic work spaces. Structurally this bore down on some frail construction work of 1902 on the second floor and rendered the house by 1948, in serious danger of partial collapse. President Harry S. Truman, having built his unpopular south balcony in 1947, now authorized a total reconstruction of the interior of the White House. He insisted, however, that the original stone walls remain untouched; it might be said that the vessel was emptied from within. A new interior was built in steel and concrete. The only old materials reused were some window sash and part of the panelling McKim had put in the State Dining Room. A new sub-basement system was built, and the original count of some sixty-four rooms was increased to one hundred thirty-two, counting about every space. Air conditioning, new security systems, and every modern convenience as then known created a modern White House, yet one with no apparent change to the architecture. Except for the inevitable redecoration of the interior, Truman's rebuilt White House, looking outside as it did in 1830, and inside, more or less as McKim had remodeled it in 1902, is the White House of the late twentieth century.

The White House Complex. The White House is the oldest continually occupied official residence of a chief of state in the Western World. Obviously it has not remained the vast but simple country house James Hoban built for George Washington. Security considerations preclude the publication of plans of office and residential sections of the White House and too-detailed descriptions of remote parts of the building. Broadly speaking, the White House has three parts: the central block; the West Wing, which includes the President's office; and the East Wing, which includes an entrance and offices to support the FIRST LADY's social responsibilities.

The central block. This is what is usually identified as the White House—the center section with the columns north and south. It contains the historic rooms open to the public and all the family's private living quarters. On the ground floor, (the basement before 1902) the kitchen and pantries and the doctor's office are on the west end of a long central corridor, while on the east are the library (established by Franklin D. Roosevelt), the Diplomatic Reception Room, the Map Room (so-called for its use by President Roosevelt and Winston Churchill during WORLD WAR II), the China Room (with past White House tableware), and the Vermeil Room (with a large collection of gold-plated silver table service objects presented to the house during the Eisenhower administration). The groin-vaulted corridor of the basement floor accommodates lines of tourists that call during visiting hours and connects the East and West wings.

Extending north from the ground floor, under the north lawn, are a series of underground rooms devoted mostly to the landscaping work of the White House, the florist office, with its great refrigerators, and maintenance storage rooms. Beneath the ground floor are two levels of basements, heavily built in concrete and steel. The dimensions of the walls were thickened by President Truman during the reconstruction of the house in 1950, on the request of the Secret Service. This area includes rooms for domestic services, utilities, and storage as well as the air conditioning and heating system.

The main floor, above the ground floor, is the state floor containing the great public rooms. This, together with hallways in the East Wing and ground floor, is the part of the White House that tourists see. Basically the plan is the same Hoban completed two centuries ago. From the north one enters a large entrance hall, with the grand stair to the left, and, directly ahead, a screen of Doric columns (the originals were Ionic) that divides this hall from the transverse hall off which the state rooms open. At opposite ends of the house, and rather like bookends, the East Room and the State Dining Room flank the row of three parlors, the Green, Blue, and Red Rooms. In general, Charles McKim's Beaux-Arts luster still prevails in the various state rooms, but most notably in the paneled East Room and State Dining Room, with their glossy painted surfaces and rich parquet floors. The parlors are more intimate. Since the late 1920s they have been furnished with a mixture of antique furnishings and reproductions, and, while the configuration changes from time to time, this is more or less the rule today.

James Monroe's gilded French furniture is still seen in the Blue Room. The Red Room, which contains a bust of Martin Van Buren by Hiram Powers, is furnished largely in "Grecian" and neoclassical chairs, tables, and sofas made dating from before about 1840. Earlier pieces are in the Green Room, where are also James Madison's candlesticks and John Quincy Adams's coffee pot. Most notable, if somewhat overpowering at times, is the presence in the state rooms of portraits of the early Presidents and their wives. By relatively recent tradition, portraits of modern presidents and wives hang in the transverse hall and ground floor corridor, in a more or less chronological arrangement beginning at the East Room.

The living quarters of the President and his family are on the second and attic, or third, floors. These provide a comfortable, if confining, area in which to live with some privacy and entertain personal friends and family. Like the state floor, the second floor has a long transverse hall; there are three sitting rooms. The most popular sitting room for the First Family is the west hall with its great arched window, built-in bookshelves, and adjacent family kitchen and dining room. Central to the second floor is the Yellow Oval Room, a very formal, private drawing room for the President, designed during the Kennedy administration. This room opens onto the Truman balcony, with its panoramic views.

On the west end there are four bedrooms. Other bedrooms are on the floor above, with a central hall used for sitting, a small solarium atop the South Portico, and a suite of rooms for live-in servants, as well as a small greenhouse.

On the east end of the second floor are the President's private study (from 1962 until 1991 called the Treaty Room) and several rooms of historical interest. The Lincoln Bedroom, which was originally Lincoln's office, contains the large rosewood bed his wife, MARY TODD LINCOLN, purchased in Philadelphia in 1861, but in which Lincoln never seems to have actually slept. The EMANCIPATION PROCLAMATION was signed in this room and a copy in Lincoln's handwriting on foolscap is displayed before the fireplace.

The Lincoln Bedroom is a guest room, as is the Queen's Bedroom, across the hall, so-named because royalty has used it in the past. A large high-post bed dominates the Queen's Bedroom, the bed, presented to Theodore Roosevelt as Andrew Jackson's. Historically this room had been the bedroom of the President's secretary, but in 1865 Andrew Johnson made it into an office. Artists liked this room for its north light, and most of the early portraits painted in the White House were painted here. Ralph E. W. Earle, friend and companion of Andrew Jackson, did a thriving business from this room painting portraits of the President and his late wife.

The West Wing. The popular name "West Wing" today refers to the President's office complex, derived from the 1902 building. The earlier West Wing, one of the two Jefferson built as service rooms for the house, with its colonnade facing the Rose Garden, is now incorporated into the functions of the West Wing and contains the Press Room, where the President and his aides meet the press. The press room was built in the Nixon administration over the swimming pool installed by Franklin D. Roosevelt, who used funds raised for the purpose primarily by New York school children.

The West Wing office building contains the OVAL OFFICE, the Cabinet Room, the Situation Room—a top-secret information center for the President—and various offices for the President's closest aides, including the WHITE HOUSE CHIEF OF STAFF, PRESS SECRETARY, and NATIONAL SECURITY ADVISER. Callers to the President go to the north door of the West Wing, where they are received in a lobby, before being ushered to the President for their appointment. Beneath the West Wing are various restaurant-style dining rooms for the convenience of those who work there. Two other buildings serve the some six thousand executive employees, the OLD EXECUTIVE OFFICE BUILDING to the west of the White House and the New Executive Office Building a block away on 17th Street.

The East Wing. This is the social and general entrance to the residence. Here, high-security systems check all callers, no matter what their purpose, before they are allowed to proceed along the broad inner hallway to the glassed-in east colonnade. In that area they have a full view of the east garden on the south, and on the north the doors to the coat box, or coat room, which is now used for a household movie theater. From the colonnade callers pass into the ground floor, from which a stair gives access to the state floor above.

Within the complex of the White House, the East Wing houses the social offices. Once under the direction of the Office of Protocol at the State Department, social management of the White House is now conducted from within the White House. The office of the First Lady's chief of staff is here, including aides, secretaries, and calligraphers. Here the guest lists are made and approved, social functions and ceremonies are planned, and all the details of these various endeavors are determined and put into effect. Press functions of the First Lady are also managed through the East Wing. [*See* First Lady's Office.]

The White House proper is under the direction of the chief usher, who functions as an executive officer, and answers directly to the President. The usher interacts when necessary with the chiefs of staff of the East and West Wings and the three officials comprise a sort of triumvrate, managing the three major parts of the house. Under the chief usher are the grounds management and the office of the curator of the White House, an office of research and stewardship over the vast collections of art, antiques, and memorabilia in the White House.

BIBLIOGRAPHY

Seale, William. *The President's House: A History.* 1985.
Seale, William. *The White House: The History of an American Idea.* 1992.
Singleton, Esther. *The Story of the White House.* 1907.
White House Historical Association. *The White House: An Historic Guide.* 5th ed. 1991.

WILLIAM SEALE

WHITE HOUSE ADVISERS. A modern President has several hundred men and women who are personal advisers and assistants—comprising the senior and central part of the much larger White House staff community. Despite labels in the annual Budget Appendix such as "Office of Policy Development" and "National Security Council," which imply that these units are part of the professional Executive Office of the President, the policy assistants in those sections, like the others in the "White House Office" itself, are in reality part of the President's personal staff; they all serve without tenure and at the President's pleasure.

The Need for Advisers. In the late twentieth century the American nation is a cacophonous, no-consensus society; not only are its dissensions reflected in Congress and throughout the federal system, but its pluralism is mirrored in the President's own enormously diverse executive branch. Demarcations between matters "foreign" and "domestic" are

disappearing, and boundaries separating cabinet departments are increasingly irrelevant. The principal policy issues facing a modern President—for example, the eradication of illegal drugs—stretch across all those borders; they are interdepartmental, intergovernmental, and international.

Article II of the Constitution, however, remains unchanged: in the executive branch, ultimate responsibility still rests in one person's hands. The President's personal White House staff bridges this gap between a raucously plural executive establishment and a determinedly singular President and manages the now-indispensable coordination of the President's business. It is not clear that cabinet officers or budget directors could ever have performed these very personal political functions, but nowadays they certainly could not. The Cabinet is a diverse bunch; its members, who are typically assembled to bind up the wounds of the presidential primaries, include the erstwhile feuding factions of the President's party and also encompass representatives of both sexes, of several racial and/or ethnic groups, various professions, ages, states, and religions. Cabinet officers are (and should be) antagonists: often, they not only differ vociferously with one another but also mix their considerable egos into their disputes. It is too much to expect any one of them to be a central coordinator to whose signals the others will defer.

Furthermore, department and agency heads have divided loyalties: they are always deferential—sometimes even hostage—to congressional committees, outside support constituencies, and their own bureaucracies. If, for instance, a major presidential speech is in the works, agency heads are likely to behave as supplicants rather than as integrators for the President.

Functions. Personal presidential advisers in the modern White House have five core functions. First, they coordinate the policy process across the spectrum of departments and agencies. Meetings of "task forces" or Cabinet councils (rarely of the full cabinet because of its size, pluralism, and propensity for leaks) are a frequently used technique. The White House staff sets the agenda of any White House meeting, composes whatever formal record is made of the proceedings (especially of the presidential decision), and performs the follow-up surveillance over departmental compliance. Some Presidents, however, distrust or even detest meetings; they prefer to work from option papers. Here, too, a White House adviser specifies the assignment for the paper and drafts either the last version of the option paper or the "road map" memorandum that guides the President through the paper's attachments and alerts the President to traps and pitfalls. White House advisers draft or record the chief executive's decision and mount the follow-up.

Second, policy issues occasionally arise that are of extreme sensitivity. Sometimes they must be kept secret for NATIONAL SECURITY reasons, or they may be potentially politically explosive, or they may be of such great import that the President is determined to capture the initiative by issuing a major presidential statement. The President will want absolutely no leaks, no premature dribbling out of bits and snippets of his program to be attacked piecemeal before his comprehensive argument is set forth. In such cases, the President will instruct that the preparatory work be kept deep in his advisers' pockets, from start to finish, with little or no reaching out to his Cabinet subordinates. (Examples include Richard M. Nixon's March 1970 statement on school desegregation and busing, Jimmy Carter's 1977 energy package, and Ronald Reagan's 1982 "new federalism" proposals). The President may direct one or more personal advisers to drop everything else and concentrate all their time on a single undertaking—a mandate no Cabinet officer could handle.

Third, a President cannot get through his early press conferences without being rudely asked, for example, about what he is doing to fix an operational goof-up in such-and-such an agency or about whether he agrees with yesterday's speech by Secretary So-and-so. If he confesses ignorance it is doubly embarrassing. Presidents have thus come to demand the establishment of information systems that will make sure that the White House knows about where things are going off the track. He and his staff insist on acquiring a very rare commodity in big institutions: anticipatory information. At least five such systems have been put in place: the SITUATION ROOMS into which raw and processed information of all kinds flows from the entire national security community; the daily News Summary, a twenty-page digest of important items from all U.S. television networks, wire services, East Coast newspapers (and others coming in by mail), foreign papers and foreign radio and TV stations (once a week a "Friday Follies" supplement of some sixty cartoons is appended); the regular Cabinet Report compiled by the secretary to the cabinet from individual submissions dragooned from the respective department and agency heads; weekly written reports from principal staff members summarizing all their and their subordinates' activities; and, supplementing all this, the informal, word-of-mouth networks that are maintained by each of the President's advisers and that reach throughout the bureaucracy and across the country.

Fourth, White House staffs have discovered that they must do more than assist in the development of policy; they must also mount a surveillance over the implementation, by the departments and agencies, of those presidential decisions that break new ground. Presidents are, after all, change-makers and are impatient to "turn the ship around." Although government bureaucrats, career or noncareer, do not often dig in against a President (though this does occasionally happen), 180-degree corrections in course may give rise to so many alterations in so many past practices that inertia is very difficult to overcome.

Fifth, crisis management is a special form of White House administration. Crises are always handled by the White House, usually in close detail, although the intensity of the supervision from the top is often masked at the time. In crises, all the aforementioned practices are redoubled. The staff taxes its information systems to wrest data from the very front lines of the crisis (often bypassing intermediate points); policy development is vastly accelerated but with an even higher degree of personal input from White House advisers.

The Work of Advisers. White House advisers are a brainy, aggressive, egotistical coterie, intolerant of mistakes and impatient for results. Most come from the campaign apparat, but they are not cut from the same mold, and the group is likely to include civilians and military people, young and old, men and women, whites and members of minorities, and ideologues and pragmatists. A few may be famous, most will be unknown. Out of this variety spring correspondingly different viewpoints on issues of public policy. When they are kept within the White House perimeter, staff debates are beneficial to the President, but they can be harmful if leaked to the always-encircling newspeople and columnists. With very few exceptions White House advisers are men and women of high intellectual integrity, insisting that the policy processes they manage be honest and fair; crusaders and sycophants are unwelcome and scarce. But White House advisers are not merely process-managers; they have strong convictions and are expected to express them. This means they must guard against letting their personal predilections skew their commitment and must make sure that all sides of a debate get through to the President.

White House advisers live tension-filled lives; they work such sacrificial hours that there are family strains and high divorce rates; many staffmembers quit short of the President's own four or eight years. When their President does leave office, they all depart abruptly, and while some experts recommend that there be continuity in senior White House staff ranks, these proposals hardly coincide with the reality of a new Chief Executive's housecleaning proclivities.

The most frequent accusation hurled at White House advisers is that they are not accountable. They have been called "29-year-old wimps" and accused of riding their own hobbyhorses and not representing the President. In almost every case such charges are wrong. Though it is unrecognized by the recipients of their queries or requests, they are in fact relaying or acting on the President's own general—and sometimes very specific—instructions. In fact, junior and middle-level White House advisers, who most commonly suffer from such accusations, are constantly subject to challenge and are instantly disciplined if they are caught out on a limb.

BIBLIOGRAPHY

Hess, Stephen. *Organizing the Presidency*. 2d ed. 1988.
Patterson, Bradley H., Jr. *The Ring of Power: The White House Staff and Its Expanding Role in Government*. 1988.
Pfiffner, James P. *The Managerial Presidency*. 1991.

BRADLEY H. PATTERSON, JR.

WHITE HOUSE BUREAUCRACY. The real character of the WHITE HOUSE STAFF is cloaked by two widely held but incorrect assumptions: that it is small and that the men and women who compose it function as generalists with broad, undifferentiated responsibilities. In fact, the White House staff community is large and the policy staff is subdivided into twenty specialized offices with firmly staked-out jurisdictions. These twenty, in turn, are undergirded by a sizable technical support staff. The White House (quite apart from the rest of the EXECUTIVE OFFICE OF THE PRESIDENT) is indeed a bureaucracy.

Offices and Functions. The twenty principal offices in the contemporary White House are the embodiments of the twenty major staff functions supporting the modern President. They are as follows:

1. The Assistant for National Security Affairs. Though the specific position of Assistant for National Security Affairs was created in 1953 by Dwight D. Eisenhower, the NATIONAL SECURITY staff office itself began earlier, in 1947. This unit of nearly two hundred people is the secretariat for the NATIONAL SECURITY COUNCIL and manages the President's entire national security decision-making process and apparatus, including flows of intelligence materials, policy cables to and from posts abroad, the "hot line," and two White House SITUATION ROOMS. As instructed by the President, the Assistant himself will meet and deal with foreign ambassadors in Washington, undertake personal negotiating missions to hot spots in far corners of the world, and appear on national television talk shows. He is expected to add his own policy advice into the decision system but must guard against skewing the whole process to favor his own leanings.

2. The Assistant for Domestic Policy. This office was created de jure under Richard M. Nixon, but its antecedents go back at least as far as Franklin D. Roosevelt's administration. The staff in this office performs the same review and coordinating functions for domestic affairs that the National Security Affairs office does for national security.

3. The Counsel. Franklin Roosevelt wanted a personal legal/policy adviser in addition to his ATTORNEY GENERAL; so has each succeeding President. Since almost every policy matter in the White House has a legal dimension, the WHITE HOUSE COUNSEL and a staff of nearly thirty are involved in many different areas. All bills passed by Congress cross the Counsel's desk before the final decision to sign or VETO; so do all PROCLAMATIONS, EXECUTIVE ORDERS, pardons, and drafts of major speeches. The Counsel is the ethics officer for the staff and the principal coordinator for judicial appointments. The Counsel reviews the SOLICITOR GENERAL's briefs on ultrasensitive Supreme Court cases, guards the President's EXECUTIVE PRIVILEGE, and heads off challenges to the President's constitutional powers, advises the President about his will, his papers, and, whenever he is facing surgery, about the applicability of the TWENTY-FIFTH AMENDMENT.

4. The Assistant for Legislative Affairs. A few staff members dabbled in this role during the administrations of Roosevelt and Harry S. Truman, but it was Eisenhower who elevated the head of this office and enlarged and strengthened its corps. Every later President has copied the Eisenhower model. This unit is the President's personal link with Congress—"an ambulatory bridge across a constitutional gulf," as one White House assistant put it. All congressional mail addressed to the President goes first to this office for logging and control. Using the legislative assistants in each of the departments as a network, the office of the Assistant for Legislative Affairs tracks the President's priority legislation and nominations and tries to round up the needed votes for passage or confirmation.

5. The Assistant for Political Affairs. This officer is the link between the White House and the national party and with the party's local committees in the states and territories. Under Truman, the Appointments Secretary had this responsibility, but it has become more institutionalized under later Presidents. Everything in the White House is political: a major speech, an unpopular veto message, and a presidential trip as well as plans for the reelection campaign.

6. *The Assistant for Intergovernmental Affairs.* The federal system is exceedingly plural: there are 50 states, some 3,050 counties, 19,200 cities, 17,000 townships, 15,000 school districts, 30,000 special districts, and 500 Indian tribes—the total governed by some 320,000 elected officials. Major domestic programs (drug control, education, environmental protection) involve coordination across all those governmental boundaries. The intergovernmental affairs office is the White House's contact point and ombudsman with the governors, mayors, and other principal officeholders among those 80,000-plus units of local government.

7. *The Director of Communications.* A modern President is never unaware that the White House is a splendid theater—playing to both a nationwide and worldwide audience. The Director of Communications is in effect the theater manager. Every presidential trip, speech, visit, or photo opportunity is prearranged and exploited to make the boss appear favorably in the print media and especially on the evening television news programs. The White House "theater director" makes sure that good news is released from the White House, while unwelcome announcements come from the agencies. No Cabinet officer appears on the Sunday morning talk shows without White House approval.

8. *The Press Secretary.* The President meets the press occasionally, but the WHITE HOUSE PRESS SECRETARY faces reporters' insistent questioning every working day. Close to two thousand people hold White House press passes; some fifty regulars have labeled seats in the West Terrace Briefing Room. With rare exceptions, the Press Secretary is the only responsible, on-the-record spokesperson on the White House staff. The Press Secretary consults constantly not only with the President and with staff colleagues but also with the press secretaries in the various departments (whose appointments he controls). The staff that prepares the daily White House News Summary is often attached to the Press Secretary's office, but then the News Summary editor must take care not to make his product merely the echo of the Press Secretary's pronouncements.

9. *The Assistant for Public Liaison.* Of the twenty thousand nationwide nonprofit public-interest organizations in the United States, many have Washington, D.C., headquarters staffed by power-brokers eager to present their views to the White House. At least since Nixon's time, the Public Liaison office has been their door-opener; it arranges strategically timed White House sessions at which they may set forth their views and petitions. The President gains by this arrangement as well: those same nationwide nongovernmen-

tal organizations, when they are persuaded to support his legislative initiatives, can be potent lobbying forces on the Congress.

10. *Speechwriters and the Research Office.* Except at PRESS CONFERENCES, modern Presidents make hardly any extemporaneous remarks. Speeches by the Chief Executive are often great theater and major policy simultaneously; they are accordingly the product of meticulous staff creativity. Even "Rose Garden rubbish"—for example, greeting the Turkey of the Year—is crafted ahead of time. There have been designated PRESIDENTIAL SPEECHWRITERS since Harding.

11. *The Assistant for Appointments and Scheduling.* The President has 1,461 days in his four-year term. The Appointments Secretary bestrides the voluminous flow of invitations and, sometimes backstopped by a senior-level internal White House committee, screens out low-priority requests and helps the President focus on those events that will strengthen his policy program. Once the schedule is set (though it is usually reworked every few hours), the Scheduling Office sees to it that all the other White House offices (SECRET SERVICE, photographer, speechwriters, Press Secretary, Director of Communications, etc.) are reminded of their roles in the upcoming event. Attached to the Scheduling Office is the Presidential Diarist, who gleans from the cooperating offices (the Chief Usher, White House telephone operators, the Secret Service, and so on) the details of every moment of the President's waking life: who was with him, or talked with him, for how long, and on what subject.

12. *Office of Presidential Personnel.* In addition to the White House staff (which this office does not handle), a modern President can control some five thousand political jobs, including roughly nine hundred full-time senior executive-branch positions, the two hundred judicial vacancies that will typically occur during a presidential term, more than fifteen hundred part-timers on boards and commissions, and some twenty-three hundred SCHEDULE C POSITIONS or noncareer SENIOR EXECUTIVE SERVICE jobs in various agencies. The Presidential Personnel Office has a forty-person staff that catalogues, recruits, and helps the President select appointees for this patronage universe.

13. *The Advance Office.* There is practically no extemporaneous presidential travel; every trip is planned in minute detail. The Advance Office staff comprises the planners and coordinators who mobilize and synchronize the efforts of many of the existing White House units (the Press Office, the Secret Service, the FIRST LADY'S OFFICE, communications, medical, Air Force One, speechwriters, etc.) for presidential journeys. Advance staffers visit all sites ahead of time.

14. White House "Czars." If a momentous problem slams itself onto the presidential agenda, making the nation apprehensive, provoking calls for swift response, and cutting widely across departmental jurisdictions, a President will be tempted to take quick, and at least symbolic, action—often appointing a "czar" right in the White House. Eisenhower used this technique often, and his successors have done likewise. Some positions, such as the "Drug Czar," have been authorized by Congress.

15. The First Lady. Students of the American presidency should never underestimate the policy role of the President's spouse. ELEANOR ROOSEVELT traveled widely and wrote a newspaper column; ROSALYNN CARTER attended Cabinet meetings; NANCY REAGAN hosted a world summit conference of first ladies; and BARBARA BUSH had an active schedule of public appearances. FIRST LADIES have some thirty-five assistants to help them.

16. The Vice President. After Harry S. Truman's experience of becoming President without any executive branch experience in 1945, Vice Presidents have increasingly become advisers to the President and participants in the work of the administration. Under John F. Kennedy, Lyndon Baines Johnson became the first Vice President to move his office and staff into the White House environs. Under Jimmy Carter, Vice President WALTER MONDALE was the first whose advice was truly welcomed; the Ronald Reagan and George Bush presidencies followed the Carter-Mondale model. In the early 1990s the Vice President's staff numbered about one hundred, and even the Vice President's spouse had a staff. Most of the President's information is shared with the Vice President, who has been made a statutory member of the National Security Council and participates in important White House meetings.

17. The Staff Secretary. First created under Eisenhower in 1953, the Staff Secretary regulates the flow of papers into the OVAL OFFICE, enforcing the internal system of circulating draft speeches and papers for staff comment.

18. The Office of Cabinet Affairs. This office handles external coordination with the departments and agencies, sending option memoranda and speech drafts out for comment and issuing the periodic "Cabinet Report" to which agency heads contribute. The full Cabinet meets rarely, but CABINET COUNCILS and subgroups convene constantly, and the Cabinet Secretary and assistants provide the executive secretariat services to these groups. This office also began under Eisenhower in 1953.

19. The Personal Office Assistants. One or two secretaries and a personal assistant sit outside the President's door, the former performing standard secretarial duties, the latter handling the myriad daily personal details for the boss: making sure that the schedule is being followed, that people whose presence the President is going to acknowledge will in fact be on hand, and that a presidential request, made while walking to or from the office, is put into the action system.

20. The Chief of Staff. Most centripetal of all, the CHIEF OF STAFF is the system manager, "boss of none but the quarterback of everything." The Chief of Staff does not command any other senior White House staff officer, but his personal antennae reach into every corner of the place. He enforces the indispensable coordination across all of the sixteen principal offices described above. Since it is the Chief of Staff who so often has to say "no"—to inadequate papers, beseeching visitors, or proposed appointees—he swiftly makes many more enemies than friends.

Support Staff. Undergirding these twenty offices are the professional support units of the contemporary White House, including the Secret Service details (involving eight hundred personnel, with others borrowed as needed), the thirteen-hundred-person Military Office (with ten specialized subunits, e.g., Air Force One, the doctor, the mess, CAMP DAVID, and the eight-hundred-person White House Communications Agency), the Chief Usher (who manages the mansion), the Executive Clerk, and the Correspondence, Gifts, Telephone, and Visitors offices. The number of people in the entire White House Staff community totals some thirty-four hundred. Many are assigned or detailed from other agencies. In addition, five hundred volunteers help out part time.

Every White House staff will inevitably reflect the style and working habits of the President. The offices are often renamed and the lines of supervision rejiggered. But these twenty principal functions are such basic responsibilities of the White House that future Presidents are not likely to abolish any of them outright.

BIBLIOGRAPHY

Hess, Stephen. *Organizing the Presidency.* 2d ed. 1988.
Kernell, Samuel, and Samuel L. Popkin. *Chief of Staff: Twenty-Five Years of Managing the Presidency.* 1986.
Patterson, Bradley H., Jr. *The Ring of Power: The White House Staff and Its Expanding Role in Government.* 1988.
Pfiffner, James P. *The Managerial Presidency.* 1991.

BRADLEY H. PATTERSON, JR.

WHITE HOUSE CHIEF OF STAFF. Up until the advent of WORLD WAR II the White House still served primarily as the President's residence. White House staff maintained informal relations with President Franklin D. Roosevelt: formal staff meetings did not occur, but rather key advisers often met with Franklin Roosevelt at breakfast to discuss the agenda for the day. Advisers who needed to see him during the day could readily gain access to Roosevelt in his office by going through the President's appointment secretary or his personal secretary. Roosevelt was also typically available during the afternoon cocktail hour, and he frequently spent evenings with his speechwriters.

The war increased demands on the presidency, as did the expanded role of the federal government, both internationally and domestically, after the war. By the time the war ended, the staff within the White House reporting personally to the President had grown considerably, and the White House had become a locus for policy development and decision making as well as a residence. These intensifying pressures contributed to the creation of the post of White House Chief of Staff during the Dwight D. Eisenhower administration.

Eisenhower's predecessor, Harry S. Truman, had initially intended to cut the White House staff back to its prewar size. The COLD WAR, however, expanded the role of the United States in global military and diplomatic affairs. The expanding role of the federal government in the domestic sphere can be traced back to the Great Depression of the 1930s, which had launched the country into an era of Keynesian fiscal policy, with greater government intervention in the economy. From the 1930s on, government regulation had expanded incrementally (but seemingly inevitably) to encompass regulation of business practices, management-labor relations, and consumer protection. Government's greater role, in turn, had generated greater demands by various constituencies to pursue their cases before the President. Truman therefore reversed himself and expanded the White House staff, without, however, creating a chief of staff. (One assistant did serve as a route to the President for minor agencies without other direct presidential access.)

Drawing on his military experience of managing complex and sometimes competing units in unfamiliar circumstances, Eisenhower replicated the military role of chief of staff in the White House. Although SHERMAN ADAMS retained the previously used title of Assistant to the President, his role was vastly expanded. Adams functioned in a way similar to how General Walter Bedell Smith had functioned as Eisenhower's chief of staff during the war. Eisenhower saw his Chief of Staff as his personal "son of a bitch": Adams served as a gatekeeper for all activities, issues, and constituencies

White House Chiefs of Staff

President	White House Chief of Staff
33 Truman	John R. Stedman, 1946–1952
34 Eisenhower	Sherman Adams, 1953–1958
	Wilton Persons, 1958–1961
35 Kennedy	None
36 L. B. Johnson	None
37 Nixon	H. R. Haldeman, 1969–1973
	Alexander M. Haig, 1973–1974
38 Ford	Donald Rumsfeld, 1974–1975
	Richard B. Cheney, 1975–1977
39 Carter	Hamilton Jordan, 1979–1980
	Jack Watson, 1980–1981
40 Reagan	James A. Baker III, 1981–1985
	Donald T. Regan, 1985–1987
	Howard H. Baker, Jr., 1987–1988
	Kenneth Duberstein, 1988–1989
41 Bush	John H. Sununu, 1989–1991
	Samuel K. Skinner, 1991–1992
	James A. Baker III, 1992–1993
42 Clinton	Thomas F. ("Mack") McLarty, 1993–1994
	Leon E. Panetta, 1994–

(except for those involving foreign policy) wanting to reach the President. He oversaw PATRONAGE and personnel decisions, appointments and scheduling, PRESIDENTIAL SPEECHWRITERS, and PRESS RELATIONS. He also served as the liaison to the CABINET, headed up special projects, and managed PRESIDENTIAL-CONGRESSIONAL RELATIONS. Adams held staff meetings as frequently as three times a week to coordinate White House work. Under his management the White House staff gained a valued reputation for efficiency and a less-valued reputation for rigidity. Adams wielded immense power as Chief of Staff until he was forced out in 1958 after having been accused of accepting favors from a Boston industrialist.

There was no formally appointed White House Chief of Staff under Presidents John F. Kennedy and Lyndon B. Johnson. Kennedy was more attracted to the informal managerial techniques of Roosevelt than to Eisenhower's formal organizational structure, which had been designed to meld relative strangers into an efficient working team. In contrast, most of the staff Kennedy appointed had worked with him previously and were personally loyal to him. Johnson, too, preferred personal control and informal organization. Richard M. Nixon, however, reinstituted the Chief of Staff position, appointing H. R. Haldeman to fill it. Haldeman's mismanagement of the considerable powers he was given as Chief of Staff played a major role to the disastrous WATERGATE AFFAIR. In response to this, Gerald Ford did not appoint a formal Chief of Staff, although Donald Rumsfeld, who had headed up the Ford transition team, served as a de facto Chief of Staff. At the end of the Ford Administration, DICK CHENEY was the Chief of Staff.

Jimmy Carter also initially eschewed the formal appointment of a Chief of Staff, preferring to serve as his own. This overburdened the President with minor details, however, and, by 1979, Hamilton Jordan was appointed to the position. Ronald Reagan, likewise, chose not to appoint a single Chief of Staff during his first term, instead splitting the Chief of Staff's functions among three advisers. At the beginning of his second term, he appointed a single Chief of Staff, DONALD REGAN. In contrast to his two immediate predecessors, George Bush embraced the Chief of Staff concept and appointed the bright but contentious John Sununu, former governor of New Hampshire, to the post. Both Regan and Sununu were unpopular with the public, and both were replaced before the ends of their respective Presidents' terms. Bill Clinton followed in the tradition of Eisenhower, Nixon, and Bush and appointed a chief of staff (Thomas F. McLarty) on first assuming office.

The Chief of Staff requires no Senate approval and serves at the pleasure of the President with few formal constraints. The Chief of Staff wields considerable power from serving daily at the President's elbow and may be the second most important person in an administration.

The Chief of Staff performs several functions. One primary duty is to organize the information flowing to the President. The Chief of Staff must make sure that important issues receive adequate attention and enough staff to handle their workload. Further, the Chief of Staff coordinates policy development and work across various issues. Another important function of the Chief of Staff is to take the heat for the President, serving as a buffer between the President and angry constituencies. For example, appointments are often announced by the President personally, but personnel who are dismissed will likely receive the news from the White House Chief of Staff.

The Chief of Staff manages WHITE HOUSE–DEPARTMENT RELATIONS, negotiating with members of the Cabinet over budget and personnel matters. As the President's surrogate, the Chief of Staff may be called on to massage egos and soothe hurt feelings. Besides these functions, a Chief of Staff may be asked to orchestrate policy issues, cutting across several Cabinet departments to develop policies on issues of particular interest to the President, to uncover information (sometimes embarrassing) that Cabinet officers may be reluctant to report, and to intervene in and monitor foreign and domestic crises in which the White House has a role.

BIBLIOGRAPHY

Dwight D. Eisenhower. *The White House Years: Waging Peace, 1956–1961.* 1965.

Hess, Stephen. *Organizing the Presidency.* 2d ed. 1988.

Kernell, Samuel, and Samuel L. Popkin. *Chief of Staff: Twenty-five Years of Managing the Presidency.* 1986.

Pffifner, James P. *The Strategic Presidency.* 1988.

MARCIA LYNN WHICKER

WHITE HOUSE COUNSEL. The key legal adviser to the President is known as the White House Counsel. The Counsel works in the White House Office and provides legal advice to the President on a wide array of issues; legal services performed by the Counsel and staff include legal clearance of documents for the President's signature, assistance on legal problems not provided by the Justice Department, and liaison between the President and the Justice Department. The position of White House Counsel is located in the personal office of the President. White House Counsel staff and facilities allow the President to communicate with Congress, the press, the public, and appointed department and agency heads.

Even during the Franklin D. Roosevelt and Harry S. Truman administrations, when members of the White House office were mostly generalists, the position of legal counsel was somewhat functionally specialized, although the counsel did not yet have a large staff at his disposal. Despite this relative specialization, the legal counsel continued to perform many nonlegal duties as late as the Truman administration.

Functional specialization within the White House became more pronounced during the Dwight D. Eisenhower administration. Specialized staff units were formed to handle functions (including Cabinet affairs, legislative liaison with Congress, and liaison with the President's party) previously handled by the legal counsel as well as other staff members. Under Richard M. Nixon, Gerald Ford, and Jimmy Carter, additional specialized units were created to deal with communications and to provide liaison with state and local governments and interest groups.

Some administrations have taken on additional legal advisers within the White House. By the Lyndon B. Johnson administration, the President's legal staff had grown to include not only a counsel and four special counsels but also a deputy special counsel, assistant special counsel, associate counsel, and associate special counsel. Besides serving the legal unit, these special counsels provided advice to White House speechwriting, appointments, and legislative program development units. Counsel staff were also active in executive guidance and control. More recent administrations

White House Counsels

President	White House Counsel
35 Kennedy	Theodore C. Sorensen, 1961–1963
36 L. B. Johnson	Theodore C. Sorensen, 1963–1964 Lee C. White, 1964–1966 Harry C. McPherson, Jr., 1966–1969
37 Nixon	John D. Ehrlichman, 1969 John Welsey Dean III, 1970–1973 Leonard Garment, 1973–1974 J. Fred Buzhardt, 1974
38 Ford	Philip W. Buchen, 1974–1977
39 Carter	Robert J. Lipshutz, 1977–1979 Lloyd N. Cutler, 1979–1981
40 Reagan	Fred F. Fielding, 1981–1986 Peter J. Wallison, 1986–1987 Arthur B. Culvahouse, Jr., 1987–1989
41 Bush	C. Boyden Gray, 1989–1993
42 Clinton	Bernard Nussbaum, 1993–

have followed Johnson's lead, employing a number of legal counselors on the President's personal staff.

The White House Counsel facilitates White House coordination with the Justice Department, headed by the U.S. ATTORNEY GENERAL, who is the chief law enforcement officer in the federal government. Unlike the White House Counsel, who represents the interests of the President personally, the Attorney General represents the legal interests of the United States. As a personal adviser to the President, the White House Counsel is not subject to confirmation by the U.S. Senate, and here, too, the Counsel position differs from that of the Attorney General, who as a department head and Cabinet member must be confirmed by the Senate. Moreover, the White House Counsel cannot be forced to testify before congressional committees, whereas the Attorney General is expected to appear regularly at congressional hearings and to respond to legislators' requests for information.

The White House Counsel does not appear in court on behalf of the President, but informally provides advice on litigation. By contrast, the Attorney General may appear in person in court to represent the United States in particularly important cases. (More commonly, the SOLICITOR GENERAL represents the U.S. government in cases before the U.S. Supreme Court.)

The relation of the White House Counsel to the President has varied from administration to administration. In administrations that have employed a central-management model, such as the Nixon presidency and to a lesser extent the Ronald Reagan and George Bush presidencies, counsels have had less-frequent contact with the President and have worked mainly through the WHITE HOUSE CHIEF OF STAFF. In collegially

managed White Houses (the model used by John F. Kennedy and attempted by Carter), the Counsel has had more direct contact with the President. In a competitive advisory system—the staffing arrangement preferred by Franklin Roosevelt—the President's legal counsel may have frequent access to him, but duties are more ambiguously defined and no member of the staff has proprietorship of any particular advisory role.

Organizational problems may occur when a President encounters legal difficulties in an area that has not been defined as belonging to the realm of the White House Counsel, as when legal problems arise over matters of substantive policy or electoral politics. Such problems are more likely to arise when the White House follows a central-management model than when it uses a collegial or competitive model. For example, some of the legal problems Nixon encountered during the WATERGATE AFFAIR involved election tactics rather than the legal suitability of routine government documents or laws. Similarly, the legality of actions of Reagan and Bush in the IRAN-CONTRA AFFAIR were subsequently questioned, but the decisions made in the arms-for-hostages deal with Iran to fund contra activities in Nicaragua were kept from the White House Counsel.

BIBLIOGRAPHY

Burke, John P. *The Institutional Presidency.* 1992.
Edwards, George C., and Stephen J. Wayne. *Presidential Leadership: Politics and Policy Making.* 2d ed. 1990.
Groner, Jonathan. "Counseling Clinton." *Legal Times* (1 February 1993): 1, 22–23. On Bernard Nussbaum.
Moore, W. John. "The True Believers." *National Journal* (17 August 1991): 2018–2022. On C. Boyden Gray.
Redford, Emmette S., and Richard T. McCulley. *White House Operations: The Johnson Presidency.* 1986.

MARCIA LYNN WHICKER

WHITE HOUSE–DEPARTMENTAL RELATIONS. The American presidential system differs from parliamentary systems in crucial ways that influence relations between the White House and CABINET departments. In most parliamentary systems, both the prime minister and the cabinet members are members of the parliament and serve both legislative and executive functions. In parliamentary systems, prime ministers are constrained in forming their cabinets, whose membership is limited to party colleagues, and so cabinets are likely to consist of people who have worked together on legislative elections and issues. These shared experiences, institutional linkages, and greater party accountability facilitate coordination and communication between the prime minister and the cabinet ministers.

The "American Constitution, however, prohibits most overlapping of executive and legislative functions through the principle of SEPARATION OF POWERS. Presidents are not limited to appointing departmental secretaries with the same institutional backgrounds as themselves. Nor are they even required to appoint secretaries from their own political party. Presidents may balance constituency demands when making appointments, and they often strive to achieve a broad mix of political, geographic, demographic, and ideological representation rather than shared experience and common perspective. Given the highly personalized nature of presidential elections, secretarial appointments are also used to reward people who supported the newly elected President during the campaign. All these factors diminish Cabinet cohesiveness.

Consequently, relations between the White House and the departments may sometimes become distant and strained. Cabinet secretaries may be caught between White House demands to implement presidential priorities and less vociferous but very real demands by career bureaucrats to do otherwise.

Cabinet secretaries are appointed by the President and must be confirmed by the U.S. Senate. Unlike independent regulatory commission members and federal judges, however, Cabinet members may be removed from office by the President for any reason, whether policy disagreements or simply personal differences. To keep the job, a secretary must please the President.

Tensions between departmental norms and presidential priorities may exist in any administration, but they are particularly likely to arise when the President wants change. Bureaucratic norms generally support the status quo. Presidents who want to cut federal programs inevitably run into conflict with departmental cultures that wish to maintain and even expand programs. In response to this tension, change-oriented Presidents are likely to rely more heavily on White House staff than on their Cabinets. For example, because he wished to break with many of the policies and traditions of the Eisenhower administration, John F. Kennedy expanded the White House staff and made extensive use of personal advisers. Friction between the permanent bureaucracy and the White House staff was pronounced at times, and critics have contended that this friction contributed to poor quality of information and advice from the permanent bureaucracy bolstering Kennedy's decision to back the BAY OF PIGS INVASION.

Relations between the White House and career bureaucrats in the permanent bureaucracy have not, historically, shown any improvement. Whereas career bureaucrats were regarded as civic-minded civil servants during the 1930s and 1940s, by the Ronald Reagan era the public image of career bureaucrats had become tarnished. Strong antigovernment sentiment in both the Reagan and George Bush White Houses resulted in sometimes hostile relationships between departments and White House staff. "Bureaucrat bashing" by Reagan as well as other conservative politicians contributed to the tension.

The expansion of the powers of the presidency and the centralization of policy-making in the White House have increasingly distanced the President from the bureaucracy that must formulate the regulations to implement policy. The sheer size of the bureaucracy contributes to its independence, making the bureaucracy a power in its own right. Yet Presidents do retain several key checks over federal departments and agencies.

Presidential appointment power, however, provides a greater check on the bureaucracy in theory than in practice. The notion that Presidents dominate the recruitment and appointment process is misleading. In actuality, time constraints and errors in judgment in the selection process reduce the impact that presidential APPOINTMENT POWERS might have on the bureaucracy. Too, over time, the Senate has increasingly come to view appointment powers as shared and has been less willing to rubber-stamp presidential nominees. With the expansion of Senate staffs, Senators have gained a greater capacity to examine closely the backgrounds and qualifications of nominees. Ironically, Presidents must make the greatest number of appointments early in their administrations, when their knowledge of government programs is least. Later in their terms, when they are typically more familiar with the details of various programs, the number of vacancies diminishes.

Federal EMERGENCY POWERS may help Presidents check the power of the bureaucracy, but they are used infrequently. In times of national crisis such as war or economic depression, Congress has given the President the right to create offices and to appoint officeholders without Senate confirmation, a power used in the past to regulate economic activities. Presidents may use their veto power to curb program growth desired by career bureaucrats, but the use of the veto usually carries at least some political costs.

The budget process can also be used by the President to exert control over the bureaucracy. Bureaucracies typically want to increase their appropriations, while Presidents may wish to hold them constant or even to cut funding for particular departments or agencies. In theory, Presidents can advocate sizable cuts in existing programs or even their abolition, but in reality budgeting is frequently characterized by "incrementalism," whereby budget bases (previous expenditure levels) are rarely examined or altered.

To assist the President in controlling the rate of expenditure by agencies and departments, Congress has developed and enacted the apportionments and allotments. Under these procedures, the OFFICE OF MANAGEMENT AND BUDGET (OMB) releases funds through quarterly apportionments and even smaller allotments. Presidents have also used IMPOUNDMENT to curb bureaucratic expansion.

While many presidential checks on the bureaucracy are formal, most bureaucratic checks on the President are more subtle. Recalcitrant bureaucrats frequently resort to silent resistance and foot-dragging. Without openly defying higher authority, bureaucrats may give lip service to presidential orders while finding reasons to delay, postpone, and implement presidential policies piecemeal. Before implementation can fully occur, a President and his political appointees may be out of office, while career bureaucrats continue in their posts.

Departments and their agencies are one leg of an IRON TRIANGLE in national politics that consists of bureaucrats, client beneficiaries, and members of key congressional committees. Departmental officials can often use their relationships with clients and Congress to promote their goals even when those goals conflict with the thrust of presidential policy.

CIVIL SERVICE recruitment and promotion procedures protect bureaucrats from unwarranted political interference from both the President and Congress. Under the provisions of the HATCH ACT (1939), federal bureaucrats are shielded from having to campaign for current political appointees or for other members of the political party in power. Given career-employee longevity within departments, especially compared to the government experience of political appointees, agencies typically have an institutional memory of what has been attempted and what has succeeded and failed. Bureaucratic knowledge is both broad and deep and career bureaucrats do not hesitate to use this detailed knowledge to advance their own causes.

Bureaucrats frustrated with presidential policies have also used information leaks and off-the-record comments to reporters as methods to check presidential initiatives. When all else fails, committed bureaucrats may be willing to become WHISTLE-BLOWERS on the President and his appointees.

BIBLIOGRAPHY

Cronin, Thomas E. "Everybody Believes in Democracy until He Gets to the White House." *Law and Contemporary Problems* 35 (1970): 573–625.

Cronin, Thomas E. *The State of the Presidency*. 2d ed. 1980.

Pfiffner, James P. *The President, the Budget, and Congress: Impoundment and the 1974 Budget Act*. 1979.

Pfiffner, James P. *The Strategic Presidency*. 1988.

Rose, Richard, and Ezra N. Suleiman, eds. *Presidents and Prime Ministers*. 1980.

MARCIA LYNN WHICKER

WHITE HOUSE OFFICE. One of the five original divisions of the EXECUTIVE OFFICE OF THE PRESIDENT (EOP) established by Franklin D. Roosevelt's Executive Order 8248 of 8 September 1939, the White House Office is the formal home of the personal staff of the President [*see* WHITE HOUSE STAFF]. The White House Office was intended, in the words of the executive order, "to serve the President in an intimate capacity in the performance of the many detailed activities incident to his immediate office."

Although the White House Office officially dates from 1939, there has, in effect, been a White House Office ever since President George Washington appointed Tobias Lear as his private secretary 150 years earlier. By 1937, when the BROWNLOW COMMITTEE recommended formalizing the President's personal staff as a division of the proposed EOP, the White House staff was already institutionally well established.

Executive Order 8248 envisaged three kinds of staff in the White House Office. One group consisted of the secretaries to the President—those senior presidential staff positions that had existed prior to the Brownlow Report. They were "to facilitate and maintain quick and easy communication with the Congress, the heads of executive departments and agencies, the press, the radio and the general public"—a job description that merely recognized what the post of Secretary to the President had become by the early twentieth century. The second group comprised the institutional support staff in the White House Office and included those, like the Executive Clerk and his assistants, who were responsible for clerical services and the official routines of the presidency. The third category covered the six new administrative assistants that the Brownlow Report had recommended adding to the presidential staff. Their role was described, and circumscribed, in much the same way as it had been in the Brownlow Report, which is not surprising given that Louis Brownlow also drafted Executive Order 8248 for President Roosevelt. The administrative assistants were "to assist the President in such matters as he may direct, and at the specific request of the President, to get information and to condense and summarize it for his use." These positions were clearly intended to be of less importance than the secretaries to the President, and the role prescribed for the administrative assistants in the both the Brownlow Report and the executive order envisioned them as information-gatherers and messengers, but little else.

Those titles have long gone, and the functional distinction between the secretaries to the President and the administrative assistants has been eroded over time. Today, a substantial number of White House Office staff carry senior positions as Assistant, Deputy, or Special Assistant to the President. In fact, the growth of senior positions in the White House Office, and the high salaries that went with them, so disturbed some members of Congress that in 1978 Congress passed the WHITE HOUSE PERSONNEL AUTHORIZATION ACT, imposing a ceiling on the number of senior staff a President would be permitted to employ in the White House Office.

The clerical and support staff still remain as a distinct group, largely because they are not considered political appointees (although they are not protected under CIVIL SERVICE regulations) and they continue to serve in the White House Office irrespective of who is President. Their number has been declining over the last three decades, however, as successive Presidents have been inclined to bring more of the institutional support services under political direction. Today, the institutional memory of the White House Office resides largely in the offices of the Executive Clerk and the Records Manager, but even their existence as nonpolitical, professional staff is vulnerable to any incoming administration's failure to make the distinction between institutional and personal staff within the White House Office.

One other aspect of Brownlow's blueprint for the White House Office also went unrealized. In proposing the six additional administrative assistants, Brownlow suggested that some might be recruited from executive branch departments, do a tour of duty in the White House Office, and then return to their former assignments. This was analogous to the recruitment method used for staffing the secretariat in the British Cabinet Office—an institution Brownlow much admired and had hoped to imitate, at least in part, in the White House Office.

But the attempt to give the White House Office a professional, career civil-service staff was not to be. Presidents have preferred to staff their personal office with loyal, devoted, and highly political individuals who often possess little or no prior experience of Washington and who see their role as serving the interests of their President rather than satisfying the longer-term concerns of an institutional presidency. The staff in the White House Office are an extension of the President himself. Their appointments are not subject to Senate confirmation (as are a number of senior posts in other EOP units); they do not usually testify before congressional committees; and they are answerable to no one but the President. When the President's term is over, so is theirs. Furthermore, Congress does not normally interfere with the structure and functions of the White House Office, whereas it has shown a remarkable propensity to intervene in the development of the rest of the EOP and to tell the President what staff units he needs to have, or ought not to have, irrespective of his wishes. In that sense, the White House Office is marked off from the other EOP units as a highly personal staff that is subject to congressional scrutiny only in the most exceptional circumstances.

The nature and size of the White House Office have developed far beyond the scope of Executive Order 8248 [*see* WHITE HOUSE BUREAUCRACY]. Successive post-Brownlow Presidents have made the White House Office into a highly responsive, politically powerful, personal staff unit that has become the directing force of the EOP and the hub of the presidential policy-making process. Therein lies its strength. The White House Office extends the reach of the President into the executive branch and Congress, which are not always inclined to respond to presidential leadership and direction without persuasion or pressure. But the intensely personal nature of much of the White House Office is also its institutional weakness. Institutional memory and continuity are at risk each time the presidency changes hands, and the collective lack of experience in a new White House Office can be a potential source of weakness, even damage, in the early days of a new administration. Most staff in the White House Office have to learn while on the job—and learn very quickly. What is surprising is that this institutionally weak body, located at the very center of presidential government, generally performs as well as it does.

BIBLIOGRAPHY

Burke, John P. *The Institutional Presidency.* 1992.
Hart, John. *The Presidential Branch.* 1987.
Hess, Stephen. *Organizing the Presidency.* 2d ed. 1988.
Kernell, Samuel, and Samuel L. Popkin. *Chief of Staff: Twenty-five Years of Managing the Presidency.* 1986.
Patterson, Bradley H., Jr. *The Ring of Power: The White House Staff and Its Expanding Role in Government.* 1988.

JOHN HART

WHITE HOUSE OFFICE OF COMMUNICATIONS. Although the precise structure and jurisdiction of the White House Office of Communications, created by President Richard M. Nixon in 1969, have changed from administration to administration, its functions have remained constant. The office develops long-term public relations planning, coordinates news flow from the entire executive branch, and orchestrates direct appeals to the public through television, radio, town meetings, surrogate speakers, and outreach to local media.

The goal of the Office of Communications is to set the public agenda, to make sure that all parts of the presidential team (the WHITE HOUSE STAFF, Cabinet officers, and other executive-branch officials) adhere to that agenda, and to promote the public agenda through aggressive mass marketing. Communications Office staff use data drawn from focus groups and polls to fashion presidential messages, make sure that the public pronouncements of the President and his underlings contain sound-bites that clearly articulate those messages, choreograph public appearances so that the messages are reinforced by visual images, and enforce the White House viewpoint through the "line of the day," to prevent the articulation of conflicting messages. Technological developments have made such efforts easier. For instance, communications satellites allow the office to target messages to specific media markets in congressional districts where the White House needs support. Similarly, presidential spokespeople around the country can use their personal computers to obtain the line of the day before talking with reporters.

The Office of Communications' functions are different from those of the more visible White House Press Office, which is primarily concerned with providing information from the White House itself, not the entire executive branch. Also, the Press Office avoids long-term public relations management, seldom moving beyond disseminating the news of the day and responding to reporters' queries. And rather than targeting local media outlets and engaging in other tactics to circumvent the elite media, the Press Office caters almost exclusively to the needs of the WHITE HOUSE PRESS CORPS. Thus, the Office of Communications is primarily proactive, while the Press Office is primarily reactive. The two offices have often been completely distinct entities, but in the Bill Clinton White House, as during parts of the Gerald Ford and Ronald Reagan administrations, the Press Office has fallen under the jurisdiction of the Office of Communications.

Before the Office of Communications was created, its functions were carried out either in a sporadic, ad hoc manner by the WHITE HOUSE PRESS SECRETARY or by a few formal structures for coordinating the flow of news from the executive branch. The most notable of these structures was the Committee on Public Information, chaired by George Creel, that was established during WORLD WAR I. Such structures were short-lived and were almost always created in response to national emergencies.

By the 1960s it was obvious that communications functions needed to be institutionalized through the creation of a permanent office. With the rise of electronic media, Presidents were no longer as dependent on newspaper reporters to convey their messages to the public. Increasingly, Presidents and their surrogates took messages directly to the people in an effort to mold mandates for their policy initiatives. The strategy for increasing presidential power via such appeals is known as "going public." As defined by Samuel Kernell, this understanding of presidential power assumes that the elite bargaining community that implements policy is neither as insulated from public pressure nor as tightly bound together by established norms of elite behavior as it used to be. According to this scenario, policymakers became increasingly susceptible to the influence of public opinion, and the ability to harness or manufacture that opinion became a key to presidential power. This atmosphere created new institutional demands on the White House that were filled by the Office of Communications.

During the earlier years of the Nixon administration, under its first director, Herbert G. Klein, the Office of Communications was a respected, professional operation. During the WATERGATE AFFAIR, however, the office degenerated into a hard-line political operation designed to shore up the image of the embattled President. At times, the office stepped over the line that separates legitimate appeals for public support from illegitimate tactics to induce or fabricate that support through the use of administration-spon sored letters and telegrams, the creation of supposedly independent citizens' committees to praise administration policy, and even threats of Internal Revenue Service investigations and antitrust suits against media organizations that painted the White House in an unfavorable light.

The discredited Office of Communications was significantly cut back when Nixon resigned in 1974, but in 1976, during the Gerald Ford administration, it reemerged as a powerful and professional office under the direction of David Gergen. Jimmy Carter, as part of his effort to create an "open" White House, all but abolished the office in 1977, but he was forced by his sinking approval rating to recreate the office a year later under the direction of Gerald Rafshoon. The office played a major role in the Ronald Reagan administration, especially under the directorships of Gergen, who returned as director of communications in 1981, and of Patrick Buchanan, and it became even more visible in the Clinton White House, largely because of the high profile of Clinton's first communications director, George Stephanopoulos, and the highly publicized restaffing of the office when Gergen unexpectedly joined the Democratic administration as Counselor to the President in June 1993.

Increasingly, the Office of Communications has become an umbrella term for a variety of offices that fall under its jurisdiction. The Press Office, the Planning Office, the Speechwriting Office, the Advance Office, the Public Liaison Office (which handles outreach to special interest groups), the Media Affairs Office (covering outreach to local media), and the Public Affairs Office (serving as liaison with public information officers throughout the executive branch), among others, have all fallen under the purview of the Office of Communications.

BIBLIOGRAPHY

Grossman, Michael Baruch, and Martha Joynt Kumar. *Portraying the President.* 1981.

Kernell, Samuel. *Going Public: New Strategies of Presidential Leadership.* 2d ed. 1993.

Maltese, John Anthony. *Spin Control: The White House Office of Communications and the Management of Presidential News.* 1992.

Tulis, Jeffrey K. *The Rhetorical Presidency.* 1987.

JOHN ANTHONY MALTESE

WHITE HOUSE PERSONNEL AUTHORIZATION ACT

(1978). The White House Personnel Authorization Act (P.L. 95-570) was signed into law by President Jimmy Carter on 2 November 1978 and stands as the only attempt by Congress to improve its capacity to oversee the activities of the presidential staff in the aftermath of the WATERGATE AFFAIR. It was the first time in thirty years that Congress had formally authorized an increase in the size of the President's personal staff in the White House Office (notwithstanding the substantial increase since the last authorization in 1948), and it attempted to make the President accountable for the number of staff employed while also limiting presidential ability to expand the senior staff at will.

The act authorizes the President to appoint to the White House Office not more than twenty-five employees at executive-level II, nor more than twenty-five at executive-level III [*see table accompanying* SALARIES, EXECUTIVE], and not more than fifty at the supergrade (GS 16–GS 18) level. Below the GS 16 level, the President can appoint as many staff as desired. There is no upper limit on the total size of the White House staff, but the legislation does place a ceiling on the number of senior staff a President can appoint. It similarly limits the number of senior appointments in the executive residence, the Office of the Vice President, the Domestic Policy Staff, and the OFFICE OF ADMINISTRATION. The act also regulates the practice of detailing, or borrowing, staff from executive branch departments and agencies for White House duties.

Section 113 of the act requires the President to submit a personnel report to Congress that must show the number of staff employed in the White House Office in each fiscal year. It also requires the President to account for the number of detailees and temporary consultants employed in the White House and certain other EXECUTIVE OFFICE OF THE PRESIDENT agencies.

The White House Personnel Authorization Act was the culmination of a five-year effort, beginning in 1973, to regulate some of the worst abuses of White House staffing exposed by the events of Watergate. It has, however, proved to be an innocuous piece of legislation with little impact on presidential staffing practices or on congressional oversight of the White House staff. Much of the force of the original legislation was watered down during a tortuous passage through Congress, including a provision to limit the total size of the White House staff. Furthermore, although the act did limit the number of senior positions on the White House staff, the ceilings it imposed were considerably in excess of the numbers of senior staff actually employed at the time the act was passed and, consequently, it actually permitted President Carter to increase the number of appointees in those categories. There are also significant loopholes in the provisions regulating the practice of detailing departmental and agency staff to the White House.

The least effective provision of the 1978 act is the reporting requirement. The information yielded is of little value to members of Congress charged with oversight of the White House Office, and congressional attempts to strengthen this section of the act have been singularly unsuccessful. The major shortcoming is that nothing in the personnel report gives any indication of who does what in the White House. No individuals are named and no functions are described. (A provision to this effect was included in the House version of the bill but was removed at the insistence of the Senate in the conference committee).

There are two principal explanations for the weakness of this legislation. First, Vice President WALTER MONDALE was very successful in persuading members of the relevant Senate committee that the legislation would be making President Carter pay for President Richard M. Nixon's mistakes and that this would be unfair. The House Post Office and Civil Service Committee had taken a much tougher stand on the problems of White House staffing, but the Senate's position (and that of the Carter administration) prevailed in most of the disputes during legislative passage. Second, the original legislative proposals challenged the historic tradition of comity between the legislative and executive branches of government, whereby one branch does not interfere with the housekeeping arrangements of the other. Presidential staffing, just like congressional staffing, is considered to be a housekeeping issue. The pervasiveness of the tradition and principle of comity in the contemporary Congress, even in the aftermath of Watergate, is a major constraint on its capacity to make the presidential staff more accountable and a significant factor in the gutting of the white House Personnel Authorization Act.

BIBLIOGRAPHY

Hart, John. *The Presidential Branch.* 1987.

JOHN HART

WHITE HOUSE PHOTOGRAPHER.

The White House photographer is responsible for providing official photographs to news organizations and to others selected by the President. The photographer represents just one of the resources in the well-stocked presidential publicity arsenal. Photographs released by the White House almost invariably portray the President in a positive light.

The official White House photographer and his staff (of about a dozen) are responsible for recording the photographic history of an administration. Often that history is compiled by the White House photographic staff alone. In crisis situations, for example, only the presidential photographer is allowed to record the historic moments. Such a situation occurred when President Gerald Ford was making the decision to free the crew of the freighter *Mayaguez* [*see* MAYAGUEZ INCIDENT]. Other images typically controlled by the photographic unit include those recording presidential illnesses, CAMP DAVID meetings, daily presidential life, and the President and his family relaxing. Whenever the President welcomes visitors to his office, he and they are photographed together. Over the course of an administration, thousands of such pictures are taken and given away.

President Lyndon B. Johnson appointed Yoshi Okamoto the first official White House photographer. Not all administrations have appointed a photographer. Presidents Jimmy Carter and George Bush chose to let a group of staff photographers document their presidencies, with no one of them designated as the official photographer. President Ford relied on David Kennerly, Pulitzer Prize–winning photographer from *Time* magazine.

BIBLIOGRAPHY

Cornwell, Elmer. *Presidential Leadership of Public Opinion.* 1965.
Grossman, Michael Baruch, and Martha Joynt Kumar. *Portraying the President: The White House and the News Media.* 1981.
Maltese, John. *Spin Control: The White House Office of Communications and the Management of Presidential News.* 1992.
Patterson, Bradley H. *The Ring of Power: The White House Staff and Its Expanding Role in Government.* 1988.
Pollard, James E. *Presidents and the Press.* 1964.

MARTHA KUMAR

WHITE HOUSE PRESS CORPS.

The presidency has become the central media drama of our national life and members of the White House press corps, a cranky cast of seventeen hundred, have become supporting actors. The press corps consists of correspondents and support crews from the major newspapers, wire services, magazines, and radio and television networks. The original purpose of the press corps—to convey accounts of the activities of the President—is still the central task of these journalists and they do it competently. The White House press corps acts as a group of contentious voyeurs trying to poke holes in the slick imagery that the President concocts and projects directly to the people through television. But as often as not, the true news of the inside of the White House comes from sources beyond its guarded confines: for instance, the account of President John F. Kennedy's sexual involvement with Judith Exner, a woman with gangster connections, emerged from Senate hearings on abuses of the CENTRAL INTELLIGENCE AGENCY; the failure of the VIETNAM WAR from reporters in the battlefields and from the Pentagon itself; and the WATERGATE AFFAIR from political campaign workers, court documents, and congressional investigations. The White House press corps was left to record how the Presidents responded to these revelations from outside.

The charter of the White House press corps is to report the President's speeches, PRESS CONFERENCES, messages, ceremonies, and meetings, and even a good deal on his time with friends and family as well as his health. The President, after all, is the most powerful individual in the world and everything about him—including his mood and manner—affects everyone to some degree. Knowing about him is vitally important.

In the presidency mistakes and misjudgments are inevitable. The incessant search for political success encourages Presidents and their staffs to burnish good news and ignore the bad. Balancing the record is a critical function of the press corps, and that often leads to harsh adversarial bickering between reporters and White House sources. The corps fights a minute-by-minute battle for undoctored information in order to tell the presidential story as best it can.

The press corps has been around since the beginning of the presidency. George Washington had a small retinue of scribblers who went with him on his 1791 tour of the South, a carriage being his version of Air Force One. In those early years most of the journalists writing on the White House were editors and publishers of political flyers, devoted to tirades against their enemies and lavish praise of their friends. Distrust abounded. The press corps had grown to about fifty and had become more diligent and thoughtful by the time of the CIVIL WAR; many of the reporters were intensely interested in President Abraham Lincoln as a person. President William McKinley, who had been friends with many reporters when he was in the House of Representatives, continued his friendships when he came to the White House, which eventually led to the institutionalization of the White House press corps. McKinley, however, left the press corps outside the White House. In 1901 President Theodore Roosevelt gave the journalists a room inside the White House and talked to them frequently to get his muscular declarations out to the world. The press corps was part of his BULLY PULPIT.

On 6 August 1945, when the press corps was alerted for a major announcement, a dozen reporters and photographers showed up in the press office. The prepared statement of President Harry S. Truman (he was at sea returning from the POTSDAM CONFERENCE) announced that an atomic bomb had successfully been dropped on Hiroshima, Japan. It was one of the biggest stories of modern times. So inexpert and overwhelmed by the event was the press corps that the person taking dictation at the *Washington Evening Star* heard "Adam bomb" and the mistake went through several editions.

Today a normal White House briefing has fifty to one hundred participants from among the seventeen hundred accredited writers, reporters broadcasters, photographers, and technicians. The least hint of special news will bring two hundred. The day President Ronald Reagan was shot an estimated four hundred journalists rushed to the small press room in the West Wing of the White House, which President Richard M. Nixon had had converted from the swimming pool put in by Franklin D. Roosevelt. When the President travels, he is often accompanied by some two hundred fifty of the corps, who charter their own airplane. When American hostages were released by Iran in 1981, about one thousand reporters were on the South Lawn of the White House to see Reagan greet them.

In the 1940s the White House press corps was 80 percent print, the rest radio. By 1990 the ratio was about 60 percent electronic (television and radio) to 40 percent print. The White House lawns have become television studios, and the North Portico is a familiar backdrop for news flashes from 1600 Pennsylvania Avenue.

The White House press corps and the presidency have enlarged one another's importance, as the White House has become a focus of instant information and guidance for almost any event around the world.

[*See also* PRESS AND PRESIDENCY, HISTORY OF; PRESS RELATIONS.]

BIBLIOGRAPHY

Hess, Stephen. *Organizing the Presidency*. 1988.
Hess, Stephen. *The Washington Reporters*. 1981.
Seale, William. *The President's House: A History*. 1987.

HUGH SIDEY

WHITE HOUSE PRESS SECRETARY. The first White House aide to have PRESS RELATIONS as his sole responsibility—the equivalent of being Press Secretary to the President—was George Akerson, who served (not very successfully) from 1929 to 1931 under Herbert Hoover. Presidential press relations, of course, predated the institution of a full-time Press Secretary, and some earlier White House assistants, notably William Loeb during Theodore Roosevelt's administration and Joseph Tumulty during Woodrow Wilson's administration, had been skillful at explaining their Presidents' actions to reporters.

The role of the Press Secretary came of age during the administration of Franklin D. Roosevelt; Stephen Early ran Roosevelt's press office. While later changes in the office resulted from new communications technologies and the growth of the WHITE HOUSE PRESS CORPS, the Press Secretary's basic functions remained relatively constant, and included conducting daily briefings for reporters on the White House beat, helping the President prepare for PRESS CONFERENCES, handling press arrangements for presidential trips and vacations, responding to reporters' individual requests for interviews and information, and putting out press releases and the texts of presidential speeches and messages.

Strictly speaking, the Press Secretary is not a policy adviser, although the law of propinquity—the power that can emanate from being close to the powerful—has from time to time affected staffers who have occupied the press relations slot. For example, Bill Moyers, Press Secretary to Lyndon Baines Johnson, was one of six officials composing what was known as the Tuesday Cabinet, which held weekly VIETNAM WAR decision-making sessions.

The Press Secretary's domain largely involves the handling of Washington-based reporters, with other MEDIA relations handled by other White House offices. The Press Office staff had grown to seventeen by 1991, with three Deputy Press Secretaries, one of whom was in charge of foreign policy issues and also served as the spokesperson for the NATIONAL SECURITY ADVISER. Junior staff, responsible for turning out press releases, are housed in what is called the Lower Press Office, which is adjacent to the White House Briefing Room. During Richard M. Nixon's first term the White House swimming pool, located between the President's residence and his office in the West Wing, was decked over to create this working area for reporters.

There were eighteen presidential Press Secretaries from Akerson through Marlin Fitzwater, who served under Ronald Reagan and George Bush. All were white males, usually of early middle years. The average age at time of appointment was forty-two; the youngest, Ronald Ziegler, who served under Nixon, was thirty; the oldest, Charles Ross, sixty, died in office during the presidency of Harry S. Truman. Half had served as Washington correspondents; five had never

been journalists. Interestingly, those whose entire careers had been in journalism were among the least successful Press Secretaries. The most successful, on the other hand, were either very close to the Presidents they served regardless of their previous occupations or had had some previous experience in public affairs or political press relations.

Perhaps the most successful was JAMES HAGERTY, who served under Dwight D. Eisenhower. Hagerty had been a *New York Times* reporter, press secretary to a governor of New York, and spokesman for the 1952 Republican presidential campaign. Hagerty is credited with creating new rules for frankness when Eisenhower suffered a heart attack in 1955. For three weeks he held five briefings a day, releasing such intimate details as the number of bowel movements recorded on the President's medical chart. (At the other extreme, press secretaries do not always offer the whole truth; for example, Ronald Reagan's Press Secretary Larry Speakes said that an invasion of Grenada was "preposterous" on the day before the United States invaded that island in 1983.)

At Hagerty's first meeting with White House reporters in 1953, he told them, "When I say to you, 'I don't know,' I mean I don't know. When I say, 'No comment,' it means I'm not talking, but not necessarily any more than that. Aside from that, I'm here to help you get the news. I am also here to work for one man, who happens to be the President. And I will do that to the best of my ability." Being between President and press creates what Walter Wurfel, a Deputy Press Secretary under President Jimmy Carter, has called "the fundamental duality to the role of the White House press secretary." Wurfel wrote that the Press Secretary is "a government official paid by the taxpayers and is responsible for supplying information to the public. On the other hand, he is a political appointee answerable only to the president, and the president views the spokesman's job to be that of putting the most favorable light on his administration." Some of the Press Secretaries who came directly from journalism were the most conflicted by this "fundamental duality." Jerald terHorst, who left the Washington bureau of the *Detroit News* to become Gerald Ford's first Press Secretary, lasted only thirty days, resigning when he could not support Ford's decision to pardon former President Nixon.

Thirty-nine White House reporters, interviewed in the summer of 1991 about their preferences among the Press Secretaries they had known, often mentioned desirable personal and professional qualities. Among the personal qualities they appreciated were friendliness, an unwillingness to embarrass reporters,

Press Secretaries

Number	President	Press Secretary
31	Hoover	George Akerson, 1929–1931 Theodore Joslin, 1931–1933
32	F. D. Roosevelt	Stephen Early, 1933–1945
33	Truman	Charles Ross, 1945–1950 Joseph Short, 1950–1952 Roger Tubby, 1952 James Hagerty, 1953
34	Eisenhower	James Hagerty, 1953–1961
35	Kennedy	Pierre Salinger, 1961–1963
36	L. B. Johnson	Pierre Salinger, 1963–1964 George Reedy, 1964–1965 Bill Moyers, 1965–1967 George Christian, 1967–1969
37	Nixon	Ronald Ziegler, 1969–1974 Jerald terHorst, 1974
38	Ford	Ronald Nessen, 1974–1977
39	Carter	Jody Powell, 1977–1981
40	Reagan	James Brady, 1981 Larry Speakes, 1981–1987 Marlin Fitzwater, 1987–1989
41	Bush	Marlin Fitzwater, 1989–1993
42	Clinton	Dee Dee Myers, 1993–

a sense of humor, and honesty. Professional qualities they admired included an understanding of journalists' needs, a lack of favoritism, and good briefing skills. But overwhelmingly what they wanted in a White House Press Secretary was confidence that what he told them came from an intimate and immediate knowledge of what the President was thinking. They appreciated, for example, the almost father-son relationship between Carter and Press Secretary Jody Powell. Reporters also enjoyed Pierre Salinger's company, but they knew that John F. Kennedy had kept him in the dark in advance of the BAY OF PIGS INVASION, and they respected George Reedy's intelligence, but they knew that Lyndon Johnson withheld information from him. Ultimately, then, as George Christian, another of Johnson's Press Secretaries, once said, Press Secretaries' "style will be shaped by the Presidents they work for, or they won't be there long."

BIBLIOGRAPHY

Hess, Stephen. *The Government/Press Connection: Press Officers and Their Offices.* 1984.

Spragens, William C., with Carole Ann Terwoord. *From Spokesman to Press Secretary: White House Media Operations.* 1980.

Wurfel, Walter. "The White House: Center Stage for Government." In *Informing the People.* Edited by Lewis M. Helm, Ray Eldon Hiebert, Michael R. Naver, and Kenneth Rabin. 1981.

STEPHEN HESS

WHITE HOUSE SECRETARIES. From the beginning, Presidents have relied on aides possessed of what Franklin D. Roosevelt called "a passion for anonymity." The early Presidents depended on well-recommended younger men to be their assistants and amanuenses and to run political errands. These were secretaries in the older meaning of the word: people entrusted with secrets. For this kind of service, Martin Van Buren leaned on his sons Abraham and Martin, Jr. Millard Fillmore's son Millard Powers Fillmore also served as his father's secretary.

As presidential responsibilities grew, the pool of qualified men was enlarged. (Women were not yet considered for the work.) Abraham Lincoln chose as his private secretary John Nicolay, a German-born acquaintance from Lincoln's Springfield days. Nicolay, only twenty-nine years old in 1861, had become a close friend of JOHN HAY, then twenty-three years old. When Nicolay was named, he obtained the appointment of Hay as assistant secretary. Nicolay and Hay shared a room in the White House, and few people enjoyed closer relations with the President, whom they lovingly referred to as "Tycoon" or "the Ancient."

Secretary to the President. With the rise of modern office-keeping (including especially the widening use of the typewriter in the 1880s) and an increase in the volume of mail, secretaries who knew shorthand became indispensable. Presidents were entitled by statute to one private secretary. Still, they continued to have the need for other trustworthy right-hand men who were adroit at political maneuvering as well as paper-pushing. Consequently, the position of Secretary to the President was authorized by Congress in 1897. To the new post William McKinley appointed J. Addison Porter, a wealthy newspaper owner from Hartford, Connecticut—"a tall, thickset dude with pince-nez on a black cord." He was succeeded by his assistant, George B. Cortelyou, a New Yorker, recommended to McKinley by Grover Cleveland, for whom Cortelyou had done stenography. Cortelyou continued as Secretary under Theodore Roosevelt until he joined Roosevelt's Cabinet, after which Roosevelt designated William Loeb, Jr., to the post. Loeb was on hand on many memorable occasions, taking notes, for example, at the critical meeting settling the coal strike of 1902. Roosevelt, who had brought Loeb to the White House from New York, said of him, "When I was Governor . . . I was as erratic about hours as I am here, and when I was seized with a desire to work Loeb was the only stenographer or secretary whom I could ever find after office hours, and it is the same now. He is always on the spot, and that means everything to me."

But stenography ceased to be a requirement for the office as the presidents came to rely on female clerks for that service. Woodrow Wilson's Secretary, Joseph P. Tumulty, came with Wilson to Washington from New Jersey, where Tumulty had served on Wilson's gubernatorial staff. Tumulty, a reforming Democrat, had demonstrated considerable political cunning in helping to engineer Wilson's nomination for President. The first Roman Catholic to hold the post of Secretary, Tumulty was in charge of PATRONAGE, appointments, PRESS RELATIONS, and in-house editing of presidential papers—functions that a few years later would be assigned to separate appointees.

The last person to hold the post of Secretary to the President was JAMES C. HAGERTY, a New Yorker who handled press relations under President Dwight D. Eisenhower. The title was dropped by legislation passed in 1956. Since President Richard M. Nixon, the title WHITE HOUSE CHIEF OF STAFF has been used given to that person in the administration who fills the role formerly filled by the Secretary to the President.

Private Secretaries. In the twentieth century a number of private presidential secretaries became familiar to the public. One was Franklin Roosevelt's secretary Marguerite ("Missy") LeHand. Roosevelt had met her in 1920, and she served him through the years that followed, living at the Executive Mansion in Albany when he was Governor of New York, and then at the White House. Because ELEANOR ROOSEVELT was often out of town, LeHand could sometimes be found at the President's side as his hostess, resulting in persistent rumors about their relationships. Serving as the "number two girl"—her own words—was Grace Tully, whom Eleanor Roosevelt had become acquainted with during the presidential campaign of 1928. Tully was in charge of the President's mail and did the typing and stenographic chores that "Missy" LeHand generally dodged. Tully was with Roosevelt when he died in 1945.

Eisenhower's secretary, Ann Whitman, joined his staff just before the 1952 presidential campaign got underway. Intending to stay only "a few days," she remained with him to the end of his presidency. He relied on her probity and good judgment. The devotion of Evelyn Lincoln, John F. Kennedy's private secretary, was legendary. One day, after making an urgent request of the unflappable Lincoln over the telephone, Kennedy commented to his aide THEODORE SORENSEN, "No matter what I do or say, Mrs. Lincoln will be sweet and unsurprised. If I had said just now, 'Mrs. Lincoln, I have just cut off Jackie's head, would you please send over a box?' she would have replied, 'That's wonderful, Mr. President, I'll send it right away. . . . Did you get your nap?' " The fidelity of Rose Mary Woods, private secretary to Richard Nixon, whose employ with him had begun when he became a Senator in 1951, was also celebrated. She gained notoriety during the WATERGATE AFFAIR, when it was claimed, rightly or wrongly, that an erasure of eighteen minutes and fifteen seconds on one of the critical subpoenaed tapes was her responsibility.

Many subordinate secretaries in the White House have made their work a lifelong career. For instance, Toinette ("Toy") Bachelder, whom Franklin Roosevelt had met at the spa at Warm Springs, Georgia, where he was treated for polio, and who like Roosevelt wore a leg brace, came to Washington in 1933. She participated in the preparation of the President's speeches and, at the cocktail hour, of his old-fashioneds. She served his successors and their wives until well into the Lyndon B. Johnson administration.

First Ladies' Secretaries. First Ladies have their own secretaries, who have increasingly performed more than just social duties, which at first was their chief task. Two of the best known to the public were Letitia ("Tish") Baldridge, social secretary to JACQUELINE KENNEDY, and Elizabeth ("Liz") Carpenter, staff director and press secretary to LADY BIRD JOHNSON. HILLARY RODHAM CLINTON's secretarial requirements were almost as substantial as President Bill Clinton's. [See FIRST LADY'S OFFICE.]

Executive Clerk. An indispensable secretarial institution of the White House is that of Staff Secretary, the person responsible for preparing all of the President's documents. But the Staff Secretary—as well as the WHITE HOUSE PRESS SECRETARY, the Director of Presidential Personnel, and the WHITE HOUSE COUNSEL—depend unceasingly on the Office of the Executive Clerk, today located in the OLD EXECUTIVE OFFICE BUILDING next door to the White House. First created in 1857, the Office of the Executive Clerk in 1993 consisted of six employees. The Executive Clerk is responsible for reviewing, processing, making final preparations of, and recording all Presidential documents in order to ensure their correct form, conformity to legal requirements, and proper disposition. The office maintains the regulations governing all who work in the EXECUTIVE BRANCH and oversees the continuous business of the Presidency that runs from one administration to the next regardless of party. Housing an extensive record of presidential precedent, the office serves as the institutional memory of the Presidency. When delivering reports of the President to Congress, members of the Office of the Executive Clerk serve in the capacity of "private secretary to the President"—and are the only persons in the White House bureaucracy who are granted access to the floor of the Senate and the House of Representatives.

From Franklin Roosevelt's days through Richard Nixon's time the Executive Clerk was William J. Hopkins, a Kansan who had begun his career as a stenographer for Herbert Hoover. Eisenhower said that Hopkins "knew more about . . . procedure in all areas of government than anyone else with whom I have come in contact." In 1956, President Johnson honored Hopkins with the additional title Executive Assistant to the President of the United States. In 1993 the Executive Clerk was Ronald R. Geisler, a Pennsylvanian who had held the post since 1981. He had been detailed from the Pentagon in 1964 to work under Hopkins.

BIBLIOGRAPHY

Lash, Joseph. *Love, Eleanor: Eleanor Roosevelt and Her Friends.* 1982.

Lincoln, Evelyn. *My Twelve Years with John F. Kennedy.* 1965.

Medved, Michael. *The Shadow Presidents: The Secret History of the Chief Executives and the Top Aides.* 1979.

"The Office of the Executive Clerk." Typescript. Issued by the White House.

Tully, Grace. *FDR: My Boss.* 1949.

Tumulty, Joseph P. *Woodrow Wilson As I Know Him.* 1921.

HENRY F. GRAFF

WHITE HOUSE STAFF. The term "White House staff" is often popularly used to refer to anyone working in the EXECUTIVE OFFICE OF THE PRESIDENT (EOP), but its proper usage refers specifically to the staff working close to the President in the White House Office, a division incorporated into the newly established Executive Office in 1939. But formal titles and dates of origin should not mask the fact that the White House staff is as old as the presidency itself.

Private Secretaries. Its beginnings can be traced to the very first congressional appropriation for presidential expenses in 1789, which included an unspecified amount for secretarial and clerical assistance. Tobias Lear, whom President George Washington appointed as his private secretary, might appropriately be considered the first White House staffer (even though the WHITE HOUSE had not been completed during Washington's administration). However, congressional funding for presidential staff assistance soon proved to be totally inadequate and, for the first half of the nineteenth century at least, most Presidents were forced to rely on young relatives as private secretaries and clerks and, even then, found their expense allowance insufficient to cover staff costs.

It was not until 1857 that Congress approved a specific appropriation to fund the position of private secretary and it then took another ten years before additional assistance, in the form of an assistant secretary, a shorthand writer, and four clerks, was added to the White House staff payroll. Congressional funding increased slowly and erratically during the latter half of the nineteenth century and, by 1900, the complement of administrative and clerical staff in the White House totaled thirteen. But the level of support still did not satisfy presidential needs. The status of the private secretary was low, as was his salary, and Presidents often experienced difficulty finding competent people to assist them. President Rutherford B. Hayes's first two choices for private secretary turned down his job offer because they considered the position beneath their dignity and President James A. Garfield once confided to a friend that he was "at a loss to find just the man for Private Secretary than for any place I shall have to fill."

The practice of appointing relatives to the position of private secretary virtually ceased with President Ulysses S. Grant's administration, and the increased congressional funding for presidential staff in 1867, particularly the creation of the executive clerks' positions, freed the private secretary from the most basic and routine clerical chores enabling him to perform more weightier tasks on behalf of the President. The additional posts also permitted the beginning of some degree of institutional continuity within the White House staff. When President Hayes took office, he retained three of President Grant's assistants and two of them, O. L. Pruden and W. H. Crook, eventually ended their service as executive clerks under Theodore Roosevelt's presidency. To this day, the executive clerk continues to hold his position even when the presidency changes hands and changes parties.

James Garfield's presidency marked the beginning of a succession of very able and talented private secretaries—Stanley Brown (Garfield), Daniel Lamont (Cleveland), George Cortelyou (McKinley), and William Loeb (Theodore Roosevelt)—all of whom helped to develop and broaden the role of private secretary and gradually turned it into a more politically important position. By the turn of the century, the private secretary (whose title had been changed by President William McKinley to Secretary to the President) was much more than the administrative clerk he had been at the beginning of the century and was active as a speechwriter, political adviser, and as an intermediary between the President and key constituencies, particularly Congress, party officials, and the rapidly expanding world of political journalism.

The heightened political role of the secretary to the

President also began to transform the position into a much more visible one and, consequently, made prior political experience an important prerequisite for the job. Of the nineteenth-century secretaries, only Cleveland's Daniel Lamont had any substantial background in politics before coming to the White House, but, this became more usual in the twentieth century beginning with President Woodrow Wilson's appointment of Joseph Tumulty as his secretary. There were even occasions when the political profile of the secretary to the President generated public opposition to his appointment. Tumulty, for example, became the target of Protestant bigots who feared the consequences of having a Roman Catholic so close to the President of the United States, and C. Bascom Slemp's appointment as President Calvin Coolidge's secretary drew criticism from the DEMOCRATIC PARTY and the National Association for the Advancement of Colored People because of Slemp's prior reputation as a member of the House of Representatives and chairman of the Virginia REPUBLICAN PARTY.

Although the role of the Secretary to the President was expanding significantly, the size and shape of the White House staff hardly changed at all during the early years of the twentieth century. Some increase took place in the early 1920s to bring the staff total to thirty-one, but all the new positions were at the lower end of the staff hierarchy. Traditionally, Presidents had circumvented the limits on White House staff positions by borrowing, or detailing, staff from the executive branch departments and agencies, a practice first begun by President Andrew Jackson, but even that did not meet the President's need for more high-level assistance in the White House. In 1929, Congress did agree to increase the number of secretaries to the President from one to three, which permitted some division of labor between the President's top aides. It enabled President Herbert Hoover, for example, to designate one of his three secretaries to the specialized job of PRESS SECRETARY, a position that has been part of the White House bureaucracy ever since.

The Brownlow Model. Neither the additional two secretaries, nor the large number of detailed staff working in the White House satisfied President Franklin D. Roosevelt who forcefully drew attention to the President's inadequate staff resources through the publication of the BROWNLOW COMMITTEE Report in 1937. That report led to the creation of the Executive Office of the President and the formalization of the White House Office within it. In terms of resources, the Brownlow Report recommended that the White House Office was to be provided with an additional six executive assistants who were to be the President's direct aides in dealing with the new managerial agencies established within the EOP.

The importance of the Brownlow Report lay not so much in the extra staff it recommended, but rather in the considerable effort it made to delineate carefully the appropriate role and function of the White House staff. "These aides would have no power to make decisions or issue instructions in their own right," wrote Brownlow. "They would not be interposed between the President and the heads of departments. They would not be assistant Presidents in any sense." The report placed special emphasis on the necessary personal attributes of the staff.

> Their effectiveness in assisting the President will . . . be directly proportional to their ability to discharge their function with restraints. . . . They should be men in whom the President has personal confidence and whose character and attitude is such that they would not attempt to exercise power on their own account. They should be possessed of high competence, great physical vigor, and a passion for anonymity.

That passage from the Brownlow Report is frequently regarded as a model for how White House staff ought to function and how staffers ought to behave in a position so close to the center of power in American government. It was based on what Louis Brownlow saw when he visited the British Cabinet Office in London and so deeply was he influenced by the British Cabinet secretariat that he tried to transpose it to Washington, D.C., but unsuccessfully. The history of the White House staff since 1939 has been a history of departures and deviations from the Brownlow blueprint and the report now serves primarily as a yardstick by which to measure how far post-Brownlow White House staffs have moved away from the norm.

Both the size and the power of the White House staff increased steadily after 1939. There are various estimates of the current number of the White House staffers, but it is impossible to calculate the total with precision. The number of budgeted White House staff positions in 1991 was 381, but there were also approximately another 80 staff detailed from departments and agencies to the White House Office and about a dozen temporary consultants who also ought to be included in the staff total. Aggregate totals do, however, overstate the problem of the growth of the White House staff because they do not differentiate between the clerical and the professional staff working in the White House. It has been estimated that only about half the total White House staff are professionals, and post-WATERGATE AFFAIR efforts to curb presidential staff expansion have been directed at this group rather than the totality of White House employees.

Functions and Powers. Perhaps more important than the sheer growth in numbers is the change in the function and the power of the presidential staff. Since the 1970s, senior White House staffers have regularly done what Brownlow said they should not do. They do make decisions, they do interpose themselves between the President and heads of departments, they do exercise power on their own account, and they tend not to discharge their functions with restraint. Some have clearly lacked the high competence Brownlow thought was essential and few have displayed much passion for anonymity. The White House staff is now a powerful political body operating at the very center of public policy-making, and its activities have, at times, resulted in serious abuses of power, as manifested in the events of Watergate and the IRAN-CONTRA AFFAIR.

Watergate, particularly, generated considerable criticism of the role of the White House staff and led to attempts by Congress to regulate the growth of the staff and make it more accountable. Four years after President Richard M. Nixon's resignation, Congress passed the WHITE HOUSE PERSONNEL AUTHORIZATION ACT of 1978, which imposes a limit on the number of senior White House staffers and requires the President to report the total number of employees in the White House Office each year. It is, however, a weak piece of legislation that has had little subsequent impact on the nature of the White House staff or on the ability of Congress to exercise oversight of the presidential staff.

The power of the modern White House staff derives from its political and policy responsibilities. These have been acquired over a period of time as a consequence of the increasing power of the presidency itself and the fact that Presidents have preferred to delegate these responsibilities to their personal staffs rather than members of their Cabinets, career civil servants, or any other body. Senior White House staff, such as SHERMAN ADAMS (Eisenhower), THEODORE SORENSEN (Kennedy), Joseph Califano (Johnson), HENRY A. KISSINGER (Nixon), Hamilton Jordan (Carter), JAMES A. BAKER III (Reagan), and John Sununu (Bush) achieve power and fame, and sometimes notoriety, in their own right.

But an active, prominent, and powerful White House staff is now a fact of life in American government, and the nature of the development of the presidential staff since the end of the nineteenth century is unlikely to be changed in the foreseeable future. White House staffers have the capacity to bring considerable talents and strengths to the conduct of government, but they can also do great damage to the modern presidency, as the Watergate and Iran-contra affairs proved. Today, few White House staffers take much notice of Brownlow's strictures, as desirable as they might be, and all too often in the post-Brownlow period, we are reminded of what President Harry S. Truman once wrote in his diary about his White House staff. "Some of my boys who came in with me are having trouble with their dignity and prerogatives. It's hell when a man gets in close association with the President."

BIBLIOGRAPHY

Burke, John P. *The Institutional Presidency.* 1992.
Hart, John. "Eisenhower and the Swelling of the Presidency." *Polity* 24 (1992): 673–691.
Hart, John. *The Presidential Branch.* 1987.
Hess, Stephen. *Organizing the Presidency.* 2d ed. 1988.
Medved, Michael. *The Shadow Presidents.* 1979.
Mondale, Walter F. *The Accountability of Power: Toward a Responsible Presidency.* 1975.
Wildavsky, Aaron. "Salvation by Staff: Reform of the Presidential Office." In *The Presidency.* Edited by Aaron Wildavsky. 1969.

JOHN HART

WIENER v. UNITED STATES 357 U.S. 349 (1958). This case was one of several Supreme Court rulings concerning the President's REMOVAL POWER. In *Wiener,* the specific question concerned whether a President may remove an official of a quasi-judicial agency in the absence of a statutory provision qualifying the presidential removal power. In an earlier case, HUMPHREY'S EXECUTOR V. UNITED STATES (1935), the Supreme Court had upheld a statutory provision that limited the President's power to remove a commissioner of an independent agency. But what if there were no statutory provision?

In 1948 Congress had created the War Claims Commission to adjudicate claims against Axis powers made by internees, prisoners of war, and religious organizations. The President was to appoint, by and with the ADVICE AND CONSENT of the Senate, three commissioners. Myron Wiener, appointed commissioner by President Harry S. Truman in 1950, was removed in 1953 by President Dwight D. Eisenhower, who wanted "personnel of my own selection." Wiener sued in the Court of Claims for back pay from the date of his dismissal to the date of the end of his term. That court dismissed the case, holding that absent a limitation on removals placed in a statute, the intent of Congress could be taken to mean that the President retained the power of removal (1956). The Supreme Court reversed, concluding that in the case of an independent commission given substantial adjudicatory power "to act according to law" and possessing an "intrinsic judicial character," the removal power is for Congress to determine. The President possesses no removal power over such officials unless Congress explicitly confers it. No grant to the President can be implied from the fact that Congress failed to limit removal for cause.

The Court held that it was the function of the office—in this case a position involving quasi-judicial powers—that provided the protection against presidential removal and not the presence or absence of statutory provisions. It stated that officials in agencies vested with significant quasi-judicial functions, serving for a fixed term, may not be removed by the President except for cause even if Congress has not explicitly protected their tenure by statute. By implication, the President may still remove commissioners for inefficiency, neglect of duty, or malfeasance in office, even if no provision for removals for cause is made in the statute. Together with the *Humphrey* decision, *Wiener* freed many agencies from direct presidential supervision. Commissioners were protected from what the Court referred to as the "Damocles' sword of removal." Agencies such as the Federal Trade Commission, the Federal Communications Commission, the Federal Power Commission, and the Securities and Exchange Commission all had statutory bases that were silent on the removal of commissioners, and all seemed to come under the combined *Humphrey-Wiener* rule. The two rulings allow Congress to create independent agencies outside the departmental structure and free of the constraints of the executive branch. But they may not free officials exercising purely or primarily administrative functions from presidential control simply because their agencies are declared "independent." Rather, the nature of their functions determines whether officials are free from the presidential removal power.

BIBLIOGRAPHY

Healy, Joseph F., Jr. "Decisions—*Wiener v. United States.*" *Georgetown Law Journal* 47 (1958):395–398.

Ingle, John R. "Constitutional Law—President's Power to Remove Non-Executive Officeholders." *North Carolina Law Review* 37 (1959):144–148.

Jones, Norvill. "Law Notes—Constitutional Law." *George Washington Law Review* 27 (1958):129–132.

RICHARD M. PIOUS

WILLKIE, WENDELL (1892–1944), Republican presidential nominee in 1940. Wendell Willkie, a lawyer and businessman, gained national prominence in the 1930s as one of the more articulate critics of the NEW DEAL, but in the 1940s he became a valuable ally of Franklin D. Roosevelt in Roosevelt's struggle to move the United States beyond ISOLATIONISM.

The grandson of German immigrants, Willkie was born and reared in Indiana, where he graduated from the state university. After serving in WORLD WAR I as an army lieutenant, he practiced law in Akron, Ohio. A Democrat until 1939, Willkie held views that were influenced by Woodrow Wilson. His first political involvement was as a campaigner for ratification of the TREATY OF VERSAILLES and for U.S. participation in the LEAGUE OF NATIONS. Willkie also aggressively fought the KU KLUX KLAN in Ohio. He was a delegate to the 1924 Democratic National Convention from Ohio and supported ALFRED E. SMITH for the presidency.

Willkie did not become a major player on the national political stage until after he moved to New York in 1929 as the lawyer for Commonwealth and Southern, a large utility holding company. In 1933, he became president of the holding company, which controlled midwestern and southern utilities. In this position, Willkie led the opposition to two major initiatives of Franklin D. Roosevelt's New Deal: the PUBLIC UTILITY HOLDING COMPANY ACT and the TENNESSEE VALLEY AUTHORITY ACT, which provided for cheap electrical power in competition with private utilities. Willkie and his allies carried their fight to Congress and to the Supreme Court, losing in both arenas. In 1939, when he became a Republican, he sold his company's Tennessee Valley properties to the TVA for $78.6 million.

In the process of fighting these losing battles, Willkie gained recognition as a strong new voice for the business community. Broad-shouldered and handsome, he was a powerful speaker and a compelling personality. Encouraged by *Time* and *Life* magazine publisher Henry Luce and by Russell Davenport, the managing editor of *Fortune*, one of Luce's magazines, Willkie launched a long-shot bid for the 1940 Republican presidential nomination. Although he had been identified with domestic issues, Willkie moved into serious contention because of his strong views on foreign policy. The leading Republican candidates—THOMAS E. DEWEY, Robert A. Taft, and Arthur H. Vandenberg—were isolationists who were not greatly concerned about the threat of Nazi Germany. In contrast, for months Willkie had been warning about the threat of a Hitler-dominated Europe. Just before the Republican convention, Germany conquered Denmark, Norway, the Low Countries, and France. Public opinion dramatically shifted away from isolationism, and the Republican convention deadlocked. Influenced by world events and a pro-Willkie propaganda blitz led by the *New York Herald-Tribune* and by Luce's magazines, Republicans nominated Willkie on the sixth ballot. Roosevelt, who viewed Willkie as a serious rival, called his nomination a "godsend" because it united the country against fascism. "Second only to the Battle of Britain," wrote Walter Lippmann, "the sudden rise and nomination of Willkie was the decisive event, perhaps providential, which made it possible to rally the free world when it was almost conquered. Under any other leadership but his, the REPUBLICAN PARTY would in 1940 have turned its back on Great Britain, causing all who still resisted Hitler to feel that they were abandoned."

During the 1940 campaign, Willkie provided critical support for the Selective Service Training Act of 1940 and for aid to Britain, also delivering the support of his running mate, Senate Minority Leader Charles L. McNary, who had been aligned with the isolationists. In the campaign, Willkie criticized New Deal programs and, in what he later would dismiss as campaign oratory, accused Roosevelt of leading the United States into a world war. Willkie lost by about 5 million votes but received a larger vote than any previous Republican candidate.

Following his defeat, Willkie grew in stature as a leader of Republican internationalists and as an outspoken champion of civil rights. "After the campaign, having failed to defeat the administration, I decided that I would do all I could to support its foreign policy," Willkie said. In 1941 he flew to England, then under German attack, to demonstrate American support for the democratic cause. On his return, Willkie testified before the Senate in support of lend-lease aid to the Allies [see LEND-LEASE ACT], which was approved. Willkie also aided Roosevelt in pushing for a revision of the neutrality act.

In 1942, Roosevelt named Willkie as a special envoy and sent him to promote goodwill in the Middle East, China, and the Soviet Union. On his mission, Willkie promoted Allied cooperation. In China, Willkie called for an end to Western imperialism. "The colonial days are past," he said. "We believe this war must mean an end to the empire of nations over other nations." His best-selling book *One World* (1943) chronicled his global tour and supported the nationalist movements then emerging in underdeveloped countries. Willkie also urged the creation of a UNITED NATIONS organization that would promote world peace. Through the force of his personality and ideas, Willkie got the Republican National Committee to endorse an international organization with U.S. participation.

On the domestic front, Willkie became the conscience of American politics. He urged Roosevelt to issue an EXECUTIVE ORDER ending segregation of the armed forces. He also called for a federal antilynching law and a repeal of the poll tax. He criticized Allied cooperation with fascists in war zones liberated by the Allies.

He made a second bid for the presidency in 1944, winning the New Hampshire primary but withdraw-ing after losing the Wisconsin and Nebraska primaries. Thomas E. Dewey, who won the GOP presidential nomination, disliked Willkie and denied him a role at the party convention. Willkie's support was courted by Roosevelt, though Willkie made no endorsement. He was responsive to Roosevelt's overtures about joining forces to form a liberal third party after the 1944 election. Less than a month before Roosevelt's reelection to a fourth term, Willkie died of a heart attack at fifty-two. Willkie was arguably the most influential defeated presidential nominee of the twentieth century.

BIBLIOGRAPHY

Barnard, Ellsworth. *Wendell Willkie: Fighter for Freedom.* 1966.
Barnes, Joseph F. *Willkie.* 1952.
Neal, Steve. *Dark Horse: A Biography of Wendell Willkie.* 1984

STEVE NEAL

WILMOT PROVISO. By the summer of 1846 James K. Polk had achieved a number of his domestic goals (reducing the tariff and creating an INDEPENDENT TREASURY) and diplomatic objectives (acquiring Oregon and Texas). The President, however, paid a high price for success. Often secretive and manipulative, Polk alienated many politicians, even within his own majority DEMOCRATIC PARTY, through his management style, principled stands, and controversial patronage policy. When war erupted with Mexico in April 1846, suspicious Whigs and northern Democrats wanted clarification of Polk's territorial ambitions. The Democrats, often supporters of former President Martin Van Buren, sought guarantees that the MEXICAN WAR was not a Trojan horse, designed to extend the bounds of SLAVERY.

On 8 August 1846, Polk presented a $2 million appropriation bill to the House of Representatives, a sum designed to facilitate peace negotiations with the Mexican government. Since the President remained vague about acquisition of land, Congressman David Wilmot of Pennsylvania, a Van Buren dissident, attached a clarifying amendment—or proviso—to the measure. Slavery could not exist in any territory acquired from Mexico through the appropriation.

Surprisingly, the amended bill generated little excitement in the House and passed by a bipartisan sectional vote on 8 August. The administration hoped to rush the appropriation, stripped of the proviso, through the Senate before adjournment on 10 August. Antislavery members, however, grasped the strategy and filibustered the measure until the session expired.

Inspired by political opportunism and genuine antislavery feeling, Whigs and many northern Democrats supported the reintroduction in January 1847 of the $2 million appropriation bill with Wilmot's proviso attached. Led by Congressman Preston King of New York, free soil again triumphed in the House on 15 February. Two weeks later, proadministration Democrats allied with southerners to defeat the measure. Although the appropriation (increased to $3 million) soon passed without the proviso, slavery in the territories had became a sectionally explosive issue.

Congress never endorsed a territorial free-soil bill before the CIVIL WAR. The Wilmot Proviso had a powerful impact, however, and contributed to the division of the major parties in 1848. It argued that Congress could prohibit slavery in the territories, prompting a call by JOHN C. CALHOUN for a southern party, generating the alternative solution of popular sovereignty, and promoting the formation of the FREE-SOIL PARTY. That party (in 1848 and 1852) and the REPUBLICAN PARTY (1856 and 1860) utilized the proviso as a fundamental plank in their platforms.

BIBLIOGRAPHY

Bergeron, Paul. *The Presidency of James K. Polk.* 1987.
Going, Charles B. *David Wilmot, Free Soiler.* 1924.
Morrison, Chaplain. *Democratic Politics and Sectionalism: The Wilmot Proviso Controversy.* 1967.

JOHN M. BELOHLAVEK

WILSON, EDITH (1872–1961), First Lady, second wife of Woodrow Wilson. Edith Bolling Galt Wilson is an important figure in the evolution of the presidency as an example both of the problems that presidential disability poses and of the ill-defined role of the First Lady. A Virginia native who grew up in modest circumstances, Edith Bolling had an unsuccessful marriage to Norman Galt that ended with his death in 1908. As a widow with a profitable jewelry business, she became friendly with female members of Woodrow Wilson's circle and was introduced to the President in March 1915. His first wife had died in August 1914, and the lonely President found Edith Galt physically and intellectually attractive. He pursued her ardently. They were married on 18 December 1915.

Mrs. Wilson became a trusted confidante and personal aide to her husband. He shared state papers and secrets with her. She accompanied him to the Paris Peace Conference in 1919. He listened to her advice but made his own decisions. After the President suffered a disabling stroke on 2 October 1919, Mrs. Wilson's role became more important and historically controversial. She agreed with the doctors that Wilson should not resign. She screened the documents and letters that the President saw. She also decided who was allowed to see Wilson in his sickroom. The First Lady maintained that she did not make any independent political judgments for the President while he was ill. Nonetheless, her role as a political gatekeeper for the President prevented Wilson from receiving the broadest possible range of advice. Most important, she contributed to the sense of political paralysis that characterized the last months of Wilson's administration. She became a symbol of the dangers of allowing FIRST LADIES too much influence, and has been labeled inaccurately as "the first woman President."

BIBLIOGRAPHY

Maddox, Robert J. "Mrs. Wilson and the Presidency." *American History Illustrated* 7 (1973): 36–44.
Weaver, Judith. "Edith Bolling Wilson as First Lady: A Study in the Power of Personality, 1919–1920." *Presidential Studies Quarterly* 15 (1985): 51–76.
Wilson, Edith Bolling. *My Memoir.* 1939.

LEWIS L. GOULD

WILSON, HENRY (1812–1875), Senator, eighteenth Vice President of the United States (1873–1875). Henry Wilson, who served as Vice President under Ulysses S. Grant from 1873 until his death on 22 November 1875, was born on 16 February 1812 on a farm near Farmington, New Hampshire. He shared a poverty-stricken life with his parents. For ten years, he worked as an apprentice for a local farmer. Upon turning twenty-one, he walked to Natick, Massachusetts, where he entered the shoemaking business. Although he became a successful businessman, his real interest lay in politics; and despite his lack of formal education, he soon became a respected speaker and debater.

Wilson ran as a Whig in the campaign of 1840 and was elected to the Massachusetts legislature, where he served a total of eight terms in both houses. During these years he developed the legislative skills that he would later use to great advantage in Washington. He proved adept at engineering compromises, building coalitions, and corralling votes.

Wilson's constant manipulation of the political process revealed his intense ambition, but it also revealed an equally intense hostility to slavery. He became an abolitionist at the age of twenty-five, devoting his political career to overthrowing the institution and securing equal rights for blacks. When the WHIG PARTY proved unresponsive to his abolitionist views, Wilson left it in 1848 to help organize the FREE SOIL PARTY; six years later he moved to the KNOW-NOTHING (AMERICAN) PARTY, whose followers rewarded him for his efforts by electing him in 1855 to the United States Senate. Secure in his new position, Wilson turned his political talents to the organization and promotion of the Republican Party, remaining loyal to it for the rest of his life; the party, in turn, rewarded him by electing him to two additional Senate terms and eventually to the vice presidency.

Since the Republicans did not gain control of Congress until 1861, Wilson and his party colleagues spent much of their time attempting to thwart the initiatives of Democratic Presidents Franklin Pierce and James Buchanan. After the CIVIL WAR began, Wilson defended the executive actions of newly elected Republican President Abraham Lincoln from congressional criticism, but as the war continued, he became more protective of legislative prerogatives. As chairman of the Senate Military Affairs Committee, Wilson became one of that body's premier legislators. Lincoln played little role in setting congressional agendas or proposing legislation, which gave Wilson a relatively free hand in devising the many measures, including the first national conscription act, that the Union implemented to raise and supply its armies. Wilson was also a key member of the group of RADICAL REPUBLICANS that pushed a variety of antislavery measures through Congress and urged Lincoln to issue the EMANCIPATION PROCLAMATION. Although Wilson was sometimes critical of Lincoln's use of his executive powers and although he remained jealous of congressional prerogatives, he and his Republican colleagues cooperated effectively with the President to help save the Union and overthrow slavery.

During RECONSTRUCTION this cooperation between Congress and the executive branch broke down completely. Senator Wilson played a major role in drafting and securing the passage of the more important Reconstruction measures, most of which were designed to protect the freedom and equal rights of the former slaves. President Andrew Johnson repeatedly vetoed these laws; consequently, Wilson became an ardent supporter of Congress's attempt to impeach the President and was therefore bitterly disappointed when the effort failed.

On the other hand, his efforts in 1868 to help elect U. S. Grant as President were successful, and after that time rivalry between the President and Congress diminished. Wilson did become increasingly dissatisfied with Grant's Southern policy and with growing evidence of corruption in his administration, but he did not publicly voice his concerns and refused to join the Liberal Republican revolt against Grant in 1872. In nominating Wilson for Vice President that year, the Republican Party recognized him for his loyalty as well as for his contributions to preserving the Union, ending slavery, and securing equal rights for freedmen. The following year Wilson left the Senate to take up his new office, which he found gave him little influence with the President or with Congress. He spent much of his time writing a multivolume history of the nation's struggle with slavery. Wilson, who was openly critical of proposals to secure Grant a third term in 1876, harbored dreams of running for President himself, an ambition cut short by his death at the age of sixty-three.

BIBLIOGRAPHY

Abbott, Richard H. *Cobbler in Congress: The Life of Henry Wilson, 1812–1875.* 1972.

McKay, Ernest. *Henry Wilson: Practical Radical.* 1971.

RICHARD H. ABBOTT

WILSON, JAMES (1742–1798), signer of the Declaration of Independence and the Constitution, Associate Justice of the Supreme Court. Wilson was one of the most influential members of the founding generation. Born in Scotland and educated as a classical scholar at the University of St. Andrews, he migrated to America in 1765 and studied law with the celebrated John Dickinson. His keen and perceptive mind, superior classical education, and excellent legal training prepared him to play a major role in the creation of the new American republic. He was one of six men who signed both the Declaration of Independence and the Constitution and is widely regarded as second only to James Madison in his contributions to the deliberations of the CONSTITUTIONAL CONVENTION. He produced what was probably the most widely distributed and discussed defense of the new Constitution in his statehouse speech of 6 October 1787 and was the principal figure in the efforts to secure Pennsylvania's ratification of the Constitution. He was one of the six original Justices of the United States Supreme Court, and he was the only Framer to formulate a general theory of government and law (in his lectures on law, delivered in 1791–1792).

Wilson's influence was nowhere more keenly felt than in the creation of the executive branch. Wilson was the first delegate at the Constitutional Convention to propose "that the Executive consist of a single person." He argued that the executive, no less than the legislature, needed to be restrained and controlled. But, "in order to control the legislative authority, you must divide it. In order to control the Executive, you must unite it." The advantage of clear-cut responsibility would reinforce and assure those other "very important advantages" that are also obtained from a single executive, including energy, vigor, dispatch, firmness, consistency, and stability. Wilson was also the first delegate to suggest that the President be elected directly by the people. When this proposal failed to gain general support, he was then the first to propose a scheme for an ELECTORAL COLLEGE, a modification of which ultimately found its way into the Constitution. He also favored a relatively brief presidential tenure of three years and reeligibility. These features were crucial to Wilson, for they would ensure that the President would become and remain "the Man of the People."

Wilson's "Man of the People" was to be more than simply a person derived from their midst; he was also to be capable of acting vigorously on their behalf. As Wilson stressed in the Pennsylvania ratifying convention, the President was to be the Captain of the Ship of State, holding firmly to the helm and allowing the vessel to "proceed neither in one direction nor another without his concurrence." He was to be powerful and independent enough to serve the people and to protect them from the excesses, instabilities, and injustices of legislative dominance. Although the President was to be the Captain; nonetheless, Wilson argued, he was still to take his bearings from the people and set his course according to their dictates. Unlike ALEXANDER HAMILTON in FEDERALIST 71, Wilson would not have the President provide the people with direction or resist them when they are wrong. He did not believe that the people would be easily misled; therefore, he perceived no need for the President to check or lead them. As with the other branches of government, whatever checking or leading must be done could be accomplished through institutions whose primary purpose was to preserve the fidelity of the various branches of the government—in this case, the presidency—to the people.

Among the principal Framers, Wilson was the most committed to, and trusting of, unmitigated majoritarian democracy. He favored the simplicity of immediate consent and self-restraint over the complexity of procedural protections and constitutional contrivances. Relying heavily on the Scottish moralists (especially Thomas Reid), Wilson argued that men are naturally social; imbued with a sense of goodness, veracity, and benevolence; and possessed of a progressive intuitive sense that can be improved with practice as to carry society "above any limits which we can now assign." As a consequence, he trusted them to elect leaders—and especially the President—who would

govern soberly and well over the large and "comprehensive Federal Republic" created by the Constitution. The people's participation in the election of the President not only affirmed Wilson's confidence in the people but also contributed to their future improvement; in Wilson's words, it was "a rich mine of intelligence and patriotism" and "an abundant source of the most rational, the most improving, and the most endearing connection among the citizens."

BIBLIOGRAPHY

McCloskey, Robert Green, ed. *The Works of James Wilson.* 2 vols. 1967.

Rossum, Ralph A. "James Wilson and the 'Pyramid of Government': The Federal Republic." *Political Science Reviewer* 6 (1976): 113–142.

Smith, Charles Page. *James Wilson: Founding Father.* 1956.

RALPH A. ROSSUM

WILSON, WOODROW (1856–1924), twenty-eighth President of the United States (1913–1921). Born in Staunton, Virginia, on 29 December 1856, Thomas Woodrow Wilson was the only President to earn the Ph.D. degree and to write extensively about the presidency and the American constitutional system. He was well trained in American constitutional law at the University of Virginia, and his preparation in political science, history, and economics at Johns Hopkins University (1883–1885) was about the best he could have obtained anywhere. Wilson was one of the founders of the discipline of political science in the United States and one of the first presidents of the American Political Science Association.

Evolving Views of the Presidency. From his undergraduate days at Princeton onward, Wilson was intensely interested in the problems of modern democracy, particularly in the role and functions of leadership. He believed that forceful and effective leadership on the federal level would be possible only were the United States to adopt the British form of cabinet government—that is, were the United States to make the President and his CABINET responsible to Congress and their tenure dependent on retaining a majority in the legislative branch.

In light of Wilson's later political career, probably the most notable feature of his first book, *Congressional Government* (1885), was its treatment of the presidency. Wilson virtually wrote off the President as an unimportant third wheel of the federal system—in short as, a nonentity. Ignoring the examples set by Andrew Jackson, James K. Polk, and Abraham Lincoln, Wilson claimed that since Thomas Jefferson, the prestige and power of Presidents had declined to such an extent that the power of Congress had become predominant and could be held in check only by the judicial branch. *Congressional Government* was a subtle argument for reform of the executive branch. It was also a realistic analysis of how the federal government functioned in 1885. Between Andrew Johnson and Grover Cleveland, the presidency was at a nadir; Congress was then the predominant branch. The book is still rightly regarded as a classic.

Although Wilson later radically altered his view of the potentialities of the presidential office, he never ceased to believe that the parliamentary system was the best instrument for responsible leadership and government in a modern democracy. As late as 1913 we find him writing that sooner or later the President had to "be made answerable to opinion in a somewhat more informal and intimate fashion,—answerable, it may be, to the Houses whom he seeks to lead, either personally or through a cabinet, as well as to the people for whom they speak." Some later examples of Wilson's efforts to adapt the parliamentary system to American practice included his plan to resign immediately if he had lost the presidential election of 1916, to allow his Republican opponent, CHARLES EVANS HUGHES, to assume the presidency as soon as possible; his ill-fated appeal for the election of a Democratic Congress in 1918; and his attempt to make the election of 1920 a "great and solemn referendum" on the issue of American membership in the LEAGUE OF NATIONS.

But throughout his life Wilson was an instrumentalist, not an ideologue, and to him it mattered only that there be leadership that could educate the public and galvanize opinion behind reforms that would make for progressive development. Wilson's views on the possibility of effective national leadership under an unamended Constitution changed radically, however, during the early 1900s in response to two of the most important developments of the time. One was the United States' entry onto the stage of world politics, a development that Wilson knew would have profound impact on the location of authority and leadership in the federal government. The second development that caused Wilson to view the possibilities of presidential leadership in a new light was the revivification of the presidency of Theodore Roosevelt (1901–1909). Roosevelt demonstrated the potential powers of the CHIEF EXECUTIVE by asserting a national leadership through education of public opinion and by bludgeoning Congress into enacting significant reform legislation [see BULLY PULPIT]. In his last scholarly lectures, published as *Constitutional Government in the United States* in 1908, Wilson consequently saw the President

as being potentially the single powerful party leader and national spokesman.

Events between 1907 and 1913, notably Roosevelt's continued success and President William Howard Taft's failure as a popular leader, only reinforced Wilson's new view of the presidency. The President, he wrote in early 1913,

> is expected by the nation to be the leader of his party as well as the chief executive officer of the government, and the country will take no excuses from him. He must play the part and play it successfully, or lose the country's confidence. He must be prime minister, as much concerned with the guidance of legislation as with the just and orderly execution of law; and he is the spokesman of the nation in everything, even the most momentous and most delicate dealings of the government with foreign nations.

As President-elect, Wilson let it be clearly understood that an activist would soon occupy the White House.

Wilsonian Style and Practice. An activist was exactly the kind of President that Wilson intended to be after his victory in the election of 5 November 1912 over the Republican incumbent, Taft, the Republican insurgent (or Progressive), Theodore Roosevelt, and the Socialist, EUGENE V. DEBS [see ELECTION, PRESIDENTIAL, 1912]. In fact, Wilson entered the White House not only equipped with theory but also experienced in leadership skills he had gained as president of Princeton University from 1902 to 1910 and governor of New Jersey from 1911 to 1913. During this decade of apprenticeship, he had worked out and applied all the methods of leadership that he would use so successfully from 1913 to 1919.

The extraordinary circumstances prevailing during these years greatly facilitated Wilson's style and practice of presidential leadership. The reform impulses and movements that had shattered party alignments in the 1890s and disrupted the REPUBLICAN PARTY from 1910 to 1912 were pulsating at an even faster tempo during Wilson's first presidential term. Then came war from 1917 to 1918, during which he still had a Democratic Congress behind him and a large measure of Republican support. In addition, there was no congressional machine headed by the Speaker to thwart him, as there had been during the Roosevelt presidency. In fact, a large number of the Democratic members of the House of Representatives during Wilson's first term were newcomers, putty in their leader's hands, while a probable majority of Senators, Democratic and Republican, were advanced progressives, as much in touch with reform sentiment as Wilson himself. Circumstances therefore made it comparatively easy for Wilson to be the spokesman and guide of a cooperative Congress, at least until 1919.

Wilson's contributions to this, the parliamentary

style, were very great. His first move, an innovation, was to hold regularly scheduled PRESS CONFERENCES with the Washington press corps. Although he said that he wanted reporters to interpret PUBLIC OPINION to him, he, like other Presidents after him, really wanted to control the flow of information from Washington to the country and to use it to shape public opinion. He usually succeeded. He prepared well for the press conferences, bantered with the newsmen, and was as open and frank with them as circumstances would permit.

Wilson also sought to educate the public by speeches, state papers, and public letters. As an articulator of national ideals, he was rivaled in the use of noble language only by Jefferson, Abraham Lincoln, and Franklin D. Roosevelt. Wilson was a sensitive poet able to translate American ideals into words so lofty that he helped to change the course of history, particularly during WORLD WAR I.

Wilson made his most significant contribution to the parliamentary presidency in the methods he used to maintain firm control over his party members in Congress. He began soon after his inauguration. On 9 March 1913, the White House announced that the new President would help to frame important legislation; ten days later it said that he would confer frequently with congressional leaders in the President's room in the White House, which he did. (He was the only President to use this room frequently.) But Wilson's most spectacular assertion of personal leadership came on 8 April 1913, when he delivered his message on tariff reform in person. Not since John Adams had a President delivered a message to Congress in other than written form. Before the United States entered the war and Wilson had to rely on a bipartisan coalition for support, he also used the Democratic caucus in the House of Representatives very effectively to discipline and control Democrats, and presidential intervention among Democratic Senators was usually successful.

In dealing personally with congressional Democrats, whether individually or in committees, Wilson never once asked anyone to do something as a personal favor. He always took the high ground of national need and party honor and responsibility. On several critical occasions, he compromised important points to gain larger goals and won his objectives by leading instead of by driving. Even so, Wilson was always the master in the showdown, determined and able to bend Democrats in Congress to his will. As one reporter wrote: "The Democratic party revolves round him. He is the center of it; the biggest Democratic in the country—the leader and the chief."

The important fact is that Wilson substantially trans-

formed the presidency, or, as George Will has put it, "redefined" the presidency. When Franklin Roosevelt later recovered the full powers of national and party leadership for that office, he was only following the example of the President under whom he had served for nearly eight years as Assistant Secretary of the Navy.

The Wilson Administration. Wilson's Cabinet was well representative of both the geographical distribution of his party across the country and its various factions. Wilson usually worked harmoniously with his departmental heads, gave them almost total freedom of initiation and action, and rarely overruled them. Secretary of State William Jennings Bryan and Secretary of War Lindley M. Garrison resigned on points of principle—Bryan because he thought Wilson's second *Lusitania* note carried the risk of war with Germany, Garrison because he could not accept the President's compromise with House Democrats on the terms of the Military Reorganization bill of 1916. Wilson was very ill when he dismissed Bryan's successor, Robert Lansing. Cabinet meetings, which usually took place once a week, were informal affairs, where Wilson sought the counsel of his advisers.

The Wilson Cabinet was one of the strongest in the history of the presidency. The members were all activists who carried out initiatives that were as important as the legislative policies of the Wilson presidency. Wilson, however, insisted on being his own Secretary of State.

One kind of initiative by Cabinet members raised a public furor and remains a stain upon the record of the Wilson administration. Wilson permitted the acceleration of racial segregation in the Post Office and its institution in one bureau of the Treasury Department. But Wilson quietly killed bills in Congress to institute segregation on street cars in Washington and to prohibit interracial marriages. He also appointed more African Americans to federal positions than any President before him.

The New Freedom. During the presidential campaign of 1912, Wilson advocated a program that he called the NEW FREEDOM. It envisaged unleashing the economic energies of the American people, particularly small businessmen.

Tariff reform. The first item on his reform agenda when Wilson came to the White House in 1913 was inevitably tariff reform, for the Republican PAYNE-ALDRICH TARIFF ACT of 1909 stood as the single most glaring symbol of the power of special-interest groups over legislative policy since the TARIFF OF ABOMINATIONS of 1828. On 3 May 1913, the House of Representatives speedily passed a measure, drawn up by Oscar W.

Underwood of Alabama, chairman of the Ways and Means Committee, that greatly expanded the free list (including sugar and wool, at Wilson's insistence), reduced the Payne-Aldrich rates on other imports from 40 to 29 percent, and imposed a small income tax, the first under the Sixteenth Amendment, which had just been ratified. Wilson signed what is known as the UNDERWOOD TARIFF ACT on 3 October 1913.

Much more complex and difficult than tariff reform was the second item on the New Freedom agenda—restructuring the banking and currency systems so as to ensure a money supply adequate for the needs of a growing economy and a workable reserve system, to replace the then currency, which was based on the bonded indebtedness of the United States, and a rudimentary reserve system that did not work in times of financial panic. Wilson wanted a number of regional reserve banks owned and controlled by member banks, with a capstone provided by a Federal Reserve Board, to control the money supply and interest rates and perform all the functions of a central bank. The Federal Reserve banks would issue a new currency, Federal Reserve notes, based on both gold and commercial paper so that the money supply could expand or contract according to need.

Nothing is so important in a capitalist economy as money and banking, and the completion of the Federal Reserve bill in 1913 by Carter Glass, chairman of the House Banking Committee, set off controversies that sorely tested Wilson's leadership. Radical spokesmen, led by Secretary of the Treasury William McAdoo, demanded a reserve system that would be an adjunct of the Treasury Department. Secretary of State Bryan and agrarians objected because the Glass bill gave minority membership on the Federal Reserve Board to private bankers, did not provide for short-term credits to farmers, and stipulated that Federal Reserve notes would be obligations of the Federal Reserve banks, not of the government. Wilson conceded all of Bryan's points, and the House approved a revised Glass bill on 18 September 1913. The Federal Reserve bill, probably the most important piece of economic legislation in the history of the United States, finally passed intact on 19 December. The act has been amended significantly only once, in 1935; the FEDERAL RESERVE SYSTEM is still the most important economic instrumentality of the United States.

Antitrust. The third and last cornerstone of the New Freedom program—antitrust legislation—proved to be also immensely difficult and complicated to achieve. Wilson originally thought that it would suffice merely to strengthen the SHERMAN ANTITRUST ACT of 1890. But his critics in the small-business community convinced him that it was impossible to define every conceivable restraint of trade in statutory form. Wilson then fell back upon a plan that Theodore Roosevelt had advocated during the presidential campaign of 1912—to create a federal trade commission to monitor business practices and issue cease and desist orders, which would take effect like court injunctions, to stop restraint of trade in its tracks. This was effectuated in the FEDERAL TRADE COMMISSION ACT of 1914. The CLAYTON ACT gave private parties the benefit of decisions in antitrust suits won by the government, imposed criminal penalties for violations of the antitrust laws, and gave labor unions some measure of relief from the application of the Sherman Act to activities that the courts since 1895 had said violated that statute.

Rounding out the New Freedom. Wilson and the Democrats had won control in Washington in 1912 mainly because of the split in the Republican Party between conservatives under President Taft and insurgents who nominated Roosevelt on the third-party Progressive ticket. The congressional election of 1914 showed that the PROGRESSIVE (BULL MOOSE) PARTY had already been relegated to the dustbin of history and that Wilson's only hope of reelection in 1916 lay in winning a goodly portion of former Progressives—and advanced progressives in general—to his side.

The pace of Wilsonian reform quickened as the two great parties prepared for the presidential campaign of 1916. Wilson pushed through to adoption a comprehensive program to aid farmers. He advocated and obtained approval of the Federal Tariff Commission, and he appointed the preeminent foe of Wall Street, Louis D. Brandeis of Boston, to the Supreme Court. Soon after the adjournment of the Democratic national convention in June 1916, which renominated him and Vice President THOMAS R. MARSHALL of Indiana, Wilson won approval of two pieces of advanced progressive legislation—the Child Labor and Model Federal Workmen's Compensation bills—which had been stalled in the Senate. Finally, in early September, in order to avert a nationwide railroad strike, he obtained passage of the Adamson Act, which imposed the eight-hour day on interstate railroads. He also approved a tax bill that drastically increased taxes on incomes and estates.

Foreign Affairs. Among all the statesmen of the modern era, Wilson stands as the preeminent champion of liberal humanitarian international ideals and practices. Such ideals sprang from his conviction that God had created the United States to serve mankind. Wilson detested IMPERIALISM and the very suggestion that the strong and ruthless had a right to exploit helpless people. Wilson also believed in the right of all clearly defined nationalities to self-determination and in the peaceful settlement of all international controversies. Secretary of State Bryan shared Wilson's views; together they determined to make a new beginning in colonial and foreign policies.

Self-determination and peace. Following Democratic doctrine since the Spanish-American War, Wilson was determined to give independence to the Philippines. After a struggle, he accepted a compromise measure, the Jones Act of 1916, which conferred dominion status and full internal self-government on Filipinos. In the second Jones Act (1917), Wilson again fulfilled his party's pledges by giving territorial status to Puerto Rico and conferring American citizenship and internal self-government on the inhabitants of that island. Wilson was the first decolonizer among the statesmen of the modern world.

Wilson and Bryan were determined to unite the Western Hemisphere by generous policies and bonds of international friendship. Their first step was to try to repair the moral damage done by Roosevelt's complicity in 1901 in the Panamanian "revolution," which tore the province of Panama from its mother country, Colombia. In the Treaty of Bogotá (1914), the United States not only awarded Colombia reparation of $25 million but also expressed "sincere regret" that anything should have happened to impair good relations between the two countries. Roosevelt's friends were able to block ratification of this treaty (the administration of Warren G. Harding put through an amended treaty in 1921).

Wilson's great personal goal was a pact to unite all the American republics in an alliance binding them to guarantee one another's territorial integrity and political independence and to settle all disputes among themselves by peaceful means. This, the most radical pan-American proposal by an American President before Franklin Roosevelt, failed because Chile, which had a boundary dispute with Peru that it would not submit to arbitration, would not accept it.

The Caribbean. When it came to the Caribbean, Wilson and Bryan were as much realists as idealists. The construction of the Panama Canal, the new lifeline of the nation, demanded that the United States dominate its approaches from the Caribbean. Since 1898 Germany had been trying to obtain a naval base in the area; that danger to American security became more acute after the outbreak of war in Europe in 1914.

There were four Caribbean danger spots from 1913 to 1916—Nicaragua, Haiti, the Dominican Republic, and the Danish West Indies (Virgin Islands). In Nicaragua, Bryan simply continued to support a corrupt and conservative pro-American regime. Haiti, where German interests were involved and which had one of the best harbors in the Caribbean, was so racked by revolution that it descended into chaos in 1915. Wilson saw no alternative but to occupy the island and establish peace through intervention of the U.S. Marines. This action also forestalled German intervention at a later date. Under a Dominican-American treaty of 1905, the United States collected the Dominican customs revenues, paid the foreign debt of the Dominican Republic, and was at least indirectly responsible for political stability in that small republic. When a cycle of revolution threatened to devastate the Dominican Republic in 1916, Wilson saw no other recourse than to impose peace by military occupation. As for the Danish West Indies, when rumors began to circulate that Denmark might sell them to Germany, Wilson moved quickly and bought the islands—which became the U.S. Virgin Islands—for the inflated price of $25 million in 1916.

Mexico: The acid test. Wilson fought his first battle against imperialism while dealing with the Mexican revolution. Wilson supported the Constitutionalists because he believed they were fighting to free their country from the grip of foreign imperialists and their Mexican surrogates, which in fact was true. Wilson's problem by the spring of 1914 was that Victoriano Huerta, the military dictator, was growing stronger, not weaker. Wilson sent marines and soldiers into Veracruz, Mexico's largest port, in 1914. Cut off from his customs revenues and beleaguered by the Constitutionalists, Huerta fled to Spain, and the Constitutionalists entered Mexico City.

At this moment of triumph, the Mexican revolution seemed about to devour itself. Francisco (Pancho) Villa had started a rebellion in the northern part of the country. After Villa murdered Americans, Wilson sent General John J. Pershing with a so-called punitive expedition to capture Villa. But the wily Villa drew Pershing deep into Mexico. Wilson agreed to the face-saving device of a joint high commission and called the punitive expedition back to the United States. He then recognized the constitutional government.

Throughout the long ordeal in Mexico, from 1913 to 1917, Wilson never ceased to believe that the Mexican revolution was "a revolution as profound as that which occurred in France." He never ceased to believe that the Mexican people had an inalienable right to self-determination. Without his support, the Constitutionalists probably could not have triumphed when they did.

The Ordeal of Neutrality. The outbreak of war in Europe and the Far East in the summer of 1914 raised challenges to Wilson's leadership in FOREIGN AFFAIRS such as no President since Jefferson and James Madison had faced. Wilson was usually his own Secretary of State, and in dealing with problems arising from relations with the belligerents, he took complete control, conferred personally with ambassadors, and wrote (or rewrote) all important correspondence with the warring governments. As it turned out, the fate of the world depended on his actions and policies.

Although he was emotionally an Anglophile, Wilson sternly subdued his personal feelings because he profoundly believed that NEUTRALITY was the right policy for the United States and the world. As he said many times, the United States could best serve mankind by standing as the hope of peace. In addition, he knew that the vast majority of Americans wanted to stay clear of the carnage in Europe so long as they could do so without loss of national honor.

With these thoughts in mind, Wilson appealed to his fellow countrymen to be "impartial in thought as well as in action" and put the United States in a position of strict neutrality under INTERNATIONAL LAW, which entitled the belligerents to buy whatever they pleased and borrow as much money as they could raise from private sources in the United States. International law also roughly defined three categories of exports of American merchants that could and could not be seized by belligerents: the free list of "innocent" goods (food, raw materials, items not susceptible to military use) that were exempt from capture; conditional contraband, which might or might not be susceptible to military use and might or might not be captured on the high seas (this question to be determined by a prize court); and absolute contraband, most specifically weapons of war, which could be captured by belligerent warships.

Since Great Britain controlled the seas, under international law Britain and its Entente allies had free access to private American supplies and credit. The British were also able to block the leader of the Central Powers, Germany, from access to American markets. Thus a booming trade between the United States and Britain, France, and Italy developed from 1914 to 1917—entirely the consequence of the operation of international law and British naval supremacy.

On the other hand, the Germans enjoyed great advantages as the superior military power in Europe. They overran Belgium and northern France and moved through Poland into Russia. Wilson accepted the fact of German military predominance. For example, he did not protest against the German invasion of Belgium, which was a gross violation of international law and brought Great Britain into the war. With the British navy in control of the seas and the Germany

army predominant on the continent, American neutrality seemed secure.

The decision of the German government in early 1915 to use an untried weapon, the submarine, against allied and, perhaps accidentally, American maritime commerce threatened to upset the nice balance of power favorable to the United States. When the Germans announced a submarine bogus (because it could not be effective) blockade in a broad war zone on 4 February 1915, Wilson replied that he would hold them to a "strict accountability" for the destruction of American ships and lives by submarine attack. Actually, before 1917 Germany always conceded the right of American ships to immunity from unwarned attack, and there would have been no serious German-American crisis had submarines confined themselves to allied merchant vessels. Crises occurred because the Germans, in the spring of 1915, began a campaign of terror against the unarmed allied passenger ships on which Americans had to travel.

The first great crisis occurred when a submarine, without warning, torpedoed the pride of the White Star passenger ship line, the *Lusitania*, on 7 May 1915, causing the death, among others, of 128 Americans. In the ensuing diplomatic controversy, Wilson took the high moral ground and appealed to the German government to abandon its campaign against unarmed passenger ships and merchantmen. The Germans replied by sinking another British liner, the *Arabic*, without warning on 19 August 1915, again with the loss of American lives. This time the President issued an ultimatum: he would break diplomatic relations with the German government if it did not cease to kill Americans on unarmed passenger ships. The German emperor, Wilhelm II, secretly issued orders to this effect to submarine commanders.

When a submarine torpedoed the *Sussex*, another unarmed ship, in 1916, with heavy loss of life, Wilson sent another ultimatum to Berlin: unless the Germans abandoned their ruthless submarine campaign at once, he would break diplomatic relations with them. Since they did not have enough submarines to justify the risk of war with the United States, the Germans returned the pledge that Wilson demanded. In the same note, they warned that they would feel free to revoke it if Wilson did not force the British to observe international law in their blockade practices.

Wilson had rallied the country and Congress behind a limited augmentation of the army and a significant expansion of the navy. He also pushed through Congress a comprehensive program that pleased farmers and social progressives. He was thus able to go to the nation in the presidential campaign of 1916 against his

Republican opponent, Charles Evans Hughes, on a platform of prosperity, progressivism, and peace. In what was a great personal triumph (for the country was still Republican), Wilson narrowly won reelection on 7 November 1916 [*see* ELECTION, PRESIDENTIAL, 1916].

Wilson's thoughts now turned again toward mediation. The war was increasing in ferocity. The British were becoming reckless in their economic warfare against Germany. The Germans were still honoring the *Sussex* pledge, but Wilson knew that they would revoke it if they could win by doing so. What Wilson feared most was that the United States might be sucked willy-nilly into the war's vortex, knowing neither why it fought nor what the outcome might be. Thus on 18 December 1916, Wilson appealed to the belligerents to disclose the terms on which they would end the bloody struggle. He thought that the Allies would have to reply forthrightly, so dependent were they on American supplies and credit for continuation of their war effort. The President had no such power over Germany. He could offer and did offer, however, the Germans his cooperation in a drive for a status quo ante bellum peace and a postwar league of nations to guarantee the settlement. Wilson laid his cards before the world in a speech to the Senate on 22 January 1917. The United States, he said, was prepared to work for a "peace without victory," one without annexations and indemnities, above all, one based upon a league of nations to preserve the peace.

Of course, neither side wanted a peace without victory after such an enormous loss of material resources and the lives of so many young men. But the Allies were not prepared to defy Wilson, while the Germans were. By 1917 they had enough submarines to enable naval authorities to guarantee that an all-out submarine campaign against all shipping—belligerent and neutral—would bring Britain to her knees within six months and that it did not matter whether the United States entered the war. On 31 January, the German government announced that the following day it would begin such a ruthless campaign against all maritime commerce.

Wilson broke diplomatic relations with Germany on 3 February, but he continued to hope that submarines would spare American ships. Then, in late February, incontrovertible evidence came from the American ambassador in London that the German government had instructed its minister in Mexico City, in the event the United States entered the war against Germany, to offer an alliance by which Mexico would go to war against the United States and would receive in return "the lost territory in Texas, New Mexico, and Arizona." Publication of this, the so-called Zimmermann telegram, caused the first significant outcry for war in the United States. But Wilson still held back and resorted only to putting naval gun crews on merchant ships. When submarines sank a large British liner without warning on 26 February and three American merchant ships, one without warning, on 19 March, however, Wilson concluded that belligerency was the only instrumentality to defend and vindicate the dignity, sovereignty, and rights of the United States and its citizens. Therefore, reluctantly but eloquently, on 2 April he asked Congress for a declaration of war against Germany. Congress complied with overwhelming majorities on 6 April 1917. The long ordeal of neutrality was over.

Commander in Chief and Peacemaker. With only recent British experience to guide him, Wilson led his administration, Congress, and the entire American people in one of the speediest and most successful mobilizations for war in history. As a student of American history, Wilson was keenly aware of the wartime problems that had confronted previous administrations, particularly Lincoln's. He sought to avoid, or at least to minimize, such problems during the war against Germany. One result of this, as well as of his personal style of leadership, was that Wilson played a direct and decisive role in all major decisions relating to the war effort. Of course the President could not do everything himself. During the first year of belligerency, he worked through his Cabinet and the heads of the war agencies. But this machinery proved inadequate once domestic mobilization began to move into high gear. Thus he called into being the so-called war cabinet, or council, an unofficial body that met with him regularly on Wednesdays, beginning 20 March 1918.

Running the war. At Wilson's urging, a reluctant Congress approved a selective service bill on 18 May 1917, and the War Department and civilian selective service boards across the country set about raising an army of three million men. Congress gave Wilson full power over the production, distribution, and prices of food and fuel supplies in the Lever Act of 10 August 1917. Food and fuel administrations mobilized and stimulated production to such an efficient degree that there was never a shortage of food for the American people, the army, and the Allies, and no shortage of fuel except for a few weeks in the winter of 1917–1918. The War Industries Board maintained a steady supply of raw materials to war industries by a system of priorities. Substantial labor peace was maintained by the DEPARTMENT OF LABOR and in 1918 through the National War Labor Board. Wilson launched massive aircraft and shipbuilding programs at the outset of belligerency, but both encountered difficulties and took until the autumn of 1918 to get into high gear. Wilson took control of the railroads in December; Secretary of the Treasury McAdoo headed the United States Railroad Administration. To rally public support behind the war effort, Wilson established the Committee on Public Information (CPI), which carried on the most gigantic propaganda campaign in American history.

Finally, to stamp out opposition to the war, Congress, at Wilson's request, adopted the Espionage Act of 15 June 1917. It provided prison terms and/or fines for persons who committed sabotage, obstructed recruiting and the draft, opposed the sale of war bonds, and in other ways opposed the war effort. Congress added an amendment known as the Sedition Act, in the spring of 1918. It extended the power of the government over seditious speech. Other legislation empowered the Postmaster General to deny second-class mailing privileges to publications that he deemed seditious. Finally, Attorney General Thomas Gregory established a vast extralegal network, the American Protective League, to assist federal agents in maintaining internal security.

Nations involved in modern total wars have never been tolerant of dissent, and the United States was no exception in 1917–1918. Actually, the number of persons indicted under the Espionage and Sedition acts was small—2,168 altogether, and of those only 1,055 were convicted, which shows that a modicum of due process was observed in federal courts. Moreover, in early 1918 Wilson beat back a strong movement in Congress to establish military courts to try and execute opponents of the war. But the combined effect of the CPI's propaganda and the government's repression of dissent was to encourage a public hysteria that reached alarming proportions. German Americans were the chief victims.

Wilson was also COMMANDER IN CHIEF of the armed forces in fact as well as in name. He left tactics and strategy to the military, but, through daily meetings with Secretary of War Newton D. Baker and members of the general staff as necessary, the President maintained personal control of the military establishment. Only once did he disagree with his commander in France, General John J. Pershing. During discussions concerning an armistice, Pershing pressed strenuously to refuse an armistice and to march instead into Germany. Wilson overruled him. He was equally watchful over the navy and gave full support to the Navy Department's insistence on adopting the convoy system and constructing a line of mines from Norway to Scotland to bottle up German submarines.

In his management of diplomacy with the Allies, in enunciating American war aims, and in rallying his own and allied peoples to the defense of freedom and the rights of small nations, Wilson worked almost alone. He first made it clear that the United States was fighting as an associate and not a member of the Entente allies, unembarrassed by any secret agreements they might have made. Thus when the Bolsheviks under V. I. Lenin seized power in Russia in November 1917 and called for a general peace of no indemnities and no annexations, Wilson replied with his FOURTEEN POINTS address of 8 January 1918—a comprehensive statement of liberal war aims—and with his own effort to achieve a negotiated settlement. It failed only because the Germans answered him with a final drive on the western front. Its failure, combined with the great augmentation of American troops in France, enabled the American and allied armies to press to the German frontier and caused the Berlin government to sue for peace in October 1918. Since the Germans appealed to him personally, Wilson was the exclusive manager of the first stage of the negotiations that ended in the armistice of 11 November 1918.

The concept of parliamentary responsibility still strong in his mind, Wilson in October 1918 appealed for the election of a Democratic Congress in the November elections. For various reasons, most of them domestic, the voters returned a House and Senate that were Republican. Both Wilson, who by now believed that achievement of a good peace settlement depended largely on himself, did not resign, as he had arranged to do if Hughes had won in 1916. On the contrary, Wilson appointed himself as head of the commission to go to the peace conference that met in Paris in January 1919.

Making peace. By all accounts, Wilson was the only disinterested leader at that conference. He wanted nothing for the United States except a just peace that would endure and a world organization that could maintain peace in the future. Wilson fought as hard as any person could to achieve these objectives. But since he had only one voice and vote in the councils at Paris, his only alternative to yielding or to compromise when the British and French opposed him was to leave Paris and make a separate peace with Germany. But, as Wilson knew, the cure in that case would be worse than the disease, for withdrawal would wreck his plans for a world organization and result in a repressive settlement imposed by the French on Germany. Even so, Wilson was able to win most of his Fourteen Points. Belgium, brutally overrun and occupied by Germany, was restored. The western part of Germany was not dismembered, as the French had wanted, though Alsace-Lorraine was restored to France. An independent Poland with access to the sea came back into the family of nations, and the claims of central European peoples to self-determination were satisfied. Wilson's most important achievement at Paris was the creation of the League of Nations, whose constitution, or covenant, was included in the TREATY OF VERSAILLES, signed on 28 June 1919 by representatives of the United States, the Allies, and Germany.

In retrospect, Wilson, from his mediation effort of 1916 and 1917 through the Paris peace conference, thrust American influence and power to the front stage of European affairs for the first time. He was the President who effectually ended American isolation.

The Treaty Fight and Collapse of Wilson's Presidency. Wilson had suffered from malignant hypertension, carotid artery disease, and small strokes since at least the 1890s. The White House physician's imposed regime of a low-fat diet and regular exercise and recreation brought considerable remission from 1913 to 1917. But the stress and strain of the war and the peace conference revived his severe hypertension. Wilson was a sick man when he returned to the United States on 8 July 1919. What was undoubtedly another small stroke (he had suffered one in Paris in April) on 19 July greatly worsened his physical and mental condition. The recurrence of his old medical problems could not have come at a more portentous time, for Wilson now faced the formidable challenge of winning the Senate's consent to the ratification of the Versailles treaty.

When Wilson presented the treaty to the Senate on 10 July, a large majority of Americans probably favored its ratification, including membership in the League of Nations. There was no opposition to the treaty's military, economic, and territorial terms, but there was a strong undercurrent of opposition to membership in the League, because it would mean entanglement in world affairs. A minority of Republicans in the Senate, led by Henry Cabot Lodge, chairman of the Foreign Relations Committee, wanted ratification only with strong reservations to protect American sovereignty, the MONROE DOCTRINE, and congressional control of the WAR POWER. The majority of Republican Senators favored ratification with only a few (so-called) mild reservations. Almost all Democratic Senators favored ratification without reservations.

Instead of rallying moderate Republican reservationists and Democrats into an unbeatable phalanx, Wilson decided, against the advice of his physician, to go on a month-long speaking tour of the Midwest and West. The stress and strain of travel and speechmaking was too much for his frail constitution. He collapsed in the early morning of 26 September 1919 on the train in Colorado, his tour unfinished. Back in Washington, he suffered a massive stroke on 2 October that paralyzed his left side and that effectually left him unable to carry on the duties of the presidency in more than a minimal way for the balance of his term. The stroke also adversely affected Wilson emotionally and mentally and destroyed his reservoir of acumen and judgment.

It was certainly the longest if not the worst crisis of the presidency, at least before the WATERGATE AFFAIR. The Cabinet, in conjunction with Wilson's chief of staff, Joseph P. Tumulty, carried on the business of government almost entirely by themselves from 2 October 1919, to about 1 February 1920. (Contrary to myth, the President's wife, EDITH WILSON, played no part in running the government.) The one exception was foreign policy. By this time, Wilson had a paranoid suspicion of Secretary of State Lansing, whom he thought was disloyal. Wilson simply refused to allow Lansing to do anything. Experiencing some recovery in early February 1920, Wilson dismissed Lansing and appointed the pliant Bainbridge Colby in his stead.

Against this backdrop of PRESIDENTIAL DISABILITY, the struggle in the Senate over the Versailles treaty was played out. By the time that the treaty first came up for a vote on 19 November 1919, the Republicans had united on a platform of ratification with fourteen reservations, none of which was important except the one that reserved for Congress the right to determine when American forces should be used to support the peacekeeping efforts of the League of Nations. In the Senate's first vote on the treaty, Democrats, at Wilson's command, defeated ratification-with-reservations, while Republicans defeated ratification-without-reservations. A healthy Wilson would probably have accepted the Republican reservations or at least have sought a compromise. But the sick Wilson only grew more stubborn and rejected any compromise when the treaty came up for a second vote on 19 March 1920. It went down to defeat. Wilson actually had the fantasy that he would run for a third term on a pro-League platform and would win.

The years 1919 and 1921 were not barren of legislative accomplishments. The Army Reorganization Act, the Transportation Act (which returned the railroads to private ownership under strict federal control), the Water Power Act, and the General Leasing Act, all of 1920, were milestone pieces of legislation, but Wilson had very little to do with them directly. He left the presidency on 4 March 1921, after it seemed that the voters had repudiated him and all he stood for in the Harding landslide of the preceding November.

But historians, taking a longer view, know better. They have usually ranked Wilson high on the PRESIDENTIAL GREATNESS scale because of his contributions to the maturation of the presidential office, his achievements in domestic reform, his humanitarianism and love of peace, his valor and decency in war, and his efforts to win a lasting peace for the world. Historians remember, also, that the new political economy that Wilson instituted from 1913 through 1916 still stands in bedrock fashion, and that Wilson laid down an agenda in FOREIGN AFFAIRS that the United States would follow during WORLD WAR II and afterward.

BIBLIOGRAPHY

Ambrosius, Lloyd E. *Woodrow Wilson and the American Diplomatic Tradition: The Treaty Fight in Perspective.* 1987.

Clements, Kendrick A. *The Presidency of Woodrow Wilson.* 1992.

Cooper, John Milton, Jr. *The Warrior and the Priest: Woodrow Wilson and Theodore Roosevelt.* 1983.

Heckscher, August. *Woodrow Wilson: A Biography.* 1991.

Levin, N. Gordon, Jr. *Woodrow Wilson and World Politics: America's Response to War and Revolution.* 1968.

Link, Arthur S., et al., eds. *The Papers of Woodrow Wilson.* 69 vols. 1966–1993.

Link, Arthur S., ed. *Woodrow Wilson: Revolution, War and Peace.* 1979.

Link, Arthur S., and John Whiteclay Chambers II. "Woodrow Wilson as Commander in Chief." In *The United States Military under the Constitution of the United States, 1789–1989.* Edited by Richard H. Kohn. 1991.

Thorsen, Niels A. *The Political Thought of Woodrow Wilson, 1875–1910.* 1988.

Weinstein, Edwin A. *Woodrow Wilson: A Medical and Psychological Biography.* 1981.

ARTHUR S. LINK

WILSON-GORMAN TARIFF ACT (1894).

Grover Cleveland construed the election of 1892, in which Democrats achieved control of the presidency and of Congress for the first time since 1859, as a mandate for tariff reform. Nevertheless, prospects for tariff reform were uncertain. Democrats were split between those advocating revenue-only tariffs and others, including Cleveland, who favored only moderate revisions to the protective system.

Cleveland worked closely with William Wilson, who chaired the House Ways and Means Committee, to fashion the tariff bill. The committee bill added numerous raw materials to the free list (including coal, iron ore, wool, lumber, and copper) and modestly reduced duty levels. To cure budget deficits that had developed under the McKINLEY TARIFF ACT of 1890,

the committee also sought to reimpose duties on sugar and to tax corporate income. The full House then amended the committee bill, voting to remove the duties on sugar and to tax both corporate and individual incomes.

Democrats controlled the Senate by a narrow majority. As the Senate considered the tariff bill, certain Senate Democrats, including Arthur Gorman of Maryland, insisted on rate modifications favoring their home states' products. The resulting compromise bill incorporated more than six hundred amendments to the Wilson bill, increasing many duties and removing such key items as sugar, coal, and iron ore from the free list. Nevertheless, Cleveland encouraged the Senate to approve its version, hoping that momentum for tariff reform could be restored in the House-Senate conference committee.

In conference, however, Cleveland's last vestige of influence over the Senate evaporated. In an effort to break through the apparent deadlock, Cleveland denounced those Senate Democrats who had insisted on favoring their home states' products. This effort to influence the Senate backfired, as Senate Democrats refused to consider any amendments to the Senate bill, and the House capitulated. Although the bill mildly decreased tariff duties, Cleveland perceived it as a failure. He briefly considered a veto but allowed the measure to become law without his signature.

BIBLIOGRAPHY

Nevins, Allan. *Grover Cleveland: A Study in Courage.* 1932.

Stanwood, Edward. *American Tariff Controversies in the Nineteenth Century.* Vol. 2. Repr. 1967.

Welch, Richard E., Jr. *The Presidencies of Grover Cleveland.* 1988.

RALPH MITZENMACHER

WIRETAPPING. See ELECTRONIC SURVEILLANCE.

WIRT, WILLIAM (1772–1834), lawyer, author, Attorney General.

When appointed Attorney General by President James Monroe in October 1817, William Wirt of Virginia was already well known. In 1800 he had assisted in the defense of James Thomas Callendar in his trial under the ALIEN AND SEDITION ACTS; in 1807 he had taken part in the prosecution of AARON BURR for treason. He was the author of the popular *Letters of a British Spy*, and, more recently, *Sketches of the Life and Character of Patrick Henry.*

It was as Attorney General, however, that Wirt left his mark on American law and politics. He is rightly considered the first great Attorney General. He served for twelve years, from 1817 to 1829, longer than any person before or since. He instituted the practice of reporting and compiling the *Opinions of the Attorney General.*

Wirt argued a number of important cases while Attorney General, both for the United States government and (consistent with the practice of the day) as a private attorney. He argued unsuccessfully on behalf of the state of New Hampshire (and against DANIEL WEBSTER) in the famous contract-clause case of *Dartmouth College v. Woodward* (1819). He was more successful with Webster on his side, arguing on behalf of the national government's interests in *McCulloch v. Maryland* (1819) and *Gibbons v. Ogden* (1824). He was also on the winning side in *Brown v. Maryland* (1827), an important commerce case that established the "original package" doctrine.

Wirt, who had been retained in office by John Quincy Adams, left office upon the election of Andrew Jackson and was later retained as counsel by the Cherokee Indians in their dispute with the state of Georgia. A committed opponent of Jackson, Wirt was nominated for President by the ANTI-MASONIC PARTY in 1832, carrying only Vermont.

BIBLIOGRAPHY

Robert, Joseph C. "William Wirt, Virginian." *The Virginia Magazine of History and Biography* 80 (1972): 387–441.

WILLIAM LASSER

WITNESSES, PRESIDENTS AND FORMER PRESIDENTS AS. Gerald R. Ford made history on 17 October 1974, when he became the first incumbent President to testify formally before a congressional committee. Only the oft-told, but fictitious accounts of President Abraham Lincoln defending his wife's good name on Capitol Hill were offered as precedents. His appearance, as Ford recognized, was "an unusual historic moment—one that [had] no firm precedent in the whole history of presidential relations with congress." He was not there, however, "to make history, but to report on history." In actuality, he did both.

Ford's testimony before the House Judiciary Subcommittee on Criminal Justice was in response to questions posed in two resolutions of inquiry regarding the pardon of his predecessor, Richard M. Nixon. His motivation for issuing the pardon, Ford explained, was to change the "national focus" and shift attention "from the pursuit of a fallen President to the pursuit of the urgent needs of a rising nation." Most observers have concluded that Ford's historic gesture did little to change the various preconceived notions of why he had issued the pardon.

Informal Testimony. Although Gerald Ford's testimony was unique, a number of other Presidents have afforded Congress the opportunity to question them under less formal circumstances. Several of these instances are particularly noteworthy. Early in his first term, President George Washington and Secretary of War Henry Knox visited the Senate chamber on Saturday, 22 August 1789, to gain the advice and consent of the Senators on a treaty involving the Creek INDIANS. Since few of the Senators were familiar with the subject, a decision was made to defer a decision until the following Monday. Ultimately, the Senate approved the Creek Indian Treaty, but the experience convinced Washington that formal, in-person consultations with Congress were ill-advised. While technically Washington was not a witness, his gesture established possible model for future CHIEF EXECUTIVES. Not for 185 years would another incumbent President return to the halls of Congress as a potential witness.

At least two enduring stories, however, have placed Abraham Lincoln before congressional inquisitors on Capitol Hill. The initial account of Lincoln's alleged session with the Joint Committee on the Conduct of the War to discuss rumors of his wife leaking important military secrets to the Confederacy first appeared in a 1905 newspaper. Subsequently, it was repeated by several Lincoln biographers who further embellished the story. Despite a lack of primary documentation, it has endured, at least in part, because of MARY TODD LINCOLN's historic image as an erratic woman, and its usefulness as a standard for Presidential accountability.

As equally intriguing, but apocryphal story places Lincoln before the House Judiciary Committee in February 1862 to dispel rumors that his wife had given presidential documents to an informant of the *New York Herald.* Lincoln apparently visited the Capitol that day, but met only informally with the Republican members of the committee. This was neither the first nor would it be the last time Lincoln used an informal session with a congressional committee to make a point. On at least eight different occasions during the CIVIL WAR, he discussed military matters at the White House with various members of the Joint Committee on the Conduct of the War.

Woodrow Wilson's challenge of 26 February 1919 was quite different when he hosted a White House dinner for the Senate Foreign Relations Committee and the House Foreign Affairs Committee. Less than two weeks earlier, he had presented the completed draft of the LEAGUE OF NATIONS Covenant to the Paris Peace Conference and now had to convince the Senate of its merits. The following morning, the *New York*

Times reported that Wilson had "submitted himself to the very widest range of questions and was remarkably frank in his replies." Although congressional reaction to the session was not necessarily one of unanimous approval, those who had attended were "impressed with the idea that the President did not impose secrecy upon them, but that, rather, he was disposed to have the whole country know his ideas, as conveyed to them."

Subsequently, Wilson met with the Senate Foreign Relations Committee to discuss the TREATY OF VERSAILLES in a three-hour White House conference on 19 August that shattered "all tradition and defying all precedent," according to the *Washington Post*. Wilson "submitted himself to public cross-examination by the committee, in hope of smoothing the way of the League of Nations covenant and the treaty with Germany through the Senate."

Only President Washington's Senate appearance to explain the Creek Indian Treaty, Washington's *Evening Star* dramatically exclaimed, equaled Wilson's disclosure of the "inside details of the peace conference, [and] how the league of nations covenant was drawn." It was a striking "contrast to the time-honored procedure of secrecy." The *New York Tribune* viewed the occasion as "probably the most searching inquiry ever directed, for a public record, at any President of the United States, or for that matter any other head of a great power."

Former Presidents. Far less dramatic, were the congressional testimonies former Chief Executives John Tyler, Theodore Roosevelt, Gerald R. Ford, and Jimmy Carter delivered regarding their respective presidencies. Early in 1846, a year after he had left the White House, Tyler became the first and only incumbent or former Chief Executive to receive a congressional subpoena. That May, he appeared before two House select committees investigating DANIEL WEBSTER's alleged "fraudulent misapplication and personal use of public funds" while Secretary of State. Tyler's testimony was probably the decisive factor in disproving the charges against Webster.

A special House investigation of U.S. Steel's 1907 acquisition of the Tennessee Coal and Iron Company prompted former President Theodore Roosevelt's initial Capitol Hill appearance. Despite Roosevelt's 5 August 1911 testimony that his action in approving the transaction was not a violation of antitrust laws, the administration of William Howard Taft began antitrust proceedings against U.S. Steel two months later. Although the committee was highly critical of Roosevelt's approval of the purchase, the Supreme Court ruled in 1920 that the transaction was not in violation of the Sherman Antitrust Act (*United States v. United States Steel Corporation*, 1920).

On 4 October 1912, Roosevelt returned to the witness table to refute charges that he had approved questionable corporate fund-raising activities during his 1904 presidential campaign. Roosevelt told a Senate Privileges and Elections Subcommittee that he "had asked no man to contribute to the campaign fund," and had made "no promises" in connection with any contribution. A formal report on Roosevelt's 1904 campaign role was never published.

Hearings held by a subcommittee of the Senate Foreign Relations Committee, on a possible revision of the WAR POWERS RESOLUTION (1973), brought former President Gerald Ford to Washington in September 1988. Ford responded by expressing his long-held belief that the resolution "violated the SEPARATION OF POWERS between the executive and legislative branches," and "was impractical."

Subsequently, Ford and former President Jimmy Carter participated in executive session briefings during a 1989–1990 review of the resolution by a subcommittee of the House Armed Services Committee. Ford reiterated his criticism of the resolution as an unconstitutional "encroachment on the prerogatives of the President as COMMANDER-IN-CHIEF." As President, he had on at least six occasions gone through all of the reporting procedures, but "never conceded that the War Powers Act was applicable."

Jimmy Carter conversely told the subcommittee during a congressional hearing in Atlanta that he had "never contemplated initiating any military invasion or confrontation without close consultation with Congress." Only once during his "presidency was there an instance when the resolution seemed to apply. This was when the attempt was made to rescue the hostages in Iran. Afterwards, [he] immediately called in the House and Senate leadership and informed them of everything that had happened."

Still, Carter believed the resolution was "basically flawed" and felt the provision requiring Congress to take positive action within sixty days to continue any military action, "should be removed." No President wants "to face a debate with Congress, possible legal action, or a necessity to get the majority of votes in both houses in order to keep military forces in action."

Other twentieth-century congressional testimony by former Presidents, William Howard Taft (seventeen times), Herbert Hoover (nineteen), Harry S. Truman (seven), and Gerald Ford (two), focused on a broad range of matters unrelated to their presidencies.

Judicial Testimony. Participation by Presidents in judicial proceedings has been rare. Only five incumbent Chief Executives, and one former President, have made voluntary contributions, either written or oral to a court. The most celebrated case stemmed from former Vice President AARON BURR's alleged efforts to separate the western states from the Union.

Burr's 1807 request for documents held by Thomas Jefferson relating to the conspiracy resulted in Chief Justice John Marshall, sitting in circuit capacity as a trial judge, issuing the first judicial subpoena to an American President. On 17 June, Jefferson, in response, turned over a sizeable number of documents relating to the case, prepared written responses to questions asked by the court, and offered to submit a deposition to the Federal Circuit Court in Richmond. However, personally appearing before the court, Jefferson felt, might establish a precedent that would, in the future, expose him to being subpoenaed to appear at trials throughout the country.

Similarly, President James Monroe, in response to a subpoena issued by a navy court martial in 1818, declined to attend the Philadelphia proceedings because his official duties rendered it impracticable. He did respond to eleven interrogatories approved by the court. The defendant, Dr. William P. C. Barton, a naval surgeon, was charged with having solicited the removal of another surgeon in order to gain a position for himself at the Philadelphia naval hospital. In pursuit of the appointment, Barton allegedly approached a number of federal officials, including the President. Ironically, the court reached a verdict before Monroe's responses arrived in Philadelphia.

A judicial inquiry of a very different nature penetrated the White House in 1875 when Orville E. Babcock, President Ulysses S. Grant's confidential secretary, was implicated in a scheme to defraud the federal government of millions of dollars in whiskey taxes. Initially, the President told his Cabinet that he would go to Saint Louis to testify in behalf of his embattled secretary. After the Cabinet dissuaded him from testifying, Grant settled on a three-hour legal deposition, which was taken by the defendant's counsel in February 1876. Babcock was acquitted following President Grant's declaration that he had neither seen nor heard anything remotely connecting the defendant with the WHISKEY RING.

With far less fanfare, President Nixon, in a July 1974 letter to U.S. District Judge Gerhard A. Gesell, responded to six questions posed by defense attorneys for former White House aide, John D. Ehrlichman, who had been charged with conspiring to burglarize the office of Daniel Ellsberg's psychiatrist. Ellsberg, the prosecution contended, had become a target of the White House in 1971, after leaking the "Pentagon Papers" to the *New York Times*. Nixon emphasized that he had never authorized anyone in the White House to search the files of Ellsberg's psychiatrist.

Late in June 1975, ten months after his resignation as President, Nixon ended nearly two years of refusals to submit to questioning under oath about his role in the WATERGATE AFFAIR. During an extraordinary grand jury session at a Coast Guard station adjacent to his San Clemente home, the former President voluntarily testified for eleven hours before Watergate prosecutors and two Watergate grand jurors. By this time, however, most of the litigation surrounding Watergate was already over.

Twice in the 1970s, incumbent Presidents—Gerald R. Ford and Jimmy Carter—provided videotape testimony to the courts. Later in 1975, President Ford, in a small conference room in the Executive Office Building next to the White House, was questioned as a defense witness in the trial of Lynette Alice Fromme. The nineteen-minute videotape session was seen two weeks later by the Sacramento court considering the fate of Fromme, who had been charged with attempting to assassinate the President the previous September.

Ford's successor, President Jimmy Carter, delivered videotape testimony in April 1978 as a government witness in the trial of Edward Culver Kidd, a Georgia state senator, who had been indicted on charges of perjury and conspiracy to obstruct the enforcement of state gambling laws. Despite Carter's strong statements against Kidd, the jury, two days after listening to the President's videotaped testimony, acquitted Kidd.

Testifying under oath behind the locked and guarded doors at a U.S. district courthouse in Los Angeles, former President Ronald Reagan on 16–17 February 1990 responded to nearly eight hours of questioning in the trial of former national security adviser John M. Poindexter. In his videotaped disposition, which was released to the public on 22 February 1990, the former Chief Executive denied that he had ever instructed his subordinates to violate the law in the IRAN-CONTRA AFFAIR. Reagan had also been formally questioned about Iran-contra in early 1987 when he twice appeared before the TOWER COMMISSION.

BIBLIOGRAPHY

Neely, Mark E., Jr. "Abraham Lincoln Did NOT Defend His Wife before the Committee on the Conduct of the War." *Lincoln Lore* No. 1643 (January 1975): 1–4.

Stathis, Stephen W. "Executive Cooperation: Presidential Recognition of the Investigative Authority of Congress and the Courts." *The Journal of Law and Politics* 3 (Fall 1986): 183–294.

Stathis, Stephen W. "Former Presidents as Congressional Witnesses." *Presidential Studies Quarterly* 13 (Summer 1983): 458–481.

STEPHEN W. STATHIS

WOMEN'S RIGHTS. As early as 31 March 1776, ABIGAIL ADAMS wrote to her husband John, who later was to become the second President of the United States: "In the new Code of Laws . . . I desire you would Remember the Ladies, and be more generous and favourable to them than your ancestors. Do not put such unlimited power into the hands of the Husbands. Remember all men would be tyrants if they could." Adams's admonitions to her husband had little impact on the Articles of Confederation, which he helped draft, or on the subsequent United States Constitution. And, in spite of having such a staunchly feminist wife, as President, John Adams did little to further the status of women's rights in the United States.

Emancipation and Suffrage. Adams's son, John Quincy Adams, however, was one of the first elected officials to speak out publicly on behalf of women's rights. In 1834, the Congregational church vehemently criticized the activities of women who were speaking out against SLAVERY, and in 1835 a fierce debate arose in Congress over the propriety of women's actions including their efforts at collecting signatures for the thousands of antislavery petitions that flooded Congress. Congressman Adams led the debate in favor of the women's actions. Throughout his public life he advocated an expanded role for women, calling women's public participation in politics "a virtue of the highest order."

Public pronouncements like Adams's were encouraging to women and in 1848 two women active in the antislavery movement, Elizabeth Cady Stanton and Lucretia Mott, called a meeting in Seneca Falls, New York. At that meeting and one held a week later in Rochester, New York, attended by Susan B. Anthony, a series of resolutions and a Declaration of Sentiments were drafted calling for expanded rights for women in all walks of life. Both documents reflected women's dissatisfaction with certain moral codes, divorce, and criminal laws, and the limited opportunities for women to obtain an education, participate in the church, and to enter careers in medicine, law, and politics.

Work for women's rights all but came to a stop during the CIVIL WAR as women turned their energies to volunteer activities to help the war effort. In fact, many hoped that they would be rewarded for their actions by congressional or presidential support for a suffrage amendment. But, as they saw the Thirteenth, Fourteenth, and Fifteenth Amendments added to the Constitution and were told "Now is the Negro's hour," their hopes for immediate expanded rights on the national level were dashed. In fact, passage of the Fourteenth Amendment was opposed by Stanton and Anthony because, as proposed, it introduced the word *male* into the Constitution for the first time. Although Article II of the Constitution refers to the President as "he," the use of the word *male* to limit suffrage was infuriating to many as prior to that time voting qualifications had been left to the states. These women were concerned that the text of the proposed amendment would necessitate an additional amendment to enfranchise women. How right they were. Soon after passage of the Fourteenth Amendment, the Fifteenth Amendment was proposed to enfranchise black males previously ineligible to vote. Feverish efforts to have the word *sex* added to the amendment's list of "race, color, or previous condition of servitude" specifications were unsuccessful.

In 1890, the two leading women's rights groups that had been founded shortly after the Civil War, the National Woman Suffrage Association and the American Woman Suffrage Association, joined forces to become the National American Woman Suffrage Association (NAWSA). Few advances had been made in the cause and no President had yet taken up the cause of women's rights. Leaders in both groups concluded that their combined forces would better enable them to press for reforms.

Unlike earlier efforts for women's rights that had targeted improved conditions for women in all spheres of life, NAWSA devoted its activities exclusively to the cause of female suffrage. Still, most of its efforts were focused on obtaining the vote at the state and not the federal level. By 1915, however, these efforts as well as those of several other like-minded women's rights groups had but little success. In 1917, the most radical of the prosuffrage groups, the National Woman's Party (NWP), began to picket the White House to draw attention to President Woodrow Wilson's refusal to endorse a constitutional amendment to give women the right to vote. NWP members were arrested for obstructing the sidewalk in front of the House and were carted off to jail by exasperated police. Newspaper accounts about how some of the women were beaten and force fed shocked the nation. Capitalizing on this sympathy, NAWSA used the clout of its two million members to try to convince President Wilson to support a suffrage amendment, which he finally endorsed in a meeting with the chairman of the House Committee on Suffrage on 9 January 1918. The House adopted the amendment the next day.

In September when the amendment came before the Senate for debate, succumbing to pressure by NAWSA, President Wilson went to the Senate to appeal personally to that body to adopt the amendment. It was not until 4 June 1919, however, that the Senate finally approved the Nineteenth "Susan B. Anthony" Amendment, and, after three-fourths of the states approved it, it became part of the Constitution on 26 August 1920.

Legal Changes. Passage of the Nineteenth Amendment did little for the cause of women's rights in the short run. In fact, it was not until the 1960s that additional protracted efforts to obtain improved rights for women was to begin. And, like the first women's rights movement that occurred in the 1840s, many of the women active in this new cause had been active in the move for civil rights for blacks.

Women who had been active in the presidential campaign of John F. Kennedy, a Democrat, were angered by the successful candidate's failure to appoint women to high governmental positions. In an effort to appease his supporters, President Kennedy set up a President's Commission on the Status of Women (headed by former First Lady Eleanor Roosevelt) to investigate the "prejudice and outmoded customs [that] act as barriers to the full realization of women's basic rights" and to make recommendations in a wide variety of areas that affect women's lives. Its report, *American Women*, was issued in 1963 and was the first comprehensive investigation of the status of women's rights in the United States. Moderate in tone, the report concluded that women faced pervasive discrimination in all walks of life. In fact, the recommendations of the commission were not that much different than the Declaration of Resolves drafted by the women who attended the Seneca Falls Convention in 1848.

Around the same time the report was issued, three important legal changes occurred. In 1963, Congress passed the Equal Pay Act to outlaw unequal pay for equal work. The next year, at the urging of President Lyndon B. Johnson, Congress passed the sweeping Civil Rights Act of 1964 that barred (among its many provisions) discrimination in the workplace on account of sex. Three years later, President Johnson issued Executive Order (EO) 11375 as an amendment to an earlier order banning federal government and any federal contractors from discriminating on account of sex as well as other grounds.

Although President Kennedy was never considered a strong supporter of women's rights, his establishment of the commission had a profound impact on the course of women's rights in the United States. For the first time since ratification of the Nineteenth Amendment, women across the country were afforded a means of communication and an opportunity to air their grievances in a supportive environment when governors around the nation—mimicking the President—established state commissions on the status of women. Thus, shortly before the issuance of Executive Order 11375, the National Organization for Women (NOW) was formed by irate commission members when it appeared that little was being done to listen to the recommendations of the President's Commission on the Status of Women and that the Equal Employment Opportunity Commission (EEOC), the executive agency charged with implementing provisions of the 1964 Civil Rights Act, was not taking complaints of sex discrimination seriously. NOW's demand for immediate passage of an equal rights amendment (ERA) and subsequent call for the repeal of all restrictive ABORTION statutes attracted a considerable amount of press attention and a new women's rights movement was born as other women's rights groups were created and older women's groups reinvigorated.

Women's rights activists immediately began to pressure the federal government for better enforcement of existing statutes. They also pressured the EEOC and the Office of Federal Contract Compliance to draft strong sex-discrimination guidelines for federal contractors and to enforce them rigorously. Women's rights groups also began to turn to the courts seeking expanded rights under the Fifth and Fourteenth Amendments.

From 1972, when they won congressional passage of the proposed Equal Rights Amendment (ERA), women's-rights activists fought long and hard for ratification in the states. Although Presidents Richard M. Nixon and Gerald Ford supported the amendment (as did a majority of Americans according to public opinion polls) passage was stalled in the wake of the Supreme Court's decision in *Roe v. Wade* (1973), which granted the right to abortion. Anti-amendment forces led by Phyllis Schlafly, the founder of STOP ERA, were able to associate the ERA with the Supreme Court's abortion decision and, joined by the "pro-life" movement, were able to defeat the amendment in several key state legislatures.

Conflict and Criticism. Conflict over the potential ramifications of the ERA including its affect on the all-male draft and on family law and the whole issue of expanded rights for women came to a head in 1977 at a national conference on women that was held in Houston, Texas, as part of observances of the United Nations International Women's Year. President Jimmy Carter appointed Bella Abzug to chair the commission and replaced several conservative Republican members of the President's Commission on the Status of Women with more liberal Democrats, including Lynda Bird Robb, the daughter of former President Lyndon B. Johnson. Carter appointees were caught off guard by the number of attendees opposed to the goals of the Carter administration.

The decade of the 1970s was disappointing for advocates of women's rights. Hopes for ratification of the ERA were illusory and little had been done on the national level to expand women's rights. The courts, which had provided little relief in earlier rulings, to women, however, issued a number of landmark decisions under the political pressure of the ERA. Beginning in 1971 in *Reed v. Reed*, the Supreme Court ruled that the equal protection clause of the Fourteenth Amendment could be interpreted to ban some kinds of gender-based discrimination. Although women's rights activists had first tried to convince the Court to apply the Fourteenth Amendment to prevent gender-based discrimination as early as 1873, it took nearly a century for the Court to come around to that view. By 1976, in fact, the Supreme Court had carved out a new test for gender-based discrimination. According to the Court's decision in *Craig v. Boren* (1976) no state could discriminate against women in any of its laws or practices unless the state could should that "classifications by gender must serve important governmental objectives and must be substantially related to achievement of those objectives."

On the national level, the 1980s did not offer much hope for women's rights activists. Ronald Reagan—a candidate openly opposed to the ERA and many of the rights sought by women—won a landslide victory in 1980. The Reagan administration did little to advance the cause of women although Reagan did appoint the first women, Sandra Day O'Connor, to the Supreme Court in 1981. Few women were appointed to key positions in the administration and the Reagan administration usually appeared in court to argue against further rights for women. Both Presidents Reagan and George Bush appointed conservative justices to the Supreme Court. Women's rights activists were particularly enraged by President George Bush's appointment of Clarence Thomas to the Supreme Court. The politically conservative Thomas, the former chair of the EEOC during the Reagan administration, was not known as a strong supporter of women's rights. When a former employee at the EEOC, Professor Anita Hill of the University of Oklahoma, charged that Thomas had subjected her to several episodes of sexual harassment many years before, the whole topic of the Bush administration's insensitivity to women's rights was resurrected.

The Bush administration also drew fire from women's rights activists over the abortion issue. George Bush campaigned vigorously on anti-abortion platforms in 1988 and 1992, and, although he made family values a key theme on his 1992 reelection bid he vetoed legislation that would have provided unpaid family leave to employees with family emergencies, legislation strongly favored by women's rights groups.

In contrast, President Bill Clinton campaigned as a strong supporter of women's rights. He appointed the first female Attorney General, Janet Reno, and more women to his first Cabinet than any other President. He also strongly advocates legislation to enhance women's rights and quickly signed the Family and Medical Leave Act of 1993.

BIBLIOGRAPHY

Davis, Flora. *Moving the Mountain: The Women's Movement in America since 1960.* 1991.
Evans, Sara M. *Born for Liberty.* 1989.
Freeman, Jo. *The Politics of Women's Liberation.* 1985.
McGlen, Nancy E., and Karen O'Connor. *Women's Rights.* 1983.
Papachristou, Judith. *Women Together.* 1976.

KAREN O'CONNOR

WORKS PROGRESS ADMINISTRATION. Empowered by the Emergency Relief Appropriation Act, President Franklin D. Roosevelt established the Works Progress Administration (WPA) by EXECUTIVE ORDER in May 1935. Roosevelt's appointment of HARRY HOPKINS as agency head reflected his desire to achieve quick results by allocating WPA funds, initially $1.4 billion, primarilyt to wages for small-scale programs. Roosevelt hoped that rapid and widespread WPA employment would provide a quick infusion of spending power and help spur the economy. By its end in 1943 the WPA (renamed the Works Projects Administration in 1939) expanded more than $11 billion.

The WPA limited hours and wages to avoid competition with private enterprise. Thus by paying more than relief stipends but less than private employment, it provided an intermediate station between relief and regular employment. Wages usually were as much as $55 monthly.

Like other work-relief programs, the WPA represented Roosevelt's preference for work over assistance. He viewed these programs as temporary emergency acts designed to get the country rolling again. Additionally, Roosevelt recognized the potential political gains available in this arena; in fact, the WPA provided Roosevelt political strength in the 1936 campaign, partly by aiding development of Democratic organizations in the cities.

Abundant political opposition to the WPA existed, with conservatives not only objecting to its aid to the arts, but complaining that workers often were lazy, inefficient, and engaged in unnecessary projects. Business leaders complained of unfair competition, and organized labor contended that the WPA undercut prevailing wages. Nevertheless, millions of Americans, including blacks and women, benefited from opportunities available through the WPA. Furthermore, the country benefited by the WPA's construction of 350 airports, more than 500,000 miles of roads, 40,000 new buildings, 78,000 new bridges, 8,000 new parks, and much more.

BIBLIOGRAPHY

Biles, Roger. *A New Deal for the American People.* 1991.
Freidel, Frank. *Franklin D. Roosevelt: A Rendezvous withDestiny.* 1990.
Leuchtenburg, William E. *Franklin D. Roosevelt and the New Deal.* 1963.

NICHOLAS AHARON BOGGIONI

WORLD WAR I. The First World War (1914–1918) both enhanced and destroyed EXECUTIVE POWER. In Europe as well as the United States, the war dramatically changed the previous modes of leadership. In some countries civilians concentrated power in their hands, while in others military officers controlled the government. Prime Minister David Lloyd George and Premier Georges Clemenceau emerged as the dominant leaders in the United Kingdom and France. But in Imperial Germany, with Kaiser Wilhelm II's acquiescence, Field Marshal Paul von Hindenburg and General Erich Ludendorff forced aside both the civilian chancellors and other generals. Where neither civilian nor military rulers proved effective, as in Russia under Tsar Nicholas II by 1917, the collapse of authority culminated in revolution. Military defeat produced revolutions in the German and Austro-Hungarian empires at the war's end. In general, democratic governments demonstrated somewhat greater capacity to function under civilian executives, while autocratic governments succumbed to military rule and revolution.

Presidential Power. President Woodrow Wilson expanded executive leadership in the United States during the war. Like Lloyd George and Clemenceau, he retained civilian control. But he, too, experienced the limits of his power, notably in the congressional elections of 1918 and the Senate's rejection of the TREATY OF VERSAILLES in 1919–1920. He had fostered a new wartime relationship between the United States and Europe, but could not convince U.S. voters to elect Democrats to Congress. Nor could he persuade Re-

publican Senators to approve the peace treaty with Germany, including the LEAGUE OF NATIONS. Wilson enhanced his presidential power during the war, but then lost much of it during the postwar years.

In foreign affairs, the President held a great advantage over Congress. Because he could speak with one voice, while the Senate and House of Representatives were divided between the Democratic and Republican Parties and among various other factions, Wilson succeeded in setting the agenda and defining the issues. In August 1914, when Europe plunged into a war that would spread throughout the world, he proclaimed U.S. NEUTRALITY and refused to join either the Allies or the Central Powers. He steadfastly adhered to this policy until 1917, when he finally led the United States into war on the side of the Allies against Imperial Germany.

Despite German submarine attacks on Allied and U.S. ships, resulting in the loss of lives as well as commerce, Wilson had avoided military intervention. After the sinking of the British liner *Lusitania* on 7 May 1915, he stated that the United States was "too proud to fight." This response, which former President Theodore Roosevelt and Massachusetts Senator Henry Cabot Lodge mocked, allowed Wilson both to register a moral protest against Germany's submarine warfare and to maintain official U.S. neutrality. His moral condemnation of Germany, without a similar stance against the British naval blockade, caused WILLIAM JENNINGS BRYAN to resign as secretary of state. Bryan still advocated strict neutrality rather than a pro-British tilt. Wilson replaced him with the more compliant State Department counselor Robert Lansing. Although the President favored the Allies with his definition of U.S. neutrality, he still wanted to keep the United States out of the war. He retained the initiative in policymaking.

By early 1917, Germany's new policy of unrestricted submarine warfare against both neutral and belligerent shipping compelled the United States to enter the European war. The President had defined U.S. policy in such a way as to end further neutrality without humiliation. Wilson had warned Germany in 1915, and again in 1916, to refrain from using its submarines, or the United States would hold it accountable. In the *Sussex* pledge of 4 May 1916, the German government had promised in effect to halt submarine attacks against Allied shipping. Its decision to resume this new form of warfare ended U.S. neutrality. Even if Wilson or Congress were reluctant to resort to war, neither had much choice now in view of the warnings he had delivered.

Also by 1917, the United States was somewhat better prepared for war. The President had launched a preparedness campaign in 1915–1916 to win congressional support for expanding the U.S. armed forces. Others, especially Republicans, had already advocated military and naval preparedness, but Congress did not act until Wilson joined the campaign. The United States was just beginning to enlarge its army and navy when it entered the war. Recognizing at this time that volunteers could not supply sufficient recruits, Wilson requested and Congress passed the Selective Service Act in May 1917 to allow the drafting of young men into the U.S. armed forces. The President obviously played the key role in defining and implementing the requirements of NATIONAL SECURITY.

When Wilson finally resolved to take the nation into war, he went before Congress on 2 April 1917, to recommend this action. Giving the war a larger purpose than retaliation against submarine warfare, he urged U.S. intervention to make the world "safe for democracy." He advocated a partnership of democratic nations between the United States and the Allies, and anticipated the postwar creation of the League of Nations. Four days later, on 6 April, Congress voted to declare war against Germany. Later that year, Wilson also asked Congress to declare war against the Austro-Hungarian empire. Congress complied on 7 December 1917. In both cases, the President determined the action.

Wilson's Leadership. Wilson's war message epitomized a new style of presidential leadership. It followed a pattern that he had initiated in his first term. In the nineteenth and early twentieth centuries, U.S. Presidents had merely submitted written messages to Congress. No President since John Adams had appeared in person. Wilson had broken this precedent in 1913 by addressing Congress on behalf of one of his NEW FREEDOM reforms. He had used this same rhetorical technique not only to advocate domestic reforms, but also in foreign affairs, notably in his "peace without victory" address on 22 January 1917. Wilson launched what would become known in the Ronald Reagan era of the 1980s as the RHETORICAL PRESIDENCY.

Wilson's war message was also notable as the last time a President requested Congress to declare war prior to U.S. military involvement. In 1941, when President Franklin D. Roosevelt called for DECLARATIONS OF WAR against the Axis Powers, Japan had already attacked PEARL HARBOR, and Germany and Italy had joined in the war against the United States. After WORLD WAR II, Presidents from Harry S. Truman to George Bush ordered U.S. armed forces into combat in Korea, Vietnam, and the Persian Gulf without requesting formal declarations of war by Congress. Wilson had contributed to what would eventually become known as the IMPERIAL PRESIDENCY by sending U.S. armed forces into several Central American and Caribbean countries without congressional authorization. But in the case of World War I, he still adhered to the procedure stipulated in the U.S. Constitution.

Wilson redefined the U.S. presidency. His progressive concept of the office expressed a new political philosophy. He abandoned the traditional focus on the constitutional principles of balanced representative government. His statecraft emphasized, instead, the general will of the people, or public opinion. Twentieth-century presidents, beginning with Wilson, devoted less attention to constitutional principles concerning SEPARATION OF POWERS among the branches of government and more to the executive management of public opinion. They sought to rule by fostering the general will through rhetorical appeals directly to the people.

Employing this new style of leadership during World War I, Wilson appealed to the peoples in the Central Powers to reject their autocratic rulers and join his democratic crusade. He delivered the same message to the Russian people after the 1917 revolution. In his FOURTEEN POINTS address on 8 January 1918, the President heralded an open diplomacy to replace the old diplomacy of secret treaties. He wanted to create a new world order that would supplant the old balances of power and alliances. Seeking to formulate the general will at the Paris Peace Conference and to institutionalize it in the League of Nations, he repudiated the old idea of a global balance of power among competing nations.

Wilson's vision of a new world order was the international counterpart to U.S. political culture. His contribution to the imperial presidency coincided with his pursuit of U.S. hegemony in world affairs. Instead of a balance of power, either among the branches of government at home or among nations abroad, he favored a new type of community based on the general will as he perceived it. This was his concept of democracy.

Wilson did not ignore Congress, however, even when he expanded presidential power. Rather than claim WAR POWERS as the exclusive prerogative of the executive branch, he generally accepted the role of Congress. He usually requested its authorization for the powers that he needed to mobilize the nation. When Republicans condemned him for inefficient administration after a year of mobilization, he turned this issue against his critics by asking Congress to grant him discretionary authority to reorganize executive agencies. The passage of the Overman Act on 20 May 1918, which gave him this authority, significantly expanded presidential power.

Wilson also asserted his constitutional role as COMMANDER IN CHIEF. Soon after the U.S. entry into the war, he ordered General John J. Pershing to command the American Expeditionary Forces in France. Once it was organized and trained, the President expected the AEF to join the Allies in combat on the western front. The War and Navy departments, headed by secretaries NEWTON D. BAKER and Josephus Daniels, mobilized the AEF and transported it to Europe. By summer and autumn 1918, Pershing's forces contributed to the Allied victory over the Central Powers.

Persuasion and Control. Whenever possible, Wilson preferred to rely on persuasion. By an EXECUTIVE ORDER in April 1917, he established the Committee on Public Information to manage public opinion. Under George Creel's direction, the CPI conducted extensive propaganda campaigns in the United States and overseas. It used various techniques, including school lessons, public speakers, pamphlets, and motion pictures, to convey the message that the United States was fighting a just war. It delivered this message not only at home and in Allied countries, but also behind enemy lines. Wilson's democratic crusade depended upon this kind of persuasion.

When persuasion proved inadequate even in the United States, the President employed other methods of social control. Congress granted him extensive power to suppress dissent under the Espionage Act of June 1917, the Trading with the Enemy Act of October 1917, and the Sedition Act of May 1918. He used this authority to silence radical critics of the war, such as the Socialist Party and the Industrial Workers of the World, and to coerce supposedly disloyal ethnics, such as German Americans and Irish Americans. Under Postmaster General Albert S. Burleson and Attorney General Thomas W. Gregory, the Post Office and Justice departments became actively involved in restricting free speech and preventing the circulation of dissenting opinions.

With the authorization of Congress, Wilson also mobilized the U.S. economy. The Lever Food and Fuel Control Act of August 1917 enabled him to regulate the use of vital raw materials. For this purpose, he established the Food Administration under Herbert Hoover and the Fuel Administration under Harry Garfield. In December 1917 he acted to solve the country's transportation crisis by nationalizing the railroads and placing them under the Railroad Administration's management. He named Treasury Secretary William Gibbs McAdoo to head this operation. When earlier attempts by the War Industries Board to mobilize key industries for wartime purposes proved inadequate, the President placed BERNARD BARUCH in charge of this agency in March 1918 and gave him extensive executive authority to set priorities for production. A National War Labor Board, headed by

former President William Howard Taft and attorney Frank P. Walsh, mediated labor disputes to avoid strikes. As a consequence of these various actions, the U.S. government exercised unprecedented powers over all sectors of the economy.

Wilson's wartime leadership at home and abroad generated a backlash by the war's end. As soon as the fighting ended with the armistice on 11 November 1918, Americans reasserted what they had traditionally understood as their democratic rights to individual freedom and local control. They resisted further centralization of power in the national government, and especially in the presidency. Farmers and industrialists who had resented government regulation, but who tolerated it while reaping financial rewards during the war, demanded the end of controls once the wartime contracts and purchases stopped. Suppression of dissent seemed less justifiable after the war, although it continued during the red scare of 1919–1920. Disillusionment with the war's failure to make the world safe for democracy in Germany or elsewhere, or even to produce harmony among the victorious Allies, created a political climate in which the Senate rejected the Treaty of Versailles, thereby preventing U.S. membership in the postwar League of Nations.

Presidential power that Wilson had wielded during World War I eroded quickly in the postwar years. Voters repudiated his progressive leadership in 1920. They preferred the normalcy that Republican presidential candidate Warren G. Harding promised. They rejected Wilson's legacy of diplomatic and military involvement abroad and of social control and economic regulation at home. The United States had experienced the growth of executive power during the war, followed by its rapid demise in the postwar era.

BIBLIOGRAPHY

Ambrosius, Lloyd E. *Wilsonian Statecraft: Theory and Practice of Liberal Internationalism during World War I.* 1991.

Ferrell, Robert H. *Woodrow Wilson and World War I, 1917–1921.* 1985.

Hilderbrand, Robert C. *Power and the People: Executive Management of Public Opinion in Foreign Affairs, 1897–1921.* 1981.

Karl, Barry D. *The Uneasy State: The United States from 1915 to 1945.* 1983.

Kennedy, David M. *Over Here: The First World War and American Society.* 1980.

May, Christopher N. *In the Name of War: Judicial Review and the War Powers since 1918.* 1989.

Schaffer, Ronald. *America in the Great War.* 1991.

Tulis, Jeffrey K. *The Rhetorical Presidency.* 1987.

LLOYD E. AMBROSIUS

WORLD WAR II. It is a truism that the challenges the United States faced during World War II produced such sweeping changes that this conflict, rather than the Great Depression, constitutes the watershed event of the twentieth century. World War II was also a laboratory for radical social, economic, and political transformations that affected all aspects of life in America. However, World War II's lasting effects on the presidency—its significance for extending the CHIEF EXECUTIVE's constitutional prerogatives and for broadening the President's extraconstitutional functions—are less certain. The period 1939–1945 witnessed a substantial expansion of presidential functions, but it is not clear whether this expansion should be attributed to the special circumstances of World War II or to trends long underway.

The enormous power associated with America's war effort has contributed to this confusion. Even mired in depression the United States stood first in world industrial production and at its peak in 1943 was outproducing the Axis powers and generating 60 percent of total Allied war supplies. Did President Franklin D. Roosevelt acquire and wield near-dictatorial powers? Is the IMPERIAL PRESIDENCY a legacy of World War II?

For many years the view that dominated was that the wartime presidency of Franklin D. Roosevelt reflected a temporary, episodic expansion of presidential powers, that the Chief Executive merely inspired the sacrifices and strategic decisions that won the war. President's Roosevelt's genius for politics permitted the American people to apply their inventiveness, entrepreneurial skills, and unequaled talent for improvisation to the task of creating the tools of victory. The "democracy rises to any challenge" explanation of America's mobilization has proved remarkably durable. Those who found fault with the Roosevelt administration's wartime performance, who argued that failures of coordination and lack of systematic planning had retarded the pace of mobilization and risked the Allied battle plan and the lives of American soldiers, have been dismissed as naysayers and statist ideologues.

Equity or Efficiency. During 1938–1945 the Roosevelt administration zigzagged between equity and efficiency and maximizing output and minimizing inequalities of wealth and power. Those metronomic lurches—from the antimonopoly, prolabor zeal of 1935–1939, to a stance offering the olive branch to big business in 1941 as bribe for conversion to war production, to the egalitarian rhetoric of Roosevelt's January 1944 "Economic Bill of Rights," to that final swerve toward political and fiscal conservatism in spring-summer 1944—cloaked an all-embracing commitment to productivity as the solution to the dilemmas and divisions besetting American society.

This amorphous notion was an outcome of the inability to achieve consensus about essential matters. Whether one's allegiance was to conflict or consensus, to a "broker state" (with the national administration playing off competing interests) or to a "corporatist" model grounded in the appeal that continued growth would provide larger and larger slices of the economic pie for all at America's banquet table, that rhetorical expression, "arsenal of democracy," offered a commanding vision of the U.S. role in World War II.

As a result, America's wartime experience differed in basic ways from that of its principal allies. Only Americans could describe World War II as a "good war," bringing an improved standard of living and requiring few real sacrifices by the great majority. Even the tide of state intervention in the economy proved moderate and temporary. It was not that Americans cared less about defeating the Axis powers. Both the public and its leaders were united in that purpose but, except for those months of self-doubt and military disaster in winter-spring 1942, the Axis threat remained an abstraction.

Efforts to devise policies for the most efficient and equitable use of manpower proved the most glaring failure of American wartime mobilization. The Selective Service Act of 1940 conferred authority to conscript males for military service as well as to give deferments for those occupations that were vital to the nation's economy. Only, in late 1941, however, did the huge expansion of production fueled by the LEND LEASE ACT and the army's "victory program," a blueprint for building a 215-division ground force, begin to raise concern about allocating manpower as any scarce resource. How to do so, unfortunately, became ensnarled in awkward philosophical issues (the historic American commitment in theory to universal male military obligation and its aversion in practice to comprehensive national service), thorny social questions involving the utilization of blacks and women, and the partisan and bureaucratic political imperatives that flowed from labor shortages. From a total population of slightly over 130 million, 66 million Americans either were in uniform or performing war-related civilian jobs during the peak year of 1944. The armed forces increased from some 1.5 million in 1941 to 11.4 million at war's end.

The years of combat overseas meant full employment and high earnings at home. The nature of America's mobilization left largely intact prewar social and political patterns of behavior and reinforced, via such devices as cost-plus contracts, wage-price freezes, and raw materials and manpower allocation policies, the power of large corporations. Living standards for most Americans apparently rose as well. Average weekly earnings, benefiting from heavy overtime, in-

WORLD WAR II 1667

creased by 70 percent. There is also evidence that a permanent if modest redistribution of income had taken place. Of course, many were denied the benefits (actual or perceived) flowing from wartime mobilization. Full employment, higher wages, improved living conditions were not enjoyed by all and for some the "benefits" proved transitory. The detention of Japanese Americans in War Relocation Centers remains a tragic blot on the presidency of Franklin D. Roosevelt [see JAPANESE AMERICANS, TREATMENT OF].

With hundreds of thousands of eighteen-year-old males each month being called into military service, a manpower crisis was inevitable unless the linkage of manpower and production goals was acknowledged. The government sought to put in place adequate mechanisms to deal with occupational deferments in critical industries, wage differentials, labor standards, prohibition of racial discrimination in employment, and other problems. These alleviated some bottlenecks, but administrative confusion and the government's unwillingness to confront the issue of work assignments (no strikes, no changing jobs without approval) meant that competition for skilled workers, wholesale work force disruptions, and wildcat strikes were the norm. For individuals and families, war work often mean intolerable strains, repeated relocations, and inadequate living conditions in the boom towns.

The government's dilemma represented a choice between voluntarism and compulsion. On one side were the tender minded, convinced that the American people were prepared to give their utmost to make the "arsenal of democracy" a reality and that patriotic rhetoric and education would suffice to create an aroused citizenry. On the other side stood the tough minded, such as Robert Patterson and General Brehon B. Somervell, convinced that compulsion and sacrifice were essential to the nation's moral welfare. Generally, the advocates of persuasion and a passive approach triumphed, though whether a policy of national service would have proved more effective in the America of 1941–1945 continues to be debated.

Wielding Presidential Power. The ambiguities associated with World War II ultimately come down to whether the presidency emerged from the war with greatly expanded powers, and the presidency, as locus of policy initiative and moral arbiter, acquired its contemporary character. Any assessment of Roosevelt's wielding of presidential powers during World War II offers an uncertain and contradictory picture. The desperate international situation of 1940 led to the precedent-shattering decision of Roosevelt to seek a third term; his sweeping victory seemingly confirmed the DEMOCRATIC PARTY's unchallengeable position. However, in 1944, Roosevelt's campaign for a fourth term proved the NEW DEAL's death knell and, arguably, foreshadowed the downplaying of ideology and party alignments in COLD WAR presidential politics.

Roosevelt made use of war's exigencies to assert his prerogatives as COMMANDER IN CHIEF far more aggressively than had, for example President Woodrow Wilson. Anxious to avoid a repetition of America's 1917–1918 mobilization, the WAR DEPARTMENT had undertaken planning for wartime economic expansion during the 1920s. After many drafts, a summary version of this Industrial Mobilization Plan (IMP) was released in October 1939. A crucial assumption was that existing executive departments would prove unable to add wartime functions to their normal routines. Thus, the 1939 IMP provided for creation, when war was imminent, of a War Resources Administration under a distinguished civilian to oversee the various temporary agencies charged with administering the nation's mobilization. To the planners, both textbooks on administration and the historical record argued that the President would be so immersed in his duties as Commander in Chief, party head, and cheerleader that he could not give sustained attention to mobilization issues.

The President objected vehemently on both political and constitutional grounds to the interposition of some appointed expert between him and agencies responsible for such critical activities as labor, prices, and industrial production. Roosevelt complained that War Department planners wanted him to abdicate. In July 1939 he imposed control by a military order that transferred the Joint Army-Navy Board, Munitions Board, and various procurement agencies to the new EXECUTIVE OFFICE OF THE PRESIDENT. This action had huge implications for mobilization and for strategic policy-making.

Dealing with the Economy. Roosevelt's rejection of a superagency and a war cabinet ironically ushered in the worst nightmare of liberals and some conservatives—significant military involvement in the economy. A host of alphabet agencies emerged over the next two years—the Office of Price Administration, Office of Defense Transportation, War Food Administration, War Production Board, War Manpower Commission, to name but a few—but in the interim somebody had to take responsibility for placing orders, pushing plant expansion, and monitoring contract compliance. In the absence of any civilian agency with adequate authority, the War Department developed its own mechanisms by trial and error. Unfortunately, the trials and errors were numerous.

The administrative apparatus simply did not exist to control the economy's expansion. By EXECUTIVE ORDER on 7 January 1941 the Office of Production Management (OPM) assumed responsibilities over production, raw materials, and manpower; OPM, moreover, was supposed to ensure a close relationship between civilian agencies and those handling military procurement, but as OPM had no authority to decide major policy questions, such authority remained with the President.

For the duration of the war, debate focused on the relative balance between military and civilian needs. Critics spoke of the War Department's gargantuan appetite. The Truman Committee zeroed in on cost overruns in camp construction and challenged such costly ventures as a $134 million pipeline from the Arctic Circle across Alaska to pump oil that no one needed. As food and other items disappeared from stores, many questioned the huge stockpiles of tires, canned meat, and numerous other commodities. The Pentagon's stated policy of acquiring 200 percent of projected requirements provoked widespread irritation.

The Roosevelt administration approached the tasks of financing the war and imposing controls over wages, profits, and prices as interrelated aspects of the challenge to sustain public confidence in the American economy. At the same time, Roosevelt's advisers were acutely aware of the political need to assure each important constituent group—labor, business, farmers, housewives, draftees, retired people—that it was bearing no more than its fair share of the war's burdens and reaping its fair share (or a little more) of the benefits. Though the imposition of controls and the government's preemptive claim upon resources restricted choices, the marketplace remained (or was perceived to be) dominant in almost all areas of economic activity of concern to the average citizen. Nowhere was the abstract concept of a command economy more plainly called for than here, and in no case was the door to absolute coercion slammed so quickly and with such force.

Directing Global Strategy. A quite different pattern evolved regarding the President's role in devising America's global strategy. Roosevelt made use of his powers as Commander in Chief to assert general supervision of military planning. He intervened on numerous occasions to ensure adherence to the policy of Europe First, all-out support of the U.S.S.R., primacy to the air war, and limiting American casualties.

Because Roosevelt disliked the highly structured JOINT CHIEFS OF STAFF, preferring to consult individually with favorite military chieftains such as General Henry H. Arnold and Admiral Ernest J. King, the official record contains few instances of direct presidential meddling in military matters. Nevertheless, the President's desires, often politically motivated, proved crucial. Kent Roberts Greenfield once compiled a list of twelve important presidential initiatives affecting the conduct of the war and twenty occasions when President Roosevelt overruled his military advisers. Though the view that Roosevelt as Commander in Chief stood aloof from the daily challenges of running the war still finds advocates, most scholars today agree with Warren F. Kimball's conclusion that Roosevelt was actively and centrally involved in strategic-military policymaking.

The structural changes Roosevelt imposed on the war-navy administrative apparatus foreshadowed and, indeed, made possible the postwar evolution of a fully fledged national security bureaucracy. However, such misuses of presidential powers as the wholesale confinement of Japanese Americans, enlarged controls over dissemination of information, and domestic surveillance of radicals had origins that long predated World War II. As well, the pressures to create a war cabinet and a civil service establishment directly linked to the White House proved temporary.

World War II gave President Roosevelt abundant opportunity to showcase his talents as moral leader and political wizard. In the process of displaying those skills, he transformed the institution of the presidency.

BIBLIOGRAPHY

Blum, John M. *V Was for Victory: Politics and American Culture during World War II.* 1976.

Burns, James MacGregor. *Roosevelt: The Soldier of Freedom.* 1970.

Emerson, William. "Franklin Roosevelt as Commander-in-Chief in World War II." *Military Affairs* 22 (Winter 1958–1959).

Janeway, Eliot. *Struggle for Survival: A Chronicle of Economic Mobilization in World War II.* 1951.

Kimball, Warren F. "Franklin D. Roosevelt: 'Dr Win the War.'" In *Commanders in Chief: Presidential Leadership in Modern Wars.* Edited by Joseph G. Dawson III. 1993.

Larrabee, Eric. *Commander-in-Chief: Franklin Delano Roosevelt, His Lieutenants, and Their War.* 1987.

THEODORE A. WILSON

X Y

XYZ AFFAIR. See Quasi War with France.

YACHTS, PRESIDENTIAL. For nearly a century—from the administrations of Rutherford B. Hayes to Jimmy Carter—yachts were maintained and operated by the U.S. Navy for the President of the United States. Before there were official presidential yachts, Abraham Lincoln used the revenue cutter *Miami* and occasionally the steamer *River Queen* for important Civil War meetings. A decade later, the *River Queen* conveyed President Ulysses S. Grant to Martha's Vineyard where he was greeted with fireworks, banners, and a parade.

Although presidential yachts were often used for pleasure cruises and private working sessions, they also afforded an impressive setting for ceremonial occasions, discussions of state, and hosting visiting dignitaries. Beginning in 1880, the 174-foot steamer U.S.S. *Despatch* served as a presidential yacht for Rutherford B. Hayes, Chester A. Arthur, Grover Cleveland, and Benjamin Harrison. In the 1890s, the *Despatch* was replaced by the steel cruiser U.S.S. *Dolphin*.

Early in the twentieth century, both the U.S.S. *Sylph*, a sleek steam-powered yacht, and the gunboat U.S.S. *Mayflower*, were used by Presidents William McKinley, Theodore Roosevelt, William Howard Taft, and Woodrow Wilson. The *Mayflower* served Warren G. Harding and Calvin Coolidge as well.

Franklin D. Roosevelt used three different yachts during his twelve years as chief executive—the U.S.S. *Sequoia*, *Potomac*, and *Williamsburg*. While abroad his favorite, the *Potomac*, Roosevelt planned wartime strategy, recorded several of his fireside chats, and frequently sailed the Atlantic Coast.

President Harry S. Truman favored the *Williamsburg*, traveling to Florida, Bermuda, the British West Indies, Cuba, and the Virgin Islands. Dwight D. Eisenhower, opted for two smaller yachts—the *Barbara Anne* and *Susie E.* When John F. Kennedy became President, the *Barbara Anne* was renamed the *Honey Fitz*, the *Susie E.* became the *Patrick J.* The two yachts were known as he *Patricia* and *Julie* under President Richard M. Nixon's tenure, before both were decommissioned in 1969.

The U.S.S. *Sequoia*, the last of the presidential yachts, was used by nine successive Presidents before Jimmy Carter sold it for $286,000 in 1979 as an economy measure. It was a particular favorite of Presidents Nixon and Gerald R. Ford, who in their terms entertained more than 14,000 guests on its deck. President John F. Kennedy celebrated his last birthday on the *Sequoia*, and it was there that Nixon told his family he was resigning the presidency.

BIBLIOGRAPHY

Crockett, Fred E. *Special Fleet: The History of the Presidential Yachts.* 1985.

Lawford, Valentine. "The Presidential Yacht U.S.S. *Sequoia.*" *Architectural Digest* 40 (January 1983): 60–67.

Scott, Frank D. "Presidential Yachts." *Nautical Research Journal* 20 (April 1974): 119–128.

STEPHEN W. STATHIS

YAKUS v. UNITED STATES 321 U.S. 414 (1944). *Yakus* is an important Supreme Court case in the evolution of constitutional law concerning the DELEGATION OF LEGISLATIVE POWER. The Emergency Price Control Act of 1942 (56 Stat. 23), as amended by the Inflation Control Act of 1942 (56 Stat. 765), was enacted to prevent wartime inflation, "profiteering, hoarding, manipulation, speculation, and other disruptive practices resulting from abnormal market conditions or scarcities caused by or contributing to the national emergency." It established an Office of Price Administration, headed by a Price Administrator appointed by the President.

The administrator was authorized to consult with industry representatives and to promulgate regulations to fix the prices of commodities that "in his judgment will be generally fair and equitable and will effectuate the purposes of this Act." The administrator was to act when, in his judgment, prices "have risen or threaten to rise to an extent or in a manner inconsistent with the purposes of this Act," and was to give "due consideration" to prices that prevailed during the base period designated by law and was to "make adjustments for such relevant factors as he may determine and deem to be of general applicability." The 1942 act authorized the President to stabilize prices, wages, and salaries "so far as practicable" on the basis of levels that existed on 15 September 1942.

Petitioners had been tried and convicted for selling wholesale cuts of beef at prices that exceeded the levels set by regulations issued under the statute. In response to their claim that the statute represented an unconstitutional delegation of power, the Court concluded that "the boundaries of the field of the Administrator's permissible action are marked by the statute. . . . Congress has stated the legislative objective, has prescribed the method of achieving that objective—maximum price fixing—and has laid down standards to guide the administrative determination of both the occasions for the exercise of the price-fixing power, and the particular prices to be established."

In distinguishing this case from SCHECHTER POULTRY CORP. v. UNITED STATES (1935), where the Supreme Court voided statutory provisions that were an impermissible delegation of power, the Court in *Yakus* argued that "the Constitution as a continuously operative charter of government does not demand the impossible or the impracticable. It does not require that Congress find for itself every fact upon which it desires to base legislative action or that it make for itself detailed determinations which it has declared to be prerequisite to the application of the legislative policy to particular facts and circumstances impossible for Congress itself properly to investigate." All Congress needed to do was to satisfy the "essentials of the legislative function," which included the "determination of the legislative policy and its formulation and promulgation as a defined and binding rule of conduct."

The Court was not troubled that the delegation called for the "exercise of judgment," by the administrator or that an administrative officer have "ample latitude . . . to ascertain the conditions which Congress has made prerequisite to the operation of its legislative command." Judicial review is to be limited to "ascertain whether the will of Congress has been obeyed. This depends not upon the breadth of the definition of the facts or conditions which the administrative officer is to find but upon the determination whether the definition sufficiently marks the field within which the Administrator is to act so that it may be known whether he has kept within it in compliance with the legislative will."

The Court found irrelevant the fact that Congress could itself have prescribed maximum prices: "Congress is not confined to that method of executing its policy which involves the least possible delegation of discretion to administrative officers." For the Court, a key criterion for assessing delegations is whether Congress, the courts, and others can determine if the agency is conforming to legislative standards: "Only if we could say that there is an absence of standards for the guidance of the Administrator's action, so that it would be impossible in a proper proceeding to ascertain whether the will of Congress has been obeyed, would we be justified in overriding its choice of means for effecting its declared purpose of preventing inflation."

The delegation to fix prices was judged by the Court to be no broader than the "power to fix just and reasonable rates . . . or the power to approve consolidations in the 'public interest,' . . . or the power to regulate radio stations engaged in chain broadcasting 'as public interest, convenience or necessity requires,' . . . or the power to prohibit 'unfair methods of competition' " that it had upheld in other cases.

BIBLIOGRAPHY

Corwin, Edward S. *The President: Office and Powers, 1787–1984.* 1984.
"American Economic Mobilization: A Study in the Mechanism of War." *Harvard Law Review* 55 (1942): 427–536.

GARY C. BRYNER

YALTA CONFERENCE. Leaders of the WORLD WAR II coalition against Hitler—Franklin Roosevelt, Winston Churchill, and Joseph Stalin, collectively known as the Big Three—met at the Crimean seaport, Yalta, 3–11 February 1945, to resolve issues central to the postwar peace. Germany was near defeat. As Yalta opened, Soviet armies controlled Poland and were thirty-five miles from Berlin; Anglo-American armies, on the other hand, had just reached the German border. On 6 February, Stalin, while at Yalta, canceled the planned Berlin assault and concentrated on coalition diplomacy.

Decisions entered into by Roosevelt did not legally bind the United States until the Senate consented to a peace treaty; rather they were EXECUTIVE AGREEMENTS, morally binding only on the CHIEF EXECUTIVE who concluded the agreement. At the conference major European issues were discussed: for Germany dismemberment, occupation zones, reparations payments, and moving the eastern border westward; Poland's borders and a government required to be "friendly" to the Soviet Union; the postwar role of liberated France in Europe; and the UNITED NATIONS Organization (replacing the LEAGUE OF NATIONS), designated as the postwar instrument maintaining international peace and order. A decision concluded easily was the Soviet-American agreement on Soviet entry into the war against Japan, stipulating a "restoration" of Russia's losses in the Russo-Japanese war (1905), and acquisition of the Kurile Islands.

Each nation left Yalta having achieved its primary objective. The United States secured agreement to its voting formula for the U.N. Security Council, the list of original members attending the San Francisco Conference, and territorial trusteeship. Great Britain succeeded in restoring France to major-power status with a zone of occupation in Germany and membership on the Allied Control Council governing Germany. The Soviet Union received partial satisfaction: a Polish government based on the current Lublin (as opposed to the London exile) government, although one to be "democratically broadened" prior to holding general elections; a Polish-Soviet border running along the Curzon line recommended after WORLD WAR I; two Soviet republics in the U.N. General Assembly; and the United States' promise to support $10 billion in reparations from Germany for the U.S.S.R. when the Reparations Commission met. The coalition would jointly control Germany and Berlin, each temporarily divided into four zones of occupation. Left unsettled were Germany's eastern border with Poland and a final composition for the future Polish government, although a formula was established to create it. The Declaration on Liberated Europe was as easily supported as the word *democracy* on Poland, but their meanings were interpreted differently.

The Yalta agreements reflected both a high degree of cooperation and the traditional compromises of diplomacy. Yet "Yalta," after Roosevelt's death, became a focal point for censuring the Soviet Union.

Myths grew up about Yalta. The first held that the United States honored the agreements and threatened the Soviet Union if it did not; the later myth shifted blame to Roosevelt, who was accused of selling out to the Russians. Neither myth was true. Some Yalta decisions went into effect, some did not, and Truman renegotiated others at the POTSDAM CONFERENCE. "Yalta," however, remained a derogatory term condemning negotiation or cooperation with the Soviet Union throughout the COLD WAR.

BIBLIOGRAPHY

Clemens, Diane Shaver. *Yalta.* 1970. Repr. 1978.
Stettinius, Edward R., Jr. *Roosevelt and the Russians: The Yalta Conference.* 1949.
U.S. Department of State. *Foreign Relations of the United States: Diplomatic Papers: The Conferences at Malta and Yalta, 1945.* 1955.

DIANE SHAVER CLEMENS

YOUNGSTOWN SHEET & TUBE CO. v. SAWYER 343 U.S. 579 (1952). In *Youngstown Sheet & Tube Co. v. Sawyer* the Supreme Court held that the federal government's seizure of the nation's steel mills, as directed by President Harry S. Truman in EXECUTIVE ORDER 10340, was unconstitutional. After the President issued the seizure order, the steel companies immediately brought suit for a preliminary injunction to restrain the Secretary of Commerce, Charles Sawyer, from taking possession of the mills. The Supreme Court's decision affirmed a federal district court ruling in favor of the steel companies and against the President's exercise of INHERENT POWERS. President Truman justified his action by relying on his institutional obligation to act in the public interest—to prosecute the KOREAN WAR effectively and protect the safety of American troops—and did not cite any statutory authorization in support of his seizure order.

Constitutional Issues. From the beginning, attorneys for the government displayed a surprising inability to articulate any limits on the theory of inherent executive power, which appeared to reduce their argument to the proposition that the ends justified the means. Both the government and the STEWARDSHIP THEORY of the presidency received a sharp rebuke from Federal District Judge David A. Pine. Declaring that the federal government was one only "of limited, enumerated, and delegated powers," he held that the seizure was unconstitutional because it was not authorized by an express grant of power in the Constitution. Of even greater import was Judge Pine's attempt to rivet into the Constitution William Howard Taft's theory of the LITERALIST PRESIDENT.

Rejecting the proposition that the President possessed a "broad residuum of power" on which he could draw when statutory authorization was lacking, Judge Pine wrote,

> The non-existence of this "inherent" power in the President has been recognized by eminent writers, and I cite in this connection the unequivocal language of the late Chief Justice Taft in his treatise entitled "Our Chief Magistrate and His Powers" (1916) wherein he says: "The true view of the Executive function is, as I conceive it, that the President can exercise no power which cannot be fairly and reasonably traced to some specific grant of power or justly implied and included within such express grant as proper and necessary to its exercise. Such specific grant must be either in the Federal Constitution or in an Act of Congress passed in pursuance thereof. There is no undefined residuum of power which he can exercise because it seems to him to be in the public interest. . . . [H]is jurisdiction must be justified and vindicated by affirmative constitutional or statutory provision, or it does not exist."

On expedited review, bypassing the federal appeals court, the Supreme Court affirmed the lower court's decision but largely ignored the emphasis it gave to the literalist theory of presidential power. Speaking for the Court, Justice Hugo Black asserted that "the President's power, if any, to issue the order must stem from an act of Congress or from the Constitution itself" and he pointed out that "no statute . . . expressly authorizes the President to take possession of property as he did here" and, further, that there was no statute "from which such a power [could] fairly be implied." Indeed, he noted, Congress had specifically rejected government seizure as a means of dealing with labor-management disputes when it passed the Taft-Hartley Act.

Absent any statutory basis for the President's action, Justice Black continued, justification would have to be found in the Constitution itself. He rejected the contention that the President's power as Commander in Chief sufficed. Although he conceded that "theater of war" was an "expanding concept," he explained that it could not be stretched to encompass presidential seizure of private property to prevent a production stoppage and still manifest allegiance to the principle of constitutionalism.

Nor could adequate justification be squeezed from the President's constitutional role as Chief Executive. Wrote Justice Black, "In the framework of our Constitution, the President's power to see that the laws are faithfully executed refutes the idea that he is to be a lawmaker. The Constitution limits his functions in the lawmaking process to the recommending of laws he thinks wise and the vetoing of laws he thinks bad. And the Constitution is neither silent nor equivocal about who shall make laws which the President is to execute."

Constitutionally speaking, the fatal flaw in Executive Order 10340 was that "[t]he President's order does not direct that a congressional policy be executed in a manner prescribed by Congress—it directs that a presidential policy be executed in a manner prescribed by the President." To be sure, seizure could be ordered if authorized by a Congress willing to pay just compensation, but it could not be ordered simply on presidential say so.

***Youngstown*'s Value as Precedent.** Controversy persists, however, about the force of the Court's holding in *Youngstown* and whether it actually amounts to the effective limitation on the presidential power that it purports to be. Critics of *Youngstown*'s value as precedent argue that it only shows the Court's capacity to check the actions of a politically vulnerable incumbent and point to numerous features of the decision that blunt its constitutional edge.

Since the Court speaks most forcefully when it speaks unanimously and with one voice, there is the foremost fact that *Youngstown* was a 6 to 3 decision, in which every Justice voting in the majority wrote his own opinion, a point that was not overlooked by the vigorous dissenting opinion of Chief Justice Fred Vinson. It is therefore unclear whether Justice Black's opinion, which functioned as a lowest common denominator of sentiments among the majority of Justices, faulted the President's seizure order because of its inherent illegality or because it flew squarely in the face of Congress's expressed rejection of seizure as a way of resolving labor-management disputes.

Furthermore, if the Court is to function as an effective check on Executive Power, it must articulate a conception of the presidency that imposes limitations. After all, that was the point of Judge Pine's opinion in the lower court. Yet none of the Justices' opinions in *Youngstown* articulated any theory of the office of the presidency. Indeed, in his concurring opinion, Justice Felix Frankfurter declared, "The issue before us can be met, and therefore should be, without attempting to define the President's powers comprehensively." Deciding cases on the narrowest possible ground surely minimizes the exercise of judicial power.

If any Justice in the majority ventured a view of presidential power larger than the facts of the case at hand, it was Justice Robert Jackson. In a concurring opinion still considered a masterpiece of political analysis of Presidential-Congressional Relations, he gave at best half-hearted support to the Court's judgment. As a former legal adviser to Truman's predecessor, Franklin D. Roosevelt, in crisis times, Justice Jackson began by openly confessing sympathy for "the poverty of really useful and unambiguous authority applicable to concrete problems of executive power as they actually present themselves." Brushing off legal quotations and precedents on presidential power because they "largely cancel one another," he observed that court decisions were likely to be unhelpful "because of the judicial practice of dealing with the largest questions in the most narrow way." Instead, his concurring opinion was devoted to marking out three categories of presidential actions: where the President acts pursuant to an act of Congress, where the President acts but Congress is silent, and where the President acts contrary to the expressed will of Congress. In the first category, he asserted, the President stands on the strongest constitutional grounds since he then exercises not only his own powers under Article II but also those powers of Article I gives to Congress. Regarding the second category of circumstances, Justice Jackson observed that "any actual test of power is likely to depend on the imperatives of events and contemporary imponderables rather than on abstract theories of law." In the last category—the one into which the facts in the *Youngstown* fell—Justice Jackson described the President's constitutional footing as being at its shakiest, since the powers on which he could rely were only his own minus any possessed by Congress.

His concurrence was free of any pretense that the Court could bury the stewardship theory of presidential power even if it chose to do so. Justice Jackson maintained

no illusion that any decision by this Court can keep power in the hands of Congress if it is not wise and timely in meeting its problems. A crisis that challenges the President equally, or perhaps primarily, challenges Congress. If not good law, there is worldly wisdom in the maxim attributed to Napoléon that "The tools belong to the man who can use them." We may say that power to legislate for emergencies belongs in the hands of Congress, but only Congress itself can prevent power from slipping through its fingers.

In the struggle of legislative institutions to maintain their power, he added, "Such institutions may be destined to pass away. But it is the duty of the Court to be last, not first, to give them up."

BIBLIOGRAPHY

Banks, Robert F. "Steel, Sawyer, and the Executive Power." *University of Pittsburgh Law Reivew* 14 (1953): 467–537.

Kauper, Paul G. "The Steel Seizure Case: Congress, the President and the Supreme Court." *Michigan Law Review* 51 (1952): 141–182.

Lea, L. B. "The Steel Case: Presidential Seizure of Private Industry." *Northwestern University Law Review* 47 (1952): 289–313.

Marcus, Maeva. *Truman and the Steel Seizure Case: The Limits of Presidential Power.* 1977.

Schubert, Glendon A., Jr. "The Steel Case: Presidential Responsibility and Judicial Irresponsibility." *Western Political Quarterly* 6 (1953): 61–77.

Westin, Alan F. *The Anatomy of a Constitutional Law Case.* 1958.

Williams, Jerre. "The Steel Seizure: A Legal Analysis of a Political Controversy." *Journal of Public Law* 2 (1953): 29–40.

CRAIG R. DUCAT

The Constitution of the United States

Spelling, capitalization, and punctuation conform to the text of the engrossed copy.

WE THE PEOPLE of the United States, in Order to form a more perfect Union, establish Justice, insure domestic Tranquility, provide for the common defence, promote the general Welfare, and secure the Blessings of Liberty to ourselves and our Posterity, do ordain and establish this Constitution of the United States of America.

ARTICLE. I.

SECTION. 1. All legislative Powers herein granted shall be vested in a Congress of the United States, which shall consist of a Senate and House of Representatives.

SECTION. 2. The House of Representatives shall be composed of Members chosen every second Year by the People of the several States, and the Electors in each State shall have the Qualifications requisite for Electors of the most numerous Branch of the State Legislature.

No Person shall be a Representative who shall not have attained to the Age of twenty five Years, and been seven Years a Citizen of the United States, and who shall not, when elected, be an Inhabitant of that State in which he shall be chosen.

Representatives and direct Taxes shall be apportioned among the several States which may be included within this Union, according to their respective Numbers, which shall be determined by adding to the whole Number of free Persons, including those bound to Service for a Term of Years, and excluding Indians not taxed, three fifths of all other Persons. The actual Enumeration shall be made within three Years after the first Meeting of the Congress of the United States, and within every subsequent Term of ten Years, in such Manner as they shall by Law direct. The Number of Representatives shall not exceed one for every thirty Thousand, but each State shall have at Least one Representative; and until such enumeration shall be made, the State of New Hampshire shall be entitled to chuse three, Massachusetts eight, Rhode-Island and Providence Plantations one, Connecticut five, New-York six, New Jersey four, Pennsylvania eight, Delaware one, Maryland six, Virginia ten, North Carolina five, South Carolina five, and Georgia three.

When vacancies happen in the Representation from any State, the Executive Authority thereof shall issue Writs of Election to fill such Vacancies.

The House of Representatives shall chuse their Speaker and other Officers; and shall have the sole Power of Impeachment.

SECTION. 3. The Senate of the United States shall be composed of two Senators from each State, chosen by the Legislature thereof, for six Years; and each Senator shall have one Vote.

Immediately after they shall be assembled in Consequence of the first Election, they shall be divided as equally as may be into three Classes. The Seats of the Senators of the first Class shall be vacated at the Expiration of the second Year, of the second Class at the Expiration of the fourth Year, and of the third Class at the Expiration of the sixth Year, so that one third may be chosen every second Year; and if Vacancies happen by Resignation, or otherwise, during the Recess of the Legislature of any State, the Executive thereof may make temporary Appointments until the next Meeting of the Legislature, which shall then fill such Vacancies.

No Person shall be a Senator who shall not have attained to the Age of thirty Years, and been nine Years a Citizen of the United States, and who shall not, when elected, be an Inhabitant of that State for which he shall be chosen.

The Vice President of the United States shall be President of the Senate, but shall have no Vote, unless they be equally divided.

The Senate shall chuse their other Officers, and also a President pro tempore, in the Absence of the Vice President, or when he shall exercise the Office of President of the United States.

The Senate shall have the sole Power to try all Impeachments. When sitting for that Purpose, they shall be on Oath or Affirmation. When the President of the United States is tried, the Chief Justice shall preside: And no Person shall be convicted without the Concurrence of two thirds of the Members present.

Judgment in Cases of Impeachment shall not extend further than to removal from Office, and disqualification to hold and enjoy any Office of honor, Trust or Profit under the United States: but the Party convicted shall nevertheless be liable and subject to Indictment, Trial, Judgment and Punishment, according to Law.

SECTION. 4. The Times, Places and Manner of holding Elections for Senators and Representatives, shall be prescribed in each State by the Legislature thereof; but the Congress may at any time by Law make or alter such Regulations, except as to the Places of chusing Senators.

The Congress shall assemble at least once in every Year, and such Meeting shall be on the first Monday in December, unless they shall by Law appoint a different Day.

SECTION. 5. Each House shall be the Judge of the Elections, Returns and Qualifications of its own Members, and a Majority of each shall constitute a Quorum to do Business; but a smaller Number may adjourn from day to day, and may be authorized to compel the Attendance of absent Members, in such Manner, and under such Penalties as each House may provide.

Each House may determine the Rules of its Proceedings, punish its Members for disorderly Behaviour, and, with the Concurrence of two thirds, expel a Member.

Each House shall keep a Journal of its Proceedings, and from time to time publish the same, excepting such Parts as may in their Judgment require Secrecy; and the Yeas and Nays of the Members of either House on any question shall, at the Desire of one fifth of those Present, be entered on the Journal.

Neither House, during the Session of Congress, shall, without the Consent of the other, adjourn for more than three days, nor to any other Place than that in which the two Houses shall be sitting.

SECTION. 6. The Senators and Representatives shall receive a Compensation for their Services, to be ascertained by Law, and paid out of the Treasury of the United States. They shall in all Cases, except Treason, Felony and Breach of the Peace, be privileged from Arrest during their Attendance at the Session of their respective Houses, and in going to and returning from the same; and for any Speech or Debate in either House, they shall not be questioned in any other Place.

No Senator or Representative shall, during the Time for which he was elected, be appointed to any civil Office under the Authority of the United States, which shall have been created, or the Emoluments whereof shall have been encreased during such time; and no Person holding any Office under the United States, shall be a Member of either House during his Continuance in Office.

SECTION. 7. All Bills for raising Revenue shall originate in the House of Representatives; but the Senate may propose or concur with Amendments as on other Bills.

Every Bill which shall have passed the House of Representatives and the Senate, shall, before it become a Law, be presented to the President of the United States; If he approve he shall sign it, but if not he shall return it, with his Objections to that House in which it shall have originated, who shall enter the Objections at large on their Journal, and proceed to reconsider it. If after such Reconsideration two thirds of that House shall agree to pass the Bill, it shall be sent, together with the Objections, to the other House, by which it shall likewise be reconsidered, and if approved by two thirds of that House, it shall become a Law. But in all such Cases the Votes of both Houses shall be determined by yeas and Nays, and the Names of the Persons voting for and against the Bill shall be entered on the Journal of each House respectively. If any Bill shall not be returned by the President within ten

Days (Sundays excepted) after it shall have been presented to him, the Same shall be a Law, in like Manner as if he had signed it, unless the Congress by their Adjournment prevent its Return, in which Case it shall not be a Law.

Every Order, Resolution, or Vote to which the Concurrence of the Senate and House of Representatives may be necessary (except on a question of Adjournment) shall be presented to the President of the United States; and before the Same shall take Effect, shall be approved by him, or being disapproved by him, shall be repassed by two thirds of the Senate and House of Representatives, according to the Rules and Limitations prescribed in the Case of a Bill.

SECTION. 8. The Congress shall have Power To lay and collect Taxes, Duties, Imposts and Excises, to pay the Debts and provide for the common Defence and general Welfare of the United States; but all Duties, Imposts and Excises shall be uniform throughout the United States;

To borrow Money on the credit of the United States;

To regulate Commerce with foreign Nations, and among the several States, and with the Indian tribes;

To establish an uniform Rule of Naturalization, and uniform Laws on the subject of Bankruptcies throughout the United States;

To coin Money, regulate the Value thereof, and of foreign Coin, and fix the Standard of Weights and Measures;

To provide for the Punishment of counterfeiting the Securities and current Coin of the United States;

To establish Post Offices and post Roads;

To promote the Progress of Science and useful Arts, by securing for limited Times to Authors and Inventors the exclusive Right to their respective Writings and Discoveries;

To constitute Tribunals inferior to the supreme Court;

To define and punish Piracies and Felonies committed on the high Seas, and Offences against the Law of Nations;

To declare War, grant Letters of Marque and Reprisal, and make Rules concerning Captures on Land and Water;

To raise and support Armies, but no Appropriation of Money to that Use shall be for a longer Term than two Years;

To provide and maintain a Navy;

To make Rules for the Government and Regulation of the land and naval Forces;

To provide for calling forth the Militia to execute the Laws of the Union, suppress Insurrections and repel Invasions;

To provide for organizing, arming, and disciplining, the Militia, and for governing such Part of them as may be employed in the Service of the United States, reserving to the States respectively, the Appointment of the Officers, and the Authority of training the Militia according to the discipline prescribed by Congress;

To exercise exclusive Legislation in all Cases whatsoever, over such District (not exceeding ten Miles square) as may, by Cession of particular States, and the Acceptance of Congress, become the Seat of the Government of the United States, and to exercise like Authority over all Places purchased by the Consent of the Legislature of the State in which the Same shall be, for the Erection of Forts, Magazines, Arsenals, dock- Yards, and other needful Buildings;—And

To make all Laws which shall be necessary and proper for carrying into Execution the foregoing Powers, and all other Powers vested by this Constitution in the Government of the United States, or in any Department or Officer thereof.

SECTION. 9. The Migration or Importation of such Persons as any of the States now existing shall think proper to admit, shall not be prohibited by the Congress prior to the Year one thousand eight hundred and eight, but a Tax or duty may be imposed on such Importation, not exceeding ten dollars for each Person.

The Privilege of the Writ of Habeas Corpus shall not be suspended, unless when in Cases of Rebellion or Invasion the public Safety may require it.

No Bill of Attainder or ex post facto Law shall be passed.

No Capitation, or other direct, Tax shall be laid, unless in Proportion to the Census or Enumeration herein before directed to be taken.

No Tax or Duty shall be laid on Articles exported from any State.

No Preference shall be given by any Regulation of Commerce or Revenue to the Ports of one State over those of another: nor shall Vessels bound to, or from, one State, be obliged to enter, clear, or pay Duties in another.

No Money shall be drawn from the Treasury, but in Consequence of Appropriations made by Law; and a regular Statement and Account of the Receipts and Expenditures of all public Money shall be published from time to time.

No Title of Nobility shall be granted by the United States: And no Person holding any Office of Profit or Trust under them, shall, without the Consent of the Congress, accept of any present, Emolument, Office, or Title, of any kind whatever, from any King, Prince, or foreign State.

SECTION. 10. No State shall enter into any Treaty, Alliance, or Confederation; grant Letters of Marque and Reprisal; coin Money; emit Bills of Credit; make any Thing but gold and silver Coin a Tender in Payment of Debts; pass any Bill of Attainder, ex post facto Law, or Law impairing the Obligation of Contracts, or grant any Title of Nobility.

No State shall, without the Consent of the Congress, lay any Imposts or Duties on Imports or Exports, except what may be absolutely necessary for executing it's inspection Laws: and the net Produce of all Duties and Imposts, laid by any State on Imports or Exports, shall be for the Use of the Treasury of the United States; and all such Laws shall be subject to the Revision and Controul of the Congress.

No State shall, without the consent of Congress, lay any Duty of Tonnage, keep Troops, or Ships of War in time of Peace, enter into any Agreement or Compact with another State, or with a foreign Power, or engage in War, unless actually invaded, or in such imminent Danger as will not admit of delay.

ARTICLE II.

SECTION. 1. The executive Power shall be vested in a President of the United States of America. He shall hold his Office during the Term of four Years, and, together with the Vice President, chosen for the same Term, be elected, as follows

Each State shall appoint, in such Manner as the Legislature thereof may direct, a Number of Electors, equal to the whole Number of Senators and Representatives to which the State may be entitled in the Congress; but no Senator or Representative, or Person holding an Office of Trust or Profit under the United States, shall be appointed an Elector.

The Electors shall meet in their respective States, and vote by Ballot for two Persons, of whom one at least shall not be an inhabitant of the same State with themselves. And they shall make a List of all the Persons voted for, and of the Number of Votes for each; which List they shall sign and certify, and transmit sealed to the Seat of the Government of the United States, directed to the President of the Senate. The President of the Senate shall, in the Presence of the Senate and House of Representatives, open all the Certificates, and the Votes shall then be counted. The Person having the greatest Number of Votes shall be the President, if such Number be a Majority of the whole Number of Electors appointed; and if there be more than one who have such Majority, and have an equal Number of Votes, then the House of Representatives shall immediately chuse by Ballot one of them for President; and if no Person have a Majority, then from the five highest on the List the said House shall in like Manner chuse the President. But in chusing the President, the Votes shall be taken by States, the Representation from each State having one Vote; A quorum for this purpose shall consist of a Member or Members from two thirds of the States, and a Majority of all the States shall be necessary to a Choice. In every Case, after the Choice of the President, the Person having the greatest Number of Votes of the Electors shall be the Vice President. But if there should remain two or more who have equal Votes, the Senate shall chuse from them by Ballot the Vice President.

The Congress may determine the Time of chusing the Electors, and the Day on which they shall give their Votes; which Day shall be the same throughout the United States.

No Person except a natural born Citizen, or a Citizen of the United States, at the time of the Adoption of this Constitution, shall be eligible to the Office of President; neither shall any Person be eligible to that Office who shall not have attained to the Age of thirty five Years, and been fourteen Years a Resident within the United States.

In Case of the Removal of the President from Office, or of his Death, Resignation, or

Inability to discharge the Powers and Duties of the said Office, the Same shall devolve on the Vice President, and the Congress may by Law provide for the Case of Removal, Death, Resignation or Inability, both of the President and the Vice President, declaring what Officer shall then act as President, and such Officer shall act accordingly, until the Disability be removed, or a President shall be elected.

The President shall, at stated Times, receive for his Services, a Compensation, which shall neither be encreased nor diminished during the Period for which he shall have been elected, and he shall not receive within that Period any other Emolument from the United States, or any of them.

Before he enter on the Execution of his Office, he shall take the following Oath of Affirmation:—"I do solemnly swear (or affirm) that I will faithfully execute the Office of President of the United States, and will to the best of my Ability, preserve, protect and defend the Constitution of the United States."

SECTION. 2. The President shall be Commander in Chief of the Army and Navy of the United States, and of the Militia of the several States, when called into the actual Service of the United States; he may require the Opinion, in writing, of the principal Officer in each of the executive Departments, upon any Subject relating to the Duties of their respective Offices, and he shall have Power to grant Reprieves and Pardons for Offences against the United States, except in Cases of Impeachment.

He shall have Power, by and with the Advice and Consent of the Senate, to make Treaties, provided two thirds of the Senators present concur; and he shall nominate, and by and with the Advice and Consent of the Senate, shall appoint Ambassadors, other public Ministers and Consuls, Judges of the supreme Court, and all other Officers of the United States, whose Appointments are not herein otherwise provided for, and which shall be established by Law: but the Congress may by Law vest the Appointment of such inferior Officers, as they think proper, in the President alone, in the Courts of Law, or in the Heads of Departments.

The President shall have Power to fill up all Vacancies that may happen during the Recess of the Senate, by granting Commissions which shall expire at the End of their next Session.

SECTION. 3. He shall from time to time give to the Congress Information of the State of the Union, and recommend to their Consideration such Measures as he shall judge necessary and expedient; he may, on extraordinary Occasions, convene both Houses, or either of them, and in Case of Disagreement between them, with Respect to the Time of Adjournment, he may adjourn them to such Time as he shall think proper; he shall receive Ambassadors and other public Ministers; he shall take Care that the Laws be faithfully executed, and shall Commission all the Officers of the United States.

SECTION. 4. The President, Vice President and all civil Officers of the United States, shall be removed from Office on Impeachment for, and Conviction of, Treason, Bribery, or other high Crimes and Misdemeanors.

ARTICLE III.

SECTION. 1. The judicial Power of the United States, shall be vested in one supreme Court, and in such inferior Courts as the Congress may from time to time ordain and establish. The Judges, both of the supreme and inferior Courts, shall hold their Offices during good Behaviour, and shall, at stated Times, receive for their Services, a Compensation, which shall not be diminished during their Continuance in Office.

SECTION. 2. The judicial Power shall extend to all Cases, in Law and Equity, arising under this Constitution, the Laws of the United States, and Treaties made, or which shall be made, under their Authority;—to all cases affecting Ambassadors, other public Ministers and Consuls;—to all Cases of admiralty and maritime Jurisdiction;—to Controversies to which the United States shall be a Party;—to Controversies between two or more States;—between a State and Citizens of another State;—between Citizens of different States;—between Citizens of the same State claiming Lands under Grants of different States, and between a State, or the Citizens thereof, and foreign States, Citizens or Subjects.

In all Cases affecting Ambassadors, other public Ministers and Consuls, and those in which a State shall be Party, the supreme Court shall have original Jurisdiction. In all the other Cases before mentioned, the supreme Court shall have appellate Jurisdiction, both as to Law and Fact, with such Exceptions, and under such Regulations as the Congress shall make.

The Trial of all Crimes, except in Cases of Impeachment, shall be by Jury; and such Trial shall be held in the State where the said Crimes shall have been committed; but when not committed within any State, the Trial shall be at such Place or Places as the Congress may by Law have directed.

SECTION. 3. Treason against the United States, shall consist only in levying War against them, or in adhering to their Enemies, giving them Aid and Comfort. No Person shall be convicted of Treason unless on the Testimony of two Witnesses to the same overt Act, or on Confession in open Court.

The Congress shall have Power to declare the Punishment of Treason, but no Attainder of Treason shall work Corruption of Blood, or Forfeiture except during the Life of the Person attainted.

ARTICLE IV.

SECTION. 1. Full Faith and Credit shall be given in each State to the public Acts, Records, and judicial Proceedings of every other State. And the Congress may by general Laws prescribe the Manner in which such Acts, Records and Proceedings shall be proved, and the Effect thereof.

SECTION. 2. The Citizens of each State shall be entitled to all Privileges and Immunities of Citizens in the several States.

A Person charged in any State with Treason, Felony, or other Crime, who shall flee from Justice, and be found in another State, shall on Demand of the executive Authority of the State from which he fled, be delivered up, to be removed to the State having Jurisdiction of the Crime.

No Person held to Service or Labour in one State, under the Laws thereof, escaping into another, shall, in Consequence of any Law or Regulation therein, be discharged from such Service or Labour, but shall be delivered up on Claim of the Party to whom such Service or Labour may be due.

SECTION. 3. New States may be admitted by the Congress into this Union; but no new State shall be formed or erected within the Jurisdiction of any other State; nor any State be formed by the Junction of two or more States, or Parts of States, without the Consent of the Legislatures of the States concerned as well as of the Congress.

The Congress shall have Power to dispose of and make all needful Rules and Regulations respecting the Territory or other Property belonging to the United States; and nothing in this Constitution shall be so construed as to Prejudice any Claims of the United States, or of any particular State.

SECTION. 4. The United States shall guarantee to every State in this Union a Republican Form of Government, and shall protect each of them against Invasion; and on Application of the Legislature, or of the Executive (when the Legislature cannot be convened) against domestic Violence.

ARTICLE V.

The Congress, whenever two thirds of both Houses shall deem it necessary, shall propose Amendments to this Constitution, or, on the Application of the Legislatures of two thirds of the several States, shall call a Convention for proposing Amendments, which, in either Case, shall be valid to all Intents and Purposes, as Part of this Constitution, when ratified by the legislatures of three fourths of the several States, or by Conventions in three fourths thereof, as the one or the other Mode of Ratification may be proposed by the Congress; Provided that no Amendment which may be made prior to the Year One thousand eight hundred and eight shall in any Manner affect the first and fourth Clauses in the Ninth Section of the first Article; and that no State, without its Consent, shall be deprived of it's equal Suffrage in the Senate.

ARTICLE VI.

All Debts contracted and Engagements entered into, before the Adoption of this Constitution, shall be as valid against the United States under this Constitution, as under the Confederation.

This Constitution, and the Laws of the United States which shall be made in Pursuance thereof; and all Treaties made, or which shall be made, under the Authority of the United States, shall be the supreme Law of the Land; and the Judges in every State shall be bound thereby, any Thing in the Constitution or Laws of any State to the Contrary notwithstanding.

The Senators and Representatives before mentioned, and the Members of the several State Legislatures, and all executive and judicial Officers, both of the United States and of the several States, shall be bound by Oath or Affirmation, to support this Constitution; but no religious Test shall ever be required as a Qualification to any Office or public Trust under the United States.

ARTICLE VII.

The Ratification of the Conventions of nine States, shall be sufficient for the Establishment of this Constitution between the States so ratifying the Same.

The Word "the", being interlined between the seventh and eighth Lines of the first Page, the Word "Thirty" being partly written on an Erazure in the fifteenth Line of the first Page, The Words "is tried" being interlined between the thirty second and thirty third Lines of the first Page and the Word "the" being interlined between the forty third and forty fourth Lines of the second Page.

Attest William Jackson Secretary

DONE in Convention by the Unanimous Consent of the States present the Seventeenth Day of September in the Year of our Lord one thousand seven hundred and Eighty seven and of the Independance of the United States of America the Twelfth. IN WITNESS whereof We have hereunto subscribed our Names.

G° WASHINGTON
Presid' and deputy from Virginia

DELAWARE
- GEO: READ
- GUNNING BEDFORD jun
- JOHN DICKINSON
- RICHARD BASSETT
- JACO: BROOM

MARYLAND
- JAMES MCHENRY
- DAN OF ST. THOS. JENIFER
- DANL. CARROLL

VIRGINIA
- JOHN BLAIR—
- JAMES MADISON JR.

NORTH CAROLINA
- WM. BLOUNT
- RICHD. DOBBS SPAIGHT
- HU WILLIAMSON

SOUTH CAROLINA
- J. RUTLEDGE
- CHARLES COTESWORTH PINCKNEY
- CHARLES PINCKNEY
- PIERCE BUTLER

GEORGIA
- WILLIAM FEW
- ABR BALDWIN

NEW HAMPSHIRE
- JOHN LANGDON
- NICHOLAS GILMAN

MASSACHUSETTS
- NATHANIEL GORHAM
- RUFUS KING

CONNECTICUT
- WM. SAML. JOHNSON
- ROGER SHERMAN

NEW YORK
- ALEXANDER HAMILTON

NEW JERSEY
- WIL: LIVINGSTON
- DAVID BREARLEY
- WM. PATERSON
- JONA: DAYTON

PENNSYLVANIA
- B. FRANKLIN
- THOMAS MIFFLIN
- ROBT. MORRIS
- GEO. CLYMER
- THOS. FITZSIMONS
- JARED INGERSOLL
- JAMES WILSON
- GOUV MORRIS

AMENDMENT I [1791]

Congress shall make no law respecting an establishment of religion, or prohibiting the free exercise thereof; or abridging the freedom of speech, or of the press; or the right of the people peaceably to assemble, and to petition the Government for a redress of grievances.

AMENDMENT II [1791]

A well regulated Militia, being necessary to the security of a free State, the right of the people to keep and bear Arms, shall not be infringed.

AMENDMENT III [1791]

No Soldier shall, in time of peace be quartered in any house, without the consent of the Owner, nor in time of war, but in a manner to be prescribed by law.

AMENDMENT IV [1791]

The right of the people to be secure in their persons, houses, papers, and effects, against unreasonable searches and seizures, shall not be violated, and no Warrants shall issue, but upon probable cause, supported by Oath or affirmation, and particularly describing the place to be searched, and the persons or things to be seized.

AMENDMENT V [1791]

No person shall be held to answer for a capital, or otherwise infamous crime, unless on a presentment or indictment of a Grand Jury, except in cases arising in the land or naval forces, or in the Militia, when in actual service in time of War or public danger; nor shall any person be subject for the same offence to be twice put in jeopardy of life or limb; nor shall be compelled in any criminal case to be a witness against himself, nor be deprived of life, liberty or property, without due process of law; nor shall private property be taken for public use, without just compensation.

AMENDMENT VI [1791]

In all criminal prosecutions, the accused shall enjoy the right to a speedy and public trial, by an impartial jury of the State and district wherein the crime shall have been committed, which district shall have been previously ascertained by law, and to be informed of the nature and cause of the accusation; to be confronted with the witnesses against him; to have compulsory process for obtaining Witnesses in his favor, and to have the assistance of counsel for his defence.

AMENDMENT VII [1791]

In Suits at Common law, where the value in controversy shall exceed twenty dollars, the right of trial by jury shall be preserved, and no fact tried by a jury, shall be otherwise re-examined in any Court of the United States, than according to the rules of the common law.

AMENDMENT VIII [1791]

Excessive bail shall not be required, nor excessive fines imposed, nor cruel and unusual punishments inflicted.

AMENDMENT IX [1791]

The enumeration in the Constitution, of certain rights, shall not be construed to deny or disparage others retained by the people.

AMENDMENT X [1791]

The powers not delegated to the United States by the Constitution, nor prohibited by it to the States, are reserved to the States respectively, or to the people.

AMENDMENT XI [1798]

The Judicial power of the United States shall not be construed to extend to any suit in law or equity, commenced or prosecuted against one of the United States by Citizens of another State, or by Citizens or Subjects of any Foreign State.

AMENDMENT XII [1804]

The Electors shall meet in their respective states, and vote by ballot for President and Vice-President, one of whom, at least, shall not be an inhabitant of the same state with themselves; they shall name in their ballots the person voted for as President, and in distinct ballots the person voted for as Vice-President, and they shall make distinct lists of all persons voted for as President, and of all persons voted for as Vice-President, and of the number of votes for each, which lists they shall sign and certify, and transmit sealed to the seat of the government of the United States, directed to the President of the Senate;—The President of the Senate shall, in the presence of the Senate and House of Representatives, open all the certificates and the votes shall then be counted;—The Person having the greatest number of votes for President, shall be the President, if such number be a majority of the whole number of Electors appointed; and if no person have such majority, then from the persons having the highest numbers not exceeding three on the list of those voted for as President, the House of Representatives shall choose immediately, by ballot, the President. But in choosing the President, the votes shall be taken by states, the representation from each state having one vote; a quorum for this purpose shall consist of a member or members from two-thirds of the states, and a majority of all the states shall be necessary to a choice. And if the House of Representatives shall not choose a President whenever the right of choice shall devolve upon them, before the fourth day of March next following, then the Vice-President shall act as President, as in the case of the death or other constitutional disability of the President.—The person having the greatest number of votes as Vice-President, shall be the Vice-President, if such number be a majority of the whole number of Electors appointed, and if no person have a majority, then from the two highest numbers on the list, the Senate shall choose the Vice-President; a quorum for the purpose shall consist of two-thirds of the whole number of Senators, and a majority of the whole number shall be necessary to a choice. But no person constitutionally ineligible to the office of President shall be eligible to that of Vice-President of the United States.

AMENDMENT XIII [1865]

Section 1. Neither slavery nor involuntary servitude, except as a punishment for crime whereof the party shall have been duly convicted, shall exist within the United States, or any place subject to their jurisdiction.

Section 2. Congress shall have power to enforce this article by appropriate legislation.

AMENDMENT XIV [1868]

Section 1. All persons born or naturalized in the United States, and subject to the jurisdiction thereof, are citizens of the United States and of the State wherein they reside. No State shall make or enforce any law which shall abridge the privileges or immunities of citizens of the United States; nor shall any State deprive any person of life, liberty, or property, without due process of law; nor deny to any person within its jurisdiction the equal protection of the laws.

SECTION 2. Representatives shall be apportioned among the several States according to their respective numbers, counting the whole number of persons in each State, excluding Indians not taxed. But when the right to vote at any election for the choice of electors for President and Vice President of the United States, Representatives in Congress, the Executive and Judicial officers of a State, or the members of the Legislature thereof, is denied to any of the male inhabitants of such State, being twenty-one years of age, and citizens of the United States, or in any way abridged, except for participation in rebellion, or other crime, the basis of representation therein shall be reduced in the proportion which the number of such male citizens shall bear to the whole number of male citizens twenty-one years of age in such State.

SECTION 3. No person shall be a Senator or Representative in Congress, or elector of President and Vice President, or hold any office, civil or military, under the United States, or under any State, who, having previously taken an oath, as a member of Congress, or as an officer of the United States, or as a member of any State legislature, or as an executive or judicial officer of any State, to support the Constitution of the United States, shall have engaged in insurrection or rebellion against the same, or given aid or comfort to the enemies thereof. But Congress may by a vote of two-thirds of each House, remove such disability.

SECTION 4. The validity of the public debt of the United States, authorized by law, including debts incurred for payment of pensions and bounties for services in suppressing insurrection or rebellion, shall not be questioned. But neither the United States nor any State shall assume or pay any debt or obligation incurred in aid of insurrection or rebellion against the United States, or any claim for the loss or emancipation of any slave; but all such debts, obligations and claims shall be held illegal and void.

SECTION 5. The Congress shall have power to enforce, by appropriate legislation, the provisions of this article.

AMENDMENT XV [1870]

SECTION 1. The right of citizens of the United States to vote shall not be denied or abridged by the United States or by any State on account of race, color, or previous condition of servitude.

SECTION 2. The Congress shall have power to enforce this article by appropriate legislation.

AMENDMENT XVI [1913]

The Congress shall have power to lay and collect taxes on incomes, from whatever source derived, without apportionment among the several States, and without regard to any census or enumeration.

AMENDMENT XVII [1913]

The Senate of the United States shall be composed of two Senators from each State, elected by the people thereof, for six years; and each Senator shall have one vote. The electors in each State shall have the qualifications requisite for electors of the most numerous branch of the State legislatures.

When vacancies happen in the representation of any State in the Senate, the executive authority of such State shall issue writs of election to fill such vacancies: *Provided,* That the legislature of any State may empower the executive thereof to make temporary appointments until the people fill the vacancies by election as the legislature may direct.

This amendment shall not be so construed as to affect the election or term of any Senator chosen before it becomes valid as part of the Constitution.

AMENDMENT XVIII [1919]

SECTION 1. After one year from the ratification of this article the manufacture, sale, or transportation of intoxicating liquors within, the importation thereof into, or the exportation thereof from the United States and all territory subject to the jurisdiction thereof for beverage purposes is hereby prohibited.

SECTION 2. The Congress and the several States shall have concurrent power to enforce this article by appropriate legislation.

SECTION 3. This article shall be inoperative unless it shall have been ratified as an amendment to the Constitution by the legislatures of the several States, as provided in the Constitution, within seven years from the date of the submission hereof to the States by the Congress.

AMENDMENT XIX [1920]

The right of citizens of the United States to vote shall not be denied or abridged by the United States or by any State on account of sex.

Congress shall have power to enforce this article by appropriate legislation.

AMENDMENT XX [1933]

SECTION 1. The terms of the President and Vice President shall end at noon on the 20th day of January, and the terms of Senators and Representatives at noon on the 3d day of January, of the years in which such terms would have ended if this article had not been ratified; and the terms of their successors shall then begin.

SECTION 2. The Congress shall assemble at least once in every year, and such meeting shall begin at noon on the 3d day of January, unless they shall by law appoint a different day.

SECTION 3. If, at the time fixed for the beginning of the term of the President, the President elect shall have died, the Vice President elect shall become President. If a President shall not have been chosen before the time fixed for the beginning of his term, or if the President elect shall have failed to qualify, then the Vice President elect shall act as President until a President shall have qualified; and the Congress may by law provide for the case wherein neither a President elect nor a Vice President elect shall have qualified, declaring who shall then act as President, or the manner in which one who is to act shall be selected, and such person shall act accordingly until a President or Vice President shall have qualified.

SECTION 4. The Congress may by law provide for the case of the death of any of the persons from whom the House of Representatives may choose a President whenever the right of choice shall have devolved upon them, and for the case of the death of any of the persons from whom the Senate may choose a Vice President whenever the right of choice shall have devolved upon them.

SECTION 5. Sections 1 and 2 shall take effect on the 15th day of October following the ratification of this article.

SECTION 6. This article shall be inoperative unless it shall have been ratified as an amendment to the Constitution by the legislatures of three-fourths of the several States within seven years from the date of its submission.

AMENDMENT XXI [1933]

SECTION 1. The eighteenth article of amendment to the Constitution of the United States is hereby repealed.

SECTION 2. The transportation or importation into any State, Territory, or possession of the United States for delivery or use therein of intoxicating liquors, in violation of the laws thereof, is hereby prohibited.

SECTION 3. This article shall be inoperative unless it shall have been ratified as an amendment to the Constitution by conventions in the several States, as provided in the

Constitition, within seven years from the date of the submission hereof to the States by the Congress.

AMENDMENT XXII [1951]

SECTION 1. No person shall be elected to the office of the President more than twice, and no person who has held the office of President, or acted as President, for more than two years of a term to which some other person was elected President shall be elected to the office of the president more than once. But this Article shall not apply to any person holding the office of President when this Article was proposed by the Congress, and shall not prevent any person who may be holding the office of President, or acting as President, during the term within which this Article becomes operative from holding the office of President or acting as president during the remainder of such term.

SECTION 2. This article shall be inoperative unless it shall have been ratified as an amendment to the Constitution by the legislatures of three-fourths of the several States within seven years from the date of its submission to the States by the Congress.

AMENDMENT XXIII [1961]

SECTION 1. The District constituting the seat of Government of the United States shall appoint in such manner as the Congress may direct:

A number of electors of President and Vice President equal to the whole number of Senators and Representatives in Congress to which the District would be entitled if it were a State, but in no event more than the least populous State; they shall be in addition to those appointed by the States, but they shall be considered, for the purposes of the election of President and Vice President, to be electors appointed by a State; and they shall meet in the District and perform such duties as provided by the twelfth article of amendment.

SECTION 2. The Congress shall have power to enforce this article by appropriate legislation.

AMENDMENT XXIV [1964]

SECTION 1. The right of citizens of the United States to vote in any primary or other election for President or Vice President, for electors for President or Vice President, or for Senator or Representatives in Congress, shall not be denied or abridged by the United States or any State by reason of failure to pay any poll tax or other tax.

SECTION 2. The Congress shall have power to enforce this article by appropriate legislation.

AMENDMENT XXV [1967]

SECTION 1. In case of the removal of the President from office or of his death or resignation, the Vice President shall become President.

SECTION 2. Whenever there is a vacancy in the office of the Vice President, the President shall nominate a Vice President who shall take office upon confirmation by a majority vote of both Houses of Congress.

SECTION 3. Whenever the President transmits to the President pro tempore of the Senate and the Speaker of the House of Representatives his written declaration that he is unable to discharge the powers and duties of his office, and until he transmits to them a written declaration to the contrary, such powers and duties shall be discharged by the Vice President as Acting President.

SECTION 4. Whenever the Vice President and a majority of either the principal officers of the executive departments or of such other body as Congress may by law provide, transmit to the President pro tempore of the Senate and the Speaker of the House of Representatives their written declaration that the President is unable to discharge the powers and duties of his office, the Vice President shall immediately assume the powers and duties of the office as Acting President.

Thereafter, when the President transmits to the President pro tempore of the Senate and the Speaker of the House of Representatives his written declaration that no inability exists, he shall resume the powers and duties of his office unless the Vice President and a majority of either the principal officers of the executive department or of such other body as Congress may by law provide, transmit within four days to the President pro tempore of the Senate and the Speaker of the House of Representatives their written declaration that the President is unable to discharge the powers and duties of his office. Thereupon Congress shall decide the issue, assembling within forty-eight hours for that purpose if not in session. If the Congress, within twenty-one days after receipt of the latter written declaration, or, if Congress is not in session, within twenty-one days after Congress is required to assemble, determines by two-thirds vote of both Houses that the President is unable to discharge the powers and duties of his office, the Vice President shall continue to discharge the same as Acting President; otherwise, the President shall resume the powers and duties of his office.

AMENDMENT XXVI [1971]

Section 1. The right of citizens of the United States, who are eighteen years of age or older, to vote shall not be denied or abridged by the United States or by any State on account of age.

Section 2. The Congress shall have power to enforce this article by appropriate legislation.

AMENDMENT XXVII [1992]

No law, varying the compensation for the services of the Senators and Representatives, shall take effect, until an election of Representatives shall have intervened.

Tables

TABLE 1. *Presidents: Personal Information*

No.	President	Birthdate	Age at Election	Birthplace	First Lady	Place of Death	Date of Death
1	George Washington, 1789–1797	22 Feb 1732	57	Westmoreland County, Virginia	Martha Dandridge Custis Washington	Mount Vernon, Virginia	14 Dec 1799
2	John Adams, 1797–1801	30 Oct 1735	61	Braintree (now Quincy), Massachusetts	Abigail Smith Adams	Quincy, Massachusetts	4 Jul 1826
3	Thomas Jefferson, 1801–1809	13 Apr 1743	57	Goochland (now Albemarle) County, Virginia	Widower	Charlottesville, Virginia	4 Jul 1826
4	James Madison, 1809–1817	16 Mar 1751	57	Port Conway, Virginia	Dolley Payne Todd Madison	Orange County, Virginia	28 Jun 1836
5	James Monroe, 1817–1825	28 Apr 1758	58	Westmoreland County, Virginia	Elizabeth Kortright Monroe	New York City	4 Jul 1831
6	John Quincy Adams, 1825–1829	11 Jul 1767	57	Braintree (now Quincy), Massachusetts	Louisa Johnson Adams	Washington, D.C.	23 Feb 1848
7	Andrew Jackson, 1829–1837	15 Mar 1767	61	Waxhaw, South Carolina	Widower	Nashville, Tennessee	8 Jun 1845
8	Martin van Buren, 1837–1841	5 Dec 1782	54	Kinderhook, New York	Widower	Kinderhook, New York	24 Jul 1862
9	William Henry Harrison, 1841	9 Feb 1773	68	Berkeley, Virginia	Anna Symmes Harrison	Washington, D.C.	4 Apr 1841
10	John Tyler, 1841–1845	29 Mar 1790	51	Charles City County, Virginia	Letitia Christian Tyler; Julia Gardiner Tyler	Richmond, Virginia	18 Jan 1862
11	James Knox Polk, 1845–1849	2 Nov 1795	49	Mecklenburg County, North Carolina	Sarah Childress Polk	Nashville, Tennessee	15 Jun 1849
12	Zachary Taylor, 1849–1850	24 Nov 1784	64	Orange County, Virginia	Margaret Mackall Smith Taylor	Washington, D.C.	9 Jul 1850
13	Millard Fillmore, 1850–1853	7 Jan 1800	50	Cayuga County, New York	Abigail Powers Fillmore	Buffalo, New York	8 Mar 1874
14	Franklin Pierce, 1853–1857	23 Nov 1804	48	Hillsboro, New Hampshire	Jane Means Appleton Pierce	Concord, New Hampshire	8 Oct 1869
15	James Buchanan, 1857–1861	23 Apr 1791	65	Stony Batter, Pennsylvania	Never married	Lancaster, Pennsylvania	1 Jun 1868
16	Abraham Lincoln, 1861–1865	12 Feb 1809	52	Hodgenville, Kentucky	Mary Todd Lincoln	Washington, D.C.	15 Apr 1865
17	Andrew Johnson, 1865–1869	29 Dec 1808	56	Raleigh, North Carolina	Eliza McCardle Johnson	Carter's Station, Tennessee	31 Jul 1875
18	Ulysses S. Grant, 1869–1877	27 Apr 1822	46	Point Pleasant, Ohio	Julia Dent Grant	Mount McGregor, New York	23 Jul 1885
19	Rutherford B. Hayes, 1877–1881	4 Oct 1822	54	Delaware, Ohio	Lucy Webb Hayes	Fremont, Ohio	17 Jan 1893
20	James A. Garfield, 1881	19 Nov 1831	49	Orange, Ohio	Lucretia Rudolph Garfield	Elberon, New Jersey	19 Sep 1881
21	Chester A. Arthur, 1881–1885	5 Oct 1830	50	Fairfield, Vermont	Widower	New York City	18 Nov 1886
22	Grover Cleveland, 1885–1889	18 Mar 1837	47	Caldwell, New Jersey	Frances Folsom Cleveland	Princeton, New Jersey	24 Jun 1908

TABLE 1.   *Presidents: Personal Information (Continued)*

No.	President	Birthdate	Age at Election	Birthplace	First Lady	Place of Death	Date of Death
23	Benjamin Harrison, 1889–1893	20 Aug 1833	55	North Bend, Ohio	Caroline Scott Harrison	Indianapolis, Indiana	13 Mar 1901
24	Grover Cleveland, 1893–1897	18 Mar 1837	55	Caldwell, New Jersey	Frances Folsom Cleveland	Princeton, New Jersey	24 Jun 1908
25	William McKinley, 1897–1901	29 Jan 1843	54	Niles, Ohio	Ida Saxton McKinley	Buffalo, New York	14 Sep 1901
26	Theodore Roosevelt, 1901–1909	27 Oct 1858	42	New York City	Edith Kermit Carow Roosevelt	Oyster Bay, New York	6 Jan 1919
27	William Howard Taft, 1909–1913	15 Sep 1857	51	Cincinnati, Ohio	Helen Herron Taft	Washington, D.C.	8 Mar 1931
28	Woodrow Wilson, 1913–1921	28 Dec 1856	56	Staunton, Virginia	Ellen Louise Axson Wilson; Edith Bolling Galt Wilson	Washington, D.C.	3 Feb 1924
29	Warren G. Harding, 1921–1923	2 Nov 1865	55	Corsica (now Blooming Grove), Ohio	Florence Kling De Wolfe Harding	San Francisco, California	2 Aug 1923
30	Calvin Coolidge, 1923–1929	4 Jul 1872	51	Plymouth Notch, Vermont	Grace Goodhue Coolidge	Northampton, Massachussetts	5 Jan 1933
31	Herbert C. Hoover, 1929–1933	10 Aug 1874	54	West Branch, Iowa	Lou Henry Hoover	New York City	20 Oct 1964
32	Franklin D. Roosevelt, 1933–1945	30 Jan 1882	51	Hyde Park, New York	Anna Eleanor Roosevelt Roosevelt	Warm Springs, Georgia	12 Apr 1945
33	Harry S. Truman, 1945–1953	8 May 1884	60	Lamar, Missouri	Elizabeth Wallace ("Bess") Truman	Kansas City, Missouri	26 Dec 1972
34	Dwight D. Eisenhower, 1953–1961	14 Oct 1890	62	Denison, Texas	Mamie Doud Eisenhower	Washington, D.C.	28 Mar 1969
35	John F. Kennedy, 1961–1963	29 May 1917	43	Brookline, Massachusetts	Jacqueline Bouvier Kennedy	Dallas, Texas	22 Nov 1963
36	Lyndon B. Johnson, 1963–1969	27 Aug 1908	55	Stonewall, Texas	Claudia Alta Taylor ("Lady Bird") Johnson	San Antonio, Texas	22 Jan 1973
37	Richard M. Nixon, 1969–1974	9 Jan 1913	56	Yorba Linda, California	Thelma Catherine ("Pat") Ryan Nixon	New York City	22 Apr 1994
38	Gerald Ford, 1974–1977	14 Jul 1913	61	Omaha, Nebraska	Betty Bloomer Warren Ford		
39	Jimmy Carter, 1977–1981	1 Oct 1924	52	Plains, Georgia	Rosalynn Smith Carter		
40	Ronald Reagan, 1981–1989	6 Feb 1911	69	Tampico, Illinois	Nancy Davis Reagan		
41	George Bush, 1989–1993	12 Jun 1924	64	Milton, Massachusetts	Barbara Pierce Bush		
42	Bill Clinton, 1993–	19 Aug 1946	46	Hope, Arkansas	Hillary Rodham Clinton		

TABLE 2. *Presidents and Cabinets*
This table includes Vice Presidents, heads of Cabinet departments, Solicitors General
(part of the Justice Department), and Chairmen of the Joint Chiefs of Staff (part of
the Defense Department). For the development and composition of the Cabinet, see
the table that accompanies the entry CABINET.

No.	President	Vice President	Secretary of State	Secretary of the Treasury	Secretary of War
1	George Washington, 1789–1797	John Adams, 1789–1797	Thomas Jefferson, 1789–1793 Edmund Randolph, 1794–1795 Timothy Pickering, 1795–1797	Alexander Hamilton, 1789–1795 Oliver Wolcott, Jr. 1795–1797	Henry Knox, 1789–1795 Timothy Pickering, 1795–1796 James McHenry, 1796–1797
2	John Adams, 1797–1801	Thomas Jefferson, 1797–1801	Timothy Pickering, 1797–1800 John Marshall, 1800–1801	Oliver Wolcott, Jr., 1797–1800 Samuel Dexter, 1801	James McHenry, 1797–1800 Samuel Dexter, 1800–1801 Roger Griswold, 1801
3	Thomas Jefferson, 1801–1809	Aaron Burr, 1801–1805 George Clinton, 1805–1809	James Madison, 1801–1809	Samuel Dexter, 1801 Albert Gallatin, 1801–1809	Henry Dearborn, 1801–1809
4	James Madison, 1809–1817	George Clinton, 1809–1813 Elbridge Gerry, 1813–1814	Robert Smith, 1809–1811 James Monroe, 1811–1817	Albert Gallatin, 1809–1814 George W. Campbell, 1814 Alexander J. Dallas, 1814–1816 William H. Crawford, 1816–1817	William Eustis, 1809 John Armstrong, 1813–1814 James Monroe, 1814–1815 William H. Crawford, 1815–1816
5	James Monroe, 1817–1825	Daniel D. Tompkins, 1817–1825	John Quincy Adams, 1817–1825	William H. Crawford, 1817–1825	George Graham, 1817 John C. Calhoun, 1817–1825
6	John Quincy Adams, 1825–1829	John C. Calhoun, 1825–1829	Henry Clay, 1825–1829	Richard Rush, 1825–1829	James Barbour, 1825–1828 Peter B. Porter, 1828–1829
7	Andrew Jackson, 1829–1837	John C. Calhoun, 1829–1832 Martin Van Buren, 1833–1837	Martin Van Buren, 1829–1831 Edward Livingston, 1831–1833	Samuel D. Ingham, 1829–1831 Louis McLane, 1831–1833	John H. Eaton, 1829–1831 Lewis Cass, 1831–1836

Continued down on page 1694; continued across on page 1693.

Secretary of the Navy	Chairman, Joint Chiefs of Staff	Attorney General	Solicitor General	Postmaster General	Secretary of the Interior
		Edmund Randolph, 1789–1794		Samuel Osgood, 1789–1791	
		William Bradford, 1794–1795		Timothy Pickering, 1791–1795	
		Charles Lee, 1795–1797		Joseph Habersham, 1795–1797	
Benjamin Stoddert, 1798–1801		Charles Lee, 1797–1801		Joseph Habersham, 1797–1801	
		Theophilus Parsons, 1801			
Benjamin Stoddert, 1801		Levi Lincoln, 1801–1804		Joseph Habersham, 1801	
Robert Smith, 1801–1809		Robert Smith, 1805		Gideon Granger, 1801–1809	
Jacob Crowninshield, 1805		John Breckinridge, 1805–1806			
		Caesar A. Rodney, 1807–1809			
Paul Hamilton, 1809–1812		Caesar A. Rodney, 1809–1811		Gideon Granger, 1809–1814	
William Jones, 1813–1814		William Pinckney, 1811–1814		Return J. Meigs, Jr., 1814–1817	
Benjamin W. Crowninshield, 1815–1817		Richard Rush, 1814–1817			
Benjamin W. Crowninshield, 1817–1818		Richard Rush, 1817		Return J. Meigs, Jr., 1817–1823	
Smith Thompson, 1819–1823		William Wirt, 1817–1825		John McLean, 1823–1825	
Samuel L. Southard, 1823–1825					
Samuel L. Southard, 1825–1829		William Wirt, 1825–1829		John McLean, 1825–1829	
John Branch, 1829–1831		John M. Berrien, 1829–1831		William T. Barry, 1829–1835	

Continued down on page 1695.

TABLE 2. *Presidents and Cabinets (Continued)*

No.	President	Vice President	Secretary of State	Secretary of the Treasury	Secretary of War
7	Andrew Jackson 1829–1837		Louis McLane, 1833–1834 John Forsyth, 1834–1837	William J. Duane, 1833 Roger B. Taney, 1833–1834 Levi Woodbury, 1834–1837	
8	Martin Van Buren, 1837–1841	Richard M. Johnson, 1837–1841	John Forsyth, 1837–1841	Levi Woodbury, 1837–1841	Joel R. Poinsett, 1837–1841
9	William Henry Harrison, 1841	John Tyler, 1841	Daniel Webster, 1841	Thomas Ewing, 1841	John Bell, 1841
10	John Tyler, 1841–1845	None	Daniel Webster, 1841–1843 Abel P. Upshur, 1843–1844 John C. Calhoun, 1844–1845	Thomas Ewing, 1841 Walter Forward, 1841–1843 John C. Spencer, 1843–1844 George M. Bibb, 1844–1845	John Bell, 1841 John McLean, 1841 John C. Spencer, 1841–1843 James M. Porter, 1843–1844 William Wilkins, 1844–1845
11	James Knox Polk, 1845–1849	George M. Dallas, 1845–1849	James Buchanan, 1845–1849	George M. Bibb, 1845 Robert J. Walker, 1845–1849	William L. Marcy, 1845–1849
12	Zachary Taylor, 1849–1850	Millard Fillmore, 1849–1850	John M. Clayton, 1849–1850	William M. Meredith, 1849–1850	George W. Crawford, 1849–1850
13	Millard Fillmore, 1850–1853	None	John Clayton, 1850 Daniel Webster, 1850–1852 Edward Everett, 1852–1853	William M. Meredith, 1850 Thomas Corwin, 1850–1853	George W. Crawford, 1850 Charles M. Conrad, 1850–1853
14	Franklin Pierce, 1853–1857	William R. D. King, 1853	William L. Marcy, 1853–1857	James Guthrie, 1853–1857	Jefferson Davis, 1853–1857
15	James Buchanan, 1857–1861	John C. Breckinridge, 1857–1861	Lewis Cass, 1857–1860 Jeremiah S. Black, 1860–1861	Howell Cobb, 1857–1860 Philip F. Thomas, 1860–1861 John A. Dix 1861	John B. Floyd 1857–1861 Joseph Holt, 1861

Continued down on page 1696; continued across on page 1695.

Secretary of the Navy	Chairman, Joint Chiefs of Staff	Attorney General	Solicitor General	Postmaster General	Secretary of the Interior
Levi Woodbury, 1831–1834 Mahlon Dickerson, 1834–1837		Roger B. Taney, 1831–1833 Benjamin F. Butler, 1833–1837		Amos Kendall, 1835–1837	
Mahlon Dickerson, 1837–1838 James K. Paulding, 1838–1841		Benjamin F. Butler, 1837–1838 Felix Grundy, 1838–1840 Henry D. Gilpin, 1840–1841		Amos Kendall, 1837–1840 John M. Niles, 1840–1841	
George E. Badger, 1841		John J. Crittenden, 1841		Francis Granger, 1841	
George E. Badger, 1841 Abel P. Upshur, 1841–1843 David Henshaw, 1843–1844 Thomas W. Gilmer, 1844 John Y. Mason, 1844–1845		John J. Crittenden, 1841 Hugh S. Legaré, 1841–1843 John Nelson, 1843–1845		Francis Granger, 1841 Charles A. Wickliffe, 1841–1845	
George Bancroft, 1845–1846 John Y. Mason, 1846–1849		John Y. Mason, 1845–1846 Nathan Clifford, 1846–1848 Isaac Toucey, 1848–1849		Cave Johnson, 1845–1849	
William B. Preston, 1849–1850		Reverdy Johnson, 1849–1850		Jacob Collamer, 1849–1850	Thomas Ewing, 1849–1850
William A. Graham, 1850–1852 John P. Kennedy, 1852–1853		John J. Crittenden, 1850–1853		Nathan K. Hall, 1850–1852 Samuel D. Hubbard, 1852–1853	T. M. T. McKennan, 1850 Alex H. H. Stuart, 1850–1853
James C. Dobbin, 1853–1857		Caleb Cushing, 1853–1857		James Campbell, 1853–1857	Robert McClelland, 1853–1857
Isaac Toucey, 1857–1861		Jeremiah S. Black, 1857–1860 Edwin M. Stanton, 1860–1861		Aaron V. Brown, 1857–1859 Joseph Holt, 1859–1861 Horatio King, 1861	Jacob Thompson, 1857–1861

Continued down on page 1697.

TABLE 2. *Presidents and Cabinets (Continued)*

No.	President	Vice President	Secretary of State	Secretary of the Treasury	Secretary of War
16	Abraham Lincoln, 1861–1865	Hannibal Hamlin, 1861–1865 Andrew Johnson, 1865	William H. Seward, 1861–1865	Salmon P. Chase, 1861–1864 William P. Fessenden, 1864–1865 Hugh McCulloch, 1865	Simon Cameron, 1861–1862 Edwin M. Stanton, 1862–1865
17	Andrew Johnson, 1865–1869	None	William H. Seward, 1865–1869	Hugh McCulloch, 1865–1869	Edwin M. Stanton, 1865–1867 Ulysses S. Grant, 1867–1868 Lorenzo Thomas, 1868 John M. Schofield, 1868–1869
18	Ulysses S. Grant, 1869–1877	Schuyler Colfax, 1869–1873 Henry Wilson, 1873–1875	Elihu B. Washburne, 1869 Hamilton Fish, 1869–1877	George S. Boutwell, 1869–1873 William A. Richardson, 1873–1874 Benjamin H. Bristow, 1874–1876 Lot M. Morrill, 1876–1877	John A. Rawlins, 1869 William T. Sherman, 1869 William W. Belknap, 1869–1876 Alphonso Taft, 1876 James D. Cameron, 1876–1877
19	Rutherford B. Hayes, 1877–1881	William A. Wheeler, 1877–1881	William M. Evarts, 1877–1881	John Sherman, 1877–1881	George W. McCrary, 1877–1879 Alexander Ramsey, 1879–1881
20	James A. Garfield, 1881	Chester A. Arthur, 1881	James G. Blaine, 1881	William Windom, 1881	Robert T. Lincoln, 1881
21	Chester A. Arthur, 1881–1885	None	James G. Blaine, 1881 Frederick T. Frelinghuysen, 1881–1885	William Windom, 1881 Charles J. Folger, 1881–1884 Walter Q. Gresham, 1884 Hugh McCulloch, 1884–1885	Robert T. Lincoln, 1881–1885
22	Grover Cleveland, 1885–1889	Thomas A. Hendricks, 1885	Thomas F. Bayard, 1885–1889	Daniel Manning, 1885–1887 Charles S. Fairchild, 1887–1889	William C. Endicott, 1885–1889

Continued down on page 1698; continued across on page 1697.

Secretary of the Navy	Chairman, Joint Chiefs of Staff	Attorney General	Solicitor General	Postmaster General	Secretary of the Interior
Gideon Welles, 1861–1865		Edward Bates, 1861–1863 Titian J. Coffey, 1863 James Speed, 1864–1865		Montgomery Blair, 1861–1864 William Dennison, 1864–1865	Caleb B. Smith, 1861–1863 John P. Usher, 1863–1865
Gideon Welles, 1865–1869		James Speed, 1865–1866 Henry Stanbery, 1866–1868 William M. Everts, 1868–1869		William Dennison, 1865–1866 Alexander W. Randall, 1866–1869	John P. Usher, 1865 James Harlan, 1865–1866 Orville H. Browning, 1866–1869
Adolph E. Borie, 1869 George M. Robeson, 1869–1877		Rockwood Hoar, 1869–1870 Amos T. Akerman, 1870–1871 George H. Williams, 1871–1875 Edwards Pierrepont, 1875–1876 Alphonso Taft, 1877	Benjamin H. Bristow, 1870–1872 Samuel F. Phillips, 1872–1877	John A. Creswell, 1869–1874 James W. Marshall, 1874 Marshall Jewell, 1874–1876 James N. Tyner, 1876–1877	Jacob D. Cox, 1869–1870 Columbus Delano, 1870–1875 Zachariah Chandler, 1875–1877
Richard W. Thompson, 1877–1881 Nathan Goff, Jr., 1881		Charles Devens, 1877–1881	Samuel F. Phillips, 1877–1881	David M. Key, 1877–1880 Horace Maynard, 1880–1881	Carl Schurz, 1877–1881
William H. Hunt, 1881		Wayne MacVeagh, 1881	Samuel F. Phillips, 1881	Thomas L. James, 1881	Samuel J. Kirkwood, 1881
William H. Hunt, 1881–1882 William E. Chandler, 1882–1885		Wayne MacVeagh, 1881 Benjamin H. Brewster, 1882–1885	Samuel F. Phillips, 1881–1885	Thomas L. James, 1881 Timothy O. Howe, 1882–1883 Frank Hatton, 1883 Walter Q. Gresham, 1883–1884 Frank Hatton, 1884–1885	Samuel J. Kirkwood, 1881–1882 Henry M. Teller, 1882–1885
William C. Whitney, 1885–1889		Augustus H. Garland, 1885–1889	John Goode, 1885–1886 George A. Jenks, 1886–1889	William F. Vilas, 1885–1888 Don M. Dickinson, 1888–1889	Lucius Q. C. Lamar, 1885–1888 William F. Vilas, 1888–1889

Continued down on page 1699; continued across on page 1707.

TABLE 2. *Presidents and Cabinets (Continued)*

No.	President	Vice President	Secretary of State	Secretary of the Treasury	Secretary of War
23	Benjamin Harrison, 1889–1893	Levi P. Morton, 1889–1893	James G. Blaine, 1889–1892 John W. Foster, 1892–1893	William Windom, 1889–1891 Charles Foster, 1891–1893	Redfield Proctor, 1889–1891 Stephen B. Elkins, 1891–1893
24	Grover Cleveland, 1893–1897	Adlai E. Stevenson, 1893–1897	Walter Q. Gresham, 1893–1895 Richard Olney, 1895–1897	John G. Carlisle, 1893–1897	Daniel S. Lamont, 1893–1897
25	William McKinley, 1897–1901	Garret T. Hobart, 1897–1899 Theodore Roosevelt, 1901	John Sherman, 1897–1898 William R. Day, 1898 John Hay, 1898–1901	Lyman J. Gage, 1897–1901	Russell A. Alger, 1897–1899 Elihu Root, 1899–1901
26	Theodore Roosevelt, 1901–1909	Charles W. Fairbanks, 1905–1909	John Hay, 1901–1905 Elihu Root, 1905–1909 Robert Bacon, 1909	Lyman J. Gage, 1901–1902 Leslie M. Shaw, 1902–1907 George B. Cortelyou, 1907–1909	Elihu Root, 1901–1904 William H. Taft, 1904–1908 Luke E. Wright, 1908–1909
27	William Howard Taft, 1909–1913	James Schoolcraft Sherman, 1909–1912	Philander C. Knox, 1909–1913	Franklin Mac Veagh, 1909–1913	Jacob M. Dickinson, 1909–1911 Henry L. Stimson, 1911–1913
28	Woodrow Wilson, 1913–1921	Thomas R. Marshall, 1913–1921	William Jennings Bryan, 1913–1915 Robert Lansing, 1915–1920 Bainbridge Colby, 1920–1921	William G. McAdoo, 1913–1918 Carter Glass, 1918–1920 David F. Houston, 1920–1921	Lindley M. Garrison, 1913–1916 Newton D. Baker, 1916–1921

Continued down on page 1700; continued across on page 1699.

Secretary of the Navy	Chairman, Joint Chiefs of Staff	Attorney General	Solicitor General	Postmaster General	Secretary of the Interior
Benjamin F. Tracy, 1889–1893		William H. H. Miller, 1889–1893	Orlow Chapman, 1889–1890 William Howard Taft, 1890–1892 Charles H. Aldrich, 1892–1893	John Wanamaker, 1889–1893	John W. Noble, 1889–1893
Hilary A. Herbert, 1893–1897		Richard Olney 1893–1895 Judson Harmon, 1895–1897	Lawrence Maxwell, Jr., 1893–1895 Holmes Conrad, 1895–1897	Wilson S. Bissell, 1893–1895 William L. Wilson, 1895–1897	Hoke Smith, 1893–1896 David R. Francis, 1896–1897
John D. Long, 1897–1901		Joseph McKenna, 1897–1898 John W. Griggs, 1898–1901 Philander C. Knox, 1901	John K. Richards, 1897–1901	James A. Gary, 1897–1898 Charles E. Smith, 1898–1901	Cornelius N. Bliss, 1897–1899 Ethan A. Hitchcock, 1899–1901
John D. Long, 1901–1902 William H. Moody, 1902–1904 Paul Morton, 1904–1905 Charles J. Bonaparte, 1905–1906 Victor H. Metcalf, 1906–1908 Trueman H. Newberry, 1908–1909		Philander C. Knox, 1901–1904 William H. Moody, 1904–1906 Charles J. Bonaparte, 1906–1909	John K. Richards, 1901–1903 Henry M. Hoyt, 1903–1909	Charles E. Smith, 1901–1902 Henry C. Payne, 1902–1904 Robert J. Wynne, 1904–1905 George B. Cortelyou, 1905–1907 George von L. Meyer, 1907–1909	Ethan A. Hitchcock, 1901–1907 James R. Garfield, 1907–1909
George von L. Meyer, 1909–1913		George W. Wichersham, 1909–1913	Lloyd Wheaton Bowers, 1909–1910 Frederick W. Lehmann, 1910–1912 William Marshall Bullitt, 1912—1913	Frank H. Hitchcock, 1909–1913	Richard A. Ballinger, 1909–1911 Walter L. Fisher, 1911–1913
Josephus Daniels, 1913–1921		James C. McReynolds, 1913–1914 Thomas W. Gregory, 1914–1919	John William Davis, 1913–1918 Alexander King, 1918–1920	Albert S. Burleson, 1913–1921	Franklin K. Lane, 1913–1920 John B. Payne, 1920–1921

Continued down on page 1701; continued across on page 1707.

TABLE 2. *Presidents and Cabinets (Continued)*

No.	President	Vice President	Secretary of State	Secretary of the Treasury	Secretary of War
28	Wilson				
29	Warren G. Harding, 1921–1923	Calvin Coolidge, 1921–1923	Charles Evans Hughes, 1921–1923	Andrew W. Mellon, 1921–1923	John W. Weeks, 1921–1923
30	Calvin Coolidge, 1923–1929	Charles D. Dawes, 1925–1929	Charles Evans Hughes, 1923–1925 Frank B. Kellogg, 1925–1929	Andrew W. Mellon, 1923–1929	John W. Weeks, 1923–1925 Dwight F. Davis, 1925–1929
31	Herbert C. Hoover, 1929–1933	Charles Curtis, 1929–1933	Henry L. Stimson, 1929–1933	Andrew W. Mellon, 1929–1932 Ogden L. Mills, 1932–1933	James W. Good, 1929 Patrick J. Hurley, 1929–1933
32	Franklin D. Roosevelt, 1933–1945	John Nance Garner, 1933–1941 Henry A. Wallace, 1941–1945 Harry S. Truman, 1945	Cordell Hull, 1933–1944 Edward R. Stettinius, Jr. 1944–1945	W. H. Woodin, 1933–1934 Henry Morgenthau, Jr., 1934–1945	George H. Dren, 1933–1936 Harry H. Woodring, 1936–1940 Henry L. Stimson, 1940–1945
33	Harry S. Truman, 1945–1953	Alben W. Barkley, 1949–1953	Edward R. Stettinius, Jr., 1945 James F. Byrnes, 1945–1947 George C. Marshall, 1947–1949 Dean G. Acheson, 1949–1953	Henry Morgenthau, Jr., 1945 Fred M. Vinson, 1945–1946 John W. Snyder, 1946–1953	Henry L. Stimson, 1945 Robert P. Patterson, 1945–1947 Kenneth C. Royall, 1947

					Secretary of Defense
					James V. Forrestal, 1947–1949 Louis A. Johnson, 1949–1950 George C. Marshall, 1950–1951 Robert A. Lovett, 1951–1953

Continued down on page 1702; continued across on page 1701.

Secretary of the Navy	Chairman, Joint Chiefs of Staff	Attorney General	Solicitor General	Postmaster General	Secretary of the Interior
		A. Mitchell Palmer, 1919–1921	William L. Frierson, 1920–1921		
Edwin Denby, 1921–1923		Harry M. Daugherty, 1921–1923	James M. Beck, 1921–1923	Will H. Hays, 1921–1922 Hubert Work, 1922–1923 Harry S. New, 1923	Albert B. Fall, 1921–1923 Hubert Work, 1923
Edwin Denby, 1923–1924 Curtis D. Wilbur, 1924–1929		Harry M. Daugherty, 1923–1924 Harlan F. Stone, 1924–1925 John G. Sargent, 1925–1929	James M. Beck, 1923–1925 William D. Mitchell, 1925–1929	Harry S. New, 1923–1929	Hubert Work, 1923–1928 Roy O. West, 1928–1929
Charles Francis Adams, 1929–1933		William D. Mitchell, 1929–1933	Charles Evans Hughes, Jr., 1929–1930 Thomas D. Thatcher, 1930–1933	Walter F. Brown, 1929–1933	Ray Lyman Wilbur, 1929–1933
Claude A. Swanson, 1933–1939 Charles Edison, 1939–1940 Frank Knox, 1940–1944 James V. Forrestal, 1944–1945		Homer S. Cummings 1933–1939 Frank Murphy, 1939–1940 Robert H. Jackson, 1940–1941 Francis Biddle, 1941–1945	James Crawford Biggs, 1933–1935 Stanley Reed, 1935–1938 Robert H. Jackson, 1938–1940 Francis Biddle, 1940–1941 Charles Fahy, 1941–1945	James A. Farley, 1933–1940 Frank C. Walker, 1940–1945	Harold L. Ickes, 1933–1945
James V. Forrestal, 1945–1947	General Omar N. Bradley, USA, 1949–1953	Francis Biddle, 1945 Thomas C. Clark, 1945–1949 J. Howard McGrath, 1949–1952 James P. McGranery, 1952–1953	J. Howard McGrath, 1945–1946 Philip B. Perlman, 1947–1952 Walter J. Cummings, Jr., 1952–1953	Frank C. Walker, 1945 Robert E. Hannegan, 1945–1947 Jesse M. Donaldson, 1947–1953	Harold L. Ickes, 1945–1946 Julius A. Krug, 1946–1949 Oscar L. Chapman, 1949–1953

Continued down on page 1703; continued across on page 1707.

Table 2. *Presidents and Cabinets (Continued)*

No.	President	Vice President	Secretary of State	Secretary of the Treasury	Secretary of Defense
34	Dwight D. Eisenhower, 1953–1961	Richard M. Nixon, 1953–1961	John Foster Dulles, 1953–1959 Christian A. Herter, 1959–1961	George M. Humphrey, 1953–1957 Robert B. Anderson, 1957–1961	Charles E. Wilson, 1953–1957 Neil H. McElroy, 1957–1959 Thomas S. Gates, Jr., 1959–1961
35	John F. Kennedy, 1961–1963	Lyndon B. Johnson, 1961–1963	Dean Rusk, 1961–1963	C. Douglas Dillon, 1961–1963	Robert S. McNamara, 1961–1963
36	Lyndon B. Johnson, 1963–1969	Hubert Humphrey, 1965–1969	Dean Rusk, 1963–1969	C. Douglas Dillon, 1963–1965 Henry H. Fowler, 1965–1968 Joseph W. Barr, 1968–1969	Robert S. McNamara, 1963–1968 Clark Clifford, 1968–1969
37	Richard M. Nixon, 1969–1974	Spiro Agnew, 1969–1973 Gerald R. Ford, 1973–1974	William P. Rogers, 1969–1973 Henry A. Kissinger, 1973–1974	David M. Kennedy, 1969–1971 John B. Connally, Jr., 1971–1972 George P. Shultz, 1972–1974 William E. Simon, 1974	Melvin R. Laird, 1969–1973 Elliot L. Richardson, 1973 James R. Schlesinger, 1973–1974
38	Gerald Ford, 1974–1977	Nelson A. Rockefeller, 1974–1977	Henry A. Kissinger, 1974–1977	William E. Simon, 1974–1977	James R. Schlesinger, 1974–1975 Donald H. Rumsfeld, 1975–1977
39	Jimmy Carter, 1977–1981	Walter F. Mondale, 1977–1981	Cyrus R. Vance, 1977–1980 Edward S. Muskie, 1980–1981	W. Michael Blumenthal, 1977–1979 G. William Miller, 1979–1981	Harold Brown, 1977–1981

Continued down on page 1704; continued across on page 1703.

Secretary of the Navy	Chairman, Joint Chiefs of Staff	Attorney General	Solicitor General	Postmaster General	Secretary of the Interior
	Adm. Arthur W. Radford, USN, 1953–1957 Gen. Nathan F. Twining, USAF, 1957–1960 Gen. Lyman L. Lemnitzer, USA, 1960–1961	Herbert Brownell, Jr., 1953–1958 William P. Rogers, 1958–1961	Walter J. Cummings, Jr., 1953 Simon E. Sobeloff, 1954–1956 J. Lee Rankin, 1956–1961	Arthur E. Summerfield, 1953–1961	Douglas McKay, 1953–1956 Frederick A. Seaton, 1956–1961
	Gen. Lyman L. Lemnitzer, USA, 1961–1962 Gen. Maxwell D. Taylor, USA, 1962–1963	Robert F. Kennedy, 1961–1963	Archibald Cox, 1961–1963	J. Edward Day, 1961–1963 John A. Gronouski, Jr., 1963	Stewart L. Udall, 1961–1963
	Gen. Maxwell D. Taylor, USA, 1963–1964 Gen. Earle G. Wheeler, USA, 1964–1969	Robert F. Kennedy, 1963–1965 Nicholas deB. Katzenbach, 1965–1967 Ramsey Clark, 1967–1969	Archibald Cox, 1963–1965 Thurgood Marshall, 1965–1967 Erwin N. Griswold, 1967–1969	John A. Gronouski, Jr., 1963–1965 Lawrence F. O'Brien, 1965–1968 W. Marvin Watson, 1968–1969	Stewart L. Udall, 1963–1969
	Gen. Earle G. Wheeler, USA, 1969–1970 Adm. Thomas H. Moorer, USN, 1970–1974	John N. Mitchell, 1969–1972 Richard G. Kleindienst, 1972–1973 Elliot L. Richardson, 1973 William B. Saxbe, 1974	Erwin N. Griswold, 1969–1973 Robert H. Bork, 1973–1974	Wilton M. Blount, 1969–1971	Walter J. Hickel, 1969–1970 Rogers C. B. Morton, 1971–1974
	Adm. Thomas H. Moorer, USN, 1974 Gen. George S. Brown, USAF, 1974–1977	William B. Saxbe, 1974–1975 Edward H. Levi, 1975–1977	Robert H. Bork, 1974–1977		Rogers C. B. Morton, 1974–1975 Stanley K. Hathaway, 1975 Thomas S. Kleppe, 1975–1977
	Gen. George S. Brown, USAF, 1977–1978 Gen. David C. Jones, USAF, 1978–1981	Griffin B. Bell, 1977–1979 Benjamin R. Civiletti, 1979–1981	Wade H. McCree, 1977–1981		Cecil D. Andrus, 1977–1981

Continued down on page 1705; continued across on pages 1707–1709.

TABLE 2. *Presidents and Cabinets (Continued)*

No.	President	Vice President	Secretary of State	Secretary of the Treasury	Secretary of Defense
40	Ronald Reagan, 1981–1989	George Bush, 1981–1989	Alexander Haig, 1981–1982 George P. Schultz, 1982–1989	Donald T. Regan, 1981–1985 James A. Baker, III, 1985–1988 Nicholas F. Brady, 1988–1989	Caspar Weinberger, 1981–1987 Frank Carlucci, 1987–1989
41	George Bush, 1989–1993	Dan Quayle, 1989–1993	James A. Baker, III, 1989–1992 Lawrence S. Eagleburger, 1992–1993	Nicholas F. Brady, 1989–1993	Richard B. Cheney, 1989–1993
42	Bill Clinton, 1993–	Al Gore, 1993–	Warren M. Christopher, 1993–	Lloyd M. Bentsen, 1993–	Les Aspin, 1993–1994 William Perry, 1994–

Secretary of the Navy	Chairman, Joint Chiefs of Staff	Attorney General	Solicitor General	Postmaster General	Secretary of the Interior
	Gen. David C. Jones, USAF, 1981–1982 Gen. John W. Vessey, Jr., USA, 1982–1985 Adm. William J. Crowe, Jr., USN, 1985–1989	William French Smith, 1981–1985 Edwin Meese, III, 1985–1988 Dick Thornburgh, 1988–1989	Rex E. Lee, 1981–1985 Charles Fried, 1985–1989		James G. Watt, 1981–1983 William P. Clark, 1983–1985 Donald P. Hodel, 1985–1989
	Gen. Colin L. Powell, USA, 1989–1993	Dick Thornburgh, 1989–1991 William Barr, 1991–1993	Kenneth W. Starr, 1989–1993		Manuel Lujan, Jr., 1989–1993
	Gen. Colin L. Powell, USA, 1993 Gen. John M. Shalikashvili, USA, 1993–	Janet Reno, 1993–	Drew S. Days, III, 1993–		Bruce Babbitt, 1993–

Continued across on pages 1708–1709.

TABLE 2. *Presidents and Cabinets (Continued)*

No.	President	Secretary of Agriculture	Secretary of Commerce and Labor		Secretary of Health, Education, and Welfare
22	Cleveland	Norman J. Coleman, 1889			
23	B. Harrison	Jeremiah M. Rusk, 1889–1893			
24	Cleveland	Julius Sterling Morton, 1893–1897			
25	McKinley	James Wilson, 1897–1901			
26	T. Roosevelt	James Wilson, 1901–1909	George B. Cortelyou, 1903–1904 Victor H. Metcalf, 1904–1906 Oscar S. Straus, 1906–1909		
27	Taft	James Wilson, 1909–1913	Charles Nagel, 1909–1913		
			Secretary of Commerce	Secretary of Labor	
28	Wilson	David F. Houston, 1913–1920 Edwin T. Meredith, 1920–1921	William C. Redfield, 1913–1919 Joshua W. Alexander, 1919–1921	William B. Wilson, 1913–1921	
29	Harding	Henry C. Wallace, 1921–1923	Herbert C. Hoover, 1921–1923	James J. Davis, 1921–1923	
30	Coolidge	Henry C. Wallace, 1923–1924 Howard M. Gore, 1924–1925 William M. Jardine, 1925–1929	Herbert C. Hoover, 1923–1928 William F. Whiting, 1928–1929	James J. Davis, 1923–1929	
31	Hoover	Arthur M. Hyde, 1929–1933	Robert P. Lamont, 1929–1932 Roy D. Chapin, 1932–1933	James J. Davis, 1929–1930 William N. Doak, 1930–1933	
32	F. D. Roosevelt	Henry A. Wallace, 1933–1940 Claude R. Wickard, 1940–1945	Daniel C. Roper, 1933–1938 Harry L. Hopkins, 1938–1940 Jesse H. Jones, 1940–1945 Henry A. Wallace, 1945	Frances Perkins, 1933–1945	
33	Truman	Claude R. Wickard, 1945 Clinton P. Anderson, 1945–1948 Charles F. Brannan, 1948–1953	Henry A. Wallace, 1945–1946 W. Averell Harriman, 1946–1948 Charles Sawyer, 1948–1953	Frances Perkins, 1945 Lewis B. Schwellenbach, 1945–1948 Maurice J. Tobin, 1948–1953	
34	Eisenhower	Ezra Taft Benson, 1953–1961	Sinclair Weeks, 1953–1958 Lewis L. Strauss, 1958–1959 Frederick H. Mueller, 1959–1961	Martin P. Durkin, 1953 James P. Mitchell, 1953–1961	Oveta Culp Hobby, 1953–1955 Marion B. Fulson, 1955–1958 Arthur S. Flemming, 1958–1961

Continued down on page 1708.

TABLE 2. *Presidents and Cabinets (Continued)*

No.	President	Secretary of Agriculture	Secretary of Labor	Secretary of Commerce	Secretary of Health, Education, and Welfare
35	Kennedy	Orville L. Freeman, 1961–1963	Luther H. Hodges, 1961–1963	Arthur J. Goldberg, 1961–1962 W. Willard Wirtz, 1962–1963	Abraham A. Ribicoff, 1961–1962 Anthony J. Celebrezze, 1962–1963
36	L. B. Johnson	Orville L. Freeman, 1963–1969	Luther H. Hodges, 1963–1965 John T. Connor, 1965–1967 Alexander B. Trowbridge, 1967–1968 C. R. Smith, 1968–1969	W. Willard Wirtz, 1963–1969	Anthony J. Celebrezze, 1963–1965 John W. Gardner, 1965–1968 Wilbur J. Cohen, 1968–1969
37	Nixon	Clifford M. Hardin, 1969–1971 Earl L. Butz, 1971–1974	Maurice H. Stans, 1969–1972 Peter G. Peterson, 1972–1973 Frederick B. Dent, 1973–1974	George P. Shultz, 1969–1970 James D. Hodgson, 1970–1973 Peter J. Brennan, 1973–1974	Robert H. Finch, 1969–1970 Elliot L. Richardson, 1970–1973 Caspar W. Weinburger, 1973–1974
38	Ford	Earl L. Butz, 1974–1976 John A. Knebel, 1976–1977	Frederick B. Dent, 1974–1975 Rogers C. B. Morton, 1975–1976 Elliot L. Richardson, 1976–1977	Peter J. Brennan, 1974–1975 John T. Dunlop, 1975–1976 Wille J. Usery, Jr., 1976–1977	Caspar W. Weinburger, 1974–1975 F. David Mathews, 1975–1977
39	Carter	Bob S. Bergland, 1977–1981	Juanita M. Kreps, 1977–1980 Philip M. Klutznick, 1980–1981	Ray Marshall, 1977–1981	Joseph A. Califano, Jr., 1977–1979 Patricia Roberts Harris, 1979–1981
40	Reagan	John R. Block, 1981–1986 Richard E. Lyng, 1986–1989	Malcolm Baldrige, 1981–1987 C. William Verity, Jr., 1987–1989	Raymond J. Donovan, 1981–1985 William E. Brock, III, 1985–1987 Ann D. McLaughlin, 1987–1989	
41	Bush	Clayton Yeutter, 1989–1991 Edward R. Madigan, 1991–1993	Robert A. Mosbacher, 1989–1992 Barbara A. Franklin, 1992–1993	Elizabeth H. Dole, 1989–1991 Lynn Martin, 1991–1993	
42	Clinton	Mike Epsy, 1993–	Ronald H. Brown, 1993–	Robert B. Reich, 1993–	

Secretary of Housing and Urban Development	Secretary of Transportation	Secretary of Energy	Secretary of Education	Secretary of Health and Human Services	Secretary of Veterans Affairs
Robert C. Weaver, 1966–1968 Robert C. Wood, 1969	Alan S. Boyd, 1967–1969				
George W. Romney, 1969–1973 James T. Lynn, 1973–1974	John A. Volpe, 1969–1973 Claude S. Brinegar, 1973–1974				
James T. Lynn, 1974–1975 Carla Anderson Hills, 1975–1977	Claude S. Brinegar, 1974–1975 William T. Coleman, Jr., 1975–1977				
Patricia Roberts Harris, 1977–1979 Moon Landrieu, 1979–1981	Brock Adams, 1977–1979 Neil Goldschmidt, 1979–1981	James R. Schlesinger, 1977–1979 Charles W. Duncan, 1979–1981	Shirley M. Hufstedler, 1979–1981		
Samuel R. Pierce, Jr., 1981–1989	Andrew L. Lewis, 1981–1983 Elizabeth H. Dole, 1983–1987 James H. Burnley, IV, 1987–1989	James B. Edwards, 1981–1983 Donald P. Hodel, 1983–1985 John S. Herrington, 1985–1989	Terrel H. Bell, 1981–1985 William J. Bennett, 1985–1988 Lauro F. Cavazos, 1988–1989	Richard S. Schweiker, 1981–1983 Margaret M. Heckler, 1983–1985 Otis R. Bowen, 1985–1989	
Jack F. Kemp, 1989–1993	Samuel K. Skinner, 1989–1992 Andrew H. Card, 1992–1993	James Watkins, 1989–1993	Lauro F. Cavazos, 1989–1990 Lamar Alexander, 1991–1993	Louis W. Sullivan, 1989–1993	Edward J. Derwinski, 1989–1992
Henry G. Cisneros, 1993–	Federico F. Pena, 1993–	Hazel R. O'Leary, 1993–	Richard W. Riley, 1993–	Donna E. Shalala, 1993–	Jesse Brown, 1993–

TABLE 3. *Presidents and Other Officials*

No.	President	Budget Director	Press Secretary	Chief of Staff	White House Counsel
29	Harding	Charles E. Dawes, 1921–1922 Herbert M. Lard, 1922–1923			
30	Coolidge	Herbert M. Lard, 1923–1929			
31	Hoover	J. Clawson Roop, 1929–1933	George Akerson, 1929–1931 Theodore Joslin, 1931–1933		
32	F. D. Roosevelt	Lewis W. Douglas, 1933–1934 Daniel W. Bell, 1934–1939 Harold D. Smith, 1939–1945	Stephen Early, 1933–1945		
33	Truman	Harold D. Smith, 1945–1946 James E. Webb, 1946–1949 Frank Pace, 1949–1950 Frederick J. Lawson, 1950–1953	Charles Ross, 1945–1950 Joseph Short, 1950–1952 Roger Tubby, 1952 James Hagerty, 1953	John R. Stedman, 1946–1952	
34	Eisenhower	Joseph M. Dodge, 1953–1954 Rowland R. Hughes, 1954–1956 Percival F. Brundage, 1956–1958 Maurice H. Stans, 1958–1961	James Hagerty, 1953–1961	Sherman Adams, 1953–1958 Wilton Persons, 1958–1961	
35	Kennedy	David E. Bell, 1961–1962 Kermit Gordon, 1962–1963	Pierre Salinger, 1961–1963	None	Theodore C. Sorensen, 1961–1963
36	L. B. Johnson	Kermit Gordon, 1963–1965 Charles L. Shultze, 1965–1968 Charles J. Zwick, 1968–1969	Pierre Salinger, 1963–1964 George Reedy, 1964–1965 Bill Moyers, 1965–1967 George Christian, 1967–1969	None	Theodore C. Sorensen, 1963–1964 Lee C. White, 1964–1966 Harry C. McPherson, Jr., 1966–1969

Continued down on page 1712; continued across on page 1711.

Chairman, Council of Economic Advisers	National Security Adviser	Legislative Affairs	Trade Representative	Policy Development
Edwin G. Nourse, 1946–1949 Leon H. Keyserling, 1949–1953				
Arthur F. Burns, 1953–1956 Raymond J. Saulnier, 1956–1961	Robert Cutler, 1954–1955 Dillon Anderson, 1956 Robert Cutler, 1957–1958 Gordon Gray, 1959–1961	Wilton B. Persons, 1953–1958 Bryce Harlow, 1958–1961		
Walter W. Heller, 1961–1963	McGeorge Bundy, 1961–1963	Lawrence F. O'Brien, 1961–1963	Christian A. Herter, 1962–1963	
Walter W. Heller, 1963–1964 Gardner Ackley, 1964–1968 Arthur M. Okun, 1968–1969	McGeorge Bundy, 1963–1966 Walt W. Rostow, 1966–1969	Lawrence F. O'Brien, 1963–1965 O'Brien (now Postmaster General) supported by Henry Hall Wilson and Barefoot Sanders, Jr., 1965–1969	Christian A. Herter, 1963–1967 William E. Roth, 1967–1969	

Continued down on page 1713.

Table 3. *Presidents and Other Officials (Continued)*

No.	President	Budget Director	Press Secretary	Chief of Staff	White House Counsel
37	Nixon	Robert P. Mayo, 1969–1970 George P. Schultz, 1970–1972 Caspar W. Weinberger, 1972–1973 Roy L. Ash, 1973–1974	Ronald Ziegler, 1969–1974 Jerald terHorst, 1974	H. R. Haldeman, 1969–1973 Alexander M. Haig, 1973–1974	John D. Ehrlichman, 1969 John Wesley Dean, III, 1970–1973 Leonard Garment, 1973–1974 J. Fred Buzhardt, 1974
38	Ford	Roy L. Ash, 1974–1975 James T. Lynn, 1975–1977	Ronald Nessen, 1974–1977	Donald Rumsfeld, 1974–1975 Richard B. Cheney, 1975–1977	Philip W. Buchen, 1974–1977
39	Carter	Thomas Bertram Lance, 1977 James T. McIntyre, Jr., 1977–1981	Jody Powell, 1977–1981	Hamilton Jordan, 1979–1980 Jack Watson, 1980–1981	Robert J. Lipshutz, 1977–1979 Lloyd N. Cutler, 1979–1981
40	Reagan	David Stockman, 1981–1985 James C. Miller III, 1985–1988	James Brady, 1981 Larry Speakes, 1981–1987 Marlin Fitzwater, 1987–1989	James A. Baker, III, 1981–1985 Donald T. Regan, 1985–1987 Howard H. Baker, Jr., 1987–1988 Kenneth Duberstein, 1988–1989	Fred F. Fielding, 1981–1986 Peter J. Wallison, 1986–1987 Arthur B. Culvahouse, Jr., 1987–1989
41	Bush	Richard G. Darman, 1989–1993	Marlin Fitzwater, 1989–1993	John H. Sununu, 1989–1991 Samuel K. Skinner, 1991–1992 James A. Baker III, 1992–1993	C. Boyden Gray, 1989–1993
42	Clinton	Leon E. Panetta, 1993–1994 Alice M. Rivlin, 1994–	Dee Dee Myers, 1993–	Thomas F. (Mack) McLarty, 1993–1994 Leon E. Panetta, 1994–	Bernard Nussbaum, 1993–

Chairman, Council of Economic Advisers	National Security Adviser	Legislative Affairs	Trade Representative	Policy Development
Paul W. McCracken, 1969–1971 Herbert Stein, 1972–1974	Henry Kissinger, 1969–1974	Bryce Harlow, 1969–1970 Clark MacGregor, 1971–1972 William E. Timmons, 1972–1974	Carl J. Gilbert, 1969–1972 William D. Eberle, 1972–1974	John D. Ehrlichman, 1970–1973 Kenneth R. Cole, Jr., 1973–1974
Alan Greenspan, 1974–1977	Henry Kissinger, 1974–1975 Brent Scowcroft, 1975–1977	Max L. Friedersdorf, 1974–1977	William D. Eberle, 1974–1975 Frederick B. Dent, 1975–1977	Kenneth R. Cole, Jr., 1974–1975 James M. Cannon, 1975–1977
Charles L. Schultze, 1977–1981	Zbigniew Brzezinski, 1977–1981	Frank B. Moore, 1977–1981	Robet Strauss, 1977–1979 Reubin Askew, 1979–1981	Stuart E. Eizenstat, 1977–1981
Murray L. Wiedenbaum, 1981–1982 Martin Feldstein, 1982–1984 Beryl W. Sprinkel, 1985–1989	Richard V. Allen, 1981–1982 William P. Clark, 1982–1983 Robert C. McFarlane, 1983–1986 John M. Poindexter, 1986 Frank C. Carlucci, 1986–1987 Colin L. Powell, 1987–1989	Max L. Friedersdorf, 1981–1982 Kenneth M. Duberstein, 1982–1983 M. B. Oglesby, Jr., 1983–1986 William L. Ball, III, 1986–1988 Alan M. Kranowitz, 1988–1989	William E. Brock, III, 1981–1985 Clayton Yeutter, 1985–1989	Martin Anderson, 1981–1982 Edwin L. Harper, 1982–1983 John A. Svahn, 1983–1986 Gary L. Bauer, 1987–1988 Franmarie Kennedy-Peel, 1988–1989
Michael J. Boskin, 1989–1993	Brent Scowcroft, 1989–1993	Frederick D. McClure, 1989–1992 Nicholas E. Calio, 1992–1993	Carla A. Hills, 1989–1993	Roger B. Porter, 1989–1993
Laura D'Andrea Tyson, 1993–	W. Anthony Lake, 1993–	Howard Paster, 1993–	Mickey Kantor, 1993–	Carol Rasco, 1993–

TABLE 4. *Presidential Elections, 1788–1992*

Year	Candidate[a]	Running Mate	Popular Vote[b]	Popular Percentage[c]	Electoral Vote
1788	George Washington				69
	Others				35
	John Adams				34
1792	George Washington				132
	John Adams				77
	George Clinton				50
	Others				5
1796	John Adams				71
	Thomas Jefferson				68
	Thomas Pinckney				59
	Others				48
	Aaron Burr				30
1800	Thomas Jefferson				73
	Aaron Burr				73
	John Adams				65
	Charles Cotesworth Pinckney				64
	John Jay				1
1804	Thomas Jefferson				162
	Charles Cotesworth Pinckney				14
1808	James Madison				122
	Charles Cotesworth Pinckney				47
	George Clinton				6
1812	James Madison				128
	DeWitt Clinton				89
1816	James Monroe				183
	Rufus King				34
1820	James Monroe				231
	John Quincy Adams				1
1824	Andrew Jackson (D)		153,000	42.2	99
	John Quincy Adams (D)		116,000	31.9	84
	William H. Crawford (D)		47,000	13.0	41
	Henry Clay (D)		47,000	13.0	37
1828	Andrew Jackson (D)	John C. Calhoun	647,000	56.0	178
	John Quincy Adams (NR)	none	508,000	44.0	83
1832	Andrew Jackson (D)	Martin Van Buren	688,000	54.5	219
	Henry Clay (W)	John Sergeant	473,000	37.5	49
	John F. Floyd (I)	Henry Lee			11
	William Wirt (AM)	Amos Ellmaker	101,000	8.0	0
1836	Martin Van Buren (D)	Richard M. Johnson	764,000	50.9	170
	William Henry Harrison (W)[d]	Francis Granger	550,000	36.6	73
	Others		187,000	12.4	51
1840	William Henry Harrison (W)	John Tyler	1,276,000	52.9	234
	Martin Van Buren (D)	none	1,130,000	46.8	60
1844	James K. Polk (D)	George M. Dallas	1,339,000	49.6	170
	Henry Clay (W)	Theodore Frelinghuysen	1,301,000	48.1	105

[a] All candidates who received electoral votes are shown. Other candidates are not shown when they received no electoral votes and their share of the popular vote was less than 1 percent.

[b] General election results are rounded to the nearest thousand.

[c] Percentages are rounded to the nearest tenth. Percentages do not add to 100.0 because of rounding.

[d] In 1836 the Whigs ran several candidates in various sections of the country; Harrison was the most important.

Party abbreviations: AI, American Independent; AM, Anti-Masonic; BM, Bull Moose (Progressive); CU, Constitutional Union; D, Democratic; I, Independent; IP, Independent Party; Ln, Libertarian; NR, National Republican; NUC, National Unity Campaign; Pr, Progressive; S, Socialist; W, Whig.

Continued on next page

TABLE 4.   *Presidential Elections, 1788–1992 (Continued)*

Year	Candidate[a]	Running Mate	Popular Vote[b]	Popular Percentage[c]	Electoral Vote
1848	Zachary Taylor (W)	Millard Fillmore	1,362,000	47.3	163
	Lewis Cass (D)	W. O. Butler	1,223,000	42.5	127
	Others		294,000	10.2	0
1852	Franklin Pierce (D)	William B. King	1,609,000	50.9	254
	Winfield Scott (W)	William A. Graham	1,387,000	43.8	42
	Others		169,000	5.3	0
1856	James Buchanan (D)	John C. Breckinridge	1,839,000	45.6	174
	John C. Frémont (R)	William L. Dayton	1,341,000	33.3	114
	Millard Fillmore (W)	Andrew J. Donelson	850,000	21.1	8
1860	Abraham Lincoln (R)	Hannibal Hamlin	1,867,000	39.8	180
	John C. Breckinridge (D)	Joseph Lane	854,000	18.2	72
	John Bell (CU)	Edward Everett	592,000	12.6	39
	Stephen A. Douglas (D)	Herschel V. Johnson	1,379,000	29.4	12
1864	Abraham Lincoln (R)	Andrew Johnson	2,190,000	55.2	212
	George B. McClellan (D)	George H. Pendleton	1,805,000	44.9	21
1868	Ulysses S. Grant (R)	Schuyler Colfax	3,013,000	52.7	214
	Horatio Seymour (D)	Francis P. Blair, Jr.	2,704,000	47.3	80
1872	Ulysses S. Grant (R)	Henry Wilson	3,597,000	55.6	286
	Horace Greeley (D)[c]	Thomas A. Hendricks	2,834,000	43.8	42
	Others				21
1876	Rutherford B. Hayes (R)	William A. Wheeler	4,036,000	47.9	185
	Samuel J. Tilden (D)	Thomas A. Hendricks	4,288,000	50.9	184
	Others		95,000	1.2	0
1880	James A. Garfield (R)	Chester A. Arthur	4,454,000	48.3	214
	Winfield S. Hancock (D)	William H. English	4,445,000	48.2	155
	Others		320,000	3.5	0
1884	Grover Cleveland (D)	Thomas A. Hendricks	4,876,000	48.5	219
	James G. Blaine (R)	John A. Logan	4,852,000	48.3	182
	Others		326,000	3.2	0
1888	Benjamin Harrison (R)	Levi P. Morton	5,445,000	47.8	233
	Grover Cleveland (D)	Allen G. Thurman	5,540,000	48.6	168
	Others		404,000	3.6	0
1892	Grover Cleveland (D)	Adlai E. Stevenson	5,557,000	46.0	277
	Benjamin Harrison (R)	Whitelaw Reid	5,191,000	43.0	145
	James B. Weaver (P)	James G. Field	1,030,000	8.5	22
	Others		293,000	2.4	0
1896	William McKinley (R)	Garret A. Hobart	7,114,000	51.0	271
	William J. Bryan (D)	Arthur Sewall	6,517,000	46.7	176
	Others		317,000	2.3	0
1900	William McKinley (R)	Theodore Roosevelt	7,220,000	51.7	292
	William J. Bryan (D)	Adlai E. Stevenson	6,358,000	45.5	155
	Others		396,000	2.8	0
1904	Theodore Roosevelt (R)	Charles W. Fairbanks	7,629,000	56.4	336
	Alton B. Parker (D)	Henry G. Davis	5,085,000	37.6	140
	Others		409,000	3.0	0
	Eugene V. Debs (S)	Benjamin Hanford	403,000	3.0	0
1908	William H. Taft (R)	James S. Sherman	7,679,000	51.6	321
	William J. Bryan (D)	John W. Kern	6,411,000	43.1	162
	Others		336,000	2.6	0
	Eugene V. Debs (S)	Benjamin Hanford	421,000	2.8	0
1912	Woodrow Wilson (D)	Thomas R. Marshall	6,301,000	41.9	435
	Theodore Roosevelt (BM)	Hiram W. Johnson	4,128,000	27.4	88
	William H. Taft (R)	Nicholas M. Butler	3,486,000	23.2	8
	Eugene V. Debs (S)	Emil Seidel	901,000	6.0	0
	Others		239,000	1.6	0

TABLE 4. *Presidential Elections, 1788–1992 (Continued)*

Year	Candidate[a]	Running Mate	Popular Vote[b]	Popular Percentage[c]	Electoral Vote
1916	Woodrow Wilson (D)	Thomas R. Marshall	9,132,000	49.3	277
	Charles E. Hughes (R)	Charles W. Fairbanks	8,549,000	46.1	254
	Others		270,000	1.5	0
	Allan L. Benson (S)	George R. Kirkpatrick	586,000	3.2	0
1920	Warren G. Harding (R)	Calvin Coolidge	16,154,000	60.3	404
	James M. Cox (D)	Franklin D. Roosevelt	9,147,000	34.1	127
	Eugene V. Debs (S)	Seymour Stedman	920,000	3.4	0
	Others		455,000	2.1	0
1924	Calvin Coolidge (R)	Charles G. Dawes	15,725,000	54.0	382
	John W. Davis (D)	Charles W. Bryan	8,387,000	28.8	136
	Robert M. La Follette (Pr)	Burton K. Wheeler	4,831,000	16.6	13
1928	Herbert C. Hoover (R)	Charles Curtis	21,431,000	58.2	444
	Alfred E. Smith (D)	Joseph T. Robinson	15,016,000	40.8	87
	Others		364,000	1.0	0
1932	Franklin D. Roosevelt (D)	John N. Garner	22,822,000	57.4	472
	Herbert C. Hoover (R)	Charles Curtis	15,762,000	39.7	59
	Norman Thomas (S)	James A. Maurer	885,000	2.2	0
1936	Franklin D. Roosevelt (D)	John Nance Garner	27,752,000	60.8	523
	Alfred M. Landon (R)	Frank Knox	16,679,000	36.5	8
	William Lemke (Union)	Thomas C. O'Brien	892,000	2.0	0
1940	Franklin D. Roosevelt (D)	Henry A. Wallace	27,243,000	54.7	449
	Wendell Willkie (R)	Charles L. McNary	22,334,000	44.8	82
1944	Franklin D. Roosevelt (D)	Harry S. Truman	25,612,000	53.4	432
	Thomas E. Dewey (R)	John W. Bricker	22,018,000	45.9	99
1948	Harry S. Truman (D)	Alben W. Barkley	24,104,000	49.6	303
	Thomas E. Dewey (R)	Earl Warren	21,971,000	45.1	189
	J. Strom Thurmond (Dixiecrat)	Fielding L. Wright	1,619,000	2.4	39
	Henry A. Wallace (Pr)	Glen H. Taylor	1,157,000	2.4	0
1952	Dwight D. Eisenhower (R)	Richard M. Nixon	33,937,000	55.1	442
	Adlai E. Stevenson (D)	John Sparkman	27,315,000	44.4	89
1956	Dwight D. Eisenhower (R)	Richard M. Nixon	35,589,000	57.4	457
	Adlai E. Stevenson (D)	Estes Kefauver	26,036,000	42.0	73
	Walter B. Jones	none	—	—	1
	Others		704,000	1.2	0
1960	John F. Kennedy (D)	Lyndon B. Johnson	34,221,000	49.7	303
	Richard M. Nixon (R)	Henry Cabot Lodge	34,109,000	49.6	219
	Harry F. Byrd	none	—	—	15
1964	Lyndon B. Johnson (D)	Hubert H. Humphrey	43,130,000	61.1	486
	Barry Goldwater (R)	William E. Miller	27,178,000	38.5	52
1968	Richard M. Nixon (R)	Spiro T. Agnew	31,785,000	43.4	301
	Hubert H. Humphrey (D)	Edmund S. Muskie	31,275,000	42.7	191
	George Wallace (AI)	Curtis E. LeMay	9,906,000	13.5	46
1972	Richard M. Nixon (R)	Spiro T. Agnew	47,170,000	60.7	520
	George McGovern (D)	R. Sargent Shriver	29,170,000	37.5	17
	John Hospers (Ln)	none	—	—	1
	Others		1,378,000	1.8	0

[a] All candidates who received electoral votes are shown. Other candidates are not shown when they received no electoral votes and their share of the popular vote was less than 1 percent.

[b] General election results are rounded to the nearest thousand.

[c] Percentages are rounded to the nearest tenth. Percentages do not add to 100.0 because of rounding.

[e] In 1872 Horace Greeley died between the general election and the meeting of the electoral colleges; Greeley's running mate, Thomas A. Hendricks, received forty-two of his electoral votes; twenty-one electoral votes were awarded to candidates who had not run in the general election.

Party abbreviations: AI, American Independent; AM, Anti-Masonic; BM, Bull Moose (Progressive); CU, Constitutional Union; D, Democratic; I, Independent; IP, Independent Party; Ln, Libertarian; NR, National Republican; NUC, National Unity Campaign; Pr, Progressive; S, Socialist; W, Whig.

Continued on next page

TABLE 4. *Presidential Elections, 1788–1992 (Continued)*

Year	Candidate[a]	Running Mate	Popular Vote[b]	Popular Percentage[c]	Electoral Vote
1976	Jimmy Carter (D)	Walter F. Mondale	40,831,000	50.1	297
	Gerald R. Ford (R)	Robert Dole	39,148,000	48.0	240
	Ronald Reagan	none	—	—	1
	Others		1,577,000	1.9	0
1980	Ronald Reagan (R)	George Bush	43,904,000	50.7	489
	Jimmy Carter (D)	Walter F. Mondale	35,484,000	41.0	49
	Other		1,407,000	1.6	0
	John B. Anderson (NUC)	Patrick J. Lucey	5,720,000	6.6	0
1984	Ronald Reagan (R)	George Bush	54,455,000	58.8	525
	Walter F. Mondale (D)	Geraldine A. Ferraro	37,577,000	40.6	13
	Other		621,000	0.7	0
1988	George Bush (R)	Dan Quayle	48,886,000	53.4	426
	Michael Dukakis (D)	Lloyd Bentsen	41,809,000	45.6	111
	Lloyd Bentsen	none	—	—	1
	Other		900,000	1.0	0
1992	Bill Clinton (D)	Al Gore	44,908,000	43.0	370
	George Bush (R)	Dan Quayle	39,102,000	37.5	168
	Ross Perot (I)	James B. Stockdale	19,741,000	18.9	0

[a] All candidates who received electoral votes are shown. Other candidates are not shown when they received no electoral votes and their share of the popular vote was less than 1 percent.

[b] General election results are rounded to the nearest thousand.

[c] Percentages are rounded to the nearest tenth. Percentages do not add to 100.0 because of rounding.

Party abbreviations: AI, American Independent; AM, Anti-Masonic; BM, Bull Moose (Progressive); CU, Constitutional Union; D, Democratic; I, Independent; IP, Independent Party; Ln, Libertarian; NR, National Republican; NUC, National Unity Campaign; Pr, Progressive; S, Socialist; W, Whig.

SOURCES: For elections from 1788 to 1960: Svend Petersen, *A Statistical History of the American Presidential Elections* (1968). For elections from 1964 to 1988: Richard M. Scammon and Alice V. McGillivray, *America Votes 18: A Handbook of Contemporary American Election Statistics* (1989). For the election of 1992: *Congressional Quarterly* (23 January 1993):190.

Synoptic Outline of Contents

The synoptic outline provides a general overview of the conceptual scheme of this encyclopedia, listing the entry term of each article (in capital and small capital letters).

The outline is divided into five parts:

1 The Presidency
2 Policies and Issues
3 Laws and Legal Cases
4 Historical Events and Politics
5 Biographies

Each of these parts is divided into several sections. Because the section headings are not mutually exclusive, certain entries in the encyclopedia are listed in more than one section.

1 THE PRESIDENCY

This part is divided into sections on the presidency in the Constitution, the office of the presidency, the text of the Constitution dealing with the presidency (clauses and amendments), qualifications for President and term of office, the powers of the President, theories and interpretations of the presidency, relations with the other branches of government, and the executive branch.

The Presidency in the Constitution

CONSTITUTION, PRESIDENT IN THE
CONFEDERATE CONSTITUTION
CONSTITUTIONAL CONVENTION
CREATION OF THE PRESIDENCY
THE FEDERALIST
PRESIDENT (TITLE)

Constitutional Offices

CHIEF EXECUTIVE
COMMANDER IN CHIEF
DIPLOMAT IN CHIEF

Clauses and Amendments

FAITHFUL EXECUTION CLAUSE
INCOMPATIBILITY CLAUSE

INELIGIBILITY CLAUSE
PRESENTATION CLAUSE
STATEMENT AND ACCOUNT CLAUSE
TWELFTH AMENDMENT
TWENTIETH AMENDMENT
TWENTY-FIFTH AMENDMENT
TWENTY-FOURTH AMENDMENT
TWENTY-SECOND AMENDMENT
TWENTY-THIRD AMENDMENT

Qualifications and Term

DISABILITY, PRESIDENTIAL
INAUGURATION
OATH OF OFFICE, PRESIDENTIAL
QUALIFICATIONS FOR PRESIDENT
SIX-YEAR PRESIDENTIAL TERM
TERM AND TENURE

TWO-TERM TRADITION
TYLER PRECEDENT

Removal of the President

IMPEACHMENT
IMPEACHMENT OF ANDREW JOHNSON
HIGH CRIMES AND MISDEMEANORS

Powers of the President

ACT OF STATE DOCTRINE
AMNESTY
APPOINTMENT POWER
APPOINTMENTS, RECESS
CHIEF EXECUTIVE
COMMANDER IN CHIEF
CRISIS MANAGEMENT
DECISION OF 1789

2   POLICIES AND ISSUES

*This part contains sections on foreign policy, defense and national security, civil rights and civil
liberties, domestic policy, economic policy, and fiscal policy. For acts of Congress, see below in Part 3.*

3 LAWS AND LEGAL CASES

This part includes sections on acts of Congress, bills and legislative proposals, resolutions, court cases, and executive orders.

Tariffs

Legal Cases

Executive Orders and Proclamations

4   HISTORICAL EVENTS AND POLITICS

*This part includes sections on the history of the presidency, elections and the electoral process, and
presidential relations with the public and the press.*

Historical Events and Movements

Indexes

Index of Cases

Abbreviations

aff'd   affirmed
Black   Black (United States Reports, vols. 66–67)
C.A.F.C.   Court of Appeals, Federal Circuit
C.C. Md.   Circuit Court, Maryland
C.C. Va.   Circuit Court, Virginia
Cir.   circuit
Cr.   Cranch (United States Reports, vols. 5–13)
Crim.   criminal
Dall.   Dallas (United States Reports, vols. 1–4)
D.C. Cir.   District of Columbia Circuit
D.D.C.   District Court, District of Columbia

D. Idaho   District Court, Idaho
F.Cas.   Federal Cases
F.2d   Federal Reporter, 2d series
F.Supp.   Federal Supplement
How.   Howard (United States Reports, vols. 42–65)
N.D. Cal.   Northern District, California
Pet.   Peters
S.Ct.   Supreme Court Reporter
U.S.   United States Reports
Wall.   Wallace (United States Reports, vols. 68–90)
Wheat.   Wheaton (United States Reports, vols. 14–25)

Numbers in boldface refer to the main entry on the subject.

Vol. 1: pp. 1–398; Vol. 2: pp. 399–856; Vol. 3: pp. 857–1342; Vol. 4: pp. 1343–1673

General Index

Numbers in boldface refer to the main entry on the subject.

Bank of the United States,
  continued
    as issue in election of 1800, 422
    as issue in election of 1832, 860
    as issue in election of 1836, 442
    Jackson and, 440, 859, 1542
    Jefferson and, 876
    Johnson, Richard M., and, 895
    under Jones, William, 1036
    Madison and, 1002
    revival of, 1001
Banks, Nathaniel, 928
Banning, Lance, 1211
  as contributor, 414–416, 416–418
Barbary War, **100**, 799, 879, 1573
Barber, James David, *Presidential
    Character: Predicting Performance
    in the White House, The*, 1198,
    1200–1202, 1253, 1459
Barbour, James, 432, 1036, 1576
Barbour, Philip P., 899
Barger, Harold M., 1253
Barilleaux, Ryan, *Post-Modern
    Presidency, The*, 1190
Barker, Wharton, 730
Barkley, Alben W., **100–101**, 514,
    686, 1325, 1557, 1560
Barlow, Joel, 997
Barnard, Henry, 401
Barnburners, 450, 673, 1543, 1544,
    1545
Barnett, Ross, 215, 1017
Barnum, William H., 474, 725
Barr, Joseph W., 1442, 1483
Barr, William P., 93, 816
Barrody, William J., 1120
Barry, William T., 864, 1188, 1189
Bartlett, Bruce, 1417
Bartley, Robert, 1417
Barton, William P. C., 1659
Baruch, Bernard, **101–102**, 1499,
    1665
Baruch Plan, 1500
Basic Principles of United
    States–Soviet Relations, 1087
Bates, Edward, 92, **102**, 456, 710,
    963, 970, 1310
Batista, Fulgencio, 103, 333, 694,
    1323
Bauer, Gary L., 1116, 1117
Bayard, James A., 137
Bayard, Thomas F., 78, 470, 1399
Bayh, Birch, 531, 534, 1267

Bay of Pigs invasion, **102–104**, 919
  groupthink and, 713
Beard, Charles A., 228, 543, 1403
Bear Flag Republic, 1184, 1456
Bearss, E. C., *as contributor*, 835–837
Beautification program of Lady
    Bird Johnson, 634, 887
Beck, James M., 1385
Beckely, John, 418
Beckler, David Z., *as contributor*,
    1352–1354, 1354–1356
Bedell, Robert P., 1106
Beecher, Henry Ward, 472
Beer, Samuel H., 1223
Begin, Menachem, 175, 855
  at Camp David, 170, 1541
Begs, William, 954
Belarus, 1397
Belgium
  and Brussels Pact, 86
  NATO member, 86
  Treaty of Washington
    (1921-1922), 1493
Belknap, Michal R., *as contributor*,
    210–211
Belknap, William W., 1226, 1576
  impeachment of, 706, 790–791
Bell, Daniel W., 1110
Bell, David E., 1110
Bell, Griffin B., 93, 953, 1109
Bell, John, **104**, 124, 456, 1466,
    1520, 1576
Bell, Terrel H., 402
Bell Trade Act, 1165
Belmont, Alan H., 1590
Belohlavek, John M., *as contributor*,
    341–342, 399–400, 458–461,
    673, 837–839, 1100–1101,
    1172, 1644–1645
Bemis, Samuel Flagg, 436
Benchley, Peter, 1391
Benedict, Michael Les, *as contributor*,
    454–456, 461–463, 464–466,
    547, 794–796
Benefits, presidential, **104–106**
Benefits to former Presidents,
    106–107
Benjamin, Judah P., 460, 624
Bennett, Henry Garland, 1176
Bennett, William J., 402
Benson, Allan, 494
Benson, Egbert, 352
Benson, Ezra Taft, 44, 1046

Bentley, Elizabeth, 978
Benton, Jessie, 674
Benton, Thomas Hart, 674, 858,
    866, 1183, 1356, 1390, 1608
  Texas, annexation of, 55
Bentsen, Lloyd M., 139, 539, 898,
    1483
Bergeron, Paul H., *as contributor*,
    1179–1186
Bergland, Bob S., 44
Berkowitz, Edward D., *as contributor*,
    1381–1383, 1610–1613
Berle, Adolf A., Jr., 116, 502, 1319
Berlin, John F. Kennedy in, 919
Berlin crisis (1961), **107**
  and cold war, 251–253
Berlin Resolution, 70
Berman, Larry, *as contributor*,
    714–715, 959–962
Bernstein, Irving, *as contributor*,
    916–923, 1077–1078
Berrien, John M., 92
Berube, Maurice R., *as contributor*,
    400–402, 402–405
Bethune, Mary McCleod, 213
Bevin, Ernest, 86
Bewick, Moreing, 760
Bibb, George M., 1482
Bibb, William W., 430
Biddle, Francis, 93, **107–108**, 1325,
    1384, 1385
Biddle, Nicholas, 440, 860, 864,
    1542
Biden, Joseph, 538
Biden Condition, 1384, 1494
Biggs, James Crawford, 1385
Billias, George Athan, *as contributor*,
    689–690
"Billion Dollar" Congress (1890),
    731–732
Bill of Rights, 199
  Elbridge, Gerry, and, 689
  and inalienable rights, 777
Binkley, Wilfred E., *American
    Political Parties*, 1309
Biological Weapons Convention
    (1972), 74, 190
Bipartisanship, Congress and,
    108–109
Birchard, Sardis, 739
Birney, James G., 2, 187, 448, 958,
    1466
Bishop, Maurice, 712

1439, 1518, 1541, 1542, 1544,
1557, 1558, 1559, 1575, 1576,
1645
annexation of Texas, 447, 1182,
1376, 1457
Discourse on the Constitution, The,
157
Disquisition on Government, The,
157
Monroe and, 1035
and Tariff Act of 1833, 1437,
1439
Califano, Joseph A., 387, 402,
708–709, 746, 747, 1642
as contributor, 745–747, 747–749
California, 1004
in Mexican War, 1019
Taylor and, 1446
Treaty of Guadalupe Hidalgo
(1848), 1490
Calio, Nicholas E., 952
Callaghan, James, 650, 1149
Callaway, Howard (Bo), 1317
Call to Action, A (Weaver), 1607
Call to Greatness (Stevenson), 517
Cambodia, 1565
covert operations in, 319
Mayaguez capture, 1011–1012
Cambon, Jules, 1389
Cameron, Donald, 469, 682, 684
Cameron, James D., 1576
Cameron, Simon, 456, 963, 1396,
1576
Campaign finances, **158–162**
in election of 1888, 475
in election of 1896, 481
in election of 1972, 528
fund-raising abilities and
primaries, 1234
interest groups and, 833
PACs' diminishing role, 1137
public subsidies in presidential
elections, 1978–1992 (table),
159
Campaign pledges, **162–164**
Campaign program titles, 164
Campaigns
consultants used in, 303
First Ladies and, 634–635, 887
techniques developed during
election of 1828, 439
television influence, 1450
Vice Presidents' role in, 1561

Campaign slogans, **164–166**
Campaign strategy, **166–169**
Campbell, Alan K., 224, 225, 1114
Campbell, George W., 1001, 1482
Campbell, James, 1167, 1189
Campbell, John A., 899
Campbell, Joseph, 272
Campbell, W. Glenn, 1224
Camp David, **169–170**, 1314, 1540
as presidential benefit, 105
Camp David Accords, **170–171**,
175, 855
Camp Rapidan (Camp Hoover),
1540
Canada, 86, 1343
Webster-Ashburton Treaty, 1609
Canning, George, 1038, 1039, 1040
Cannon, James M., 1116
Cannon, Joseph G., 486, 1370, 1428
Cannon, Lou, *as contributor,*
1280–1289
Cantor, Milton, *as contributor,*
1271–1273
Capital punishment, **171–173**
Caramanly, Joseph, 260, 1585
Card, Andrew H., 1478
Cardozo, Benjamin N., 669, 900
New Deal, attitude toward, 317
Panama v. Ryan, dissent in,
1140–1141
Schechter, concurring opinion in,
1351
Caribbean
American interventionism in,
797–798
dollar diplomacy in, 386
imperialism in, 796–797
Monroe Doctrine and, 1042
Wilson and, 1651
Carlisle, John G., 1483
Carlucci, Frank C., 353, 355, 1062,
1063, 1286
Carmichael, William, 1236, 1598
Carnegie, Andrew, 473
Caroli, Betty Boyd, *as contributor,*
11, 138, 180, 248–249, 413,
630–637, 637–638, 645–646,
886–887, 916, 970–971,
993–994, 1080–1081, 1280,
1603
Carpenter, Elizabeth, 638, 886,
1639
Carson, Rachel, *Silent Spring,* 561

Carswell, G. Harrold, 1424, 1425,
1426
Carter, Amy, 924
Carter, Jimmy, **173–179**, 365,
531–532, 651, 822, 902, 1044,
1155, 1175, 1222, 1234, 1235,
1283–1284, 1541, 1566
on abortion, 4
administrative reform, 30
affirmative action, 35
agricultural policy, 42
and appointment of federal
judges, 898
approval rate, 1275, 1277
arms control, 71, 1348
budget policy, 133, 134
budget summits, 135
business policy, 146
campaign pledges, 163
Camp David Accords, 170–171
and civil religion, 205–206
civil rights policy, 216–217
civil service reform, 221, 223,
1017
cold war tensions under, 253
conception of presidency, 1198
Council on Environmental
Quality, role of, 316
Crisis of confidence speech, 332
Dames & Moore, 342–343
defense policy, 358
deregulation, 369
Desert One, 370–371, 850
domestic policy, 387, 389, 1116
education policy, 401, 404, 746
energy policy, 558–560, 563
environmental policy, 563
Equal Rights Amendment, 564
Executive Order 12065, 823
federalism, 615
first use of National Emergencies
Act, 556
fiscal policy, 641
foreign affairs, 656
foreign aid, 663
groupthink and, 713
home, 754, 757
housing policy, 771, 773–774
human rights policy, 777,
778–779, 788
immigration policy, 788
imperial presidency and, 801
inaugural address, 808, 809

Chandler, Zachariah, 836, 964, 1274

Chapin, Roy D., 264

Chapman, Orlow, 1385

Chapman, Oscar L., 836

Character, presidential. *See* Presidential character

Chase, Harvey S., 1433

Chase, Salmon P., 2, **187–188**, 229, 455, 456, 459, 462, 673, 701–702, 710, 885, 899, 902, 963, 969, 970, 1274, 1309, 1482

   Bas v. Tingy, opinion in, 1007

   and Know-Nothing (American) Party, 928

   Milligan, dissent in, 1022

Chase, Samuel, 879, 899, 903, 1393, 1397

   impeachment of, 753, 791

Checkers speech (Nixon), 515, 1082, 1450

Checks and balances, **188–189**

   Cabinet, influence on, 152

   and presidential accountability, 6

Cheetham, William, 427

Chemerinsky, Erwin, *as contributor*, 1417–1421

Chemical Weapons Convention (1992), 71, 74, **189–190**

Cheney, Dick, 140, **190–191**, 353, 355, 648, 1618, 1627

Cherokee Indians, 861

   Marshall, John, and, 1009

   Monroe and, 1039

   removal, 819

   Scott, Winfield, and, 1356

   Taylor and, 1445

   Van Buren and, 1543

   Wirt, William, counsel for, 1657

   Worcester v. Georgia, 819

Chesapeake affair, 881

Cheves, Langdon, 1036

Chiang Kai-shek, 69, 409, 1127, 1326, 1503

Chicago Daily News, 942

Chicago Seven, 1027

Chicago Tribune, 1260

Chickasaw Indians, 861

Chief Executive, **191–196**, 587

   in Confederate Constitution, 273

Chief legislator, President as, 277, 588–589, 949

Chief manager, President as, 572

Chief of Staff, White House. *See* White House Chief of Staff

Chief of State, President as, 590, 1249

Chief Usher (White House), 1626

Child labor, **196–197**, 1650

Children's Bureau, 196, 933

Child Support Enforcement Administration, 747

Chile, 732, 778

   democratization of, 779

   Rio Treaty, party to, 1316

Chiles, Lawton, 1105, 1106

China, 662, 1503.

   Boxer Rebellion, 992, 1127

   dollar diplomacy in, 386

   immigrants from, 787

   Japanese interest in, 797

   Marshall, George C., peace mission to, 1008

   Nationalist, fall of, 981

   open door, 739, 797, 991

   Russian interest in, 797

   Treaty of Washington (1921-1922), 1493

   See also People's Republic of China; United States–China relations

Chinese Engineering and Mining Company, 760

Chinese exclusion acts, 47, **197**, 787

Chinese Immigration Bill (1879) Hayes, veto of, 741–742

Choctaw Indians, 861

Christian, George, 1638

Christian Bases of World Order (Wallace), 1572

Christian Century, The, 931

Christopher, Warren M., 371, 850, 1237, 1399

Church, Frank, 197, 311, 319, 531, 534, 830, 1170

Church, separation of state and, 1299–1300

Church and the City, The (Thomas), 1467

Church Committee, **197–199**, 319, 830, 1170

Churchill, Sir Winston, 405, 406, 668, 1326

   at Atlantic Conference, 86

   at Camp David, 170

   at Casablanca Conference, 180–181

   destroyers for bases, 371

   Lend Lease Act (1941), 955

   and moral philosophy, 1223

   at Potsdam Conference, 88, 1192, 1499

   at Quebec Conference, 1268

   Roosevelt, F., and, 1326

   at Teheran Conference, 1449

   United Nations Declaration, 1525

   at Yalta conference, 1670

CIA. *See* Central Intelligence Agency (CIA)

Cinquegrana, Americo R., *as contributor*, 549–551, 664–665, 912–913, 1125–1126, 1535–1536

Circuit Court of Appeals Act (1891), 904

Circuit courts of appeals. *See* Judiciary, Federal

Circuit Judge Nomination Commission, 898

Cisneros, Henry G., 770

Citizens' Commission on Compensation and Public Service, 1263, 1344, 1347

Civiletti, Benjamin R., 93

Civilian Conservation Corps (CCC), **199**, 289, 774, 1073, 1320

Civilian Conservation Corps Reforestation Relief Act (1933), 199

Civil liberties, **199–203**

   Fortas, Abe, and, 667

   Kennedy, Robert F., and, 923

   Lincoln's assaults on, 228

Civil religion, President and, **203–206**

Civil rights

   Arthur and, 80–81

   Brownell, Herbert, and, 120

   Eisenhower and, 409

   Fortas, Abe, and, 667

   Hayes and, 741

   Health, Education, and Welfare, Department of, and, 747

   and housing policy, 773

   Ickes, Harold, and, 795

   importance in election of 1948, 513

   Katzenbach, Nicholas deB., 911

Commander in Chief, *continued*
  and first use of nuclear weapons,
    638–639
  imperial presidency and, 799
  inherent powers, 823
  international law limitations, 840,
    842
  Jackson as, 1194
  Johnson, A., as, 794–795
  Lincoln as, 963–964
  McKinley as, 990
  Roosevelt, F. D., as, 1667–1668
  title origin, 1586
  Wilson as, 1654, 1664–1665
Commander in Chief power
  basis for Emancipation
    Proclamation, 552
  as basis for executive agreement,
    567
  as basis for proclamation, 1242
  Supreme Court decisions on, 1418
Command of the Army Act (1867),
  1304
Commentaries on the Constitution of the
  United States (Story), 300
Commentaries on the Laws of England
  (Blackstone), 257
Commentators on the presidency,
  261–263
Commerce, Department of, 150,
  151, 154, **263–266**, 570, 574
  economic policy, role in, 1177
  Hoover and, 760
  Secretaries of Commerce and
    Labor (table), 264
  Secretaries of Commerce (table),
    264
Commerce and Labor, Department
  of, 150, 153
Commerce Clause under Marshall,
  Taney, and Waite, The
  (Frankfurter), 670
Commerce Court, 1005
Commercial Space Launch Act
  (1984), 1479
Commercial treaties under J. Q.
  Adams, 22
Commission for Relief in Belgium,
  760
Commission of Higher Education, 403
Commission on Administrative
  Management. *See* Brownlow
  Committee

Commission on Civil Rights, 571
Commission on Debates, 168
Commission on Departmental
  Methods. *See* Keep Commission
Commission on Economy and
  Efficiency. *See* Taft Commission
Commission on Executive,
  Legislative, and Judicial
  Salaries, 1263, 1346
Commission on Federal Ethics Law
  Reform, 1131
Commission on Government
  Procurement, 1105
Commission on Indian Reservation
  Economies, 821
Commission on Industrial Relations,
  936
Commission on Law Enforcement,
  329
Commission on National Goals,
  1115
Commission on Obscenity and
  Pornography, 267
Commission on Population Growth
  and the American Future, 267
Commission on the Bicentennial of
  the U.S. Constitution, 571
Commission on the Conservation
  and Administration of the
  Public Domain, 289, 761
Commission on the Organization of
  the Executive Branch. *See*
  Hoover Commissions
Commission on Wartime Relocation
  and Internment of Civilians,
  267
Commissions, presidential, **266–269**
Committee for a Single Six-Year
  Presidential Term, 1374
Committee for Industrial
  Organization, 604
Committee for the
  Non-Participation in Japanese
  Aggressionism, 843
Committee of Equality of
  Treatment and Opportunity in
  the Armed Services, 579
Committee of Fair Employment
  Practice, 688
Committee of Principals, 74
Committee on Civil Rights, 214
Committee on Economic Security,
  1381

Committee on Equal Employment
  Opportunity, 582, 921
Committee on Equal Opportunity
  in Housing, 580
Committee on Fair Employment
  Practice, 581
Committee on Government
  Contract Compliance, 582
Committee on Government
  Employment Policy, 582
Committee on Public Information
  (World War I), 1633, 1654,
  1665
Committee on Social Trends, 1115
Committee on the Constitutional
  System, 301
Committee on Un-American
  Activities. *See* House
  Un-American Activities
  Committee
Committee to Defend America by
  Aiding the Allies, 844
Committee to Re-elect the
  President, 528, 1088, 1154,
  1603
Commodity Credit Corporation,
  696
Commodity Futures Trading
  Commission (CFTC), 570
Communications Act (1934), 1227
  televised presidential debates,
    effect on, 348–349
Communist Control Act (1954),
  1273
Communist Party of the United
  States, 503, 508
  McCarran Internal Security Act
    and, 981
  passports denied to members,
    1480
  prosecution of leaders, 1273
Communists, fear of, in election of
  1948, 513
Community Mental Health Centers
  Act (1963), 395
Community Relations Service, 908
Commutation of death sentences.
  See capital punishment
Compact of Fifth Avenue, 519
Competition in Contracting Act
  (1984), 272
Competitiveness Council, **269–270**,
  370

Comprehensive Crime Control Act (1984), 396

Comprehensive Crime Control Act (1990), 396

Comprehensive Employment and Training Act (1973), 935

Comprehensive Environmental Response, Compensation and Liability Act (1980), 1048

Compromise of 1850, **270–271**, 622–623, 1377
  Clay, Henry, and, 235
  opposition to, 723
  Pierce and, 1166

Compromise of 1876, 213

Comptroller General, 128, **271–272**, 696
  and Attorney General, 1164
  Bowsher and, 815
  General Accounting Office and, 687–688
  and removal power, 1305
  table, 272

Comstock, William A., 552

Concord Cabal, 1166

Confederate Constitution, **272–273**
  item veto in, 1549

Conference for Progressive Political Action, 939–940, 1244

Conference on Disarmament, 74

Conference on Security and Cooperation in Europe, 71

Confirmation hearings, 33

Conger, Clement, 633

Congress
  affirmative action, 34
  and Cabinet secretaries, 152
  conflict with President, sources of, 285–286
  cooperation with President, sources of, 286
  criminal contempt statute, 305–306, 845
  exclusive war power, 1573
  and executive orders, 585
  executive privilege in, 597
  foreign affairs powers, 285, 657–658
  and human rights, 778
  INS v. Chadha, opposition to, 828–829
  and international law, 841–842
  intervention in organizational management, 575

power of inquiry, 845
power to subpoena, 845
and presidential emergency powers, 555
protection of right to travel, 1481
and Puerto Rico, 1259
relations with President, 1202–1207

Congress, White House influence on, **273–277**

Congress, White House liaison with, **277–281**

Congressional administrative reform, 385

Congressional Budget and Impoundment Control Act (1974), 129, 131, 133, **281–283**, 641, 805, 1133, 1292
  amendments to, 699
  forces behind passage of, 283
  legislative veto use, 953
  See also Impoundment Control Act (1974)

Congressional Budget Office (CBO), 282, **283–284**
  and Watergate, 1605

Congressional caucus, 1093, 1232

Congressional delegation of executive power, 1419

Congressional Directory, 637

Congressional-executive agreements, 566

Congressional Government (Wilson), 261–262, 295, 800, 1316, 1559, 1647
  on Cleveland, 240

Congressional influence on President, **284–288**

Congressional investigations
  contempt of Congress used in, 305
  imperial presidency and, 801

Congressional oversight of executive, 588, 1134
  imperial presidency and, 801
  intelligence activities and procedures, 830
  investigations as means of, 844–845

Congressional Quarterly, 115

Congressional Quarterly Guide to Congress, 832

Congressional salaries, 1263, 1345

Congressional war power
  upheld in *Bas v. Tingy*, 1573
  upheld in *Little v. Barreme*, 1573, 1585
  upheld in *Talbot v. Seeman*, 1573

Congress of Industrial Organizations, 41

Conkling, Roscoe, 77, 78, 110, 467, 469, 682–685, 710, 741, 1453

Connally, John B., 146, 528, 1083, 1130, 1207, 1224, 1483, 1592

Connally Amendment (1946), **288**

Connally Resolution, 677

Connery, Lawrence J., 604

Connor, John T., 264

Conrad, Charles M., 1576

Conrad, Holmes, 1385

Conservation policy, **288–291**, 837
  Civilian Conservation Corps, 199
  under Hoover, 763
  under Roosevelt, T., 1330, 1333
  under Taft, 97–98, 1429
  Watt, James G., and, 1606

Conservatism, **291–293**

Constitution
  Cabinet, 151–152
  and covert operations, 320–321
  Electoral College, 542–543, 547
  emergency powers, 553
  enumerated powers, 1213
  executive departments, 568
  executive orders, 586
  executive power, 587
  executive prerogative, 594–595
  faithful execution clause, 605–607
  foreign affairs powers, 653, 659–661
  interpretation by Federalist Party, 617
  judges, appointment of, 897
  judiciary, federal, 904
  oath of office, presidential, 1103
  pardon power, 1145
  pocket veto, 1551
  presentation clause, 1192–1193
  and presidential signing statements, 1372–1373
  presidential succession in, 1413
  President's salary, 1346
  science policy, 1354
  silent on treaty termination, 1495
  spending power, 1392

budget formulation, role in, 132
Chairmen (table), 315
economic policy, role in, 1177
and Treasury Department, 1484
Council of National Defense, 101
Council on Environmental Quality
(CEQ), **316**, 576, 827
Council on Wage and Price
Stability, 827
Counterintelligence, 186, 829
Court-packing plan, **316–318**, 630,
775–776, 814, 906, 1074, 1322,
1421
Moley, Raymond, and, 1028
Covert expenditures, 1402
Covert operations, 186, **318–321**,
408
CIA and, 776, 829, 830
Clark Amendment, 231
Congressional approval, 1574
finding, presidential, 628–629
Hughes-Ryan Amendment and,
776, 830
Intelligence Oversight Act (1980),
830
Jefferson, by, 799
legislative oversight, 776
Lincoln, by, 799–800
Madison, by, 799
marque and reprisal, and, 1007
Monroe, by, 799
presidential approval of, 628–629
President's Foreign Intelligence
Advisory Board and, 1225
Roosevelt, F., by, 799–800
Cox, Archibald, 595, 792, 816,
1089, 1384, 1385, 1419, 1532,
1604
Cox, Jacob D., 703, 836
Cox, James M., **321–322**, 365, 495,
726, 744, 1319
Journey through My Years, 322
Coxe, Tenche, 1303
Coxey, Jacob Sechler, 322
Coxey's Army, **322**
Olney, Richard, 1126
Coy, Wayne, 1104
Cozy triangles. *See* Iron triangles
Cramer, William, 210
Cranch, William, 1519, 1522
Crawford, George W., 1447, 1576
Crawford, William H., 20–21, 51,
323, 363, 430, 433, 435, 436,

565, 1152, 1232, 1393, 1482,
1541, 1542, 1576
American Colonization Society,
and, 1038
Monroe and, 1034–1035
Creation of the presidency, 297,
323–328
James Wilson's role in,
1646–1647
Crédit Mobilier scandal, **328–329**,
683, 725
Creek Indians, 857, 861
Creek War, 861
Creel, George, 1633, 1665
Creswell, John A., 703, 1189
Crime, policy on, **329–330**
as issue in elections, 944
Criminal offenses and
impeachment, 753
Crisis management, **330–332**, 1252,
1623
Crisis of confidence speech (Carter),
332
Crittenden, John J., 92, 623, 1425,
1520
Croker, Richard, 478
Croly, Herbert, 1244
Promise of American Life, The, 263,
1075, 1078
Cronin, Thomas E.
as contributor, 1511–1513
State of the Presidency, The, 1457
"Superman: Our Textbook
President," 1462
Crook, W. H., 1640
Cross of Gold Speech (Bryan), 480
Crouse, Timothy, 166
Crovitz, Gordon, 1462
Crowe, William J., Jr., 897
Crowninshield, Benjamin, 433
Monroe and, 1035
Crowninshield, Jacob, 354
Crusade in Europe (Eisenhower), 407
Cuba, **332–334**, 1336
Adams, J. Q., and, 23
*Banco Nacional de Cuba v.
Sabbatino*, 751
Bay of Pigs invasion, 102–104,
919
Cleveland and, 1389
Eisenhower and, 411
expropriation of U.S. nationals'
property, 751

Fillmore and, 624
Fish, Hamilton, and, 642
Guantńamo Naval Base, 721
gunboat diplomacy and, 716
independence of, 991
Kennedy and, 252
McKinley and, 989, 991, 1389
Monroe and, 1038
Monroe Doctrine and, 1040
nationalization of private
interests, 751
Pierce and, 1168
Rio Treaty, party to, 1316
Roosevelt, F., and, 694, 1323
Spanish-American War and, 797,
989–990
Taylor and, 1447
travel restrictions, 1295, 1479,
1480
Cuban missile crisis, 252, **334–336**,
919–920
communication lag during, 769
groupthink and, 713
Katzenbach, Nicholas deB., 912
Cuban Resolution, 70
Cullom, Shelby M., 385
Culvahouse, Arthur B., Jr., 1629
Cumberland Road, 838, 1002, 1036
Cummings, Homer, 93, **336**, 610,
909
Cummings, Walter J., Jr., 1385
Cummins, Albert, 565
Currency Act (1863), 1304
Currency policy. *See* Monetary
policy
Curtis, Benjamin R., 899
Dred Scott, dissent in, 800
Curtis, Carl, 1382
Curtis, Charles, **336–337**, 499, 501,
1557, 1560
Cushing, Caleb, 92, 93, **337–338**,
908, 1167, 1517, 1573
Cushing, William, 899
Customs Bureau, 830
Cutler, Lloyd N., 301, 1629
Cutler, Robert, 1061, 1062, 1063,
1218
Cycles, presidential, **338–340**
Czechoslovakia, 141
Peace Corps volunteers in, 1159
Soviet invasion of, 894
Treaty of Versailles, 1492
Czolgosz, Leon F., 84, 85, **341**, 992

Dillinger, John, 610

Dillon, C. Douglas, 301, 918, 921, 1483

Dimmick, Mary Lord, 733

Dingley, Nelson, Jr., 373, 385

Dingley Tariff Act (1897), **373–374**, 989, 1439

Dinnerstein, Leonard, *as contributor*, 476–479, 930–931

Diplomatic and Consular Services, 665

Diplomat in Chief, **374–376**, 589, 1194

Diplomats, precedence order of, 1250–1251

Direct election plan, 546, 548

Director of Central Intelligence (DCI), 829

Director of Communications, 1014, 1625

Director of the CIA (DCIA), 829

Direct spending. *See* Entitlements

Dirksen, Everett M., 211, 780

Dirty tricks, **376–379**, 1603
  in election of 1800, 422
  in election of 1828, 438, 858
  in election of 1880, 471
  in election of 1884, 471, 472–473
  in election of 1928, 499
  in election of 1944, 510
  in election of 1972, 528

Disability, presidential, **379–381**, 1414–1415
  Constitutional Convention discussions, 327
  Twenty-fifth Amendment, 327
  Twenty-first Amendment, 1509–1510
  Wilson, 1010, 1655

Discourse on the Constitution, The (Calhoun), 157

Discourses on Davila (Adams), 12, 417

Discourses on Titus Livy (Machiavelli), 553

Displaced Persons Act (1948), 786

Displaced persons after World War II, 982

Disquisition on Government, The (Calhoun), 157

Disraeli, Benjamin, 1223

District courts. *See* Judiciary, Federal

District of Columbia, voting rights in, 1513–1514

District Plan, 546, 548

Divided government, 287, **381–385**
  and appointment process, 32
  and budget summits, 135
  and confirmation, 32
  effect on Nixon administration, 1154
  and electoral accountability, 7
  and legislative leadership, 950
  Presidential-congressional relations, 1206
  President's use of interest groups, 832–833
  proposed reforms, 301
  table, 382–384

Division of Protocol, 1250

Division of Public Construction, 761

Dix, Dorothea, 613, 1167

Dix, John A., 1482

Dixiecrats. *See* States' Rights Democratic Party

Doak, William N., 933, 934

Dobbin, James C., 354, 1167

Dobrynin, Anatoly, 335

Dobson, John M., *as contributor*, 474–476

Dockery, Alexander, 385

Dockery-Cockrell Commission, **385**

Dodd, William, Jr., 1532

Dodge, Grenville, 255

Dodge, Joseph M., 1110

Doenecke, Justus D., *as contributor*, 77–82

Doheny, Edward L., 728, 1448

Dolan, Tony, 1391

Dole, Elizabeth H., 934, 935, 1478, 1479

Dole, Robert, 140, 530, 538, 651, 1029, 1234, 1235, 1295

Dollar diplomacy, **385–387**, 717, 928, 1431

Dolliver, Jonathan P., 482, 485

Domestic Council, 387, 1108, 1115, 1560

Domestic discretionary spending, 132

Domestic policy, 1177
  under Adams, J., 14–15
  under Adams, J. Q., 23
  under Arthur, 78–79
  under Buchanan, 123–125

  under Bush, 140–141, 143, 387, 389, 540, 1117
  under Carter, 175, 177, 178, 387, 389, 1116
  under Cleveland, 238–240
  under Clinton, 387–388, 1117
  under Coolidge, 308
  coordination of, 1115–1117
  delegation of legislative power, 360
  under Eisenhower, 387, 407–408, 1115
  executive orders, 584
  under Fillmore, 622–624
  under Ford, 387, 649–650
  under Garfield, 684
  under Grant, 702, 703–704
  under Harding, 731–732
  under Harrison, B., 731–732
  under Harrison, W. H., 736
  under Hayes, 741–742
  under Hoover, 761–763, 1115
  interest groups, and, 832
  as issue in election of 1940, 507
  as issue in election of 1944, 509
  under Jackson, 858–864
  under Jefferson, 878–879, 880
  under Johnson, A., 882–884
  under Johnson, L. B., 387, 745–746, 889–890, 1115
  under Kennedy, 921
  under Lincoln, 962–963, 965–966, 967, 970
  McGovern, George, and, 986–987
  under McKinley, 991–992
  under Madison, 995, 997, 1002
  under Monroe, 1036–1037
  under Nixon, 1084–1086
  under Pierce, 1167
  under Polk, 1181–1182
  President's use of interest gourps, 833
  under Reagan, 387, 389, 1116, 1284, 1287
  under Roosevelt, F., 1320–1323
  under Roosevelt, T., 1332, 1333
  Supreme Court decisions on, 1418–1421
  under Taft, 1430
  under Taylor, 1446–1447
  under Truman, 1500–1501
  under Tyler, 1519–1521
  under Van Buren, 1543

under Washington, 1596–1599
under Wilson, 1649–1650
Domestic policy adviser, **387–388**
Domestic Policy Council, 30, 368.
    See also Office of Policy
Development
Domestic Policy Staff, 1116
Domestic program innovation,
    388–390
Domestic Volunteer Service Act
    (1973), 1159
Dominican Republic, **390–391**
    dollar diplomacy in, 386
    gunboat diplomacy in, 716
    intervention in, 694
    Johnson, L. B., and, 891
    occupation under Wilson, 1651
    Rio Treaty, party to, 1316
    See also Santo Domingo
Donaldson, Jesse M., 1189
Donelson, Andrew J., 454–455, 1183
Donelson, Rachel, 857
Donovan, Raymond J., 816, 934,
    935
Donovan, William, 1236
Dorchester, Lord, 872
Dorr, Thomas Wilson, 391
Dorr War, **391–392**, 1521
Dorsen, Norman, *as contributor*,
    643–644
Dotson, Donald, 939
Douglas, Davison M., *as contributor*,
    603–604
Douglas, Helen Gahagan, 1081,
    1282
Douglas, Lewis W., 1110
Douglas, Paul, 691, 707, 773
Douglas, Stephen A., 51, 123, 124,
    364, **392–393**, 452, 454, 456,
    457, 623, 1166, 1168, 1309,
    1615
    Compromise of 1850, 271
    Kansas-Nebraska Act (1854), 911
    and slavery, 1376, 1377
Douglas, William O., 101, 900, 902,
    1273, 1535
    Aptheker, opinion in, 1480
    Johnson, L. B., and, 1423
    Kennedy and, 1423
    New York Times Co., opinion in,
    1080
    Peters v. Hobby, concurring
    opinion in, 1162

Reid v. Covert, opinion in, 1298
Richardson, dissent in, 1535
Roosevelt, F., and, 1422
Truman and, 1423
U.S. v. Columbia, opinion in, 58
Youngstown, concurring opinion
    in, 1419
Douglass, Frederick, 206, 967, 968
Dow, Neal, 470, 683
Dren, George H., 1577
Drew, Elizabeth, *as contributor*,
    243–246, 694–695, 1160–1161
Drug Enforcement Administration
    (DEA), 395–396, 907
Drug policy, **394–397**, 1015
Dual federalism, 612
    and internal improvements, 612
Duane, William J., 860, 1304, 1435,
    1482
Duberstein, Kenneth M., 952, 1286,
    1627
Dubofsky, Melvyn, *as contributor*,
    196–197, 935–939
DuBridge, Lee A., 1352, 1353
Ducat, Craig R., *as contributor*,
    126–128, 580, 1671–1673
Dudley Letter, 475
Dugan, Michael, 897
Dukakis, Michael S., 50, 140, **397**,
    537–539, 644, 1155, 1209,
    1234, 1235
Duke, David, 212
Dulles, Allen W., 408, 919, 1591,
    1593
Dulles, John Foster, 26, **398**, 407,
    751, 1008, 1219, 1237, 1399,
    1564
    on ANZUS Treaty, 60
    Bricker Amendment, 118–119
    brinkmanship, 119
    negotiator of Japanese peace
    treaty, 871
    New Look defense posture, 251
    on SEATO Treaty, 1358–1359
Dumas, Charles, 1236
Dumpers, Dale, 244
Duncan, Charles W., 559
Dunlop, John T., 934, 935
DuPont, Pete, 538
DuPont, William, 1043
Durant, Thomas J., 704
Durkin, Martin P., 934
Duval, Gabriel, 899

Duval, Thomas, 704
Duvalier, François ("Papa Doc"),
    721
Duvalier, Jean-Claude ("Baby Doc"),
    721

E

Eagleburger, Lawrence S., 142,
    1399
Eagleton, Thomas F., 321, 528, 898,
    987, 1266
Early, Stephen, **399**, 1637, 1638
Earth in the Balance (Gore), 695
East Florida, **399–400**, 996
East Germany, 141
Eastland, Terry, 1462
Eaton, John H., 439, 632, 863, 927,
    1541, 1576
Eaton, Margaret (Peggy), 439, 632,
    862, 1542
Eberle, William D., 1122
Eberstadt, Ferdinand, 1060, 1063
Eccles, Marriner, 618
Economic Cooperation Act (1948).
    See Marshall Plan
Economic Defense Board, 1560
Economic destabilization efforts,
    319
Economic leadership, 640
Economic Opportunity Act (1964),
    615, 890, 1611
Economic policy, 140–141, 175,
    177, 400, 1072–1075, 1084–
    1085, 1177, 1284–1285, 1519
    agricultural policy, importance of,
    40
    American system, 53–54
    during Civil War, 229
    coordinating committees, 1056,
    1264
    Employment Act (1946), 556
    and federal courts, 906
    full employment, 557
    Hamilton, Alexander, and, 722
    as issue in election of 1868, 462
    New Deal, 1072–1075
    use of proclamations, 1242
Economic Recovery Tax Act (1981),
    1443
Economic Report of the President,
    314, 557

Executive orders, 194, **584–587**
  classified information system, 232
  FBI and, 767
  proclamations compared, 1241
  regulatory policy, effect on, 1297
Executive power, **587–594**
  Anti-Federalist criticism of, 57
  Article II of Constitution, 702
  broad interpretation by strong
    President, 1411
  definition in *Neagle*, 1070
  foreign policy and, 750
  inherent powers and, 824
  as interpreted during Barbary
    War, 100
  invalidation in *Youngstown*, 1070
  lame-duck Presidents' reliance on,
    941
  Lincoln's use of, 229
  literalist Presidents' use of, 971
  Myers v. U.S., 1052
  support in *Debs*, 1070
  World War I effect on,
    1663–1664
Executive prerogative, **593–595**
  as basis for emergency powers,
    554
  national security as basis for,
    1059
  in political crisis, 330
  use in stewardship theory, 1409
Executive privilege, **595–598**
  claimed by Nixon, 7, 1604
  congressional investigations and,
    845
  independent counsel and, 817
  limited in *U.S. v. Nixon*, 7, 789,
    793, 845, 1419
  Nixon's use of, 801
  presidential immunity and, 789
  Reagan, claim by, 1048
Executive Protective Service, 1248,
  1360
Executive Residence staff, **598–599**
Executive responsibilites, growth of,
  592
Executive Schedule, 1993 (table),
  1344
Exner, Judith, 1636
Exon, James, 948
Expansionism
  Cass, Lewis, and, 182
  defining boundaries, 1004

in inaugural addresses, 809
isolationism and, 852–854
as issue in election of 1844, 447
manifest destiny and, 1004–1005
Polk and, 1180
Expenses, unvouchered. *See*
  Unvouchered expenses
Explorer 1, 1387
Export-Import Bank of the United
  States, 571
Export Trading Company Act
  (1982), 266
*Exposition of the Motives for Opposing
  the Nomination of James
  Monroe...*, 431
Extra Globe, 446

F

Fahrenkopf, Frank, 1155
Fahy, Charles, 579, 1384, 1385
Fairbanks, Charles W., 484, 486,
  601–602, 1557, 1560
Fair Campaign Practices
  Committee, 378
Fairchild, Charles S., 1483
Fair Deal, **602–603**, 707, 1502
Fair Employment Board, 581
Fair employment policy, 581, 582
Fair Employment Practice
  Committee, 213, **603–604**
Fairfield, John, 723, 1544
Fair Housing Act (1968), 773
Fair Labor Standards Act (1938),
  197, **604–605**, 933, 938, 1160,
  1323
Fair Warning Act (1966), 1029
Faithful execution clause, **605–607**
Fall, Albert B., 309, 727, 728, 820,
  836, 837, 1448
Fallows, James, 1391
Family and Medical Act (1993),
  1662
  Family Assistance Plan, 1612
Family Assistance Program,
  1084–1085
Family Support Act (1988), 1613
Farewell Address (Eisenhower),
  411–412, 1021
Farewell Address (Jackson), 865,
  1435

Farewell Address (Washington),
  255, 418–419, **607–608**, 1065,
  1602
  civil religion in, 204
  defense policy, 356
Farley, James A., 63, 502, 503, 506,
  507, **608–609**, 774, 1153, 1189,
  1320, 1506
Farm Credit Administration, 571
Farm Credit System, 697–698
Farmer, James, 210
Farmer-Labor Party, 502, 1463
Farmers, Eugene McCarthy and,
  983
Farmers Home Administration, 770
  impoundment impact, 805
Farmers' Union, 41
Farm Loan system, lending powers
  of, 762
Farm Security Act (1937), 41
Farm Security Administration, 1323
Farragut, David, 460
Farrand, Max, 326
Fast, Howard, 1273
Fast-track authority, **609**, 1473
Faubus, Orval E., 214, 311, 410,
  972–973, 1405
FBI. *See* Federal Bureau of
  Investigation (FBI)
Fechner, Robert, 199
Federal Acquisition Regulation,
  1105
Federal Advisory Committee Act
  (1972), 269
Federal Agricultural Mortgage
  Association, 697
Federal Aviation Administration,
  574, 697
Federal Bureau of Investigation
  (FBI), 570, **609–611**, 766, 907,
  943
  congressional investigation of,
    846
  counterintelligence branch, 830
  and electronic surveillance, 792
  Hoover, E., as Director of, 766
  intelligence units, 829–830
  internal security, 766, 830
  unvouchered expenses, 1537
Federal Communications Act
  (1934), 549
  interpretation in *Nardone*, 1126
  wiretapping ban, 766

Ford, Gerald R., *continued*
  Office of Communications, 1634
  and Panama, 1140
  pardon of Nixon, 1604–1605
  pardon power, 1147
  personnel recruitment, 1118
  and Philippines, 1165
  pocket veto, 1552
  President's Foreign Intelligence
    Advisory Board, 1225
  President's Intelligence Oversight
    Board, 1225
  press conferences, 1229
  public support, 759, 1257, 1275
  relations with Congress, 833
  religion, 1303
  retreats, presidential, 1314
  savings and loan industry, 1349
  science adviser, 1353, 1355
  science and technology, 1121
  seal, presidential, 1358
  tax policy, 1443
  testimony, 1657, 1658, 1659
  Time to Heal, A, 646, 1198
  travel abroad, 375
  United Nations, policy toward,
    1524
  veto, use of, 1554
  and Vietnam, 1565
  War Powers Resolution, and,
    1588
  and White House Counsel, 1628
  White House liaison with
    Congress, 278
Ford, Henry, 308, 1016
Ford, Henry Jones
  *Cost of Our National Government,
    The*, 262
  *Rise and Growth of American
    Politics, The*, 295
Fordney, Joseph W., 652
Fordney-McCumber Tariff Act
  (1922), **652–653**, 1440
Foreign Affairs, 304
Foreign affairs, 589, 1177–1178
  under Adams, J., 13, 14–19
  under Adams, J. Q., 21–22
  Alliance for Progress, 48–49
  area resolutions, 69–70
  arms sales as instrument of, 75,
    76
  under Arthur, 81–82
  Bricker Amendment, 118

  brinkmanship, 119–120
  under Buchanan, 125–126
  under Bush, 141–142, 540, 656,
    853, 1216
  under Carter, 174–175, 656
  Chief Executive's role, 295
  under Cleveland, 240
  Clifford, Clark, and, 242
  Congress's role in, 1055–1056
  under Coolidge, 310, 775
  delegation of legislative power in,
    359–360
  division of powers, 257
  Dulles, John Foster, 398
  under Eisenhower, 410–411, 656,
    707
  executive orders, 584
  executive power and, 750
  as factor in election of 1900, 481
  under Fillmore, 623–624
  Fish, Hamilton, 642
  under Ford, 650–651
  under Garfield, 684
  Good Neighbor Policy, 694
  under Grant, 705
  under Harding, 775
  under Harrison, B., 732
  Hay, John,, 1336
  under Hoover, 763–765
  House, Edward M., and, 769
  imperial presidency, 798
  implied powers and, 803
  in inaugural addresses, 808
  increasing specialization, 1401
  inherent powers and, 823–824
  interventionism, 843
  isolationism, 852–854
  under Jackson, 864–865
  under Jefferson, 653, 655, 877,
    879, 881
  under Johnson, A., 886
  under Johnson, L. B., 656,
    891–894
  under Kennedy, 918–919
  Kissinger, Henry, and, 926–927
  under Lincoln, 969
  Lodge, Henry Cabot, and, 1336
  Logan Act, 976
  McGovern, George, 987
  under McKinley, 989, 991
  under Madison, 995, 996, 997
  Mahan, Alfred T., and, 1336
  military as instrument of, 1578

  under Monroe, 1037
  under Nixon, 1086–1088
  under Pierce, 1167–1168
  under Polk, 1182–1185
  under Reagan, 1285, 1286
  regional collective security, 1546
  religious liberty abroad, 1299
  religious missionaries, protection
    of, 1299
  Republican Party and, 1311
  under Roosevelt, F., 1323–1327
  under Roosevelt, T., 1195, 1330,
    1333
  Root, Elihu, and, 1336
  State, Department of, and, 1398,
    1400
  Supreme Court decisions on,
    1417–1418, 1529, 1534
  under Taft, 1430–1431
  under Taylor, 1447
  under Truman, 251, 656,
    1498–1500, 1501–1502
  under Tyler, 1521
  use of proclamations, 1242
  under Van Buren, 1544
  Vandenberg Resolution,
    1545–1546
  under Washington, 1600–1601
  under Wilson, 1650–1656
Foreign affairs: an overview,
  653–659
Foreign affairs: original intent,
  659–661
Foreign affairs power
  ambassadors, receiving and
    appointing, 52–53, 653, 803
  as basis for proclamation, 1242
  Curtiss-Wright, 824, 1529
  Dames & Moore, importance of,
    342
  international law limitations,
    840–841
  support in *Pink*, 1534
  war power, confused with, 1574
Foreign Agents Registration Act,
  977
Foreign Agricultural Service, 666
Foreign aid, **661–664**, 751, 1400
  human rights observance and, 777
  Point Four Program, 1176–1177
Foreign Assistance Act (1961), 663
  Hughes-Ryan Amendment, 76,
    232, 319, 628, 776, 830

Hayes, Lucy, 631, 632, 634, 739, 743, 756

Hayes, Rutherford B., 78, 466, 467, 547, 683, **739–743**, 1294, 1311, 1453

Chinese exclusion policy, 197

Civil Rights Act of 1875, 207

on Cleveland, 241

conception of presidency, 1195

dark-horse candidate, 343

Harlan, John Marshall, and, 704

home, 756

immigration policy, 787

inaugural address, 808

on item veto, 1549

legislative riders, 68

library, 1044, 1142

religion, 1302

seal, presidential, 1358

use of troops in labor disputes, 936

veto threats, 1555

Wheeler, William, and, 1613

Hayes, Sophia Birchard, 739

Hayes, Webb, 756

Hayne, Robert, 1608

Haynsworth, Clement F., Jr., 898, 1424, 1425, 1426

Hay-Pauncefote Treaty (1901), 739, **743**, 991

Hays, Will H., 1189

Hazlitt, Henry, 301

Head Start, 404, 708, 745, 890

Johnson, Lady Bird, and, 887

Health, Education, and Welfare, Department of, 151, 154, 745

First Hoover Commission, 573

Secretaries of Health, Education, and Welfare (table), 746

Health, presidential, **743–745**

Health and Human Services, Department of, 151, 154, 570, 574, **745–747**

domestic policy, role in, 1177

Inspectors General, and, 825

Secretaries of Health and Human Services (table), 746

Health Care Financing Administration, 746

Health insurance plans, federal, 748

Health policy, **747–749**, 1177

interest groups and, 832

New Frontier, 1077

Hearst, William Randolph, 311, 485, 490, 502, 504, 685–686, 941, 1148, 1227

Heckler, Margaret M., 746

Heclo, Hugh, 283, 852, 1461

as contributor, 855–856, 1109–1114

Heineman, Ben, 29

Heineman task force. *See* Task Force on Governmental Organization (1966)

Heller, Walter W., 315, 918, 921

Helms, Jesse, 32

Helms, Richard, 1273

Helsinki Accords (1975), 71, 372, 651

Helvidius-Pacificus debate, 654, **749–750**, 1242, 1584

inherent powers, 824

international law, and, 840

Hemings, Sally, 377

Henderson, David B., 1369–1370

Hendricks, Thomas A., 462, 464, 466, 468, 472, **750–751**, 1414, 1557, 1558, 1559

Henkin, Louis, *as contributor*, 10–11, 98–99, 653–659, 751

Hennings, Thomas, 119

Henry, John (British spy), 1580

"Henry, Patrick," 157

Henshaw, David, 354

Hepburn Act (1906), 486, 1332

Herbert, Hilary A., 354

Heritage Foundation, 37, 1363

Hermitage, 755, 757, 866, 1043, 1313

Herndon, William H., 1213

Herrera, José Joaquín, 1378

Herrington, John S., 559

Hersh, Seymour M., 198, 1169

Herter, Christian A., 517, 1122, 1398, 1399

Hertzberg, Arthur, *as contributor*, 854–855

Hess, Stephen, *as contributor*, 1230–1232, 1636–1638

Hewitt, Abram S., 476

Hickel, Walter J., 563, 836

Hickenlooper, Bourke B., 751

Hickenlooper Amendments (1963, 1964), 11, 98, **751**

Hickerson, John D., 86

Hickey, Donald R., *as contributor*, 617–618, 1490, 1580–1582

Hidden-hand President, **751–752**, 1211–1212

High crimes and misdemeanors, **752–753**, 790–791, 793–794

Higher Education Facilities Act (1963), 922

Highlands, 755, 1039

Highway Beautification Act (1965), 290, 891

Hill, Anita, 142, 1662

Hill, David B., 476, 1147

Hillman, Sidney, 510, 511, 604

Hills, Carla A., 648, 770, 1122

Himmelberg, Robert F., *as contributor*, 1044–1045

Hinckley, John W., Jr., 84, 85, 1284

Hindenburg, Paul von, 1663

Hines, Walker, 565

Hiroshima, 87, 89, 1004, 1499

Hirsch, Mark G., *as contributor*, 471–474

Hiss, Alger, 407, 984, 1503

Hitchcock, Ethan A., 836

Hitchcock, Frank H., 913, 1189

campaign manager for Taft, 487, 488

Hitler, Adolf, 843–844, 1324

Hitt, Robert R., 601

Hoar, Ebenezer Rockwood, 703–704, 1425

Hoar, George F., 472, 1414

Hoar, Rockwood, 92

Hoban, James, 755, 1618, 1619

Hobart, Garret A., 480, 482, **753–754**, 988, 991, 1557, 1558, 1559, 1560

Hobby, Oveta Culp, 746, 1382

Ho Chi Minh, 251, 891

Hochman, Steven H., *as contributor*, 1042–1043

Hodel, Donald P., 559, 836

Hodges, Luther H., 264

Hodgson, Godfrey, *All Things to All Men*, 1462

Hodgson, James D., 934, 935

Hoff, Joan, *as contributor*, 112–113, 499–501, 1081–1090, 1603–1606

Hoffa, James (Jimmy), 923

Hoffman, John T., 464

Hoffman, Walter E., 39

Hogan, Harry L., *as contributor*, 394–396

legislative role, 1204
liberalism, 956
Louisiana Purchase, 977–978
Madison and, 994
on maintaining separation of
    powers, 1366
Manual of Parliamentary Procedure,
    876
Marbury v. Madison, 1005–1006
Marshall, John, and, 1009
Monroe, and, 1033–1034, 1038,
    1040
Mount Rushmore National
    Memorial, 1050
national university, 402
and neutrality, 749
on neutrality proclamation,
    1600–1601
Notes on the State of Virginia, 873,
    875
as party leader, 1152, 1194
and political parties, 361, 1151
presidential greatness, 1211–1212
presidential immunity and, 789
presidential papers, 1141
and the press, 1226, 1256
relations with Congress,
    1203–1204, 1205, 1213
religion, 1301
removal power, 1303–1304
retreats, presidential, 1313
as Secretary of State, 1398, 1399
State of the Union Messages,
    written, 1402
and states' rights, 1404, 1405
*Summary View of the Rights of
    British America, A*, 875
Supreme Court, conflict with,
    1004–1005
two-term tradition, 1454, 1455,
    1516
on vice presidency, 1558
as viewed by Rufus King, 925
on war power, 1573
and war powers, 799, 1579
on Washington, 1602
Washington and, 153, 1596,
    1598, 1599, 1600
and White House (building),
    1618, 1619
Jeffersonian, 709
Jeffersonian Republican Party. *See*
    Democratic Party

Jefferson Memorial, 1044
Jefferson National Expansion
    Memorial, 1044
Jeffrey, Robert C., *as contributor*,
    692–693
Jenks, George A., 1385
Jenson, Richard, 732
Jeritza, Maria, 1362
Jewell, Marshall, 1189
Jimmy Carter Library, Museum, and
    Presidential Center, 179, 960
Job Corps, 708, 890, 935
Job Training and Partnership Act
    (1983), 935
Job Training Partnership Act
    (1982), 1268
John F. Kennedy Center for the
    Performing Arts, 1044
Johnson, Andrew, 113, 188, 459,
    882–886, 902, 970, 1044, 1189,
    1213, 1453, 1509, 1557, 1558,
    1559
  Alaska Purchase Treaty, 46
  amnesty granting, 55
  capital punishment, 171
  civil rights policy, 206–207, 212
  conception of presidency, 1195
  Freedmen's Bureau, opposition
      to, 671
  Hamlin, Hannibal, and, 724
  home, 755
  impeachment of. *See*
      Impeachment of Andrew
      Johnson
  Mississippi v. Johnson, 1024
  public support, 701
  Radicals, opposition to, 1274
  Reconstruction, approach to, 613,
      1293
  religion, 1302
  removal power controversy, 153,
      791, 1304
  Stanton, Edwin M., and, 1396
  State of the Union Message, 1403
  use of veto, 1554
Johnson, Cave, 1181, 1189
Johnson, Eliza, 631
Johnson, Harriet Lane, 757
Johnson, Herschel V., 457
Johnson, Hiram W., 493, 495, 496,
    501, 1335
Johnson, Hugh S., 102, 116, 1058,
    1321

Johnson, Jack, 610
Johnson, John A., 487
Johnson, Lady Bird, 631, 634, 635,
    637, 638, **886–887**, 889, 891,
    924
  beautification, 290
Johnson, Loch K., *as contributor*,
    181–182, 184–187, 197–199,
    231–232, 311, 628–629,
    829–830, 1169–1171,
    1401–1402, 1534–1535
Johnson, Louis A., 353, 1008
Johnson, Lyndon B., 365, 517, 519,
    520–524, 647, 702, 833,
    887–895, 1044, 1222, 1308,
    1352, 1509, 1523, 1557, 1560,
    1561, 1566
  administrative reform, 29
  affirmative action, 34–36
  agricultural policy, 42, 44
  and appointment of federal
      judges, 897
  arms control, 71, 1347
  budget policy, 134
  business policy, 146
  civil rights policy, 208, 209, 210,
      215
  Clifford, Clark, and, 242
  cold war policy, 252
  conception of the presidency,
      1197
  crime, policy on, 329
  deregulation, 369
  domestic policy, 387, 1115
  and Dominican Republic, 390,
      391, 694, 716
  drug policy, 395
  education policy, 401, 404
  environmental policy, 290, 562
  fair employment practices, 581
  Federal Bureau of Investigation
      and, 767
  federalism, 615
  fiscal policy, 641
  foreign affairs, 656
  foreign aid, 663
  Fortas, Abe, and, 667–668
  Great Society program, 745–746
  groupthink and, 713
  Gulf of Tonkin Resolution, 70
  health, 745
  health policy, 748
  home, 757

Fillmore and, 625
Wilson, Henry, and, 1646
Knox, Frank, 354, 508, 942, 1324, 1407
Knox, Henry, 16, 1575, 1576, 1657
Indian policy, 818–819
on neutrality proclamation, 1600–1601
Washington and, 153, 1597, 1598
Knox, Philander, 93, 486, **928**, 1062, 1066, 1330, 1399
dollar diplomacy, 385–387
drug policy, 394
ineligibility clause and, 821–822
Knudsen, William, 1119
Knutson, Harold, 510
Koed, Elizabeth, *as contributor*, 504–506, 1057–1058, 1072–1075, 1452
Koenig, Louis W., *as contributor*, 313–314, 706–707, 769, 971–972, 1017, 1024–1025, 1148–1150, 1239–1240, 1408–1409, 1411–1412
Koerner, Gustave, 1042
Koh, Harold Hongju, *as contributor*, 111–112, 370–371, 849–851, 1471
Kolb, Charles E. M., 1117
Koop, C. Everett, 747
Kopechne, Mary Jo, 1234
Koplow, David A., *as contributor*, 1, 187, 189–190, 822, 1128, 1347–1348, 1357–1358, 1397
Korea, 796, 1122
Korean War, 251, 706, **928–930**
Acheson and, 9
Eisenhower and, 407
executive justification of war-making power, 801
groupthink and escalation of, 713
McCarran Internal Security Act and, 981
McCarthyism during, 984
Marshall, George C., role in, 1008
Truman and, 1504
Kosygin, Aleksey N., 252, 894
Kraft, Tim, 816
Kranowitz, Alan M., 952
Kreps, Juanita M., 264
Kristol, Irving, 1417
Krock, Arthur, 507, 510
Krug, Julius A., 836

Ku Klux Klan, 466, 645, **930–931**
and election of 1868, 1369
and election of 1924, 346, 497–498
law enforcement and, 705
as political force in the 1920s, 365
Ku Klux Klan Act (1870). *See* Force Act (1870)
Kumar, Martha, 1231
as contributor, 831–835, 1119–1120, 1228–1230, 1390–1391, 1635
Kurds, 779
Kurtz, Stephen G., *as contributor*, 11–20, 674–675
Kutler, Stanley I., *as contributor*, 1008–1009
Kuwait, 142, 1578
Bush and, 779
Gulf War and, 715
Kyvig, David E., *as contributor*, 1245–1246, 1247

L

Labor, Department of, 150, 151, 154, 570, 574, **933–935**
law enforcement responsibility, 942
Secretaries of Labor (table), 934
Labor Injunction, The (Frankfurter and Greene), 670
Labor-management relations, 1058
Labor-Management Relations Act. *See* Taft-Hartley Act (1947)
Labor policy, 494, **935–939**
labor-management relations, 1058
Labor's Non-Partisan League, 604
Labovitz, John R., *as contributor*, 752–753, 790–794
Laffer, Arthur, 1417
La Follette, Robert M., 50, 345, 486, 489, 497, 498, 728, **939–940**, 1243, 1448, 1464, 1466, 1467
Progressive Party (1924), 1244
La Follette Seamans Act, 494
LaGuardia, Fiorello, 1468
Laingen, L. Bruce, *as contributor*, 665–666
Laird, Melvin R., 353, 355, 368, **940**, 1083, 1084

Lake, W. Anthony, 1062
Lamar, Joseph R., 900, 1432
Field v. Clark, dissent in, 621
Lamar, Lucius Q. C., 836, 900
Lame-duck Presidents, 732, **940–941**
Lamont, Daniel S., 1577, 1640, 1641
Lamont, Robert P., 264
Lance, Thomas Bertram, 174, 1110
Land Act (1841), 838
Landis, James M., 250, 814, 1258, 1296
Business of the Supreme Court, The, 670
Land Management, 837
Landon, Alfred M., 49, 50, 504, **941–942**, 1074, 1322, 1381
Landrieu, Moon, 770
Landrum-Griffin Act (1959), 937
Lane, Franklin K., 836, 837
Lane, Harriet, 634
Lane, Joseph, 117, 457
Langdon, John, 416, 428, 998
Lange, David, 61
Langley, Lester D., *as contributor*, 102–104, 332–334, 716–717, 721, 1138–1139, 1139–1140
Lanham Act (1940), 773
Lansing, Robert, 380, 669, 1399, 1649, 1655, 1663
Lard, Herbert M., 1110
Larkin, John A., *as contributor*, 1164–1166
Larkin, Thomas O., 1019
LaRouche, Lyndon, 1207
Lash, Joseph, 924
Lasser, William, *as contributor*, 107–108, 116–117, 147–148, 250, 313, 344, 608–609, 629–630, 785, 866–867, 911–912, 923, 1028, 1258, 1336–1337, 1656–1657
Latin America
Arthur and, 81
covert operations in, under Madison, 799
foreign aid limitation, 778
Good Neighbor Policy and, 694
gunboat diplomacy and, 716
Hoover and, 763
human rights and, 778
immigrants from, 788

and Hoover Commission, 767
Hopkins, Harry, and, 769
human rights policy, 777
Ickes, Harold, and, 785
Immigration Act, 786
immigration quota system, 982
immmigration policy, 788
imperial presidency and, 800–801
inaugural address, 807, 808, 809
inauguration, 1013
independent commissions, 814
Indian policy, 820
initiating acts of war, 260–261
interventionism, 844
and Israel, 854
and Joint Chiefs of Staff, 896
Korean War, 706, 800–801, 929
labor policy, 934, 937
liberalism, 958
Loyalty Order, 578
McCarran Internal Security Act,
    veto of, 981–982
McCarran-Walter Act, veto of,
    786, 788, 982
McCarthy, Joseph, and, 984
and Manhattan Project, 1003
Marshall, George C., and, 1008
Marshall Plan, 1010–1011
Memoirs, 1221
national disability insurance, 1382
national health insurance, 1382
National Security Council's role,
    1063
national security system,
    development of, 356
NATO Treaty, 1546
pardon power, 1147
personnel recruitment, 64, 1118
and Philippines, 1165
Point Four Program, 1176
at Potsdam Conference, 1192
presidential commissions, 266
and presidential flag, 643
presidential papers, 1142
presidential succession,
    1221–1222, 1414
and the press, 1227, 1636
press conferences, 1230
Progressivism and, 767
and Puerto Rico, 1259
pump priming, 1261
radicals, attitude toward, 1272
religion, 1302

reorganization power, 1307
retreats, presidential, 1314
science adviser, 1352, 1355
science and technology, 1121
seal, presidential, 1358
steel mills seizure (E.O. 10340),
    580, 1671
Stimson, Henry L., and, 1409
Taft-Hartley Act veto, 1434
tariff policy, 1440
tax policy, 1442
Thanksgiving proclamations,
    1458
travel abroad, 375
and Twenty-second Amendment,
    1512
United Nations, creation of, 1524
and Vietnam, 1564
Wallace, Henry A., and, 1572
and war powers, 260–261, 314
welfare policy, 1610
and White House Counsel, 1628
Truman Committee, 1668
Truman Doctrine, 9, 256, 304, 662,
    1501, **1505–1506**, 1564
Truman Library, 757
Trumbull, Lyman, 465, 1539
Truncated majority, 287
Tsongas, Paul, 245, 541
Tubby, Roger, 1638
Tubman, William, 1252
Tuchman, Barbara, *Guns of August,*
    The, 331
Tuck, Dick, 378
Tufte, Edward, *Political Control of*
    the Economy, 1460
Tugwell, Rexford G., 116, 238, 301,
    502, 775, 1319, 1452, **1506**
Tulis, Jeffrey K., 1202, 1222
    as contributor, 1315–1316
Tully, Grace, 1639
Tumulty, Joseph P., 1230, 1637,
    1639, 1641, 1655
Tunis, 100
Tunney, John, 232
Tunney Amendment. *See* Clark
    Amendment
Ture, Norman, 1417
Turkey, 662
    U.S. aid to, 1501, 1505
Turner, Michael, *as contributor,*
    1316–1318
Turnure, Pamela, 638

Tushnet, Mark, *as contributor,*
    212–217
Tuttle, Holmes, 1283
Tuyll, Baron de, 1040–1041
Twain, Mark, 472
Tweed, William Marcy, 77, 1369,
    1469
Twelfth Amendment, 300, 326,
    544, 547, 925, 1093, 1151,
    1413, **1506–1507**
    qualifications for President, 1266
    as result of election of 1800, 423,
    1558
Twentieth Amendment, 300, 326,
    811, 1413, 1454, 1456,
    1507–1509
Twentieth Century Fund's
    Taskforce, 349–350
Twenty-fifth Amendment, 327, 380,
    381, 646, 745, 1413, 1414,
    1415, 1562
Twenty-first Amendment, 1246,
    1509–1510
Twenty-fourth Amendment, **1511**
Twenty-second Amendment, 6, 300,
    326, 794, 800, 1264, 1454,
    1455, **1511–1513**
Twenty-seventh Amendment, 1263
Twenty-third Amendment, 545,
    1513–1514
Twenty Years of Congress (Blaine),
    471
Twining, Nathan F., 897
Twohig, Dorothy, *as contributor,*
    1051
Two-party system, general ticket
    system and, 545
Two presidencies, 589, 1461,
    1514–1516
Two Sicilies, Kingdom of the, 865
Two-term tradition, 1511,
    1516–1517
    Washington and, 1602
Tydings-McDuffie Act (1934), 256,
    1165
Tydings Rehabilitation Act, 1165
Tyler, Elizabeth, 930
Tyler, John, 364, 445, 447, 639,
    736–737, 1376, **1517–1522,**
    1544, 1557, 1559
    Bell, John, and, 104
    Clay, Henry, and, 1615
    conception of presidency, 1195

Tyler, John, *continued*
  and Cuba, 333
  Dorr War, 391
  Gallatin, Albert and, 681
  home, 754, 755
  immigration policy, 786
  and Independent Treasury, 818
  and internal improvements, 838
  nominees confirmation, 32
  presidential commissions, 266
  presidential papers, 1141
  and presidential succession, 1413
  religion, 1301
  testimony, as former President,
    1658
  Texas, annexation of, 5, 1182,
    1456
  unvouchered expenses, 1537
  use of veto, 1554
  Webster, Daniel, and, 1608
  Webster-Ashburton Treaty, 1608
  See also Tyler precedent
Tyler, Julia Gardiner, 631, 632,
    1521
Tyler, Letitia, 631, 1521
Tyler precedent, 379, 1103,
    1413–1414, 1509, **1522**, 1559
Tyner, James N., 1189
Tyson, Laura D'Andrea, 315
Tzu-wen Soong, 1525

U

Udall, Morris, 531
Udall, Stewart, 562, 836, 837, 918,
    1523
  1976: Agenda for Tomorrow, 1523
  Quiet Crisis, The, 1523
Uelman, Gerald F., *as contributor*,
    171–173
Ukraine, 1397
Un-American Activities Committee.
    See House Un-American
    Activities Committee
Underwood, Oscar W., 490, 498,
    1009, 1523, 1649–1650
Underwood Tariff Act (1913), 491,
    1076, 1439, **1523–1524**, 1650
Unified executive office, 591
Uniformed Division of the Secret
    Service, 1248, 1360
Unilateral agreements, 567

Union of Soviet Socialist Republics,
    141, 662, 1499
  Afghanistan, invasion of, 177,
    180
  arms control treaties with, 74
  Basic Principles of United
    States–Soviet Relations, 1087
  Berlin crisis (1961), 107
  and cold war, 251–253
  diplomatic recognition of, 764
  effect of dissolution on nuclear
    arms control, 1397
  Ford and, 650, 651
  Lend Lease Act and, 955
  Marshall Plan and, 1010
  Nixon's policy toward, 1087
  nuclear testing, 1097–1098
  Roosevelt, F., and, 1326–1327
  and Yalta conference, 1671
Union Pacific Railroad, 328
Union Party, 504
Unitary executive, 297
United Kingdom. *See* Great Britain
United Mine Workers, 1500
United Nations, 769, **1524–1525**
  Charter for International Trade
    Organization (ITO), 687
  Cuban missile crisis, 920
  Gulf War and, 715
  Israel and, 854
  Korean War and, 801
  Mayaguez capture, 1012
  neutral rights, curtailment of,
    1072
  Resolution 665, 715
  Rhodesia and, 778
  Roosevelt, F., plans for, 1327
United Nations Charter, 677
  colonialism, 256
  and declaration of war, 1578
United Nations Declaration, **1525**
United Nations International
    Women's Year, 1661
United Nations Participation Act
    (UNPA), **1525–1527**
United Nations Relief and
    Reconstruction Agency, 662
United States Agricultural Society,
    43
United States-Canadian relations
  reciprocity agreement attempted
    by Taft, 1430–1431
  Saint Lawrence Seaway, 1343

United States–China relations, 796
  Carter, role in, 803
  imperialism and, 797
  Nixon, role in, 1015
United States Geological Survey,
    836
  Reclamation service, 837
United States George Washington
    Bicentennial Commission, 1142
United States Postal Service, 571,
    696–697, 1192, **1527–1528**
  law enforcement responsibility,
    942
United States Sentencing
    Commission, 1026–1027
United States–Soviet relations, 175,
    410, 411, 855, 1015, 1286,
    1499
  détente, 1348
  INF Treaty, 822
United States' Telegraph, 438
University of Alabama, 1571
Unruh, Jesse M., 1283
Untermeyer, Chase, 1118
Unvouchered expenses, **1536–1537**
Upshur, Abel P., 354, 447, 1399,
    1457, 1521
  *Brief Inquiry into the Nature and
    Character of Our Federal
Government, A*, 1304
Uranium Enrichment Program, 697
Urban policy. *See* Housing policy
Urban renewal programs. *See*
    Housing and Urban
    Development,
Department of
Urgent Deficiency Appropriations
    Act (1943), 1531–1532
Uruguay, 778, 1316
Uruguay Round, 687, 1122, 1123,
    1473, 1474
U.S. Arms Control and Disarma-
    ment Agency (ACDA), 571
U.S. Army, 985
U.S. Civil Service Commission's War
    Service Regulations (1942), 978
U.S. Commission on Federal
    Paperwork, 1144
U.S. Court of Veterans Appeals,
    1547, 1548
U.S. Housing Authority, 770
U.S. Information Agency (USIA),
    571, 666